Family Violence

Family Violence: Legal, Medical, and Social Perspectives examines the entire spectrum of family violence, focusing on social processes and social relationships. The eighth edition is a multidisciplinary introduction to the study of domestic violence that guides readers to a better understanding of the challenges involved in reducing or eliminating violence. The new edition includes more information on PTSD and head trauma, a new section in children witnessing domestic violence, more international perspectives, which allow students to understand that family violence crosses borders and cultures, and a series of Promising Practices boxes that bring professional knowledge and accomplishments into the classroom.

Harvey Wallace and Cliff Roberson

Harvey Wallace (1944–2007) was a Professor in the Criminology Department, California State University, Fresno. He served as Chairman of the Department of Criminology. During his tenure as Chairman, the department embarked on a number of innovative programs. He was the Associate Dean for the College of Social Sciences at California State University, Fresno from 2003 to 2005.

Professor Wallace received a Jurist Doctorate Degree from California Western School of Law, an MPA from Golden Gate University and a BS in Criminology from California State University, Fresno.

He was considered a subject matter expert by the U.S. Department of Justice in Family Violence and Victimology. He was the author or co-author of nine college texts and has been published in a number of referred and scholarly journals, as well as presented his research at a variety of international and national conferences. Professor Wallace was an attorney licensed to practice law in the State of California and his professional experience includes appointment as the City Attorney of the City of Fresno, service as the County Counsel for the County of Butte, private practice in a media law firm and experience as a Deputy District Attorney in San Diego, California.

In 2008, the Northern California Mock Trial Regional was renamed the Harvey Wallace Northern California Mock Trial Regional in his memory.

Cliff Roberson LLM, Ph.D. is an Emeritus Professor of Criminal Justice at Washburn University, Topeka, Kansas and a retired Professor of Criminology at California State University, Fresno, California. Dr. Roberson's non-academic experience includes U.S. Marine Corps service as an infantry officer, trial and defense counsel and military judge as a marine judge advocate; and Director of the Military Law Branch, U.S. Marine Corps. He has authored or co-authored numerous books and texts on legal subjects and victims' issues. His previous academic experiences include Associate Vice-President for Academic Affairs, Arkansas Tech University; Dean of Arts and Sciences, University of Houston, Victoria; Director of Programs, National College of District Attorneys; Professor of Criminology and Director of Justice Center, California State University, Fresno; and Assistant Professor of Criminal Justice, St. Edwards University.

Other legal employment experiences include Trial Supervisor, Office of State Counsel for Offenders, Texas Board of Criminal Justice and judge *pro tem* in the California courts.

Eighth edition

Family Violence

LEGAL, MEDICAL, AND SOCIAL PERSPECTIVES

Harvey Wallace
Cliff Roberson
Washburn University

Routledge
Taylor & Francis Group

LONDON AND NEW YORK

Eighth edition published 2016

By Routledge
711 Third Ave, New York, NY 10017

and by Routledge
2 Park Square, Milton Park, Abingdon, Oxon, OX14 4RN

Routledge is an imprint of the Taylor & Francis Group, an informa business

First edition published 1996 by Pearson Education, Inc.

Seventh edition published 2014 Pearson Education, Inc.

Library of Congress Cataloging-in-Publication Data
Names: Wallace, Harvey. | Roberson, Cliff, 1937- Title: Family violence / by Harvey Wallace and Cliff Roberson. Description: 8 Edition. | New York : Routledge, 2016. | Revised edition of the authors' Family violence, 2014. | Includes bibliographical references and index. Identifiers: LCCN 2015038756| ISBN 9781138642331 (hardback : alk. paper) | ISBN 9781138642348 (pbk. : alk. paper) | ISBN 9781315628271 (ebook) Subjects: LCSH: Family violence—United States. | Family social work—United States. | Family violence—Law and legislation—United States. | Victims of family violence—Mental health—United States. | Victims of family violence—Health and hygiene—United States. | Victims of family violence—Legal status, laws, etc.—United States. Classification: LCC HV6626.2 .W35 2016 | DDC 362.82/92— dc23LC record available at http://lccn.loc.gov/2015038756

ISBN: 978-1-138-64233-1 (hbk)
ISBN: 978-1-315-62827-1 (pbk)
ISBN: 978-1-138-64234-8 (ebk)

Typeset in Minion Pro
by Cenveo Publisher Services

Printed and bound in the United States of America by
Edwards Brothers Malloy on sustainably sourced paper

To Elena

CONTENTS

FOREWORD

In preparing the eighth edition and attempting to improve on our text, I received extensive support and encouragement from Dr. Elena Azaola of Centro de Investigaciones y Estudios Superiores en Antropologia Social. Thanks Elena.

Cliff Roberson, LLM, Ph.D.
Emeritus Professor of Criminal Justice, Washburn University

PREFACE

The eighth edition of *Family Violence* is an updated and revised text from the seventh edition.

As noted by Professor Wallace in the first edition, the study of family violence is a complex, multifaceted experience. By its very nature, family violence involves physicians, nurses, psychiatrists, psychologists, family counsellors, educators, social workers, attorneys, judges, and law enforcement officials. All of these professionals have expertise in their own areas of specialization. However, they may not understand or appreciate the difficulties experienced by others in their areas of interest. For example, a member of the medical profession may be able to diagnose physical injuries but not understand the complexities of the courtroom.

As a nation, we are becoming more aware of the extent and nature of family violence. Nationally broadcast trials have brought family violence into our front rooms. Judith Leekin of West Palm Beach, Florida, was charged in June 2007 with abusing eleven adopted children by keeping them handcuffed and forcing them to soil themselves, while lining her pockets with $1.26 million in stipends she was supposed to use to care for them. A 2007 study financed by the Pentagon found that mothers in Army families were about four times as likely to neglect their children and more likely to physically abuse them when their soldier husbands were deployed in Iraq and Afghanistan than when the fathers were home. And who can forget Mary Winkler, who killed her husband Matthew, a church minister in Selmer, Tennessee. Mary Winkler's father claims that his daughter was a victim of domestic abuse. The sexual violence occurring at the U.S. Air Force Academy focused us on sexual violence in the military.

Many states require students in certain fields of study to take courses in specific areas of family violence as a condition of receiving a license to practice. Law enforcement agencies are not required by statute in some jurisdictions to respond in certain ways to domestic abuse cases. Many times, members of the medical profession are the first to come in contact with victims of family violence. They must not only recognize the physical and emotional symptoms of the victims but also understand how their own role relates to law enforcement and the legal system. Criminal justice professionals, including law enforcement personnel, are becoming more involved in cases of family violence.

Mandatory arrest of spousal or partner abusers, temporary restraining orders, vertical prosecution teams, and victim impact statements are all developments that have appeared in response to a recognized need to protect the victims of family violence. In our society, many forces continue to allow violence to occur in the home. As this text discusses, no single cause or factor contributes to family violence. This, however, should not deter students and professionals from understanding the existing controversies in the field. These factors must be understood to appreciate fully the consequences of family violence.

Family violence courses are becoming more common at the junior and community college level. Many of these courses are offered in the areas of sociology, nursing, and law enforcement. They are providing students with a much-needed perspective on a topic that for too long has been left in the area of upper-division courses or graduate study. The study of family violence does not belong only in the rarified atmosphere of select university classes. Rather, it is a subject with which more people should become familiar.

A survey of law enforcement agencies indicated their desire for new recruits to receive formal training in family violence. In addition, professionals are becoming more aware that they must adopt an interdisciplinary approach to this problem, and more and more seminars are being offered in the area of family violence. These developments are both a blessing and a curse. On one hand, as we learn more about family violence, we are better able to respond to it. At the same time, the more we learn, the more we must be aware that there are increasing data in this field and that we can be overwhelmed with studies and their results. We are rapidly approaching an overload of information based on this research and yet have failed to agree on something as simple as a definition for the term *family violence*.

The study of family violence has many excellent texts that completely cover specific areas of this topic. There are comprehensive treatises on intimate partner abuse, child abuse, treatment, intervention, and legal issues of family violence. Because this area is so fragmented and complex, the problem arises of finding one source that provides an overview or introduction while supplying references that allow the reader to expand his or her knowledge in a specific area. This text is an attempt to examine the more commonly discussed topics of family violence from medical, social, and legal perspectives. It addresses specialized topics, such as sexual harassment, stalking, and victims' rights, that are normally not found in many family violence texts. This text is an introduction to this complex area, and it provides the reader with sufficient knowledge to understand the various dynamics involved in family violence.

Since the publication of the first edition of this text in 1996, many aspects of family violence have changed. Numerous states have passed additional laws affording victims of family violence more protection. New textbooks and academic journals provide additional research into this complex area. However, the dilemmas faced by professionals in the field remain the same. New and important research is being conducted even as this text goes to print. I have attempted to add new information that affects professionals in the field. We must strive to understand how to deal with victims of family violence who are different from you and me. We must also understand the impact and consequences of family violence.

This eighth edition continues to change and adapt, as does the knowledge and research in this evolving area. Rather than undertaking a complete rewrite of the text, I have relied on comments from other academics, researchers, and reviewers to update and modify this edition. I have added a series of Promising Practices boxes that bring professional knowledge and accomplishments into the classroom. These are not the only promising practices in the field; rather, space dictated that I limit the number and type of procedures that are currently being used by professionals in the field. I have also included a number of International Perspectives in this edition. These perspectives allow students to understand that family violence crosses borders and cultures. A number of additional updates and new material are spread across this edition, including child homicide, family violence in the military, churches' responses to family violence, and an expanded section on police officers who abuse their spouses. Also new to the eighth edition is that each chapter begins with a list of objectives that should be understood after a study of the subject matter of that chapter.

Suggestions for improvement, corrections, etc. may be submitted to cliff.roberson@ washburn.edu.

ACKNOWLEDGMENTS

Over the long period of time it has taken to complete this revision, I have become indebted to many people who provided advice, support, resources, and encouragement. First and foremost, I would like to thank Samantha Barbaro, my editor and Drew Acuff, the editorial assistant, who coordinated the many details of getting the eighth edition of the text into print.

Professor Wallace's students, at both the graduate and the undergraduate levels at California State University, Fresno (CSUF), as well as those attending the Victim Services Institute and the National Victim Assistance Academy, provided him with insight into the teaching of family violence.

Harvey's colleagues at CSUF were especially helpful and supportive to Harvey in the development and publication of the first five editions of *Family Violence*. Those colleagues include Steve Walker, Ph.D.; John Dussech, Ph.D.; Arthur Wint, J.D.; and Eric Hickey, Ph.D. of the Criminology Department. Bernadette Muscat, Ph.D., another colleague and friend of Harvey, reviewed the earlier editions. Her suggestions and recommendations were invaluable. Christine Edmonds, special consultant with the Office for Victims of Crimes, furnished Harvey with material and data on a variety of topics. Al Stickler of Santa Rosa, California, provided much-needed editorial assistance. The following reviewers provided Harvey or me with invaluable suggestions and corrections that helped to improve this text: Bonnie Black, Mesa Community College; David Briscoe, University of Arkansas at Little Rock; Lisa Nored, University of Southern Mississippi; Chuck Baker, Delaware County Community College; Patricia O'Brien, Elgin Community College; and Beverly Stiles, Midwestern State University. Finally, a special word of thanks to a long-time friend and former colleague at Washburn University, Nancy Palmer who provided me with insight, comments, and recommendations regarding teaching a course in family violence and her use of the text in her classes.

NEW TO THE EIGHTH EDITION

- The eighth edition was revised at the suggestion of the reviewers. It is now divided into four sections; domestic partner abuse, elder abuse, child abuse, and special issues in family violence.
- New discussions on the effects of children observing family violence.
- New discussions on how children exposed to violence may respond differently to law enforcement.
- Added discussions on the effects on children who are involved in family violence.
- New material on children observing the arrest of their parents.
- New discussions on gay and lesbian partner abuse.
- New material and extended discussion on the mental health issues associated with family violence.
- Expanded and revised discussion questions.
- Elder abuse among LGBT partnerships.
- New Section on physical disabilities and partner violence.
- New material on family violence courts.
- New material on rape and sexual violence on campuses.
- New material on parents who reject their children.
- Discussions on the new controversy regarding shaken baby syndrome.

Characteristics and Consequences of Family Violence

CHAPTER OBJECTIVES

After studying this chapter, you should be able to:

- Explain what acts or conduct is considered to constitute family violence;
- Discuss the consequences of family violence;
- List and explain the mandatory reporting laws on child abuse;
- Recognize the extent of family violence in today's society;
- Understand the widely used intervention strategies used in dealing with family violence;
- Recognize and explain the controversies in family violence.

Detailed Look at What You Should Know About Family Violence

- It is difficult to define what constitutes family violence.
- There are inherent problems in attempting to measure the extent of family violence.
- The study of family violence is still in its infancy.
- There are numerous myths and misconceptions that surround family violence.
- The concept of family violence is a wide-ranging concept that must remain flexible to adaption as we learn more about its scope and impact.
- The term *serious injury* may involve physical or emotional harm or a violation of another family member's rights and freedom of choice.
- Intervention strategies vary widely in dealing with family violence.
- The most commonly relied on data on the extent of family violence are reports by local law enforcement agencies, the American Humane Society, the Uniform Crime Reports (UCR), and the National Crime Victimization Surveys.

- Since the adoption of the mandatory reporting laws for child abuse, and in some states mandatory arrest of those accused of intimate partner abuse, local agencies have been able to provide researchers with a wealth of information regarding family violence.

- The Violence against Women Act provides a fundamental change in the criminal justice system's gathering of information on violent crimes committed against women.

- The UCR program is a nationwide statistical compilation involving more than 1,600 cities, counties, and state law enforcement agencies that voluntarily report data on reported crimes.

- The psychiatric model tries to understand family violence by analyzing the offender's personality traits and mental status.

- The **psychopathology theory** is grounded on the concept that certain individuals suffer from mental illness, personality disorders, and other dysfunctions that cause them to engage in aggressive acts within the family.

- The **substance abuse theory** accepts the proposition that drugs or alcohols cause or contribute to family violence.

- The social-psychological model analyzes external environmental factors that affect the family unit. Factors such as stress, family structure, the intergenerational transmission of violence, and family interactions are all considered as primary causes of family violence.

- The social learning theory assumes that the type of behavior most frequently reinforced by others is the one most often exhibited by the individual.

- The **exchange theory** is based on the premise that persons act according to a system of rewards or punishments.

- The **frustration-aggression theory** is based on the premise that human beings display aggression toward objects that impede their achievement of certain goals.

- The **ecological theory** is based on an analysis of the organism and the environment, the interacting systems in which family development occurs, and the environment in which the family resides.

- The **sociobiology or evolutionary theory** is based on the concept that parents display aggressive acts toward children who are not their own or do not have the potential to reproduce.

- The sociocultural model of family violence focuses on the roles of men and women in our society as well as on the cultural attitudes toward women and the acceptance of violence as a cause of family violence.

- The **culture of violence theory** is based on the premise that violence is unevenly distributed within our society, and that violence is more prevalent in the lower socioeconomic sectors of society.

- The patriarchy theory views society as dominated by men, with women in subordinate positions, treated by men as possessions and things.

- The **general systems theory** views the maintenance of violence as a result of the social system in which families live.

- This **social conflict theory** analyzes large-scale conflicts, marriages, and the communication process.

- The **resource theory** is based on the proposition that the one who controls resources, such as money, property, or prestige, is in the dominant position in a relationship.

- The intergenerational transmission of violence theory was formerly known as the cycle of violence theory.

- One of the most obvious consequences of family violence is the physical injuries suffered by victims. These injuries are easy to observe and treat.

- There are four general classifications of physical injuries inflicted on victims of family violence: immediate injuries that heal leaving no trace, injuries that leave visible scars, unknown longterm physical injuries, and long-term catastrophic injuries.

- The types of physical injuries suffered by victims of family violence can cover the entire spectrum of illness, from simple bruises to deadly gunshot wounds to the head.

- **Acute stress disorder** (ASD) is acute stress that is experienced in the immediate aftermath of a traumatic event.

- **Posttraumatic stress disorder** is defined as the development of characteristic symptoms following a psychologically distressing event that is outside the range of usual human experience.

- Victims of family violence may suffer a wide variety of mental disorders as a result of their victimization.

INTRODUCTION

The study of **family violence** as a discipline is still in its infancy. In U.S. society, numerous myths and misconceptions are present when examining family violence issues and prevention techniques. Many laypersons, students, and professionals are skeptical regarding the dynamics involved in family violence. It is not uncommon to hear "Persons who molest children are mentally deranged," and "Women who stay with abusive partners must really like it or deserve it." Otherwise knowledgeable individuals display an alarming lack of understanding regarding the various aspects and issues involved.

The media including the television and popular magazines have brought the specter of family violence into our living rooms on a daily basis. For example, in 2007 Court TV covered the trial of Mary Winkler, a former schoolteacher accused of killing her pastor husband. During the three days of jury selection, the defense lawyers and prosecutors used phrases such as "spousal abuse," "brainwashed," and "fog of war." Through questions from Winkler's lawyers about battered wife syndrome and posttraumatic stress disorder, the defense painted a picture of the defendant as an abused spouse whose role as a minister's wife elevated her status in the community while isolating her from it within a "fishbowl." Her lawyers suggested that her situation rendered her incapable of seeking help or escaping the abusive marriage. During jury selection, defense attorney asked potential jurors: "Do you all agree with me that people, especially women, will live in an abusive relationship for a variety of reasons?" Two prospective female panelists, who said they were once victims of domestic violence, agreed that abandoning the abusive relationships was not as easy as it seemed.[1]

From May to July 2011, CNN and other news media brought the investigations and court proceedings involving the death of two-year-old Caylee Marie Anthony into our living

Most researchers believe that the best way to reduce partnership violence is through education, awareness, and prevention.

rooms with numerous updates each hour. Caylee's mother Casey Anthony was charged with killing Caylee. Casey was acquitted on July 5, 2011. The verdict was greeted with public outrage, and was both attacked and defended by media and legal commentators. Some complained that the jury misunderstood the meaning of reasonable doubt, while others said the prosecution relied too heavily on the defendant's allegedly poor moral character because it had been unable to show conclusively how the victim had died. *Time* magazine described the case as "the social media trial of the century."

Numerous controversies in the area of family violence are discussed in this textbook. No definition of the term *family violence* has been universally accepted by all scholars, researchers, and other professionals. The full extent and nature of the subject is still being debated. However, statistics gathered from independent research as well as projections from state and federal agencies clearly establish its widespread existence.

DEFINITION

Simply defining the term *family violence* causes debate. Some argue that the use of the word *family* is too restrictive and should be replaced with the term *intimate,* because current research includes studies of couples who cohabitate but are not necessarily married. However, most professionals now accept the idea that a family unit may exist without any formal sanction such as a marriage ceremony. Therefore, the term *family* will be used to include situations in which

Focus

Ninety percent of the time, the best predictor of domestic violence is past behavior.

Source: B. Auchter, "Men Who Murder Their Families," *NIJ Journal*, No. 266, (2010), page 11.

individuals are living together regardless of whether they are legally married. The term family violence is also used to include gay and lesbian couples who are living together as a family.

Violence implies physical acts that result in injuries to the victim. As will be discussed, some forms of family violence involve the withholding of physical or emotional support and can have devastating long-term consequences for the victim. Therefore, violence within this context includes physical or mental acts or omissions that result in injuries to the victim. Violence may also be directed at restricting or denying another person certain rights or liberties.

The concept of family violence includes several subtopics, such as child abuse, intimate partner abuse, and elder abuse. It is therefore a wide-ranging concept that must remain flexible to adaption as we learn more about its scope and impact. The definition of *family violence* for purposes of this textbook is: *any act or omission by persons who are cohabiting or living together as a family that results in serious injury to other members of the family.* This definition includes those who live together or are married. It also includes same gender couples living together as a family regardless of their martial status. The term *serious injury* may involve physical or emotional harm or a violation of another family member's rights and freedom of choice. As will be seen, the great majority of victims of family violence are females or children. This is not to say that men are not battered.[2] However, they are in the minority, and the reasons for this disparity are discussed in detail in Chapter 2, which deals with intimate partner abuse. This definition is broader than Straus, Gelles, and Steinmetz's approach to family violence because their study did not include neglect.[3] It goes beyond Pagelow's definition in that it specifically applies to those who live with other persons.[4]

Family violence includes criminal offenses, behavioral acts, and medical problems. Each of these factors has its own proponents and advocates, and each defines family violence from its own perspective. Despite the need for an acceptable definition from which research and treatment can proceed, each of these interest groups claims its view or approach as the only true alternative. A quick review of the literature in the field highlights this disparate approach to family violence. Some textbooks deal with legal issues and child abuse, policing of intimate partner abuse, medical interventions for victims, and psychological treatment for survivors of abuse. While a few textbooks attempt to take a global approach to family violence, these are in the minority, and professionals continue to specialize within subgroupings of this form of aggression.

Focus

Prevalence of Domestic Violence in the United States

- On average more than three women a day are murdered by their husbands or boyfriends in the United States.
- One in four women in the United States reports experiencing violence by a current or former spouse, life partner, or boyfriend at some point in her life.
- Women are much more likely than men to be victimized by a current or former intimate partner. Women are 84 percent of spouse abuse victims and 86 percent of victims of abuse at the hands of a boyfriend or girlfriend. About three-fourths of the persons who commit family violence are male.
- Women ages 20 to 24 are at the greatest risk of experiencing nonfatal intimate partner violence.[5]

As the preceding discussion indicates, conflict exists among scholars, academics, and professionals regarding the definition of the term *family violence.* However, this should not hinder further study of this form of aggression. It simply means that we must remain flexible in evaluating all forms of aggression to determine whether they fall within the realm of family violence. Defining the term *family violence* is only one of many controversies in this area.

CONTROVERSIES IN FAMILY VIOLENCE

Numerous controversies are present when studying family violence.[6] Specific controversies are addressed in chapters that deal with specific forms or types of family violence. However, an overview of issues that affect the study of family violence provides a basis for understanding that this form of aggression requires additional research before we can determine all of its ramifications.

Family violence has several distinct subgroupings, such as child physical and sexual abuse, intimate partner abuse, and elder abuse. Many scholars have focused on these specific areas and ignored the broader view of family violence. Conversely, others have attempted to view family violence from a broad perspective by creating models of research that are so vague as to be difficult, if not impossible, to test or validate. How does one accurately study or research a phenomenon if a definition cannot be agreed on because the definition of any act both sets limits and focuses research within certain boundaries? The lack of agreement in defining *family violence* has led to confusion and disarray in attempts to determine factors that cause or contribute to family violence.

Just as there are numerous definitions for the term *family violence,* so are there myriad competing and conflicting theories on the causes. The psychological approach, the social-psychological approach, and the sociocultural approach are but a few of the more popular models or theories of family violence. Although feminist perspectives may fall within parts of these models, some authors argue that it is another valid method of classifying family violence. These approaches are discussed later in this chapter, but it must be remembered that no one approach or theory has yet to gain universal acceptance within the field of professionals who deal with this phenomenon.

Intervention strategies vary widely in dealing with family violence. There is widespread agreement that in many instances a child should be removed from the home immediately to prevent further harm or injury. However, in some situations experts argue that removal from the family is a very traumatic experience for the child and should be avoided at all costs. Intervention may also be challenged by defense attorneys who claim that some therapists have brainwashed or planted the thought of abuse in the minds of impressionable children. This technique is commonly used by a number of defense attorneys today, although it is unknown how effective this strategy is in convincing juries.

Reporting and law enforcement's mandated response to child abuse, elder abuse, and intimate partner abuse is a current topic of controversy. Some authorities argue that mandatory reporting of child abuse and elder abuse should be expanded. Others believe that mandatory arrest of intimate partner abusers leads to increased risk to the victim. Still other professionals would expand some laws to require terms of incarceration for those who abuse their spouses.

If no agreement can be reached on the cause of family violence, how can the factors present in a violent relationship be addressed? Depending on the study one reads, different factors are found to exist in family violence. This chapter examines four common factors present in families that have experienced violence. This does not mean that these are the only factors that may exist in every form of abuse, only that these factors are the most common.

Does ritual abuse of children really occur? Probably no subject in family violence has generated as much controversy as the topic of ritual abuse of children does. Some critics have suggested that the symptoms are therapist enhanced, whereas others claim that ritual abuse clearly exists and is more widespread than believed.

As the prior discussion indicates, many controversies exist in the field of family violence. Where appropriate, these subjects are examined in more detail in the chapters that deal with the specific form of abuse. These controversies should not create anxiety or apprehension, but they present a series of exciting and stimulating ideas that should cause healthy discussion and debate among all those interested in this topic.

NATURE AND SCOPE OF THE PROBLEM

The National Family Violence Surveys

Two of the most comprehensive studies of family violence were carried out by Murray Straus and Richard J. Gelles in 1975 and 1985.[7] Both surveys involved interviews with a nationally representative sample of 2,143 respondents in 1975 and 6,014 respondents in 1985. The results of these landmark surveys continue to provide information and data for the study of family violence. Even though the surveys are dated, they are continually cited as authoritative in numerous textbooks, articles, and research projects.

In both surveys, *violence* was defined as an act carried out with the intention or perceived intention of causing physical pain or injury to another person. Acts of violence that had a high probability of causing injury were included even if injury did not occur. Violence was measured by using the Conflict Tactics Scale (CTS). This tool was developed at the University of New Hampshire in 1971 and is still used today in many studies of family violence. The CTS measures three variables: use of rational discussion and agreement, use of verbal and nonverbal expressions of hostility, and use of physical force or violence. Respondents were asked how many times within the last year they used certain responses that fell within one of the three classifications when they had a disagreement or were angry with family members.

Both studies were judged to be reliable because of the sampling procedure, the large number of respondents, and the validity of the CTS as a measuring instrument. The studies surveyed families from all fifty states and assessed many different relationships: parent to child, child to parent, wife to husband, husband to wife, and sibling interactions. Interviews were conducted by trained investigators and lasted about one hour in the 1975 study and thirty minutes in the 1985 survey.

Other Sources of Data on Family Violence

Other social surveys have added to our knowledge of family violence. *Rape in America,* conducted by the National Victims Center, shed new light on this form of aggression, and a survey of Boston residents examined elder abuse. Both surveys are discussed in detail later.

Clinical studies are another source of information regarding family violence. These studies are carried out by practitioners in the field—medical professionals, psychiatrists,

Focus

Conflict Tactics Scale

The conflict tactics scale (CTS) is the most widely used instrument in conducting research on family violence. It is also one of the most widely criticized instruments. There are two versions of the scale; the CTS2 which is an expanded version of the original scale and the CTSPC (CTS parent-child) version. The scales are based on the premise that conflict is an inevitable aspect of all human association. The CTS focuses on conflict tactics and measures one's own interest within a conflict as a behavior. It also measures the conflict tactics of both the victim and the abuser.

The revised CTS2 uses a total of 39 behaviors which are subdivided into five categories and each category is further subdivided into two subscales.[8] CTS2 questions are presented in pairs. The first question in the pair asks respondents to indicate how often they carried out each item, in a range from never to more than 20 times, in the referent period. The second asks how often the partner carried out each item within the same referent period. Referent periods are usually 12 months, but other spans of time may be used. Subscales measuring the degree of severity of less severe and more severe behaviors are included for all CTS scales, based on the presumed greater harm resulting from acts in the severe subscale.

The severity of behaviors can also be measured by analyzing the frequency of the acts and by whether an injury was reported by the respondent. For example, in the sexual coercion category a question may include the following choices: Have you ever insisted on sex with your partner when the partner did not want sex (considered as minor) or forced your partner to engage in sex (considered as major). The possible answers that can be selected are: never, once, twice, 3–5 times, 6–10 times, 11–20 times, and more than 20 times.[9]

psychologists, and counselors—all of whom use samples gathered from actual cases of family violence. These researchers collect information from hospitals, clinics, and therapy sessions. Clinical studies normally have small sample sizes, and therefore, caution must be used when drawing any conclusions. However, these studies provide valuable data on the nature of abuse and assist in evaluating the different types of interventions used in family violence as well as pointing out areas for further research.

Many different types of official reports are compiled by private or public agencies in the form of statistical data. These provide a much-needed resource for further research into family violence. The most commonly relied on are reports by local law enforcement agencies, the American Humane Society, the Uniform Crime Reports (UCR), and the National Crime Victimization Survey (NCVS).

Since adoption of the mandatory reporting laws for child abuse, and in some states mandatory arrest of those accused of intimate partner abuse, local agencies have been able to provide researchers with a wealth of information regarding family violence. This information is usually limited to a specific geographic location and therefore does not reflect any national perspective.

The Violence against Women Act provided a fundamental change in the criminal justice system's gathering of information on violent crimes committed against women. A 1996 report of Congress indicated that both the federal government and most states are collecting data on family violence.[10] This report points out two continuing controversies: the need for

Focus

Data Collection: National Crime Victimization Surveys (NCVS)

NCVS is the nation's primary source of information on criminal victimization. Each year, data are obtained from a nationally representative sample of about 90,000 households, comprising nearly 160,000 persons, on the frequency, characteristics, and consequences of criminal victimization in the United States. Each household is interviewed twice during the year. The survey enables BJS to estimate the likelihood of victimization by rape or sexual assault, robbery, aggravated and simple assault, theft, household burglary, and motor vehicle theft for the population as a whole as well as for segments of the population such as women, the elderly, members of various racial or ethnic groups, city dwellers, and other groups. The NCVS provides the largest national forum for victims to describe the impact of crime and characteristics of violent offenders.

Source: U.S. Bureau of Justice Statistics Web site, accessed September 1, 2015 at www.bjs.gov/index.cfm?ty=dcdetail&iid=245.

uniform definitions and the need to include data from other parts of the criminal justice system.[11]

The UCR is this country's oldest form of criminal statistics. During the 1920s, the International Association of Chiefs of Police (IACP) formed the Commission on Uniform Crime Reports to develop a uniform system of reporting criminal statistics. The committee evaluated various crimes on the basis of their seriousness, frequency of occurrence, commonality across the nation, and likelihood of being reported to the police. In 1929, the committee finished its study and recommended a plan for crime reporting that became the foundation of the UCR program. Eight crimes were chosen to serve as an index for determining fluctuations in the overall rate of crime. These crimes became known as the "crime index" and included the following: murder, manslaughter, forcible rape, robbery, aggravated assault, burglary, larceny-theft, and motor vehicle theft. In 1979, Congress mandated that arson be added to the index. In 1930, Congress enacted federal law that authorized the attorney general to gather crime information.[12] The attorney general designated the FBI as the national clearinghouse for all data, and since that time data based on this system have been obtained from the nation's law enforcement agencies.

The UCR program is a nationwide statistical compilation involving more than 1,600 cities, counties, and state law enforcement agencies that voluntarily report data on reported crimes. Law enforcement agencies in the UCR program represented more than 245 million inhabitants, or about 95 percent of the total population of the United States. The program is administrated by the FBI, which issues assessments on the nature and type of crime. The program's primary objective is to generate a set of reliable criminal statistics for use in law enforcement administration, operation, and management.[13]

The FBI administers the UCR program and issues periodic reports addressing the nature and type of crime in the United States. While the UCR's primary objective is to issue reliable statistics for use by law enforcement agencies, it has also become an important social indicator of deviance in our society.

The UCR prepares an annual crime index composed of selected offenses used to gauge changes in the overall rate of crime reported to law enforcement agencies. The crime index is composed of the index crimes discussed previously. Therefore, the index is a combination of violent and property crimes. Approximately 14 percent of the index offenses are violent crimes, and 86 percent are property crimes.

The UCR is an annual report, which includes the number of crimes reported by citizens to local police departments and the number of arrests made by law enforcement agencies in a given year. This information is of somewhat limited value as the data are based on instances of violence classified as criminal and reported to the local law enforcement agencies. Many serious acts of violence are not reported to the police and therefore do not become part of the UCR. The UCR does not provide detailed information needed to document the full extent of family violence-related events known to law enforcement agencies.

With the exception of the Hate Crime Statistics Act of 1990, the UCR remained virtually unchanged for fifty years. Eventually, various law enforcement agencies began to call for an evaluation and redesign of the program. Because the UCR lists only crimes that are reported to it, this presents a serious problem, as not all police agencies report crimes to the FBI and the Department of Justice. Also, because the UCR relies on law enforcement agencies to report crimes voluntarily, underreporting by some agencies for political reasons is possible.[14] The UCR generally provides only tabular summaries of crime and does not provide crime analysts with more meaningful information. In addition, the method of counting crimes causes problems. For example, only the most serious crime is reported. If a person is robbed and his car has been stolen, police agencies are instructed to report only the robbery. Finally, some crimes, such as white-collar crime, are excluded from the UCR system. After several years of study, the FBI began to institute various modifications to the UCR program. These changes established a new, more effective crime-reporting system.

The redesigned UCR program is called the National Incident-Based Reporting System (NIBRS). In 1989, the FBI began accepting data, and nine states started supplying information in the new format. The NIBRS collects data on each single incident and arrest within twenty-two crime categories. Incident, victim, property, offender, and arrestee information is gathered for each offense known to the local agency. The NIBRS provides much-needed detailed information regarding family violence-related offenses. Although the NIBRS standard includes a major data collection system specifically related to the relationship between family violence and victim-offender, it does not measure other aspects of family violence.[15] The goal of the redesigned system was to modernize crime reporting information by collecting data presently maintained in law enforcement records. The enhanced UCR program is a byproduct of modern law enforcement records systems that have the capability to store and collate more information regarding criminal offenses. While it has taken almost 30 years, NIBRS is gradually replacing the UCRs as the primary program used by law enforcement for measuring crime.

The NCVS attempts to correct the problems on non-reporting inherent in the UCR by contacting a nationwide sample and by interviewing citizens regarding victimization. The report was originally called the National Crime Survey (NCS) but was renamed to reflect more clearly its emphasis on the measurement of victimizations experienced by citizens. Since 1972, the NCVS has collected detailed information about certain criminal offenses, both attempted and completed, that concern the general public and law enforcement. These offenses include the frequency and nature of rape, robbery, assault, household burglary, personal and household theft, and motor vehicle theft.[16] The NCVS does not measure homicide or commercial crime.

A single crime may have more than one victim. For example, a bank robbery may involve several bank tellers. Therefore, a single incident may have more than one victimization. A victimization, the basic measure of the occurrence of crime, is a specific criminal act because it affects a specific victim. The number of victimizations, however, is determined by the number of victims of each specific criminal act.

The NCVS is an annual survey of citizens conducted by the U.S. Bureau of the Census in cooperation with the Bureau of Justice Statistics of the U.S. Department of Justice. Census Bureau personnel conduct interviews with all household members over the age of twelve. These households stay in the sample for three years and are interviewed every six months. The total sample size of this survey is about 66,000 households with 101,000 individuals.[17]

The NCVS provides data regarding the victims of crime, including age, sex, race, ethnicity, marital status, income, and educational level as well as information about the offender. Questions covering the victim's experience with the justice system, details regarding any self-protective measures used by the victims, and possible substance abuse by offenders are included in the survey. Periodic supplemental questionnaires address specific issues, such as school crime.

The NCVS has been modified by the Bureau of Justice Statistics as a result of a number of problems, including the underreporting of family violence and sexual violence incidents.[18] The revised survey was fully implemented for the 1993 data set, and the first data from the survey became available in 1994. The first analysis of this information became available in 1996. The report now covers trends in intimate violence, characteristics of victims, types of crimes, and trends in reporting to the police. Intimate victimizations measured include rape and sexual assault, robbery, aggravated assault, and simple assault. A recent report of the NCVS shows that violent victimization has decreased. This should not stop us from continuing to research family violence because the report also points out that among 5.7 million violent victimizations in 2001, most female victims faced someone they knew. Intimate violence and violence by friends and acquaintances continue to be a critical issue we must address.[19]

The NCVS continues to suffer from problems that mitigate its validity, such as respondents underreporting or over reporting crimes. The NCVS is based on an extensive scientific sample of American households. Therefore, every crime measure presented in the NCVS report is an estimate based on results of the sample. Because measures are only estimates, they will have a sampling variation or margin of error associated with each sample. In addition, these estimates are only of criminal activity and do not mean that the crime actually occurred.

Another survey measuring family violence was the National Violence against Women (NVAW) Survey, a national telephone survey of adults coordinated by the National Institute of Justice and the Centers for Disease Control and Prevention (CDC). The NVAW focused on the relationship between certain types of violence against women (child abuse) and later victimization as adults. It also examined minority women's experiences with violence and attempted to address the consequences of violence. The NVAW was different from other studies in that both men and women were surveyed, both prevalence rates (number of victims) and incidence rates (number of incidents) were gathered, and it used behaviorally specific questions to minimize any misunderstanding about the type of information sought. The information supplied by the report has led to a number of publications, including one by the Department of Justice and the CDC. The impact of its information is still being studied.

Each of the methods of collecting data on family violence presents a different perspective and has its own validity problems. What is certain is that family violence occurs on all social and economic levels in our nation. Its toll on victims is severe and long-lasting. No matter which statistic or sample is used, professionals agree that further research is necessary.

Focus

Serious Intimate Partner Violence Against Females Declined 72 Percent From 1994 to 2011

In a November 21, 2013 press release, the Bureau of Justice Statistics announced that:

From 1994 to 2011, the rate of serious intimate partner violence, such as rape, sexual assault, robbery, or aggravated assault, declined 72 percent for females. During the same time, the percentage of female intimate partner victims who were physically attacked, attacked with a weapon, injured, or required medical treatment remained relatively stable.

Nonfatal intimate partner violence includes serious violence and simple assault committed by an offender who is the victim's current or former spouse, boyfriend, or girlfriend. The severity of intimate partner violence is measured by the type of violent crime, type of physical attack, whether the victim was threatened before the attack, presence of a weapon, victim injury, and medical treatment. Estimates of nonfatal violence are based on data from the National Crime Victimization Survey, which collects self-reported information from victims of crime.

During the most recent 10-year period (2002–11), the offender physically attacked the victim in more than two-thirds of intimate partner victimizations against females (67 percent). In about half of female victimizations (52 percent), the intimate partner threatened to harm the victim prior to the physical attack. In addition, about 5 percent of female victims were hit by an object their intimate partner held or threw at them, 36 percent were grabbed, held, tripped, jumped on or pushed, and 8 percent suffered sexual violence.

In 2011, 18 percent of intimate partner victimizations against females involved a weapon, similar to the percentage observed in 1994. In 2002–11, about 4 percent of nonfatal female intimate partner victims were shot at, stabbed, or hit with a weapon. About half of intimate partner victimizations against females resulted in physical injury, with 13 percent suffering serious physical injury such as gun shot or knife wounds, internal injuries, unconsciousness, or broken bones.

Between 2002 and 2011, about 18 percent of female intimate partner victimizations resulted in medical treatment for victim injuries.

In addition to estimates for nonfatal female victimizations, the report includes for comparison the number of homicides committed by intimates, estimates of nonfatal male intimate partner violence, and non-intimate partner violence.

Estimates of male intimate partner violence include:

- From 1994 to 2011, the rate of serious violence (rape, sexual assault, robbery, and aggravated assault) committed by an intimate partner declined 64 percent for males.
- During the most recent 10-year period (2002–2011), nonfatal serious violence accounted for more than a third of intimate partner violence against males (39 percent).
- Aggravated assault (22 percent) accounted for the largest percentage of serious intimate partner violence against males, followed by robbery (16 percent).

(continued)

- Rape or sexual assault (1 percent) accounted for the smallest percentage of intimate violence experienced by males.
- Sixty-five percent of male victims of intimate partner violence were physically attacked by the offender, and in almost a third of male victimizations (31 percent) the intimate partner threatened to harm the victim before the physical attack.
- A weapon was present in 27 percent of male intimate partner victimizations, and about 8 percent of males victimized by an intimate partner were shot at, stabbed, or hit with a weapon.
- Of the 3,032 homicides involving female victims in 2010 (the most recent year), 39 percent were committed by an intimate, 37 percent by a non-intimate, and 24 percent by an offender with an unknown relationship to the victim. Among the 10,878 homicide incidents involving male victims in 2010, 3 percent were committed by an intimate, 48 percent by a non-intimate, and 50 percent by an offender with an unknown relationship to the victim.

The Rate of Intimate Partner Violence Remained Stable From 2013 to 2014

The rate of domestic violence, which includes crime committed by intimate partners and family members, remained stable from 2013 to 2014 (4.2 per 1,000). No measurable change was detected from 2013 to 2014 in the rate of intimate partner violence (2.4 per 1,000), which includes victimizations committed by current or former spouses, boyfriends, or girlfriends.

From 2013 to 2014, no statistically significant change was observed in the rate of violent victimizations committed by a stranger (8.1 per 1,000). However, the rate of violence committed by a stranger in 2014 was 30 percent lower than the rate 10 years earlier in 2005 (11.6 per 1,000). No statistically significant difference was found in rates of serious violent crime involving weapons (4.9 per 1,000) or resulting in physical injury to the victim (2.6 per 1,000) from 2013 to 2014. Like violent victimizations committed by a stranger, the rate of serious violent crime involving weapons in 2014 was 28 percent lower than the rate in 2005 (6.8 per 1,000).

Source: S. Catalano "Intimate Partner Violence: Attributes of Victimization, 1993–2011" (NCJ 243300) (2013), available on the BJS Web site at /www.bjs.gov/, accessed September 1, 2015, and J. Truman and L.Langton "Criminal Victimization, 2014" (August 2015). Available on BJS Web site, accessed September 7, 2015.

FACTORS THAT CONTRIBUTE TO FAMILY VIOLENCE

Researchers have interviewed, tested, observed, and evaluated thousands of people in an attempt to discover the factors that contribute to family violence. Unfortunately, to date no one authority has discovered the single correct answer. However, it is incumbent on all professionals to have at least a cursory knowledge of the more commonly cited theories of family violence. These theories may be grouped into three main models or categories: the psychiatric classifications, the social-psychological models, and the sociocultural models.

The Psychiatric Model of Family Violence

The psychiatric model tries to understand family violence by analyzing the offender's personality traits and mental status. Some professionals also include individual characteristics of the victim in this approach. This model characterizes personality disorders, mental illness, and substance abuse as the primary causes of family violence.

THE PSYCHOPATHOLOGY THEORY.   The **psychopathology theory** is grounded on the concept that certain individuals suffer from mental illness, personality disorders, and other dysfunctions that cause them to engage in aggressive acts within the family. This mental disorder, or illness, causes the individual to react violently within the family.[20] It is not surprising that this theory was first proposed by those in the medical profession. Psychiatrists, clinicians, and psychologists were exposed to family violence because of their close association with the medical personnel who treated the victims. Although this is still a popular theory, researchers have failed to isolate any particular mental disorder common to those who abuse that distinguishes those who engage in violent behavior from the rest of the population. In addition, attempts to distinguish the personality traits of those who engage in family violence and to compare those characteristics with individuals who are not abusive have been inconsistent and difficult to apply in practice.[21] Furthermore, many individuals who suffer from various forms of mental illness do not engage in aggressive behavior.

The problem with the psychopathology model is its failure to explain which personality traits are associated with family violence. In addition, focusing on mental illness as a cause of violence ignores the fact that many violent individuals are not considered mentally ill.

THE SUBSTANCE ABUSE THEORY.   Many laypersons and nonprofessionals believe that alcohol or drugs cause family violence. The **substance abuse theory** accepts the proposition that drugs or alcohols cause or contribute to family violence. This theory is based on the concept that these substances impair judgment and lessen inhibitions and thereby allow violent acts to occur. Some authorities believe that these substances do not cause family violence. Rather, they are used as an excuse for violent acts.[22]

Numerous studies have linked alcohol or drugs to violent behavior, but no concrete evidence establishes that these substances directly cause family violence. In addition, this theory fails to explain why everyone who uses alcohol or drugs does not engage in violent acts.

The Social-Psychological Model of Family Violence

The social-psychological model analyzes external environmental factors that affect the family unit. Factors such as stress, family structure, the intergenerational transmission of violence, and family interactions are all considered as primary causes of family violence. Because of the controversy surrounding the intergenerational transmission of violence theory, it is discussed in more detail later in this chapter.

THE SOCIAL LEARNING THEORY.   This theory assumes that the type of behavior most frequently reinforced by others is the one most often exhibited by the individual. The **social learning theory** is an integration of differential associations with differential reinforcements so that the people with whom one interacts are the reinforcers of behavior that results in learning both deviant and nondeviant behavior.[23]

The social learning process is accomplished by two important mechanisms: modeling and reinforcement. Modeling is an important tool in learning behavior. Children learn by watching and imitating others. This role-model situation results in children adopting the behavior they observe in adults, including aggressive acts. Reinforcement occurs when certain behavior is rewarded and other behavior is punished. Studies have shown that behavior can be modified by praise more effectively than by punitive actions. Social learning continues as children mature and enter school and begin to interact with other children and adults. This process of interaction results in modification of behavior as the individual ages.

The social learning theory has been criticized as failing to explain certain kinds of spontaneous acts of aggression within the family, such as a frustrated parent who suddenly slaps a crying child.

THE EXCHANGE THEORY.   The **exchange theory** is based on the premise that persons act according to a system of rewards or punishments.[24] The exchange theory argues that family violence is based on a determination of costs and rewards. Gelles accepted the basic premise of the exchange theory and modified it to apply to family violence situations. He entitled this approach the *exchange/social control theory*.[25] As Gelles has stated, "To put it simply, people hit family members because they can."[26] Interaction within the family is based on a pursuit of rewards and an avoidance of costs or punishments. Family members resort to violence to obtain goals as long as what they achieve is outweighed by the cost of aggression. The absence of social controls over family relations increases the likelihood that family members will engage in violence. The privacy of the family unit and the subsequent low risk of intervention decrease the cost of violence, thereby allowing it to occur.[27]

THE FRUSTRATION-AGGRESSION THEORY.   The **frustration-aggression theory** is based on the premise that human beings display aggression toward objects that impede their achievement of certain goals.[28] In a family situation, there are many instances in which parties attempt to obtain certain goals or objectives. Frustration may result when the attainment of those goals is blocked. Failure to attain desired goals can lead to aggression within the family by the frustrated party.

This theory does not explain the complexities of modern society. All of us at one time or another become frustrated. However, we do not automatically react with aggressive actions. The socialization process teaches people how to react to frustration. This process varies from culture to culture and group to group, so that what is accepted as an appropriate response to frustration by one culture may not be condoned by another group.

THE ECOLOGICAL THEORY.   The **ecological theory** is based on an analysis of the organism and the environment, the interacting systems in which family development occurs, and the environment in which the family resides.[29] Garbarino established two conditions that must be present under this theory for child abuse to occur: The environment in which the family lives must accept the use of force against children, and the family must be isolated from supporting community services or systems.[30] The ecological theory assumes that family violence occurs when the parent, child, and family are mismatched with the neighborhood and community. According to this theory, children who are disabled or otherwise below the expected norm in a society face the highest risk of abuse.[31] The interaction between spouses having to deal with the stress of parenting a disabled child increases the tension within the family. The final aspect of this theory views the total environment and suggests that if no agencies are available to support or assist the family, then the risk of abuse is greatly increased.

THE SOCIOBIOLOGY OR EVOLUTIONARY THEORY.   The **sociobiology or evolutionary theory** is based on the concept that parents display aggressive acts toward children who are not their own or do not have the potential to reproduce. This concept postulates that individuals behave in certain ways so as to increase their chances of reproducing. One scholar theorizes that male aggression against females illustrates the effects of the male reproductive urges.[32] Male humans and primates use aggression as a form of intimidation against females so that they will not resist efforts to mate with them. The sociobiology or evolutionary theory assumes that parents will not emotionally attach or invest themselves to children with low reproductive potential.[33] Under this theory, stepchildren or children with low reproductive potential, such as children with disabilities, are at a higher risk of abuse than normal, healthy children. Thus, the risk of abuse is higher where there is a lack of bonding between the child and the parent.

The Sociocultural Model of Family Violence

The sociocultural model of family violence focuses on the roles of men and women in our society as well as on the cultural attitudes toward women and the acceptance of violence as a cause of family violence. This is a macrolevel of analysis that focuses on the variables that cause violence.

THE CULTURE OF VIOLENCE THEORY.   Wolfgang and Ferracuti argue that certain subcultures within the United States accept values that justify the use of force.[34] The **culture of violence theory** is based on the premise that violence is unevenly distributed within our society, and that violence is more prevalent in the lower socioeconomic sectors of society.[35] These subcultures use force as a response more often than the general population. This theory assumes that violence is a learned response and reflects a socialization or acceptance of violence as appropriate behavior.

One of the main limitations of this theory is that it does not explain how subcultural values originate or are modified. Furthermore, this theory limits the learning of violence to certain socioeconomic subcultures. However, violence portrayed in the media is received by all classes within our society.

As shocking as television violence is, it graphically illustrates how prevalent violence is within our society today. For the most part, our society glamorizes violence. This approval of violence and aggression is primarily a male perspective. Males believe it is macho to be strong, assertive, and aggressive.[36] As is discussed in later chapters, this view of violence and masculinity contributes to aggression toward women.

Violence is an everyday part of our existence. Sporting events, children's toys, cartoons, video games, movies, television, and the media's graphic depiction of violence all contribute to our desensitization to the effects of violence and contribute to an attitude that aggressive behavior is rewarded and condoned by society.[37]

Sporting events are often displays of violence. Professional wrestling is not so much a contest of strength and agility as it is entertainment featuring uncontrolled aggression, women clad in revealing bathing suits escorting the wrestlers, and frenzied crowds yelling

Focus

Worldwide Violence Against Women

"This is what statistics tell us that up to seven in ten that means of course 70 per- cent of women globally will be beaten, raped, abused, or mutilated in their lifetime. This pandemic strikes the lives of millions of women, fractures families and communities, and impedes development, costing also countries billions of dollars each year in health care cost and lost productivity. And I really cannot say strongly enough: the 21st century has no place for violence against women."

The head of the United Nations Entity for Gender Equality and the Empowerment of Women posted on UN Women's Web site at www.unmultimedia.org/radio/english/2013/03/twentieth-century-has-no-place-for-violence-against-women-un-women, accessed July 25, 2015.

for the champion to destroy the contender. Fights between players are a common occurrence in football, ice hockey, baseball, and basketball. Some international soccer matches end with hundreds of fans fighting each other on the field. Aggressive behavior and violence are rewarded by large signing bonuses, and those athletes who display it are accorded the status of celebrities.

Children's toys and the advertisements that promote them are a study in violence and marketing. Young children can buy toy soldiers, monsters that fire futuristic weapons, cars that crash into buildings, and all sorts of other violent playthings. As children mature, they "graduate" from toy soldiers to toy guns. The M-16 assault rifle made of plastic and painted in camouflage colors is a favorite for the preteen age group. The real M-16 has been used in a number of shootings across the nation.

Cartoons animate violent behavior. The "Roadrunner" series is an excellent example of how violent acts are interwoven into cartoons. In other cartoons, make-believe characters fight evil by attacking with weapons, fists, hands, feet, and elbows. On any Saturday morning, the airwaves are filled with animated violence.

Video games and arcades promote and reward superior skills in violence. If players can destroy the enemy ships, persons, or planes, they are rewarded with an additional free game. Martial arts are used by the hero in his attempt to either rescue the lady or prevent the world from being destroyed.

VIOLENCE AND THE MEDIA.   Television, music, and video games have a direct impact on our everyday lives. This is especially true regarding children and teenagers. Physicians who treat children are aware of this aspect of modern life. Concerns regarding the effect of violence in the media on the public health are not a new phenomenon. In 1952, when television was in its infancy, an editorial in *The Journal of the American Medical Association* raised this issue.[38] At the same time, Congress began holding hearings on juvenile delinquency and violence in the media. In the late 1960s, the top public health official in the United States, the U.S. surgeon general, researched this issue and concluded that violence in the media did in fact adversely affect some children.[39]

Just as other technological changes have affected our society, so have the increased tempo and changes in our communications systems and technology altered our beliefs and approaches to problems. The positive effects of television and videos on children can be classified as follows:[40]

Cognitive Skills. Television can be effective in the development of a variety of academic skills, such as reading, math, and other skills. Anyone who has watched *Sesame Street* is familiar with the presentation of these skills.

Academic Content. Many different forms of knowledge are presented over television. Shows on networks such as the Discovery Channel and the History Channel are just two examples.

Prosocial Behavior. A number of studies support the proposition that children can learn positive behavioral patterns, such as cooperation and other traits, from public and private television.

Nutrition and Health. Television can provide a wide range of information regarding various public health issues, from closure of beaches due to pollution to advances in medicine.

Social and Political Issues. The nature of democracy is explored on television every four years when the major networks cover the presidential elections.

Just as there are major beneficial aspects to television, so are there detrimental effects or adverse impacts from this medium. The following is a summary of the more common negative effects discussed by various experts:[41]

Lack of Exercise. Watching television is inherently sedentary. It takes time from more healthy activities, such as walking, sports, and so on.

Unhealthy Eating Habits. We, as a society, are growing larger and fatter. Many people who watch television snack and do not exercise, leading to increased weight.

Solitary in Nature. Television is a solitary activity and reduces meaningful social interaction with family, friends, and others.

Behavioral Messages. There is a growing body of research that supports the proposition that television desensitizes youth to violence and other forms of unacceptable social behavior.

Is it any wonder that we as a society accept violence as part of our culture? It is nearly impossible to avoid. We would have to live in the mountains, refuse to purchase certain toys for our children, never read the local paper, and refrain from watching television to escape being inundated with our society's violent and aggressive acts.

THE PATRIARCHY THEORY.   Dobash and Dobash have advanced the **patriarchy theory** to explain violence toward women. The patriarchy theory views society as dominated by males, with women in subordinate positions, treated by men as possessions and things.[42] According to the feminist perspective, social and economic norms directly and indirectly support a patriarchal structure within our society. The patriarchy theory holds that laws and customs combine to uphold this difference in power between men and women and legitimize their different status. This approach views male domination as explaining the historical pattern of violence toward women throughout the ages.

TABLE 1.1	Major Theories of Family Violence	
Psychiatric Theories	**Social-Psychological Theories**	**Sociocultural Theories**
Psychopathology	Social Learning	Culture of Violence
Substance Abuse	Exchange	Patriarchy

THE GENERAL SYSTEMS THEORY. The **general systems theory** views the maintenance of violence as a result of the social system in which families live. It assumes that violence within the family is a result of a system rather than individual pathology of the family member.[43] This family system operates to maintain, increase, or decrease levels of violence within the family. Straus proposes that a general system of family violence contain three elements: alternative courses of action, a method of feedback, and system goals.[44] Under Straus's approach, violence within the family has many causes. Whenever a family member engages in violence, there is or may be positive feedback because the violence produced the desired results. Finally, Straus points out that whenever violence occurs, family members who engage in these acts fulfill their own self-concept of being violent.

THE SOCIAL CONFLICT THEORY. This **social conflict theory** analyzes large-scale conflicts, marriages, and the communication process.[45] It proposes that unacknowledged alienation and shame generate violence within the family. A theory of escalation is central to this concept and holds that escalation of conflict or violence occurs when anger and shame within a relationship are not acknowledged.

THE RESOURCE THEORY. The **resource theory** is based on the proposition that the one who controls resources, such as money, property, or prestige, is in the dominant position in a relationship.[46] It holds that the use of violence within a relationship depends on the resources a family member controls. The more resources one commands, the more force or power he can muster. Because men hold higher-paying jobs with more prestige, they will have more power in relationships than women. Some authorities argue that the more resources available to the male, the more force he can use. With this abundance of power, however, there is less likelihood of his employing force. Those males who have no resources such as high-paying jobs or status tend to resort to violence more often as a way of controlling the spouse.[47]

Common Features of Family Violence

As the preceding discussion illustrates, numerous theories exist on the causes of family violence. These theories approach family violence from a variety of perspectives. No one theory, however, is accepted by all scholars as the cause of this form of aggression. Other researchers have attempted to isolate certain factors that are common in all forms of family violence.[48] Still others have focused on the distinctions between family violence and other forms of violence. Tolan's work lists several factors that make family violence unique:

- First, in contrast to other forms of violence, family violence requires a relationship between the parties.

- Second, these relationships usually exist between the parties before, during, and after incidents of family violence.
- Third, certain forms of violence are more common in families than in other contexts of violence.
- Fourth, in some societies, family violence has a different legal meaning than other forms of violence.[49]

Each of these characteristics is discussed in more detail in the chapters that examine specific forms of family violence. However, to aid in understanding the dynamics of this form of aggression, the following discussion briefly examines some of the more common forces present in all forms of family violence.

ISOLATION.   Family violence is the most private form of aggression. The concept of the privacy of the family, coupled with isolation, diminishes outside social control, lessens input from others, and increases the opportunity for violence. Whether it is a child who is physically or sexually abused or a spouse who is battered, the assault occurs in private, and the victims are isolated from the normal support systems in our society. As the level of privacy in a family increases, the level of social control decreases. What one person may do in private is different from what that same person will do in public.

Isolation is a common characteristic of intimate partner abuse. The abuser will curtail the spouse's outside contacts and, eventually, she will believe that she is alone and helpless to prevent his assaults. Child abuse does not occur in a public environment. Children who are

Continued efforts are needed to stop family violence.

Focus and Practicum

Violence in the Media

In September 2000, the chairman of the Federal Trade Commission (FTC) addressed a United States Senate committee regarding the marketing of violent entertainment. The following is a summary of his remarks.

The FTC report on marketing violence by the entertainment industries addresses two questions: (1) Do the motion picture, music recording, and electronic game industries promote products they themselves acknowledge warrant parental caution in venues where children make up a substantial percentage of the audience? (2) Are these advertisements intended to attract children and teenagers? The commission has found that the answer to both questions is plainly yes. Although all three industries studied have self-regulatory systems that purport to rate or label their products to help parents make choices about their children's entertainment, the commission found that members of all three industries routinely target advertising and marketing for violent entertainment products directly to children.

The FTC is the federal government's primary consumer protection agency. On June 1, 1999, following the horrifying school shooting in Littleton, Colorado, President Bill Clinton requested that the Federal Trade Commission and the Department of Justice conduct a study of whether violent entertainment material was being advertised and promoted to children and teenagers. Revelations that the teenaged shooters at Columbine High School in Littleton had been infatuated with extremely violent movies, music, and video games reinvigorated public debate about the effects of violent entertainment media on youth.

The Study

If you were researching the two questions the Federal Trade Commission was examining, what type of information/data would you attempt to gather? How would you go about this research?

The commission collected information from the principal industry trade associations, and from the motion picture, music recording, and electronic game industries regarding their self-regulatory systems and marketing practices. In addition, the commission contacted interested government agencies, medical associations, academics, and parent and consumer advocacy groups. It reviewed a substantial amount of information collected from consumers through various surveys and polls, and it also designed and conducted its own surveys for this study. The FTC also conducted an undercover survey of retail stores and movie theaters to see whether unaccompanied children under seventeen could purchase or gain access to products labeled as inappropriate or warranting parental guidance. Finally, the commission reviewed Internet sites to study how they are used to market and directly access these products.

The Findings

In 2004, in a follow-up to the original study, the commission found that on the whole the industry continues to comply with their self-regulatory limits on violence in the media. However, the commission found that all three industries continue to advertise violent R-rated movies, explicit-content labeled recordings, and mature (M-rated) games in media with large teen audiences. In addition, the commission found that youth can still purchase rated or labeled entertainment products at a significant number of stores and theaters.

Movies

The movie industry continues to advertise and promote R-rated films in some media and venues popular with youth. In addition, retailers do not appear to be effectively restricting youth from purchasing R-rated DVDs, despite the existence of policies adopted by some retailers. Movie

(continued)

theaters have shown some improvement in barring unaccompanied children under seventeen from purchasing tickets to R-rated films.

Music

Although industry members continue to advertise explicit-content labeled recordings on cable music channels and wrestling programs popular with teens, advertising on other television shows is almost nonexistent. Retailers need to take additional steps to limit the sale of music with parental advisories to children.

Games

The electronic game industry has adopted numerous standards that limit children's exposure to ads for M-rated products. The industry is actively enforcing those standards and penalizing those companies found to be in noncompliance. Yet, these standards still permit and industry members continue to place advertisements in television and print media with substantial youth audiences. Retailers still routinely make sales of M-rated products to most buyers without regard to age.

Recommendations

If you were making recommendations, what would you focus on?

The commission believes that all three industries should take additional action to enhance their self-regulatory efforts, including the following:

1. Establish or expand codes that prohibit target marketing to children and impose sanctions for noncompliance.
2. Increase compliance at the retail level.
3. Increase parental understanding of the ratings and labels.

The commission emphasizes that its proposal to improve self-regulations is not designed to regulate or even influence the content of movies, music lyrics, or electronic games. The First Amendment generally requires that creative decisions about content be left to artists and their distributors.

Arguments Against the Commission's Report

What arguments or positions can you advance to counter the commission's report?

1. The commission is condemning an entire industry for the acts of a few members.
2. Simply targeting a population does not mean that an industry believes they should be admitted without parental supervision. That is why the ratings state minors must be accompanied by an adult.
3. The industry is being blamed for lack of control by parents and retail outlets such as stores and theaters.
4. The First Amendment prohibits restrictions that regulate expression of ideas, and restrictions on R-rated movies might infringe on First Amendment rights.

Sources: Based on the statement of Chairman Robert Pitofsky on "Marketing Violent Entertainment to Children: A Review of Self-Regulation and Industry Practices in the Motion Picture, Music Recording, and Electronic Game Industries," before the Committee on Commerce, Science, and Transportation, United States Senate, Washington, D.C., September 13, 2000, www.ftc.gov/os/2000/violencerepttest.html, accessed September 15, 2000; and *Marketing Violent Entertainment to Children: A Fourth Follow-up Review of Industry Practices in the Motion Picture, Music Recording and Electronic Game Industries, A Report to Congress* (Federal Trade Commission, Washington, D.C., July 2004).

molested are told to keep the act secret, or they will be punished. Elders suffer abuse in their own homes at the hands of their caretakers.

A support system within the community and among other family members may, for some persons, act as a regulator or inhibitor of family violence. If the victim receives input from others outside the immediate family, she may have the courage to leave the abuser. Social interaction may also provide a means to defuse potentially hostile situations by allowing the parties to talk with others whom they respect and love.

POWER DIFFERENTIALS.   The persons with the most power or resources have the ability to impose their will on other members of the family. This difference in power allows the spouse or parent to use force on the less powerful mate or child. This characteristic of power differentials is present in both intimate partner and child abuse. Finkelhor points out that abuse tends to gravitate toward relationships with the greatest power differential[50]

Many professionals argue for reducing this power differential. As a result of a number of forces in society, the power differential in relationships is decreasing. More and more women are leaving their home to take positions in government and industry, and as a result they are slowly beginning to raise their power level to that of men. Children are taught that they have the right (power) to say "no" to sexual advances. Child victims are now represented in some court hearings by attorneys who must look out for the children's best interests. Battered women's shelters have been established, and laws have been passed in some states that mandate the arrest of any spouse who batters the other. These accomplishments have not diminished the difference in power between men and women to any great degree, but they represent a trend that society must continue to encourage.

POWER/POWERLESSNESS.   This characteristic occurs when a person perceives that he or she has a lack of power or control in the work or social environment but has power in relationship to other persons in his family. The person has power over less powerful individuals. Power in this context is defined as the ability to control the behavior of others, with or without

Family violence, also known as domestic violence, takes many forms.

their consent.[51] Applying these concepts to a family environment, it is easy to see that within the family a man usually has the most power. Many men, however, work in jobs outside the home where they perceive or believe themselves to be powerless to control their environment. Therefore, after being powerless all day at work, a man can return home and dominate the family. This control and power may take the form of abuse. When a mother needlessly disciplines her child, she may be reacting to the fact that her spouse and others are controlling her. By disciplining the child, she can exert power or control over another person.

SUBSTANCE ABUSE.   In 2005, there were 2.4 million persons who were currently using cocaine. Crack users increased from 467,000 in 2004 to 682,000 in 2005. There were 136,000 users of heroin. There were approximately nine million persons aged twelve and older who were current users of illicit drugs *other* than marijuana in 2005.[52] Those who engage in violent acts within the family also use and abuse these substances.

Drug and alcohol dependency was discussed briefly earlier in this chapter. It will be explored in more depth in relation to intimate partner abuse. Drug and alcohol abuse is a common characteristic of all forms of family violence. Although substance abuse may be present in family violence situations, as indicated above, no causal link has been established to date. However, the concept that drugs and alcohol contribute to or cause family violence continues to be a popular and enduring belief among both victims and abusers.

The excuse of substance abuse is an attractive explanation for both the victim and the abuser. From the victim's point of view, the abuser is not really a bad person, but the drugs or alcohols cause him to commit the acts. The perpetrator can deny responsibility by claiming a lack of control caused by drugs or alcohol. This approach allows both parties to point to an external influence that "caused" the abuse. Although it would be convenient to blame substance abuse as the cause of family violence, to do so would be to overlook all the interlocking dynamics that are involved in both substance abuse and family violence.

Frequently alcohol or drug abuse issues are involved in family violence incidents.

EFFECT ON VICTIMS.   The full consequences of abuse are examined in more detail in later chapters. Family violence has a profound, long-lasting effect on its victims. All victims report a sense of loss of self-esteem. Battered spouses, maltreated children, and abused elders all feel shame and helplessness as a result of the abuse. Many victims of abuse blame themselves, feeling that if they had only pleased the abuser, he or she would not have had to resort to violence.

Low self-esteem is common for victims of physical and sexual child abuse. These children do not have the capacity to understand the dynamics of child maltreatment and therefore develop a negative view of themselves. Many victims of sexual abuse not only blame themselves but also develop a self-hatred that leads to increased vulnerability and problems in adjusting as they mature. Victims of intimate partner abuse are commonly degraded as unfit and unworthy by the abuser. Constant criticism and the abused person's inability to break the intergenerational transmission of violence lead to a lack of confidence in themselves and a feeling of inferiority. The elderly are already disadvantaged because of the aging process, and abuse only increases their loss of self-confidence.

Victims of family violence have difficulty trusting others. There is perhaps no greater betrayal of trust than that experienced by children who are sexually abused by family members. Not only did a family member commit sexual acts with the child, but also other family members may have known about the abuse and failed to protect the child. Survivors of sexual abuse have trouble developing close relationships as they mature. Victims may believe that by not trusting others, they can avoid being betrayed or hurt again.[53] Many women who have suffered intimate partner abuse during a marriage are naturally hesitant to enter into another relationship.

Psychological problems in adjusting, even after the abuse has ended, are a common characteristic of victims of family violence. Emotional maladjustment and personality and character disorders have been reported among those who have suffered abuse in the family environment.[54] Some abuse is so severe that victims learn to dissociate from the trauma and develop alternate personalities and are later diagnosed as suffering from multiple personality disorder.[55]

Isolation, power differentials, power/powerlessness, substance abuse, and the effects on victims are common characteristics found in all forms of family violence. How these dynamics occur is explored in more detail later. At this stage, it is important to remember that victims of family violence are no different from anyone else. They are human beings who, through no fault of their own, have become trapped in a nightmare of violence from which they believe there is no escape.

THE INTERGENERATIONAL TRANSMISSION OF VIOLENCE THEORY

The intergenerational transmission of violence theory was formerly known as the cycle of violence theory. The quotation in the Focus box "The Intergenerational Transmission of Violence Theory Continues" is not from some ancient research conducted in the 1950s or 1960s. Rather, it comes from respected scholars in a 1993 textbook on family violence. Because of its popularity and complexity, the intergenerational transmission of violence formally considered as the inter-generational transmission of violence theory is discussed as a distinct

Focus

The Intergenerational Transmission of Violence Theory Continues

"Physical punishment of children is perhaps the most effective means of teaching violence, and eliminating it would be an important step in violence prevention."

Source: R. J. Gelles, "Family Violence," in R. L. Hampton et al., eds., *Family Violence: Prevention and Treatment* (Sage, Newbury Park, Calif., 1993), p. 20.

and separate theory of family violence. Simply separating it from the other theories should not imply that this is the definite answer as to why people commit aggressive acts. Rather, it is singled out for examination because professionals and laypersons constantly refer to it as a scientifically accepted fact. As with other causes or theories of family violence, there is no way to prove or disprove the intergenerational transmission of violence theory. However, because there is a widespread acceptance of this theory, it is necessary to fully explore both the premises it is founded on as well as the criticisms directed to it.

The intergenerational transmission of violence concept has generated continuing controversy among researchers for several decades. Scholars have attempted to determine whether violent tendencies can be inherited from the family of origin as a result of observing it or being a victim of it. Other scholars have attempted to explain criminal behavior by reference to this cycle.[56]

Definitions of the Intergenerational Transmission of Violence

The most commonly used term to describe the process involved in this concept is *intergenerational transmission of violence*. This theory is also known as the *intergenerational transmission of violence theory*. Since many authors, researchers, and commentators use the former, which is the term that is used in this textbook. The **intergenerational transmission of violence theory** asserts that violent behavior is learned within the family and bequeathed from one generation to the next. This theory holds that children who are victims of child abuse or who witness violent aggression by one spouse against the other will grow up and react to their children or spouses in the same manner. The childhood survivor of a violent family thus develops a predisposition toward violence in his or her own family. Therefore, so this theory holds, we have a never-ending chain of violence that is passed from one generation to the next. Numerous studies on the inter-generational transmission of violence have been conducted, and the results of these studies are discussed later in this section.

The Intergenerational Transmission of Violence and Family Violence

The sources for most studies of the intergenerational transmission of violence theory are case studies, clinical interviews, self-reporting, and agency records. As discussed above, each of these approaches suffers from defects in methodology and definitions.

One of the most widely cited studies in support of the intergenerational transmission of violence theory is Steele and Polick's research, which appeared in Helfer and Kempe's *The*

Battered Child Syndrome in 1968.[57] Their study involved sixty parents who were referred to them as a result of their children being treated for child abuse. Steele and Polick gathered data by testing and interviewing the parents. The parents stated that as children they had experienced intense, pervasive, continuous demands from their own parents. Lost within the conclusions of the study was the fact that some parents were physically abused and others were not. While the researchers had cautioned against drawing too many inferences from their research, their study is constantly cited as evidence supporting the intergenerational transmission of violence theory.

Strauss conducted an extensive study by interviewing 1,146 families with children.[58] The results of the study indicated an 18 percent rate of generational transmission of violence. This percentage may be low because the researchers limited the definition of abuse to physical acts that occurred during adolescence. As is discussed in Chapter 2, child abuse is more likely to occur at a younger age, with a gradual tapering off in incidents as the child reaches the teenage years.

During this same time period, Hunter and Kilstrom interviewed 282 parents of newborn infants.[59] These researchers followed the parents and determined that the intergenerational transmission of violence was 18 percent. However, 82 percent of the parents who were abused as children did not abuse their offspring. Those parents appeared to be able to break the intergenerational transmission of violence because of social support, healthy children, and a more supportive relationship with one of their own parents. Hunter and Kilstrom's study is suspect, because it examined only infants who had been admitted to an intensive care nursery. In addition, there was no extended follow-up of the families or their children.

In 1984, Egeland and Jacobvitz concluded a major study of 160 single-parent mothers.[60] Each mother had at least one child under the age of five years. The sample was divided into three groups: severe physical child abuse, including being struck by objects or burned; borderline child abuse, including weekly spankings; and those children who were being raised by another caretaker. The researchers found a 70 percent intergenerational transmission of violence for those mothers who had suffered severe abuse as a child.

In 1990, Cappell and Heiner analyzed 888 child-rearing families, measuring the incidence of aggression in each respondent's family.[61] The presence or absence of aggression was classified into family member relationships: husband-to-wife aggression, wife-to-husband aggression, and respondent-to-child aggression. These researchers found that women who witnessed or experienced violence as children were more likely to aggressively discipline their own children. Perhaps more important, these scholars suggested that children who are raised in a violent family learn or inherit vulnerability. Cappell and Heiner theorize that this intergenerational transmission of vulnerability causes men and women to provoke violence, accept violence as natural, and select aggressive partners. These scholars rightfully point out that this research is limited because the group was composed only of intact couples.

In 1997, Loos and Alexander examined 247 female and 155 male undergraduates at a large public mid-Atlantic university.[62] The focus of their study was to determine the longterm effects of parental physical abuse, verbal abuse, and emotional neglect on children. While the study did not directly address the intergenerational transmission of violence, its conclusions add weight to this theory. These researchers found that physical abuse by parents is significantly related to anger and aggression by the survivors in adulthood. Perceived parental emotional neglect resulted in feelings of loneliness and social isolation in the survivors. These feelings of social isolation suggest that these survivors may have difficulty in establishing satisfying relationships with others. Although this study has potential problems because it used retrospective self-reports, which are always subject to inaccuracy, it does support the intergenerational transmission of violence theory by indicating that survivors of childhood abuse may feel anger and aggression as well as loneliness or isolation. These feelings may cause these survivors to enter into abusive relationships as adults.

In a 1999 publication regarding the intergenerational transmission of violence, Jennifer Clarke and her colleagues surveyed persons seeking medical assistance for intravenous drug use. They found that individuals with a history of childhood abuse were four times more likely to assault family members or sexual partners than those individuals who did not report any history of family violence.[63]

The Intergenerational Transmission of Violence and Aggression

Dodge and his associates examined the effect of the intergenerational transmission of violence on development of aggressive tendencies in children.[64] They studied a representative sample of 309 children in kindergarten. This research was multisite in nature, and children were selected from Nashville and Knoxville, Tennessee, as well as from Bloomington, Indiana. The researchers interviewed the mothers, evaluated the children, and received responses regarding the children's behavior from school personnel, peer ratings, and direct observation.

They found that children who had been physically abused were more aggressive toward other children than those who had not been harmed.[65] The teacher-rated aggression index for abused children was 93 percent higher than that for nonabused children. The researchers also found that abused children were less able to process information and solve interpersonal problems. Although the authors accurately point out several caveats to their study, it does demonstrate the harm inflicted on children by abuse.

This harm may translate into future acts of aggression that take the form of crimes against society. One of the most comprehensive studies in this area of child abuse and delinquency was completed by Widom in 1989.[66] She followed 1,575 individuals from childhood through young adulthood. The study compared arrest records of two groups:

- One group consisted of 908 children with documented histories of abuse or neglect.
- The control group consisted of 667 children with no reported incidents of child abuse.

These groups were tracked through official records over the next fifteen to twenty years. The children were eleven years or younger at the time of the abuse. Therefore, an inherent weakness in the Strauss research was avoided. The study classified abuse into three distinct areas: physical, sexual, and neglect cases. Court and probation records were the source of data for the initial acts of abuse, and subsequent arrest data were obtained from federal, state, and local law enforcement agencies.

The study found that children who had been abused were more likely to commit crimes as juveniles and adults than were those in the control group. Furthermore, these children were arrested more often for violent crimes (11% versus 8%) than the nonabused children. Those children who were physically abused were more likely to be arrested for a violent crime. Interestingly, this study pointed out that the next biggest arrest rate for violent crimes comprised those children who had been neglected.

In one of the most detailed studies of its type, the National Institute of Justice sponsored research that found childhood abuse and neglect increased the odds of future delinquency and adult criminal behavior overall by 29 percent. The study followed 1,575 cases from childhood through young adulthood. One group was composed of 908 children who experienced substantiated cases of childhood abuse and neglect, and the other group was a comparison group of 667 children who did not have any official record of being abused or neglected. The study followed these children for approximately twenty-five years. Although there were children in both groups who had no juvenile or adult record, being abused or neglected as a child increased the likelihood of arrest as a juvenile by 59 percent, as an adult by 28 percent, and as a result of a violent crime by 30 percent.[67]

As this discussion illustrates, the intergenerational transmission of violence theory continues to dominate the family violence literature. This and other theories of family violence will continue to be researched in an attempt to find the cause of family violence, predict its occurrence, and search for a cure.

CONSEQUENCES OF FAMILY VIOLENCE

Physical Consequences

One of the most obvious consequences of family violence is the physical injuries suffered by victims. These injuries are easy to observe and treat. They are also the ones we are the most knowledgeable about, because most of us know someone who has suffered a broken arm or leg or other injury.

Types of Injuries

There are four general classifications of physical injuries inflicted on victims of family violence: immediate injuries that heal leaving no trace, injuries that leave visible scars, unknown long-term physical injuries, and long-term catastrophic injuries.

Immediate injuries include bruises, contusions, cuts, and broken bones. These injuries generally heal quickly and are not perceived as serious by most people. In fact, many of us have suffered these same types of injuries on a vacation trip. However, some family violence victims face more serious consequences as a result of these types of injuries. As Chapter 5 points out, certain types of bruises represent a serious form of child abuse. An elderly person who suffers a broken hip as a result of a shove by a caretaker may have significant complications during the healing process that could lead to death. A diabetic patient suffering from a stab wound inflicted during a domestic dispute may take two to three times as long to heal as another person.

Injuries that leave visible scars include those that result in facial scars; loss of teeth, fingers, or toes; scars on the neck, arms, or legs; and loss of mobility due to incomplete healing. The injuries are not considered catastrophic, but can cause changes in life activities. For example, a stalker might inflict scars on the face of his victim that may result in a model being unable to pursue her career.

Unknown long-term physical injuries can include a potential exposure to HIV and AIDS. These types of diseases can result in the loss of life or a complete change in life activities. Other sexually transmitted diseases (STDs) may occur as a result of a sexual attack, including, but not limited to, gonorrhea, syphilis, and the herpes simplex viruses.

Practicum

What Is a Crime Worth?

Stephanie is a thirty-five-year-old schoolteacher who lives by herself in a modern condominium project in an upper-middle-class section of her city. One night at approximately 1:00 A.M., she heard a sound of breaking glass. Before she could reach her phone to dial 911, a man dressed in black entered the bedroom and shoved a knife against her chest. The perpetrator wore a ski mask and latex gloves. He said, "You do what I want and I won't cut you." He proceeded to rape and sodomize her over the next hour.

Afterward, as he was preparing to leave, he saw a cameo brooch laying on Stephanie's night-stand. As he picked it up and placed it in his pocket, Stephanie pleaded with him not to take it because it had belonged to her deceased mother. The perpetrator merely laughed and struck her on the side of her head with the butt of his knife, stating that it would remind him of her.

The perpetrator, who was a wealthy play-boy, was eventually arrested, charged with a number of similar sexual assaults, and convicted on all counts by a jury. At sentencing, Stephanie asked to speak regarding her losses. She asked the court to order the defendant to pay for her counseling ($5,000), the time she lost at her job ($2,000), her medical expenses ($3,000), pain and suffering ($10,000), and the fair market value of her brooch, which was never recovered ($750).

What should the perpetrator pay? Supposing that he didn't have enough money to pay all the victim's claims, which one is the most important? The least important?

Long-term catastrophic injuries include those that restrict a victim's physical movements. For example, a person struck by a drunk driver may become a paraplegic or may lose an arm or a leg. Some victims of intimate partner abuse have suffered loss of liver function as a result of repeated beatings by their abuser. These severe injuries often result in family members having to alter their lifestyles in order to care for the victim, whereas others may result in a reduction in the life span of the victim, a change in identity, and altered quality of life.

Medical Aspects

The types of physical injuries suffered by victims of family violence can cover the entire spectrum of illness, from simple bruises to deadly gunshot wounds to the head. Although professionals in this area are not expected to be physicians, they should have a basic understanding of the various types of injuries that family violence victims may suffer. The next section briefly examines the medical aspects of some of the more common traumatic injuries.[68]

GUNSHOT WOUNDS.   The civilian population in the United States is the most heavily armed in history.[69] More than 850,000 civilians were killed by bullets in the twentieth century.[70]

The science of ballistics is complex, but a few basic rules will assist in understanding the nature of injuries that result from gunshot wounds. The magnitude of the injury is proportional to the amount of kinetic energy impacted by the bullet striking the victim. This kinetic energy is determined by a variety of factors, including the distance between the assailant and the victim, the muzzle velocity, and the various characteristics of the bullet. At medium velocity, the missile has an explosive impact and creates a temporary passage in the tissue along its course. Bone and tissue may be fractured and torn without being directly struck by the missile. High-velocity missiles cause additional problems, including the possibility of fragmentation, which will cause additional multiple trajectories and injuries. Medical personnel are interested in obtaining information regarding the type of weapon used, the distance from the assailant when the victim was shot, the suspected number of shots, the blood lost at the scene, and any type of fluids administered prior to arrival at the hospital.

Shotgun wounds present special types of problems. The shotgun was designed to strike a small, fast-moving target at close range. Because of the design of the pellets inside the round, the shotgun is not an effective weapon at long range. However, when used at close range, a shotgun is extremely lethal. Shotgun wounds have been classified into three groups according to the range, the pattern of the pellets, and the depth of penetration. Type I wounds involve long range (greater than seven yards) and basically result in a penetration of subcutaneous tissue and deep fascia only. Type II wounds involve medium range (between three and four yards) and may create a large number of perforated wounds. Type III wounds involve short or point-blank range (less than three yards) and involve a massive destruction of tissue. Type III wounds are very lethal, carrying a mortality rate of 39 to 65 percent.

STABBING WOUNDS.   Knives are not the only instrument used in stabbings. Ice picks, pens, coat hangers, screwdrivers, broken bottles, and other sharp objects have all been used as weapons by assailants. Stabbing wounds usually result in lacerations or punctures. These injuries may be only a minor inconvenience, or they may be life-threatening, depending on the location and depth of the wound. Frequently, more than one stab wound is sustained. Medical personnel are interested in obtaining information regarding the type and size of the weapon, the estimated blood loss at the scene of the crime, the time of injury, and whether the victim had ingested any drugs or alcohol.

BURNS.   As it will be discussed in Chapter 5, burns are one of the most painful and devastating types of physical injury. They are classified into first, second, or third degree, according to the depth of the burned area. First-degree burns involve the epidermal tissue and may exhibit red or pink skin accompanied by hyperesthesia and tingling. The more common causes of first-degree burns are sunburn and brief contact with hot liquids. Second-degree burns involve the epidermal and dermal tissues and may exhibit red or mottled skin with blisters, considerable swelling, wet surfaces, pain, and sensitivity to cold air. The most frequent cause includes scalds and flash flames. Third-degree burns involve dermal or deeper tissues and may exhibit a pale white or charred appearance with a dry surface. Body fat may be exposed, and systemic symptoms include shock, hematuria, and hemolysis. The most common causes include fire, contact with hot objects, and electrical and chemical burns.

The severity of burns is based on both the extent and the type of burn. The American Burn Association classifies burns as major, moderate, and minor. Major burns include second-degree burns over more than 25 percent of an adult's body and 20 percent of a child's body; third-degree burns involving 10 percent of the body surface; all burns involving hands, eyes, face, ears, and feet; and all inhalation injuries and all burns complicated by other injuries. Moderate burns include second-degree burns over 15 to 25 percent of an adult's body and 10 to 20 percent of a child's body and all third-degree burns of 2 to 10 percent not involving eyes, ears, face, hands, or feet. Minor burns include second-degree burns over less than 15 percent of an adult's body and less than 10 percent of a child's body and third-degree burns of 2 percent or less and not involving eyes, ears, face, hands, or feet.

TRAUMA TO THE HEAD.   A significant portion of all emergency department work involves the care of people suffering from trauma to the head. Vehicle accidents, including drunk driving incidents, account for a significant percentage of this form of injury. Other acts, such as child abuse and intimate partner abuse, also constitute another important cause of head trauma. Often, people who sustain head injuries also have other associated major traumatic injuries that they received at the same time.

One of the effects of trauma to the head may be the inducement of a coma. Comas may be a result of a subdural hematoma, epidural hematoma, traumatic intracerebral hemorrhage, contusion, or concussion. Defining a coma is difficult, but for the purposes here it is an altered state that exists in a person manifesting inappropriate responses to external stimuli and who maintains eye closure throughout the stimuli.

The victim's ability to relate the course of events leading to the injury may be compromised by injury, alcohol, drugs, hysteria, or any number of factors. Medical personnel will want to know whether the victim was struck on the head by the assailant and, if so, what the object was. Police and firefighters will be questioned about whether the victim was awake on their arrival. Any changes in consciousness between the incident and arrival at the emergency room should be noted.

OTHER MEDICAL CONCERNS.   In addition to the different types of physical injuries suffered by victims of violent crimes, victims of sexual assault endure a specific trauma that results in specialized medical issues. Rape victims will undergo a very particular type of examination intended to assist in prosecuting the perpetrator. In the recent past, these medical examinations were conducted by hospital staff with little or no specialized training regarding the effects of rape on the victim. In addition, there were times when a male police officer remained in the examination room to conduct questioning of the victim during the examination. Fortunately, we have progressed in our medical treatment of sexual assault victims, and in many jurisdictions, rape crisis counselors are available and present during this examination. They have been trained to provide support to the victim during this and other phases of the criminal justice process.

The rape victim should discuss the issue of pregnancy with hospital staff. If she was pregnant prior to the assault, the possible effects on the fetus should be discussed. If she was not pregnant, the possibility that the assailant impregnated her should be evaluated. The victim should discuss all aspects of this issue at the earliest possible time with the medical staff at the hospital or her own physician.

The possibility of contracting an STD must be evaluated. Many of these diseases can be successfully avoided if treated immediately after the assault; however, many STDs will not show up during the physical examination, so rape victims should be tested for several weeks after the attack. It is therefore critical that victims discuss this possibility with medical personnel.

With the threat of AIDS/HIV so much a part of our lives today, the possibility of contracting the disease is perhaps one of the most frightening aspects of sexual assaults. HIV causes AIDS, which is a disease that attacks the body's immune system, rendering the person vulnerable to infections and diseases and ultimately resulting in death. A victim may contract HIV in a variety of ways. Victims should be tested immediately for the virus and request appropriate periodic follow-up testing.

MENTAL CONSEQUENCES

Crisis

Eric Lindemann is considered by many scholars to be one of the leading pioneers in the study of the effects of crisis on the mental health or emotional being of humans.[71] Lindemann offered both a new understanding of the dynamics of crisis and a systematic approach to treating those suffering from it.[72] His study dealing with the grieving process of the survivors in the Cocoanut Grove fire in Boston in 1942 has become the foundation on which much of the knowledge concerning the grief process has been built. Lindemann believed that acute grief was a natural and necessary reaction to significant loss. Another scholar, Gerald Caplin, extended Lindemann's theories to include all human reactions to traumatic events, not just the grieving process as a result of loss.[73]

Individuals react differently to different situations, and what may be a crisis to one person may only be a minor annoyance to another. As a result, the term *crisis* has many valid meanings. In medicine, *crisis* has one meaning; in psychiatry, it has another meaning. Rather than adopting a sociological, medical, psychological, or legal definition of *crisis,* here it will be viewed from the perspective of a family violence victim's reactions to violence. **Crisis,** therefore, is defined as a specific set of temporary circumstances that results in a state of upset and disequilibrium, characterized by an individual's inability to cope with a particular situation using customary methods of problem solving.[74]

Although some authorities may differ regarding the number of steps in the crisis reaction, one of the most common approaches describes this process as involving three stages: impact, recoil, and reorganization.

THE IMPACT STAGE.   This phase occurs immediately after the violence. Victims feel as if they are in shock. Some cannot eat or sleep, whereas others may express disbelief that the violence actually occurred. Statements such as "I can't believe this happened to me!" are common during this stage. Many victims feel exposed and vulnerable or express feelings of helplessness.

The impact phase may last for several hours to several days after the crime and is often punctuated by episodes of severe mood swings. One moment the victim may appear to be in control, and the next moment he or she may exhibit disorganized and uncontrolled emotions. A family violence victim is especially vulnerable at this time and susceptible to the influence of others. What may appear to be innocent statements offered by friends may be interpreted by the victim as a blame for being the victim.

THE RECOIL STAGE.   During this phase, victims attempt to accept or adapt to the violence and begin to reintegrate their personalities. Victims commonly experience a wide variety of emotions, including guilt, fear, anger, self-pity, and sadness. Some victims struggle to accept the painful feelings caused by the violence; at other times, they deny experiencing any of these feelings at all. Caplin explains this process as involving victims who need opportunities to rest from wrestling with their situations, but who must eventually awake and return to consider the problem.[75] In essence, after trying to cope with their feelings regarding the violence, victims become emotionally exhausted and put these feelings aside so that they can rest, recover, and begin the healing process. Later, they are able to examine their feelings regarding the violence with renewed emotional resources.

Many victims will be in denial during this phase. This emotional detachment can be an extension of the shock of the impact phase. Such detachment allows victims to develop a gradual immunity to the feelings that would overwhelm them if they faced them all at once. Victims may believe that they must seal off any feelings to get on with their lives. Some victims defend against any feeling during this phase by submerging themselves in work or other projects. Other victims accomplish the same objective by becoming almost obsessional with the criminal justice system, learning about the procedures, criminal laws, parties, and so on.

During this phase, victims begin to deal with their feelings about the violence. Some victims will reexamine every detail of the crime in their minds and may want to talk about it endlessly. Others will dream about the violence. As victims confront the reality of the violent act, they may reexperience the fear. Some victims allow themselves to feel the full intensity of emotions only after the immediate threat of the violence has passed. This feeling of fear can be immobilizing. Victims must verbalize their fears and other intense emotions associated with the violent act to begin the healing process. With time, most of the traumatic impact associated with these feelings will lessen.

Another common feeling during the recoil stage is anger toward the perpetrator. Victims may experience rage but be unable to vent this feeling. Some may spend hours thinking about revenge, especially those who have suffered from a violent attack. Victims must understand that the desire for revenge is a natural and normal part of the healing process. Many victims want to construct a reason for their victimization. These victims will search for the answer to the question "Why me?"

THE REORGANIZATION STAGE.   After a period of time, the recoil stage will give way to the reorganization stage. The victim becomes more normal as feelings of fear and rage diminish in intensity, and the victim has energy left over to confront life's daily activities. The victim becomes more normalized, as the need to deny the victimization lessens and gradually is able to put the experience in perspective and commit energy to the task of living in the present.

Victims will never forget the experience, and, as indicated earlier, they will respond in a variety of ways. This discussion has focused on one method or approach to victimization. Other victims may experience different feelings. Acute stress disorder (ASD) is another reaction that family violence victims may experience.

Acute Stress Disorder

Acute stress disorder is acute stress that is experienced in the immediate aftermath of a traumatic event. This is a newly categorized disorder that was first listed in the *Diagnostic and Statistical Manual of Disorders,* fourth edition (DSM-IV), in 1994.[76] The characteristic feature of ASD is the development of anxiety, dissociative symptoms, and other manifestations that occur within one month after exposure to the traumatic event. To receive a diagnosis of ASD, the victim must have experienced, have witnessed, or have been confronted with an event that involved actual or threatened death, serious injury, or a threat to the physical safety of the victim or others. In addition, the victim's response to such a condition must involve intense fear, helplessness, or horror. This diagnosis requires that the victim experience several symptoms of posttraumatic stress disorder (PTSD), and that he or she must experience three of five PTSD dissociative symptoms during or immediately after the traumatic incident. These symptoms must persist for at least two days but last not more than thirty days. The dissociative symptoms are derealization, depersonalization, dissociative amnesia, subjective sense of numbing, and reduction in awareness of surroundings. If these symptoms last longer than thirty days, the victim may be suffering from PTSD.

Posttraumatic Stress Disorder

Posttraumatic stress disorder (PTSD) was first identified when some Vietnam War veterans began experiencing flashbacks of events that occurred during combat. **Posttraumatic stress disorder** is defined as the development of characteristic symptoms following a psychologically distressing event that is outside the range of usual human experience.[77] Traumatic events include, but are not limited to, military combat, violent personal assault, kidnapping, being taken hostage, terrorist attack, torture, incarceration as a prisoner of war, natural or manmade disasters, severe automobile accidents, or diagnosis of a life-threatening illness. The characteristic symptoms involved require that the person experience, witness, or be confronted with an event or events that involved actual or threatened death or serious injury or a threat to the physical integrity of self or others and the person's response involved intense fear, helplessness, or horror. Symptoms may include reexperiencing the traumatic event, avoiding stimuli associated with the event, or numbing of general responsiveness and increased agitation.[78]

Victims of many forms of family violence can experience PTSD. However, several scholars have carried out research regarding the effect of rape on victims.[79] Victims of rape have reported or been diagnosed as suffering from PTSD. Rothbaum's study found that 94 percent of rape victims displayed classic symptoms of PTSD one week after the assault. This figure dropped to 47 percent twelve weeks after the incident.[80] Kilpatrick and colleagues' study *Rape in America* reported that 11 percent of all women raped suffer from PTSD, and the authors estimated that 1.3 million women in the United States are currently suffering from PTSD as a result of a rape or multiple rapes.[81]

Long-Term Crisis Reaction

Long-term crisis reaction is the name of a condition identified by the National Organization for Victim Assistance (NOVA), which is considered one of the early leaders in the victims' rights movement. They have responded to a number of crises throughout the world. Professionals from NOVA working with crisis victims have observed this reaction on a number of occasions. Long-term crisis reaction is a condition that occurs when victims do not suffer from PTSD but may reexperience feelings of the crisis reaction when certain events trigger the recollection of the trauma in their lives.[82] The trigger event may be a number of situations, including the anniversaries of the crisis, birthdays, or holidays of loved ones lost during the trauma; significant life events such as marriage, divorces, births, and graduations; media events that broadcast similar types of incidents; and involvement in the criminal justice system.

The intensity and frequency of long-term crisis reactions usually diminish with the passage of time. As the victim develops coping mechanisms to deal with the trauma, these resources may lessen the victim's reaction to triggering events. The victim must learn to continue to function despite these reactions.

Other Mental Disorders

Victims of family violence may suffer a wide variety of mental disorders as a result of their victimization. They are going through a process of attempting to regain their mental equilibrium that is off-center as a result of the traumatic event. The following is a brief discussion of two of the more common mental problems faced by victims of crime.

DEPRESSION.   Depression consists of a major depressive episode lasting at least two weeks, during which there is either a depressed mood or the loss of interest or pleasure in nearly all activities. Possible symptoms include changes in appetite, weight, sleep, and psychomotor activity; decreased energy; feelings of worthlessness or guilt; difficulty in thinking, concentrating, or making decisions; and recurrent thoughts of death or suicide. The victim must experience clinically significant distress or impairment in social, occupational, or other important areas of functioning.

SUBSTANCE ABUSE.   The essential feature of this disorder is a maladaptive pattern of substance use, leading to significant adverse consequences related to the repeated uses of substances. Normally, these substances are drugs or alcohol. The victim may suffer repeated failure in fulfilling major role obligations, repeated use of substances in situations in which it is physically dangerous, legal problems related to the use of the substance, and social and interpersonal problems.

Other Effects

Different victims of family violence suffer different reactions to that event, and, conversely, victims of different forms of family violence may suffer similar reactions. There is no "clear bright line" that professionals can look to and determine which symptoms victims will suffer. However, researchers have attempted to establish broad general categories of problems suffered by victims of certain crimes. Susman and Vittert's textbook *Building a Solution: A Practical Guide for Establishing Crime Victim Service Agencies* lists certain crimes and typical reactions.[83]

With the passage of time and other intervention techniques, the mental and/or emotional consequences associated with the trauma of a criminal act may lessen or be alleviated, but the victim may never be the same person he or she was before the crime. Moreover, in addition to the mental effects that victims endure as a result of the crime, they also suffer fiscal consequences.

FINANCIAL CONSEQUENCES

In 1996, the National Institute of Justice released *Victim Costs and Consequences: A New Look,* an in-depth study of the costs of victimization.[84] This study raises serious questions regarding previous estimates of the cost of crime. Using the data from the Bureau of Justice Statistics and including "quality of life" or intangible losses, this study concludes that the cost of crime is higher than it was previously suggested. The following sections examine the results of this study.

Introduction

It is fairly easy to establish tangible costs of crime such as medical care, police services, and other items that have a specific monetary value. However, it not so easy to value the loss of quality of life or intangible losses suffered by victims of family violence. How much is a murdered spouse's life worth? What is the cost for the pain and suffering experienced by a rape victim? In addition, costs associated with society's response to crime are difficult if not impossible to measure. Society's response to crime includes a variety of items that are not normally considered when discussing costs of crime. Measuring our actions and resulting costs on the basis of our fear of crime is difficult.[85] On the other hand, measuring items (e.g., filing fees paid for a protective order are typical of the precautionary expenditures associated with protecting ourselves from an abusive partner) is relatively easy. In addition, everyone understands the costs associated with running the criminal justice system and keeping offenders incarcerated. Thus, it can be observed that society's response to crime includes both tangible and intangible costs.

The cost-of-crime section also includes tangible and intangible losses suffered as a result of family violence. These costs include tangible items such as medical and mental health treatment cost. The intangible costs include quality of life and loss of companionship.

Tangible Losses

Family violence costs taxpayers, businesses, and victims in medical costs, lost earnings, and public programs related to family violence prevention or assistance. These tangible losses do not account for the full impact of crime on victims of family violence, because they ignore pain and suffering and the reduced quality of life that many victims suffer as a result of the violence.

Victims of family violence usually suffer three types of losses: out-of-pocket expenses such as medical costs and property loss, reduced productivity at work because of sick days and so on, and nonmonetary losses such as pain and suffering and loss of quality of life. Although some of these losses are easily quantified, even the intangible losses may be valued in dollars. Tangible losses include property damage and loss, medical care, mental health care, police and fire services, victim services, and productivity.

Property damage and loss. This includes the value of the property damaged during a violent act. It also includes insurance claims and administration costs that arise as a result of compensating the victim under an insurance policy.

Medical care. This includes payments for hospital and physician care, emergency medical transportation, rehabilitation, prescriptions, allied health services, medical devices, and related insurance claim-processing costs. Managed care systems are changing health care payments and are not reflected in these costs. Recent research findings point out that medical care may take the form of multiple visits to a health care provider for one incident of family violence. For example, a family violence victim may require an ambulance to transport him or her to the emergency room. They may be admitted to the hospital for observation or receive outpatient care and may require physical therapy for their injuries after discharge.[86] More study is necessary in this area as medical costs adapt to changing circumstances.

Mental health care. This provides funding for services to family violence victims by psychiatrists, psychologists, social workers, and counselors. This cost has been one of the least-researched areas in crime victimization. Similar to medical costs, one victimization may require multiple visits to a therapist. For example, the CDC states that one-third of all rapes result in the victim speaking with a psychologist, psychiatrist, or other mental health professional. Overall, each incident requires approximately twelve mental health care visits, with a mean cost of $78.86 per visit.[87]

Police and fire services. This includes initial police and fire responses as well as follow-up investigations. The costs of other components of the criminal justice system are not included in this element. Generally speaking, police and fire costs are a relatively small portion of the cost of family violence, averaging $100 per case.

Summary

Family violence is a multifaceted phenomenon. It includes abusive acts toward children, significant others in a cohabitating relationship, and the older people. These acts may be sexual, physical, emotional, or psychological, or involve neglect or a denial of rights to the other person. It has existed for centuries but has only recently come to the consciousness of the public. Numerous studies have been done in an attempt to find answers to this form of aggression. We have yet, however, to agree on a definition that all professionals can accept.

Several measuring techniques are used to determine the extent of family violence. Surveys, official reports, and clinical studies all offer professionals insight and information into the nature and extent of this form of aggression. Unfortunately, each of these measures has internal flaws that are acknowledged by those who use them.

Just as a number of significant controversies still exist in the study of family violence, so do a number of theories attempt to explain how or why one person would act aggressively toward another within the family environment. No one theory that identifies a single cause or multiple causes of family violence has yet gained total acceptance by all the professionals in this area.

All professionals must have an understanding of various types of family violence and be able to respond to this form of aggression in a manner that protects the victims. In addition, society must examine its attitude toward women and strive to make them equal partners so as to avoid situations in which males may take advantage of superior power and resources. Only by moving forward on a variety of fronts can we hope to diminish or stop this form of aggression that leaves its victims physically and mentally injured.

We have known for years that victims of family violence suffer from specific types of physical injuries as a result of their victimization. These are, for the most part, easy to recognize and treat. The broken arm or jaw may be repaired, and it is hoped that the victim will regain full use of his or her physical faculties.

More recently, society has acknowledged that victims of family violence may also suffer mental problems as a consequence of their victimization. They may experience a wide variety of mental problems, including acute stress disorder, posttraumatic stress disorder, long-term crisis reaction, or other mental disorders. These reactions do not mean that family violence victims are insane or crazy; rather, these are normal reactions to an abnormal event. Victim service providers and professionals who deal with family violence victims must understand these dynamics in order to work with and assist victims of crimes.

In addition to the physical and mental injuries suffered by victims are the financial consequences. Recent studies have begun to address this long-overlooked aspect of victimization. The consequences of family violence are multifaceted and, like a stone dropped in a calm pool of water, move out in ever-widening circles, affecting victims, their families, and society as a whole. Professionals in the field must understand all the consequences of family violence victimization to function effectively.

Family Violence–related Web Links

There are numerous family violence-related web links. List below are a few of the most popular web links that were active when this edition of the text was published.

Adult Victims of Crime and Abuse in Residential Care Facilities
www.trynova.org/victiminfo/elderly/

Aeqiotas: The Prosecutors' Resource on Violence Against Women
www.aequitasresource.org/

AgingStats.gov
www.agingstats.gov

AMBER Alert
www.amberalert.gov

AmberVision
www.ambervision.org/

American Association for Retired Persons (AARP)
www.aarp.org/

American Association of Retired Persons (AARP): Money
www.aarp.org/money/

American Association of Retired Persons (AARP): Scams & Fraud
www.aarp.org/money/scams-fraud/

American Bar Association (ABA) Commission on Law and Aging
www.americanbar.org/groups/law_aging.html

American Humane Association (AHA) Children's Division
www.americanhumane.org/children/

American Professional Society on the Abuse of Children (APSAC)
www.apsac.org/

Anti-Slavery International (ASI)
www.antislavery.org

Arte Sana
www.arte-sana.com/

Association of Missing & Exploited Children's Organizations (AMECO)
www.amecoinc.org/

Battered Women's Justice Project
www.bwjp.org/menu.htm

Captive Daughters
www.captivedaughters.org/

Chadwick Center for Children and Families
www.chadwickcenter.org/

Child Abduction: Resources for Victims and Families
www.ojjdp.gov/childabduction.html

Child Abuse Prevention Association (CAPA)
www.childabuseprevention.org/

Child Abuse Prevention Network
www.child-abuse.com/

Child Centre: The Expert Group for Cooperation on Children at Risk
www.childcentre.info/

Child Crisis Network
www.childcybersearch.com/index.shtml

Child Find of America
www.childfindofamerica.org/

Child Labor Public Education Project
www.continuetolearn.uiowa.edu/laborctr/child_labor/

Child Welfare Information Gateway
www.childwelfare.gov/

Child Welfare Information Gateway: State Statutes Search
www.childwelfare.gov/systemwide/laws_policies/state/

Child Welfare League of America (CWLA)
www.cwla.org/default.htm

Child Witness to Violence Project (CWVP)
www.childwitnesstoviolence.org/

Children's Defense Fund (CDF)
www.childrensdefense.org/

Children's Exposure to Violence Evidence-Based Guide
www.cevresearch.org/EvidenceBasedGuide.htm

Clearinghouse on Abuse and Neglect of the Elderly (CANE)
www.cane.udel.edu/

Coalition Against Trafficking in Women (CATW)
www.catwinternational.org/

Cyber Tipline
www.missingkids.com/missingkids/servlet/PageServlet?LanguageCountry=en_US&PageId=2936

Defending Childhood
www.justice.gov/ag/defendingchildhood/

Department of Veterans Affairs (VA): Center for Women Veterans
www.va.gov/womenvet/

Doe Network
www.doenetwork.org/

Domestic Abuse Helpline for Men and Women
dahmw.org/

Dougy Center for Grieving Children and Families
www.dougy.org/

Elder Abuse Forensic Center
www.elderabuseforensiccenter.com/

End Child Prostitution, Child Pornography and Trafficking in Children (ECPAT)
www.ecpat.net/EI/index.asp

Foundation Aiding the Elderly (FATE)
www.4fate.org/

Futures Without Violence
www.futureswithoutviolence.org/

International Network for the Prevention of Elder Abuse (INPEA)
www.inpea.net/

International Organization for Migration (IOM)
www.iom.int/jahia/jsp/index.jsp

International Women's Rights Center "La Strada"
www.lastradainternational.org/?main

Maiti Nepal
www.maitinepal.org/

Ministry of Justice of the Republic of Korea
www.moj.go.kr/HP/ENG/index.do

MiraMed
www.miramed.org/

National Center for Children Exposed to Violence (NCCEV)
www.nccev.org/

National Center for Missing and Exploited Children (NCMEC)
www.ncmec.org

National Center on Elder Abuse (NCEA)
www.ncea.aoa.gov/

National Network to End Domestic Violence (NNEDV)
www.nnedv.org/

NCJRS: Elder Abuse Special Feature
www.ncjrs.gov/elderabuse

Nursing Network on Violence Against Women International (NNVAWI)
www.nnvawi.org/

Nursing Response to Elder Mistreatment
  Curriculum
www.iafn.org/displaycommon.
  cfm?an=1&subarticlenbr=459

Office on Violence Against Women (OVW)
www.ovw.usdoj.gov/

Office on Violence Against Women (OVW):
  National Hotlines
www.ovw.usdoj.gov/areas-focus.html

Polaris Project
www.polarisproject.org/

Sacred Circle: National Resource Center to End
  Violence Against Native Women
www.sacred-circle.com/

Scandinavian Research Council for Criminology
www.nsfk.org

Shared Hope International
www.sharedhope.org/

Start by Believing
www.startbybelieving.org/

Stop Violence Against Women (STOPVAW)
www.stopvaw.org/

U.S. Department of Justice (DOJ):
  Child Exploitation and Obscenity Section (CEOS)
www.justice.gov/criminal/ceos/

United Nations Development Fund for Women
  (UNIFEM)
www.unwomen.org/

Vital Voices Global Partnership
www.vitalvoices.org/

White House: 1 is 2 Many
www.whitehouse.gov/1is2many

Women Aid International
www.womenaid.org/

Women's Commission for Refugee Women &
  Children
www.womensrefugeecommission.org/

Womenshealth.gov
www.womenshealth.gov/

Key Terms

family violence—any act or omission by persons who are cohabitating that results in serious injury to other members of the family.

psychopathology theory—certain individuals suffer from mental illness, personality disorders, and other dysfunctions that cause them to engage in aggressive acts within the family.

substance abuse theory—accepts the proposition that drugs or alcohols cause or contribute to family violence.

social learning theory—an integration of differential associations with differential reinforcements so that people with whom one interacts are the reinforcers of behavior that results in learning of both deviant and nondeviant behavior.

exchange theory—argues that family violence is based on a determination of costs and rewards.

Frustration-aggression theory—based on the premise that individuals react aggressively when some goal is blocked or frustrated.

ecological theory—assumes that family violence occurs when the parent, child, and family are mismatched with the neighborhood and community.

sociobiology or evolutionary theory—assumes that parents will not emotionally attach to or invest themselves in children with low reproductive potential.

culture of violence theory—is based on the premise that violence is unevenly distributed within our society, and that violence is more prevalent in the lower socioeconomic sectors of society.

patriarchy theory—views society as being dominated by males, with women and children in subordinate positions in which they are treated as possessions by men.

general systems theory—assumes that violence within the family is a function of a system rather than an individual pathology of the family member.

social conflict theory—proposes that unacknowledged alienation and shame generate violence within the family.

resource theory—holds that the use of violence within a relationship depends on the resources that a family member controls.

intergenerational transmission of violence theory—asserts that violent behavior is learned within the family and bequeathed from one generation to the next.

crisis—a specific set of temporary circumstances resulting in a state of upset and disequilibrium, characterized by an individual's inability to cope with a particular situation using customary methods of problem solving.

acute stress disorder—acute stress that is experienced in the immediate aftermath of a traumatic event.

posttraumatic stress disorder—the development of characteristic symptoms following a psychologically distressing event that is outside the range of usual human experience.

long-term crisis reaction—a condition that occurs when victims do not suffer from posttraumatic stress disorder, but may reexperience feelings of the crisis reaction when certain events trigger the recollection of the trauma in their lives.

Discussion Questions

1. Based on your reading of this chapter, how would you define *family violence?* Draft a definition and justify your answer.
2. What is the most accurate method to measure the incidence of family violence? Why is this method more reliable than others?
3. Which of the theories discussed in this chapter appears to offer the most hope for understanding the cause of family violence? Why is that theory more complete or acceptable than the others?
4. What should we do about violence in the media? Which argument carries the most weight? Why?
5. Is the intergenerational transmission of violence theory valid? Why? Why not?
6. In your own words, describe why you think people abuse others in the family. Keep this assignment and compare it with your understanding of family violence after you have finished reading this textbook.
7. What are the four stages of physical injury? How do they differ from one another?
8. What is acute stress disorder? How is it different from a crisis reaction?
9. Explain the symptoms of posttraumatic stress disorder.
10. List other mental effects of family violence on victims. In your opinion, which effect is the most serious? Justify your answer.

Suggested Readings

American Psychiatric Association. *Understanding Mental Disorders: Your guide to DSM-5* (American Psychiatric Association, Washington, D.C., 2015)

Akers, R. L. *Deviant Behavior* (Wadsworth, Belmont, Calif., 1973).

Bard, M., and D. Sangrey. *The Crime Victim's Book,* 2nd ed. (Brunner/Mazel, New York, 1986).

Blau, P. M. *Exchange and Power in Social Life* (Wiley, New York, 1964).

Caplin, G. *Principles of Preventive Psychiatry* (Basic Books, New York, 1964).

Coser, L. A. *Continuities in the Study of Social Conflict* (Free Press, New York, 1967).

Covell, K., and B. Howe. *Children, Families and Violence: Challenges for Children's Rights.* (Kingsley, London, 2009)

Dobash, R. E., and R. P. Dobash. *Violence against Wives* (Free Press, New York, 1979).

Dollard, J., L. W. Doob, N. E. Miller, O. H. Mowrer, and R. R. Sears. *Frustration and Aggression* (Yale University Press, New Haven, Conn., 1939).

Finkelhor, D., R. J. Gelles, G. T. Hotaling, and M. A. Straus, eds. *The Dark Side of Families: Current Family Violence Research* (SAGE, Beverly Hills, Calif., 1983).

Gelles, R. J. *The Violent Home* (SAGE, Beverly Hills, Calif., 1974).

_____. *Family Violence,* 2nd ed. (SAGE, Newbury Park, Calif., 1987).

_____. "Family Violence." In R. L. Hampton, D. F. Schwarz, J. A. Grisso, and C, Miles, eds., *Family Violence: Prevention and Treatment* (SAGE, Newbury Park, Calif., 1993).

_____. *The Violent Home* (SAGE, Newbury Park, Calif., 1993).

Gelles, R. J., and D. R. Loseke, eds. *Current Controversies on Family Violence* (SAGE, Newbury Park, Calif., 1993).

Gil, E. M. *Outgrowing the Pain: A Book for and about Adults Abused as Children* (Launch Press, San Francisco, 1983).

Giles-Sims, J. *Wife-Beating: A Systems Theory Approach* (Guilford, New York, 1983).

Helfer, R., and C. H. Kempe, eds. *The Battered Child Syndrome,* 4th ed. (University of Chicago Press, Chicago, 1987).

Helfer, R. E., and R. S. Kempe, eds. *The Battered Child,* 4th ed. (University of Chicago Press, Chicago, 1987).

Miller, J. *Family Abuse and Violence: A Social Problems Perspective* (AltaMira Press, Lanham, Md, 2006).

Ohlin, L., and M. Tonry, eds. *Family Violence* (University of Chicago Press, Chicago, 1989).

Pagelow, M. D. *Family Violence* (Praeger, New York, 1984).

Reiss, A. J. Jr., and J. A. Roth, eds. *Understanding and Preventing Violence* (National Academy Press, Washington, D.C., 1993).

Retzinger, S. M. *Violent Emotions: Shame and Rage in Marital Quarrels* (SAGE, Newbury Park, Calif., 1991).

Richards, L. *Family Violence (Social Issues Firsthand)* (Greenhaven Press, Farmington Hills, Mich., 2006).

Roberts, A. R., ed. *Crisis Intervention and Time-Limited Cognitive Treatment* (SAGE, Thousand Oaks, Calif., 1995).

Siegal, L. J. *Criminology,* 3rd ed. (West, St. Paul, Minn., 1989).

Straus, M. A., R. J. Gelles, and S. K. Steinmetz. *Behind Closed Doors* (Anchor, Garden City, New York, 1980).

Walker, L. E. *The Battered Women* (Harper & Row, New York, 1979).

Wing, C. P. *Crisis Intervention as Psychotherapy* (Oxford University Press, New York, 1978).

Weber, M. *The Theory of Social and Economic Organization,* trans. A. M. Henderson and T. Parsons (Free Press, New York, 1964).

Wolfgang, M. E., and F. Ferracuti. *The Subculture of Violence: Toward an Integrated Theory of Criminology* (SAGE, Beverly Hills, Calif., 1982).

Endnotes

1. Court TV, www.courttv.com/trials/winkler/041007_ctv.html, accessed August 8, 2007.

2. P. W. Cook, *Abused Men: The Hidden Side of Domestic Violence* (Praeger, Westport, Conn., 1977).

3. M. A. Straus, R. J. Gelles, and S. K. Steinmetz, *Behind Closed Doors* (Anchor, Garden City, N.Y., 1980), p. 22.

4. M. D. Pagelow, *Family Violence* (Praeger, New York, 1984), p. 21.

5. Futures Without Violence Webpage at www.futureswithoutviolence.org/resources-events/get-the-facts/, accessed June 16, 2015.

6. See, for example, R. J. Gelles and D. R. Loseke, eds., *Current Controversies on Family Violence* (SAGE, Newbury Park, Calif., 1993).

7. See M. A. Strauss, R. J. Gelles, and S. K. Steinmetz, *Behind Closed Doors: Violence in the American Family* (Anchor/Doubleday, New York, 1980), for an in-depth discussion of the 1975 survey, and M. A. Strauss's "Is Violence toward Children Increasing? A Comparison of the 1975 and 1985 National Survey Rates," in R. J. Gelles, ed., *Family Violence* (SAGE, Newbury Park, Calif., 1987), for an analysis of the 1985 survey.

8. M. A. Straus, S. L. Hamby, S. Boney-McCoy, and D. B. Sugarman, "The Revised Conflict Tactics Scales (CTS2): Development and Preliminary Psychometric Data" (PDF), *Journal of Family Issues* 17 (3): 308–309, May 1996.

9. "Measuring Intimate Partner (Domestic) Violence," *National Institute of Justice*, May 12, 2010. Retrieved May 20, 2015.

10. *Domestic and Sexual Violence Data Collection: A Report to Congress under the Violence Against Women Act* (National Institute of Justice and the Bureau of Justice Statistics, Washington, D.C., July 1996).

11. Ibid., p. 1.

12. 28 USC 534 (1930).

13. "Crime in the United States, 1996," *Uniform Crime Reports* (Superintendent of Documents, Washington, D.C., 1997), p. 1.

14. M. E. Milakovich and K. Weis, "Politics and the Measure of Success in the War on Crime," *Crime and Delinquency* 21 (January 1975), pp. 1–10.

15. *Domestic and Sexual Violence Data Collection: A Report to Congress under the Violence Against Women Act* (National Institute of Justice and the Bureau of Justice Statistics, Washington, D.C., July 1996), pp. 26–28.

16. The UCR states that the NCVS started in 1973. See "Crime in the United States, 1996," *Uniform Crime Reports* (Superintendent of Documents, Washington, D.C., 1997).

17. The UCR presents a different estimate of households than the NCVS. See www.fbi.gov, accessed September 7, 2006.

18. *Domestic and Sexual Violence Data Collection: A Report to Congress under the Violence against Women Act* (National Institute of Justice and the Bureau of Justice Statistics, Washington, D.C., July 1996), p. 31.

19. Callie Rennison, "Criminal Victimization 2001: Changes 2000–01 with Trends 1993–2001," *National Crime Victimization Survey* (Bureau of Justice Statistics, Washington, D.C., September 2002).

20. B. Steele, "Psychodynamic Factors in Child Abuse," in R. E. Helfer and R. S. Kempe, eds., *The Battered Child*, 4th ed. (University of Chicago Press, Chicago, 1987).

21. D. J. Caplin et al., "Toronto Multiagency Child Abuse Research Project: The Abused and the Abuser," *Child Abuse and Neglect* 8(3) (1984), pp. 343–351.

22. R. J. Gelles, *The Violent Home* (SAGE, Beverly Hills, Calif., 1974).

23. R. L. Akers, *Deviant Behavior* (Wadsworth, Belmont, Calif., 1973).

24. P. M. Blau, *Exchange and Power in Social Life* (Wiley, New York, 1964).

25. R. J. Gelles, "An Exchange/Social Theory," in D. Finkelhor et al., eds., *The Dark Side of Families: Current Family Violence Research* (SAGE, Beverly Hills, Calif., 1983), pp. 151–165.

26. R. J. Gelles, *Family Violence*, 2nd ed. (SAGE, Newbury Park, Calif., 1987), p. 17.

27. Ibid., p. 158.

28. J. Dollard et al., *Frustration and Aggression* (Yale University Press, New Haven, Conn., 1939).

29. J. Garbarino, "The Human Ecology of Child Maltreatment," *Journal of Marriage and the Family* 39 (November 1977), pp. 721–735.

30. Ibid.

31. S. Porter, J. C. Yuille, and A. Bent, "A Comparison of the Eyewitness Accounts of Deaf and Hearing Children," *Child Abuse and Neglect* 19(1) (1995), pp. 51–62.

32. B. Smuts, "Male Aggression against Women: An Evolutionary Perspective," *Human Nature* 3 (1992), pp. 1–44.

33. R. L. Burgess and P. Draper, "The Explanation of Family Violence: The Role of Biological Behavioral, and Cultural Selection," in L. Ohlin and M. Tonry, eds., *Family Violence* (University of Chicago Press, Chicago, 1989).

34. M. E. Wolfgang and F. Ferracuti, *The Subculture of Violence: Toward an Integrated Theory of Criminology* (SAGE, Beverly Hills, Calif., 1982).

35. L. A. Coser, *Continuities in the Study of Social Conflict* (New York Free Press, New York, 1967).

36. For an excellent analysis of Australian male violence, see K. Polk's "Male-to-Male Homicides: Scenarios of Masculine Violence," paper presented at the annual meeting of the American Society of Criminology, San Francisco, November 18–23, 1991.

37. See M. D. Pagelow, *Family Violence* (Praeger, New York, 1984), pp. 127–138.

38. "Influence of TV Crime Programs on Children's Health," *JAMA* 150 (1952), p. 37.

39. Surgeon General's Scientific Advisory Committee on Television and Social Behavior.

Television and Growing Up: The Impact of Televised Violence (U.S. Department of Health, Washington, D.C., 1972).

40. D. Walsh, L. S. Goldman, and R. Brown, *Physicians Guide to Media Violence* (American Medical Association, Chicago, July 1996).

41. Ibid.

42. R. E. Dobash and R. P. Dobash, *Violence against Wives* (Free Press, New York, 1979).

43. J. Giles-Sims, *Wife-Beating: A Systems Theory Approach* (Guilford, New York, 1983).

44. M. A. Straus, "A General Systems Theory Approach to a Theory of Violence between Family Members," *Social Science Information* 12 (1973), pp. 105–125.

45. S. M. Retzinger, *Violent Emotions: Shame and Rage in Marital Quarrels* (SAGE, Newbury Park, Calif., 1991).

46. R. L. Warner, G. R. Lee, and J. Lee, "Social Organization, Spousal Resources, and Marital Power: A Cross-Cultural Study," *Journal of Marriage and the Family* 48 (1986), pp. 121–128.

47. R. Gelles, *The Violent Home* (SAGE, Newbury Park, Calif., 1993).

48. See D. Finkelhor, "Common Features of Family Abuse," in D. Finkelhor et al., eds., *The Dark Side of Families* (SAGE, Beverly Hills, Calif., 1983), pp. 17–18; and M. D. Pagelow, *Family Violence* (Praeger, New York, 1984).

49. P. Tolan, D. Gorman-Smith, and D. Henry, "Family Violence," *Annual Review of Psychology* 57 (2006), pp. 557–583.

50. D. Finkelhor, "Common Features of Family Abuse," in D. Finkelhor et al., eds., *The Dark Side of Families* (SAGE, Beverly Hills, Calif., 1983), pp. 17–18.

51. M. Weber, *The Theory of Social and Economic Organization*, trans. A. M. Henderson and T. Parsons (Free Press, New York, 1964), p. 152.

52. Results from the National Survey on Drug Use and Health, www.oas.samhsa.gov/NSDUH/2k5results.htm, accessed September 7, 2006.

53. E. M. Gil, *Outgrowing the Pain: A Book for and about Adults Abused as Children* (Launch Press, San Francisco, 1983).

54. M. L. Blumberg, "Character Disorders in Traumatized and Handicapped Children," *American Journal of Psychotherapy* 33(2) (1979), pp. 201–213.

55. G. E. Dunn, "Multiple Personality Disorder: A New Challenge for Psychology," *Professional Psychology: Research and Practice* 23(1) (1992), pp. 18–23.

56. L. J. Siegal, *Criminology*, 3rd ed. (West, St. Paul, Minn., 1989), p. 188.

57. B. Steele and V. Pollock, "A Psychiatric Study of Parents Who Abuse Infants and Small Children," in R. Helfer and C. H. Kempe, eds., *The Battered Child Syndrome* (University of Chicago Press, Chicago, 1968). It is interesting to note that later editions of this classic book on child abuse do not contain the article. For example, see the fourth edition, published in 1987.

58. M. Straus, "Family Patterns in a Nationally Representative Sample," *International Journal of Child Abuse and Neglect* 3(23) (1979).

59. R. Hunter and N. Kilstrom, "Breaking the Cycle in Abusive Families," *American Journal of Psychiatry* 136(1320) (1979).

60. B. Egeland and D. Jacobvitz, "Intergenerational Continuity of Parental Abuse: Causes and Consequences," paper presented at the Conference on Biosocial Perspectives in Abuse and Neglect (York, Maine, 1984).

61. C. Cappell and R. B. Heiner, "The Intergenerational Transmission of Family Aggression," *Journal of Family Violence* 5(2) (1990), p. 135.

62. E. Loos and P. C. Alexander, "Differential Effects Associated with Self-Reported Histories of Abuse and Neglect in a College Sample," *Journal of Interpersonal Violence* 12(3) (1997), p. 340.

63. J. Clarke et al., "Victims as Victimizers: Physical Aggression by Persons with a History of Childhood Abuse," *Archive of Internal Medicine* 159 (1999), p. 1920.

64. K. A. Dodge, J. E. Bates, and G. S. Pettit, "Mechanisms in the Cycle of Violence," *Science* 250 (December 1990), p. 1678.

65. Ibid., p. 1681.

66. C. S. Widom, "The Cycle of Violence," *Research in Brief* (National Institute of Justice, U.S. Department of Justice, Washington, D.C., October, 1992).

67. C. S. Widon and M. G. Maxfield, "An Update on the Cycle of Violence," *Research in Brief*

(Office of Justice Programs, National Institute of Justice, Washington D.C., February 2001).

68. Much of this information was gathered from interviewing members of the Fresno Valley Medical Center emergency room staff. Barbara Miller, R.N., was of significant assistance in providing guidance for material in this section.

69. J. D. Wright, "The Demography of Gun Control," *The Nation*, September 20, 1976, p. 241.

70. L. Adelson, "The Gun and the Sanctity of Human Life: or the Bullet as a Pathogen," *The Phasos* (Summer 1980), p. 15.

71. A. R. Roberts and S. F. Dziegielewski, "Foundation Skills and Applications of Crisis Intervention and Cognitive Therapy," in A. R. Roberts, ed., *Crisis Intervention and Time-Limited Cognitive Treatment* (SAGE, Thousand Oaks, Calif., 1995).

72. E. Lindemann, "Symptomatology and Management of Acute Grief," *American Journal of Psychiatry* 101 (1994), pp. 141–148.

73. C. P. Wing, *Crisis Intervention as Psychotherapy* (Oxford University Press, New York, 1978); and G. Caplin, *Principles of Preventive Psychiatry* (Basic Books, New York, 1964).

74. See A. R. Roberts, *Crisis Intervention Handbook: Assessment, Treatment and Research* (Wadsworth, Belmont, Calif., 1990); and M. Bard and D. Sangrey, *The Crime Victim's Book*, 2nd ed. (Brunner/Mazel, New York, 1986).

75. G. Caplin, *Principles of Preventive Psychiatry* (Basic Books, New York, 1964), p. 46.

76. *Diagnostic and Statistical Manual of Mental Disorders*, 4th ed. (American Psychiatric Association, Washington, D.C., 1994).

77. Ibid., pp. 427–429

78. Ibid.

79. For an excellent discussion of the effects of rape on victims, see Bruce Taylor, "The Role of Significant Others in a Rape Victim's Recovery: People Who Are More Likely to Be Harmful Than Helpful," paper presented at the 1996 ACJS Annual Meeting, Las Vegas, Nevada, March 1996.

80. B. O. Rothbaum et al., "A Prospective Examination of Posttraumatic Stress Disorder in Rape Victims," *Journal of Traumatic Stress* 5 (1992), pp. 455–475.

81. D. G. Kilpatrick, C. N. Edmunds, and A. K. Seymour, *Rape in America: A Report to the Nation* (National Victim Center, Arlington, Va., 1992).

82. M. A. Young, "Crisis Response Teams in the Aftermath of Disasters," in Roberts, ed., *Crisis Intervention and Time-Limited Cognitive Treatment* (SAGE, Thousand Oaks, Calif., 1995), pp. 151–187.

83. J. Susman and C. H. Vittert, *Building a Solution: A Practical Guide for Establishing Crime Victim Service Agencies* (National Council of Jewish Women, St. Louis, Mo., 1980).

84. T. R. Miller, M. A. Cohen, and B. Wiersema, *Victim Costs and Consequences: A New Look* (National Institute of Justice, U.S. Department of Justice, Washington, D.C., February 1996). This section is based on the material presented in this study.

85. M. A. Cohen and T. R. Miller, "The Cost of Mental Health Care for Victims of Crime," *Journal of Interpersonal Violence* 13(1) (1998) p. 93.

86. *Costs of Intimate Partner Violence against Women in the United States* (Centers for Disease Control and Prevention, Atlanta, Ga., April, 2006).

87. Ibid., p. 30.

2

Intimate Partner Abuse and
Relationship Violence

CHAPTER OBJECTIVES

After studying this chapter, you should be able to:

- Explain what constitutes intimate partner abuse;
- List reasons why an abused partner stays in the relationship;
- Describe why battered persons have feelings of powerlessness;
- Discuss how violence is often used as a means of gaining a power advantage over the abused partner;
- Explain battered spouse syndrome.

Detailed Look at What You Should Know About Intimate Partner Abuse and Relationship Violence

- Questions always arise in the beginning of any discussion of partner and relationship abuse as to why the abused person stays in the relationship.
- Both modern and ancient history are replete with a generalized domination of women by men.
- Women are the victims in nearly three out of four victims of the murders attributable to intimate partners.
- The impact of repetitive violence on an individual's health often brings domestic violence into the medical setting.
- Family violence is a major health concern in the medical profession, with approximately 10 to 40 percent of female patients disclosing abuse by their partners to their physicians when screened in a primary care setting.

- There is no clear definition of intimate partner abuse.
- Violence against women has long-term health effects.
- Approximately one-third (31%) of all women have been kicked, hit, or punched, choked, or otherwise physically assaulted by a spouse or partner in their lifetime.
- *Family* is a group of persons who cohabit. Marriage is not a requirement. Within this living arrangement, forces converge to cause stress. Stress does not cause violence; instead, violence is one of the many responses available to persons who suffer from stress.
- Power is the ability to impose one's will on another and make life decisions. Partners who share power or are equals in the decision-making process have the lowest level of both conflict and violence.
- Battered partners report a feeling of powerlessness as a result of the partner abuse they have suffered.
- Marital dependency is a multifaceted concept that involves economic, emotional, and societal forces that result in a woman being dependent on her spouse for support.
- Studies have attempted to determine whether alcohol causes partner abuse. At this stage, there is no definitive answer, but a link does seem to exist between alcohol and partner abuse.
- Pregnancy and intimate partner abuse is a controversial subject, and studies indicate that a relationship exists between the two.
- In partner abuse, many times the abuser will use violence as a means of gaining a power advantage over the abused partner.
- Dependency is associated with economics. The abuser may cut off the partner's financial support system. He or she may not have the financial ability to leave the relationship.
- Determining who has suffered what type of abuse is more of an art than a science. Two major types or techniques are relied on in assessing partner abuse: self-reporting and interviews.
- Physical aggression may take the form of minor acts that escalate over time. It may begin with grabbing an arm, throwing a dish, or slapping an arm or face.
- Physical violence is often accompanied by sexual abuse. Sex on demand or after physical assaults is very common.
- Emotional abuse includes many different acts that all contribute to a feeling of helplessness and inability.
- Emotional abuse may take the form of humiliation.
- Using fear, guilt, and isolation, the abuser will promote a feeling of helplessness within the spouse that further ties the victim to the abuser. She believes that there is no way to break the cycle and feels trapped.
- Most states and the District of Columbia allowed the use of expert testimony on the subject of battered spouse syndrome.
- Gay couples can face the same kind of violence that sometimes occurs in heterosexual relationships.

INTRODUCTION

The costs of intimate partner rape, physical assault, and stalking exceed $5.8 billion each year, nearly $4.1 billion of which is for direct medical and mental health care services.[1]

Intimate partner violence (IPV) is violence committed by a spouse, ex-spouse, or current or former boyfriend or girlfriend. IPV occurs among both heterosexual and same-sex couples. It is often a repeated offense. It can occur to both men and women, but the literature indicates that women among heterosexual or same-sex couples are much more likely than men to suffer physical, and probably psychological, injuries from IPV.

This chapter examines the dynamics of intimate partner abuse and relationship violence. The term *intimate partner* is used to describe not only those couples living together in traditional marriage but also those individuals living together or those involved in serious relationships, but not necessarily living together on a daily basis. In this text, intimate partner violence includes violence among same gender partners.

Questions always arise in the beginning of any discussion of partner and relationship abuse as to why the abused person stays in the relationship. This issue is explored here, as well as other misconceptions and characteristics of the traditional form of family violence.

The Focus box "Acknowledging Domestic Violence" indicates the turmoil that partner and relationship violence is generating within the professions. If well-educated and knowledgeable individuals such as physicians are having difficulty with partner abuse, it stands to

---

Focus

Partner Abuse Facts

- More than one in three women (35.6%) and more than one in four men (28.5%) in the United States have experienced rape, physical violence, and/or stalking by an intimate partner in their lifetime.
- Nearly half of all women and men in the United States have experienced psychological aggression by an intimate partner in their lifetime (48.4% and 48.8%, respectively).
- More than one in three women experienced multiple forms of rape, stalking, or physical violence; 92.1 percent of male victims experienced physical violence alone, and 6.3 percent experienced physical violence and stalking.
- Nearly one in ten women in the United States (9.4%) has been raped by an intimate partner in her lifetime, and an estimated 16.9 percent of women and 8.0 percent of men have experienced sexual violence other than rape by an intimate partner at some point in their lifetime.
- Nearly half of all women and men in the United States have experienced psychological aggression by an intimate partner in their lifetime (48.4% and 48.8%, respectively).
- Most female and male victims of rape, physical violence, and/or stalking by an intimate partner (69% of female victims; 53% of male victims) experienced some form of intimate partner violence for the first time before twenty-five years of age.

Source: The National Intimate Partner and Sexual Violence Survey: 2010 Summary Report (National Center for Injury Prevention and Control, the Centers for Disease Control and Prevention, Atlanta, Ga, 2011).

reason that many other professionals still harbor doubts, misconceptions, and half-truths about this form of family violence.

Throughout this chapter, the word *her* will often be used to denote the victim or abused party. This is not to indicate that men are not victims of partner abuse; they are, and, as will be seen, some studies indicate that this type of abuse is far more common than it is imagined. However, generally the abuse visited on women is more severe and long-lasting than the type of abuse men suffer. In addition, research has shown that men have far greater opportunities to leave the abusive situation than women.

PARTNER ABUSE

Both modern and ancient history are replete with a generalized domination of women by men. In early times, women were looked on as property and as a method of ensuring that a man's heritage and line continued. Husbands were allowed to beat, torture, and even kill their wives. In Rome, where the first laws of marriage were enacted, a husband was the absolute ruler who controlled all properties and persons in his household. The wife was required to obey her husband, and he was given the legal right to punish her for any misbehavior.[2] Even today, many marriage ceremonies still include instructions for the wife to love, honor, and obey her future husband.

In France, Napoleon Bonaparte enacted the Civil Code, which stated that women were property. They were first "owned" by their fathers, then in marriage that ownership transferred to their husbands.[3] Under English common law, wives and children were property of the husband.[4] The famous legal commentator Blackstone stated that husbands had a right and duty to "chastise" their wives like apprentices or children for "correctional" purposes.[5]

THE RULE OF THUMB

Recent research reveals a form of urban legend regarding the phrase, accuracy, and use of the term *Rule of Thumb*. Many victim advocates, researchers, and professionals have accepted without question that in early England and America a man might legally beat his wife so long as he used a stick that was no thicker than his thumb.

One authority relies on Blackstone for the origin of the Rule of Thumb, but that is in error. Blackstone allowed for moderate discipline, but never discussed or authorized the use of a stick the size of a man's thumb.[6] The existence of the Rule of Thumb gained further acceptance with the publication in 1824 of a Mississippi case, *Bradley v. State,* in which the court stated that other states allow for chastisement that was referred to as the Rule of Thumb.[7] The court cited two sources, Prosser and Stedman, for its position. Prosser in the first edition of his famous law treatise, *Prosser on Torts,* actually states:

A husband or father, as the head of the household, was recognized by the early law as having authority to discipline the members of his family. He might administer to his wife "moderate correction," and "restrain" her by "domestic chastisement" [citing Blackstone and Stedman], although there is probably no truth whatever in the legend that he was permitted to beat her with a stick no thicker than his thumb.[8]

Focus

Violence Against Women

- In 2007, women were nearly three out of four victims of the murders attributable to intimate partners.
- Considered by age category, women aged sixteen to twenty-four experienced the highest per capita rates of intimate violence (19.7 per 1,000 women).

- Only about half the intimate partner violence against women was reported to the police.
- About four out of ten female victims of intimate partner violence lived in households with children under the age of twelve.

Source: Intimate Partner Violence (Bureau of Justice Statistics, Washington, D.C., May 2008).

However, Stedman in his classic law review article, "Right of Husband to Chastise Wife," does state that a husband may inflict moderate personal chastisement on his wife provided he uses a switch no larger than his thumb.[9] Stedman cites as his authority *State v. Oliver* and *State v. Rhodes*, in which neither court specifically endorsed the Rule of Thumb. In *Rhodes*, the court stated "the standard to use was the effect produced, and not the manner of producing it, or the instrument used."[10] In *Oliver*, the defendant (Oliver) was found guilty of assault and battery and fined $10.00 for beating his wife with two switches, one of which was about half as large as a man's little finger. In *Oliver*, Judge Settle stated:

> We may assume that the old doctrine, that a husband had a right to whip his wife, provided he used a switch no larger than his thumb, is not law in North Carolina. Indeed, the courts. . . have reached the position, that the husband has no right to chastise his wife, under any circumstances.[11]

Sommers was one of the first to question the existence and origin of the Rule of Thumb.[12] She traced the history of the term and points out that it relies on a misreading of Blackstone and a lack of understanding of the two cases discussed earlier.

It would therefore seem that the concept of the husband beating his wife using a stick no larger than the circumference of his thumb is an example of an urban legend. However, this does not mean that partner abuse did not occur during this time. It simply means that the Rule of Thumb was not an accepted form of punishment.

This section is not a defense of beating of women. Rather it is an attempt to inform and ensure that when advocates and other professionals discuss partner abuse they do so based upon accurate research rather than faulty folklore. Even if the Rule of Thumb did not exist, partner abuse did. Partner abuse has existed since the beginning of recorded time, and only of late have we as a society begun to address it.

It took a constitutional amendment in the United States to allow women the right to vote. Even after women were granted this privilege, they continued to be viewed as extensions of their husbands. It wasn't until the 1960s and 1970s with the explosive growth of the women's movement that women began to be viewed as equals. During this time, women began to seek help and protection from abusive spouses, and the first shelters for battered women opened. In 1974, a feminist organization known as Women's Advocates opened Women's

Focus

Same Sex Relationship Violence

- Some people believe that women are not likely to abuse each other. But experts believe that abuse happens as often in same-sex relationships as in heterosexual relationships.
- A woman in a same-sex relationship who experiences dating violence or domestic violence may face many of the same issues as an abused heterosexual woman. Her partner may hit her, try to control her, or force her to have sex.
- A woman in a same-sex relationship may also face additional issues, including:
  - o Fear of being "outed" as gay
  - o Thinking that you have to be married to be considered a victim of domestic abuse
  - o Concern that people who should help will instead be anti-gay
- Lesbians who abuse another women may do so for reasons similar to those that motivate heterosexual male batterers. Lesbians abuse their partners to gain and maintain control. Lesbian batterers are motivated to avoid feelings of loss and abandonment. Therefore, many violent incidents occur during threatened separations.
- There are several similarities between lesbian and heterosexual partner violence. Violence appears to be about as common among lesbian couples as among heterosexual couples. However, there also are several differences. In lesbian relationships, the "butch" (physically stronger, more masculine, or wage-earning) member of the couple may be as likely to be the victim as the batterer, whereas in heterosexual relationships, the male partner (usually the stronger, more masculine, and wage-earning member) is most often the batterer. Some lesbians in abusive relationships report fighting back in their relationship.
- Violence that abusive gay men inflict on domestic partners is no less serious than the violence inflicted by abusive heterosexual men on their domestic partners. One study found 79 percent of gay victims had suffered some physical injury, with 60 percent reporting bruises, 23 percent reporting head injuries and concussions, 13 percent reporting forced sex with the intention to infect the victim with HIV, 12 percent reporting broken bones, and 10 percent reporting burns.
- Experts believe that domestic violence occurs in the lesbian, gay, bisexual, and transgender community with the same amount of frequency and severity as in the heterosexual community.

Sources: Office on Women's Health, U.S. Department of Health and Human Services Web site at www.womenshealth.gov, accessed June 17, 2015; National Coalition Against Domestic Violence Web site at www.uncfsp.org, accessed June 17, 2015; University of Missouri's National Violence Against Women Web site at https://mainweb-v.musc.edu/vawprevention,accessed June 17, 2015; and Introduction to Gay Male Domestic Violence Web site at www.psychpage.com, accessed June 17, 2015.

House in St. Paul, Minnesota. This was the first unrestricted shelter for abused women in the United States.[13] From this humble beginning, women's shelters have sprung up in every major metropolitan center in the United States. This is not to imply that the establishment or maintenance of these shelters has been easy or painless. Traditionally, these shelters rely on contributions or grants from local, state, or federal sources. Today, these funds are in short supply, and many social programs for the establishment and maintenance of women's shelters are viewed as less of a priority than funding police and fire operations. Part of the reason for this cutback on funding is the general public's lack of understanding of the exact nature and extent of partner abuse. The following sections examine these issues.

DEFINITION

No clear definition of intimate partner abuse exists. Different authorities include different acts within their definitions, and some have established levels of partner abuse. They categorize partner abuse into two forms of violence. The lesser forms include yelling and throwing things, and the more severe forms include striking and hitting.

Focus

Acknowledging Domestic Violence—Opening Pandora's Box

The impact of repetitive violence on an individual's health often brings domestic violence into the medical setting. Family violence is a major health concern in the medical profession, with approximately 10 to 40 percent of female patients disclosing abuse by their partners to their physicians when screened in a primary care setting.

Recently, concern about physicians' responsiveness to domestic violence has been expressed. Several studies have shown that even with knowledge of the underlying cause of the trauma, many physicians fail to respond to the battering. Repeatedly, the image of opening Pandora's box was used by physicians to describe their reactions to exploring domestic violence with patients. This metaphor suggests the fear of unleashing a myriad of evils. The close identification that physicians have with their patients may preclude them from considering the possibility of domestic violence in their differential diagnoses. Physicians who come from white, middle-class backgrounds with no experience of domestic violence often assume that their patients with similar characteristics would likewise not be at risk for violence. Although most physicians intellectually acknowledge that domestic violence cuts across all races, classes, and ethnic groups, the socioeconomic status of the patient was

clearly used as a marker for determining whether abuse was likely.

Fear of offending the patient was one of the strongest concerns expressed by physicians. This discomfort often arose from areas that are culturally defined as private. Physicians felt that by broaching the subject of violence, the patient would take offense at the implications of the question. It appeared that to suggest the diagnosis of domestic violence was to accuse the partner of being a batterer.

Many physicians voiced frustration and feelings of inadequacy when discussing what would constitute appropriate interventions. Several pointed to the complexity of the problem and the fact that they had no tools to help. There was a strong sense of powerlessness when physicians described their inability to "fix it."

Pediatricians face the same obstacles as other doctors when asked to address the issue of family violence. The American Academy of Pediatrics has recently suggested that all pediatricians incorporate family violence screening as part of anticipatory guidance. However, the real issue is whether pediatricians have the resources, time, and knowledge to screen patients in a community setting.

Sources: Based on N. K. Sugg and T. Inui, "Primary Care Physicians' Response to Domestic Violence, Opening Pandora's Box," *Journal of American Medical Association* 267(23) (17, 1992), pp. 3157–3160; and Robert M. Siegal et al., "Screening for Domestic Violence in the Community Pediatric Setting," *Pediatrics* 104 (October 1999), p. 878.

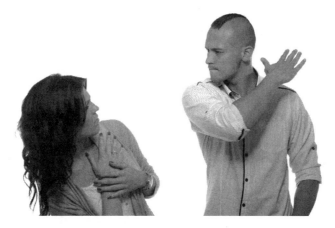

An example of physical partner violence, an angry man slapping his partner.

Shades of gray exist in any situation, and reasonable people may disagree as to what constitutes partner abuse. For purposes of this chapter, **partner abuse** is defined as any intentional act or series of acts that cause injury to the partner. These acts may be physical, emotional, or sexual. *Spouse* is gender-neutral, and therefore the abuse may occur to a male or female. The term includes those who are married, cohabiting, or involved in a serious relationship. It also encompasses individuals who are separated and living apart from their former spouse. Although some disagreement exists regarding the exact definition of partner abuse, all scholars and authorities agree that it exists. The next section examines the extent of this form of family violence.

EXTENT OF THE PROBLEM

Depending on which study is reviewed, the extent of partner abuse varies. In their landmark study of 8,145 families, Straus and Gelles estimated that just over 16 percent, or one in six, American couples experienced an incident of physical assault during 1985. Projecting that number to the 54 million couples in the United States in that year leads to a startling figure of approximately 8.7 million couples who were involved in partner abuse.[14] Other scholars point out that 20 percent of all women who go to emergency rooms for treatment have been battered.[15]

The Bureau of Justice Statistics reports that approximately 85 percent (588,490 out of 691,710) of victimizations by intimate partners in 2001 were against women. This is a decline in the number of crimes by intimate partners against females. In 1993, the total of such nonfatal violent crimes was 1.1 million. By 2001, it had decreased to 588,490.[16] Although this is a significant decrease, partner abuse still remains a serious problem in our society.

The figures cited pertain to physical violence. As the definition presented previously indicates, partner abuse includes psychological and sexual abuse as well. When a person is emotionally abused, she may not go to an emergency room or even report the acts because

Practicum

Which of the Following in Your Opinion Would Be Considered Partner Abuse?

- A boy is upset at his girlfriend who is late for a date. He calls her lazy and irresponsible.
- During a date, the male takes his date's arm and steers her to an entrance, commenting that she is stupid for not seeing that this is the fastest way to leave the theater.
- A couple who is living together while attending college get into a yelling match, each calling the other names.
- The same couple's argument escalates, and one partner throws a textbook at the other partner. It misses and strikes the television.

- During a heated argument, one partner grabs the other partner by the arms and shakes the partner.
- A husband slaps his wife after she overdraws the bank account, causing him to bounce a check.
- The husband does not allow his wife access to any funds after she bounced three checks and almost caused him to lose his job at the bank.
- The one partner is tired and wants to sleep, but the other partner forces the tired partner to engage in sex.

she may believe she deserved the treatment, and therefore it is not abuse. "After all, he didn't hit me" is a common refrain in some partner abuse cases.

Violence against women has long-term health effects. Approximately one-third (31%) of all women have been kicked, hit, punched, choked, or otherwise physically assaulted by a spouse or partner in their lifetime. Three percent—a figure representing approximately three million women in the United States—reported experiencing recent incidents of partner abuse. *The Commonwealth Fund 1998 Survey of Women's Health* confirms that violence and abuse cut across all regions of the country, races, and incomes.[17]

As stated, a surprising result of some of these studies is the indication that partner abuse may have declined by as much as 20 percent in recent years. Several explanations exist for this apparent decline. One is the availability of shelters for women who are abused. This escape valve allows them a way to leave an abusive relationship. Another is the widespread publicity that has occurred in recent years about partner abuse. A third possible explanation is more effective punishment and better treatment for the assaultive partner.[18] Even though the incidence of partner abuse may be declining, many scholars believe that its severity is increasing. Even with a decline in the number of reported cases in recent years, this form of family violence is still prevalent and requires any professional to be familiar with the nature and dynamics of partner abuse.

THEORIES OF PARTNER ABUSE

If professionals knew the causes of partner abuse, they could correct it. To date, no one has yet come forward with a definitive answer to this question. However, numerous scholars in different professions have studied this form of family violence and come up with a variety of reasons or causes for this type of abuse. These causes are specific to the phenomenon of partner abuse and must be considered and evaluated in light of the earlier discussion in Chapter 1, which dealt with the general characteristics of family violence. Although there are many

Focus

Domestic Violence and LGBT Relationship Protections

According to the National Coalition Against Domestic Violence Web site, in 2006 there were 3,524 Lesbian, Gay, Bisexual, and Transgender Relationship (LGBT) domestic violence incidents in only ten cities and two states. The Web site also states that LGBT domestic violence is vastly underreported.

The Web site notes that in three states (Delaware, Montana, and South Carolina) explicitly exclude same-sex survivors of domestic violence from protection under criminal laws on domestic violence.

As of 2015, 30 states and the District of Columbia have domestic violence laws that are gender neutral and include persons living together or dating. Eighteen other states have domestic violence laws that are gender neutral but apply only to household members.

The coalition list the below barriers to addressing LGBT intimate partner violence include:

- The belief that domestic violence does not occur in LGBT relationships and/or is a gender based issue;
- Societal anti-LGBT bias (homophobia, biphobia, and transphobia);
- Lack of appropriate training regarding LGBT domestic violence for service providers;

- A fear that airing of the problems among the LGBT population will take away from progress toward equality or fuel anti-LGBT bias;
- Domestic violence shelters are typically female only, thus transgender people may not be allowed entrance into shelters or emergency facilities due to their gender/genital/legal status.

In addition to the traditional forms of domestic abuse, there are additional forms of abuse that may be present in LGBT partnerships. Under transgender abuse the forms of abuse include:

- Using offensive pronouns such as "it" to refer to the transgender partner;
- Ridiculing the transgender partner's body and/or appearance;
- Telling the transgender partner that he or she is not a real man or woman;
- Ridiculing the transgender partner's identity as "bisexual," "trans," "femme," "butch," "gender queer," etc.;
- Denying the transgender partner's access to medical treatment or hormones or coercing him or her to not pursue medical treatment.

Source: National Coalition Against Domestic Violence Web site at www.uncfsp.org, accessed August 27, 2015.

theories and studies in the area of partner abuse, space dictates that only a few of the more well-known ones be discussed here.

Social Stress

The family system in the United States is a system of contradictions. Citizens retreat from the city streets to their homes and install bars on their windows to keep out the violence. Yet the family structure is one of the most violent settings a person is likely to encounter.

For purposes of this discussion, a **family** is a group of persons who cohabit. Marriage is not a requirement. Within this living arrangement, forces converge to cause stress. This increased level of stress in turn leads to a high rate of violence within the family. Many times this violence is directed at the spouse in the form of physical assaults. It should be pointed out that stress does not cause violence; instead, violence is one of the many responses available to persons who suffer from stress.

Family life has a different set of behaviors than other social settings. How the members within a family setting dress, talk, and act in their home is different from how they act when they attend social functions. In addition, violence in the form of physical punishment is accepted by many as a characteristic of the family. Parents can and do slap infants' hands to teach them, for example, not to touch the hot coffee pot. Such a form of physical violence may be used on loved ones for their own benefit. Therefore, when stress occurs, there is already a preconditioned response or behavior that has been used and is easy to use when one is under pressure.

Power

Power is the ability to impose one's will on another and make life decisions. Couples who share power or are equals in the decision-making process have the lowest level of both conflict and violence.[19] When a conflict arises, these families display the greatest resistance to the use of violence. As indicated in Chapter 1, one of the characteristics of family violence is the use and abuse of power. In addition, battered partners report a feeling of powerlessness as a result of the partner abuse they have suffered.

Dependency

As the introduction to this chapter indicated, our society has fostered women's dependency. Women's financial and social success in many instances has been dependent on the men they marry. Although this is beginning to change, the "glass ceiling" still remains, for the most part, an impenetrable barrier (this phenomenon is discussed in more detail later). A few examples bring home this point. In 2009, there were only two female U.S. Supreme Court justices, only ten women are U.S. senators, and only a small percentage of women are chief executive officers of major corporations.[20] Statistically, after a divorce a man's standard of living increases, whereas a woman's declines.[21]

The meaning of marital dependency is subject to debate, but the most common meaning includes economic dependency. The female spouse often has little or no earning power and is therefore dependent on her male partner for the necessities of life.[22] A variation on this theme of economic dependency is the presence of children. Although a female may be able to leave an abusive relationship and make ends meet, the addition of children multiplies the difficulties inherent in any separation. A third factor in dependence is society's expectation of women as caregivers and the further hidden message that a woman is not whole until she is married.[23]

Thus, **marital dependency** is a multifaceted concept that involves economic, emotional, and societal forces that result in a woman being dependent on her spouse for support. This dependency on a man and marriage for economic, emotional, and other support increases a woman's tolerance for physical abuse.

Straus and Gelles and their associates conducted an in-depth study of dependency and violence and reported that women whose dependency on marriage is high tend to suffer more physical violence than women whose dependency is low. Dependent wives have fewer alternatives to marriage and fewer resources within the marriage with which to cope or modify their husband's behavior.[24] This dependency is a pair of "golden handcuffs" that binds the spouse to the abusive partner.

A drunken partner beating his partner.

Alcohol

A common perception is that males who drink alcohol beat their spouses. Therefore, so the reasoning goes, alcohol causes violence. Movies, books, and to some extent our own personal experiences support the concept that alcohol causes problems in relationships. The relationship between alcohol and abuse has been studied extensively, and several theories have been formed regarding alcohol and its relationship to violence. A few of the more common theories follow:

> *Disinhibition theory:* This theory is based on the principle that alcohol releases inhibitions and alters judgment. Medical evidence regarding the effects of alcohol on the central nervous system supports this theory. However, recent research into disinhibition theory reveals that alcohol interacts with individuals depending on varying individual expectancies, which is only one aspect of the alcohol–violence equation.[25]

> *Social learning and deviance disavowal theory:* Coleman and Straus have argued that individuals learn violence by observing others who drink and become violent. This violent behavior is excused, pardoned, or justified because the individual was drunk and, therefore, not accountable for his actions.[26] Other scholars have suggested that individuals use alcohol to increase their sense of power and as an excuse for the exercise of unlawful force against others.[27]

> *Integrated theoretical models:* Pernanem's research into alcohol and violence indicates numerous factors that interact in alcohol and violence. These factors may include the inherent conflict present in marriages.[28] A second factor is society's belief that drinking is an acceptable and expected form of male behavior.

All these theories and studies have attempted to determine whether alcohol causes partner abuse. At this stage, there is no definitive answer, but a link does seem to exist between alcohol and partner abuse. However, some people drink and do not abuse their spouses, so it would appear that alcohol by itself cannot be defined as the cause of partner abuse.

Pregnancy

Pregnancy and partner abuse is a controversial subject, and studies indicate that a relationship exists between the two.[29] Despite this linkage, the question remains of whether pregnancy causes domestic violence or whether it is just another factor to be considered. Most of the studies are based on small samples and have internal validity problems. However, the Straus and Gelles survey of violence, using the National Family Violence Survey, determined that the rates of violence were higher for households in which the female partner was pregnant.[30] Subsequently, the authors concluded that previously reported associations between pregnancy and violence were not valid and that age is a more critical factor in determining violence than pregnancy. Young women have higher pregnancy rates and experience violence more often than older women. Females under the age of twenty-five appeared to be at the highest risk.

Marriage

"The marriage license as a hitting license" concept was adopted in the early 1970s by Gelles and Straus when they discovered that married couples suffered assault at a much greater rate than strangers.[31] They reasoned that the common-law tradition that allowed a husband to discipline his wife was alive and well. However, more recent studies indicate that the highest rate and greatest severity of assault is among cohabiting couples.[32]

Age may also be a factor because dating and cohabiting couples tend to be younger than married couples. However, other research indicates that age and marital status have no relationship to violence. Therefore, significant relationships, whether they involve dating, cohabitation, or marriage, place women at risk. As indicated previously, cohabiting couples may be at a higher risk than married couples. In a more recent evaluation of the National Family Violence Surveys, Straus and Gelles set forth the following factors as having more impact on the degree of risk a women faces in a cohabiting relationship:

Isolation: Couples who are living together without being married may be more isolated than married couples. Part of this isolation may be because of the stigma that society in some parts of the country attaches to cohabitation before marriage. This isolation may promote partner abuse because there are a lack of supporting network of friends or family available for help.

Autonomy and control: Some people prefer cohabitation over marriage with the thought that they can retain their independence. However, any living arrangement brings with it duties, obligations, tensions, and the resulting disagreements. Some authorities point out that when the issue of control arises, violence occurs.[33] As the relationship becomes more serious, the issue of control becomes more important, and violence is more likely to occur.

Investment in the relationship: Cohabiting couples may share some characteristics that trigger violence while lacking others shared by married couples that stop the conflict from escalating into physical violence.[34]

As with other theories of partner abuse, more study needs to be done before researchers can understand whether women who enter into any significant relationship are at risk of partner abuse. This section has discussed various theories of partner abuse, and it is clear that professionals have not yet discovered a cure for this type of abuse. Because the cause of this type of violence may never be determined, professionals must understand some of the characteristics of partner abuse.

CHARACTERISTICS OF PARTNER ABUSE

Various factors or characteristics may indicate a higher probability of partner abuse. These characteristics may take the form of personality traits in men or women or present themselves as situations. Distinctions should be made between theories regarding partner abuse and situations that may increase the likelihood of this form of family violence. In the previous section, various theories were set forth that attempted to explain why partner abuse occurs; this section deals with factors or characteristics that are present when partner abuse happens.

Anderson and her associates presented a series of factors that characterize abusive relationships. Although their study concerned psychological abuse of spouses, psychological and physical abuse are usually intertwined in partner abuse. Therefore, these characteristics or situations are deemed applicable to all forms of partner abuse. These factors include traumatic bonding, psychological entrapment, social isolation, economic stress, alcohol abuse, power imbalance, and intergenerational transmission.[35]

Traumatic bonding: In partner abuse, many times the abuser will use violence as a means of gaining a power advantage over the abused partner. This is accomplished by control over the spouse's time, contacts, and perception of herself. The battering may be followed by a period of calm, which is then followed by another incident of violence. This intermittent reinforcement creates a traumatic bond in which the abused partner becomes progressively more attached to the abuser and intent on modifying him.

Psychological entrapment: This situation occurs when the woman begins the relationship with the intent of making it work. When incidents of abuse occur, she tries harder to maintain the relationship and thereby invests more of herself in it. Abusers seek out partners who are easily victimized, willing to take responsibility for the relationship, and whose passivity fits the self-sacrificing role.

Social isolation: The abuser isolates the spouse so that no family or support system is available to give her feedback on the acts of the abuser. Her entire world is limited to the values and actions of her spouse. This in turn leads to domination and control by the abuser.

Economic stress: Dependency is associated with economics. The abuser may cut off the spouse's financial support system. She may not have the financial ability to leave the relationship.

Alcohol abuse: Alcohol does not cause abuse but is present in many abusive relationships. The spouse may believe that if the abuser simply did not drink, the abuse would stop. This faulty logic may lead the spouse to believe that alcohol is the cause of the problem.

Power imbalance: If the male or abuser is threatened by the other's achievements, this imbalance of power may lead to abuse. Traditionally, abusive partners want to maintain control over their victims.

Partners involved in violence.

Intergenerational transmission: The cycle of violence theory discussed in Chapter 1 may apply in partner abuse. Some authorities believe that if the batterer witnessed violence as a child, there is an increased chance that violence will be present in his adult life.

Other authorities such as Pagelow have established a list of factors that may indicate the possibility of increased violence in an intimate relationship. These factors are danger signals or early warnings that women should examine when entering into or maintaining an intimate relationship.

Although individuals who abuse or are abused may suffer from mental disorders, mental classifications have not been established for either group. Neither from a psychological point of view has a clear diagnosis been developed that deals with the dynamics involved in an abusive relationship. The following sections highlight some of the more common characteristics of each of the parties—the abuser and the abused.

The Abuser

Why does he hit her? Is the partner abuser some sort of sadistic, overbearing bully? Is he a person who enjoys inflicting pain? Did she drive him over the edge and cause him to react in the only way he knows how? These and other questions are often asked by people when they first hear about partner abuse. Unfortunately, no established physical characteristics of a partner abuser exist. Casual scrutiny will not reveal who will become violent in an intimate relationship, nor will it explain why the abuse occurs. Scholars have conducted many studies and dedicated years of research in an effort to understand this phenomenon. Several approaches have been developed as a consequence of this effort.

The *feminist* approach in evaluating partner abuse is to view it as a reflection of the sexist culture and sexist institutions that perpetuate the oppression of women. The male abuser is sexist, dominating, and controlling in intimate relationships with women.[36] The *systematic* approach attempts to determine the patterns of anger arousal, problem-solving deficits, and miscommunication that occur between couples in an intimate relationship.[37]

The *psychopathological* perspective examines potential mental disorders or processes and attempts to identify psychological sources of violence for the abuser.[38]

As indicated previously, no clear diagnosis has been established for those who batter. In reality, they can be anyone. However, researchers have attempted to define some general characteristics of the batterer. The following is a summary of some of the more popular profiles of batterers. As with all characterizations, however, caution should be used because batterers are not a homogeneous group.

Rosenbaum and Maiuro have established the following common backgrounds and characteristics of those who batter:

Exposure to violence in the family of origin: This characteristic is consistently associated with partner abuse. The batterers may have been subjected to corporal punishment or witnessed violence in their families as children. Although violence in the family of origin and partner abuse are strongly related, there does not seem to be a requirement that a person be raised within a violent family for him to become a batterer.

Sex role and self-image: A lack of self-identity on the part of the male may be associated with partner abuse. Those with defective self-images may exhibit more aggression than other males with positive self-images. One study pointed out that males with low self-esteem are more prone than others to interpret their spouses' actions as damaging to their self-image.

Verbal skills deficits: Abusers may have verbal skills that are inferior to those of their wives. They may resort to violence as a method of compensating for this deficit.

Psychopathology: As indicated earlier, research is still being conducted in this area. However, Rosenbaum believes that batterers may demonstrate more psychopathology than the general population.

Alcohol abuse: As with other forms of violence, alcohol has been identified as a common denominator in family violence. Several alternatives regarding alcohol and family violence need further study.[39]

Pagelow presents the following as some of the factors responsible for men abusing their spouses:

Violence in home of orientation: For many, the father figure was violent toward his spouse or children.

Low self-esteem: Abusers believe that they are losers. Although they gain a great deal of satisfaction from their spouses' achievements, this also causes them to feel threatened, and they respond with violence.

Alcohol dependency: Many abusers accept the use and consumption of alcohol.

Traditionalist: Abusers believe in male supremacy and the stereotyped role of males as the head of the family.

Emotionally inexpressive: Abusers are incapable of expressing certain emotions. They can and do express anger and jealousy and will resort to violence as a form of communication.

Lack of assertiveness: Individuals who are incapable of asserting themselves often resort to violence.

Social isolation: Abusers have difficulty maintaining social relationships.

Employment problems: Abusers may be unemployed or underemployed. Job dissatisfaction adds stress to the relationship and may lead to violence.

Authoritarian personalities: These individuals defer to higher authority but will scapegoat others.

Moody: Abusers may have wide mood swings alternating between happy and sullen from moment to moment.

Wall punchers: They may demonstrate frustration by punching walls, kicking chairs, or hitting animals.[40]

Anderson and her associates list the following characteristics of those who batter:

Personality disorder: Many batterers display antisocial personality disorders. Some studies have found that although a percentage of batterers have no evidence of personality disorders, the great majority have demonstrated personality types that involve aggressive behavior.

Easily threatened masculinity: Abusers have more traditional views of women. Some may resort to violence when they believe their masculinity is challenged.

Low self-esteem: Abusers may have low self-esteem and resort to violence to compensate for these feelings of inadequacy.

Lack of assertiveness: Abusers lack communication skills and may resort to violence as an alternate form of expression.

Excessive, hostile attachment to wife: Abusers may make strong demands on their spouses and respond with anger when these demands are not met.

Need for power and control: The abuser's fear of loss of control or power may trigger abusive behavior.

Pathological jealousy: The batterer may be extremely jealous and demand absolute loyalty from his spouse.

Alcohol or drug abuse: The abuser may have a drug or alcohol dependency.

Violence in his family of origin: This approach focuses on assaultive behavior that either attempts to control the spouse or is a method of harming her. In either case, these reactions may have been learned from experiences observed in the family of origin.

Coping by minimizing abusiveness: Abusive partners will minimize the seriousness and extent of their abusive behavior.[41]

A review of these theories indicates that certain traits characterize an abuser, and many studies have revealed similar hallmarks of behavior. Table 2.1 illustrates these findings.

As the previous discussion indicates, no clear picture emerges of a person who abuses his spouse. However, a series of characteristics should alert professionals to the possibility of abuse. More research may help to define clearly the profile of the partner abuser.[42]

The Abused

Just as no definite set of characteristics defines the abuser, little if any agreement exists concerning the personality traits of those who are abused. In addition, the issue of men who may be abused adds confusion to this area of family violence.

In 1977, Suzanne Steinmetz presented a paper entitled "The Battered Husband Syndrome," which became the basis for an article dealing with battered husbands.[43] Steinmetz's research, which was widely publicized in the media, claimed that men were abused at a far greater rate than previously believed. Steinmetz went further and claimed that wives abused their husbands more often and more severely than vice versa. This claim was attacked by feminists, professionals, and scholars. In 1988, Steinmetz and Lucca published a follow-up article that discussed husband battering in more detail.[44] In this article, they continued to assert that husbands are battered and concluded that all forms of violence must be prevented by placing greater emphasis on changing the attitudes and values of a society that glorifies violence.

One result of Steinmetz's position is the acknowledgment that both parties in an abusive relationship need to be evaluated. Studies have indicated that there are higher levels of female aggression toward their spouses than previously thought.[45] For example, in California, the percentage of males arrested for domestic violence decreased from 94.0 percent of the total in 1988 to 83.5 percent of the total in 1998. Conversely, the percentage of females arrested for domestic violence increased from 6.0 to 16.5 percent during the same period.[46]

TABLE 2.1   Abuser Traits

Characteristic	Rosenbaum and Maiuro	Pagelow	Anderson and Associates
Violence in family of origin	x	x	x
Alcohol abuse	x	x	x
Low self-esteem	x	x	x
Verbal skills deficits	x		
Psychopathology	x		x (personality disorders)
Traditionalist		x	x (easily threatened masculinity)
Emotionally inexpressive		x	
Lack of assertiveness		x	x
Isolation		x	
Employment problems		x	
Authoritarian personalities		x	
Moody		x	
Wall punchers		x	
Excessive attachment to wife			x
Need for power or control			x
Coping by minimizing abusiveness			x

However, most authorities agree that the type and severity of aggression is different from that experienced by women.[47]

Although it may be true that some men are abused by women in an intimate relationship, the majority of all abuse is inflicted by men. The abuse inflicted on women is more severe and life threatening than those instances of husband battering. The remainder of this section examines the abused from the perspective of women as the victims.

Dynamics of Battering

One of the most often asked questions is why the victim stays in an abusive relationship. The reasons why women stay with abusive partners are complex and multifaceted, and a number of theories attempt to explain the dynamics involved in battering. This section briefly discusses some of the more well-known concepts in this area.

Lenore E. Walker, one of the leading authorities in the area of partner abuse,[48] coined the term *cycle theory of violence* as a result of her research in the area of battered women. This concept does not attempt to explain the cause of partner abuse; rather, it examines the dynamics of this form of family violence.

The cycle theory of violence sets forth the dynamics of battering in partner abuse. Walker's theory has three distinct phases: the tension-building phase; the explosion, or acute battering, phase; and the calm, loving respite phase. These phases can vary in length and intensity, depending on the relationship.

THE TENSION-BUILDING PHASE.   As the name of this phase implies, tension increases within the relationship, at which time the husband may engage in minor battering of his spouse. The wife attempts to calm him by agreeing to his demands, becoming more nurturing or simply attempting to stay out of his way during this phase. The victim may rationalize that perhaps she is really at fault and deserves the abuse, accepting the batterer's faulty logic as her own. Women who have been in a battering relationship for any extended period of time know only too well that the minor battering will increase in time. She may try to withdraw more from the abuser in an attempt to avoid more conflict, but the tension in the relationship will continue to increase until the batterer explodes in a fit of rage.

THE EXPLOSION OR ACUTE BATTERING PHASE.   During this phase, the abuser loses control and engages in major incidents of assaultive behavior. This intense violent aggression is what distinguishes this phase from the minor or occasional battering that takes place in the first phase. When the first serious attack is over, both parties may feel shock, disbelief, and denial. For example, the woman may attempt to minimize her injuries.

THE CALM, LOVING RESPITE PHASE.   This phase is characterized by contrite loving acts on the part of the abuser. The batterer may understand that he has gone too far during the previous phase and will beg forgiveness and promise never to let it happen again. The woman will want to accept the abuser's promises that he can change and that his loving behavior is an inducement for her to stay in the relationship.

Walker's theory is generally accepted in both academia and the legal system. Her explanation for the dynamics of battering has been cited in numerous court decisions that deal with battered spouses.

Walker also presented the concept of the battered woman syndrome.[49] Some authorities prefer the term *battered women's experiences* because they believe (1) the former term implies that there is one syndrome that all battered women develop and (2) carries with it pathological connotations that suggest that battered women suffer from some sort of sickness; (3) expert testimony on domestic violence refers to more than women's psychological reactions to violence; and (4) the former term focuses attention on the battered woman rather than on the batterer's coercive behavior and (5) creates an image of battered women as suffering victims rather than active survivors.[50] However, because most court cases and most experts still refer to this experience as battered woman syndrome, that term will be used in this textbook.

Walker theorized that victims of partner abuse gradually become immobilized by fear and believe that they have no other options. As a result, these women stay in the abusive relationships, coping the best they can. The **battered woman syndrome** involves one who has been, on at least two occasions, the victim of physical, sexual, or serious psychological abuse by a man with whom she has an intimate relationship. It is a pattern of psychological symptoms that develop after someone has lived in a battering relationship. This is a gradual process of conditioning in which the victim feels both helpless and hopeless and, according to Walker, is one of the main reasons why spouses stay in these situations longer than people would expect. The abuse tends to follow the three-stage cyclical pattern of tension building, acute explosion, and loving contrition. The following responses are typical of women suffering from battered woman syndrome: (1) traumatic effects of victimization induced by violence, (2) learned helplessness deficits, and (3) self-destructive coping responses to the violence.[51]

Very similar in dynamics to battered woman syndrome is a condition referred to as the **Stockholm syndrome.** This phenomenon occurs when persons who are held as hostages, captives, or prisoners of war begin to identify with their captors.[52] These victims are isolated, mistreated, and in fear of their lives. They become helpless, confined to the area they are ordered to stay in, and dependent on their captors to supply everything they need to survive. They begin to develop positive feelings for their captors. The syndrome was named after an incident in Stockholm, Sweden, in which four bank employees were held hostage in the bank's vault for 131 hours by two perpetrators. When the victims were finally freed, they expressed gratitude toward the offenders for sparing their lives.

NiCarthy indicated that the dynamics of partner abuse are very similar to techniques used to control or brainwash prisoners of war: "As stated in a report published by Amnesty International, these techniques induce 'dependency, dread, and debility.' To the extent that a person is victimized by these techniques, she or he tends to become immobilized by the belief that she or he is trapped, cannot escape."[53] This heightening of fear, helplessness, dependency, and dread are all intertwined in the definition and dynamics of partner abuse.

Dutton and Painter developed the traumatic bonding theory to explain why battered women stay in abusive relationships.[54] This theory holds that when a woman finally leaves an abusive partner, her immediate fears begin to diminish and her hidden attachment to her abuser begins to manifest itself. Emotionally drained and vulnerable, she becomes susceptible to her partner's loving contrite pressure to return. As her fears lessen and the needs previously provided by her partner increase, she may decide to give him another chance.[55]

Dutton's theory is based on the concepts of power distribution and emotional bonding that focus on the dynamics of the abusive relationship rather than on any personality defect or socioeconomic status of the victim. Dutton states that these two features—the existence of a power imbalance and the intermittent nature of the abuse—can explain why abused women stay with their abusers or even return to the relationship.

Dutton theorized that when power imbalances exist in a relationship, the person of low power feels more negative in her self-appraisal and more incapable of fending for herself and thus in need of the person with more power. This cycle of dependency and lowered self-esteem repeats itself over and over and eventually creates a strong affective bond to the high-power person.[56]

The second factor in traumatic bonding is the intermittent nature of the abuse. This occurs when the abusive partner periodically abuses the submissive partner by threats or physical acts. The time between these incidents is normally characterized by normal, socially acceptable behavior. Thus, the victim is subjected to negative arousal and the relief or release associated with its removal. This situation of alternating negative and pleasant conditions is known in learning theory as partial, or intermittent, reinforcement. Dutton states that this situation is highly effective in producing persistent patterns of behavior that are associated with strong emotional attachment to the abuser that is hard to change or modify.[57]

Another theory is that women develop a distinct set of beliefs during the abusive process. These beliefs may be classified on the basis of the time of the abuse: preexisting beliefs, beliefs that develop during the abusive relationship, and beliefs that occur as a result of the violence experienced. Preexisting beliefs are formed as a result of early childhood experiences. The woman may have been raised in a violent household and believe that all women are abused, or she may confuse abuse with love. Beliefs developed during the abusive relationship may involve a sense of fear, low self-esteem, learned helplessness, or other dynamics that prevent the spouse from leaving the abuser. Beliefs that result because of the battering may include posttraumatic stress syndrome, depression, and other symptoms that affect women's ability to function normally in society. All these beliefs influence the abused spouse and contribute to her decision to stay in the relationship.[58]

One approach examines the subjective feelings of women and lists a series of factors that explain why women stay in these relationships:[59]

Fear: The most commonly expressed feeling for staying in an abusive relationship is fear that the batterer will come after the victim if she leaves. The abuser may threaten not only the spouse but also her child and other family members. Because she has lived with his violence, she believes the threats and rightfully fears for her family's safety.

Helplessness: Many abused women feel trapped and cannot envision a way out of their situations. A feeling of being completely alone with no one to turn to is common. The abuser takes on bigger-than-life proportions and becomes all-powerful.

Guilt and feelings of failure: Many women have been raised to believe that it is their responsibility to make the marriage work and that leaving the abusive situation would be an admission of failure. In addition, some women believe that they caused or deserved the punishment.

Lack of resources: Battered spouses are isolated and have little if any ability to access funds or social support systems. Even if they would like to leave, they do not have the financial ability to do so.

Anderson and her associates list a series of factors that are characteristic of battered spouses and also help explain why spouses stay in these relationships:[60]

Traumatic bonding and entrapment: Once the abuse starts, the woman may believe that the spouse will get through this rough time and return to normal behavior again. As the battering continues and increases in severity, the woman may believe that she has too much invested in the relationship to leave. This leads her to deny the intensity or frequency of the abuse.

Fear and terror: The battered spouse may respond with fear or terror to her husband's threats of punishment. She will always try to be alert and sense his feelings, dreading any action that may lead to aggressive behavior.

Learned helplessness: The abused spouse may believe that there is no way for her to prevent the violence. Therefore, she simply gives up and accepts the abuse. Learned helplessness usually follows entrapment and is more likely as the violence increases and the isolation becomes more complete.

Guilt and self-blame: Many battered spouses develop a sense of self-blame, as do most victims of severe violence who cannot control it or the situation that causes it. They attempt to invest more in the relationship to make it work and blame themselves for its failure.

Low self-esteem: Increased violence is associated with low self-esteem among battered women. As the battering continues, the spouse's value of herself declines.

Violence in her family of origin: Some authorities have suggested that the battered spouse has learned to stay in the relationship by observing violence in her own family or by experiencing it during childhood.

Coping by minimizing her abuse: All the previously listed factors contribute to a battered spouse's resistance to leaving her husband. She has learned to cope with the abuse by minimizing its extent, severity, or cause.

As the previous discussion indicates, women stay in battering relationships for a number of reasons. Although some might question some of these reasons or their validity, women living with men who kick, choke, beat, and rape them on a regular basis are totally invested

---

Focus

The Use of Expert Testimony in Establishing the Existence of Battered Woman Syndrome

Excerpts from *People v. Martin*

2012 WL 1758723 (Mich.App.2012)

Expert testimony is necessary when a witness's actions or responses are incomprehensible to the average person. Thus, where a witness or a defendant is a battered woman, an expert may testify about the generalities or characteristics of battered-woman syndrome for the limited purpose of describing the uniqueness of a specific behavior brought out at trial. The Michigan Supreme Court has held that a child sexual-abuse expert may testify regarding the typical symptoms of child abuse for the limited purpose of explaining the victim's specific behavior that might be construed by the jury as inconsistent with that of a sexual-abuse victim.

with these factors. Because many women do stay in these relationships, professionals need to be able to recognize the symptoms of abuse so that assistance can be offered.

Pagelow developed a list of factors that professionals, friends, or family members may observe that might indicate that a spouse is involved in a battering relationship. As with all checklists, care must be taken when evaluating the factors.

This section has examined the characteristics and personality traits of both those who abuse and those who are abused. Unfortunately, professionals cannot predict when partner abuse will occur or who the parties to this violence will be. However, some factors may indicate that certain persons may be at risk of either abusing or being abused. Because researchers cannot explain why it occurs or predict who it will happen to, it is crucial to understand the different types of partner abuse.

TYPES OF PARTNER ABUSE

As with other subjects in the area of partner abuse, authorities disagree on the different types of partner abuse. Many studies have focused solely on physical abuse, documenting the number of times a husband strikes his wife, whereas others have looked at sexual violence in a marriage. Still others examine the psychological or emotional abuse a spouse suffers at the hands of her tormenter. Finally, some classify abuse as a property form and discuss the financial dependence imposed by the abuser. No matter how many types or variations employed, it is important to realize that they all work together to form a net that completely encompasses the woman in a world of physical, sexual, or emotional violence.

For clarity, partner abuse in this chapter is classified as physical, sexual, or emotional abuse. Within each area are degrees of severity and differences. A woman may suffer from one or all forms of partner abuse.

Determining who has suffered what type of abuse is more of an art than a science. Two major types or techniques of gathering information are relied on in assessing partner abuse: self-reporting and interviews. The Conflict Tactics Scale, a self report, developed by Straus, contains eighteen items that measure or assess reasoning and aggression during conflicts within a family. Another self-report is the Spouse Specific Aggression Scale, which measures psychological but not physical aspects of abuse. These inventories allow a quick and confidential screening of physical and verbal abuse. In addition, they are checklists that provide answers or information that may not be obtained in a clinical setting. A disadvantage of these inventories is that they fail to provide information on how aggression is related to or interacts with control and power in the relationship.

Another form of gathering information is the clinical interview. For any interview to be successful, it requires the interviewer be knowledgeable in the various forms of partner abuse. The interview process assesses the effects of abuse as well as the dynamics of power and control in the relationship. The main disadvantage to the interview process should be obvious—the spouse or spouses must agree to be interviewed. Because one of the characteristics of partner abuse is isolation, the interview process is limited to those situations in which one or both of the spouses have come forward and agreed to be interviewed.

Physical Abuse

Physical aggression may take the form of minor acts that escalate over time. It may begin with grabbing an arm, throwing a dish, or slapping to the arm or face. This aggression increases in severity until the victim has no way out of the relationship. The following is a list of the more common forms of physical abuse suffered by spouses:

Striking acts. The abuser may strike the face, arms, body, or legs of the spouse. The violence may be delivered with an open or closed hand. These acts include punching with the fist.

Throwing or destroying property. The abuser may throw dishes, small appliances, or other objects at the spouse, or he may go on a rampage and destroy household property.

Control or choking acts. Choking is a common form of abuse. It sends a very clear message that the abuser is stronger and more powerful. Choking allows the batterer to control the spouse and have her beg for mercy.

Repeated beating using objects. The use of belts, sticks, or other objects during the assault is not uncommon. Using the same object allows the abuser to completely control the victim simply by laying his hand on the object.

Humiliation violence. Some abusers will require their victims to assume certain positions for the imposition of violence. Having the victim undress before yelling and beating her adds to the feeling of helplessness.

Physical violence takes many forms. The results of these acts will leave certain physical marks or injuries on the women. In the event that they require medical treatment, the physician should be alert to the possibility of abuse if an injury is not consistent with the medical history given by the spouse. The second form of partner abuse is even harder to detect.

Promising Practices

Partner Abuse

The Advocacy for Women and Kids in Emergency (AWAKE) program at the Children's Hospital in Boston was the nation's first hospital-based program to offer advocacy and support to abused mothers while the hospital is providing protection to their abused children. AWAKE was formed to provide intervention on behalf of battered women and to coordinate services that are often offered separately to women and children and can conflict with each other. An advocate develops a safety plan designed to keep mothers and children together and safe. Long-term support is also offered to these families.

The Los Angeles Commission on Assaults Against Women (LACAAW) has a temporary restraining order fax service that allows victims to file for a temporary restraining order through the LACAAW office rather than going to the courthouse. To increase accessibility, there are advocates who know Spanish or American Sign Language.

The Family Violence Intervention Model for Dental Professionals Project has developed comprehensive curricula and educational videos for dentists and dental ancillary staff that provide information about the dynamics of family violence and appropriate intervention strategies by dental professionals.

Source: Based on U.S. Department of Justice, *National Victim Assistance Academy Text* (Washington, D.C., 2003).

Sexual Abuse

Physical violence is often accompanied by sexual abuse. Sex on demand or after physical assaults is very common. Since the woman does not believe that she has any choice or free will, she will submit to the abuser's demands. In addition, she may fear that a refusal to engage in sexual activity will cause the abuser to react violently.

Sexual acts that humiliate or degrade the wife are not uncommon. The husband may demand oral sex without any regard for his spouse's feelings or beliefs. Anal intercourse is a common form of sexual abuse. The abuser may say things to the spouse or require her to say things that are degrading to her. Some abusers may require their spouses to share sex with friends or coworkers.

Violence during the sexual act may occur. The abuser may engage in sexual activities in a violent and forceful manner intended to injure or hurt his spouse.

Sometimes, *sex will occur after a physical altercation.* This may be loving and caring and an attempt by the abuser to make up for the aggression. This offers false hope to the abused spouse and is intended to make her believe that the abuser is really sorry and that the physical acts will not occur again.

Sexual abuse may provoke intense emotional and physical reactions in the abused spouse. This intensity and humiliation may become addictive and be looked on as a form of release. It may on occasion take on a narcotic effect for the abused spouse.

At one time in our history, a man was believed to have a right to sex with his wife. There was no such thing as partner rape. Today, laws prevent this form of assault. Sexual abuse may not leave physical scars visible to the naked eye, but it will certainly leave emotional scars that may be even longer lasting and more devastating.

Emotional Abuse

Emotional abuse is far more than a husband simply calling his wife degrading names. This form of partner abuse has far-reaching consequences for the victim and leaves scars that require long-term treatment. Emotional abuse includes many different acts that all contribute to a feeling of helplessness and inability.

The batterer may engage in *verbal dominance.* At first, the spouse may believe this is simply ego or a strong person speaking. However, in time she learns her opinions, feelings, and thoughts carry no weight, and if she expresses herself at all, she is subject to verbal and possibly physical abuse.

Isolation is a common form of emotional abuse. The abuser may isolate the victim by limiting her access to money, use of the car, or other normal activities. He talks negatively about her family and friends, thereby making it uncomfortable for the spouse to maintain outside relationships. Isolation prevents feedback. The only feedback she receives is from the abusing partner who distorts both his and her realities, leaving her feeling dumb, lazy, and unattractive. After a period of time, the abused spouse comes to accept these statements as true.

Guilt is also common. The abuser usually blames the partner for his or her assaultive behavior with the rationale that if the partner had only carried out his or her duties better, the abuser would not have had to hit him or her. After a period of time, the abused spouse begins to accept these pronouncements and blames himself or herself for the battering.

Fear is a form of emotional abuse as well. The abuser may threaten to reveal secrets or private information to family and friends, or the batterer may threaten the spouse with a beating when he gets home. The spouse then waits hours for the expected assault. The abuser may threaten to harm her or her family if she ever leaves him or does anything else he does not approve of.

Emotional abuse may take the form of *humiliation.* The spouse may be put down in front of friends, family, or children. In extreme cases, the abuser may require her to perform degrading acts in public, such as having sex in front of friends or her children or requesting permission before leaving the room or going to the bathroom. This type of emotional abuse destroys the spouse's sense of self-worth and ability to resist further acts of control by the abuser.

Using fear, guilt, and isolation, the abuser will promote a *feeling of helplessness* within the spouse that further ties the victim to the abuser. She believes that there is no way to break the cycle and feels trapped.

One aspect of emotional abuse that deserves special attention is *financial dependence.* The abuser may require the spouse to work and turn her check over to him. He will control all finances and ensure that she never has any funds that he does not approve of. The abuser may control the funds to isolate the spouse, deny her opportunities to improve herself, or demean her. This financial dependence adds to the spouse's feelings of helplessness and entrapment. Even if she wanted to leave, she would have no money to support herself or even rent a room for a night.

Emotional abuse is a serious form of partner abuse. Although it leaves no physical scars, it can bind the abused spouse to the perpetrator far more effectively than chains or ropes. The next section examines a controversial aspect of partner abuse—police officers who abuse their spouses.

FAMILY VIOLENCE BY POLICE OFFICERS

Just as the issue of partner abuse had to move from behind closed doors, so has the issue of partner abuse by police officers recently become a topic among researchers, elected officials, and the media.[61] Several academic scholars have examined the high level of stress and dysfunction in law enforcement families.[62] DePue studied the high-risk lifestyle of police officers and the accompanying increase of stress on family.[63] Maslach and Jackson researched police burnout and stress.[64] Johnson is credited with conducting the first study of family violence by police officers, in which 40 percent of all respondents in that survey admitted to committing family violence within the last six months.[65] This study suffers from several methodical criticisms, however, including the issue of the definition of abuse, failure to discern levels of severity, and the lack of a control group.

Neidig and his colleagues examined rates of family violence by police officers by administering a series of surveys to 385 male officers, 40 female officers, and 115 female spouses attending a national law enforcement conference.[66] Their findings were consistent with Johnson's research, indicating that approximately 40 percent of all the officers reported at least one incident of violence within the last year. Significantly, the 115 spouses' responses correlated with officers' self-reports.

Neidig and colleagues conducted a second survey of 891 officers, 32 female officers, and 119 spouses attending another conference.[67] However, this group was of a higher rank than those surveyed in the first study. Although the results indicated a lower percentage of violence, it was still significant in that 24 percent of the male officers and 22 percent of the female officers reported at least one incident of violence in their relationship within the last year.

The Southwestern Law Enforcement Institute evaluated family violence by police officers by surveying the internal affairs policies of departments.[68] The institute found that no department had carried out any formal analysis of domestic violence incidents and pattern with regard to age or length of service. It concluded that many agencies tend to regard partner abuse by police officers as more a private wrong than a criminal matter.

Policing and partner abuse have been pulled into the open by the passage of the Omnibus Consolidated Appropriations Act of 1997, known as the Lautenberg Amendment to Title 18 United States Code 922(d)(9). This law prohibits any person convicted of family violence from ever owning a firearm or ammunition. It also specifically prohibits possession of a firearm by a police officer with a prior misdemeanor conviction of family violence. This law applies to all local, state, and national law enforcement agencies and to all convictions, including those that occurred before its enactment on September 30, 1996.

The International Association of Chiefs of Police has examined this issue and developed a series of principles that address family violence within the law enforcement community. The policy is intended to assist departments in effectively preventing and responding to incidents of police officer domestic violence. The *Model Policy on Police Officer Domestic Violence* states in part:

> This policy takes a continuum approach, seeking first to educate at all phases of an officer's career, then prevent, or interdict, domestic abuse situations early on in order to reduce victimization of the partner and increase the chances of officer career stability.
>
> When incidents of domestic violence are alleged to have occurred, the department will act quickly to protect the victim, arrest the perpetrator, and conduct parallel administrative and criminal investigations.
>
> This policy delineates a position by the department of absolute intolerance (i.e., zero tolerance) of domestic violence. An officer found guilty of domestic violence, either through criminal court or administrative hearing, shall have his/her police powers revoked.
>
> Once implemented, the policy will apply to past convictions and existing and future police officer domestic violence crimes.[69]

Many victims of partner abuse by police officers do not call their law enforcement agency because they fear that the case will be handled by officers who know the abuser and that these officers will side with their colleague and fail to properly investigate the crime.[70] In some instances, these are well-founded concerns. In one study, Lott found that most law enforcement agencies typically handled allegations of family violence by police officers informally, without an official complaint or record being maintained.[71]

As discussed above, although the International Association of Chiefs of Police has prepared a Model Policy on Police Officer Domestic Violence, there is little if any evidence that a great majority of the departments have done anything more than including the process in their manuals.[72] For example, between 1990 and 1997, the Los Angeles Police Department investigated 227 cases of alleged abuse by police officers. Only ninety-one of these cases were classified as sustained or proven. Of these ninety-one cases, only four were convicted of criminal charges. Of the four convictions, one was suspended from duty for a mere fifteen days and another had his conviction expunged.[73] The Office of Inspector General went on to state that the discipline imposed on these officers was exceedingly light when the facts of the case were examined.[74]

Another more recent study by Erwin and her associates supports this lack of follow-up by law enforcement agencies when one of their own is accused of partner abuse. Erwin studied a large urban police department having about 2,400 sworn officers. The final administrative actions against the majority of officers (92%) accused of partner abuse resulted in no action.[75]

What causes this alarming rate of family violence within police families? Do the same theories of family violence apply, or are we looking at a new and different aspect of family violence? Several researchers have examined the factors that impact those who serve as police officers, attempting to find specific influences that may contribute to the high rate of violence with their families.

Having evaluated police stress, Reese points out that it has no limits or boundaries.[76] The continuous exposure to trauma and tragedy experienced by victims of crime, the attitude of perpetrators, and the ever-present risk of physical danger in police work constitute the primary stressors for police officers. White and Honig argue that whatever stressed the officer on the job will stress the family system as well.[77] They theorize that officers appear to take home the anger and frustration related to their job.

Honig and White also examined the possibility that certain personality styles or behavioral characteristics of officers lend themselves to violence within the family.[78] These researchers believe that officers rank high in cognitive functioning, responsibility, and self-confidence but that officers also are guarded, moralistic, rigid, and authoritarian. Other authorities state that because of the nature of their work, officers are overly protective and restrictive of their spouses and children. This in turn leads to isolation and a lack of support systems for the spouse who is battered.

Is there no hope for victims of family violence by police officers? Although these victims face many barriers in responding to this form of violence, progress is being made in this area. For example, there is a comprehensive handbook specifically for victims of police domestic violence. Published by LifeSpan, it sets forth rights and processes available to these victims. LifeSpan was founded in 1978 and provides services to victims of family violence. The Police Domestic Violence Program is a unique program, which provides counseling and legal services for victims of violence by police officers.[79]

The Chicago Police Department has implemented a series of progressive policies to handle family violence committed by its employees. The department has established an independent unit under civilian control to investigate these crimes. Free counseling is available for any employee whose abusive behavior comes to the attention of the department, and cases are thoroughly investigated and referred to the District Attorney's Office for prosecution when appropriate.[80]

The Public Agency Training Council has also addressed the issue of family violence by police officers. It suggests that law enforcement leaders set the example by establishing clear expectations for behavior of those who serve under them. Agencies should undertake better screening and background investigations aimed at discovering those who might have engaged in family violence prior to becoming a law enforcement officer. Policies should explicitly state that there is "zero tolerance" for any domestic violence. Training should be focused on the dynamics of family violence, and this training should continue throughout the officer's career. Finally, there should be a formalized investigative response to any allegations of family violence.[81]

Partner abuse by police officers is another aspect of family violence that needs to have more research and discussion. We must hold officers just as accountable as the average citizen, but because of the nature of their profession, we must also make every effort to provide support systems for them and their families to ensure that we prevent this form of family violence.

PARTNER HOMICIDE

Women do strike back and kill their abusers. As professionals become more knowledgeable about partner abuse and battered woman syndrome, they will hear more about women who kill their abusive partners. The next section examines this topical aspect of partner abuse.

Self-Defense

Self-defense is the right of a person to use reasonable force to defend herself from physical violence. Traditionally, a person could use deadly force to protect his home from an intruder. The common law and many statutes today do not require a person to retreat in his own home before using deadly force on an intruder. If this is the law, what prevents a spouse who is in fear for her life from killing her husband and claiming self-defense? The problem is that the self-defense plea also requires the victim to be placed in fear of immediate injury. A percentage of spouses who have killed their abusers testified that their abusers were not in the process of striking them or hurting them at that moment.

The two issues that cause problems with a self-defense plea are proof that the spouse reasonably believed that she was in danger of death or great bodily injury and that injury or death was imminent. Both of these issues have been discussed by various courts that have considered cases of partner homicide.

In *State v. Gallegos,* Anita Gallegos was charged with the murder of her ex-husband and long-time companion George Gallegos by shooting him at close range while he was lying in bed, then stabbing him numerous times in the neck.[82] Mrs. Gallegos suffered a long history of physical and sexual abuse prior to meeting her husband. As a child, she had been sexually and physically abused by her brother and one of her mother's lovers. She met and married George Gallegos and began to be subjected to abuse in the marriage. George drank heavily and beat her, leaving scars on her nose, near her eyes, and on her forehead. At one time, he displayed a knife and threatened to cut off her breasts if they grew any larger. When she was pregnant with their second child, he picked her up and threw her against a wall, causing the premature birth of the child.

On the day of the killing, George sodomized the defendant against her will, causing rectal bleeding. When Mrs. Gallegos threatened to leave, George pulled out his gun and said that he would kill her if she left. After another argument later that day, the husband went into the bedroom and called for Mrs. Gallegos to come into the room. She testified that she didn't know whether she was going to be killed, raped, or beaten. Mrs. Gallegos picked up her husband's rifle, walked into the room, and shot him as he lay on the bed. She then grabbed a knife and stabbed him numerous times in the neck.

She was charged and convicted of voluntary manslaughter. The trial court refused to instruct the jury on the issue of self-defense or to allow testimony on battered woman syndrome. The New Mexico Court of Appeals reversed the conviction, holding that, under these facts, the issue of self-defense was proper and that the trial court erred in refusing to allow testimony regarding the term *battered woman syndrome.*

One of the most notable cases involving a battered woman and self-defense was the case of *People v. Aris.*[83] Brenda Denise Aris was married to her husband for ten years. During that time, he threatened and beat her numerous times. On the night of the killing, he beat her and threatened to kill her in the morning. Suffering from bruises, Mrs. Aris went next door to a neighbor's house to get some ice to ease the pain of the blows. While there, she saw a revolver and took it back with her to the bedroom. While her husband was asleep, she shot him five times in the back. She was charged and tried for the crime of murder.

During the trial, the defense called Dr. Lenore E. Walker, author of *The Battered Woman* and *Terrifying Love,* as an expert witness to testify about battered woman syndrome and Mrs. Aris's state of mind.[84] Although Dr. Walker was able to testify generally about battered women, she was precluded from stating her opinion that Mrs. Aris was suffering from battered woman syndrome at the time she shot her husband. Thus, the trial court allowed evidence that Mrs. Aris was battered and believed that her life was in danger but refused to allow Dr. Walker to testify as to the *reasonableness* of that belief.

The trial court also instructed the jury on the issue of imminent danger of death or great bodily injury, stating:

> *Imminent peril,* as used in these instructions, means that the peril must have existed or appeared to the defendant to exist at the very time the fatal shot was fired. In other words, the peril must appear to the defendant as immediate and present and not prospective or even in the near future. An imminent peril is one that, from appearances, must be instantly dealt with.[85]

Several times the jury asked for clarification on the term *imminent.* After having the instructions repeated to them, the jury found the defendant guilty of second-degree murder. The appeals court upheld the lower court decision, and Brenda Denise Aris was sentenced to state prison.

Fortunately, the case of Brenda Aris was not over. In 1993, California governor Pete Wilson reduced Aris's sentence of fifteen years to life to twelve years to life—a move that under California's complex sentencing laws made her eligible for parole in July 1994. Wilson, a strong law-and-order governor, stated, "The test of whether clemency should be considered in cases where the request is based upon battered women's syndrome must be: Did the petitioner have the option to leave her abuser, or was the homicide realistically her only chance?"[86]

The case of *Bechtel v. State,* decided in 1992, gives some insight into the continuing lack of understanding of the issues of self-defense and battered woman syndrome by some trial judges.[87] Donna Lee Bechtel and Ken Bechtel were married in 1982. From that date until the day of the killing in September 1984, Donna was battered twenty-three different times. These assaults occurred when her husband was drinking and included grabbing Donna by her ears or hair and pounding her head on the ground, wall, door, cabinet, or other available objects.

On the day of the killing, Ken returned home drunk, beat her, sexually assaulted her, and threatened to kill her. After a final assault in which he first choked her and then passed out, Donna obtained a gun and shot him. The trial court refused to admit testimony regarding battered woman syndrome and how it related to the requirement of imminence in self-defense. The jury convicted Mrs. Bechtel of first-degree murder, and she was sentenced to life imprisonment.

The Oklahoma Court of Criminal Appeals reversed the conviction, stating that expert opinion regarding battered woman syndrome and how it related to the issue of imminence of death or danger should have been admitted. The court held that thirty-one states and the District of Columbia allowed the use of expert testimony on the subject of battered woman syndrome. It went further by stating that battered woman syndrome is a substantial, scientifically accepted theory.

Although not dealing specifically with partner homicide, another court opinion illustrates how far courts are now willing to extend the concept of battered woman syndrome. In *People v. Romero,* Debra Romero was charged with one count of second-degree robbery and four counts of attempted robbery.[88] Debra met, and began living with, Terrance Romero in March 1989. They were both cocaine addicts, and Terrance soon began hitting Debra if she didn't somehow get the money for his habit. From the day she moved in, Debra testified that he hit her almost every day. He would get angry and rip screens off the windows, throw things out the windows, and threaten to kill her if she left.

From May 28 until July 23, 1989, Terrance and Debra engaged in one actual and several attempted robberies. They were caught and convicted on all counts, and Debra was sentenced to state prison for five years. During the trial, Debra testified that she was afraid of Terrance and committed the crimes under duress. Duress is very similar to self-defense in that it requires the party committing the crime to prove that they acted out of an immediate or imminent fear of injury. The defense attorney did not call any experts to testify regarding battered woman syndrome.

Debra appealed her conviction and claimed that she was denied effective counsel because her attorney did not raise the issue of battered woman syndrome to support her claim of duress. The appeals court reviewed the history of battered woman syndrome and its growing acceptance in homicide trials. The court reversed the conviction, stating that the defense attorney should have presented evidence to corroborate Debra's testimony and informed the jury of the dynamics of her mental state. Failure to do so, the appeals court reasoned, denied Debra her right to effective counsel.

In 1996, the California Supreme Court addressed the issue of battered woman syndrome and self-defense in *People v. Humphrey.*[89] Evelyn Humphrey was forcefully molested by her father from the time she was seven until she was fifteen. She had three previous abusive relationships before she met Albert Hampton. Her relationship with Hampton involved frequent arguments and beatings. Hampton once broke her nose by throwing a beer can at her face. He hit her in the back of the head because, he told her, it wouldn't leave bruises. On March 27, 1992, the evening before the killing, he grabbed his gun and fired one round at her, which missed. The next day they continued to argue, and in the evening he hit her and stated that this time when he shot at her, he wouldn't miss. She grabbed the gun and backed him into the kitchen. As he was reaching for her hand, she shot him in the chest. The police arrived, and she admitted shooting Hampton. He died in the hospital, and Evelyn was charged with murder and with use of a firearm during the commission of a crime.

In 1991, the California legislature adopted Evidence Code 1107, which provides that expert testimony is admissible regarding battered woman syndrome in criminal cases. Relying on this statute and other case law, Humphrey's attorney presented both expert and lay witness evidence regarding her experiences. The expert testified that Evelyn was suffering from battered woman syndrome and believed that she was in mortal danger from Hampton. Evelyn also testified about her experiences with Hampton. The prosecutor argued that she could have left the victim on the evening before the killing when he shot and missed her. At the end of the trial, the court dismissed the charge of first-degree murder but allowed the second-degree charge and the manslaughter charge to remain. Although the court allowed evidence regarding battered woman syndrome, it refused to allow the jury to consider whether a reasonable person in the defendant's circumstances would have perceived a threat of imminent injury or death. The jury convicted Evelyn of voluntary manslaughter. The Supreme Court reversed the decision, holding that expert testimony that Evelyn was suffering from battered woman syndrome was generally admissible in homicide cases, not only on the question of whether the defendant actually believed that it was necessary to kill in self-defense but also on the question of reasonableness of that belief.[90]

In 1997, in *State v. Thomas,* the Ohio Supreme Court reaffirmed its position on self-defense and battered woman syndrome.[91] On September 15, 1993, Teresa Thomas shot and killed Jerry Flowers, her live-in boyfriend. They had lived together two years prior to the shooting. Flowers continually abused Teresa, including hitting, pushing, and choking her. He would purposefully soil his clothes and demand that she clean them. Two days before the shooting, he forcibly sodomized her. On the day of the killing, Flowers returned home and advanced toward Teresa. She ran into the bedroom, grabbed Flowers's gun, and shot him six times. The jury convicted her of murder with a firearm specification.

The Ohio Supreme Court upheld the jury instruction dealing with self-defense, stating that it combines both an objective and a subjective test. The jury must first consider the defendant's situation objectively to determine whether a reasonable person would believe she was in imminent danger and then consider subjectively whether this particular defendant had an honest belief that she was in danger. The court reversed the decision on other grounds.

In 1997, in *People v. Morgman,* a California appellate court upheld using battered woman syndrome to impeach the victim's recantation of her previous statements to the police.[92] Julie Parker and David Morgman were dating for approximately three years. On February 5, 1995, neighbors called regarding screams coming from Julie's apartment. When the police arrived, Julie ran naked from her apartment and stated that Morgman had hit her and punched her in the face. Morgman was arrested, and Julie was taken to the hospital. An examination at the emergency room revealed multiple blunt injuries to her face, wrist, and shoulder. Three days later, Julie reaffirmed the abuse to a police detective. By the time of the trial, Julie and Morgman were back together, and she recanted her testimony on the stand. Julie testified that the injuries occurred as a result of hallucinating from drugs and alcohol, and Morgman was simply trying to restrain her and prevent more serious injuries.

The prosecutor then called an expert witness to testify about battered woman syndrome and why some victims stay with the abuser. The defense objected, but the trial court allowed

Focus

People v. Brown, 33 Cal. 4th 892 (Cal. 2004)

Defendant and Kimberly Pipes, the victim, had been dating on and off for about eleven years. On April 17, 2001, they were living together in an apartment with Pipes's four children and Carrie Miller, a woman who took care of the children when Pipes worked.

Pipes rented the apartment from Leland Jordan, defendant's cousin. At 2:00 A.M. on April 17, Jordan came to the apartment to demand payment of back rent. When Pipes refused because Jordan had not fixed the water system, Jordan told Pipes to vacate the apartment. After Jordan left, Pipes and defendant began arguing. Pipes was upset because she thought defendant should have taken her side in the argument with Jordan.

Shortly thereafter, Deputy Sheriff James Wheeler responded to a telephone call from Pipes and found her with Carrie Miller in a parked car near the apartment. Pipes told Wheeler she had been assaulted. She said she tried to leave the apartment after an argument with defendant, but he put his arm around her neck and dragged her to the bedroom. Defendant then went to the living room and returned to the bedroom with a steak knife and a barbeque fork, telling Pipes he would kill her if she left. She was afraid. When she said she wanted to leave, defendant replied, "I don't want you having my baby," and punched her in the stomach. Miller told Deputy Wheeler that defendant had threatened to kill both her and Pipes if they left. He also threatened to have some women come over to beat up Miller and

Pipes. Deputy Wheeler arrested defendant and found the steak knife where Pipes said it was.

Defendant appealed from a judgment of the Court of Appeal of California, Second Appellate District, Division Six, which affirmed his conviction on charges relating to domestic violence.

At trial, the complaining witness's testimony differed from what she had told a police deputy earlier. The prosecution offered testimony from an expert witness to explain that domestic violence victims often later deny or minimize the assailant's conduct. Defendant contended such testimony did not fall within the scope of Cal. Evid. Code § 1107. He argued that the prosecution had failed to show that the victim was a battered woman because it offered no proof that defendant had abused her on more than one occasion. The court held that neither the expert's testimony nor the prosecutor's argument was premised on the admissibility of her testimony under § 1107. There was an adequate foundation for the expert testimony because evidence presented at trial suggested the possibility that defendant and the complaining witness were in a "cycle of violence" of the type described by the expert. To assist the jury in evaluating this evidence, the trial court properly admitted the expert testimony under Cal. Evid. Code § 801. There was no rule requiring a preliminary finding that the charged act of abuse occurred before the jury could consider the evidence relating to credibility.

The Appellate Court affirmed (approved) the conviction.

the testimony. The jury convicted Morgman on five counts. The appellate court upheld this use of battered woman syndrome, stating that such testimony assisted the jury in understanding Julie's motive to recant her previous testimony. This evidence allowed the jury to evaluate Julie's credibility in light of her conflicting stories and the dynamics of battered woman syndrome.

In 1999, the Florida Supreme Court addressed the issue of self-defense and battered woman syndrome in *Weiand v. State*.[93] Kathleen Weiand was charged with murder for the 1994 shooting of her husband, Todd Weiand. Kathleen shot her husband during a violent argument in their apartment where they were living with their seven-month-old daughter.

At trial, Kathleen presented battered woman syndrome as a defense to the killing. She testified her husband had beaten her and choked her during their three-year marriage. In addition, he had threatened her if she tried to leave him. Two experts, including Dr. Lenore Walker, testified that Kathleen was suffering from battered woman syndrome, with Dr. Walker explaining why Kathleen did not believe that she could leave the home during the argument. However, during the closing argument, the prosecutor stressed as critical that the killing could not be considered justifiable homicide unless Kathleen had exhausted every reasonable means to escape the danger, including fleeing her home. The jury found Kathleen guilty of second-degree murder, and the court sentenced her to eighteen years' imprisonment.

The Florida Supreme Court reversed the decision, holding that a battered spouse has no duty to retreat from the home before using deadly force to defend herself. The court acknowledged the fact that victims of partner abuse are at greater danger when attempting to leave the abuser and found that there are sound policy reasons for not imposing a duty to retreat from a residence shared with another on victims of domestic abuse. (As a note of interest, the court decided to hear this case even though Kathleen had been granted executive clemency by the governor of Florida.)

Many states are now establishing jury instructions that attempt to address the issue of partner homicide. For example, California has what is called the "Imperfect Self Defense Jury Instruction," which reads as follows:

> A person who kills another person in the actual but unreasonable belief in the necessity to defend against imminent peril to life or great bodily injury, kills unlawfully, but does not harbor malice aforethought and is not guilty of murder. This would be so even though a reasonable person in the same situation seeing and knowing the same facts would not have had the same belief.
>
> Such an actual but unreasonable belief is not a defense to the crime of [voluntary] or [involuntary] manslaughter.
>
> As used in this definition, an "imminent" [peril] or [danger] means one that is apparent, present, immediate and must be instantly dealt with, or must so appear at the time to the slayer.
>
> However, this principle is not available, and malice aforethought is not negated if the defendant by [his][her][unlawful] or [wrongful] conduct created the circumstance, which legally justified [his][her] adversary's [use of force], [attack] [or] [pursuit].[94]

A careful reading of the California Statute indicates that it is gender-neutral. More and more courts and state legislatures are beginning to frame battered woman syndrome in a gender-neutral fashion, and some are calling it "Battering and Its Effects."[95] Although there are many who do not agree with this approach, there are others who claimed the gendered battered woman syndrome enforced stereotypes that women were weak or unable to care for themselves.[96] Thus, what started out as a means of helping women who were abused by their spouses has evolved into a method of addressing battering in all relationships.

As these cases illustrate, courts are now accepting testimony of experts regarding battered woman syndrome. This testimony allows the jury to understand the dynamics involved in these situations. In addition, it allows them to find that the abused spouse felt in imminent danger and was therefore justified in striking back at the abuser, even to the point of killing the abuser in his or her sleep.

Use of Experts

If a woman kills her abusing partner, she may be charged with homicide. As the previous discussion indicates, it is necessary to present evidence during the trial to prove that a woman suffered from battered woman syndrome. Simply having her testify that she was beaten and afraid of her partner does not educate the jury to the dynamics of the situation.[97]

The first hurdle in admitting expert testimony is to prove to the court that the testimony is relevant to the facts in the case. This is normally accomplished by showing that the expert will testify regarding the battered spouse's belief that she was in immediate or imminent peril. This raises the issue of self-defense, and the expert's testimony becomes relevant.

The next obstacle to overcome is proof that the expert use of methodology has gained general acceptance within the scientific community and permits a reasonable opinion to be expressed by the expert. In *People v. Torres,* the court held that

> the theory underlying the battered woman's syndrome has indeed passed beyond the experimental stage and gained a substantial enough scientific acceptance to warrant admissibility. . . . [N]umerous articles and books have been published about the battered woman's syndrome; and recent findings of researchers in the field have confirmed its presence and thereby indicated that the scientific community accepts its underlying premises.[98]

The court must only be satisfied that the methodology used is accepted by the scientific community, not the individual opinion based on that methodology. Therefore, once the expert has satisfied the court that his or her research is sound, any opinion is admissible.

As indicated in earlier chapters, an *expert* is someone with special training or education who can assist the jury on issues that are beyond the range of normal understanding. Doctors, psychiatrists, and psychologists would naturally qualify as experts in their fields. However, to testify regarding battered woman syndrome, they should have some special education or experience dealing with family violence in general and battered spouses specifically. Even those without advanced degrees may qualify as experts in this area if they have special training or knowledge in the area. In *Commonwealth v. Craig,* the director of a women's shelter with a master's degree in counseling, five years' experience working with battered women, and previous experience as an expert witness in this area was deemed qualified to testify regarding the defendant and battered woman syndrome.[99]

Although one study has indicated that jurors may have more knowledge about partner abuse than previously believed, an expert witness can ensure that they understand the dynamics of partner abuse.[100] The witness should be able to dispel myths, stereotypes, and misconceptions regarding partner abuse. The witness can use the courtroom to educate the judge, jury, and even the prosecutor as to why the spouse did not leave the relationship and believed that killing her partner was the only way out of the situation. Most important, the expert witness can answer the unasked question, "Why didn't she simply leave or call the police?"

When a battered woman kills her spouse, the battle has just begun. The justice system may decide that she could have left the abuser and charge her with homicide. If this occurs, it is essential that an expert witness testify regarding battered woman syndrome. Such testimony will assist in educating the jury regarding why the woman acted the way she did instead of pursuing other alternatives.

Focus

Same Gender Love and Betrayal

Duane Rath at the age of fifty-one retired from the family business as a millionaire. For fourteen years he shared his life and love with his male partner, Ted Hurdman. They lived the life of the rich and famous, traveling across the country to posh resorts, attending opening ceremonies of AIDS clinics, being acknowledged by movie stars such as Elizabeth Taylor, and donating large sums of money to political campaigns.

One day, a groundskeeper at Rath's thirteen-acre estate in Janesville, Wisconsin, found his half-clothed body covered with blood in the master bedroom of his Tudor-style mansion. Rath had been stabbed at least twelve times.

One wound had punctured the main artery in his chest, causing him to bleed to death in a matter of seconds. Hurdman's body was discovered in the three-car garage where he had evidently turned on the engines of both a Mercedes Sports Coupe and a Toyota Land Rover, causing him to asphyxiate on the exhaust fumes of the cars.

No police reports of domestic violence between the couple were on file with the local police department. However, some locals and other knowledgeable friends suspect that increased tension in the relationship may have led to the fight that escalated into a murder/suicide.

Source: Based on J. Morales, "Sleeping with the Enemy," *The Advocate*, November 24, 1994, p. 41.

SAME GENDER PARTNER ABUSE

While some may argue that including a discussion of same gender abuse in a textbook dealing with 'family violence' degrades the term family, to accept that premise is to deny marriage equality and reality. It also fails to anticipate issues that affect many professionals who work in the area of family violence. The fact is that individuals do live with, work with, and love same-sex partners. These living arrangements sometimes result in one of the members becoming a victim of violence by the other partner. Many of these individuals simply live together, and others have formalized an arrangement by declaring themselves to be married.

As explained in more detail later in this chapter, gays or lesbians who are victims of abuse by their partners fall within the definition of family violence used in this textbook. As more and more gays and lesbians acknowledge this form of violence, it will be incumbent on professionals to understand the dynamics that are involved and to offer support and treatment to the victims.

Gay couples can face the same kind of violence that sometimes occurs in heterosexual relationships. When gays or lesbians live together as a family, some authorities refer to this as a **non-traditional family.** By some estimates, several million nontraditional families live in the United States.[101] Many of these families include children from previous marriages, adoptions, or artificial insemination of a lesbian partner. These are family units in every aspect except for the issuance by the state of a marriage license. Polikoff proposes that these nontraditional families are defined by their sharing of emotions and by their financial interdependence in the relationship.[102]

History and Attitudes

The history of the gay and lesbian struggle for equal treatment does not necessarily belong in a text on family violence. However, society's reactions to same-sex living arrangements do need to be explored so that professionals can understand some of the dynamics involved in a gay or lesbian relationship and can, in turn, react properly when faced with a situation involving gay or lesbian abuse.

Historically, homosexual behavior can be traced back to ancient Greece, where homosexuality was viewed as natural in many segments of Greek society. Plato's *Symposium* extolled the virtues of homosexual behavior, indicating that homosexual lovers would make the best soldiers.[103] One scholar indicates that homosexuality was not considered socially deviant behavior until Thomas Aquinas and St. Augustine argued that it was unnatural because it did not lead to conception.[104] In 1980, the *Diagnostic and Statistical Manual of Disorders,* third edition-revised (DSM-III-R) reclassified homosexual behavior as an alternative sexual lifestyle rather than as deviant behavior. This view is not accepted by all members in society, however. Even in the medical community, the opinion sometimes persists that homosexuality is unnatural sexual behavior.

Gay and lesbian couples have struggled for years to be accepted in society and accorded the same rights as heterosexual couples, including those afforded by marriage. Controversy continues surrounding the issue of marriage between gay and lesbian couples, but this does not stop the formation or continuation of these relationships. The U.S. Census Bureau's 1990 survey revealed 4.47 million households of unmarried adults, with 1.6 million of this number composed of members of the same sex.[105] One of the most complex issues facing these couples is gay and lesbian abuse.

Definitions

Homosexual, Gay, and Lesbian. These terms standing by themselves evoke strong emotional responses from certain segments of society. However, to discuss gay and lesbian abuse accurately, one must start with a clear understanding of what these terms mean.

- **Homosexuality** is defined as the manifestation of sexual desire toward a member of one's own sex.
- **Gay** is defined as a male homosexual or a socially integrated group oriented toward and concerned with the welfare of homosexuals.
- **Lesbian** is defined as a female homosexual.[106] Lesbianism is believed to have been named for the Isle of Lesbos, where the practice of lesbianism was reputed to have been the norm in ancient days.

These terms are subject to debate and interpretation, especially among members of the gay and lesbian community. If the gay and lesbian community cannot agree on what certain terms mean, and if the heterosexual community cannot agree on what the term *family violence* means, it becomes very difficult to define abuse within the gay and lesbian communities.

In comparison to other forms of family violence, very little research has been done in the area of lesbian and gay abuse. However, some leaders within the profession have set

Focus

Some Myths and Facts About Gay and Lesbian Abuse

Myth: Battering and abuse do not exist in the lesbian community as only men abuse women.
Fact: Domestic violence does exist in the lesbian community. This is not a problem limited to heterosexual relationships.
Myth: Domestic violence affects only certain groups of lesbians.
Fact: Violence and abuse are found in all parts of the lesbian community.
Myth: The problem in lesbian relationships is really fighting or mutual battering and not domestic violence.

Fact: The issue in domestic violence is control.
Myth: Domestic violence is not a problem for gay men.
Fact: Because men traditionally have been encouraged to use violence and power to control others, it is difficult for gay men to identify violence in their lives.
Myth: Domestic violence affects only certain groups of gay men.
Fact: Violence and abuse are found in all parts of the gay community.

Source: Based on New York City Gay and Lesbian Anti-Violence Project, "Behind Closed Doors: Battering and Abuse in Lesbian Relationships" and "Behind Closed Doors: Battering and Abuse in Relationships for Gay Men."

forth definitions of gender-specific abuse. For example, Hart defines **lesbian battering** as that pattern of violent and coercive behaviors whereby a lesbian seeks to control the thoughts, beliefs, or conduct of her intimate partner or to punish the intimate for resisting the perpetrator's control over her.[107] Island and Letellier have published one of the first studies on gay abuse, and they define **gay domestic violence** as any unwanted physical force, psychological abuse, or material or property damage inflicted on one gay man by another.[108] Both of these definitions involve dynamics that have been discussed in other chapters dealing with partner abuse. Some authorities might argue that *gay and lesbian abuse* should have its own definition because of the nature of the relationship. However, if one accepts that position, then heterosexual couples who live together but are not married should have their own definition of abuse. Using this approach would be to splinter all relationships into separate groups and lose sight of the overall dynamics that are involved in an abusive relationship.

The definition of *family violence* established in Chapter 1 does not require that the parties be married or even of different sexes. **Family violence** was defined as any act or omission by persons who are cohabiting that results in serious injury to other members of the family. Because this term covers gay and lesbian abuse, it will be used to promote the fact that this type of aggression is in fact a form of family violence.

NATURE AND SCOPE OF THE PROBLEM

To acknowledge that lesbian and gay couples face many of the same problems as heterosexual couples is to accord a legitimacy to their status. Some refuse to accept same-sex relationships as a legitimate expression of society's values. This viewpoint is only one of the reasons that very little research has been done in this area of family violence. Many other reasons are unique to the lesbian and gay community and are discussed later in this chapter.

Extent of the Problem

The true extent of lesbian and gay family violence has never been accurately determined. Some researchers argue that battering within same-sex relationships is the same as it is for heterosexual couples, approximately 25 to 35 percent.[109] Other authorities have stated that domestic violence is the third most severe health problem facing gay men.[110]

For the last several years, the National Coalition of Anti-Violence Programs (NCAVP) has published a report entitled *Anti-Lesbian, Gay, Transgender and Bisexual Violence,* which provides facts and information to be used to advocate for the health, safety, and well-being of the homosexual community.[111] The 2002 final edition reports a continuing epidemic of violence against lesbian, gay, transgender, and bisexual (LGTB) individuals in the United States. Public response to this form of violence is denial and poor coordination among local, state, and federal agencies. Despite high-profile incidents such as the murder of Matthew Shepard in Wyoming in 1998, there is still no federally sponsored research to investigate this problem.

Twelve NCAVP members collected detailed information about anti-LGBT incidents occurring in their regions for 2003 and 2004.[112] The total number of incidents increased from 1,720 in 2003 to 1,792 in 2004, a 4 percent increase. The number of victims also rose 4 percent from 2,042 in 2003 to 2,131 in 2004.

Fifty-nine percent of the victims were male. With respect to sexual orientation, a significant number of victims (17%) identified themselves as heterosexual. Anecdotal information from participating programs indicates that a majority of these victims are simply heterosexual men and women who were mistaken for gay men and lesbians.

Another troubling aspect of the report concerns law enforcement's response to incidents of violence within the gay and lesbian communities. A significant number of victims reported physical abuse and anti-LGBT slurs by the police. Other victims reported law enforcement's response as "indifferent."

The lesbian and gay communities themselves have contributed in some instances to a lack of hard scientific evidence concerning this form of family violence.[113] Lesbian communities may be reluctant for ideological reasons to admit that one woman can batter another. To do so is contrary to the idea of a peaceful, women-centered world. However, more discussion occurs in the lesbian community regarding battering than in the gay community. Gays may be reluctant to discuss gay abuse because, as one scholar put it, "The gay community would rather not know."[114]

When Yale University conducted a study dealing with battered women and the effectiveness of restraining orders, researchers discovered that gay and lesbian abuse was so extensive that they needed to include this segment of the population in the study.[115] A great deal of conflict exists among authorities as to whether gay men or lesbians are the more violent of the two groups. Some researchers claim that lesbians seem to be more aggressive than gay men or heterosexual women.[116] Other authors state that there is some evidence that violence may occur more frequently between gay men than between lesbians.[117] However, all parties to this debate agree that these conclusions are tentative at best and that more empirical research needs to be conducted in this area.[118]

Types of Abuse

Lesbian and gay abusers typically use the same or similar types of violence on their victims. This includes techniques of physical and psychological terror, such as rape, beatings, strangulation, humiliation, economic deprivation, and isolation. Hart has established the following list of violent and coercive behaviors that are used in lesbian battering:

- **Physical:** assaults with weapons; assaults with the abuser's own body such as biting, scratching, and so on; and deprivation of sleep, heat, or food;
- **Sexual:** rape, sex on demand, forced sex with others, physical assaults during sexual encounters, and sexually degrading language;
- **Property:** arson, slashing of belongings, pet abuse or destruction, and breaking household items;
- **Threats:** threats against the victim or her family or friends, stalking, and harassment
- **Economic control:** control over income and assets of the partner, and not working and requiring the victim to support the abuser;
- **Psychological or emotional abuse:** humiliation, lying, isolation, bursts of fury, pouting, and mind manipulation;
- **Homophobic control:** threatening to tell friends or family that the victim is a lesbian, telling the victim that she deserves all she gets because she is lesbian, and reminding her that she has no options because the homophobic world will not help her.[119]

Although no definitive study has been done on the different types of abuse suffered by gay couples, there is support for the proposition that they suffer the same types of abuse as lesbian couples do. An additional aspect to gay abuse deals with forced sex.[120] In the past thirty years, a considerable body of knowledge and research has accumulated on sexual coercion in heterosexual relationships (marital rape is discussed in depth in this textbook in Chapter 13). However, there is very little research into the area of gay men as victims of nonconsensual or forced sex.[121] Waterman and her associates conducted one of the first studies of sexual coercion in gay male and lesbian relationships.[122] The results of their research indicate that forced sex is a considerable problem for gay men. Hickson and his associates, reviewing incidents of nonconsensual sexual activity among 930 gay men living in England and Wales, point out that most research dealing with sexual assault on males has focused on prison populations.[123] The

A physically abused female partner.

presumed sexual orientation of men who rape other men has been subject to some debate. Hickson and colleagues correctly state that men rape other men for the same reasons that they rape women and state that male rape is rarely, if ever, a homosexual problem. Of the 930 men interviewed, 257, or 27 percent, stated that they had been subjected to nonconsensual sex at some point in their lives. After excluding ten of the men who were assaulted by women and twenty-eight respondents who declined to discuss the event or could not remember the details, the remaining 219 subjects' sexual histories were examined. Hickson and colleagues found a broad range of different types of sexual assaults on gay males, including older men touching younger boys, sexual assault of the victim by a heterosexual male after the victim had identified himself as gay, and a large number of assaults between gay males.

LEGAL AND JUDICIAL RESPONSES

This section examines some of the legal aspects and other responses that are specific to lesbian and gay abuse within the context of family violence. Other chapters in this textbook have discussed responsibilities of professionals as well as law enforcement activities as they relate to child abuse and partner abuse. This section points out that victims of gay and lesbian abuse face additional obstacles in reporting these crimes.

Reporting of Abuse

Just as female victims of male battering are reluctant or incapable of reporting or leaving the abusing spouse, so are same-sex victims.[124] However, gay and lesbian victims face additional problems when it comes to disclosure or detachment from the abuser. Many of these issues are unique to the lesbian or gay community and in the past have contributed to a lack of academic research in this area of family violence.

A great deal of misinformation exists regarding AIDS, its effects, and how it may be acquired. Gay or lesbian victims who are HIV-positive may feel that they do not have any support system available to them other than the abusing partner. Also, if the abuser has AIDS or is HIV-positive, victims may feel a great deal of remorse at the thought of reporting their partners to law enforcement agencies or otherwise abandoning them.[125]

The abuser may also prevent the victim from disclosing the abuse or leaving the relationship by threatening to "out" the victim. **Outing** is disclosure of the victim's sexual preference. The abuser may threaten to tell the victim's friends, family, or others unless the victim agrees to conceal the abuse. Even if the victim is open about his or her sexual preference, the batterer may exploit fears of sexist and heterosexual stereotypes to convince the victim that reporting the incident is useless.[126]

Lesbian and gay victims face additional pressure from their peers within the gay community. Some authorities point out that the gay community's failure to acknowledge family violence within its ranks is based on a fear that acknowledgment of such behavior will lead to increased derision from the heterosexual community because it will add credence to the homophobic attitude that gay men and lesbians are deviates.[127]

Another problem facing lesbian and gay victims is the critical shortage of support services and organizations that offer support for same-sex victims of family violence.[128] Specialized counseling services for gay and lesbian victims of family violence are available in only a few cities: New York, San Francisco, Seattle, and Minneapolis.[129] No city has established an emergency shelter specifically for gay men or lesbian victims of family violence.[130] Although some lesbian victims may be able to use battered women's services or shelters, this option is not available to gay men.

In discussing justifications for a separate screened group for victims of abuse, Girshick argues that (1) a lesbian batterer might drop in to see whether her partner was attending a group (if a male showed up at a shelter, it would automatically raise warning flags—not so if a female "visited" the shelter), (2) a lesbian victim might feel uncomfortable talking about her female counterpart in a group of heterosexual females, and (3) a lesbian might not go to the shelter unless she feels it is free from homophobia.[131]

Legal Aspects of Gay and Lesbian Abuse

Gay and lesbian victims face additional hurdles when they attempt to prevent further abuse by their partners. These obstacles include outdated and, in many cases, homophobic attitudes by law enforcement officers, attorneys, and members of the judiciary. Simply reporting the incident may cause the victims to suffer more humiliation and pain from a system that is ill equipped to deal with this form of family violence.

Law enforcement officers and members of the judicial system have historically been reluctant to acknowledge gay and lesbian abuse. In many instances, this leaves the victims without assistance from the legal system. Therefore, abused gays and lesbians are generally less likely to report incidents of domestic violence to the police.

There are reported cases in which members of the judiciary have made comments reflecting their negative feelings toward gay and lesbian couples. In *Constant A. v. Paul C. A.,* for example, the court awarded custody of the children to the father stating, "Once the father

---

Focus

Reporting Barriers

Some Barriers to Reporting Incidents to Homosexual Support Organizations

- The victim's fear of reprisals
- The victim's desire to move "ahead" and get on with his or her life
- The belief that no good can come from reporting the incident
- The sense that the local homosexual organization caters or helps other kinds of individuals who do not have the same sexual orientation as the victim; a transsexual may believe that a center helps only lesbians, for example.

Some Barriers to Reporting Incidents to the Police

- Feelings of personal shame, fear of reprisal, fear of being "outed," fear of being mistreated by the police, and the supposition that nothing will be done to help them
- The supposition that the offender, even if arrested, will still "get away" with the crime
- Fear of being harassed by the police
- Fear of being arrested oneself

Source: Based on *Anti-Lesbian, Gay, Transgender and Bisexual Violence in 1999* (New York City Gay and Lesbian Anti-Violence Project, New York, 2000).

established the mother's lesbian relationship and his own legitimate and stable heterosexual relationship, a presumption arose favoring the preferability of the traditional relationship."[132]

Although many professionals in the criminal justice system are aware of the dynamics involved in male battering of women, they may be unwilling to accept the fact that these same kinds of dynamics are operating in same-sex abuse. This lack of knowledge on the part of the police and the judicial system works to the advantage of the abuser; it is not uncommon for the abuser to claim that he is in fact the victim. Because many gay and lesbian couples maybe the same size physically, the stereotypical view that the larger person is always the aggressor in a relationship may prevent professionals from seeing the facts as they are. Assuming professionals within the criminal justice system are willing to act on allegations of same-sex battering, the laws in sixteen states do not cover same-sex, nonrelated cohabitants.

In June of 2003, the U.S. Supreme Court handed a long-sought victory to advocates of private adult consensual sexual activities. In *Lawrence and Garner v. Texas,* the court struck down a Texas state statute that prohibited private consensual sexual activities between adults of the same sex.[133] The six to three ruling reverses the famous seventeen-year-old case of *Bowers v. Hardwick,* which upheld the anti-sodomy laws. The case immediately generated controversy with spokesperson Ruth Harlow of the Lambda Legal Defense Fund, who represented the two defendants, stating that the ruling was a giant step forward for gays. Conservatives responded that the ruling would undermine family values.[134]

INTERVENTION ISSUES

Professionals can support victims of lesbian and gay family violence in a variety of ways. Friman suggests the following intervention techniques for these types of survivors:

- *Acknowledge the violence:* Violence can occur in same-sex relationships. In addition, same-sex victims may not receive the same type of support from their own communities as heterosexual victims of family violence.
- *Encourage the victim to report the violence:* Many victims have not come out and fear the repercussions of reporting the incident. In addition, many victims believe that efforts to get assistance from law enforcement are futile.
- *Acknowledge the effects of religious oppression:* Some members of the gay and lesbian community have been told that the life they lead is immoral because it violates traditional religious tenets. Those victims may believe that family violence is part of the punishment meted out against them for their lifestyle.
- *Focus on empowerment:* Many same-sex partners already feel disempowered because of their lifestyle. Attempt to explain that power imbalances may also exist in heterosexual family violence.
- *Become part of a support network and act as a referral resource:* Many gays and lesbians live in isolation and do not have any support system or knowledge of where to turn for help and assistance. Professionals in this field should be aware of same-sex support groups or agencies that will assist these victims.
- *Don't blame and shame:* Many lesbians and gays have a heightened fear of abandonment. It is never appropriate to blame an individual for staying in an abusive relationship, even if the professional or others would terminate it.

- *Gain cultural sensitivity:* Professionals should seek out opportunities to educate themselves about gay and lesbian cultures and issues. Without such insight, it is almost impossible to provide support activities.[135]

Some positive signs impacting intervention are beginning to emerge. Therapists are discussing gay and lesbian relationships more often.[136] Those in academia continue researching issues of gay and lesbian abuse.[137] Local programs to support victims of gay and lesbian abuse are emerging, such as the New York City Gay & Lesbian Anti-Violence Project. This program provides a number of services for victims of this type of family violence, including the following:

- Telephone counseling and crisis intervention;
- Short-term in-person counseling;
- Assistance in obtaining orders of protection;
- Police advocacy and precinct accompaniment;
- Crime victims' compensation filing and advocacy;
- Court advocacy, monitoring, and accompaniment;
- Information and referrals;
- Community education and outreach;
- Volunteer training;
- Hospital accompaniment;
- Advocacy with other service agencies.

These services are very similar to those offered to heterosexual victims of family violence by a number of social service agencies.

The New York City Gay and Lesbian Anti-Violence Project is one of the fortunate LGTB organizations that have received funding that allows them to act on these issues. Funding for LGTB outreach is a serious and ongoing issue. The main source of funding for this form of family violence is government grants. However, many organizations compete for a limited amount of dollars; thus, foundation support for LGTB organizations is extremely limited. Some foundations are reluctant to fund family violence programs that turn the traditional concept of partner abuse around and target women as the abuser (in lesbian relationships) and men as the victim (in gay relationships).[138] As more gays and lesbians accept the fact that it is all right to come out of another closet and admit that they have been victims of abuse, society will come to accept this form of aggression as a part of the totality of the circumstances involved in family violence.

MENTAL HEALTH AND DISABILITY ISSUES

Mental Health and Partner Abuse

Victims who suffer violence at the hands of a spouse, boyfriend or girlfriend, or other intimate partner aren't only brutalized physically; they also suffer disproportionately higher rates of mental health distress, according to a policy brief from the UCLA Center for Health Policy Research[139]. Frequently family violence results from mental health issues. As noted in one research study, 54 to 84 percent of battered women suffered from PTSD. In addition, the report noted that about 70 percent of battered women experience depression and anxiety.[140]

It is also noted that according to the National Institute of Mental Health, about one of every four adults suffer from a diagnosable mental disorder. Chapter 12 includes an extension discussion on the various types of mental disorders.

Rates of anxiety and depression are higher among victims of IPV compared to non-victims. In particular, victims often report that they replay the abuse in their minds, feel emotionally detached, experience sleep disturbance, and have anxiety about entering intimate relationships. IPV also contributes to social isolation, as victims may withdraw from friends and loved ones out of a sense of shame or embarrassment. This social isolation further increases their vulnerability to recurrent physical or psychological abuse.[141]

Physical Disability and Partner Abuse

According to a study of domestic violence in Australia, women with a physical or intellectual disability are more likely than women without disability to experience intimate partner violence and the violence they experience is also likely to be more severe and extend for longer periods of time. Research has shown that many women with physical disabilities who experience domestic violence do not seek help, have limited access to appropriate support and fewer opportunities to leave violent relationships.

The Australian report also noted that women may be at increased risk of domestic violence during pregnancy. Almost 60 percent of women who had experienced violence perpetrated by a former partner were pregnant at some time during the relationship; of these, 36 percent experienced the abuse during their pregnancy and 17 percent experienced it for the first time when they were pregnant. In addition, the frequency and severity of violence has been found to be higher among pregnant women and the onset of pregnancy has been found to increase the rate of psychological abuse among those women who had previously reported being abused. The risk to pregnant women has found to be greatest among those women with lower levels of education, from disadvantaged communities and with unintended or unwanted pregnancies. The consequences of abuse while a woman is pregnant can include stress, drug and alcohol use, and physical injuries, which can further impact upon a woman's health during pregnancy, the birth outcome, and the health of their baby. There is also an increased risk in the period immediately after a baby is born, due to the additional stress that may be placed on a relationship and each partner's mental health, wellbeing, and lifestyle.[142]

Summary

Although intimate partner abuse has been intensely researched in the past years, it is still one of the most commonly misunderstood issues within the study of family violence. Society has placed women in inferior and subordinate positions throughout history, and even today the glass ceiling exists in both public and private institutions. These factors contribute to the interpersonal dynamics that result in violence against women. The nature and extent of partner abuse are staggering. Current figures indicate that women today are being brutalized in alarming numbers.

Numerous theories try to explain why men batter women; in fact, there are so many theories that entire textbooks are devoted to explaining them. Yet no theory is accepted by all scholars, practitioners, or professionals in the field as the only theory that explains partner abuse. Even though no theory prevails, professionals should be aware of the more common and well-known studies of partner abuse that consider social stress, power, dependency, alcohol, pregnancy, and marriage.

The characteristics of those who abuse and those who are abused have been researched by well-known and respected scholars. Unfortunately, no set of personality traits can be listed that automatically indicates who will be an abuser or who will be abused. Although no agreement exists regarding the theories or characteristics of partner abuse, all professionals acknowledge that there are three basic types of partner abuse: physical, sexual, and emotional. We are beginning to discuss another aspect of partner violence—police officers' battering of their spouses. More study needs to occur on this emerging topic.

When a spouse who has been abused finally reacts, she may kill her abuser. The secret of abuse thus comes out into the open and enters the judicial arena. The most common defense used in these cases is self-defense. Expert witnesses are necessary to educate the jury regarding battered woman syndrome and to explain why the spouse did not leave her abuser. Even today that question is being asked by those who should know better.

Gay and lesbian abuse is slowly being recognized as a form of family violence. Although the true nature and extent of this type of aggression is unknown, more research is being conducted in this area. Some studies place the incidence of same-sex abuse at the same level of abuse experienced by heterosexual couples. Gay and lesbian victims of family violence face special problems that heterosexual victims do not. One of these is the lack of services for parties to this type of domestic violence.

Professionals in the field of family violence are just now awakening to the fact that gay and lesbian victims need assistance and support. Law enforcement officers and some members of the judiciary may still reflect homophobic attitudes when dealing with victims of gay and lesbian abuse. However, the fact that it is now being discussed in professional journals, conferences, and college textbooks indicates a new awareness and openness to deal with this covert form of family violence.

Key Terms

partner abuse—any intentional act or series of acts that cause injury to the spouse. These acts may be physical, emotional, or sexual. The term *spouse* is gender-neutral; therefore, the abuse may occur to a male or female. The term includes those who are married, cohabitating, or involved in a serious relationship. It also encompasses individuals who are separated and living apart from their former spouses.

family—a group of persons who cohabit.

power—the ability to impose one's will on another and make life decisions for that person.

marital dependency—a multifaceted concept that involves economic, emotional, and societal forces that results in a woman's being dependent on her spouse for support.

battered woman syndrome—one who has been, on at least two occasions, the victim of physical, sexual, or serious psychological abuse by a man with whom she has an intimate relationship. It is a pattern of psychological symptoms that develop after a woman has lived in a battering relationship.

Stockholm syndrome—a phenomenon that occurs when persons who are held as hostages, captives, or prisoners of war begin to identify with their captors.

nontraditional family—gays or lesbians living together as a family.

homosexuality—the manifestation of sexual desire toward a member of one's own sex.

gay—a male homosexual or a socially integrated group oriented toward and concerned with the welfare of homosexuals.

lesbian—a female homosexual; lesbianism is believed to have been named for the Isle of Lesbos, where the practice of lesbianism was reputed to have been the norm in ancient days.

lesbian battering—that pattern of violent and coercive behaviors in which a lesbian seeks to control the thoughts, beliefs, or conduct of her intimate partners or to punish the partner for resisting the perpetrator's control over her.

gay domestic violence—any unwanted physical force, psychological abuse, or material or property damage inflicted on one gay man by another.

family violence—any act or omission by persons who are cohabitating that results in serious injury to other members of the family.

outing—the disclosure of the victim's sexual preference.

Discussion Questions

1. Should we call this form of family violence partner abuse, wife abuse, or intimate partner abuse? Justify your answer.
2. Is it important to understand the different theories regarding why the abuse occurs?
3. List what you think are the most important aspects of our society that cause relationship abuse or allow it to happen.
4. If your spouse or partner grabbed your arm during an argument and squeezed it very tightly, would you leave him or her? Why or why not?
5. Which, in your opinion, is the most severe form of abuse—physical, sexual, or emotional? Why?
6. Have you ever known a friend who you had reason to believe may have been or is now being abused? What were the characteristics you observed?
7. Should the justice system charge women who kill their abusers with homicide? Why? Why not?
8. Should there be a separate definition for gay abuse and lesbian abuse?
9. Are the dynamics involved in abuse of same-sex partners different from those that occur within heterosexual relationships? Justify your answer.
10. List the various stereotypes regarding gay and lesbian couples. Why do you think these stereotypes exist?
11. What can we do to limit or decrease the stereotypes that exist regarding gay and lesbian relationships?
12. Should victims of same sex partnership violence be admitted to battered women's shelters? What alternatives would you recommend for victims of same sex partnership violence?

Suggested Readings

Ammerman, R. T., and M. Hersen, eds. *Case Studies in Family Violence* (Plenum, New York, 1991).

Ammerman, R. T., and M. Hersen, eds. *Treatment of Family Violence* (Wiley, New York, 1990).

Bancroft, L. *Why Does He Do That? Inside the Minds of Angry and Controlling Men* (Berkley Trade, New York, 2003).

Berrill, K. T., and G. M. Herek, eds. *Hate Crimes: Confronting Violence against Lesbians and Gay Men* (SAGE, Newbury Park, Calif., 1992).

Boswell, J. *Christianity, Social Tolerance, and Homosexuality* (University of Chicago Press, Chicago, 1980).

Collins, J. J., Jr., ed. *Drinking and Crime: Perspectives on the Relationships between Alcohol Consumption and Criminal Behavior* (Guilford, New York, 1981).

Costanzo, M., and S. Oskamp, eds. *Violence and the Law* (SAGE, Thousand Oaks, Calif., 1994).

Dawes, C. *Domestic Violence: Both Sides of the Coin* (Trafford Publishing, Victoria, BC, Canada, 2006).

Dobash, R. E., and R. P. Dobash. *Violence against Wives: A Case against the Patriarchy* (Free Press, New York, 1979).

Gonsiorek, J. C., ed. *Breach of Trust* (SAGE, Thousand Oaks, Calif., 1995).

Gottheil, E., K. A. Druley, T. E. Skoloda, and H. M. Waxman, eds. *Alcohol, Drug Abuse, and Aggression* (Thomas, Springfield, Ill., 1983).

Hasselt, V. B., R. L. Morrison, A. S. Bellack, and W. Frazier, eds. *Handbook of Family Violence* (Plenum, New York, 1988).

Hotaling, G. T., D. Finkelhor, J. T. Kirkpatrick, and M. A. Straus, eds. *New Directions in Family Violence Research* (SAGE, Beverly Hills, Calif., 1988).

Island, D., and P. Letellier. *Men Who Beat the Men Who Love Them* (Harrington Park, New York, 1991).

Jaggar, A. M., and P. S. Rothenberg, eds. *Feminist Frameworks*, 3rd ed. (McGraw-Hill, New York, 1993).

Lobel, K., ed. *Naming the Violence: Speaking Out about Lesbian Battering* (Seal, Seattle, 1986).

Ludwig, R., and M. Birkbeck. *Till Death Do Us Part: Love, Marriage, and the Mind of a Killer Spouse* (Atria Books, New York, 2006).

Martin, D. *Battered Wives* (Glide, San Francisco, 1976).

Masters, W., V. Johnson, and R. Kolodny. *Masters and Johnson on Sex and Human Loving* (Little, Brown and Company, Boston, 1968).

McClelland, D. C., W. N. Davis, R. Kalin, and E. Wanner. *The Drinking Man* (Free Press, New York, 1972).

Merlo, A. V., and J. M. Pollock. *Women, Law, and Social Control* (Allyn & Bacon, Boston, 1995).

NiCarthy, G. *Getting Free: A Handbook for Women in Abusive Relationships* (Seal, New York, 1986).

Pagelow, M. D. *Family Violence* (Praeger, New York, 1984).

Penfold, R. *Dragonslippers: This Is What an Abusive Relationship Looks Like* (Grove, Press, Berkeley, Calif., 2006).

Renzetti, C. M. *Violent Betrayal: Partner Abuse in Lesbian Relationships* (SAGE, Newbury Park, Calif., 1992).

Roy, M., ed. *A Psychological Study of Domestic Violence* (Van Nostrand Reinhold, New York, 1977).

Roy, M., ed. *Battered Women: A Psychosociological Study of Domestic Violence* (Van Nostrand Reinhold, New York, 1977).

Sonkin, D. J., ed. *Domestic Violence on Trial* (Springer, New York, 1982).

Stone, L. *The Family, Sex, and Marriage in England 1500–1800* (Harper & Row, New York, 1977).

Straus, M. A., and R. J. Gelles. *Physical Violence in American Families* (Transaction, New Brunswick, N.J., 1990).

Walker, L. E. *Terrifying Love* (Harper & Row, New York, 1987).

Walker, L. E. *The Battered Women* (Harper & Row, New York, 1979).

Endnotes

1. *Costs of Intimate Partner Violence against Women in the United States* (National Center for Injury Prevention and Control, Centers for Disease Control and Prevention. U.S. Department of Health and Human Services, March 2003). Available at www.cdc.gov/Violence-Prevention/pub/IPV_cost.html, accessed June 27, 2012.

2. R. E. Dobash and R. P. Dobash, "Wives: The 'Appropriate' Victims of Marital Violence," *Victimology* 2(3/4) (1978), p. 426.

3. T. Davidson, "Wifebeating: A Recurring Phenomenon throughout History," in M. Roy, ed., *Battered Women: A Psychosociological Study of Domestic Violence* (Van Nostrand Reinhold, New York, 1977).

4. For an excellent historical overview of this area, see L. Stone, *The Family, Sex, and Marriage in England 1500–1800* (Harper & Row, New York, 1977).

5. T. Davidson, "Wifebeating: A Recurring Phenomenon throughout History," in M. Roy, ed., *Battered Women: A Psychosociological Study of Domestic Violence* (Van Nostrand Reinhold, New York, 1977).

6. N. Oppenlander, "The Evolution of Law and Wife Abuse," *Law & Policy Quarterly* 3 (1981), p. 135–167.

7. 1 Miss (1 Walker) 155 (1824).

8. W. L. Prosser, *Handbook on the Law of Torts*, 4th ed. (West Publishing, St. Paul, Minn., 1971).

9. 3 Va. L. Reg. 241 (1917).

10. See 61 N.C. (Phil. Law) 453 at 459 (1868).

11. 70 N.C. 60 (1874).

12. C. H. Sommers, *Who Stole Feminism* (Simon & Schuster, New York, 1994).

13. D. Martin, *Battered Wives* (Glide, San Francisco, 1976), pp. 197–198.

14. M. A. Straus and R. J. Gelles, *Physical Violence in American Families* (Transaction, New Brunswick, N.J., 1990), pp. 96–98.

15. E. Stark and A. Flitcraft, "Violence among Intimates: An Epidemiological Review," in V. B. Hasselt et al., eds., *Handbook of Family Violence* (Plenum, New York, 1988), pp. 293–317.

16. C. M. Rennison, *Intimate Partner Violence, 1993–2001, Crime Date Brief* (Washington, D.C., February 2003).

17. The Commonwealth Fund, New York (1999).

18. E. W. Gondolf and E. R. Fisher, "Wife Battering," in R. T. Ammerman and M. Hersen, eds., *Case Studies in Family Violence* (Plenum, New York, 1991), pp. 273–274.

19. D. Kurz, "Battering and the Criminal Justice System: A Feminist View," in E. S. Buzawa and C. G. Buzawa, eds., *Domestic Violence: The Changing Criminal Justice Response* (Auburn House, Westport, Conn., 1992).

20. For an excellent discussion of these issues, see K. Spiller, "The Feminist Majority Report: Corporate Women and the Mommy Track," in A. M. Jaggar and P. S. Rothenberg, eds., *Feminist Frameworks*, 3d ed. (McGraw-Hill, New York, 1993), pp. 316–318.

21. See K. Newman, "Middle-Class Women in Trouble," in Jaggar and Rothenberg, eds., *Feminist Frameworks*, pp. 319–323.

22. This does not imply that middle-class women are not abused. See H. Johnson and F. G. Hermelin, "The Truth about White-Collar Domestic Violence," *Working Woman* 20(3) (1995), pp. 54–62.

23. M. Roy, "A Current Study of 150 Cases," in M. Roy, ed., *A Psychological Study of Domestic Violence* (Van Nostrand Reinhold, New York, 1977).

24. D. S. Kalmuss and M. A. Straus, "Wife's Marital Dependency and Wife Abuse," in Straus and Gelles, eds., *Physical Violence in American Families*, pp. 379–380.

25. K. J. Sher, "Subjective Effects of Alcohol: The Influence of Setting and Individual Differences in Alcohol Expectancies," *Journal of Studies on Alcohol* 46 (1985), pp. 137–146.

26. D. H. Coleman and M. A. Straus, "Alcohol Abuse and Family Violence," in E. Gottheil et al., eds., *Alcohol, Drug Abuse, and Aggression* (Thomas, Springfield, Ill., 1983), pp. 104–124.

27. D. C. McClelland, W. N. Davis, R. Kalin, and E. Wanner, *The Drinking Man* (Free Press, New York, 1972).

28. K. Pernanem, "Theoretical Aspects of the Relationship between Alcohol Use and Crime," in J. J. Collins Jr., ed., *Drinking and Crime: Perspectives on the Relationships between Alcohol Consumption and Criminal Behavior* (Guilford, New York, 1981).

29. A. Helton, "Battering during Pregnancy," *American Journal of Nursing* 86 (1986), pp. 910–913.

30. R. J. Gelles, "Violence and Pregnancy: Are Pregnant Women at Greater Risk of Abuse?" in Straus and Gelles, eds., *Physical Violence in American Families*, p. 282.

31. M. A. Straus and R. J. Gelles, "How Violent Are American Families? Estimates from the National Family Violence Survey and Other Studies," in G. T. Hotaling et al., eds., *New Directions in Family Violence Research* (SAGE, Beverly Hills, Calif., 1988).

32. J. E. Sets and M. A. Straus, "The Marriage License: A Comparison of Assaults in Dating, Cohabitating, and Married Couples," in Straus and Gelles, eds., *Physical Violence in American Families*, pp. 227–244, published earlier in *Journal of Family Violence* 4 (1989), pp. 161–180.

33. J. E. Sets and M. A. Pirog-Good, "Violence in Dating Relationships," *Social Psychology Quarterly* 50 (1987), pp. 237–246.

34. See Sets and Straus, "The Marriage License."

35. S. M. Anderson, T. R. Boulette, and A. H. Schwartz, "Psychological Maltreatment," in R. T. Ammerman and M. Hersen, eds., *Case Studies in Family Violence* (Plenum, New York, 1991), pp. 304–308.

36. R. E. Dobash and R. P. Dobash, *Violence against Wives: A Case against the Patriarchy* (Free Press, New York, 1979).

37. D. Everstein and L. Everstein, *People in Crisis: Strategic Therapeutic Interventions* (Brunner/Mazel, New York, 1983).

38. B. M. Quigley and Ken E. Leonard, "Desistance of Husband Aggression in the Early Years of Marriage," *Violence and Victims* 11(4) (Winter 1996), p. 355.

39. A. Rosenbaum and R. Maiuro, "Perpetrators of Spouse Abuse," in R. T. Ammerman and M. Hersen, eds., *Treatment of Family Violence* (Wiley, New York, 1990), pp. 280–309.

40. M. D. Pagelow, *Family Violence* (Praeger, New York, 1984).

41. S. M. Anderson, T. R. Boulette, and A. H. Schwartz, "Psychological Maltreatment of Spouses," in Ammerman and Hersen, eds., *Case Studies in Family Violence* (Plenum Press, New York, 1991), pp. 293–327.

42. See C. A. Bersani et al., "Personality Traits of Convicted Male Batterers," *Journal of Family Violence* 7 (1992), p. 123, for a study regarding personality traits of abusers and an acknowledgment that further study needs to occur in this area.

43. S. Steinmetz, "The Battered Husband Syndrome," *Victimology* 2(3/4) (1978), pp. 499–509.

44. S. K. Steinmetz and J. S. Lucca, "Husband Battering," in V. B. Van Hasselt et al., eds., *Handbook of Family Violence* (Plenum, New York, 1988).

45. K. D. O'Leary et al., "Prevalence and Stability of Physical Aggression between Spouses: A Longitudinal Analysis," *Journal of Consulting and Clinical Psychology* 57 (1989), pp. 263–268.

46. *Report on Arrests for Domestic Violence in California, 1998* (Office of the Attorney General, Bureau of Criminal Information and Analysis, Sacramento, Calif., August 1999), p. 8.

47. Kevin Hamberger et al., "An Empirical Classification of Motivations for Domestic Violence," *Violence against Women* 3(4) (August 1997), pp. 401–423.

48. L. E. Walker, *The Battered Women* (Harper & Row, New York, 1979).

49. L. E. Walker, *The Battered Woman Syndrome* (Springer, New York, 1984).

50. See *People v. Humphrey*, 96 Daily Journal D.A.R. 10609 at 10612, in which the California Supreme Court addressed this issue.

51. M. A. Douglas, "The Battered Women Syndrome," in D. J. Sonkin, ed., *Domestic Violence on Trial* (Springer, New York, 1982).

52. Pagelow, *Family Violence*, p. 308.

53. G. NiCarthy, *Getting Free: A Handbook for Women in Abusive Relationships* (Seal, New York, 1986), pp. 117–118.

54. D. G. Dutton and S. L. Painter, "Traumatic Bonding: The Development of Emotional Attachments in Battered Women and Other Relationships of Intermittent Abuse," *Victimology* (1981), p. 139.

55. D. G. Dutton, *The Domestic Assault of Women* (UBC Press, Vancouver, British Columbia, 1995).

56. Ibid., p. 190.

57. Ibid., p. 191.

58. W. Webb, "Treatment Issues and Cognitive Behavior Techniques with Battered Women," *Journal of Family Violence* 7 (1992), p. 205.

59. Pagelow, *Family Violence*.

60. S. M. Anderson, T. R. Boulette, and A. H. Schwartz, "Psychological Maltreatment of Spouses."

61. This section has been based on D. C. Sheehan, ed., *Domestic Violence by Police Officers* (Behavioral Science Unit, FBI Academy, Quantico, Va., 2000).

62. V. E. Bibbens, "The Quality of Family and Marital Life of Police Personnel," in J. T. Reese and H. A. Goldstein, eds., *Psychological Services for Law Enforcement* (Government Printing Office, Washington, D.C., 1986).

63. R. DePue, "High Risk Lifestyle: The Police Family," *FBI Law Enforcement Bulletin* 50 (1981), p. 8.

64. C. Maslach and S. Jackson, "Burned Out Cops and Their Families," *Psychology Today* 12 (1979), p. 59.

65. L. B. Johnson, Testimony to U.S. House Select Committee on Children, Youth, and Families: Police Stress and Family Well-Being (May 1991).

66. P. H. Neidig et al., "Interspousal Aggression in Law Enforcement Families: A Preliminary Investigation: 15 Police Studies," *International Review of Police Development* 30 (1992).

67. P. H. Neidig et al., "FOP Marital Aggression Survey: Interspousal Aggression in Law

Enforcement Personnel Attending the FOP Biennial Conference," *National Fraternal Order of Police Journal* 5 (1992).

68. *Domestic Violence among Police: A Survey of Internal Affairs Policies* (Southwestern Law Enforcement Institute, Richardson, Tex., 1995).

69. *Model Policy on Police Officer Domestic Violence* (IACP, Alexandria, Va., June 1999).

70. A. Levinson, "Abusers behind the Badge," *Arizona Republic* (June 29, 1997).

71. See L. D. Lott, "Deadly Secrets: Violence in the Police Family," *FBI Law Enforcement Bulletin*, p. 12 (November 1995). See also "Domestic Assaults among Police: A Survey of Internal Affairs Policies, Arlington, Texas Police Department and Southwestern Law Enforcement Institute," Southwestern Law Enforcement Institute (1995).

72. See *Police Family Violence Fact Sheet,* National Center for Women and Policing, www.womenandpolicing.org, accessed November 19, 2002.

73. "Domestic Violence in the Los Angeles Police Department: How Well Does the Los Angeles Police Department Police its Own?" Domestic Violence Task Force, Office of the Inspector General (1997).

74. "Domestic Violence in the Los Angeles Police Department."

75. M. J. Erwin et al., "Reports of Intimate Partner Violence Made Against Police Officers," *Journal of Family Violence* 20(1) (2005), p. 13.

76. J. T. Reese, "Family Therapy in Law Enforcement: A New Approach to an Old Problem," *FBI Law Enforcement Bulletin* 51 (1982), p. 7.

77. E. K. White and A. L. Honig, "Law Enforcement Families," in M. I. Kurke and E. M. Scrivner, eds., *Police Psychology into the 21st Century* (Erlbaum, Hillsdale, N.J., 1995).

78. A. L. Honig and E. K. White, "Violence in the Law Enforcement Family," in M. I. Kurke and E. M. Scrivner, eds., *Law Enforcement Families: Issues and Answers* (Government Printing Office, Washington, D.C., 1994).

79. See *Police Family Violence Fact Sheet.*

80. See *Police Family Violence Fact Sheet.*

81. K. J. Kruger and N. G. Valitos, *Dealing with Domestic Violence in Law Enforcement Relationships,* Public Agency Training Council, www.patc.com.

82. 719 P. 2d 1268 (1986).

83. 215 Cal. App. 3d 1178 (1989).

84. L. E. Walker, *The Battered Women, and Terrifying Love* (Harper & Row, New York, 1987).

85. 215 Cal. App. 3d 1187.

86. V. Ellis, "Battered Wives Granted Clemency," *Fresno Bee,* May 29, 1993, p. A-18.

87. 840 P. 2d 1 (Okl. Cir. 1992). The delay between the time of the killing in 1982 and the appellate court decision was a result of an earlier murder trial that required the state to retry the defendant.

88. 13 Cal. Rptr. 2d 332 (1992).

89. 13 Cal. 4th 1073, 56 Cal. Rptr. 2d 142 (1996).

90. The court noted that some experts do not advocate using the phrase "battered woman syndrome" for a variety of reasons, including the fact that it implies that this is only a syndrome battered women develop. However, the court pointed out that others continue to use the term, and the California legislature adopted a statute in 1991 using the term.

91. 673 N.E.2d 1339 (1997).

92. 97 Daily Journal D.A.R. 13497 (October 31, 1997).

93. 732 So. 2d 1044 (March 11, 1999).

94. CALJIC Jury Instruction No. 5.17, 6th ed. (1996). Brackets in original.

95. G. R. Hatcher, "The Gendered Nature of the Battered Woman Syndrome: Why Gender Neutrality Does Not Mean Equality," *New York University Annotated Survey of American Law* 59 (2003), p. 21.

96. See for example, Paula Finley Mangum, "Reconceptualizing Battered Women Syndrome Evidence: Prosecution Use of Expert Testimony on Battering," *19 B.C. Third World L.J.* 594 (1999).

97. R. Schuller, "Juror's Decisions in Trials of Battered Women Who Kill: The Role of Prior Beliefs and Expert Testimony," *Journal of Applied Psychology* 24 (1994), p. 316.

98. 128 Misc. 2d 129 at 134–135, 488 N.Y.S.2d 358 at 363 (1985).

99. 783 S.W.2d 387 (Ky 1990).

100. E. A. Raitz Greene and H. Lindblad, "Jurors' Knowledge of Battered Women," *Journal of Family Violence* 4(2) (1989), p. 105.

101. N. D. Hunter and N. D. Polikoff, "Custody Rights of Lesbian Mothers: Legal Theory and Litigation Strategy," *Buffalo Law Review* 25 (1976), p. 691.

102. N. Polikoff, "This Child Does Have Two Mothers: Redefining Parenthood to Meet the Needs of Children in Lesbian-Mother and Other Nontraditional Families," *Georgia Law Review* 78 (1990), p. 459.

103. W. Masters, V. Johnson, and R. Kolodny, *Masters and Johnson on Sex and Human Loving* (Little, Brown and Company, Boston, 1968).

104. J. Boswell, *Christianity, Social Tolerance, and Homosexuality* (University of Chicago Press, Chicago, 1980).

105. A. E. Saluter, "Marital Status and Living Arrangements: March 1990," *U.S. Bureau of the Census,* Series P-20, No. 450 (May 1991), p. 73.

106. *Webster's New Collegiate Dictionary* (Merriam, Springfield, Mass., 1981).

107. B. Hart, "Lesbian Battering: An Examination," in Kerry Lobel, ed., *Naming the Violence: Speaking Out about Lesbian Battering* (Seal, Seattle, 1986), p. 173.

108. D. Island and P. Letellier, *Men Who Beat the Men Who Love Them* (Harrington Park, New York, 1991), p. 27.

109. C. M. Renzetti, *Violent Betrayal, Partner Abuse in Lesbian Relationships* (Sage, Newbury Park, Calif., 1992), pp. 17–18.

110. Island and Letellier. *Men Who Beat the Men Who Love Them,* p. 14.

111. *Anti-Lesbian, Gay, Transgender and Bisexual Violence in 1999* (New York City Gay and Lesbian Anti-Violence Project, New York, 2000).

112. C. Patton and R. Baum, *National Coalition of Anti-Violence Programs, 2005 Release Edition* (New York, 2005).

113. V. Jenness, "Social Movement Growth, Domain Expansion, and Framing Processes: The Gay/Lesbian Movement and Violence against Gays and Lesbians as a Social Problem," *Social Problems* 42(1) (1995), p. 145.

114. Island and Letellier, *Men Who Beat the Men Who Love Them,* pp. 10 and 36.

115. G. Brown et al., "Starting a TRO Project: Student Representation of Battered Women," *Yale Law Review* 96 (1987), p. 1985.

116. M. D. Hunter, "Homosexuals as a New Class of Domestic Violence Subjects under the New Jersey Prevention of Domestic Violence Act of 1991," *University of Louisville Journal of Family Law* 31 (1992/93), p. 86.

117. D. Bricker, "Fatal Defense: An Analysis of Battered Women's Syndrome, Expert Testimony for Gay Men and Lesbians Who Kill Abusive Partners," *Brooklyn Law Review* 58 (Winter 1993), p. 1379.

118. A recent conference on family services indicates the need for more scientific research in this area. The handout material and program material did contain a section on "Domestic Violence Service Applications for Lesbian, Gay, Transgender, and Bisexual Persons." Unfortunately, most of the material was anecdotal in nature. Seventh Annual Family Strengths Family-Centered Conference, August 28–29, 2000, Sacramento, California.

119. B. Hart, "Lesbian Battering: An Examination," in Lobel, ed., *Naming the Violence,* pp. 188–189.

120. A. W. Coxwell and M. B. King, "Male Victims of Rape and Sexual Abuse," *Sexual and Marital Therapy* 11(3) (August 1996), p. 297.

121. L. K. Waldner-Haugrud and L. Vaden-Gratch, "Sexual Coercion in Gay/Lesbian Relationships: Descriptives and Gender Differences." *Violence and Victims* 12(1) (Spring 1997).

122. C. K. Waterman, L. J. Dawson, and M. J. Bologna, "Sexual Coercion in Gay Male and Lesbian Relationships: Predictors and Implications for Support Services," *Journal of Sex Research* 26(1) (1989), p. 118.

123. F. C. I. Hickson et al., "Gay Men as Victims of Nonconsensual Sex," *Archives of Sexual Behavior* 23(3) (1994), p. 281.

124. K. Snow, "The Violence at Home," *The Advocate,* June 2, 1992, p. 60.

125. "Violence against People with HIV/AIDS." Pamphlet prepared by the New York City Gay and Lesbian Anti-Violence Project (New York, 1991).

126. R. C. Savin-Williams, "Verbal and Physical Abuse as Stressors in the Lives of Lesbian, Gay Male, and Bisexual Youths: Associations with School Problems, Running Away, Substance Abuse, Prostitution, and Suicide," *Journal of Consulting and Clinical Psychology* 62(2) (1994), p. 261.

127. M. Benowitz, "How Homophobia Affects Lesbians' Response to Violence in Lesbian Relationships," in Lobel, ed., *Naming the Violence,* p. 200.

128. L. Margolies and E. Leeder, "Violence at the Door: Treating Lesbian Batterers," *Violence against Women* 1(2) (1995), p. 139.

129. P. Winfield, "Rare Program Aids Battered Lesbians, Gays: Violence Mirrors Heterosexual Incidents," *Seattle Times,* September 24, 1990, p. E3.

130. J. Mann, "A Grant in Trouble," *Washington Post,* July 5, 1995, p. C3.

131. L. B. Girshick, "Program Notes: Descriptions and Analyses of Innovative Programs and Strategies," *Journal of Gay & Lesbian Social Services* 9(1) (1999), p. 83.

132. 496 A.2d 1 at 7 (1985).

133. USSC No. 02–0102 (2003).

134. "Supreme Court Strikes Down Texas Sodomy Law," *CNN.com,* June 27, 2003.

135. K. Friman, "Intimate Partner Violence in Same Sex Relationships: Implications for Community Response," paper presented at the Twenty-Third North American Victim Assistance Conference (Houston, August 17–22, 1977).

136. See, for example, a special section entitled "Gay and Lesbians Are Out of the Closet," *The Family Therapy Networker* (January/February 1991).

137. G.-Y. Lie and S. Gentlewarrier, "Intimate Violence in Lesbian Relationships: Discussion of Survey Findings and Practice Implications," *Journal of Social Service Research* 15 (1/2) 1991, p. 41.

138. *Lesbian, Gay, Bisexual, and Transgender Domestic Violence in 1998* (New York City Gay and Lesbian Anti-Violence Project, New York, October 1999).

139 "Victims of intimate partner violence more likely to develop mental health disorders" at News Medical website at www.news-medical.net, accessed July 23, 2015.

140 Florida Coalition Against Domestic Violence web site at www.fcadv.org/proj, accessed July 23, 2015.

141 PsychCentral website at www.psychcentral.com assessed on July 23, 2015.

142 A. Morgan and H. Chadwick, "Research in Practice Summary Paper No. 7. Key Issues in Domestic Violence." Canberra, Australia: Australian Institute of Criminology (December 2009).

3

The Criminal Justice Response to Intimate Partner Abuse and Relationship Violence

CHAPTER OBJECTIVES

After studying this chapter, you should be able to:

- Explain the various responses to intimate partner abuse that may be taken by criminal justice agencies;
- Discuss the effects of arrest on those who batter their spouse;
- Explain the "smart policing" approach;
- Discuss the goals of the Violence Against Women Act;
- Explain the issues involved with the use restraining orders.

Detailed Look at What You Should Know About the Criminal Justice Response to Intimate Partner Abuse and Relationship Violence

- The term *partner assault* is used to distinguish this form of family violence from partner abuse.
- From a legal perspective, the term *partner assault* is inaccurate. An assault does not involve any physical injury to the victim. It is actually a battery that is being discussed.
- To be consistent with other professionals and writers in the field of family violence, partner assault is used instead of partner battery and defined as the act of intentionally inflicting physical injury on a spouse or other person who is cohabitating with the abuser.
- If partner assault were like any other crime, the police response would be fairly simple: Investigate, arrest, charge, and cooperate with the district attorney in the prosecution of the perpetrator.
- Partner assault is one of the most common forms of violence in the United States.

- Although partner assault can occur in all economic groups, the rate of partner battering was five times higher in lower-income families than in the higher-income brackets.

- The stresses of unemployment, poverty, and inner-city living conditions appear to increase the risk of partner assault.

- Similar to other forms of domestic violence, alcohol use is present in a high percentage of partner assault cases.

- Law enforcement's acknowledgment and response to partner assault has been slow in coming. Even today, some police officers would rather not get involved in a "family matter."

- Special women's police stations, staffed with multidisciplinary female teams equipped to respond to the different needs of victim survivors, have been set up in several countries as an attempt to make police stations more accessible to women.

- In recent years, victims of partner abuse have turned to the courts in an attempt to force police departments to arrest the perpetrators of this form of family violence. Increasingly, courts have begun to listen to and rule in favor of the abused on both constitutional and tort grounds.

- In the area of policing and domestic violence, probably no more controversial a study has been conducted than the Minneapolis experiment, which dealt with the effect of arrest on those who batter their spouses.

- The Minneapolis experiment acted as an agent for change within the criminal justice system. Armed with its results, advocates of mandatory arrest and other sanctions were able to find support in various state legislatures for long overdue reform of criminal statutes dealing with domestic violence.

- In *Raucci v. Town of Rotterdam*, a federal court ruled that the municipality owed a battered woman a special duty to protect her from her estranged husband because of actions by the police department that had assured her of protection.

- Another alternative to arresting the abusive spouse is the concept called "smart policing." This approach is based on research involving the analysis of arrest and its effect on future violence.

- Violent Crime Control and Law Enforcement Act, Title IV of which is called the Violence Against Women Act (VAWA) mandates that various professions form partnerships and work together to respond to all forms of violence against women.

- Restraining orders (protective orders) are court orders that prohibit the offender from having any contact with the victim. They are civil versus criminal and require a judge to rule that sufficient evidence supports the issuance of such an order.

- The effectiveness of restraining orders depends on a variety of factors, including how specific and comprehensive the orders are and how well they are enforced.

- Partner assault does not end with an arrest or with the issuance of a restraining order. A necessary part of this process is the court's and prosecutor's responses to this form of family violence.

■ **Prosecution** can be defined as a proceeding instituted and carried on by due course of law before a competent tribunal for the purpose of determining the guilt or innocence of a person charged with a crime.

INTRODUCTION

This chapter explores law enforcement and criminal justice responses to intimate partner assault. Excellent texts and research material can be found that discuss police and domestic violence.[1] That material provides an in-depth scholarly examination of the causes, effects, and police responses in this area. The purpose of this chapter is to acquaint readers with an overview of policing and prosecution of partner assault cases. This will facilitate an understanding of some of the existing controversies in this highly debated area of domestic violence.

The term **partner assault** is used to distinguish this form of family violence from partner abuse. From a legal perspective, the term *partner assault* is inaccurate. An assault does

---

Focus

Thurman v. City of Torrington

Tracey Thurman was a motel maid who was married to Charles "Buck" Thurman. Tracey tried to file complaints against her husband for domestic abuse, but city officials ignored her. Finally her husband was arrested after attacking her in full view of a policeman and after a judge had issued an order prohibiting him from going to his wife's home. According to Tracey, the police ignored her pleas for help. Her husband violated the order and came to her house and threatened her. When she asked the police to arrest him for violating his probation and threatening her life, they ignored her again. She filed suit in federal district court based on police inaction after her husband had stabbed her at least thirteen times. She successfully claimed that the conduct of the Torrington Police Department deprived her of her right to equal protection.

In *Thurman v. City of Torrington (1984)*, a U.S. District Court for Downstate Connecticut stated: City officials and police officers are under an affirmative duty to preserve law and order, and to protect the personal safety of persons in the community. This duty applies equally to women whose personal safety is threatened by

individuals with whom they have or have had a domestic relationship as well as to all other persons whose personal safety is threatened, including women not involved in domestic relationships. If officials have notice of the possibility of attacks on women in domestic relationships or other persons, they are under an affirmative duty to take reasonable measures to protect the personal safety of such persons in the community.

A police officer may not knowingly refrain from interference in such violence, and may not automatically decline to make an arrest simply because the assailant and his victim are married to each other. Such inaction on the part of the officer is a denial of the equal protection of the laws.

The federal district court awarded Tracey Thurman $2.3 million in compensatory damages. After this court decision, the Connecticut legislature adopted a comprehensive domestic violence law. In the twelve months after the new law took effect, the number of domestic violence assaults reported increased by 92 percent and arrests for domestic assaults doubled.

Source: Thurman v. City of Torrington, 595 F. Suppl. 1521 (Conn. 1984).

not involve any physical injury to the victim. It is actually a battery that is being discussed. However, to be consistent with other professionals and writers in the field of family violence, *partner assault* is used instead of partner battery and is defined as the act of intentionally inflicting physical injury on a spouse or other person who is cohabitating with the abuser. It is distinct from and yet a part of partner abuse in that all the dynamics that cause partner abuse may be present in partner assault. However, this form of assault may occur without the existence of the other forms of abuse, such as emotional or psychological injury, that typically accompany partner abuse.

Similar to many other areas of domestic violence, police response to partner assault is still being researched and studied. Like so much of domestic violence and other criminal acts, professionals simply do not have the answers to the problems. Scholars such as Cynthia Bowman would argue that they do not even know which questions to ask.[2]

If partner assault were like any other crime, the police response would be fairly simple: Investigate, arrest, charge, and cooperate with the district attorney in the prosecution of the perpetrator. Unfortunately, partner assault involves certain factors that make it a special problem. These factors are explored in detail in this chapter. These forces interact to cause law enforcement agencies to respond differently to partner assault than they would to robberies, rapes, and other crimes of violence.

Partner assault can have serious consequences for both the victim and any professionals who are involved with either the abuser or the victim. Partner assault is one of the crimes society has ignored. Part of the reason for society's delayed reaction to this form of domestic violence is the perceived difficulty in responding to physical assaults between adult family members. Another factor is the apparent inability to classify those who assault their spouses into any identifiable category. Finally, as with other forms of family violence, professionals cannot predict with any certainty who will be the aggressor or who will be the victim in a partner assault. The following sections examine a risk profile that attempts to identify potential abusers and briefly discuss a new typology of husbands who assault their spouses.

EXTENT OF THE PROBLEM

Partner assault is one of the most common forms of violence in the United States.[3] Lawrence Sherman estimates that two to eight million incidents come to the attention of police each year in which a victim has been beaten by a spouse or lover.[4] Using Straus's figures, Sherman speculates the actual rate of partner assault may be as high as eighteen million incidents per year.[5]

The National Institute of Justice and the Centers for Disease Control and Prevention (CDC) conducted a comprehensive survey to determine the nature and extent of partner abuse. Between November 1995 and May 1996, they contacted 8,000 women and 8,000 men via telephone. The results of this survey support previous samples that indicate partner abuse is a serious and ongoing phenomenon. This survey, entitled the National Violence Against Women Survey, indicated that approximately 7.7 percent of all the female respondents have been raped by their intimate partner sometime in their life. Using the U.S. Bureau of the Census population statistics, this translates into nearly 7.8 million women who have been raped by an intimate partner at some time. The survey found that 22.1 percent of all female respondents had been physically assaulted by their intimate partner sometime during their lives.[6]

As difficult as it is to predict the rate of partner assault accurately in the United States, it is equally difficult to establish a profile of individuals who assault their spouses. Saunders has established a profile that is specific to partner assault.[7] This "risk profile" includes childhood violence, low socioeconomic status, and alcohol use. Although no causal relationship has been established on the basis of these factors, their presence distinguishes husbands who assault their spouses from those who do not engage in this type of aggressive behavior.

Childhood violence: The cycle of violence theory was discussed in Chapter 1. Saunders utilizes this concept and indicates that a consistent risk factor for those who engage in partner assault is a history of witnessing parental violence or being physically assaulted as a child.

Low socioeconomic status: Although partner assault can occur in all economic groups, the rate of partner battering was five times higher in lower-income families than in the higher-income brackets. The stresses of unemployment, poverty, and inner-city living conditions appear to increase the risk of partner assault.

Alcohol use: Similar to other forms of domestic violence, alcohol use is present in a high percentage of partner assault cases.

Saunders lists other factors that increase the risk of partner assault. These factors include youth, behavioral deficits, personality disorders, anger, stress, depression, and low self-esteem.[8] He has also explored the characteristics of those who assault their spouses and has established a typology of three types of males who engage in partner assault. This typology, although tentative, may be the starting point for further research in this area.

Generalized aggressor: This type of abuser has long-term chronic mental problems. He may be invested in holding onto his aggression and uses alcohol as a method of keeping his childhood abuse covered. This type of aggressor has rigid sex-role beliefs. He is unable to empathize with his victim and thus shows little or no remorse for his actions.

Family-only type: This aggressor lacks communication skills and is unable to express his anger in an appropriate manner. He therefore turns to assaultive behavior as a means of expressing his frustration. This type of aggressor also abuses alcohol.

Emotionally volatile: This type of abuser reaction is clouded by anger. He has rigid sex-role expectations and little self-control.

As the preceding discussion indicates, researchers are still learning about the extent of partner assault and its characteristics. However, partner assault is not a new form of aggression. It has existed for years, and society has turned away from it. The following section examines some of the social forces that affected law enforcement's response to partner abuse.

FACTORS AFFECTING POLICE RESPONSE

Law enforcement's acknowledgment and response to partner assault has been slow in coming. Even today, some police officers would rather not get involved in a "family matter." This situation should not be surprising because the battering of women has existed for thousands of years. As indicated in Chapter 2, women were once considered chattel, and it was perfectly proper to discipline spouses as long as no permanent injury was inflicted on the wife.[9] Clear evidence exists that numerous early laws accorded men rights and power over women.[10] The privacy that families enjoyed behind the closed doors of the home continued into modern times.

The *Journal of Marriage and the Family* did not even discuss partner assault until 1971.[11] Slowly, however, scientific data emerged that indicated criminal violence occurred in the home.[12] By the mid-1970s, numerous other studies began to elevate partner abuse to the status of a national social problem.

Feminist groups, scholars, and others raised the hue and cry in response to this form of criminal conduct. Between 1975 and 1980, forty-four states passed some sort of legislation on domestic violence. Despite the existence of laws regarding partner abuse, studies have indicated that the police have been reluctant to enforce violations of this type of criminal conduct.[13]

No single factor has resulted in this hesitation or reluctance to enforce partner assault laws.[14] Scholars have examined this phenomenon in detail and have noted a series of influences that have affected police agencies' enforcement of partner assault. These factors include call screening, beliefs regarding financial hardship on the family in the event of an arrest, the family argument theory, the classification of partner assault as a misdemeanor, the victim's preference not to arrest, and perceived danger to the police in domestic violence situations.

Numerous police departments have engaged in **call screening.** This is downgrading by the law enforcement agency of the service priority assigned to domestic violence calls. Call screening results in a slower response time by the police officer than for other calls of the same or similar seriousness. This dynamic allows the abuser to beat the victim and leave the scene of the crime before the arrival of the officers. In addition, the failure of police to respond in a timely manner may increase the power of the abuser over the victim and lead the victim to believe that she is truly alone and helpless.

Police officers are reluctant to arrest the abuser in the mistaken belief that an arrest would pose a financial hardship on the family. An **arrest** is the taking of a person into custody in the manner prescribed by law. In addition, many law enforcement officers believe arrest is a futile act in view of the lack of prosecution and lenient sentences imposed by the courts.

Many officers would make an arrest only if the injury to the victim were severe in their estimation. This is clearly not the law. It does, however, illustrate the thinking and reluctance of police to intervene in a "family argument."[15]

Until recently, another factor affecting the decision to arrest was the statutory limit on arrests for certain types of crimes. Traditionally, criminal violations are divided into two major classifications: felonies and misdemeanors. In the United States, this distinction is spelled out by statute or state constitution.[16] A **felony** is considered the most serious type of crime and is usually punished by imprisonment in state prison. Many statutes provide that all other crimes are misdemeanors. A **misdemeanor** is considered a less serious type of crime and is punished by incarceration in local jails not to exceed one year. Normally, police may arrest persons who have committed felonies on the basis of reasonable grounds or probable cause. **Probable cause** is that set of facts that would lead a reasonable person to believe a crime has been committed by the suspect. A felony arrest may occur even if the officers did not personally witness the offense. Misdemeanor arrests, on the other hand, require the officers to witness the crime. If they did not see the offense committed, they could request the victim to make a citizen's arrest and then on behalf of the citizen would take the perpetrator into custody.

This distinction in the nature and classification of crimes had a direct impact on the ability of police officers to make arrests for domestic violence assaults. Many domestic violence disputes involve a battery. Most statutes define a **battery** as the unlawful application of force to a person.[17] Battery is the unlawful touching of another; assault, conversely, does not require any physical touching of the other person.[18] Absent serious injury, many state laws define battery as a misdemeanor. Thus, until recently officers could not make an arrest for partner assault unless they witnessed the act or the victim was willing to make a citizen's arrest.

The victim's preference not to file charges also affects the police's decision not to arrest the offender.[19] Several studies have indicated that victims of partner assault often do not want the police to make an arrest.[20] This results in the officers merely admonishing the offender and then leaving the scene of the crime.

Many police officers perceive family disputes as potentially dangerous situations in which both the abuser and the victim may turn on the officer. Although there are conflicting studies as to whether family disputes are more dangerous to police officers, the fact that many officers believe this to be the case often results in a delayed response to these types of calls.[21] This perception may also cause officers to delay in responding to partner assault calls until they have a backup unit.

In the past several years, many states have passed mandatory arrest statutes that require the officer to arrest the suspect. These laws allow the police to make arrests for misdemeanors not committed in their presence. The passage of these laws and their effectiveness are subjects of debate within the field of criminal justice. The following section discusses the factors that resulted in the passage of these statutes.

ARREST AND OTHER ALTERNATIVES

In recent years, victims of partner abuse have turned to the courts in an attempt to force police departments to arrest the perpetrators of this form of family violence. Increasingly,

---

International Perspectives

Women in Police Stations

Special women's police stations, staffed with multi-disciplinary female teams equipped to respond to the different needs of victim survivors, have been set up in several countries as an attempt to make police stations more accessible to women. The first women's police station was established in São Paulo, Brazil, in 1985 in response to women's complaints that they could not report violations in regular police stations because they were treated with disrespect and disbelief. Brazil's success encouraged Argentina, Colombia, Costa Rica, Peru, Uruguay, and Venezuela to set up their own specialized units.

Malaysia, Spain, Pakistan, and India have also introduced their own versions. In India, each station has female civilian workers who provide advice and support, referring women to support networks and suggesting other options. However, problems are evident with the Indian model in that women are discouraged from registering complaints at other police stations and must sometimes travel great distances to file complaints with stations that do have female civilians.

Source: Based on *Domestic Violence Against Women and Girls* (UNICEF, New York, 2000).

Police arresting an individual who was involved with a family violence incident.

courts have begun to listen to and rule in favor of the abused on both constitutional and tort grounds. However, lawsuits and personal liability did not result in the amendment of various state statutes mandating arrest of abusers. This development started in 1984 with a federally funded experiment in Minneapolis.

The Minneapolis Experiment

In the area of policing and domestic violence, probably no more controversial study has been conducted than the Minneapolis experiment, which dealt with the effect of arrest on those who batter their spouses. The dean of policing and domestic violence, Lawrence Sherman, was the architect of the 1984 Minneapolis Domestic Violence Experiment. This study was the first controlled evaluation of the effect of arrest on individuals who commit assaultive types of crimes against their spouses.[22]

The Police Foundation and the Minneapolis Police Department joined forces to conduct a controlled experiment to test the effectiveness of arrest on prevention or deterrence of domestic violence. Funded in part by the National Institute of Justice, the experiment used a lottery system of three possible actions by police when dealing with domestic violence.

Police officers responding to a domestic disturbance were required to use one of the following options:

1. Arrest with at least one night incarceration;
2. Sending the offender away from the scene of the disturbance or arresting him if he refused to leave;
3. Giving the couple some form of advice, including mediation.

The officers were not allowed to select which option would be used; rather, they carried a pad of forms that listed the available options. Whenever they encountered a situation that met the experiment's criteria, they were required to use the option listed on the top form.

The experiment involved only misdemeanor batteries in which both the victim and the suspect were present when the officers arrived at the scene of the disturbance. Cases involving serious threats or danger to the victim were excluded, as were situations in which the victim demanded that the officers arrest the suspect.

After the officers finished their assignments, they turned in a brief report to the researchers for follow-up. The research staff used two measures to determine the amount of repeated violence by the offenders: official police reports and victim interviews. Official police reports were monitored to determine whether the suspect committed another similar offense within a specified time period. In addition, the research staff contacted the victims and conducted a detailed interview and subsequent interviews for a period of twenty-four weeks after the initial offense.

The experiment produced a sample of 314 cases that met all the criteria. The results indicated that the arrest option produced the lowest percentage of repeated violence of all the alternatives. Official police reports revealed that 10 percent of the arrested suspects committed a subsequent offense, 24 percent of those suspects who were sent from the home repeated acts of violence against their spouses, and 19 percent of the suspects who were advised by the officers committed another offense. Interviews with victims produced even more dramatic percentages: 19 percent of the arrest suspects, 33 percent of those suspects sent from the home, and 37 percent of those advised by the officers committed another offense.

On the basis of the results of the study, Sherman and his colleagues made three recommendations. The first and probably the least controversial of these alternatives was to change existing laws to allow the police to make warrantless arrests for misdemeanor partner assaults not committed in their presence. The second recommendation implied that mandatory arrest was the preferred option in most cases of domestic violence. The final recommendation suggested that additional experiments be conducted in other cities to validate the results of the Minneapolis study.

The Minneapolis experiment acted as an agent for change within the criminal justice system. Armed with its results, advocates of mandatory arrest and other sanctions were able to find support in various state legislatures for long overdue reform of criminal statutes dealing with domestic violence. Eleven states adopted legislation that authorized warrantless arrest in misdemeanor domestic violence cases, and another sixteen states enacted mandatory arrest laws in family violence situations.[23]

Prior to the experiment, only 10 percent of police departments serving cities over 100,000 in population encouraged their officers to make arrests in domestic violence situations. Within five years of the announcement of the results of the experiment, 84 percent of all major police departments in the United States had adopted a policy that stated arrest was the preferred option in domestic violence situations.[24]

The Minneapolis experiment was hailed as a breakthrough study of domestic violence as well as criticized by a number of prominent scholars as inadequate and flawed.[25] In retrospect, it may not matter whether the results of the study were accurate. Its greatest contribution may be that it generated an incredible amount of debate within academia and the law enforcement profession as to how to respond to domestic violence.

Focus

The Use of Courts as a Last Resort

In recent years, victims of family violence have turned to the courts in an attempt to require law enforcement departments to provide effective intervention and protection against partner assault.

In *Raucci v. Town of Rotterdam*, a federal court ruled that the municipality owed a battered woman a special duty to protect her from her estranged husband because of actions by the police department that had assured her of protection.[*] In spite of these assurances, the husband killed their six-year-old son and wounded the wife. The court upheld a verdict awarding the wife damages.

In *Watson v. City of Kansas City*, a federal court ruled that the victim could proceed with her suit against the police department.[†] Nancy Watson was married to a Kansas City police officer who abused her and her son on numerous occasions. When she requested assistance from the police, they refused to help and threatened to take her child away and arrest her. After being raped and battered by her husband, she escaped and he committed suicide. She sued the police department for a denial of equal protection.

In *Calloway v. Kinkelaar*, the Supreme Court of Illinois discussed municipalities' liability for willful and wanton conduct on the part of its agents.[‡] The victim had obtained a restraining order that had been served on her husband. He violated the order by calling her and threatening her and her child. She notified the sheriff's department of the threats and his location, but they failed to take the abuser into custody. He subsequently kidnapped the victim, but she was able to escape when state troopers stopped the perpetrator at a roadblock. She sued the county and the county sheriff, alleging willful and wanton conduct for failing to protect her from being abducted by her husband. The Supreme Court of Illinois allowed the action, stating that the state's Domestic Violence Act allowed such an action for civil damages.

In *Campbell v. Campbell*, the plaintiff sued her former husband, certain police officers, and the city of Plainfield.[§] The victim brought a negligence suit against the city and its police officers after they responded to a disturbance call and failed to arrest the estranged husband. The police told the abuser to leave and he did, but a short time later he returned and shot the victim. There was a restraining order on file, and a copy had been served on the husband and the police department. The New Jersey court held that the city and police had constructive notice of the existence of the restraining order and that they were negligent in failing to arrest the perpetrator.

Simpson v. City of Miami involved a wrongful death lawsuit filed against the City of Miami and its police department.[‖] The victim called the police department to complain that the perpetrator was violating a restraining order. A Miami police officer showed up and arrested the abuser but later released him after he promised not to contact the victim. The next day, the perpetrator shot and killed the victim. The heir filed suit, claiming that the city of Miami had violated a duty of care owed to the victim. The Florida Supreme Court agreed, holding that once an officer had taken the perpetrator into custody because of a violation of a domestic abuse restraining order, a special relationship was formed that required the officer to act in a manner to protect the victim from injury by that perpetrator.

The U.S. Supreme Court may have weakened a victim's recovery in the area of failure to protect when it decided *Castle Rock v. Gonzales*.[#] This case concerned a local municipality's failure to enforce a valid restraining order. This case is discussed in more detail in the following section dealing with restraining orders.

---

[*]902 F. 2d 1050 (1990).

[†]520 N.Y.S. 2d 352 (1987).

[‡]659 N.E. 2d 1322 (1995).

[§]682 A. 2d 272 (1996).

[‖]22 *Florida L. Weekly* D2313 (Fla. App. 3d Dist., October 1, 1997).

[#]125 S. Ct. 417 (2005).

Focus

Update on Arrests in Domestic Abuse Cases

According to the National Institute of Justice (NIJ), when victims and offenders were intimate partners, police make no arrests in 50.1 percent of incidents, one or more arrests in 48.0 percent of incidents, and dual arrests in 1.9 percent of incidents. In regards to same-sex relationships, the arrest rates for domestic violence were the same as those for heterosexual couples. For all intimate partner relationships, offenders were more likely to be arrested if the incident of violence was a serious aggravated assault. The NIJ also reports that "arrest occurred more frequently in cases involving intimate partners if the offender was white" and "cases involving intimate partners and acquaintances were more likely to result in arrest if the offender was twenty-one or older."

Source: Domestic Violence Cases: What Research Shows about Arrest and Dual Arrest Rates (Office of Justice Programs, National Institute of Justice, July 25, 2008).

Other Replications

One of the direct results of the Minneapolis experiment was the funding of additional replications by the National Institute of Justice. Five additional studies were undertaken in the following locations: Metro-Dade (Miami), Colorado Springs, Milwaukee, Omaha, and Charlotte. What was consistent about these additional studies was the finding of inconsistency in the deterrent effect of arrest.

The Metro-Dade experiment established two major categories with two subgroups under each of these categories. The two major subdivisions were those suspects who were arrested and those who were not arrested. Each of these groups was further divided into subgroups that did or did not receive follow-up counseling by specially trained police officers.[26] The Metro-Dade experiment clearly supports the theory that arrest is a deterrent to future domestic violence.

The Colorado Springs experiment employed four options in its replication: arrest and issuance of a restraining order, counseling for the offender and issuance of a restraining order, issuance of a restraining order, and restoring order at the scene of the crime without arrest or use of a restraining order. The Colorado Springs study supports the hypothesis that arrest in some situations does in fact act as a deterrent to future violence.[27]

The Milwaukee experiment was carried out in a city that in May 1986 had adopted a city-wide policy of mandatory arrest for domestic violence cases.[28] However, the study did not involve arrests of all offenders. Rather, it utilized three options: full arrest, short arrest, and warning. The full arrest involved taking the suspect into custody pursuant to existing policy and allowing him bail in the amount of $250. The short arrest required officers to arrest the suspect but allowed him to be released on his own recognizance, preferably within two hours after arrest. The last option used a standard warning of arrest, being that if the officers had to return to the location any time during the same day, an arrest would be made.

The results were obtained by a review of police records and follow-up interviews with the victims. The researchers found a clear initial deterrent in both the full-arrest and the short-arrest situations. However, this deterrence did not last, and there appeared to be no long-term difference between the arrest options and the warning option.

The original Minneapolis study and these three replications might lead one to conclude that arrest does in fact deter either short-term or long-term partner assault. Unfortunately, the Omaha and Charlotte replications came to the opposite conclusion. These studies were conducted in the same manner as the other replications but indicated that arrest does not deter future violence.

The Omaha experiment randomly assigned eligible police calls regarding domestic violence into three categories when both the suspect and the victim were present: arrest, separation, or mediation.[29] In those cases in which the suspect had already left the scene of the crime when the police arrived, the police randomly assigned him to a warrant group or a no-warrant group.

The results of the experiment were measured in two ways: review of police reports and victim interviews. Contrary to the Minneapolis experiment, the Omaha study concluded that arrest of a suspect at the scene of the domestic assault was not a greater deterrent than the other two options.[30] However, the issuance of a warrant for an offender who was absent from the scene of the crime at the time the officers arrived did appear to extend significantly the time frame in which the victim was free from further violence.

The Charlotte experiment tested three distinct alternatives to domestic violence.[31] Police responses included advising the couple, issuing a citation to the offender, or arresting the offender. Excluded from the study were situations in which the victim insisted on the arrest of the suspect, the suspect threatened or assaulted the officer, or the officer believed the victim to be in imminent danger. Similar to the other replications, the Charlotte study evaluated the effect of these alternatives using only two methods: police reports and victim interviews. The results indicated that no significant difference existed among advising, citing, or arresting the offender.

In 2001, the National Institute of Justice and the CDC conducted a scientific evaluation of the results of the 1984 Minneapolis Experiment and its five replications.[32] Because of the inconsistent and conditional findings of the previous studies, scholars and policy makers reevaluated the deterrent effect of arrest using an approach that was more statistically sound. The study pooled incidents from the five replications, computed comparable independent and outcome measures from common data intentionally embedded in each experiment, and standardized the experimental design and statistical models.

This method of reevaluating the data produced the following significant results:

- Arresting batterers was consistently related to reducing subsequent aggression against female partners.
- Arresting the perpetrator had no relationship to an increased risk of subsequent aggression against the female partner.

This study reexamined the Minneapolis replications and found evidence of a consistent and direct, though modest, deterrent effect of arrest on aggression by males against their female partners. This effect existed for the first several days after the incident regardless of the length of incarceration and lasted up to one year after the incident. The research also pointed out that a minority of perpetrators continued their violence regardless of the intervention that occurred.

What is needed is more study in this area of domestic violence. If arresting the offender does not prevent partner assault, other alternatives must be sought to determine whether other mechanisms can stop this form of family violence.

Alternatives to Arrest

Most people know someone who has "talked their way out of a speeding ticket." This doesn't mean that the individual did not violate a law or that he or she is especially glib. Rather, it means that, for whatever reason, the police officer decided to exercise discretion not to give the offender a ticket. This exercise of discretion is an integral part of police work.

In the area of partner assault, at least one authority has examined the use of police discretion and mediation as an alternative solution to family violence.[33] **Mediation** is a private, informal dispute resolution process in which a neutral third person, the mediator, helps disputing parties reach an agreement. Prior to the Minneapolis study, Lerman points out that most law enforcement agencies used mediation in an attempt to deal with partner abuse. Law enforcement agencies across the United States trained their officers in dispute resolution techniques specifically in the area of domestic violence. Officers attempted to use crisis intervention techniques to solve the problem in the home rather than take any formal action.

Although mediation is an excellent dispute resolution technique for business and labor, it was doomed to failure in domestic violence situations. Mediation assumes that each party is equal or nearly equal in power, status, or need. Furthermore, mediation requires that parties negotiate as equals and reach an agreement that will serve their own best interests. Informal mediation does not result in an enforceable agreement. Therefore, either party, specifically the abuser, can break this agreement without facing any sanctions.

Thus, informal mediation does not work as a method of decreasing or ending partner assault. However, a variation of the mediation concept is now employed in some jurisdictions that does establish accountability and attempts to place the parties in a more equal bargaining position. Using the court system, law enforcement officials and prosecutors are able to require counseling of both the abuser and the victim. This concept will be discussed in more detail later in this chapter.

In *Confronting Domestic Violence*, Goolkasian recommends a series of steps that all police officers can take on arrival at the scene of the crime, whether or not the suspect is arrested.[34] The following steps provide the victim of the crime with support and encouragement that are critical to her:

Medical care: Often, the officer will be able to observe that the victim needs medical attention. On other occasions, the victim may claim that she needs medical attention although no injuries are visible. Many abusers are adept at inflicting injuries that are not visible to the naked eye. Officers should always inquire whether the victim needs medical attention, and, if the answer is yes, they should arrange for transportation of the victim to an emergency room.

Transportation: In addition to transporting the victim for medical assistance, officers can provide for transportation of the victim to a battered women's shelter. Officers may either personally transport the victim to these shelters or make arrangements to meet staff from the shelter and turn the victim over to their care.

Requiring the suspect to leave the residence: In the event that the suspect cannot be arrested, officers should at a minimum request that the offender leave the premises. If he refuses to leave and the victim, rather than the offender, is entitled to possession of the residence, officers can then arrest the suspect on trespassing charges.

Ensuring the victim's safety if she leaves the residence: If the victim desires to leave the premises, officers should stand by to ensure that she can leave with her personal property without interference from the suspect.

Advising the victim on her legal options and community resources: Many departments have developed handbooks, brochures, and other materials that officers can give to victims of partner assault. This information provides a list of resources that specialize in assisting battered spouses. Caution must be used when adopting this alternative because many victims will be highly emotional and incapable of reading the material.

Case follow-up information: In addition to advising the victim of community support resources, officers should leave their cards and other information with the victim so that she can request follow-up information.

None of these options will stop or deter future partner abuse. However, they do provide support to the victim and offer her alternatives to staying in an environment that places her at risk.

Another alternative to arresting the abusive spouse is the concept Sherman calls "smart policing."[35] This approach is based on his analysis of arrest and its effect on future violence. Sherman would have legislatures and police take the following steps:

1. Authorize police to make warrantless arrests in domestic violence situations. Although most states now allow police to make such arrests, several states have not enacted this type of legislation. Because some evidence suggests that arrest deters partner assault, police should be empowered to take this step if they believe it is necessary.

2. State statutes that mandate arrest should be amended to require mandatory action from a list of alternatives. Sherman argues that there is evidence that in some cases arrest may cause more harm to the victim. He would repeal mandatory arrest policies and substitute a list of actions that allow the officers more discretion.

3. The range of options in domestic assault cases should include the following:

   a. Offering to transport the victim to a shelter;
   b. Transporting the victim or the suspect to a detoxification treatment center;
   c. Allowing the victim to decide whether arrest should be made;
   d. Mobilizing the victim's own social network to provide short-term protection.

4. Police and prosecutors should develop offender-absent warrant procedures. Although Sherman urges caution in this approach, he points out that many domestic violence calls involve situations in which the suspect has already left the scene of the crime by the time the police arrive. In view of the results, though tentative, of the Omaha replication, offender-absent arrest warrant procedures should be pursued by police and prosecutors.

5. Police should not be held civilly liable for failure to prevent domestic homicide or serious injury because of failure to make arrests in partner assault situations. Sherman cites statistics to support his position that not one of the victims in the Minneapolis experiment was murdered.

6. Police should continue to examine various alternatives in an effort to identify chronically violent couples and their residences. Sherman argues that this is an area that needs

special attention by the police and suggests that every large department detail at least one officer to identify chronically violent couples and work with them.

7. Police should advise victims that restraining orders may have limited value and not provide the victim with any substantial protection. Sherman states that the administration of restraining orders is still experiencing major problems and that officers should not offer false hope to victims by suggesting that a restraining order will solve their problems or keep the suspect at bay.

8. Police and victim rights advocates should continue to lobby Congress for additional funds to continue research in this area.

Although Sherman's approach has its supporters, several of its steps seem to ignore basic constitutional principles and other accepted research about family violence. For instance, the idea of using the victim's own social network may not be feasible because many abusers isolate their victims, and thus the victim has nowhere or no one to turn to in times of crisis. Additionally, the granting of immunity from civil action to police for failure to respond in certain situations goes against the existing U.S. Supreme Court decisions that cannot be changed by merely amending certain statutes. The Supreme Court has found that citizens have certain constitutional rights, and these rights cannot be abridged by legislative or other action.[36]

Alternatives other than arrest of the offender are possible. These include social support systems that may provide either short- or long-term relief to the victim. Police officers should be aware of these resources so that they can properly advise the victim regarding such support systems.

Many cities and agencies have established telephone hotlines for battered spouses. These hotlines are often operated by shelters and provide the victim with information on alternative housing, employment, financial aid, legal aid, counseling, and other forms of emotional support. Hotlines are often a spouse's first attempt to reaching out from her isolation in an effort to save herself from further battering.

Shelters provide a safe haven for victims of partner assault. These shelters are operated by charities or other private groups. They may offer counseling, child care, or even have a victims' rights advocate on staff. The victim may find the support in these shelters necessary to make the final break with the abuser.

Numerous other community groups provide support for victims of partner assault. These groups may work with shelters to provide counseling and advocacy for victims of partner assault.

The San Diego and Phoenix police departments are examples of law enforcement agencies that are taking a holistic approach to partner abuse. These agencies involve social workers and prosecutors who work with law enforcement officers from the start of the case. Services are housed in a central location, and some cities include child protection services (CPS) workers, physicians, sexual assault experts, and various victim service providers.[37]

It should be obvious that none of the alternatives to arrest will completely stop or deter future partner assault. Sufficient information is not available at this stage in research to propose a single approach to this problem. However, recent changes in the law do offer victims other options.

Federal Legislation

In 1994, Congress enacted the Violent Crime Control and Law Enforcement Act, Title IV of which is called the Violence Against Women Act (VAWA). Congress mandated that various professions form partnerships and work together to respond to all forms of violence against women.

The U.S. attorney general is required to make a report to Congress annually on the grants that are awarded under the Act and ensure that research examining violence against women is encouraged. The report must include the number of grants, funds distributed, and other statistical information. Additionally, the report must assess the effectiveness of any programs that are funded under VAWA.

The Act provides funding for a variety of research-based studies. It also requires that federal agencies engage in research regarding violence against women. For example, the National Institute of Justice is mandated to conduct four important projects: the development of a research agenda that will address violence, with particular emphasis on underserved populations; the assessment of establishing state databases to record the number of sexual and domestic violence incidents; a study to determine how abusive partners obtain addresses of their victims; and examination with other agencies of battered woman syndrome.[38]

The National Domestic Violence Hotline (800-799-SAFE) was established in 1996 under the authority set forth in VAWA. The hotline was cited by President Bill Clinton in his 1997 National Crime Victims' Rights Week proclamation as having already responded to 73,000 calls for assistance from across the United States.

It is now a federal crime to enter or leave Native American reservations or cross state lines to injure and intimidate a partner. The injury must be physical, and the abuser must have intended to commit the crime when he or she crossed the state line.[39] It is also a federal crime to cross a state line or to enter or leave Native American reservations and violate a restraining order. This law also requires that the perpetrator intended to violate the order when crossing the state line.[40] One of the most far-reaching and controversial laws makes it a federal crime to possess a firearm after conviction of a qualifying misdemeanor crime of domestic violence. The controversial aspect of this law is that it applies to law enforcement officers.[41] In some jurisdictions, police officers have been placed on light duty or terminated because they had a prior conviction and now cannot carry a weapon.

Although not a federal statute, model codes have affected the practice of law for many years. The Model Domestic Violence Code, drafted by the National Council of Juvenile and Family Court Judges, was presented to the National Conference of State Legislatures in 1994.[42] Several portions of the model code have been enacted into law in some jurisdictions.

RESTRAINING ORDERS

Restraining orders (protective orders) are court orders that prohibit the offender from having any contact with the victim.[43] They are civil versus criminal and require a judge to rule that sufficient evidence supports the issuance of such an order. These orders are now available in forty-eight states and the District of Columbia. They offer the option of preventing contact such as harassment or threats that might ordinarily lead to an escalation of emotions and future violence. As the following discussion indicates, research is inconclusive regarding the effectiveness of this unique tool in preventing partner abuse.

Background and Use of Restraining Orders

In the past, problems with the use of restraining orders stemmed from lack of clarity in the law and police unfamiliarity with this civil sanction. In 1983, only seventeen states provided protection against abuse from individuals who were living together but not married. However, by 1988, twenty-two states had added such protection to their statutes authorizing restraining orders.

The use and nature of restraining orders vary from state to state. Most states now authorize persons who are married, related by blood, or cohabitants to request the issuance of such an order. Six types of behavior may be prohibited by a restraining order:

1. Physical assault;
2. Threatened physical abuse;
3. Attempted physical abuse;
4. Sexual assault of an adult;
5. Sexual assault of a child;
6. Damage to personal property of the victim.

As this list indicates, restraining orders may be issued for a wide variety of acts committed by the offender. However, simply having the order issued does not solve the problem. Due process requires that the offender be served with a copy of the order for it to be effective.

Most states provide for the issuance of temporary or emergency restraining orders. These orders are issued by a judge and usually require the threat of immediate injury to the victim. The U.S. Supreme Court has upheld the issuance of these ex parte type of orders if the request includes specific facts that justify the relief, the notice and opportunity for a full hearing are given as soon as practicable, and the order is issued by a judge.[44]

In most jurisdictions, police officers or process servers are responsible for serving restraining orders. There are five basic methods of service of a temporary or emergency restraining order: carrying out personal service, informing the offender of the existence of the order, leaving a copy with the victim so that she can serve the offender, posting of the notice and order at the residence of the victim, and mailing a copy of the order via certified mail to the offender.

Some police departments have established procedures in which officers can contact judges while they are at the scene of a domestic dispute and have the judge authorize the issuance of such an order by telephone. The officer then serves the suspect at the scene and requires him to leave the premises. Once a temporary order is issued, it becomes effective immediately and is valid until a formal hearing can be held, at which time the abuser has a right to contest the allegations made by the victim. However, the issuance of the temporary order prevents the offender from having any contact with the victim until the formal hearing.

Restraining orders may provide different forms of relief for the victim of partner assault. The traditional and most common form of relief is a no-contact order that prevents the offender from having any form of contact with the victim at her residence, work, or anywhere else. This no-contact order includes telephonic, written, and physical contacts. Many orders will set forth specific conditions regarding the visitation of any children that may be involved in the situation. Some will designate certain locations for the visit, and others will require that the offender not consume any alcohol or drugs prior to the visit. Most statutes authorize the court to require counseling for both parties. Even if the counseling does not solve the immediate problem, it is a very visible sign of the authority of the court and should serve as a constant reminder to the offender of the power that the court now has over his existence.

In the event that the abuser violates the restraining order, many statutes authorize charging the offender with civil contempt, criminal contempt, or a misdemeanor violation of a court order. Although police officers cannot normally arrest a person charged with civil contempt, the court may order that the offender pay a fine and serve a period of incarceration. Criminal contempt, if authorized by state statute, would allow officers to arrest the offender if they found him in violation of the order. Criminal contempt in many jurisdictions is treated as a misdemeanor. However, many restraining order statutes allow officers to make warrantless arrests in these situations. If the violation of the order is considered a misdemeanor, many statutes also authorize the warrantless arrest of the offender.

Temporary restraining orders do not solve partner abuse. As the next section discusses, problems continue to exist with the use of this form of sanction.

Advantages and Disadvantages of Restraining Orders

Restraining orders provide the victim with another option in lieu of arrest. The use of restraining orders has several advantages.[45] Most arrests result in the offender being released in a matter of hours or within a few days at the most. A restraining order can be valid for an extended period of time, up to a year in most cases.

Arrests may result in the loss of employment, which might increase the tension that already exists in the relationship. Restraining orders do not preclude the offender from continuing his employment but do prevent him from living with the victim.

Restraining orders carry the weight and gravity of a judicial edict, and some offenders may think twice before violating a court order. Although some offenders may have had numerous contacts with police and the judicial system, most have not been involved with a direct order from a judge banning certain conduct. The specter of facing a judge after violating a judicial order may act as a deterrent for some abusers.

Just as there are advantages in this form of protection, so are there serious potential disadvantages in relying solely on the use of restraining orders in this area of family violence. The most obvious and threatening is that the offender may simply ignore the order, with injury to the victim resulting. A restraining order is merely a piece of paper that carries only as much force and effect as the offender attaches to it. If he chooses to ignore it, there is no protection for the victim unless she can contact the police and they can arrive and intercede before the abuser attacks and harms her.

There are additional disadvantages to the use of restraining orders, many written into the very statutes that were enacted to protect the victim. Some statutes require the payment of a filing fee prior to issuance of a restraining order. Although most jurisdictions allow for the waiver of the fee if the victim cannot afford to pay it, some include the income of the abuser in determining if the fee can be waived. The cost of such fees acts as a deterrent to requesting a restraining order.

Some statutes require court or county clerks to assist the victim in filling out the forms requesting the restraining order. However, no state provides funds or mandates special training for these clerks in this sensitive function. Most partner assault occurs in the evening or on the weekend after the courts are closed. Only twenty-three states provide for the issuance of emergency orders after normal working hours. Thus, during the victim's greatest time of need, no alternative is available to obtain restraining orders.

Most states require personal service of the order for it to become effective. However, many offenders are difficult to locate, and therefore the victim is not protected until the abuser has been served. There is a lack of monitoring of compliance with restraining orders. If the offender can convince or threaten the victim to remain silent, neither law enforcement officers nor the court will be aware if he violates the order. Although restraining orders pose serious problems, they do provide some victims of partner assault with an option that may protect them.

Although many statutes provide for civil contempt, criminal contempt, or even violation of criminal statutes, there is no guarantee that the order will be effective. In *Castle Rock v. Gonzales*, the U.S. Supreme Court addressed the issue of a municipality's liability for failure to enforce a restraining order.[46] In 1999, Jessica Gonzales obtained a protective order against her husband as part of divorce proceedings. The order listed the requirements of Colorado law, which mandated that officers use every reasonable means to enforce a restraining order, including the requirement that the officer "shall" arrest a person when there is probable cause to believe he or she has violated the order. The order provided for visitation of the children on alternate weekends.

One afternoon, while the kids were playing outside, Mr. Gonzales kidnapped them. Over the next ten hours Jessica made repeated requests to the Castle Rock Police Department to enforce her protective order, but they failed to do so. At 3:30 a.m. after he kidnapped the children, Mr. Gonzales appeared at the police station and opened fire with his weapon. He was killed by officers who returned his fire. Afterward, the officers found the dead bodies of Jessica's three children inside his truck.

Jessica Gonzales sued the City of Castle Rock for failing to enforce her protective order. However, the Supreme Court ruled that despite the mandatory arrest laws in effect in Colorado at that time, Jessica had no personal entitlement requiring the police to enforce the order. It went on to state that the statute simply required the police to enforce the order and the court refused to assume that the statute was meant to benefit victims of domestic violence.

There was a strong reaction by the victims' movement to the Castle Rock decision. In essence, it fails to recognize the dynamics and dangers of domestic violence. Some victim advocates are advising victims and their attorneys to request more specific language in their orders. Others are relying on state tort remedies to hold law enforcement agencies liable. Castle Rock has caused us to rethink our traditional responses to restraining orders. Only time will tell what will come from this landmark decision.

Effectiveness of Restraining Orders

The effectiveness of restraining orders depends on a variety of factors, including how specific and comprehensive the orders are and how well they are enforced. In an effort to understand how effective restraining orders are from the victim's perspective, scholars studied the restraining order process in three jurisdictions: the District of Columbia superior court; the family court in Wilmington, Delaware; and the county court in Denver.[47] The researchers contacted 285 women who had filed for restraining orders. They used telephone interviews, follow-up interviews, records from the civil case, and criminal records of the men named in the orders.

In most cases, victims felt that restraining orders protected them against repeated incidents of physical and psychological abuse and were valuable in assisting them in regaining a sense of well-being. However, a restraining order against an abuser with a history of violent offenses was not as likely to be effective. Before receiving a restraining order, victims experienced abuse ranging from intimidation to injury with a weapon. Researchers found that 37 percent of the women had been threatened or injured with a weapon; more than half had been beaten or choked; and 99 percent had suffered other forms of intimidation, including threats, stalking, and harassment.

A total of 72 percent of the victims in the initial interviews stated that the restraining order was effective and reported no continuing problems. However, in several instances, a small percentage of the victims experienced continuing acts of abuse ranging from continuing calls at work or home, stalking of the victim, repeated physical abuse, to continuing psychological abuse. As this research indicates, in many instances, restraining orders may prove effective; however, there are situations in which the abuser will simply ignore the order and continue or escalate the abuse.

In 2006, the *Orange County Register*, a respected Southern California newspaper, conducted an investigation into the use and effectiveness of restraining orders.[48] Key findings from the investigation revealed a system in disarray with conflicting procedures and processes from county to county. What was even more alarming was the fact that one in seven restraining orders issued by a judge is not served on the perpetrator. An order is not effective until served. The *Register* also pointed out that hundreds of restraining orders are not entered in the state database used by law enforcement agencies and without proof of a valid order, police are powerless to do anything.

COURTS AND PARTNER ASSAULT

Partner assault does not end with an arrest or with the issuance of a restraining order. A necessary part of this process is the court's and prosecutor's responses to this form of family violence. It is appropriate that the prosecution of partner assault be examined in this chapter because law enforcement and the criminal justice system are closely tied together. This section examines the judicial system's reactions to partner assault and how cases are processed, from the screening of reports to the presentation of evidence in a trial.

Introduction

Partner assault is a crime. In almost every jurisdiction, the striking of another person is a misdemeanor and may be a felony if serious physical injury occurs. However, making an act a crime does not mean that it will be prosecuted. Sherman and Berk point out that in the Minneapolis experiment, only 3 of the 136 suspects who were arrested were ever fined or incarcerated.[49] This is not the type of statistic that promotes confidence in the ability of police to protect the victim from further injury.

The fact that very few partner assault cases are prosecuted is not a newly discovered fact. The judicial system's apparent indifference to victims of family violence is well known. This indifference resulted in the U.S. Attorney General's Task Force on Family Violence recommending that prosecutors establish special units to prosecute family violence cases.[50] The report states:

> Staffed with both attorneys and victim assistance professionals or volunteers, the unit should review all law enforcement reports involving incidents of family violence whenever possible. . . . The attorneys of the unit develop an expertise in dealing with family violence that results in more accurate case evaluation and more effective prosecution. The creation of a special unit also fosters the development of an individual bond of trust and concern between the victim and a prosecutor sensitive to the complexities of family violence.[51]

Many prosecutors' offices in major cities have adopted the attorney general's recommendation. The office of the district attorney in San Francisco, for example, has established filing and charging policies that recognize the unique nature of domestic violence.[52] This policy states:

> Special care will be taken to ensure that [domestic violence] cases are treated as crimes against the state and prosecuted to the fullest extent in order to avoid continuation and escalation of the violence.[53]

The prosecution of partner assault cases requires that prosecutors understand the dynamics involved in this form of family violence and be willing to approach them in a sensitive manner. Partner assault is a crime against the state. However, the close relationship between the victim and the offender presents unique victim/witness problems.

Prosecution of Partner Assault

Prosecution can be defined as a proceeding instituted and carried on by due course of law before a competent tribunal for the purpose of determining the guilt or innocence of a person charged with a crime.[54] All criminal cases are prosecuted by an authorized agent of the state—normally, the *district attorney* or *prosecuting attorney.* Some jurisdictions have highly trained career civil servants who are attorneys admitted to practice law and whose full-time job is to prosecute cases. Other jurisdictions use attorneys who practice civil law on the side and hold office as the prosecutor on a part-time basis. Many of these smaller offices are not automated and have not had the luxury of specializing in any particular area of criminal law. These prosecutors are truly jacks-of-all-trades and prosecute any criminal violation that occurs within their jurisdictions.

The prosecution of any criminal offense, including a partner assault case, starts with a **case screening** by the prosecutor. A case may arrive at the district attorney's office in one of two ways: A private citizen—in some cases, the victim—may file a complaint, or the police may bring a case to the prosecutor. In either situation, the prosecutor assigned to screen the case will review the facts and evaluate those facts to determine whether the defendant has violated a criminal statute.

Once the police forward a case to the prosecutor's office or a citizen's complaint is received, a decision must be made whether to file the case and what type of charges, felony or misdemeanor, should be filed. That decision is a crucial one in a prosecutor's office. In deciding whether to issue the case as a felony or misdemeanor, the prosecutor should review the following facts:

1. The extent of any injuries;
2. Whether the defendant intended to inflict serious bodily injury;
3. The use of a deadly weapon;
4. Threats made to the victim, children, family, or friends of the victim;
5. Prior incidents of violence on the part of the defendant;
6. The defendant's use of drugs or alcohol;
7. The defendant's present and past mental state;
8. Any other facts that concern possible danger to the victim or others.[55]

Although some of these factors may not be admissible as evidence during the criminal trial, they are important for a prosecutor to consider in exercising his or her discretion as it relates to the type or seriousness of the charge to be filed.

One factor that is conspicuously absent from this list is the desires of the victim. Some jurisdictions take the position that if the act is a crime, the victim is merely a witness to the crime and the state is the victim. Others believe the victim should have input into the charging process and be involved in all stages of the prosecution.[56]

Once the decision has been made to file criminal charges, the normal criminal justice process begins. It is not necessary to explain in detail how the criminal justice system functions; several excellent introductory textbooks are available that discuss this facet of the legal system.[57]

During this process, the offender may have an opportunity to avoid prosecution by agreeing to counseling regarding family violence. Many jurisdictions offer a person accused of partner assault the opportunity to obtain counseling or education and avoid a criminal trial.[60] This process in many jurisdictions is known as **diversion.** Several variations on the diversion process are implemented throughout the United States. Some programs require that the defendant first plead guilty. After he successfully completes a diversion program, the guilty plea is withdrawn and the case dismissed. Other jurisdictions allow the defendant to waive his right to a speedy trial and attend counseling, and the case is then dismissed after the offender has completed the program.

It is not uncommon for victims of partner assault to be reluctant to testify against their spouses. Some of the more common reasons include fear of the offender, shame for being a victim in a close personal relationship with the assailant, distrust of the police and the court process, a desire to put the entire episode behind them and forget it occurred, and a belief that somehow their own behavior caused the attack.[61]

Almost all victims of violent crimes have a fear of the court and the perpetrator. However, victims of partner assault have other valid reasons for fearing possible retribution by the defendant. He knows her residence and work address, professional habits, friends, and family. And, she knows by experience his violent nature and the possible injuries that this person is capable of inflicting.

Therefore, some prosecutors' offices have established the following guidelines for questioning reluctant victims. These questions serve several purposes: They are a checklist that allows the prosecutor to establish the facts of the assault by asking certain questions; if the

Focus

The Criminal Justice Process

Filing of Criminal Charges

The case may be filed as either a misdemeanor or a felony, depending on the state statute and seriousness of the offense. The defendant may be in custody or surrender to the police at this time. An arrest warrant may be issued for his apprehension at this time.

Arraignment

This is the first formal appearance of the defendant in the criminal justice system. At this hearing, he will enter a plea to the charges. The defendant may enter a plea of not guilty, guilty, or *nolo contendere*.[58] At this hearing, an attorney will be appointed to represent him if he cannot afford to hire an attorney.

Bail Hearing

In many jurisdictions, this hearing occurs at the same time as the formal arraignment. At this hearing, the court will establish bail to ensure the future appearances of the defendant.[59]

Trial

This may be a trial in front of a judge or a jury, depending on the desires of the defendant. After the prosecution has presented its evidence, the defendant may present any evidence he desires.

Verdict: Guilty or Not Guilty

After considering the evidence, the trier of fact, being either the judge or the jury, will render a verdict of guilty or not guilty.

Sentencing

If the defendant is found not guilty, the process ends. If he is found guilty, the judge may ask for a presentencing report from the probation department. After receiving this report, the court will impose whatever sentence it considers appropriate.

victim has changed her story, these questions may explain why that has occurred; and, finally, they inform the judge or jury of the victim's feelings and fears.

- Would you prefer to talk with the judge privately in his or her chambers?
- Are you aware that you are under oath to tell the truth?
- Are you aware that the People of the State of California are bringing these charges and that the decision to prosecute the defendant is up to the prosecutor rather than you?
- (If the victim is subpoenaed) You don't want to be here, do you? Why are you here? ("Because I was subpoenaed by you"—this helps protect the victim from the defendant.)
- Are you aware that the fact that you have been subpoenaed means that you have been called as a witness, that you must testify, and that you may be held in contempt if you do not do so?
- Why do you feel reluctant to (or refuse to) testify?
- When did you become reluctant (or decide to refuse) to testify?
- Were you living with the defendant when the incident happened?
- Are you now living with the defendant or with the defendant's family?
- (If not) Does the defendant know where you are staying?
- Are you financially dependent on the defendant?
- Do you and the defendant have children together?
- Have you discussed the case with the defendant?

- Has the defendant made any promises to do something for you if you do not testify?
- Is that promise to do something the reason you do not wish to proceed or testify?
- Has the defendant or anyone else threatened you or told you not to testify or told you to tell us a different version of what really happened?
- Has the defendant or anyone else threatened your children, family, or close friends?
- Is there some other reason why you are afraid of the defendant?
- Are you aware that this court can issue an order telling the defendant to stay away from you and have no contact with you or your family?
- Are you aware that if the case is prosecuted, the defendant can be required to get counseling, pay for your damages, and stay away from you and your family?
- (If injuries are alleged or visible) How did you receive the injuries? (Allude to police reports, medical reports, photos, injuries still visible in court, etc.)
- Have you talked about your desire not to testify or to change your version of what happened with the victim/witness staff or staff of the local domestic violence agency?
- If not, would you be willing to talk with them now?
- Would you like the bailiff or officer to escort you when you leave court today?[62]

As with any checklist, discretion must be used when employing it. However, the items do establish guidelines that allow the prosecutor to present the evidence of the assault in a logical manner. If victims are concerned or express fear about the criminal justice system to police or other professionals, consideration should be given to referring them to victim advocates.

The use of family violence victim advocates is absolutely critical to the effective prosecution of partner abuse cases. These individuals, whether employed by a public agency or private social services organization, offer a personal support system for the victim. Some state statutes require prosecutors' offices to use victim advocates in this role.[63]

Victim advocates provide invaluable services to partner assault victims. The advocate can work with the victim by accompanying her to any interview, informing her of court procedures, and explaining the criminal justice operation. The advocate can also provide a source of emotional support to the victim, in effect becoming a human link between the victim and an impersonal legal system. He or she may also assist the victim by preparing her for court. The advocate might, for example, accompany the victim to a pretrial visit to the courtroom and explain the functions of the various parties. Finally, and perhaps most important, the victim advocate can supply the victim with information on community and criminal justice support providers. This information may range from the names and locations of support groups to the victim's right to file claims for compensation from the state for injuries.

Family Violence Courts

Some jurisdictions have created specialized courts to process family violence cases and intensive systemic reforms designed to revise the components of the criminal and civil systems to ensure that proper sanctions and other relief are accorded to victims of family violence.[64] Programs such as the Dade County, Florida, Domestic Violence Court (DCDVC) embed legal protections in a web of social control that reinforces the message of treatment and the threat of criminal punishment. The DCDVC is a criminal court with a civil component designed by a team of representatives from every segment of the criminal justice system to serve as a coordinated, systemic response to the treatment of family violence cases in the courts. The

Focus

Animal Abuse and Partner Abuse: Is There a Relationship?

Several researchers have examined this issue and found various relationships between abuse of animals by the perpetrator and abuse of the intimate partner. Ascione in 1998 reported that female victims of partner abuse consistently reported that their adult partner had threatened or actually hurt or killed one or more of their pets. In 2000, he conducted a replication of the first study. This replication involved 100 female victims and a companion group of 117 nonbattered females. Both groups had pets. Ascione's figures are chilling. He found that 54 percent of the battered females, as compared to 5 percent of the nonbattered females, reported that their partner had hurt or killed their pets. Flynn found a similar pattern when he studied females with pets who were victims of abuse. These studies point out the necessity of authorities considering the overlap between abuse of animals and abuse of an intimate partner.

Source: Based on Frank R. Ascione, *Animal Abuse and Youth Violence* (Office of Juvenile Justice Programs, Washington, D.C., September 2001).

DCDVC represents an innovative, interdisciplinary, and integrated systemwide approach, consisting of a team of criminal justice system professionals, to the treatment of misdemeanor cases, civil protection orders, and the violation of those orders.

The members of the court, led by the judiciary, work together as a team toward the shared goal of reducing family violence. From arrest to the completion of a sentence, only judges who are specially trained in family violence handle these cases. The founders of DCDVC believe that the combination of intensive victim services, treatment for the abusers, and an active informed judiciary can improve the control of misdemeanor family violence cases. The court is based on the following principles:

- The administration of justice should expand the traditional role of the criminal justice system, which has traditionally been concerned with punishment but which has failed to consider the role of treatment in family violence cases.
- Emphasis is on the needs of children who live in violent homes. Parents are educated about the effects of family violence on their children.
- The members of the court acknowledge and accept the responsibility to educate the general public about family violence and the fact that it is a crime.
- The court serves as a catalyst for change as a community leader by coordinating a community-wide approach to combat family violence.
- Judicial education and training in family violence is mandatory for all judges and prosecutors and some public defenders assigned to the DCDVC.

Although the DCDVC represents a giant step forward, much more needs to be accomplished with the court system. For example, the DCDVC deals only with misdemeanors, leaving felonies to the regular criminal court system. Additionally, some judges and prosecutors still do not understand the dynamics of family violence. The court system, by its nature, is tradition bound and slow to change. We must continue to educate our judges, prosecutors, public defenders, and the general public regarding partner abuse.

Focus

Family Violence Courts in Australia

It appears that on many points, Australia Family Violence Courts should provide us with ideas on how the courts in the United States may improve in handling partner violence. The Australian Family Violence Courts (AFVC) focus on the safety of victims and seek to address the causal factors of an offender's violent behavior.

AFVCs attempt to end the cycle of family violence by providing the option of programs to address the offender's violent behavior before sentencing.

These courts can produce better outcomes for victims of family violence and help reduce the damaging intergenerational and societal effects that family violence causes.

Participating in the Australian Family Violence Courts

Offenders are only eligible for the Family Violence Court case management program if they admit to their actions by pleading guilty, which demonstrates a willingness to address their behavior. Note the family violence courts are open to same gender couples.

Following a guilty plea, the dedicated Community Justice Services officer conducts further assessment to identify the offender's level of willingness to address their behavior and the level of risk that they pose to the victim and community.

This is carried out in a more thorough process of interviewing, harm assessment, case needs assessment, and spousal assault risk assessment. Once this is completed, referrals to specialized intervention programs are then carried out.

The success or otherwise of offenders engaged in programs designed to address their behavior is taken into account by the judiciary when they are sentenced at the completion of the court based regime.

Offenders may enter the Family Violence Court program by either being bailed directly to appear in the dedicated court by police or by being referred to the court upon pleading guilty in the Magistrates Court.

How Australian Family Violence Courts Work

The court process operates on a collaborative case management model involving the Department of the Attorney General, Department of Corrective Services, Western Australia Police, and Department for Child Protection.

The Family Violence Court Case Management model involves:

- Early review by the integrated case management team to assess an individual's suitability for inclusion in the court case management process;
- Deferral of sentencing to enable the offender to participate in an identified family and domestic perpetrators program and the case management process;
- Once accepted into the Family and Domestic Violence Court case management process, the offender is subject to ongoing case management and review by the integrated case management team. This involves:

  - a progress review by the integrated case management team;
  - the offender appearing in court before the family and domestic violence magistrate. A community justice services (CJS) officer also attends the court.

    The CJS represents the integrated case management team and reports the offender's progress in case management and the perpetrator program.

  - all relevant agencies in the integrated case management process as it gives a holistic review of the individual's progress.

(continued)

The Family Violence Court provides customized programs and support to meet the needs of Aboriginal people and other cultural groups. The court engages with existing support services located throughout the metropolitan regions.

Australian Family Violence Service

Each of the Family Violence Courts is supported by a Family Violence Service which provides support and advice to victims of family violence.

All Family Violence Courts provide services and programs that are culturally appropriate for Aboriginal people.

Each court also has a Family Violence Support Service which can provide:

- referrals that allow victims access to counseling, crisis care, and health services;
- help with violence restraining order applications and hearings;
- information on safety planning, victim support, court processes, and family violence services;
- help with victim impact statements.

Source: Australia Department of the Attorney General Web site, accessed August 30, 2015 at www.courts.dotag. wa.gov.au/F/family_violence_court.aspx and a personal email from the Australia Department of the Attorney General dated September 1, 2015.

Summary

Law enforcement's responsibilities to victims of partner assault are continually evolving. In the past and in many police departments today, officers are reluctant to become involved in "family disputes."

Several experiments have attempted to gauge the effectiveness of arrest in deterring future partner assault. Although they often raise more questions than they answer, it is clear that partner assault is a crime and that professionals must come to some sort of resolution on how to respond to it.

The judicial system is closely linked to law enforcement. In recent years, most states have passed laws in an attempt to protect victims of partner assault. These laws have ranged from mandatory arrest to the use of restraining orders.

Restraining orders are intended to protect the victim from future injury by the offender. However, some serious shortcomings remain with their operation and effectiveness. These problems can be addressed only by changes in state laws.

Arrest of the defendant in a partner abuse case is only the first step in the judicial system. Occasionally, victims are reluctant to testify against the defendant. These fears are normal and in most situations justified and valid. Prosecutors must be sensitive to these issues and, if necessary, frame questions in such a manner as to educate the judge or jury of these fears. The case must be issued and tried and the defendant convicted of a crime if the criminal justice system is to fulfill its responsibilities to the victim.

Key Terms

partner assault—the act of intentionally inflicting physical injury on a spouse or other person who is cohabiting with the abuser.

call screening—downgrading by police departments of the service priority assigned to domestic violence calls.

arrest—the taking of a person into custody in the manner prescribed by law.

felony—considered the most serious type of crime and usually punished by imprisonment in state prison.

misdemeanor—considered a less serious type of crime and punished by incarceration in local jails not to exceed one year.

probable cause—that set of facts that would lead a reasonable person to believe a crime has been committed by the suspect.

battery—the unlawful application of force to a person.

mediation—a private, informal dispute resolution process in which a neutral third person, the mediator, helps disputing parties reach an agreement.

restraining orders (protective orders)—court orders that prohibit the offender from having any contact with the victim.

prosecution—a proceeding instituted and carried on by due course of law before a competent tribunal for the purpose of determining the guilt or innocence of a person charged with a crime.

case screening—a review and evaluation of facts to determine whether the defendant has violated a criminal statute.

diversion—allows the offender to attend an education or counseling program rather than being processed in the criminal justice system.

Discussion Questions

1. What is the best indicator of the potential for partner assault? Why do you believe that this indicator is more important than any other factor?
2. Do you believe that arrest deters future partner assault? Explain your reasons.
3. Is the use of human subjects without their consent in an experiment ethical? The suspects in the policing and partner assault experiments were unaware that they were part of the experiment.

Would it change your answer if they had been informed of this fact? As a practical matter, how would you inform them?
4. Does your community have victim's advocates? How do they operate? Do you believe that they serve a purpose?
5. Should individuals who assault their spouses be subjected to mandatory imprisonment? Why?
6. Do you believe that diversion works?

Practical Application

A professor in your university has received a grant to do a follow-up study on the effects of arrest and prosecution on deterring future partner assault in your community. Assume that the local police chief and the prosecuting attorney have agreed to cooperate in this study.

Your community has a population of 300,000 residents, 1,000 sworn police officers, and 80 deputy district attorneys. Your professor has asked for your input in the following areas of the experiment:

1. How many arrest categories would you recommend? Why?

2. How would the police officers select one of the alternatives?
3. Would you request that the prosecuting attorney participate in the study by not filing charges on some offenders? What are the advantages of this course of action? What are some of the disadvantages?
4. Certain members of the medical profession have objected to this study on ethical grounds. List possible objections and your responses to them.

Suggested Readings

Black, D. *The Manners and Customs of Police* (Academic Press, New York, 1980).

Bolton, F. G., and S. R. Bolton. *Working with Violent Families* (SAGE, Newbury Park, Calif., 1987).

Buzawa, E. S., and C. G. Buzawa. *Domestic Violence: The Criminal Justice Response* (SAGE, Newbury Park, Calif., 1990).

Buzawa, E. S., and C. G. Buzawa, eds. *Domestic Violence: The Changing Criminal Justice Response* (Auburn House, Westport, Conn., 1992).

Fellmeth, R., and M. Ventrell. *Child Rights and Remedies: How the U.S. Legal System Affects Children*, 2nd ed. (Clarity Press, ON, Canada, 2006).

Hilton, N. Z., ed. *Legal Responses to Wife Assault* (Sage, Newbury Park, Calif., 1993).

LaFave, W. R., and A. W. Scott Jr. *Criminal Law*, 2nd ed. (West, St. Paul, Minn., 1986).

Lemon, N. K. D., and M. Kandel. *Domestic Violence: The Law and Criminal Prosecution*, 2nd ed. (Family Violence Project, San Francisco, 1990).

Merlo, A. V., and J. M. Pollock. *Woman, Law, and Social Control* (Allyn & Bacon, Boston, 1995).

Ohlin, L., and M. Tonry, eds. *Family Violence* (University of Chicago Press, Chicago, 1989).

Perkins, R. M., and R. N. Boyce. *Criminal Law*, 3rd ed. (Foundation Press, New York, 1982).

Schmalleger, F. *Criminal Justice Today*, 2nd ed. (Prentice Hall, Upper Saddle River, N.J., 1993).

Sherman, L. W. *Policing Domestic Violence* (Free Press, New York, 1992).

Siegel, L. J. *Criminology*, 3rd ed. (West, St. Paul, Minn. 1989).

Steinman, M., ed. *Women Battering: Policy Responses* (Anderson, Cincinnati, 1991).

Straus, M. A., R. J. Gelles, and S. K. Steinmetz. *Behind Closed Doors: Violence in the American Family* (Anchor, New York, 1980).

Ursel, J. *Family Violence Court* (University of Toronto Press, Toronto, 2006).

Endnotes

1. See, for example, L. W. Sherman, *Policing Domestic Violence* (Free Press, New York, 1992); F. G. Bolton and S. R. Bolton, *Working with Violent Families* (SAGE, Newbury Park, Calif., 1987); and E. S. Buzawa and C. G. Buzawa, eds., *Domestic Violence: The Changing Criminal Justice Response* (Auburn House, Westport, Conn., 1992).

2. See C. G. Bowman, "The Arrest Experiments: A Feminist Critique," *Journal of Criminal Law and Criminology* 83(1) (1992), pp. 201–208, in which Bowman argues that current research in the area of spousal assault is flawed because it is usually conducted from the abuser's perspective, ignores feminist thinking, and does not consider various social factors.

3. *Violence between Intimates* (Bureau of Justice Statistics, Washington, D.C., November 1994).

4. Sherman, *Policing Domestic Violence*, p. 6.

5. M. A. Straus, R. J. Gelles, and S. K. Steinmetz, *Behind Closed Doors: Violence in the American Family* (Anchor, New York, 1980), p. 32.

6. *Costs of Intimate Partner Violence against Women in the United States* (Department of Health and Human Services, Centers for Disease Control and Prevention, Atlanta, Ga., March 2003).

7. D. G. Saunders, "Husbands Who Assault, Multiple Profiles Requiring Multiple Responses," in N. Z. Hilton, ed., *Legal Responses to Wife Assault* (SAGE, Newbury Park, Calif., 1993), pp. 9–34.

8. Ibid., pp. 11–16.

9. L. A. Frisch, "Research That Succeeds, Policies That Fail." *Journal of Criminal Law and Criminology* 83(1) (1992), p. 209.

10. For an excellent discussion of these laws, see A. Binder and J. Meeker, "The Development of Social Attitudes toward Spousal Abuse," in Buzawa and Buzawa, eds., *Domestic Violence*.

11. J. E. O'Brien, "Women Abuse: Facts Replacing Myths," *Journal of Marriage and the Family* 33 (1971), pp. 362–398.

12. One of the earliest studies in this area was the breakthrough discussion of child abuse by Kempe discussed in Chapter 5.

13. E. Erez, "Intimacy, Violence, and the Police," *Human Relations* 39 (1986), pp. 265–281.

14. S. Bourg and H. V. Stock, "A Review of Domestic Violence Arrest Statistics in a Police Department Using a Pro-Arrest Policy: Are Pro-Arrest Policies Enough?" *Journal of Family Violence* 9(2) (1994), p. 177.

15. E. S. Buzawa and C. G. Buzawa, *Domestic Violence: The Criminal Justice Response* (SAGE, Newbury Park, Calif., 1990), p. 44.

16. W. R. LaFave and A. W. Scott Jr., *Criminal Law*, 2nd ed. (West, St. Paul, Minn., 1986), p. 30.

17. R. M. Perkins and R. N. Boyce, *Criminal Law*, 3rd ed. (Foundation Press, New York, 1982), p. 152.

18. LaFave and Scott, p. 684.

19. E. S. Buzawa and T. Austin, "Determining Police Response to Domestic Violence Victims: The Role of Victim Preference," *American Behavioral Scientist* 36(5) (1993), p. 610.

20. See D. Black, *The Manners and Customs of Police* (Academic Press, New York, 1980), p. 189.

21. For an excellent discussion of this area, see Sherman, *Policing Domestic Violence*, pp. 30–31.

22. L. W. Sherman and R. A. Berk, "The Specific Deterrent Effects of Arrest for Domestic Assault," *American Sociological Review* 49 (1984), p. 261.

23. J. R. Clark, "The Minneapolis Study: Policy Gets Made Despite Cautions," *Law Enforcement News*, March 31, 1993, p. 9.

24. J. D. Hirschel and I. Hutchinson, "Police-Preferred Arrest Policies," in M. Steinman, ed., *Women Battering: Policy Responses* (Anderson, Cincinnati, 1991), p. 59.

25. See D. S. Elliot, "Criminal Justice Procedures in Family Violence Crimes," in L. Ohlin and M. Tonry, eds., *Family Violence* (University of Chicago Press, Chicago, 1989), p. 458, which cites the study as a landmark work on the effectiveness of alternative police responses to family violence, and compare that position with Richard Lempert, "Humility Is a Virtue," *Law and Society Review* 23 (1989), p. 146, which argues that the experiment lacked a scientific basis.

26. A. Pate, E. E. Hamilton, and A. Sampson, *Metro-Dade Spouse Abuse Replication Project, Draft Final Report* (National Institute of Justice, Washington, D.C., 1991).

27. R. A. Berk et al., "A Bayesian Analysis of the Colorado Springs Spouse Abuse Experiment," *Journal of Criminal Law and Criminology* 83(1) (1992), p. 170.

28. L. W. Sherman et al., "The Variable Effects of Arrest on Criminal Careers: The Milwaukee Domestic Violence Experiment," *Journal of Criminal Law and Criminology* 83(1) (1992), p. 137.

29. F. W. Dunford, D. Huizinga, and D. S. Elliot, *The Omaha Domestic Violence Police Experiment: Final Report to the National Institute of Justice* (National Institute of Justice, Washington, D.C., 1989).

30. Ibid., p. 34.

31. J. D. Hirchel et al., *Charlotte Spouse Assault Replication Project, Final Report to the National Institute of Justice* (National Institute of Justice, Washington, D.C., 1991).

32. This section is based on C. D. Maxwell, J. H. Garner, and J. A. Fagan, *The Effects of Arrest on Intimate Partner Violence: New Evidence from the Spouse Assault Replication Program* (National Institute of Justice, Washington, D.C., June 2001).

33. L. G. Lerman, "Mediation of Wife Abuse Cases: The Adverse Impact of Informal Dispute Resolution on Women," *Harvard Women's Law Journal* 7 (1984), p. 57.

34. G. A. Goolkasian, *Confronting Domestic Violence: A Guide for Criminal Justice Agencies* (National Institute of Justice, Washington, D.C., 1986), pp. 41–51.

35. Sherman, *Policing Domestic Violence*, pp. 253–260.

36. See, for example, the cases discussed in Chapter 15 in which some of the decisions reflect the constitutional requirement that all persons be granted equal protection under the law.

37. See "Message to Batterers: If You Hit, We'll Arrest," *Law Enforcement News*, September 15, 1997, p. 7.

38. J. Travis, "Violence against Women: Reflections on NIJ's Research Agenda," *National Institute of Justice Journal* (February 1996).

39. 18 U.S.C. 2261 (a) (1) and (2) (1996).

40. 18 U.S.C. 2262 (a) (1) and (2) (1996).

41. 18 U.S.C. 992 (g) (9) (1996).

42. See *Family Violence: A Model State Code* (National Council of Juvenile and Family Court Judges, Reno, Nev., January 1994).

43. This section has been based on P. Finn and S. Colson, *Civil Protection Orders: Legislation, Current Court Practice and Enforcement* (National Institute of Justice, Washington, D.C., March 1990).

44. *Mitchell v. W. T. Grant Co.*, 416 U.S. 600 (1974).

45. For an excellent discussion of the advantages to using restraining orders, see E. Topliffe, "Why Civil Protection Orders Are Effective Remedies for Domestic Violence but Mutual Protective Orders Are Not," *Indiana Law Journal* 67 (Fall 1992), p. 1039.

46. 125 S. Ct. 417 (2005).

47. This section has been based on S. L. Keillitz et al., "Civil Protection Orders: Victim's View on Effectiveness," *National Institute of Justice Journal* (September 1997), pp. 23–24.

48. Monica Rhor, "Orders Often Fail to Restrain Violence," *Orange County Register*, www.ocregister.com/ocregister, accessed March 20, 2006.

49. L. W. Sherman and R. A. Berk, "The Specific Deterrent Effects of Arrest for Domestic Assault," *American Sociological Review* 49 (1984), p. 261.

50. *Attorney General's Task Force on Family Violence* (U.S. Department of Justice, Washington, D.C., 1984).

51. Ibid., p. 29.

52. See *Domestic Violence: The Law and Criminal Prosecution*, 2nd ed. (Family Violence Project, San Francisco, 1990), p. 12.

53. San Francisco Office of the District Attorney Protocol for the Handling of Domestic Violence (undated).

54. *U.S. v. Reisinger*, 128 U.S. 398, 9 S. Ct. 99, 32 L. Ed. 489 (1888).

55. *Domestic Violence: The Law and Criminal Prosecution*, p. 13.

56. *Domestic Violence: The Law and Criminal Prosecution*, pp. 13–14, which states, "The case should be filed when a provable case exists regardless of the victim's stated wishes. Victims should not be asked if they want the case prosecuted. Nor should they be told the DA will prosecute only if requested, or only if the victim signs the complaint.

57. F. Schmalleger, *Criminal Justice Today*, 2nd ed. (Prentice Hall, Upper Saddle River, N.J., 1993).

58. *Nolo contendere* is a Latin phrase, which means "I will not contest it." It has the same force and effect as pleading guilty. The principal difference between a guilty plea and one of *nolo contendere* is that the latter pleas may not be used against the defendant in any subsequent civil trial. *Hudson v. U.S.* 272 U.S. 451, 47 S. Ct. 127, 71 L. Ed. 347 (1926).

59. See *Domestic Violence: The Law and Criminal Prosecution*, pp. 20–26, which has an excellent discussion of bail and domestic violence.

60. See L. J. Siegel, *Criminology*, 3rd ed. (West, St. Paul, Minn., 1989), p. 214.

61. Goolkasian, *Confronting Domestic Violence*, fn. 31.

62. Based on N. K. D. Lemon and M. Kandel, *Domestic Violence: The Law and Criminal Prosecution*, 2nd ed. (Family Violence Prevention Fund, San Francisco, 1990), pp. 79–80. Production was funded in part by the Office of Criminal Justice Planning.

63. See, for example, California Penal Code Section 273.82(a)(2). Unfortunately, the legislature never provided funds to implement this requirement.

64. This section has been based on J. Fagan, *The Criminalization of Domestic Violence: Promise and Limits* (National Institute of Justice, Washington, D.C., January 1996).

4

Elder Abuse

CHAPTER OBJECTIVES

After studying this chapter, you should be able to:

- Discuss the need to treat elder abuse problems and the consequences if left untreated;
- List and explain the reporting laws involving elder abuse;
- Explain the neutralization theory;
- Discuss the power of the state to intervene in elder abuse cases;
- Distinguish between active and passive abuse;
- Discuss the issues in dealing with elder LGBT partnership abuse.

Detailed Look at What You Should Know About Elder Abuse

- Elder abuse can, if left untreated, have serious and often deadly consequences for victims.
- It wasn't until the 1980s that elder abuse came to widespread public attention.
- Although several problems persist in the study of elder abuse, defining the term itself and determining its extent are two of the most controversial.
- The term *elder abuse* was first used during congressional hearings in the late 1970s.
- Elder abuse may be classified into five areas: physical abuse, psychological abuse, material abuse, active neglect, and passive neglect.
- Elder abuse can occur in a domestic or an institutional setting.
- There is a continuing failure to report and act on elder abuse.
- Alzheimer's disease is a relatively recently recognized disability that affects persons as early as the age of forty.

- Most scholars distinguish between active and passive abuse of the elderly.

- Although authorities may disagree as to the exact cause of elder abuse, there is general agreement that it is similar to other forms of family violence and that it crosses all social and economic lines.

- One of the most accepted theories of elder abuse, the family stress theory, is based on the premise that providing care for an elder induces stress within the family.

- The neutralization theory was originally developed by Sykes and Matza to explain juvenile delinquency in society. This theory views delinquents as being affected by the norms and values of a larger social system rather than a counterculture.

- Most reporting laws require certain designated professionals to report to a specific agency if they have reason to believe an elder has been the victim of abuse. The professionals included in these laws are medical personnel, educators, and others who might come into contact with elder clients on a regular basis.

- The power of the state to intervene and care for those who cannot care for themselves is a recognized principle of the sovereignty of the state. In the case of elders, the state acts by means of establishing either a guardianship or a conservatorship.

INTRODUCTION

Elder abuse can, if left untreated, have serious and often deadly consequences for victims. Although the public became aware of certain forms of family violence in the 1960s and 1970s, it wasn't until the 1980s that elder abuse came to widespread public attention. This chapter examines various aspects of this complex form of family violence.

One of the first studies of elder abuse was published in 1979 by Block and Sinnott. They contacted twenty-four agencies in Maryland and surveyed 427 professionals and 443 elders. They found twenty-six cases of elder abuse. Unfortunately, the study went no further, but it was the first step in the long process of recognizing that elders can be victims of family violence.[1] By 1988, scholars had identified more than 200 research papers examining elder abuse.[2] Today, that number continues to expand rapidly. Although several problems persist in the study of elder abuse, defining the term itself and determining its extent are two of the most controversial.

DEFINITION

The term *elder abuse* was first used during congressional hearings in the late 1970s. The House Select Committee on Aging, chaired by Representative Claude Pepper (The Pepper Commission), examined the mistreatment of the elderly and introduced the term *elder abuse* to the United States.[3] Simply coining a term, however, does not make it clear or acceptable to all scholars or professionals.

Some scholars examined elder abuse and included persons under the age of sixty in their research, whereas others classified elders as those over the age of sixty.[4] Well-respected authorities defined elder abuse as occurring only between those who share a residence with the victim, whereas in other studies out-of-home caretakers were included.[5] Because of the problems inherent in defining elder abuse, as well as what is to be studied or how a study is to be conducted, it is easy to understand the debate that encompasses the term.

In an effort to end this confusion, some authorities have developed a list of definitions by establishing typologies involving elder abuse. Unfortunately, these typologies lacked uniformity and only resulted in more puzzlement. Hudson and Johnson point out that some typologies differed considerably in defining neglect, whereas others classified withholding of personal care as physical abuse and/or psychological abuse.[6] As a result of this continuing confusion, other researchers began to frame the definition of elder abuse from a conceptional perspective. For example, some scholars attempted to place the issue of elder abuse within the broad category of inadequate care.[7] However, the same problems that were faced in attempting to establish an acceptable typology were present in the effort to conceptualize elder abuse.[8]

Several prominent scholars, including Wolf, Pillemer, and Godkin, distilled these various definitions down to a multifaceted definition that classifies elder abuse into five areas:

1. *Physical abuse* includes the infliction of physical pain or injury, physical coercion, sexual molestation, or physical restraint;
2. *Psychological abuse* includes the infliction of mental anguish;
3. *Material abuse* includes the illegal or improper exploitation and/or use of funds or resources;
4. *Active neglect* includes the refusal or failure to undertake a caretaking obligation;
5. *Passive neglect* includes the refusal or failure to fulfill a caretaking obligation.[9]

The previous discussion clearly illustrates that simply attempting to define the term *elder abuse* has generated scholarly debate and controversy. However, for purposes of

---

Focus

What Is Elder Abuse?

Elder abuse is a term referring to any knowing, intentional, or negligent act by a caregiver or any other person that causes harm or a serious risk of harm to a vulnerable adult. The specificity of laws varies from state to state, but broadly defined, abuse may be:

- *Physical Abuse*—Inflicting, or threatening to inflict, physical pain or injury on a vulnerable elder, or depriving them of a basic need.
- *Emotional Abuse*—Inflicting mental pain, anguish, or distress on an elder person through verbal or nonverbal acts.
- *Sexual Abuse*—Nonconsensual sexual contact of any kind.

- *Exploitation*—Illegal taking, misuse, or concealment of funds, property, or assets of a vulnerable elder.
- *Neglect*—Refusal or failure by those responsible to provide food, shelter, health care, or protection for a vulnerable elder.
- *Abandonment*—The desertion of a vulnerable elder by anyone who has assumed the responsibility for care or custody of that person.

Elder abuse can affect people of all ethnic backgrounds and social status and can affect both men and women. See our section on Types of Elder Abuse (pp.137–) for more information.

Source: National Center for Elder Abuse, www.ncea.aoa.gov/, accessed August 3, 2009.

Focus

Nursing Homes: Places of Healing or Factories of Death?

The nearly 1.6 million elderly and disabled residents living in nursing homes are among the sickest and most vulnerable population in the nation. More than one-fourth of the 17,000 nursing homes nationwide have had serious deficiencies that caused actual harm to residents or placed them at risk of death or serious injury. The most frequent violations causing actual harm included inadequate prevention of pressure sores, failure to prevent accidents, and failure to assess residents' needs and provide appropriate care. More important, the threat of sanctions only temporarily induced homes to correct identified deficiencies, as many were again out of compliance by the time of the next inspection.

Source: Statement of William J. Scanlon, director of Health Financing and Public Health, Education and Human Services Division, U.S. General Accounting Office, before the Senate Special Committee on Aging, GAO/T-HEHS-99-89 (General Accounting Office, Washington, D.C., March 22, 1999).

consistency with other definitions contained in this textbook, **elder abuse** is defined as conduct that results in the physical, psychological, or material neglect, harm, or injury to an elder. This definition applies to both domestic and institutional abuse. All the terms used in this definition have been clarified and explained in previous chapters with the exception of the word *material.* **Material abuse** in the context of elder abuse refers to the exploitation or use of resources. An **elder** is a person who is sixty-five years or older. The initial age determination of sixty-five is based on common acceptance of that age by most authorities, scholars, and professionals.[10] This age group may be further subdivided into those between sixty-five and seventy-five (the young–old) and those above seventy-five (the old–old).[11]

Elder abuse can occur in a domestic or an institutional setting. Pillemer and Moore point out that despite two decades of state and federal regulation of nursing homes, abuse of the elderly continues to occur on a regular basis.[12] The focus of this chapter is on domestic abuse because it is related to the concept of family violence. However, abuse of the elderly in nursing homes and long-term care institutions is a fact of modern life and should not be forgotten or overlooked when considering the overall plight of the elderly in society.

EXTENT OF THE PROBLEM

How pervasive is elder abuse? Domestic elder abuse, like other forms of family violence, occurs behind closed doors in the privacy of the home. One of the breakthrough studies of elder abuse, published in 1988 by Pillemer and Finkelhor, involved 2,020 Boston elders aged sixty-five and older living by themselves or with their families. The authors found a rate of 32 abused elders per 1,000, which would translate into more than a million abused elders in the United States in 1988.[13] Estimates on the nature, type, and prevalence of elder abuse continue to vary widely.

In February 2006, the National Committee for the Prevention of Elder Abuse and the National Adult Protective Services Association released its survey of *Abuse of Adults Age 60+.*[14] The findings show an alarming 19.7 percent increase in the total number of reported cases of elder and vulnerable adult abuse and neglect cases. In addition, the report indicates that there has been a 15.6 percent increase in sustained or provable cases since 2000. Over 52 percent of the perpetrators of abuse were female. The most common relationship of the perpetrators to the victims was adult child.

A National Institute of Justice study conducted in 2009 reported the following conclusions:[15]

- Eleven percent of elders reported experiencing at least one form of mistreatment—emotional, physical, sexual, or potential neglect—in the past year.
- Past-year prevalence was 5.1 percent for emotional mistreatment, 1.6 percent for physical mistreatment, 0.6 percent for sexual mistreatment, and 5.1 percent for potential neglect.
- Financial exploitation by a family member in the past year was reported by 5.2 percent of elders.
- The risk of elder mistreatment is higher for individuals with the following characteristics: low household income, unemployed or retired, reporting poor health, having experienced a prior traumatic event, or reporting low levels of social support.

Despite such studies, controversy continues regarding who is the abused and who is the abuser—Are they family members, the wife, or the husband? This confusion is

The photo depicts an elderly couple where one partner is threatening the other with a firearm.

Focus

Elder Abuse as a Criminal Problem

According to the National Institute of Justice, elder abuse and neglect is an understudied problem in the United States. Historically viewed as a social rather than a criminal problem, most states did not establish adult protective services units until the mid-1980s.

Criminal justice researchers have generally paid little attention to elder abuse until recently. No uniform reporting system exists, and the available national incidence and prevalence data from administrative records are unreliable due to varying state definitions and reporting mechanisms. A 2007 nationally representative study of over 7,000 community residing elders estimated that approximately one in ten elders reported experiencing at least one form of elder mistreatment in the past year.

Research still is needed to determine the prevalence of elder abuse, neglect, and exploitation among elders with dementia and those residing in residential facilities, to identify risk factors for victimization, and to evaluate the efficacy of interventions.

The lack of research on the forensic aspects of elder mistreatment is of particular concern to criminal justice practitioners. At present, the medical community cannot easily distinguish between those types of injuries that indicate abuse or neglect and those that are the natural effects of illness or aging. Few experts are available to testify in court and limited data exist to bolster cases brought into the system.

In addition, little is known about the financial exploitation of seniors in the United States, as these crimes are difficult to detect, definitions vary, and no national reporting mechanism now exists. Such cases are often not reported. Adding to the problem, some victims of financial exploitation may be unaware of being exploited owing to cognitive disabilities or dementia. Likewise, dependence on the perpetrator for care or shelter, fear of retaliation, or fear of the loss of independence if their exploitation should become known keeps many elders from reporting financial abuse.

Source: National Institute of Justice Web site, www.nij.gov/nij/topics/crime/elder-abuse/criminal-problem.htm, accessed June 27, 2012.

illustrated by the fact that some authorities believe that elderly victims are females over the age of seventy-five,[16] whereas others believe that the wife is the one who perpetrates the abuse.[17] Other scholars argue that adult children inflict abuse on their parents, as shown in the 2006 *Abuse of Adults Age 60+* survey. The Boston survey, however, indicated that elders were abused more by their spouses than by their children. This result is plausible once it is understood that elders live with spouses more than with adult children; therefore, the chance of being abused by a spouse is greater than that of being abused by an adult child. Although both males and females may be victims of elder abuse, the abuse inflicted by husbands is more severe than that inflicted by wives. More research is necessary to determine the extent and nature of elder abuse, but the central issue is that abuse is likely to be inflicted by the people with whom the elder is living.

In addition, methodology and sampling procedures differ from study to study. Some research focuses on the elderly population, and other studies examine agency records. Still other investigations poll professionals. As a result, no clear-cut figures exist that are accepted by all scholars and researchers.

Focus

Elderly Abuse

A recent study of elderly abuse victims in the State of Michigan indicates that:

- Three out of ten elderly victims of reported violence were victimized by their own child or grandchild.
- More than a third of violent victimizations of elderly women (37.8%) involved the victim's child or grandchild, compared to less than a quarter of victimizations of elderly men (22.5%).
- The rate of reported violence against elderly men (247.7 per 100,000 males age sixty-five or older) was 1.4 times higher than the rate for elderly women (172.9 per 100,000 women age sixty-five or older).
- The rate of reported violent victimization by a stranger was more than two times

greater for elderly men (65.5 per 100,000 males age sixty-five or older) than for elderly women (29.2 per 100,000 women age sixty-five or older).
- Elderly victims were more likely to be victimized by young adult offenders ages eighteen to twenty-four than by offenders of other ages.
- More than two-thirds (69.5%) of violence against elderly victims known to law enforcement in Michigan was perpetrated by one offender against one victim.
- Among reported violent victimizations of the elderly, women were more likely than men to be victimized by a spouse or ex-spouse (12.4% of elderly female victims compared to 7.4% of elderly male victims).

Source: Erica Smith, *Violent Crime against the Elderly Reported by Law Enforcement in Michigan, 2005–2009* (U.S. Department of Justice, Office of Justice Programs, Bureau of Justice Statistics, May 2012).

Finally, there is a continuing failure to report and act on elder abuse, due in part to two major factors:

1. Understanding the size, severity, and nature of the problem is difficult because of the conflicting definitions of elder abuse.
2. The number of controlled studies and the case reporting methods that are used in most of the research in this area have produced difficulties in estimating the true extent of the various acts of abuse and neglect.[18]

TYPES OF ELDER ABUSE

Previous chapters have already discussed the different types of abuse that are inflicted on children, women, and even strangers. Elder abuse is very similar to these other forms of family violence, but the age, mental condition, and perspective of the victim make this form of abuse distinct from other forms of family violence. As discussed earlier, elder abuse may involve physical, psychological, or material abuse or neglect that results in injury to the victim.

Physical Abuse

In many instances, the victim may deny abuse or may not even remember the acts that resulted in the injury. It is therefore important that any professional carefully examine any

An elderly couple involved in an argument that could escalate into violence.

unexplained or suspicious physical injury to an elder. This form of elder abuse may include any of the following signs, symptoms, or classifications:

> ***Bruises:*** Any unexplained bruise or bruising that forms a pattern or shape of another object such as cords, belts, or hands should be carefully investigated. Bruising that

---

Focus

Warning Signs of Elder Abuse

While one sign does not necessarily indicate abuse, some tell-tale signs that there could be a problem are as follows:

- Bruises, pressure marks, broken bones, abrasions, and burns may be an indication of physical abuse, neglect, or mistreatment.
- Unexplained withdrawal from normal activities, a sudden change in alertness, and unusual depression may be indicators of emotional abuse.
- Bruises around the breasts or genital area can occur from sexual abuse.
- Sudden changes in financial situations may be the result of exploitation.

- Bedsores, unattended medical needs, poor hygiene, and unusual weight loss are indicators of possible neglect.
- Behavior such as belittling, threats, and other uses of power and control by spouses are indicators of verbal or emotional abuse.
- Strained or tense relationships, frequent arguments between the caregiver and elderly person are also signs.

Most important is to be alert. The suffering is often in silence. If you notice changes in personality or behavior, you should start to question what is going on.

Source: National Center for Elder Abuse, www.ncea.aoa.gov/, accessed August 3, 2009.

occurs after visits by relatives should be carefully examined. Bite and teeth marks should immediately raise suspicion in any professional.

Burns: Cigarette burns, burns with distinctive shapes or patterns, immersion burns, or burns from ropes or other restraints should be carefully evaluated.

Fractures: The aged have fragile bones. Unlike the young child whose bones are limber, elderly people's bones are stiffer and more apt to break. However, injuries to the head, multiple breaks, or spiral fractures should be carefully noted, and a specific inquiry regarding the circumstances surrounding these injuries should be made by any professional who observes them.

Lacerations, abrasions, or hair loss: Injuries to the lips, ears, face, or extremities should be examined and documented. Loss of hair may be simply a natural occurrence of increasing age or may indicate that the abuser has grabbed the victim by the hair.

Sexual activity: Any evidence of forced sexual activity should be examined. This includes genital or rectal bleeding, difficulty in walking or sitting, pain or itching in the genital area, and evidence of any newly acquired sexually transmitted disease.

Psychological Abuse

This type of elder abuse is more difficult to identify than physical abuse. The injury to the victim may not leave marks that can be documented. However, as with psychological abuse to women and children, the effects of this type of abuse can be long-lasting and in some cases more severe than physical abuse. The victim may feel deprived of family support, may be fearful of further continued rejection by the caretaking relative, and may believe that there is no further purpose in continuing to live or function.[19]

Depression: Many of the elderly may display symptoms of depression. However, extreme depression in the absence of other factors should prompt an inquiry into the area of abuse.

Overly anxious or fearful of younger adults: An elder who shrinks from contact with younger adults or is withdrawn may have been ridiculed by a family member or caretaker in the past. This experience can make the victim fearful of any contact with other younger adults. The victim may also have been threatened with harm if the abuser is disclosed and therefore avoids contact with others.[20]

Neurotic traits: Sleep disorders, speech disorders, and other activities not associated with a physical cause should be carefully evaluated.

Psychoneurotic behavior: Hysteria or obsession or hoarding food or other material items may indicate that the elder is being denied certain essentials, such as food, water, toilet paper, and other common amenities. This type of abuse, closely associated with neglect, is discussed later in this section.

Material Abuse

A common form of elder abuse, material abuse involves the exploitation of the elder's finances and resources. It may be as obvious as taking money from the elder's bank account or as subtle

Focus

Alzheimer's Disease—A Case of Abuse Waiting to Happen

Alzheimer's disease is a relatively recently recognized disability that affects persons as early as the age of forty. The disease has three major facets: intellectual deficits, personality deficits, and stress tolerance deficits.[21] Intellectual deficits are characterized by inattention to time, difficulty in making decisions, inability to make decisions or plan activities (e.g., dressing, bathing, or eating), and, most commonly, the loss of memory. Personality deficits include inappropriate affection, lack of inhibitions, delusions, paranoia, hallucinations, and social withdrawal. Stress tolerance deficits commonly include confusion, nighttime awakening, pacing and wandering, fatigue, anxiety, and violence.

In the final stage of Alzheimer's disease, the patient no longer recognizes himself, relatives, or close friends. He becomes bedridden, and any activity may consist of random movements.

Verbal communications cease. However, he may cry out or scream without a reason. He will have lost control of his bowel movements and will require feeding, changing, and constant care.

It is easy to see how individuals suffering from Alzheimer's disease can become victims of elder abuse. They may not remember acts of abuse, are very easy to manipulate, and, because of their wandering, need to be restrained for their own protection. These elders may be subjected to all forms of abuse and never even be aware that it has occurred. The stress that is generated in caring for an Alzheimer's patient may lead a caretaker to engage in acts that are considered abusive. Tying the patient down at night, sedating the patient so that he or she does not require constant attention, and slapping the patient to vent frustration are common forms of abuse.

as unduly influencing the elder in the disposition of her property. This undue influence may pressure the elder to transfer property to the abuser or change her will to leave that property to the perpetrator when the elder dies.

Lack of clothing: The elder's clothing may have been sold or appropriated by the caretakers for their own use. Lack of proper clothing for a particular season may mean the elder's resources have been depleted by a caretaker.

Lack of food: The caretaker may be using the elder's normal food allowance for other purposes and thereby starving the elder. The victim may be losing weight or constantly snacking or eating when away from the caretaker.

Loss of residence: The sudden unexplained transfer of ownership of the elder's home or apartment to the caretaker should prompt an immediate inquiry regarding the reasons for the transfer.

Lack of funds: The elder's Social Security or retirement checks may be converted to the caretaker's own use without approval or knowledge of the elder. The elder's savings or checking account should be checked to determine whether any unusual withdrawals have occurred in the recent past.

Loss of personal property: The elder may claim to have lost jewelry or other personal items. The unexplained loss of expensive jewelry should be investigated.

Neglect

Most scholars distinguish between active and passive abuse of the elderly.[22] Neglect may be an action or a failure to act on the part of the caretaking relative, including these forms:

Failure to care for the elder: Neglect includes failure to feed, clothe, or bathe the elder. Improper diet, lack of supervision of the elder, and other acts that expose the elder to possible injury fall within this classification.

Misuse of medication: Some caretakers will not provide or administer necessary medications to the elders. Others use medication as a form of restraint and overmedicate the elder so that he or she becomes less of a caretaking problem.

Failure to seek medical care: Many caretakers will not take time or effort to transport the elder to a physician's office or outpatient clinic even when there are clear signs of injury or other symptoms that require medical intervention.

Not all injuries to an elderly person indicate abuse, but professionals who come into contact with the elderly must be aware of that very real possibility and be prepared to pursue any signs of abuse. Because of the confusion regarding a definition of elder abuse, no clear-cut protocol exists on exactly what to look for or how to diagnose elder abuse.

All activities undertaken by relatives or caretakers should not be automatically categorized as elder abuse. Elders may have valid tax reasons for transferring ownership of property to family members. Elderly persons are, in fact, injured more easily than middle-aged adults. In addition, they may be used to wearing certain types of clothing and are resistant to change, even with the coaxing of relatives. However, professionals cannot afford to ignore the possibility of elder abuse and need to take reasonable actions to assure themselves of the physical and emotional well-being of the elderly client or patient.

THEORIES OF ELDER ABUSE

Although authorities may disagree as to the exact cause of elder abuse, there is general agreement that it is similar to other forms of family violence and that it crosses all social and

Focus

If You Suspect Elder Abuse, Neglect, or Exploitation

If you suspect elder abuse, neglect, or exploitation, call 1-800-677-1116. If someone is in immediate danger, call 911 or the local police for immediate help. The National Center on Elder Abuse (NCEA), directed by the U.S. Administration on Aging, is committed to helping national, state, and local partners in the field be fully prepared to ensure that older Americans will live with dignity, integrity, independence, and without abuse, neglect, and exploitation. The NCEA is a resource for policy makers, social service and health care practitioners, the justice system, researchers, advocates, and families

For state reporting numbers, visit the NCEA Web site at www.ncea.aoa.gov or call the *Elder-care Locator* at 1-800-677-1116.

economic lines. Most researchers agree that elder abuse is not an isolated event; rather, it is a repetitive pattern of acts by the abuser toward the victim.

Intergenerational Transmission of Violence Theory

The intergenerational transmission of violence theory, formerly considered as the cycle of violence, was discussed in detail in Chapter 1. Galbraith argues that it has proven ineffective in predicting elder abuse.[23] Wolf and Pillemer also pointed out that those who abuse elders did not necessarily grow up in families characterized by violence.[24]

Psychopathology

The **psychopathology theory** is based on the premise that abusers have mental disorders that cause them to be abusive. Douglas indicates that the flawed development of the abuser is one of the causes of elder abuse. Wolf found a high prevalence of mental illness among elder abusers.[25] This approach seems to have greater validity in explaining elder abuse than in explaining either child or spousal abuse. Researchers have found psychopathology present in cases of physical and verbal abuse of elders.[26] Other scholars indicate that a number of abusers have previous hospitalizations for serious psychiatric disorders, such as schizophrenia and other psychoses.[27]

Social Exchange Theory

The **social exchange theory** assumes that dependency in relationships contributes to elder abuse. One social exchange theory proposes that the victim's increased dependency on the abuser results in acts of abuse. Several scholars have found support for this theory in their studies.[28] Financial dependency of the abuser on the victim also has been found to be present in a number of studies of elder abuse.[29]

When there is a loss of mutual sharing of resources between the elder and the caretaker, the quality of the relationship degenerates. This results in the caretaker's perceiving the relationship as unfair with a subsequent increase in hostility toward the elder. This imbalance results in some caretakers abusing elders.[30]

A second social exchange theory assumes that the dependency of the abuser on the elder causes abuse. This concept focuses on adult children who are dependent on the elder for material rewards, such as housing and finances. Because these children perceive themselves as weaker and less powerful than the elder, abusing the elder is a way to equalize the balance of power and gain control over the relationship.[31]

Family Stress Theory

One of the most accepted theories of elder abuse,[32] the **family stress theory** is based on the premise that providing care for an elder induces stress within the family. This stress may take many forms, including economic hardship, loss of sleep, and intrusions into normal family privacy routines and other activities, that may cause the caregiver to feel resentment toward the elder. Adult children may have to give up economic security to provide care for an aged parent or other close relative. In addition, the physical toll of caring for an ill elderly person can sometimes overwhelm the adult child, resulting in a loss of control and abuse.[33] This theory is also subject to controversy. Phillips, for example, suggests that stress levels may not be as important a factor as previously believed in causing elder abuse.[34]

Neutralization Theory

The **neutralization theory** was originally developed by Sykes and Matza to explain juvenile delinquency in society.[35] This theory views delinquents as being affected by the norms and values of a larger social system rather than a counterculture. It also holds that delinquents show guilt and shame for their antisocial behavior.[36] To commit criminal or antisocial acts, people develop techniques of neutralization. These techniques are rationalizations or justifications for their behavior. Matza has established five techniques that allow individuals to justify their acts:

1. *Denial of responsibility:* Persons may claim that something else, such as alcohol, made them commit the criminal act.
2. *Denial of injury:* Juveniles may believe that even though they violated the law, no one was really hurt. For example, theft of an automobile is acceptable because the owner's insurance company will replace it with a new model anyway.
3. *Denial of victim:* Delinquents may claim that the victim had it coming and therefore that their acts were justified under the circumstances.
4. *Condemnation of the condemners:* Juveniles may shift the blame to others, calling them corrupt or incompetent.
5. *Appeal to higher loyalty:* Some offenders will claim they violated the law to satisfy a higher authority or goal.

Tomita has applied the neutralization theory to elder abuse and suggests that, although it cannot be used to establish a direct cause, it may provide the methods employed by abusers to justify their acts.[37] Examining each of the techniques of neutralization, she explains that the perpetrators may use them to justify their abuse of elders as follows:

1. *Denial of responsibility:* In these situations, the abuser claims the mistreatment was caused by forces beyond her control, such as poverty, bad parents, and so on.
2. *Denial of injury:* The abuser will rationalize that the injury was not really that serious because the victim did not have to go to the emergency room. In material abuse situations, the abuser will justify her actions by stating that the parent can afford to give away property or assets.
3. *Denial of the victim:* Abusers may state that the victim doesn't need help or that she is just attempting to gain attention. For example, the abuser may refuse to dress the victim, claiming that the victim just wants attention, when in reality the victim cannot dress herself.
4. *Condemnation of the condemners:* In these situations, the abuser condemns protective services or other agencies for interfering with the family.
5. *Appeal to higher loyalty:* The abuser may believe that he must act a certain way to satisfy his spouse.

As the previous discussion illustrates, several theories attempt to explain why individuals abuse the elderly. Just as with other causes of family violence, no single theory is accepted by all scholars. More research needs to be done in this area to determine whether a cause can be established for this type of abuse. In the absence of definite answers, elder abuse will continue to be a problem. This type of behavior necessitates the reporting of abuse and intervention by authorities.

REPORTING AND INTERVENTION

Even with programs such as the triad program (see the Focus on p. 141), elder abuse will continue. When professionals have reason to suspect that an elder is the victim of abuse, they must take certain actions not only to protect the elder but also to notify specified authorities of the incident. These actions are normally defined in the various reporting statutes adopted by each state.

Reporting Laws

As indicated earlier, elder abuse came to public consciousness during the 1980s. As a result of congressional hearings, such as the Pepper Commission, as well as scientific publications and media attention, state legislatures passed a series of laws aimed at this aspect of family violence. Although they differ in content, all states have laws relating to elder abuse.[38] Forty-two states have specific statutes that mandate reporting of suspected abuse by certain professionals.[39] Many of these reporting statutes were modeled after existing child abuse reporting laws. The major problem with elder abuse mandatory reporting laws is the lack of research comparing the needs of the elderly to the needs of abused children. Reporting laws and their

---

International Perspectives

Elder Abuse in Canada

Adults aged sixty-five and older account for 2 percent of the victims of all violent crimes in Canada. In almost one-quarter of these cases, family members were the perpetrators. In incidents in which a family member was the accused, adult children were suspected in 40 percent of the cases, followed by spouses (36%), siblings (12%), and other extended family members (11%).

Older women were more frequently the victims of violence committed by a family member than were older men. Police statistics reveal that older men were proportionately more likely to be victimized by their children (41%) than by their spouse (28%). However, older women were victimized equally by their adult children (40%) and spouses (40%). The majority of violent offenses committed by family members against elders were physical assaults.

Some studies reveal that financial or material abuse is the most frequently reported type of elder abuse in Canada. In Ontario, nearly two-thirds (62%) of the victims of telemarketing frauds who paid out money were over the age of sixty.

Source: Family Violence in Canada: A Statistical Profile 1999 (Minister Responsible for Statistics Canada, Ottawa, June 1999).

effect on child abuse and the professionals who come into contact with abused children are discussed in detail in Chapter 11. For purposes of understanding elder abuse and reporting, this section provides a brief introductory overview of these laws.

Most reporting laws require certain designated professionals to report to a specific agency if they have reason to believe an elder has been the victim of abuse. The professionals who are included in these laws are medical personnel, educators, and others who might come into contact with elder clients on a regular basis. These laws are mandatory in nature, meaning that the professional does not have discretion in deciding whether to report the suspicious activity. The person who suspects abuse must file the report or face civil or criminal sanctions by the state. Many of these statutes provide immunity from lawsuits for the professional who reports suspected abuse.

Ehrlich and Anetzberger conducted a nationwide survey in the United States of all fifty state health departments on procedures for reporting elder abuse.[40] They found that although there is an awareness of elder abuse reporting laws, none of the fifty state agencies had developed a protocol to further their implementation. Sixty-four percent of these departments did not conduct in-service training for health care providers in the area of elder abuse. Part of the reason for the failure of these state agencies to act aggressively in this area of abuse may be the confusion and widespread diffusion of responsibility within a number of distinct agencies.

Elder abuse reporting laws authorize various local or county organizations such as human services, welfare departments, and law enforcement agencies to act, rather than state health departments. Health professionals list the following problems in reporting elder abuse: limited knowledge of the reporting requirements, difficulty in understanding the definition of elder abuse, apprehension in reporting based on denial of abuse by the victim, and a lack of a high suspicion index of this type of family violence.[41]

In a study conducted by Blakely and his associates regarding physicians' responses to elder abuse and neglect, they found a low incidence of reporting to the appropriate agencies.[42] Instead, many physicians attempted to deal with the problem themselves or recommended counseling to the parties involved.

The reasons for the lack of appropriate physician response may be attributed in part to inadequate training received in medical schools. A number of researchers have suggested that medical schools have not devoted sufficient study to the problems of the elderly. Blakely and colleagues found the following:

1. Medical schools presented limited training to physicians in preparation for treating the elderly.
2. Medical schools did not provide students with basic medical and sociological information about elders.
3. Few medical students expressed an interest in working with elderly patients.
4. Although there are several recent studies regarding the attitudes of the young toward the elderly, medical schools have failed to alter students' attitudes toward the elderly.[44]

Reporting suspected incidents of elder abuse is just the beginning. Once a report is filed, other agencies become involved with all parties: the elder, the abuser, and the reporting party. Understanding the roles of these interested parties is crucial to understanding elder abuse.

Focus

Triads—Community Involvement in Fighting Elder Abuse

A new concept that emphasizes community cooperation in combating elder victimization is succeeding in a number of areas throughout the United States. This innovative concept is called the *triad program.*

Triads are formed when the local police and sheriff's departments agree to work cooperatively with senior citizens to prevent the victimization of the elderly in the community. The three groups share ideas and resources to provide programs and training for vulnerable and often fearful elderly citizens.

A triad usually begins when a police chief, a sheriff, or a leader in the senior citizen community contacts the other two essential participants to discuss a combined effort. Although each entity may already have programs in place to reduce victimization among the elderly, the three-way involvement of triads adds strength, resources, and greater credibility.

Most triads include representatives from agencies that serve older persons, such as the Agency on Aging, senior centers, and adult protective services. Law enforcement leaders then invite seniors and those working with them to serve on an advisory council, often called Seniors and Lawmen Together (SALT).

Some triads establish programs to prevent elder abuse through education and to address the plight of seniors in personal care homes. For example, in Columbus, Georgia, the plight of some seniors in such facilities came to the attention of a very active SALT council. Learning that older residents were suffering from abuse and neglect, the SALT council devised a strategy to investigate specific situations.

To begin, the council enlisted the assistance of the sheriff's office and the police and health departments. Through these agencies, a search warrant of the homes was obtained, proper lodging and care was arranged for those seniors living in unhealthy and unsafe conditions, and a plan for more careful monitoring of such homes was initiated.

The essence of the triad is cooperation. This program allows the service providers (law enforcement) to work together with the consumers (senior citizens). Through positive programs that enhance safety and quality of life, mutual respect and appreciation evolve between the law enforcement community and citizens.

The use of triads continues to grow. In July 1992, there were fifty-six triads in twenty states. Today there are more than 739 organizations located in forty-seven states, Canada, and England. In January 2000, the National Association of Triads, Inc. (NATI) was formed as a not-for-profit, tax-exempt affiliate corporation of the Sheriffs' Association. The purpose behind this reorganization was an attempt to provide a more secure funding source for triads.[43]

Sources: Based on B. Cantrell, "Triad, Reducing Criminal Victimization of the Elderly," *FBI Law Enforcement Bulletin,* February 1994, pp. 19–23; *TRIAD: Reducing Crime against the Elderly,* 4th printing (Office for Victims of Crime, Washington, D.C., 1993).

Interested Parties

One of the most important parties to interact with the elder is the health care professional.[45] This person is not only tasked with reporting the abuse but also obligated to evaluate the injuries and offer alterative courses of action. Breckman and Adelman suggest that health care professionals use the following assessment guidelines when evaluating elder abuse:

1. *Access to the victim:* There may be a reluctance to allow the professional to have contact with either the victim or the abuser. Abusers will keep their actions hidden and threaten the victim against disclosure. Elders may feel ashamed that they allowed themselves to be victims and deny that anything is wrong.
2. *Health status:* Victims may tend to dismiss injuries as accidental, or abusers may prevent victims from receiving necessary medical care in order to avoid discovery. Professionals should distinguish between nonaccidental injuries and those normally associated with advancing age.
3. *Functional status:* Abusers who care for functionally dependent elders may appear overwhelmed and frustrated. Abusers and victims may have unrealistically high expectations of each other, resulting in frustration and abuse.
4. *Financial status and living arrangement:* Victims and abusers may be financially dependent on each other and forced to live in the same household. Victims may have given the abuser control over their finances.
5. *Social support:* Victims are often isolated and have limited contact with friends, social groups, other family members, or support systems within the community.
6. *Emotional support:* Effects of abuse may include depression, fear, and withdrawal.
7. *Stress:* External factors, such as loss of employment, death, retirement, or other incidents, may lead to stress that may result in abuse.
8. *Nature of abuse:* Abuse often increases over time. Several types of maltreatment may be inflicted on the victim simultaneously, and denial of abuse is common.

In addition to health care professionals, various agencies, departments, or units are charged with enforcing statutes enacted to protect the elderly.[46] Each of these organizations carries out a needed mission to fulfill the stated goal of ensuring that aged persons are not injured by family members or by strangers. Although all these organizations serve valid purposes, this maze of interlocking and competing organizations can lead to confusion and a lack of coordination in attempts to combat elder abuse.

Various state statutes have established so-called Medicaid fraud units. These units are often located within the state attorney general's office and are charged with investigating and prosecuting violations of the state's Medicaid laws. These organizations may file criminal or civil actions against those who violate the rights of others who are entitled to receive Medicaid.

Many states have licensing divisions located in their state health departments. These divisions are authorized by statute to supervise health care providers, including nursing homes, board and care homes, and home health services. These divisions investigate allegations of violations of state and federal regulations relating to the care of the elderly.

Local legal service organizations under the umbrella of the federally established Legal Services Corporation receive state and federal funding to provide legal advice and advocacy for elders who have civil problems. These local agencies can file civil actions against those who defraud or take advantage of elders.

In addition to these widely diverse organizations, adult protective services (APS) is actively involved in caring for the elderly and is usually tasked with responding to reports of elder abuse. In response to the growing awareness of elder abuse, many states enacted laws establishing APS. These services are typically found in a local public social service agency, such as the welfare department.

Promising Practices

Elder Abuse

Elder-Sensitive Response Protocols, San Diego County, California

The Elder Crime Unit at the San Diego County District Attorney's Office has developed special response protocols for assisting the local population of 350,000 seniors in reporting elder victimization. Three prosecutors and an advocate vertically prosecute all cases. They have developed an elder-sensitive response protocol and procedures for evidence collection from elder victims. Because seniors may have difficulty providing evidence to law enforcement officers, the advocate checks all police reports daily for dates of birth and follows up with every victim over sixty-five. The unit works with hospital emergency rooms to improve detection of elder physical abuse. Prosecutors speak at banking conferences to heighten awareness of senior-related irregular money management. They monitor "boiler room" telemarketers and bogus charities that are active in the county and frequently visit retirement communities to inform them of the kinds of calls that they can expect and discuss how to respond to them.

Eldercare Locator

The Eldercare Locator is a nationwide directory assistance service sponsored by the Administration on Aging, U.S. Department of Health and Human Services, to assist seniors and caregivers in finding local community assistance for aging Americans.

Elder Victims of Crime Assistance Program, Palm Beach County, Florida

A five-county, support-to-elderly-victims program has been established in Palm Beach County at the Area Agency on Aging. The service provides crisis intervention, personal advocacy, criminal justice support and advocacy, and assistance in filing for victim compensation.

Source: Based on U.S. Department of Justice, *National Victim Assistance Academy Text* (Washington, D.C., 2000).

The goal of APS is to coordinate the delivery of social services to those over eighteen years of age.[47] Most states that have enacted this type of legislation authorize APS to intervene on behalf of the state even if the client refuses assistance.[48] These statutes often authorize special court proceedings in family or probate court and provide for the imposition of guardianships or conservatorships of adults who are incapacitated or incapable of caring for themselves.

Guardians and Conservators

The power of the state to intervene and care for those who cannot care for themselves is a recognized principle of the sovereignty of the state. In the case of elders, the state acts by means of establishing either a guardianship or a conservatorship.

Traditionally, a **conservator** is a person appointed by a court to manage the estate of one who is unable to manage his or her own affairs.[49] A **guardian** is a person appointed by a court to take care of another person who for reasons of age, lack of understanding, or self-control is unable to care for himself or herself.[50] Depending on the jurisdiction, these terms are interchangeable. For example, in California a conservatorship may be established for both the person and the property of an incompetent adult. Other states use the term *guardian* for matters affecting the person and *conservatorship* for matters affecting the property.

The initiation of a guardianship or conservatorship proceeding requires filing a petition in a court of competent jurisdiction. This petition is a formal pleading alleging that the elder is in need of the care of other persons. These pleadings usually take place in superior courts of the state and are often specialized courts such as probate or family courts that have been designated to handle these types of cases. The normal procedure requires notice to the affected elder and often his or her family. Once the notice has been served to the parties, the court holds a formal hearing on the issue of competency.

The alleged incompetent has a right to be represented by an attorney and be present at the hearing. Normally, APS or the person filing the petition presents evidence to support the allegations contained in the petition. This evidence may be an expert witness, such as a psychiatrist who can testify that the elder is incompetent or otherwise unable to care for himself or herself. Other witnesses may be called to testify as to any abuse that they may have observed.

The elder, through his or her attorney, has a right to cross-examine witnesses and present evidence in rebuttal to the charges. After hearing all the evidence, the judge or jury may find that the elder, as a result of a mental disease or defect, is incapable of providing for food, clothing, or shelter or otherwise caring for himself or herself.[51] Once the court renders this finding, it may appoint a guardian or conservator. This person may be authorized to assume total control over the fiscal and personal matters of the elder, including placement, finances, and in some cases the use of medication. The purpose of this type of action is to care for and protect the elder from abuse by others.

Other Intervention Strategies

Many elders consider Florida a very desirable retirement state; indeed, a large portion of Florida's elderly population are retirees who moved there from different states. Many of these elderly now face isolation because of the death of a spouse and the fact that they live far away from their extended families. In an effort to address elder abuse issues, the governor of Florida appointed a task force that held public hearings and made a series of recommendations to combat elder abuse.[52] These recommendations included the following:

1. Changes to state law aimed at improving the coordination of elder abuse investigations among agencies in the criminal justice system;
2. More formalized training for public guardians;
3. The establishment of elder courts with specialized training for court personnel and others in the criminal justice system.

Florida is not the only state attempting to improve its response to elder abuse. Massachusetts adopted an elder abuse reporting law in 1983. However, because of mistrust and lack of coordination among APS and the district attorney's office, very few elder abuse cases were being prosecuted. In 1988, the state and the district attorney for Middlesex County drafted a series of guidelines that established interagency protocols to increase communication and cross-agency referrals.[53] Both APS and the district attorney's offices agreed on common language, terms, and concepts. Protocols were also established to educate mandated reporters and make it clear that the decision to report was not discretionary. Cross-training between APS workers and the deputy district attorney resulted in more understanding regarding each professional's roles and responsibilities. This collaboration has resulted in cases being identified earlier and critical support services for the elderly victim better coordinated. Many other states are attempting to address the problems of elder abuse. As the U.S. population ages, it is critical that we respond to this form of family violence.

Elder Abuse among LGBT Partnerships

The National Center on Elder Abuse states that many LGBT older adults are at a higher risk for elder abuse, neglect, and exploitation than non LGBT adults. According to the Center, the fear of homophobia or transphobia keep many LGBT elders from seeking needed help and other services. In addition, many elderly LGBT adults choose to hide their identity and disclosure of that identity from their families.[54]

In one study by Metlife Mature Market Institute, 27 percent of the LGBT baby boomers reported that they had serious concerns about discrimination as they age. In a survey of 416 LGBT elders, 65 percent reported at least one victimization incident due to physical assault, sexual assault, threat of orientation disclosure, or discrimination.

In addition, many transgender older adults have experienced mistreatment in long-term care facilities. Examples include physical abuse, denial of personal care services, psychological abuse, being involuntarily "outed", and being prevented from dressing according to their gender identity. Others are refused admission into long-term care facilities.

The Center's Web site lists some tips for working with LGBT elders:

- Be familiar with the limited legal protections for LGBT elders and the potential impact. For example, an elder partner with limited income may have no legal right in many states to a portion of the abusive partner's income.
- When dealing with an elder use the name and pronoun (e.g., he, she) used by the elder, regardless of legal identification or genitalia.
- Listen especially carefully to the LGBT elder's input and desires.
- Be aware that not all couple relationships are heterosexual.
- Be prepared to be able to connect the elder to community resources for LGBT elders should they so desire (e.g., if they want to talk about being gay, lesbian, or transgendered).
- Lesbian and gay elders may have close networks of friends that may serve as a protective factor.

Summary

Elder abuse has become yet another form of family violence. Authorities cannot agree on a definition, and, as a result, the outcomes of different studies vary widely regarding its nature, cause, and extent. What can be agreed on is that it does exist and that more research is needed in this area.

Elder abuse, like other forms of family violence, is not an isolated event. Rather, it is a pattern of behavior that increases in both intensity and frequency over time. The rich, poor, college-educated, and uneducated all suffer from elder abuse. The dynamics and etiology of this type of abuse continue to spawn theories, some of which seem to hold more promise than others. Continued research is of paramount importance if professionals are to understand and treat the cause of elder abuse.

Professionals must be aware of possible instances of elder abuse and understand how to respond. Depending on the jurisdiction, a report of suspected elder abuse may have to be filed with a designated agency. The state may be required to intervene and place the elder under a guardianship or conservatorship for his or her own protection.

Key Terms

elder abuse—conduct that results in the physical, psychological, or material neglect, harm, or injury to an elder.

material abuse—the exploitation or use of resources of an elder.

elder—a person who is sixty-five years old or older.

psychopathology theory—based on the premise that abusers have mental disorders that cause them to be abusive.

social exchange theory—assumes that dependency in relationships contributes to elder abuse.

family stress theory—based on the premise that providing care for an elder induces stress within the family.

neutralization theory—views the delinquent as being affected by the norms and values of a larger social system rather than a counterculture, holding that delinquents show guilt and shame for their antisocial behavior.

conservator—a person appointed by a court to manage the estate of one who is unable to manage his or her own affairs.

guardian—a person appointed by a court to take care of another person who for reasons of age, lack of understanding, or self-control is unable to care for himself or herself.

Discussion Questions

1. In your opinion, is elder abuse more or less serious than child abuse? Justify your opinion.
2. Do you agree with the definition of elder abuse contained in this textbook? Draft another definition that you believe is more appropriate and justify your answer.
3. What is the most serious form or type of elder abuse?
4. Should elders have the right to accept abuse from a caretaker if they are competent?
5. Which of the theories discussing elder abuse do you favor? Why?
6. Are guardianships and conservatorships the best way to protect elders from abuse? What are some other alternatives?
7. Discuss the issues in dealing with elder LGBT partnership abuse.

Suggested Readings

Ammerman, R. T., and M. Hersen, eds. *Assessment of Family Violence: A Clinical and Legal Sourcebook* (Wiley, New York, 1992).

Anetzberger, G. J. *The Etiology of Elder Abuse by Adult Offspring* (Thomas, Springfield, Ill., 1987).

Block, M. R., and J. D. Sinnott, eds. *The Battered Elder Syndrome: An Exploratory Study* (University of Maryland Center on Aging, College Park, Md., 1979).

Brandi, B., C. Bitondo, and C. Heisier. *Elder Abuse Detection and Intervention: A Collaborative Approach* (Springer Publishing, New York, 2006).

Brubaker, T. H., ed. *Family Relationships in Later Life* (SAGE, Beverly Hills, Calif., 1983).

Decalmer, P., and F. Glendenning, eds. *The Mistreatment of Elder People* (SAGE, London, 1993).

Filenson, R., and S. R. Ingman, eds. *Elder Abuse: Practice and Policy* (Human Sciences Press, New York, 1989).

Finkelhor, D., G. Hotaling, R. Gelles, and M. Straus, eds. *The Dark Side of Families: Current Family Violence Research* (SAGE, Beverly Hills, Calif., 1983).

Kosberg, J. I., ed. *Abuse and Maltreatment of the Elderly: Causes and Interventions* (John Wright PSG, Boston, 1983).

Mellor, J., ed. *Elder Abuse and Mistreatment: Policy, Practice, and Research* (Haworth Social Work, Binghamton, New York, 2006).

Myers, E. B. *Myers on Evidence in Child, Domestic, and Elder Abuse* (Aspen, New York, 2005).

Pagelow, M. D. *Family Violence* (Praeger, New York, 1984).

Payne, B. K. *Crime and Elder Abuse: An Integrated Perspective,* 2nd ed. (Charles C. Thomas, Springfield, Ill., 2005).

Pillemer, K., and R. Wolf, eds. *Elder Abuse: Conflict in the Family* (Auburn House, Dover, Mass., 1986).

Schlesinger, B., and R. Schlesinger, eds. *Abuse of the Elderly: Issues and Annotated Bibliography* (University of Toronto Press, Toronto, 1988).

Short, J. F. Jr., and F. Strodtbeck. *Group Process and Gang Delinquency* (University of Chicago Press, Chicago, 1965).

Sloan, I. J. *The Law and Legislation of Elderly Abuse* (Oceana Publications, Dobbs Ferry, New York, 1983).

Steinmetz, S. K. *Duty Bound: Elder Abuse and Family Care* (SAGE, Newbury Park, Calif., 1988).

Van Hasselt, V. B., R. L. Morrison, A. S. Bellak, and M. Hersen, eds. *Handbook of Family Violence* (Plenum, New York, 1988).

Wolf, R., M. Godkin, and K. A. Pillemer. *Elder Abuse and Neglect: Report from the Model Projects* (University of Massachusetts Medical Center, University Center on Aging, Worcester, Mass., 1984).

Wolf, R. S., and K. A. Pillemer. *Helping Elderly Victims: The Reality of Elder Abuse* (Columbia University Press, New York, 1989).

Endnotes

1. M. R. Block and J. D. Sinnott, *The Battered Elder Syndrome: An Exploratory Study* (Center on Aging, University of Maryland, College Park, Md., 1979).

2. B. Schlesinger and R. Schlesinger, eds., *Abuse of the Elderly: Issues and Annotated Bibliography* (University of Toronto Press, Toronto, 1988).

3. National Victim Center, "Elder Abuse," *Infolink* 1(17) (1992).

4. K. Pillemer and J. J. Suitor, "Elder Abuse," in V. B. Van Hasselt et al., eds., *Handbook of Family Violence* (Plenum, New York, 1988).

5. Compare M. R. Block and J. D. Sinnott, *The Battered Elder Syndrome: An Exploratory Study* (Center on Aging, University of Maryland, College Park, Md., 1979), with S. Steinmetz

and D. J. Amsden, "Dependent Elders, Family Stress and Abuse," in T. H. Brubaker, ed., *Family Relationships in Later Life* (SAGE, Beverly Hills, Calif., 1983).

6. M. F. Hudson and T. F. Johnson, "Elder Abuse and Neglect: A Review of the Literature," in C. Eisdorfer et al., eds., *Annual Review of Gerontology and Geriatrics,* vol. 6 (Springer, New York, 1986).

7. T. A. O'Malley et al., "Categories of Family-Mediated Abuse and Neglect of Elderly Persons," *Journal of the American Geriatrics Society* 32(5) (1984), pp. 362–369.

8. Ibid.

9. See R. S. Wolf and K. A. Pillemer, *Helping Elderly Victims: The Reality of Elder Abuse*

(Columbia University Press, New York, 1989); and M. A. Godkin, R. S. Wolf, and K. A. Pillemer, "A Case-Comparison Analysis of Elder Abuse and Neglect," *International Journal of Aging and Human Development* 28(3) (1989), pp. 207–225.

10. R. Bachman, "Elderly Victim," *Special Report, Bureau of Justice Statistics* (U.S. Department of Justice, Washington, D.C., 1992).

11. M. D. Pagelow, *Family Violence* (Praeger, New York, 1984), p. 359.

12. K. A. Pillemer and D. W. Moore, "Abuse of Patients in Nursing Homes: Findings from a Survey of Staff," *The Gerontologist* 29(3) (1989), p. 314.

13. K. A. Pillemer and D. Finkelhor, "The Prevalence of Elder Abuse: A Random Sample Survey," *The Gerontologist* 28(1) (1988), p. 51.

14. J. M. Otto, *Abuse of Adults Age 60+* (National Committee for the Prevention of Elder Abuse and the National Adult Protective Services Association, Boulder, Colo., February 2006).

15. As reported on the National Institute of Justice Web site, www.nij.gov/topics/crime/elder-abuse/extent.htm, accessed June 27, 2012.

16. U.S. House of Representatives, Select Committee on Aging, "Elder Abuse: A Decade of Shame and Inaction" (Hearings) (Government Printing Office, Washington, D.C., May 1, 1990).

17. Pillemer and Finkelhor, "The Prevalence of Elder Abuse," p. 51.

18. P. Decalmer and F. Glendenning, eds., *The Mistreatment of Elder People* (SAGE, London, 1993), p. 35.

19. G. Taler and E. F. Ansello, "Elder Abuse," *Associations of Family Physicians* 32(2) (1985), p. 107.

20. J. S. Bloom, P. Ansell, and M. N. Bloom, "Detecting Elder Abuse: A Guide for Physicians," *Geriatrics* 44(6) (1989), p. 44.

21. J. Tackenberg, "Teaching Caregivers about Alzheimer's Disease," *Nursing* 92 (May 1992).

22. P. A. Hall, "Elder Maltreatment Patterns: Items, Sub-Groups and Types, Policy and Practical Implications," *International Journal of Aging and Human Development* 28(3) (1989), pp. 196–205.

23. M. W. Galbraith, "A Critical Examination of the Definitional, Methodological, and Theoretical Problems of Elder Abuse," in R. Filenson and S. R. Ingman, eds., *Elder Abuse: Practice and Policy* (Human Sciences Press, New York, 1989), pp. 34–42.

24. R. S. Wolf and K. A. Pillemer, *Helping Elderly Victims: The Reality of Elder Abuse* (Columbia University Press, New York, 1989).

25. R. Wolf, C. Strugnell, and M. Godkin, *Preliminary Findings from Three Model Projects on Elder Abuse* (University of Massachusetts Medical Center, Worcester, Mass., 1982).

26. T. Hickey and R. L. Douglas, "Mistreatment of the Elderly in the Domestic Setting: An Exploratory Study," *American Journal of Public Health* 71 (1981), pp. 500–517.

27. R. S. Beckman and R. D. Adelman, "Elder Abuse and Neglect," in R. T. Ammerman and M. Hersen, eds., *Assessment of Family Violence, A Clinical and Legal Sourcebook* (Wiley, New York, 1992), p. 238.

28. J. L. Davidson, "Elder Abuse," in Block and Sinnott, eds., *The Battered Elder Syndrome*, pp. 49–55.

29. R. Wolf, M. Godkin, and K. A. Pillemer, *Elder Abuse and Neglect: Report from the Model Projects* (University of Massachusetts Medical Center, University Center on Aging, Worcester, Mass., 1984).

30. S. K. Steinmetz, *Duty Bound: Elder Abuse and Family Care* (SAGE, Newbury Park, Calif., 1988).

31. G. J. Anetzberger, *The Etiology of Elder Abuse by Adult Offspring* (Thomas, Springfield, Ill., 1987).

32. Steinmetz, *Duty Bound.*

33. R. Gelles, "An Exchange/Social Control Theory," in D. Finkelhor et al., eds., *The Dark Side of Families: Current Family Violence Research* (SAGE, Beverly Hills, Calif., 1983).

34. L. Phillips, "Theoretical Explanations of Elder Abuse: Competing Hypotheses and Unresolved Issues," in K. Pillemer and R. Wolf, eds., *Elder Abuse: Conflict in the Family* (Auburn House, Dover, Mass., 1986).

35. G. M. Sykes and D. Matza, "Techniques of Neutralization: A Theory of Delinquency,"

American Sociological Review 22 (1978), pp. 664–670.

36. J. F. Short Jr. and F. Strodtbeck, *Group Process and Gang Delinquency* (University of Chicago Press, Chicago, 1965).

37. S. K. Tomita, "The Denial of Elder Mistreatment by Victims and Abusers: The Application of Neutralization Theory," *Violence and Victims* 5(3) (1990), p. 171.

38. "Geriatrics: Responding to Elder Abuse," *Nursing* 24(9) (1994), p. 76.

39. H. I. Fredriksen, "Adult Protective Services: Changes with the Introduction of Mandatory Reporting," *Journal of Elder Abuse and Neglect* 1 (1989), pp. 59–70.

40. *Triad News* 2(1) (Fall 2000).

41. P. Ehrlich and G. Anetzberger, "Survey of State Public Health Departments on Procedures for Reporting Elder Abuse," *Public Health Report No. 106* (U.S. Department of Health and Human Services, Washington, D.C., March–April 1991), pp. 151–154.

42. M. S. Lachs and K. Pillemer, "Abuse and Neglect of Elderly Persons," *New England Journal of Medicine*, 332(7) (1995), p. 437.

43. B. E. Blakely, R. Dolon, and D. D. May, "Improving the Responses of Physicians to Elder Abuse and Neglect: Contributions of a Model Program," *Journal of Gerontological Social Work* 19(3) (1993), p. 35.

44. Ibid., p. 39.

45. J. R. Matlaw and D. M. Spence, "The Hospital Elder Assessment Team: A Protocol for Suspected Cases of Elder Abuse and Neglect," *Journal of Elder Abuse and Neglect* 6(2) (Summer 1994), p. 23.

46. R. S. Wolf and K. Pillemer, "What's New in Elder Abuse Programming? Four Bright Ideas," *The Gerontologist* 34(1) (1994), p. 126.

47. J. J. Regan, "Protective Services for the Elderly: Benefits or Threat?" in J. I. Kosberg, ed., *Abuse and Maltreatment of the Elderly: Causes and Interventions* (John Wright, PSG, Boston, 1983).

48. I. J. Sloan, *The Law and Legislation of Elderly Abuse* (Oceana, Dobbs Ferry, New York, 1983).

49. See, for example, the Uniform Probate Code Section 1-201(6) and 5-401(2).

50. *Black's Law Dictionary*, 6th ed. (West, St. Paul, Minn., 1990), p. 706.

51. Regan, "Protective Services for the Elderly."

52. *Report to the Governor and Legislature on the Activities of the Governor's Elder Abuse Prevention Task Force* (Florida Department of Elder Affairs, Miami, Fla., April 1997).

53. D. M. Reulbach and J. Tewksbury, "Collaboration between Protective Services and Law Enforcement: The Massachusetts Model," *Journal of Elder Abuse* 6(2) (1994), p. 9.

54. National Center for Elder Abuse, www.ncea.aoa.gov/, accessed August 31, 2015.

5

Physical Child Abuse

CHAPTER OBJECTIVES

After studying this chapter, you should be able to:

- Define and explain battered child syndrome;
- Explain what constitutes physical child abuse;
- Define and explain Munchausen syndrome;
- Understand the state laws dealing with child abuse;
- Define and explain shaken baby (abusive head trauma) syndrome;
- Understand the current controversy regarding the diagnosis of shaken baby syndrome.

Detailed Look at What You Should Know About Child Abuse

- The term *battered child syndrome* was coined in 1961 by Dr. C.H. Kempe.
- After Kempe's study, society began to accept the fact that parents, caretakers, and siblings do in fact engage in occasional or systematic battering of young children.
- *Battered child syndrome* is a medicolegal term that describes the diagnosis of a medical expert based on scientific studies that indicate that when a child suffers certain types of continuing injuries, those injuries were not caused by accidental means.
- All states have child abuse reporting laws mandating that caretakers report suspected cases of child abuse.
- **Physical child abuse** may be defined as any act that results in a nonaccidental physical injury by a person who has care, custody, or control of a child. This definition contains two key aspects: The act is intentional or willful, and the act resulted in a physical injury. An accidental injury does not qualify as child abuse.

- The physical battering of children is not a new phenomenon. Children have suffered trauma at the hands of their parents and caretakers since the beginning of recorded history.

- The Industrial Revolution was characterized by repeated maltreatment of children. Young children were forced to work long hours under inhumane conditions in factories or other heavy industries.

- Every state now has laws preventing the physical abuse of children.

- Cynthia Crosson Tower grouped several theories into three distinct models: the psychopathological model, the interactional model, and the environmental-sociological-cultural model.

- Children of all ages, all races, both genders, and all socioeconomic backgrounds have been victims of physical abuse. Several studies have examined whether certain children are more at risk of being abused than others.

- Richard Asher coined the term *Munchausen syndrome* in 1951 to describe patients who fabricated histories of illness.

- *Munchausen syndrome by proxy* was first described in 1977 by Dr. Roy Meadow.

- **Shaken baby syndrome** (SBS) is neurological damage caused by shaking the child violently back and forth. (The term *whiplash shaken baby syndrome* was originally used by Caffey to explain and highlight this type of injury.) Many medical providers now use the term "abusive head trauma."

- Craniofacial, head, face, and neck injuries are present in more than half of all the cases of child abuse. Some authorities believe that the oral cavity may be the central focus of abuse because of its role in communication and nutrition.

- Parricide is a form of family violence that has received little attention in any research and discussion.

- The most common parricide offender may be a chronically abused child who as an adolescent kills the abusing parent.

INTRODUCTION

Many would date the acceptance of the phenomenon of child abuse from 1961 with Dr. C. H. Kempe's use of the term **battered child syndrome.** However, Kempe and his associates were not the first physicians to study child abuse. As early as 1860, Dr. Ambrose Tardieu, a forensic pathologist in France, documented thirty-two incidents of children who had died as a result of battering.[1] In 1946, Dr. John Caffey, a radiologist, reported that a study of six children with subdural hematomas (SDHs) also showed other injuries, including multiple long-bone fractures, bruising, and hemorrhages.[2] Caffey came to the conclusion that in the absence of a skeletal disease, children who have both SDHs and long-bone fractures are the victims of trauma. Others in the medical profession accepted his premise, and this condition became known as **Caffey's syndrome.**

In 1961, when Kempe and his colleagues coined the term *battered child syndrome,* society began to accept the fact that parents, caretakers, and siblings do in fact engage in

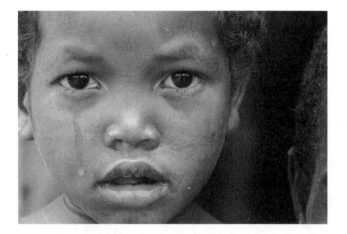

There is no justification for mistreating a young child.

occasional or systematic battering of young children.[3] Kempe and his associates wanted to use a catchy phrase to call attention to the serious medical problem they were studying. In 1961, at the meeting of the American Academy of Pediatrics in Denver, they used the term *battered child syndrome* to emphasize the problem of child abuse and point out that physical abuse was a significant cause of death and injury to children. Kempe's group stated, "The radio-logic manifestations of trauma are specific and the metaphyseal lesions in particular occur in no other disease of which we are aware."[4] *Battered child syndrome* is a medicolegal term that describes the diagnosis of a medical expert based on scientific studies that indicate that when a child suffers certain types of continuing injuries, those injuries were not caused by accidental means.[5]

Since the conference and the publication of Kempe's article "The Battered Child Syndrome" in the *Journal of the American Medical Association* in 1962, professionals have made substantial progress in understanding and diagnosing physical child abuse. Kempe's article resulted in an outpouring of concern from the general public and was the impetus for drafting a federal model child abuse reporting statute. As we discuss later in the textbook, all fifty states now have child abuse reporting laws mandating that caretakers report suspected cases of child abuse. This chapter discusses the various types of physical child abuse encountered by professional caretakers.

What is child abuse? Child abuse deals with physical force and injury to a child. The amount of force or injury to a child is the characteristic that distinguishes child abuse from normal discipline. Most of us in our younger years pledged never to use corporal discipline on our children. However, many parents acknowledge slapping a child's hand to bring attention to or correct unwanted behavior. Is this child abuse? The Practicum "Discipline of Children—Is It Child Abuse?" is designed to test values and judgments regarding corporal discipline before further discussing child abuse.

As the exercise demonstrates, there are many different views on disciplining children. Each of the acts described occurs in homes on a daily basis, and some result in children being

Practicum

Discipline of Children—Is It Child Abuse?

Assume none of the acts require the child to be hospitalized or treated by a physician. Which of the following acts are proper? Are any of them excessive? In your opinion, do any of them constitute child abuse?

Child, aged one year:

The child is reaching for the side of a hot woodstove. Which of the following acts are proper, and which are child abuse?

1. You allow the child to touch the stove to teach her a lesson.
2. You say "hot" and slap the child's hand.
3. You move the child to another part of the room without any infliction of punishment.

Child, aged two years:

The child throws food off the table during dinner.

1. You go on with dinner and tell the child not to do that anymore.
2. You require the child to pick up the food and eat it.
3. You send the child to bed without allowing him to finish dinner.

4. You pick up the food and force the child to eat it by stuffing it in his mouth.

Child, aged four years:

The child swears at you.

1. You tell the child to stop and not to do that again.
2. You wash the child's mouth out with strong soap.
3. You spank the child in a mild manner.
4. You slap the child across the face with your hand.
5. You use a belt on the child's legs and arms.

There will be differences of opinions as to which of the above reactions should be considered as child abuse. The differences highlight the problem of determining what constitutes child abuse. If you were a neighbor and observed a parent commit any of the above acts, would you report the parent to law enforcement as a child abuser? This also brings up the issue of what role should law enforcement take in the parenting of children?

treated at hospitals or walk-in clinics. If the injury is of sufficient magnitude, the medical practitioner may refer the matter to the authorities as a case of possible child abuse. The next section discusses the definition of child abuse and points out some of the problems encountered when attempting to define this concept.

DEFINITION

Is a parent considered unfit or abusive if while bathing his one-year-old daughter, she slips from his grasp and hits her head against the faucet, causing a cut over her eye that requires two stitches? Is this child abuse? While some might blame the father for not being alert to such dangers, most would not classify him as a child abuser. Accidents happen. They are a part of growing up, and painful as they may be to the parent and the child, they are part of a normal, healthy ongoing relationship. Thus, not all injuries children sustain can be classified as child abuse. If not all injuries are child abuse, and parents have a right to inflict corporal punishment on children as a form of discipline, how do we draw the line and define physical injuries to children?

Numerous authorities have defined child abuse. Part of the problem has been the continued debate on what the term *child abuse* means. Mildred Pagelow, Vincent B. Van Hasselt, Richard Gelles, and other scholars in the field have presented excellent discussions and definitions of this condition.[6] For purposes of this textbook and ease of understanding, one definition is used: **Physical child abuse** may be defined as any act that results in a nonaccidental physical injury by a person who has care, custody, or control of a child.

This definition contains two key aspects: The act is intentional or willful, and the act resulted in a physical injury. An accidental injury does not qualify as child abuse. In the example described earlier, an accidental slip in a bathtub does not qualify as child abuse even if the child received an injury that required several stitches. Child abuse as discussed in this chapter is manifested by physical injury that can be proved or documented. Simply yelling at the child is not child abuse within the meaning of this definition, nor is spanking the child on the hand, the face, or the buttocks if those acts did not result in a physical injury that can be documented. Although it is true that any form of spanking causes injury in the form of pain and some trauma to the child, unless the force is sufficient to leave marks, most medical and legal authorities do not classify these acts as child abuse. The lack of a clear definition is part of the problem of physical child abuse. The next section explores this issue and discusses the extent of child abuse in our society.

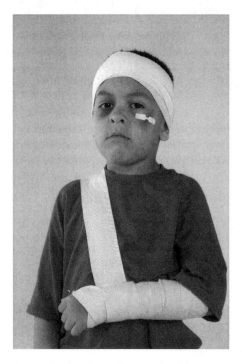

A young boy who has been beaten by his parents

Focus

Juvenile Offenders and Victims: 2014 National Report

It is estimated that one child in every twenty-five in the United States is abused or neglected. The National Center for Juvenile Justice (NCJJ) has listed the types of child mistreatment in its 2014 National Report. The NCJJ definitions are as follows:

Child maltreatment occurs when a caretaker (a parent or parental substitute such as a babysitter) is responsible for, or permits, the abuse or neglect of a child. The maltreatment can result in actual physical or emotional harm, or it can place the child in danger of physical or emotional harm.

Physical abuse includes physical acts that caused or could have caused physical injury to the child, including excessive corporal punishment.

Sexual abuse is involvement of the child in sexual activity either forcefully or without force, including contacts for sexual purposes, prostitution, pornography, or other sexually exploitative activities.

Emotional abuse refers to verbal threats and emotional assaults. It includes terrorizing a child, administering unprescribed and potentially harmful substances, and willful cruelty or exploitation not covered by other types of maltreatment.

Physical neglect is the disregard of a child's physical needs and physical safety, including abandonment; illegal transfers of custody; expulsion from the home; failure to seek remedial health care or delay in seeking care; or inadequate supervision, food, hygiene, clothing, or shelter.

Emotional neglect includes inadequate nurturance or affection, permitting maladaptive behavior, exposing the child to domestic violence or other maladaptive behaviors or environments, and other inattention to emotional or developmental needs.

Educational neglect includes permitting chronic truancy, failure to enroll, or other inattention to educational needs.

Source: M. Sickmund and C. Puzzanchera, eds., "Juvenile Offenders and Victims: 2014 National Report," *National Center for Juvenile Justice* (Pittsburgh, PA, December 2014).

EXTENT OF THE PROBLEM

One economic impact study conducted in 2007 concluded that based on data drawn from a variety of sources, the estimated annual cost of child abuse and neglect was $103.8 billion in 2007 value.[7] According to many researchers, this figure represents a conservative estimate as a result of the methods used for the calculation. The researchers also noted that children who are abused are more likely to experience adverse outcomes throughout their life span in a number of areas, including:

- Poor physical health (e.g., chronic fatigue, altered immune function, hypertension, sexually transmitted diseases, obesity);
- Poor emotional and mental health (e.g., depression, anxiety, eating disorders, suicidal thoughts and attempts, posttraumatic stress disorder);
- Social difficulties (e.g., insecure attachments with caregivers, which may lead to difficulties in developing trusting relationships with peers and adults later in life);

- Cognitive dysfunction (e.g., deficits in attention, abstract reasoning, language development, and problem-solving skills, which ultimately affect academic achievement and school performance);
- High-risk health behaviors (e.g., a higher number of lifetime sexual partners, younger age at first voluntary intercourse, teen pregnancy, alcohol and substance abuse); and
- Behavioral problems (e.g., aggression, juvenile delinquency, adult criminality, abusive or violent behavior).

Focus

Child Abuse Facts

- A report of child abuse is made every ten seconds.
- More than five children die every day as a result of child abuse.
- Approximately 80 percent of children who die from abuse are under the age of four.
- It is estimated that between 50 and 60 percent of child fatalities due to maltreatment are not recorded as such on death certificates.
- Child abuse occurs at every socioeconomic level, across ethnic and cultural lines, within all religions and at all levels of education.
- About 30 percent of abused and neglected children will later abuse their own children, continuing the horrible cycle of abuse.
- About 80 percent of twenty-one year olds who were abused as children met criteria for at least one psychological disorder.
- The estimated annual cost of child abuse and neglect in the United States for 2008 was $124 billion.

Source: Child Maltreatment 2009 (U.S. Department of Health and Human Services, Administration for Children and Families, Administration on Children, Youth and Families, Children's Bureau, 2010). Available at www.acf.h.gov/programs/cb/stats_research/index.htm#can

Focus

The Little Mary Ellen Case

In 1874, Henry Bergin, who was the founder and first president of the Society for the Prevention of Cruelty to Animals discovered that there were no laws protecting children from child abuse. He contended that children ought to be deemed just as worthy of protection from abuse that presently existed for dogs and cats. He acquired a lawyer to pursue the case involving little Mary Ellen.

Eight-year-old Mary Ellen was discovered by a social worker to have been beaten and starved by her adoptive parents. The social worker referred the case to the New York City Police Department, which refused to take any action because no laws addressed the abuse of children by their parents or caretakers. In an effort to save the child, the city filed charges against the caretakers using a statute that prevented cruelty to animals. The adoptive mother was sentenced to one year in jail, and the resulting publicity surrounding Mary Ellen's plight led to the formation of the Society for the Prevention of Cruelty to Children in 1875.

(continued)

The case, probably the first reported case on child abuse, went to court on April 10, 1874. In 1865, Mary Ellen had been orphaned as a baby. Her father was a Union soldier who died in the Second Battle of Cold Harbor, in Virginia. Her mother, who worked as a laundress, gave her up for adoption because she could not afford to care for Mary Ellen.

Mary Ellen testified in court that her adopted mother whipped her with a twisted rawhide whip. The child also testified that her adoptive mother had cut her with a pair of scissors and that child was afraid to talk in public because her mother would punish her. Mary Ellen was removed from her adoptive home. There is also evidence that Mary Ellen was not treated very well in her new home placement.

In 1875, Bergin, as the result of the Mary Ellen case, merged the Society for the Prevention of Cruelty to Animals into a new organization and formed the American Humane Association, which has pioneered standards for the protection of both children and animals.

Sources: H. Markel, "Case Shined First Light on Abuse of Children," *New York Times*, December 14, 2009, p. H-01; "The Beginnings of a Worldwide Child-Saving Crusade," American Humane Association Web site, www.american-humane.org/about-us/who-we-are/history/story-of-mary-ellen.html, accessed October 12, 2012; "Mary Ellen Wilson-America's First Recognized Child Abuse Case," Hub Pages Web site, http://hyphenbird.hubpages.com/hub/Mary-Ellen-Wilson-Americas-First-Child-Abuse-Case, accessed October 7, 2012; and Eric A. Shelman and Stephen Lazoritz, *Mary Ellen Wilson Child Abuse Case and the Beginning of Childen's Rights in 19th Century America* (McFarland Jefferson, NC, 2005).

HISTORICAL VIEW OF CHILD ABUSE

The physical battering of children is not a new phenomenon. Children have suffered trauma at the hands of their parents and caretakers since the beginning of recorded history. In Egypt, at the birth of Moses, the pharaoh ordered the death of all male children. King Herod also ordered infanticide on a large scale when Jesus was born.

Early history records the practice of burying infants alive in foundations of buildings.[8] Excavations of Canaanite dwellings have uncovered jars of infant bones in the foundations of buildings.[9] Although officially outlawed, this practice continued in seventeenth-century Europe, and children were found buried in the foundations of London Bridge.

Plato (428–348 B.C.) and Aristotle (384–322 B.C.) both urged the killing of infants born with birth defects. Children with birth defects, female infants, and the children of poor families were killed as a matter of course several hundred years before the birth of Christ. In Rome, the law of the Twelve Tables prohibited raising a child with a defect or deformity. In Sparta, infants were examined by a local council of elders who had the power to throw children considered unfit into a canyon.[10]

Infanticide was not the only form of abuse practiced by early civilizations. During the Middle Ages, families often mutilated or severed limbs from children to make them more effective beggars. The histories of the European school systems are filled with records detailing beatings and abuse that teachers inflicted on their young charges.

The Industrial Revolution was characterized by repeated maltreatment of children. Young children were forced to work long hours under inhumane conditions in factories or other heavy industries. Many were beaten, shackled, or starved to force them to work harder at their tasks.

The FBI's Uniform Crime Reports (UCR) are the accepted method for reporting crimes on a nationwide basis. The UCR publishes crime statistics reported by 16,000 law enforcement agencies. However, it provides no specific information on crimes against children. With the exception of murder, the UCR does not list the victim's age. The National Center on Child Abuse and Neglect (NCCAN), a division within the U.S. Department of Health and Human Services, has commissioned studies to provide a national estimate of the incidence of child maltreatment.

In 1986, the Prevent Child Abuse (PCA) America (formerly the National Committee to Prevent Child Abuse [NCPCA]) began collecting data from all fifty states and the District of Columbia on child abuse incidents.[11]

In August 2001, PCA America updated its 1999 Fifty State Survey.[12] This report indicates that PCA America estimates 3,244,000 children nationwide were reported to Child Protective Service (CPS) as alleged victims of child abuse or neglect. This translates into a rate of forty-six reported child victims for every 1,000 children in the United States. PCA America estimates that 1,070,000 of those reported cases of abuse or neglect were substantiated. This results in a rate of fifteen actual child victims for every 1,000 children in our nation. Nationwide, the rate of child abuse or neglect has risen 2 percent each year from 1994 through 1999.[13]

In September 2002, PCA America published a more alarming report dealing with child abuse fatalities.[14] In 2000, an estimated 1,356 children died as a result of child abuse or neglect.[15] PCA America examined three characteristics of these fatalities from 1998 through 2000. These characteristics included (1) prior or current contact with CPS, (2) types of abuse or neglect that led to the child's death, and (3) ages of the child victims. The following table illustrates the results of this investigation. These data indicate that 78 percent of the child fatalities involved children under the age of five and 40 percent under the age of one. We as a society must focus our attention on this alarming death rate among children.

Thirty-eight of the states were able to provide information regarding the causes of fatalities due to child abuse or neglect.[16] Physical abuse was the leading cause of death (51%), followed by child neglect (43%). The category of physical abuse included shaken baby syndrome (SBS), also known as abusive head trauma, blunt force trauma, suffocation or strangulation, and other intentional or dangerous acts. The category of neglect included medical neglect, lack of supervision, failure to protect, alcohol-related acts, and physical neglect.[17]

Many authorities believe that the number of reported cases of child abuse is only the tip of the iceberg. This is particularly true for those children between the ages of twelve and nineteen. This age group is far less likely than younger victims to report crimes, especially when the offender is not a stranger.[18] Part of the problem with determining the magnitude of physical child abuse may relate to the definition itself.

By defining the characteristics or hallmarks of physical child abuse differently, the research data itself can differ significantly. Researchers select their sample populations based on criteria that differ from scholar to scholar and from study to study. Some social scientists view physical child abuse in the context of determining whether the child is "at risk," whereas those working in the criminal justice field emphasize physical evidence. This multifaceted approach to understanding physical child abuse presents both problems and opportunities for growth. As mentioned earlier, the problem is how to reach consensus on the definition of physical child abuse and how we respond to it. The opportunities for growth are based on the premise that professionals can and should learn from each other. The social worker may learn of the difficulties in proving certain types of abuse while teaching the prosecuting attorney to accept the seriousness of a situation that might not otherwise be apparent from a legal perspective.

THE ABUSERS AND THE ABUSED

Both the magnitude and the definition of child abuse have caused problems in the area of family violence. Although the previous discussion defines physical child abuse, it does not establish who the perpetrators and who the victims are. This section briefly examines the parties to child abuse and how they relate to each other.

Who Are the Abusers?

As the next Practicum concerning Billy's abuse indicates, who the abuser is may vary depending on the facts. Some would argue that Julie is responsible, whereas others would lay the blame entirely on Howard. The fact that people who physically abuse children do not fit any stereotyped description further complicates the issue of physical child abuse. Abuse occurs in exclusive neighborhoods, middle-class suburbs, and inner-city slums, and it comes in all sizes, shapes, colors, and sexes. Many studies, theories, and models have been constructed in an attempt to categorize abusers but without success. One thing scholars can agree on, however, is that there is no single way of determining who a child abuser is.[19]

Rather than attempt to describe all acceptable theories of the causes of child abuse, this section sets forth one model that encompasses different theories. Cynthia Crosson Tower grouped several theories into three distinct models: the psychopathological model, the interactional model, and the environmental–sociological–cultural model.[20]

The **psychopathological model** stresses the characteristics of the abuser as the primary cause of abuse. The abuser's personality predisposes the abuser to injure the child. This model includes three separate approaches to child abuse: the psychodynamic model, the mental illness model, and the character-trait model.

The psychodynamic model is based on the work of C. Henry Kempe and Ray Helfer. It theorizes that a lack of bonding between the parent and the child is an important factor in child abuse. This model assumes that the abuser was part of a cycle of parental inadequacy. These individuals are unable to bond with children, and when a crisis occurs, they respond with abusive acts. This model also assumes that the abuser will engage in role reversal. In other words, the parents expect the child to nurture them instead of vice versa.

The mental illness model sets forth the proposition that a parent's mental illness is the primary cause of child abuse. This is a readily accepted theory because it is easy to believe that anyone who would repeatedly beat or torture a child must be crazy. Justice and Justice suggested this model as a viable category.[21] Although some scholars have found abusive parents to be mentally disturbed, many others argue that abusive parents do not fit any existing psychiatric classification. For example, Kempe found that less than 5 percent were psychotic.

The character-trait model focuses on specific traits of abusers without regard for how they acquired these traits. Scholars such as Merrill and Delsordo have categorized abusive parents by specific traits that cause child abuse.[22] Merrill's study included such traits as

Practicum

Billy M.

Julie M. is the twenty-year-old mother of Billy, aged two years. She is unmarried but has been living with Howard for the last year. Both Julie and Howard drink heavily and use cocaine. Six months ago, Julie returned from work and found a series of marks on Billy's legs. Howard stated that Billy would not quit crying, so he disciplined him with a belt. Howard believed this type of discipline was fine because his father used to beat him, and he turned out all right. While Julie wasn't happy with Howard's actions, she did not want to confront him because she was hoping they would eventually marry. Three months later, Julie and Billy were playing when Billy knocked over Howard's glass of whiskey. Howard hit Billy with the back of his hand, causing a small cut and swelling of the lip. Julie and Howard had an argument over this, but Julie took no further action, nor did she extract a promise from Howard that he would not commit similar acts in the future.

Last week, Julie was called by the emergency room at the local hospital. Billy had been brought in by Howard and was comatose. Howard did not have an adequate explanation for the injury, stating only that when he went to wake Billy up there was a bruise on his head. The nurse stated that it appeared Billy had suffered some trauma to the head.

Assuming there is a diagnosis of nonaccidental injury to Billy, who should be held responsible? Should Howard be liable? Should the fact that Howard drinks and uses narcotics enter into the picture? Is it a consideration that Howard may have been abused as a child? What about Julie? Should she have taken some action to protect Billy? If you had to proportion the blame or responsibility, how much would each party receive?

hostility, rigidity, passivity, dependence, and competitiveness. Delsordo's categorization of abusive parents' traits included mental illness, frustration, irresponsibility, severe discipline, and misplaced abuse.

The **interactional model** views child abuse as a result of a dysfunctional system. This category of abuse focuses on the following factors in child abuse: the role of the child, chance events, and the family structure.

The role of the child and the perceptions of the parent toward that child are viewed as the causes of child abuse by some scholars. Martin suggests not only that abuse requires a certain type of adult but also that certain acts of the child trigger the abuse. If the parent has certain expectations that the child does not meet, abuse may occur.[23]

"Chance events" is the somewhat inaccurate name given to events that prevent the parent from bonding with the child. This lack of attachment is viewed as a predisposition toward child abuse. Lynch suggests that difficulties in pregnancy, labor, or delivery can have a bearing on the attachment of the mother to the child.[24]

The family structure model theorizes that child abuse is a result of a dysfunctional family. The adult members of the family blame the child for their own shortcomings, and this leads to abuse.

The **environmental–sociological–cultural** model views stresses in society as the primary causes of child abuse. This category includes the following causes of child abuse: the environmental stress model, the social learning model, the social-psychological model, and the psychosocial systems model.

The environmental stress model proposes that factors such as a lack of education, poverty, unemployment, or occupational stress result in child abuse. As these outside forces build, the parent or caretaker is unable to cope and reacts by hitting or injuring the child.

The social learning model emphasizes the inadequacy of the parenting skills of abusive parents. These parents never learned appropriate responses to child rearing, and therefore their lack of skill leads to frustration. This frustration in turn causes abusive behavior.

The social–psychological model assumes that stress results from a number of social and psychological factors, including marital disputes, unemployment, and too many or unwanted children. These factors induce stress that causes the individual to react to the child in an abusive manner.

The psychosocial systems model stresses that abuse results from interactions within the family. The family as a system is out of balance and incapable of caring for the child. The child becomes the target for family members' frustration, and abuse is the result.

As the preceding discussion indicates, several theories attempt to explain who the abusers are and why they abuse children. Although no authority can point to one cause of child abuse, it is clear that it continues to occur. The causes of child physical abuse are multifaceted. Therefore, it is necessary to examine who the victims or recipients of this violence are to attempt to understand this phenomenon more fully.

The Victims

Children of all ages, all races, both genders, and all socioeconomic backgrounds have been victims of physical abuse. Several studies have examined whether certain children are more at risk of being abused than others.[25] Ammerman points out that children who are abused have a higher percentage of prematurity, low birth weight, mental retardation, and physical or sensory disabilities. In general, children who are difficult to manage or control may be at a higher risk of abuse than other children.[26]

The American Association for Protecting Children (AAPC) publishes an annual report on child maltreatment. While the use of reported incidents of child abuse has inherent problems, it does provide an overview of this phenomenon in the United States.[27] The average age of the victim is eight years. Twenty-seven percent of all child maltreatment cases involve physical abuse. Three percent of these cases involve life-threatening injuries, such as poisoning, fractures, or brain damage. Fourteen percent involve minor injuries, including bruises, cuts, or shaking. The remaining 11 percent are unspecified injuries.[28]

The National Incidence Surveys are another source for examining who the victims of physical child abuse are.[29] As with the AAPC report, problems arise in reporting and defining child abuse. Similar to the AAPC report, though, the National Incidence Surveys do provide insight into the nature and type of abuse and the most likely victims. In 1981 and 1988, two national surveys of professionals and their reporting practices provided information about the types of children who were abused or likely to be abused.

The National Incidence Surveys have clarified issues raised in earlier reports regarding duplicate reporting. This in turn has led to the elimination of the counting of duplicate reports in the NCCAN reports. These surveys, while subject to criticism, have sparked intense research efforts by professionals in the field to understand the incidence and types of physical child abuse.

Another method of determining who the victims of physical abuse are involves surveys of the general public. Some of the earliest studies of physical child abuse were conducted by surveying nationally representative samples. In 1965, Gill surveyed 1,520 adults regarding whether they had personal knowledge of a child who was injured in a nonaccidental manner.[30] Straus and Gelles conducted two surveys in 1975 and 1985 regarding physical abuse. Their survey found a decrease in the rate in which parents engage in violent acts toward their children. One explanation of the decrease may be structural changes in the families, improved living conditions, and the availability of treatment programs.[31]

This section has explored the various methods used to determine the extent and nature of physical child abuse. Different surveys and studies have attempted to provide a profile of the abused child, but to date there is no accepted method of predicting who will be the next victim. However, certain factors suggest that a child may be currently suffering from physical abuse. The next section examines those indications.

Practicum

Vallory Franklin was convicted of aggravated child abuse and sentenced to a term of twenty years imprisonment. Evidence at trial indicated that the victim was Franklin's granddaughter. The evidence also indicated that Franklin accused the five-year-old victim of cutting her brother's hair. When the child denied cutting her brother's hair, the evidence indicated that Franklin then held the victim down and poured boiling water on her arm, leg, and back. Franklin contended that the injury was an accident. As the result of the injuries, the child was transported to the Children's Hospital in Birmingham and remained there for ten days for treatment of her injuries.

On appeal, the appellate court reduced the conviction from aggravated child abuse to child abuse and returned the case to the trial court for resentencing. It appears that the jury was instructed on the elements of child abuse and not on the aggravated child abuse. The new punishment range provided for confinement from one year to ten years. If you were the trial judge at the new sentencing hearing, what range of punishment would you be inclined to assess?

Source: Franklin v. State of Alabama, 2008 Ala. Crim. App. LEXIS 216 (2008).

Focus

NFL Player Suspended for Disciplining His Son

In 2014, a National Football League star player, Adrian Peterson, was indicted on one count of injury to a child in Montgomery County, Texas. Peterson's attorney claimed that Peterson was only disciplining his son and that he had used a switch to spank his son. Peterson was suspended from the NFL for the 2014 season. The boy had suffered cuts and bruises to areas including his back, buttocks, ankles, and legs. In November 2014, Peterson pleaded no contest to misdemeanor reckless assault.

This case raising an interesting question: At what point does the act of disciplining a child become child abuse?

INDICATIONS OF PHYSICAL CHILD ABUSE

All professionals should be aware of the indications of physical child abuse. Many times, less serious injuries precede more life-threatening injuries. As discussed later in this chapter, certain specific types of physical injuries are strongly associated with physical abuse. This section reviews the more commonplace indicators of physical child abuse that may be observed by a caretaker, teacher, or other professional.

Location and Types of Injuries

The location and types of physical injuries a child suffers may suggest physical child abuse. Many times the child, parent, or person responsible for caring for the child will deny any wrongdoing or that the child is even suffering from any physical injury.[32] Although care should always be exercised when dealing with any checklist, the following facts should at the very least alert any professional to inquire further into the situation at home.

Psychological/Behavioral Symptoms

Unfortunately, many physically abused children are overlooked because the telltale marks of injuries are covered by clothing. Therefore, in addition to the physical indicators, caretakers and professionals must be aware of certain psychological or behavioral actions on the part of the child. These actions should be viewed with caution because nonabused children may exhibit some or all of the symptoms. It should raise a suspicion on the part of caretakers or professionals, however, and alert them to the possibility that the child may be a victim of physical child abuse.

Explanation of Injuries

Many times, certain physical injuries are as consistent with child abuse as they are with normal, healthy childhood development. Every practitioner must be aware of the possibility of abuse and pay particular attention to the caretaker's explanation of the child's injury. The explanation and the injury may be inconsistent and therefore suggest child abuse. Following are some of the more common explanations that should be carefully evaluated by any professional in the field.

Summary of Findings of the National Incidence Surveys

- Children from poor families—those earning less than $15,000 a year—were five times as likely to be abused and more than seven times as likely to suffer serious injury or impairment.
- Family size is associated with abuse—more children increased the chance or probability of abuse.

- Race, ethnicity, and where children live have no relationship to abuse.
- The incidence of child abuse increased with the child's age.

UNEXPLAINED INJURY.   When the caretaker claims to have no knowledge of the injury or denies any knowledge of how the injury occurred, a very strong likelihood of physical abuse exists.[33] Most nonabusive parents can explain how and why their child was injured. They will readily discuss the accident and injury with medical or professional staff.

IMPOSSIBLE EXPLANATION.   One of the strongest indicators of physical child abuse is a caretaker's statement that is implausible and inconsistent with common sense and medical judgment. Some caretakers will describe a minor accident that resulted in major or life-threatening injuries. In one case, a father stated his six-month-old daughter must have injured herself when she fell off the couch. The daughter died as a result of multiple injuries that were inconsistent with such a simple fall.[34]

DIFFERENT VERSIONS OF THE INCIDENT.   When both caretakers are present, they should be questioned separately. Many times, they will have different versions of how the accident occurred. This is a strong indication of abuse. If the child is old enough, he or she should be asked to tell what happened. If the child's version is significantly different from the caretaker's story, the injury should be carefully evaluated for signs of abuse.

DIFFERENT EXPLANATIONS.   An abusive caretaker may have difficulty keeping their story straight when it must be repeated to different persons. One story may be told to the emergency room doctor, a slightly different version to the CPS worker, and still a third scenario

TABLE 5.1 Indicators of Child Abuse	
Physical Indicators	**Behavioral Indicators**
Unexplained bruises or welts that may be in various stages of healing, in clusters of unusual patterns, or on several different areas	Easily frightened or fearful of adults and parents, physical contact, or when other children cry
Unexplained burns in the shape of a cigarette, rope, or iron or caused by immersion, which may appear socklike or glovelike	Destructive to self and/or others Extremes of behavior: aggressive or withdrawn
Unexplained lacerations to mouth, lips, arms, legs, or torso	Poor social relations Learning problems, poor academic performance, short attention span, delayed language development
Unexplained skeletal injuries, stiff or swollen joints, or multiple or spiral fractures	Runaway or delinquent behavior Reporting unbelievable reasons for injuries
Missing or loosened teeth	Complains of soreness or moves awkwardly
Human bite marks	Accident-prone
Bald spots	Wears clothing that is clearly meant to cover
Unexplained abrasions	the body when not appropriate
Appearance of injuries after school absence, weekend, or vacation	Seems afraid to go home

Source: Based on Richard Layman, *Current Issues: Volume 1. Child Abuse* (Omnigraphics, Detroit, 1990), p. 34. Originally circulated by the Children's Safety Project in Manhattan.

may be described to the investigator. Different stories should immediately alert any professional to the possibility of physical child abuse.[35]

DELAY IN SEEKING MEDICAL ATTENTION.   Concerned parents usually bring their child for medical care as soon as possible after an accident. They have nothing to hide and are seeking care for their child. Delay in seeking medical care, especially for life-threatening injuries, is an indicator of possible child abuse.

Discovery of the location, nature, and extent of injuries in a child physical abuse case is only the first step in the process. The injury must be examined, documented, and treated. The nature or type of injury often will be suggestive of certain types of abuse. The next four sections review injuries normally associated with physical child abuse.

BRUISES

Bruises come in all sizes, shapes, colors, and locations. Children are full of energy and attempt feats that they do not have the physical capability of achieving at their age. They fall when walking, trip on rugs and cut their lips, or try to climb stairs and topple down. This is part of growing up, but in some cases certain types of bruises, because of the shape and location, will suggest a darker or more sinister cause. This section examines these types of bruises.

The first two situations in the next Practicum describing the injured eighteen-month-old child are consistent with normal, healthy child rearing. However, the last situation adds facts that should alert any practitioner to potential physical abuse. Multiple injuries are described—a cut lip, bruises on the forearm and back of the legs—and, most important, the mother's dating of the last accident is inconsistent with the typical aging of bruises.

Bruises should be examined from several aspects: time of injury, location, and pattern. Each of these factors alone may indicate nonaccidental injury. On the other hand, an acceptable explanation may account for some of the injuries.

Timing of the Injury

Bruises can be a physical clock that can provide a date or time of the initial injury, because as a bruise ages it changes color. Depending on the intensity of the injury, contusion resolution varies. However, typical bruises age in the following manner:

0–5 days	Red/purple/blue
5–7 days	Green
7–10 days	Yellow
10–14 days	Brown
2–4 weeks	Clear

Location of the Bruise

As indicated previously, normal, healthy, well-cared-for children will injure themselves. Many times an injury manifests itself as a bruise. Bruises on the front portion of the arms, legs, and face may be consistent with normal childhood activities. Normal bruises occur over bony prominences such as the knees, anterior tibia (that portion of the bone that extends from the knee to the ankle on the front of the leg, sometimes called the shinbone), and forehead.[36]

Practicum

Situation 1: An eighteen-month-old child was brought to a walk-in clinic with a cut lip. He was accompanied by his mother, who stated that he had fallen against the edge of the living room table while playing. The doctor who examined the child determined it would take three stitches to close the cut. Does this fact pattern alert you to child abuse? Assume there are no more facts at this time. Justify your answer.

Situation 2: While conducting a preliminary examination of the child described above, the doctor observed pale green circular bruises on the front of the child's forearms. On questioning the mother, she replied that he had fallen approximately seven days earlier while playing on the cement patio at their apartment. Do the additional facts supplied in situation 2 change your opinion? Why? Why not? Justify your answer.

Situation 3: In addition to the pale green bruises on the front of the child's forearms, the doctor observed two large round blackish-purple colored bruises on the back of the child's legs. The mother responded that the child was very active and two weeks ago had fallen against the back of a swing set, hitting the back of his legs. Do the additional facts have any bearing on your opinion?

Bruises from falling onto objects are usually circular or oval with nondescript edges.[37] However, bruises on the back of the arms or legs or on the back, abdomen, genitals, buttocks, and other soft-tissue areas should be viewed with suspicion.[38] Careful attention should be given to any explanation offered by the parent or custodian of the child. The location of the bruise is an important indicator of nonaccidental injury. Also, the pattern or shape of the bruise may confirm this diagnosis.

Bruise Patterns

Normal bruising takes different shapes and sizes. However, some bruise patterns are strong indicators of abuse. These patterns are inflicted by objects or excessive force applied to a portion of a child's body. Schmitt describes the traditional bruises left by belts, switches, cords, or ropes:

> Strap marks are sharp-bordered, one- to two-inch wide rectangular bruises of various lengths, sometimes covering a curved body surface. These are almost always caused by a belt. Sometimes, the eyelets or buckle of the belt can be discerned. Lash marks are narrow, straight-edged bruises or scratches caused by thrashing with a tree branch or switch. Loop marks are secondary to being struck with a doubled-over lamp cord, rope, or belt. The distal end of the loop strikes with the most force, commonly breaks the skin, and may leave loop-shaped scars.[39]

These are not the only types of suspicious bruising patterns. Other typical patterns of non-accidental bruises include the following:

Eyes	Bilateral black eyes
Ear lobe	Pinch and pull marks
Cheek	Slap marks, squeeze marks, or gag marks
Upper lip	Bruises
Scalp	Bare head and broken hair, bruises

Neck	Choke marks
Upper arms	Grab marks
Chest	Fingertip encirclement marks
Inner thighs	Pressure marks and fingertip marks
Genitals	Pinch marks and wrapping of penis
Ankles/wrists	Tethering or friction burn marks
Feet	Pen or razor tattoo marks

Simply because a child is bruised does not mean that he or she is abused. Medical personnel should be requested to conduct a blood coagulation study to determine whether the child's blood composition causes him or her to bruise more easily than other children.[40] In addition, care must be given to distinguishing between Mongolian spots or allergic shiners, which are accepted physical conditions that do not indicate physical abuse. *Mongolian spots* are irregular areas of deep blue pigmentation, usually in the sacral (lower back) or gluteal (buttocks) regions, seen predominantly in newborns of African, Asian, or Latin descent.[41] *Allergic shiners*, also known as *acute contact dermatitis*, are simply an allergic reaction on the skin. If these factors are considered and ruled out, the care provider should seriously consider physical abuse as the cause of the injury.

As the previous discussion indicates, normal bruising occurs in all sizes and shapes. However, certain bruises, because of the timing, location, or pattern, should raise suspicion in any professional. As bad as bruises may seem, in the scheme of things they are probably the least serious form of physical child abuse. The next section examines a more deliberate and cruel form of abuse—intentionally burning a child.

BURNS

Burns are a common form of child abuse and are often inflicted as a form of punishment. The victim is normally an infant or child under the age of three.[42] As in the case of bruises, distinctive types of burns are highly indicative of physical child abuse.

Burns are referred to as either "partial" or "full thickness." The medical classification of burns includes *first-degree burns*, which are partial-thickness burns. These burns are characterized by localized redness, appear sunburn-like, and usually heal by themselves. They are not included when calculating burn size. *Second-degree burns* are also partial-thickness burns. They are characterized by partial skin damage, blisters containing clear fluid, and pink underlying tissue. They often heal by themselves. *Third-degree burns* are full-thickness burns. These burns exhibit full destruction of the skin, deep red tissue underlying the blister, the presence of bloody blister fluid, and sometimes muscle and bone damage. Third-degree burns require professional treatment. *Fourth-degree burns* are also full-thickness burns and are considered the most serious type of burn. They are characterized by penetration of deep tissue to fat, muscle, and bone and require immediate professional treatment.[43]

Water or Immersion Burns

Water or **immersion burns** are a common form of physical child abuse. These burns are caused by a caretaker holding the child in hot water. Many times they result from the

Focus

Establishing Child Abuse

H. A. C. (mother) brought her child, who was seven weeks old at the time, to the emergency room at Vanderbilt Hospital on February 13, 2008. The day before she brought the child to the emergency room, she had taken the child to the pediatrician because the child had been suffering from colic and was constantly crying. The pediatrician noticed a swelling in the child's leg and instructed the mother to take the child to the emergency room at Vanderbilt Hospital.

At Vanderbilt, x-rays were taken of the child's leg that revealed a fractured femur. As a result, the hospital ordered x-rays of the child's entire body, which revealed the child also suffered from two broken ribs. Due to the nature of the injuries, the Child Abuse Review and Evaluation (CARE) team was notified. The CARE team conducted an evaluation and determined the child's injuries to be consistent with nonaccidental trauma and child abuse. The physicians determined the fractured femur most likely occurred one to two days before the x-rays, and the rib fractures were a minimum of nine days old.

A social services worker and an investigator interviewed the mother and the father to determine the cause of the child's injuries. Both parents gave a series of explanations, including the child falling six inches from a "bouncy seat" the previous week, incidents with a two-year-old dog, and the mother pushing down on the child's leg while changing his diaper. After consulting with physicians, it was determined that the explanations given could not have caused the child's significant injuries. Further investigation by the CARE team resulted in explanations from both the mother and the father that could have possibly caused the child's injuries: Mother admitted to pulling the child across the bed by the leg, and the father admitted to picking up the child and squeezing him around the chest and back while frustrated.

The Department of Children's Services filed a petition against both parents to declare the child dependent and neglected based in part upon severe child abuse. Father agreed to an Order of Adjudication that the child was dependent and neglected and to a finding that he committed severe child abuse. Mother contested the petition. Following a hearing on June 17, 2008, the juvenile court found the child dependent and neglected partly based on a finding that the mother had committed severe child abuse. Following an appeal by the mother, the circuit court found the child to be dependent and neglected and that the mother had committed severe child abuse.

The appellate court noted that the evidence clearly established that the father committed severe child abuse; however, the evidence did not support that finding as to the mother. There was no direct evidence to establish that the mother knowingly abused the child or that she knowingly failed to protect the child from severe abuse by the father. The evidence did not convincingly establish that the mother knowingly failed to protect the child by not immediately seeking medical care for the child or by not reporting an event to medical providers or the authorities. The judgment of the trial court was reversed as to the finding of severe child abuse by the mother. Note: The father did not appeal the decision.

Do you agree with the appellate court that the evidence did not establish that the mother knew of the child abuse?

Source: State Dep't of Children's Servs. v. H. A. C., 2009 Tenn. App. LEXIS 241 (Tenn. Ct. App. Mar. 26, 2009).

parents' frustration over bed-wetting or potty training.[44] The child may be forcibly restrained in scalding-hot (130-degree) water. If the child is held down in a tub, many times the burn resembles a donut shape on the buttocks area. Glovelike or stocking-shaped burns indicate that the hand or foot of the child was immersed in hot liquid. An unrestrained child in hot

TABLE 5.2 Classification of Burns	
Classification	**Characteristics**
First degree	Partial-thickness burns
	• Characterized by erythema • Appear sunburnlike • Are not included when calculating burn size • Usually heal by themselves
Second degree	Partial-thickness burns
	• Part of skin has been damaged or destroyed • Have blisters containing clear fluid • Pink underlying tissue • Often heal by themselves
Third degree	Full-thickness burns
	• Full skin has been destroyed • Deep red tissue underlying blister • Presence of bloody blister fluid • Muscle and bone may have been destroyed • Require professional treatment
Fourth degree	Full-thickness burns
	• Penetrate deep tissue to fat, muscle, bone • Require immediate professional treatment

Source: Based on *Burn Injuries in Child Abuse* (U.S. Department of Justice, Washington, D.C., May 1997).

water might not be able to get out but would thrash around and create splash burns and a blurring of the outline of the burn. When a child is held down in hot water, splash burns are minimized, and the outline of the burn is clear.[45]

Pattern Burns

A second form of burn is known as the **pattern burn.** These burns are caused by holding or pressing a portion of the child's body against a hot object. The majority of these burns involve irons, stove burners, heater grates, or woodstoves. An accidental burn of this nature usually involves a brief, glancing contact with a small portion of the hot surface. Accidental burns are usually deeper and more intense on one edge of the burn. Intentional burns are characterized by symmetrical, deep imprints with clear margins of the entire burned surface.[46] Many times the actual outline of the grate or stove burner is imprinted on the child's body.

Cigarettes form another type of pattern burn. While it is possible for a small child to be accidentally burned by a lit cigarette, burns on the genitals, abdomen, and bottom of the feet are normally caused intentionally by a caretaker.[47] These burns are deep and circular and often are grouped together. Abuse is very likely if the burns are located on parts of the body that are normally covered with clothing.[48]

Some skin conditions may simulate intentional burns. Professionals should be aware that it is sometimes difficult to distinguish between burns inflicted as a form of child abuse and certain diseases and medical conditions. The following are two of the more common medical conditions that may be interpreted as intentional burns:

Cutaneous (Skin) Infections. Some infections may have patterns that resemble deliberate burn injuries. Impetigo and severe diaper rash sometimes resemble a scald injury. A careful medical history, microbiological tests, and observation of the lesion over a two- to three-week period will usually provide sufficient information to determine whether these conditions are child abuse burns or just infections.

Hypersensitivity. A substance in citrus fruits such as limes, when in contact with the skin and exposed to sunlight, may produce a pattern on the skin that resembles a splash burn. An allergic reaction may cause a severe local skin irritation that also may be mistaken for a burn. Finally, certain skin preparations such as topical antiseptics can cause a similar burn appearance. A complete medical history will allow professionals to distinguish between these conditions and child abuse.[49]

Although burns are certainly serious and may be life threatening, they are not the most serious form of physical child abuse. Munchausen syndrome by proxy (MSBP) or fictitious disorder by proxy is another type of child abuse and is discussed next.

MUNCHAUSEN SYNDROME BY PROXY

Munchausen syndrome by proxy has recently become a widely discussed type of child abuse.[50] It may be defined as a psychiatric disorder, whereby individuals intentionally produce physical symptoms of illness in their children.[51] The *Diagnostic and Statistical Manual of Disorders*, fifth edition (DSM-V) classifies this condition as "fictitious disorder by proxy" and states that the essential feature of this disorder is the deliberate production of feigned physical or psychological signs or symptoms in another person who is under the individual's care.[52] It is still being researched but has surfaced as a diagnosis in a number of cases.[53]

Munchausen syndrome by proxy (MSBP) is now considered as a mental health problem in which a caregiver makes up or causes an illness or injury in a person under his or her care, such as a child, an elderly adult, or a person who has a disability. Because vulnerable people are the victims, MSBP is considered a form of child abuse or elder abuse.

Introduction

Richard Asher coined the term *Munchausen syndrome* in 1951 to describe patients who fabricated histories of illness. These individuals described complex medical histories and often displayed symptoms of the alleged disease. These fabrications invariably led to complex medical interventions and hospitalizations. Asher named this disorder after Baron von Munchausen, born Hieronymous Karl Fredrich von Munchausen, an eighteenth-century German baron and mercenary officer in the Russian cavalry. The baron was famous for dramatizing his "amazing" adventures. Some might describe him as a world-class teller of tall tales. Adult Munchausen syndrome is characterized by a person who seeks care from doctors for symptoms that are false or self-induced. These individuals are demanding and often display rage toward the medical caretakers. One authority has characterized their rage as directed toward their parents, whom they perceive abandoned them. The medical caretakers have taken the place of the parents and now receive the brunt of the person's rage.[54]

There is some debate as to who first used the term *Munchausen syndrome by proxy*. Money used it in 1976 to describe four children who were so severely abused that they were dwarfed.[55] However, in 1977 Meadow also used the term to describe the more commonly accepted definition of this form of abuse. Meadow examined two children who were being poisoned by a parent. The parent knew what was happening but encouraged the medical professionals to search for a diagnosis. This diagnostic process was painful and dangerous to the children.[56]

Focus

Michigan v. Mathis

Defendant Mathis was convicted by a jury of involuntary manslaughter and second-degree child abuse. He was sentenced to seven to fifteen years' imprisonment on the manslaughter conviction, and two to four years' imprisonment on the child abuse conviction. Defendant appeals the convictions, arguing insufficiency of the evidence.

The case concerned the death of two-year-old Jayvon Fuller. Jayvon's father is George Taylor, and his mother is Meshell Fuller. Taylor and Fuller were never married and stopped living together around the time of Jayvon's birth. Taylor had custody of Jayvon, and although there was no formal visitation agreement, Fuller would regularly visit Jayvon. Fuller worked as a prostitute, and defendant was her pimp. Defendant Mathis and Fuller lived together, but they did not reside at any fixed residence. Rather, they would move from hotel to hotel. At times, Fuller would visit with Jayvon at whatever hotel she and defendant were currently staying. There was evidence that defendant always paid for the hotel room in which Fuller would visit with Jayvon. There was also evidence that defendant and Fuller shared the costs for Jayvon's food during visits, defendant bought shoes for Jayvon, defendant would consistently provide Fuller with money, and that he frequently helped Fuller take care of Jayvon during hotel visits. Furthermore, the record

indicated that defendant shared in the responsibility of changing Jayvon's diapers, bathing him, and disciplining Jayvon. When Fuller and defendant visited with Jayvon at the various hotels, Fuller would at times engage in acts of prostitution while defendant babysat Jayvon.

On March 25, 2006, Taylor dropped Jayvon off at the home of Fuller's mother for a visit, a regular occurrence, and Fuller and defendant thereafter picked up Jayvon from the home of Fuller's mother and took him to a local hotel, also a regular occurrence. At the beginning of this visit, Jayvon appeared happy and healthy. During the week that defendant and Fuller cared for Jayvon at the hotel, Fuller engaged in at least five acts of prostitution, at which time defendant cared for Jayvon. Several days into the visit at the hotel, on a Wednesday, defendant gave Jayvon a "whooping" for urinating on the bed, which included defendant striking Jayvon in the abdomen. According to Fuller, Jayvon's appearance and health then began to change. He started vomiting, refused to get out of bed, was lethargic, and although he attempted to eat, Jayvon could not keep any food down. Fuller and defendant, who were staying in the same hotel room along with Jayvon, did not seek medical attention for Jayvon. Fuller called her mother about the situation, and she opined that Jayvon probably had the flu. Jayvon's health continued to deteriorate

(continued)

on Thursday and Friday, yet no medical attention was sought. On that Thursday, Jayvon's abdomen began to swell, and on Friday night defendant called a pharmacist who recommended that Jayvon be given Tylenol and that Jayvon's abdomen be rubbed with ice wrapped inside a towel. Defendant administered the Tylenol to Jayvon, but no other steps were taken. Jayvon's condition further deteriorated, he continued vomiting, and on Saturday morning defendant discovered that Jayvon was no longer breathing, which he communicated to Fuller, who called 911.

A responding police officer testified that Jayvon was unresponsive, had no pulse, and was not breathing, and the officer indicated that Jayvon's abdomen was extremely distended, looking like an "overfilled basketball." The officer stated that the appearance of Jayvon's abdomen was "very abnormal" and that the distension was immediately apparent. Another responding officer testified that defendant stated that Jayvon had been vomiting for three days, and the officer further indicated that she observed vomit-stained sheets and towels in the hotel room, vomit on the room's two beds, and vomit around the beds. Marijuana was also found in the room. Jayvon did not respond to efforts by paramedics to revive him. One paramedic, who had treated children in the past, testified that Jayvon's abdomen was extremely swollen, hard, and very abnormal. He had never before observed such a severe condition in a child.

A treating physician testified that Jayvon's abdomen was extremely distended, approximating the size of a basketball, and that the extent of the distension was unusual. The physician inserted a needle into Jayvon's abdomen, resulting in a release of air and a foul smell. Medical personnel detected a shallow pulse and some blood pressure, and the treating physician found it necessary, and received approval, to perform an operation to determine the source of Jayvon's abdominal distension. During the procedure, the physician discovered that Jayvon's bowel "was all matted together and stuck." He opined that Jayvon had been suffering from the symptoms of the abdominal condition for several days.

During an interview with police, defendant stated that Jayvon had been supervised exclusively by defendant and Fuller during the previous week. Defendant denied ever hitting or otherwise striking Jayvon. Defendant conceded that he had brought marijuana into the hotel room.

As an appellate justice, would you rule that the evidence was sufficient to convict the defendant of manslaughter?

Source: *Mich. v. Gannon*, 2008 Mich. App. LEXIS 2086 (Mich. Ct. App. Oct. 21, 2008), in which the appellate court ruled that there was sufficient evidence to support the finding of guilty to the manslaughter charge upheld the conviction.

Symptoms

The warning signs of the disorder include repeated hospitalizations and medical evaluations without definitive diagnosis, inappropriate symptoms and/or medical signs that are inconsistent, signs and symptoms that disappear when the child is away from the parent, a parent who welcomes medical tests of the child even if they are painful, increased parental uneasiness as the child recovers, and a parent who is less concerned with the child's health and is more concerned about spending time with hospital staff.[57]

In 1993, Children's Healthcare of Atlanta added facilities to perform covert inpatient video surveillance of suspected cases of MSBP. The results of that procedure were published in *Pediatrics*, a respected medical journal.[58] A multidisciplinary team was formed, and the team considered monitoring patients only when they believed a diagnosis of MSBP was probable. Hidden audio and video equipment covered all areas of the patient's room except for the

TABLE 5.3 Common Presentations of Munchausen Syndrome by Proxy and the Usual Methods of Deception

Presentation	Mechanism
Apnea (breathing stops)	Suffocation, drugs, poisoning; lying
Seizures	Drugs, poisons, asphyxiation; lying
Bleeding	Adding blood to urine, vomit, etc.; opening intravenous line
Fevers, blood infection	Injection of feces, saliva, contaminated water into the child
Vomiting	Poisoning with drugs that cause vomiting; lying
Diarrhea	Poisoning with laxatives, salt, mineral oil

Source: Based on Donna Rosenberg, *Child Neglect and Munchausen Syndrome by Proxy*, 2nd printing (U.S. Department of Justice, Washington, D.C., August 1997).

bathroom. Consent was obtained by including the statement "Closed circuit monitoring of patient care may be used for educational or clinical purposes" on the admission form for consent to treat. In addition, a sign at the entrance to the hospital informed visitors and incoming patients that the facility was monitored and recorded by hidden cameras.

Focus

In the Matter of Arielle McCabe

Karrie McCabe, the mother, appealed from an order entered by a trial judge in North Carolina who determined that her minor daughter Arielle was an abused and neglected child. The mother argued that there was insufficient evidence to support the determination. The appellate court concluded that there was clear, cogent, and convincing evidence to support the trial court's findings and conclusions. The court noted that three physicians, two of whom were experts in the area of child abuse, testified that the juvenile was the victim of Munchausen syndrome by proxy, a form of child abuse with a substantial risk of morbidity and even mortality. One doctor opined that the mother potentially induced these symptoms by either smothering the juvenile or administering a toxin. Although the evidence presented by one of the doctors did raise conflicting inferences as to the cause of the juvenile's cyanotic episodes, that doctor conceded that benign paroxysmal acrocyanosis and Munchausen syndrome by proxy were not

mutually exclusive, and that the juvenile might be suffering from both. The appellate court agreed with the trial judge's findings that there was a substantial risk of serious physical injury to the juvenile and that the child lived in an environment injurious to her welfare supported the adjudication of neglect and abuse.

The appellate court noted that an expert witness, Dr. Kabeanfuller, testified during the hearing in the trial court that Munchausen syndrome by proxy ...

> was first described in 1977 by a Dr. Roy Meadow. He was the first one to put case reports out in the literature, and since then there have been hundreds of case reports and many reviews and actual books written on the subject. It is a case where we often see children where they have either a parent or a caretaker who will either simulate or induce an illness in the child, present them for medical care multiple

(continued)

times, and often deny any knowledge of the symptoms or the signs, what their etiology is and then when that child is removed from that caretaker's or parent's care, these signs and symptoms abate and no longer occur.

Dr. Kabeanfuller further stated that juvenile also potentially suffered from "vulnerable child syndrome," which she explained as

> a syndrome we sometimes see in pediatrics where a child who is otherwise well and healthy is presented multiple times for medical care by a parent or caretaker who is convinced that the child is ill or has some serious symptoms and requires a lot of reassurance by the physicians or medical

personnel but in fact there is no organic disease process going on in the child.

Dr. Kabeanfuller noted that

> there's a continuum of an illness going from vulnerable child all the way to Munchausen syndrome where you have vulnerable child where the child actually is well and the parent is just overly concerned, and then the next, it can evolve into a Munchausen syndrome by proxy, um, type situation because you can have a child whose parents or caretaker believes that they're ill when they truly are not or may evolve into a parent who creates symptoms or fabricates a history in order to present that child to various physicians and receive various medical procedures.

Source: In re McCabe, 157 N.C. App. 673 (N.C. Ct. App. 2003).

Practicum

More hospitals are considering installing hidden video cameras in certain rooms where children who are suspected to be victims of this type of abuse will be placed. The camera will monitor the activity of the child as well as the caretakers.

1. What type, if any, of notice should there be at the entrance to the hospital regarding the fact that some areas are under surveillance by video cameras?

2. What ethical issues do you see in this proposal?
3. If the cameras were installed and a parent or caretaker was filmed committing acts of abuse on the child, should law enforcement officials be allowed to use the film in any subsequent prosecution?
4. Prior to the use of the cameras, should the parents be informed that they may be monitored?

Source: D. Hall, L. Eubanks, S. Meyyazhagan, R. Kenny, and S. Johnson, "Evaluations of Covert Video Surveillance in the Diagnosis of Munchausen Syndrome by Proxy: Lessons from 41 Cases," *Pediatrics* 105 (June 2000), p. 1305.

The study also classified MSBP parents into two types: inducers and fabricators. *Inducers* were those parents who induced disease or injury directly into or onto the child. For example, a parent who smothered the child or gave the child incorrect or dangerous medication would be classified as an inducer. *Fabricators* were those parents who committed no inducement of disease but created a "disease" by lying about its presence or staging it. An example of a fabricator involved a parent who gagged and vomited and then claimed her vomit was the child's.

A diagnosis of MSBP was made in twenty-three of forty-one of the patients who were monitored in this fashion. However, in four other cases, the video conclusively established the innocence of the parents of children who were suspected to be victims of MSBP. The authors of this study recommend that all children's hospitals develop protocols and facilities to perform covert video surveillance.

Another authority classified MSBP into two different types: *simulation*, a mild and rare form in which the perpetrator feigns an illness of the victim by verbally presenting an untrue history of a nonexistent illness, and *production*, a severe and more frequent form in which the perpetrator actively produces symptoms of the illness in the victim by either internal or external manipulations.[59]

More reports continue to surface that reinforce the conclusion that MSBP is of continuing concern.[60] Some authorities predict that 10 percent of these child victims will die at the hands of their parents.[61] Professionals in the field must recognize this form of child victimization and respond accordingly.[62]

FRACTURES

The human body is an incredible machine that is supported by a series of connecting bones. Bones grow at a fast rate in the young and are very flexible, but as we mature these same bones become more brittle. Many students of family violence have experienced a broken bone or know someone who has. Most of the time this is a painful and traumatic experience. Normally, a great deal of force is needed to fracture or break one of the major bones, and although accidents may happen to young children and infants, certain types of fractures are very strong evidence of physical child abuse.

Unfortunately, this scenario occurs daily in medical institutions throughout the United States. Children are brought to walk-in clinics, emergency rooms, and family doctors with serious nonaccidental bone fractures. Certain types of fractures are strongly indicative of child abuse (see the next Practicum).

Types of Fractures

Unlike bruises and burns, fractures are internal and veiled in mystery, in part because of the Latin names associated with the different parts of the body. Professionals must have a basic understanding of the major bones in the body to understand the dynamics of physical child abuse and fractures in particular. The most common fractures in child abuse cases in order of occurrence are as follows:

1. *Rib:* The rib cage is that portion of the chest that protects the lungs and heart
2. *Humerus:* The upper bone of the arm from the elbow to the shoulder
3. *Femur:* The thigh bone extends from the hip to the knee and is one of the strongest bones in the body
4. *Tibia:* The shinbone is the inner and larger bone of the leg between the knee and the ankle
5. *Skull:* The bony framework of the head
6. *Hand:* That part of the body that is attached to the forearm at the wrist
7. *Ulna:* The inner and largest bone of the forearm, located between the wrist and the elbow on the opposite side of the thumb
8. *Radius:* The outer and shorter bone of the arm, located between the wrist and the elbow on the same side as the thumb

Fractures in children may be inflicted by hitting, shaking, or squeezing. Many times a frustrated caretaker will suddenly strike out at a child, and an injury results. As indicated earlier, the abusive parent's explanations of the injury are often not consistent with the medical evidence. This is especially true in the case of fractures.

Any time a professional suspects child abuse, consideration should be given to a complete x-ray series. Radiologists can detect multiple healed fractures by the presence of calcium deposits around them. Numerous fractures are a strong indication of physical abuse.

Because of certain distinctive characteristics, one particular type of fracture deserves special attention. Spiral fractures in children under the age of three almost always support a diagnosis of physical child abuse. The next section examines this serious form of physical abuse.

Spiral Fractures

Spiral fractures are usually a break in the humerus or femur resulting from a twisting motion. Although any adult skier may have experienced a spiral fracture on the ski slopes, it is extremely rare as an accidental injury in children under three years of age. A spiral fracture may occur during skiing when the leg is held motionless and the body twists, causing the femur to break in a turning or twisting motion. Nonaccidental spiral fractures occur when the caretaker grasps the leg or the arm at the top and the bottom and gives it a powerful twist.

Many times, parents will claim the child's foot was stuck under something and the fall caused the injury. Most medical professionals will discount this explanation because there is insufficient force with that type of fall to cause a spiral fracture in children under three. Also, young children have very limber bones that bend before they break. Other explanations may include jumping off the couch, falling while playing, slipping in the bathtub, and so on. None of these acts are capable of producing the force necessary to twist and break a bone.

Practicum

You have been called to the local emergency room by a doctor who is concerned about an eleven-month-old girl. The doctor informs you that the girl's father brought the infant to the emergency room at approximately 7:00 P.M.. The child was crying, and her left upper thigh appeared swollen. X-rays revealed a spiral fracture of the femur.

The doctor informs you that in her opinion this is a nonaccidental injury that was caused by someone who grasped the child's leg in their hands and twisted it. Based on this information, you approach the father in the waiting room, identify yourself as a representative from the county child protective services agency, and ask whether you can talk about the child's injury.

The father informs you that he just returned from a trip, and on arriving at home found his live-in girlfriend very upset and crying. The girlfriend stated that his daughter had injured herself by catching her foot in the bars and falling down inside the crib. The father immediately brought the child to the emergency room. On further questioning, the father indicated that he has been dating the girlfriend, a registered nurse, for five months, and she has never displayed any anger toward the child or himself.

Using this information, what is your next course of action? What additional information would be helpful to you in making a decision as to the proper course of action?

The More Common Types of Physical Child Abuse Fractures

Avulsion of the metaphyseal tips (chip and bucket handle)

Traction force, jerking, and twisting—most commonly observed on the humerus, radius, and femur

Skull fractures

May indicate increased intercranial pressure—the child has received blunt-force trauma of some sort to the head

Rib fractures

Blunt-force trauma—the child has been hit, punched, thrown, tossed, swung, or pummelled, resulting in compression trauma; the child has received pressure pushing inward on the rib cage or has been squeezed

Clavicle fractures

Not necessarily related to physical abuse but should be viewed with suspicion with other findings that may indicate abuse, such as multiple injuries or inconsistent stories by the caretaker

Sternum and scapula fractures

Direct blows to the body

It is hard to believe that any adult would intentionally injure a child by striking, squeezing, or twisting the child's body or limbs to the point of causing these types of injuries. However, fractures in young children are a common form of physical abuse. The final type of physical injuries may be the most dangerous form of child abuse.

HEAD AND INTERNAL INJURIES

These last two forms of physical child abuse are among the most dangerous and life threatening. Frustrated caretakers often shake, punch, or kick a child with resulting head or internal injuries. In addition, many times these caretakers postpone seeking medical treatment, which increases the life-threatening nature of the injury.

Head Injuries

Head injuries are the most common cause of morbidity and mortality in abused children.[63] Injuries to the brain are often caused by a direct blow with a blunt instrument, such as a fist, stick, or other object. Other children suffer brain injuries as a result of being thrown against the wall or onto the floor.

The brain is covered with three thin membranes (meninges). The membrane next to the brain is the *pia mater*. The next membrane is the *arachnoid*. The outer membrane is called the *dura mater*. The space between the pia mater and the arachnoid contains spinal fluid. Blood veins traverse the subarachnoid area. Violent shaking can cause bleeding in this space. The accumulation of blood in this area is called a **subdural hematoma**.[64] SDHs occur over the surface of the brain and are caused by the tearing of the bridging vessels between the brain and the dura. The acceleration–deceleration and rotational forces associated with trauma are the major causes for SDH development.[65] Bleeding may also occur within the other membranes surrounding the skull. Subarachnoid hematoma (SAH) is bleeding between the arachnoid

Focus

Child Abuse and Babysitters

Several years ago, the press had a feeding frenzy when an au pair (a live-in nanny who cares for children in exchange for living expenses) was accused of killing one of the children under her care. Louise Woodward was tried for second-degree murder in the death of eight-month-old Matthew Eappen. The jury found her guilty and imposed a life sentence. The trial court determined that there was insufficient evidence to establish that Woodward had deliberately killed Matthew and reduced the verdict to involuntary manslaughter.

Source: Commonwealth v. Woodward, 427 Mass. 659 (Mass. 1998).

Recent studies have examined the issue of crimes by babysitters against children. Finkelhor and Ormrod found that babysitters are responsible for a relatively small percentage of crimes committed against children. Approximately 4.2 percent of all crimes against children under the age of six were committed by babysitters. This is much smaller than the 53.5 percent of crimes committed against this same age group by family members.

Children most at risk for physical assault by babysitters were one to three years old, whereas children aged three to five were at risk for sex crimes by babysitters. Males committed 77 percent of all the sexual offenses, whereas females committed 64 percent of the physical assaults against children in their care.

Source: Based on D. Finkelhor and R. Ormrod, *Crimes against Children by Babysitters* (Office of Justice Programs, Washington D.C., September 2001).

Focus

How Much Force Is Necessary?

Internal injuries are not caused by simply spanking or slapping the child. A significant amount of force is necessary to rupture the liver or spleen, cause intestinal perforation, or inflict serious damage to the pancreas. Children who fall from their cribs do not sustain these types of injuries.

A Wisconsin case provides an excellent example of the use of a medical expert to establish that the force necessary to inflict the injuries far exceeded those that a child would suffer by falling from a crib. The case involved the death of a child (Shannon). The father claimed that the child was injured by falling down the stairs. The State called Dr. Robert Huntington, a forensic pathologist, who had performed the autopsy on Shannon.

Dr. Huntington's testimony regarding the cause of Shannon's death is summarized as follows: (1) He concluded that it was "a blunt force injury that tore this mesentery and from which she bled to death"; (2) the force had to be "a concentrated force" because the liver and spleen were not damaged as they would be if a person's abdomen had hit a broad surface, as in a car accident; (3) the vector or direction of the force was heading up into the abdomen and toward her back; (4) he estimated that this tear was a "quite recent injury," which would have had to occur within "four hours from the point of death," but that an injury such as this kind could kill "within a few minutes," this being the minimum amount of time from injury to death.

(continued)

He based this opinion on the medical fact that Shannon could not have survived the amount of blood she lost for a very long time; and (5) while stating that he was not sure "whether the child slammed into something or whether something slammed into the child," he stated that the kinds of objects which would have caused the concentrated force could have been "a fist or a foot or some solid object." Dr. Huntington indicated that the solid object also could have been "one of these big old fashioned round bannister ends a corner of a table or something like that." He stated that, in layman's terms, a concentrated force comparable to what Shannon experienced would result from a fifty- or sixty-mile-per-hour head-on collision.

Does the doctor's testimony regarding the cause of the injury rule out the possibility that it was caused by an accidental injury?

Source: State v. Johnson, 135 Wis. 2d 453, 460 (Wis. Ct. App. 1986).

and the pia mater. Epidural hematoma (EDH) is a collection of blood between the skull and the dura.[66]

Skull fractures result from sharp blows to the head or from throwing the child against a wall or onto the floor. In a depressed fracture, bone fragments are pressed into the skull cavity. Caretakers often claim that this type of severe head injury resulted from the child falling off the couch or bed. This type of story should be viewed with suspicion because medical research indicates that a life-threatening injury to the head requires at least a fifteen-foot fall.[67]

Two less serious forms of head injury to children are concussions and cerebral contusions. A **concussion** is a mild form of diffuse brain injury associated with the acceleration–deceleration of shaking the child's head. A **cerebral contusion** is the bruising of the brain without puncture or tearing of the pia membrane. Contusions are caused by the absorption of energy into the cerebral tissue from a blow to the head.

Shaken baby syndrome is neurological damage caused by shaking the child violently back and forth. (The term *whiplash shaken baby syndrome* was originally used by Caffey to explain and highlight this type of injury.) These injuries occur when the caretaker shakes the baby back and forth with the head being whipped from one direction to another, causing the brain to move inside the skull, which results in cerebral concussion and/or SDH. This type of abuse is largely restricted to children under three years of age, with the majority of injuries occurring in the first year.[68] Common symptoms include irritability, seizures, retinal hemorrhages, lethargy, increased or decreased tone, impaired consciousness, vomiting, and breathing difficulties.

Excerpts from a New Jersey state criminal court:

The shaken baby syndrome was first identified and named by Dr. John Caffey in his seminal article, "The Whiplash Shaken Infant Syndrome: Manual Shaking by the Extremities with Whiplash-Induced Intracranial and Intraocular Bleedings, Linked with Residual Permanent Brain Damage and Mental Retardation," 54 *Pediatrics* 396 (1974). It is a term used to connote conditions, such as those described in the title, which may typically result from vigorously shaking a young child. Since 1974, the syndrome (also referred to as *whiplash shaken infant syndrome* or *shaken infant syndrome*) has been recognized authoritatively in medical journals. See, for example, Derek A. Bruce and Robert A. Zimmerman, "Shaken Impact Syndrome," 18 *Pediatric*

Annals 482 (1989); Randell Alexander, et al., "Serial Abuse in Children Who Are Shaken," 144 *American Journal of Diseases of Children* 58 (1990); Luke J. Haseler, et al., "Evidence from Proton Magnetic Resonance Spectroscopy for a Metabolic Cascade of Neuronal Damage in Shaken Baby Syndrome," 99 *Pediatrics* 4 (1997); see also Millard Bass, et al., "Death-scene Investigation in Sudden Infant Death," 315 *New England Journal of Medicine* 100, 104, 105 (1986) (citing John Caffey, "On the Theory and Practice of Shaking Infants: Its Potential Residual Effects of Permanent Brain Damage and Mental Retardation," 124 *American Journal of Diseases of Children* 161 [1972]).

Source: State v. Compton, 304 N.J. Super. 477, 485–486 (App. Div. 1997).

The instances of shaking are directly proportional to the degree of frustration felt by the perpetrator. Men outnumber women as perpetrators of shaking by a 2 to 1 ratio. Caretakers, including babysitters, are now being examined as possible perpetrators. Risk factors of caretakers include immaturity, young age, and lack of life experience.[69] From a medical perspective, no other medical condition fully mimics all the features of SBS, which continues to take on more importance as the medical profession acknowledges its effect on children. This form of abuse is an accepted medical diagnosis. Some medical professionals argue that although there are no accurate statistics regarding its incidence, there is a consensus that head trauma is the leading killer of abused children and that SBS is involved in many of these cases.[70]

Issues Regarding the Diagnosis of Shaken Baby Syndrome

A 2015 medical research report has questioned the diagnosis of shaken baby syndrome. According to this report, shaken baby syndrome has been a recognized diagnosis for several decades, though the new label is abusive head trauma. The diagnosis is defined by a constellation of symptoms known as the triad: brain swelling, bleeding on the surface of the brain, and bleeding behind the eyes. The medical profession routinely accepted those three symptoms by themselves as evidence that a crime had been committed, even in the absence of bruises, broken bones, or other signs of abuse. Some doctors now doubt that some babies have been abused. These doctors assert that factors other than shaking, and having nothing to do with criminal behavior, may sometimes explain the existence of the triad.

About 1,600 cases involved in the diagnosis have resulted in a conviction, a rate that is higher than that for other violent crimes. In many cases, there were reports of shaking along with more obvious forms of violence that left extensive bruises and broken bones, with prosecutors alleging that babies also had been slammed, thrown, or beaten.[71]

According to forensic expert Gregory Davis, chief medical examiner in Birmingham, Alabama, and board chair of the National Association of Medical Examiners, "You can't necessarily prove [Shaken Baby Syndrome] one way or another—sort of like politics or religion. Neither side can point to compelling evidence and say, 'We're right and the other side is wrong.' So instead, it goes to trial."[72]

Oral Injuries

Craniofacial, head, face, and neck injuries are present in more than half of all the cases of child abuse. Some authorities believe that the oral cavity may be the central focus of abuse because of its role in communication and nutrition. Oral injuries may be inflicted by eating utensils, a baby bottle during forced feeding, hands, fingers, or hot liquids. One study indicated that the lips were the most common site for inflicted oral injuries. While unintended injuries to the mouth are common and must be distinguished from intentional acts of abuse, multiple injuries, injuries in different stages of healing, or insufficient explanation should arouse suspicion.[73]

Bite marks should be examined with care. Bites caused by dogs and other carnivorous animals tend to tear flesh, whereas human bites compress flesh and can cause abrasions and lacerations but rarely cause avulsions of the tissue.[74]

Internal Injuries

Chest and abdominal injuries are common physical child abuse injuries. Rib fractures may be caused by grasping a child around the chest and by shaking the child. In addition, the caretaker may strike a child with his or her fist or a blunt object.

Focus

Excerpts from the Georgia Supreme Court Decision in Whitaker v. State, 2012 S12A0640

After a jury trial, Tony Whitaker was found guilty of felony murder and cruelty to children. The trial court entered judgment of conviction for the felony murder and sentenced appellant (defendant) to life imprisonment. He appealed the denial of a motion for new trial.

Excerpts from Court's Decision

Looking at the evidence in support of the verdicts, indicates one Shonda Sweet left her thirteen-month-old twin sons with defendant while she ran errands for the day. At some point, defendant phoned his godmother, Dorothy Williams, asking her to come over to his house. Ms. Williams, noticing that Appellant sounded upset, drove to Appellant's home with her husband Dennis and her daughter Denata. Upon arriving, Appellant asked Ms. Williams to check on Darrius, one of the twins, because he could not awaken him. When Ms. Williams entered the bedroom, she saw Darrius lying face down on the corner of the bed and his lips were purple. Mr. Williams called 911, and Denata attempted to perform CPR on Darrius but had no success. Paramedics arrived and tried to revive the child.

Darrius was then taken to the hospital, but he was declared dead on arrival.

Speaking with hospital staff and law enforcement, Appellant reported that Darrius had been ill and indicated that he had heard something fall and found the child on the floor next to the bed. Appellant stated that the child was breathing and that he placed the child back on the bed. Later, when he went to check on Darrius, he saw that the baby was not breathing and that he had been vomiting out of the mouth and nose.

The forensic pathologist who performed the autopsy found swelling and a patterned injury on the back of the head, suggesting that the victim's head was struck on an uneven surface. There were circular bruises on the forehead indicating "grip marks where somebody's grabbed the child's head and squeezed vigorously, or knuckle marks where somebody's rapped a knuckle on the head, or even knuckle marks in terms of punching." The victim also had several fractures in his skull. The pathologist testified that, because the plates in the skull of a thirteen-month-old child are not yet

(continued)

fully hardened, the cause of the skull fractures must have been a sharp force. The victim also suffered damage to his brain, including hemorrhages and bruising and swelling of the brain itself. The victim had bruises along the buttocks, back, and head. The pathologist testified that these injuries were acute, meaning that they were less than three to four hours old. He concluded that the injuries were caused by blunt force trauma by shaking and impact, with the bruises along the victim's body corresponding with where the victim was likely grabbed. The pathologist also stated that the victim could not have sustained the type and severity of injuries as those found from simply falling off a bed.

Appellant (defendant) contended that the evidence against him was merely circumstantial and thus the State was required to show that the proved facts excluded every other reasonable hypothesis save that of his guilt. According to appellant, the proved facts were consistent with his theory that the victim died from injuries related to falling off the bed.

Questions as to reasonableness are generally to be decided by the jury which heard the evidence and where the jury is authorized to find that the evidence, though circumstantial, was sufficient to exclude every reasonable hypothesis save that of guilt, the appellate court will not disturb that finding, unless the verdict of guilty is unsupportable as a matter of law. It is the role of the jury to resolve conflicts in the evidence and to determine the credibility of witnesses, and the resolution of such conflicts adversely to the defendant does not render the evidence insufficient.

Here, it is undisputed that the victim did not have the physical injuries outlined above when Ms. Sweet left her house on the day of the crime. It is also undisputed that, besides the victim's baby brother, Appellant was the only person present during the hours in which the victim was physically injured and began to show signs of shaken baby syndrome. The pathologist testified that the location and severity of injuries was inconsistent with a mere fall from the bed. And the jury was not required to believe Appellant's version of events, but was authorized to weigh it against the medical testimony. Therefore, after reviewing the evidence in the light most favorable to the verdict, we conclude that the evidence is sufficient to have authorized a jury to find that the State excluded all reasonable hypotheses except that of Appellant's guilt, and to have authorized any rational trier of fact to find Appellant guilty beyond a reasonable doubt.

What is the role of a jury in a disputed child abuse case? Is the medial evidence as summarized sufficient to establish beyond a reasonable doubt that the death was caused by nonaccidental causes?

Abdominal injuries are caused by hitting a child in the stomach area. This striking may be a kick, a punch, or a blow from a blunt object. As with other forms of physical child abuse, these injuries usually result from a frustrated caretaker who lashes out at the child.

The previous discussion briefly examined head and internal injuries. Care should be taken that medical assistance is obtained as soon as possible whenever a child is suspected of being physically abused. Many of these injuries are not visible to the naked eye but, if left untreated, may become life threatening.

CHILD HOMICIDE

Children who are killed as a result of child abuse represent one of the most tragic aspects of family violence. We are still attempting to learn the true extent of this form of violence, but as

Focus

How Many Children Die from Abuse or Neglect?

Child fatalities are the most tragic consequence of maltreatment. Yet, each year many children die from abuse and neglect.

- For fiscal year 2010, fifty states reported a total of 1,537 fatalities. Based on this data, it was estimated that about 1,600 children die from abuse and neglect each year.
- Of the reported fatalities for FY 2010, the overall rate of child fatalities was 2.07 deaths per 100,000 children.
- Nearly 80 percent (79.4%) of all child fatalities were younger than four years old.

- Boys had a higher child fatality rate than girls at 2.51 boys per 100,000 boys in the population.
- Girls died of abuse and neglect at a rate of 1.73 per 100,000 girls in the population.
- More than 30 percent (32.6%) of child fatalities were attributed exclusively to neglect.
- More than 40 percent (40.8%) of child fatalities were caused by multiple maltreatment types.

Source: Child Maltreatment Report (U.S. Department of Health & Human Services, Administration for Children and Families, Administration on Children, Youth and Families Children's Bureau, 2012). Available at their Web site.

is the case with other types of family violence, we face several structural obstacles. For example, at present there is a lack of agreement on terminology when dealing with child homicide. The National Child Abuse and Neglect Data System (NCANDS) defines *child fatality* as a child dying from abuse or neglect because either (1) the injury from the abuse or neglect was the cause of death or (2) the abuse and/or neglect was a contributing factor to the cause of death.[75] Prominent academics such as Finkelhor use the term *child abuse homicide* to define child death resulting from maltreatment by a responsible caretaker.[76] Many law enforcement agencies also use the term *child abuse homicide* but include both caretaker acts and criminal acts by noncaretakers.

Most researchers agree that children under the age of three are at the highest risk. Some go farther, claiming that the majority of child deaths occur within the first year of life. Overpeck and her associates conducted a significant study of infant homicide in the United States.[77] Linking birth and death certificates for all births in the United States between 1983 and 1991, they identified 2,776 homicides during the first year of life, with half occurring by the fourth month of life. The authors examined the literature in the field and concurred with the generally accepted proposition that the relationship of the perpetrator changes with the age of the child. Homicide committed during the first week after birth is normally perpetrated by the mother, whereas the father or the stepfather is normally the perpetrator from that time until the age of three. Homicide involving children over the age of three is usually committed by a person unrelated to the child. They concur with other researchers that child homicide is probably undercounted.

Because of the problems inherent in any investigation of children who have been murdered, some agencies have established child fatality review teams.[78] These are multidisciplinary, composed of prosecutors, coroners, law enforcement officers, CPS workers, public health professionals, and others. These teams review cases of child deaths and facilitate any necessary follow-up investigation or services.

PARRICIDE

Parricide is the killing of one parent. It is a form of family violence that has received little attention in any research and discussion. Since 1976, when the FBI began reporting homicides according to victim-offender relationship, parricide is listed in 300 to 400 cases. This amounts to 1.5 to 2.5 percent of all homicides committed in the United States each year. Mones points out that except for brothers killing their sisters, parricide is the rarest form of interfamily homicide.[79]

The most common parricide offender may be a chronically abused child who as an adolescent kills the abusing parent.

Four distinct issues are raised whenever parricide is discussed:

1. Generally speaking, **parricide** refers to the killing of one's parents. Parricide may take three forms: (1) patricide, or killing one's father; (2) matricide, or killing one's mother; and (3) double parricide, or killing both parents.
2. Most parricide cases involve the existence of long-term and debilitating child abuse. Lawyers who represent parricide offenders claim that over 90 percent of all their clients have been abused.[80]
3. Sons are more likely than daughters to strike back at their parents.
4. Abuse sometimes increases during adolescence as the child experiences independence and personality changes. These changes cause some parents to feel a loss of control and power that they compensate for by increasing abuse. One authority indicates that because the teen years are a very emotional time, parricide commonly occurs during this period.[81]

Focus

Death and Demons

Larry Carrasco was convicted by a Sacramento jury of killing his five-year-old stepdaughter, Alexia, by forcing her to drink bleach in an apparent attempt to exorcise demons from her. Alexia's sister was also forced to undergo the torture. She testified that Carrasco and their mother forced them to drink bleach cocktails made from vanilla ice cream, bleach, and other ingredients, supposedly to remove demons and vampires. After Alexia died, the mother and Carrasco cut her body into pieces and burned it in the family fireplace. The ashes and cutting instruments were then dumped in the Sacramento River.

In a criminal trial court, Larry Carrasco and the mother Barbara Carrasco were convicted of murdering Barbara's daughter, Alexia.

Larry was also convicted of assault resulting in Alexia's death, and torturing, unlawfully punishing, and willfully inflicting great bodily injury on Barbara's older daughter, Jessica.

Barbara was sentenced to incarceration for fifteen years to life, and Larry was sentenced to incarceration for fifteen years to life for second-degree murder of Alexi, twenty-five years to life for assault resulting in the death of a child, and an indeterminate life term for torture of Alexia.

Source: People v. Carrasco, 2002 Cal. App. Unpub. LEXIS 2888 (Cal. App. 3d Dist. 2002).

Heide points out that parricide is typically committed by youths who fit into one or more of the following classifications: (1) the severely abused child who pushed beyond his or her limits, (2) the child with severe mental illness, or (3) the dangerously antisocial child.[82] The severely abused child may have suffered physical, sexual, or emotional abuse. The child with mental illness may be suffering from a mental disorder so severe that he or she may be unable to cooperate with the defense attorney and therefore unable to stand trial. The dangerously antisocial child may be a psychopath or sociopath who is suffering from mental disorder and yet is aware of the nature and type of his or her actions. Heide correctly concluded that some parricide offenders may represent a blend of this typology. We are still researching this form of family violence. It is controversial and steeped in misinformation and emotion. What is known about this type of homicide is sketchy and subject to debate. The next sections briefly examine parricide as it relates to child abuse.

History

Parricide is discussed in early Greek mythology. For example, Oedipus killed his father and married his mother. Alcmaeon murdered his mother, Eriphyle, to punish her for sending his father to his death, and Orestes murdered his mother, Clytemnestra, to avenge her killing of his father.[83]

Parricide is also documented in early Rome. In 59 A.D., Nero was crowned emperor of Rome. His mother, Agrippina, had plotted and maneuvered for years to secure the crown for her son. She also psychologically abused Nero during his childhood. Even after being crowned emperor, Nero was frightened and controlled by his mother. When he finally confronted her, she threatened him publicly. Aware of his mother's power over him and fearing that she would kill him, Nero ordered her death.[84]

One of the earliest recorded parricides in the United States occurred in 1867, when a seventeen-year-old girl murdered her stepfather. Prior to the killing, she disclosed to others that he had been abusing her since she was thirteen. No one reacted to her pleas for help, and when her stepfather learned of her actions, he ordered her to be silent or he would send her to a reform school. Feeling trapped and with no one to turn to, she poisoned her stepfather. She was found guilty and sentenced to an insane asylum.[85]

One of the most famous parricides involved Lizzie Borden, who, in 1892, allegedly murdered her mother and father with an ax. She and her sister were heirs to a sizable inheritance. The theory behind the prosecution case was that Lizzie killed her parents on the basis of greed and a desire to obtain their estate. The jury acquitted her on the grounds that she was a nice Christian woman who was incapable of committing such a violent crime. One author suggests that in retrospect evidence suggests that Lizzie Borden may have been a victim of sexual abuse by her father and killed her parents as a result of this long-term relationship.[86]

The relationship between child abuse and parricide was first acknowledged in the Richard Jahnke case. In 1982, after years of physical abuse, sixteen-year-old Jahnke shot and killed his father. He was convicted of voluntary manslaughter and sentenced to five to fifteen years in state prison. This case captured the nation's attention as the first case in which a parricide offender raised the issue of self-defense. The defense also used expert witnesses to support their theory of self-defense, and this may account for the jury's verdict of voluntary manslaughter instead of murder.[87]

The next widely publicized parricide case occurred in 1986, when Cheryl Pierson had her father killed. Cheryl was a sixteen-year-old high school cheerleader who was found guilty of manslaughter for hiring a classmate to murder her father. Cheryl claimed that when her mother became ill when she was twelve, her father began sexually molesting her. When her mother died, the sexual attacks intensified, and he also started to physically abuse her. As her younger sister was about to turn twelve, Cheryl was afraid she would be her father's next victim, so she hired a classmate to kill her father. Her story seemed to sway the judge who imposed a light sentence for such a crime of only six months in jail with five additional years on probation.[88]

In August 1989, brothers Lyle and Erik Menendez allegedly left their bedrooms, armed with shotguns, and entered the family room of their wealthy Beverly Hills estate, where they shot and killed both their parents as they were eating ice cream. The slaying of their parents and their subsequent trials resulted in widespread publicity regarding this form of violence. In 1993, their first trial resulted in hung juries (the brothers were tried together, but each had a separate jury). Two years later, the second trial resulted in their conviction of murder despite their claims of years of sexual abuse. The brothers claimed that they had endured years of psychological and physical abuse from both parents, and that their father sexually molested them. They claimed that they killed their parents out of fear for their own lives, because they believed that their parents were about to kill them for threatening to expose the abuse to the authorities. The prosecution alleged that the brothers were pathological liars who shot their parents in cold blood for the millions of dollars they would inherit.[89]

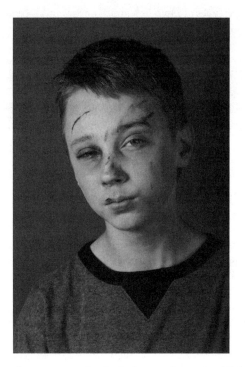

**How do we stop physical abuse of young children
such as that experienced by this young boy?**

Who Are The Killers?

Most juveniles who commit homicide kill either strangers or acquaintances. Adolescent parricide offenders are more likely than other juvenile homicide offenders to have been victims of child abuse.[90] Another study indicates that adolescent parricide offenders are mainly submissive and nonviolent with a few incidents of poor impulse control, whereas adolescents who kill strangers or acquaintances have a history of violence.[91] Simply put, most parricide offenders do not have a history of lawbreaking.

Society's reaction to parricide is still steeped in the traditional view that children should love and obey their parents. When a child kills his or her parents, we attempt to attribute this to the "bad seed" theory or argue that the child somehow is at fault. Many times, the claim of abuse is seen as an excuse for murder. However, as pointed out in other sections in this textbook, children rarely lie about abuse. We simply do not have the answers to a number of questions in this area. A great deal still needs to be done in the area of researching the dynamics and causes of parricide.

Summary

This chapter discussed the various types of physical child abuse. We cannot prevent all forms of child abuse, so we must be alert to their existence and understand how and why they occur. In addition, professionals need a basic understanding of the different types of physical abuse and how they are inflicted. We have won half the battle if we are aware that physical child abuse occurs in all segments of our society and stand ready to diagnose it when we observe it. On the other hand, we must be willing to accept reasonable explanations for injuries. Children are active human beings—they will trip, fall, and run into objects. Our goal is to be able to distinguish between a normal injury and a non-accidental one. This ability may save a child's life.

Key Terms

battered child syndrome—a medicolegal term that describes the diagnosis of a medical expert based on scientific studies that indicate that when a child suffers certain types of continuing injuries, those injuries were not caused by accidental means.

Caffey's syndrome—in the absence of a skeletal disease, children who have both subdural hematomas and long-bone fractures are the victims of trauma.

physical child abuse—any act that results in a nonaccidental physical injury by a person who has care, custody, or control of a child.

psychopathological model—stresses the characteristics of the abuser as the primary cause of abuse.

The abuser's personality predisposes the abuser to injure the child.

interactional model—views child abuse as a result of a dysfunctional system.

environmental–sociological–cultural model—views child abuse as a result of stresses in society.

immersion burns—burns caused by holding the child in hot water.

pattern burns—burns caused by holding or pressing a portion of the child's body against a hot object.

spiral fractures—usually a break in the humerus or femur resulting from a twisting motion.

subdural hematoma (SDH)—tearing of the bridging vessels between the brain and the dura occurring over the surface of the brain.

concussion—a mild form of diffuse brain injury associated with the acceleration–deceleration of shaking the child's head.

cerebral contusion—the bruising of the brain without puncture or tearing of the pia membrane.

shaken baby syndrome—neurological damage caused by shaking the child violently back and forth.

Discussion Questions

1. If a child is injured and the physician is uncertain of whether the injury is physical child abuse, should he or she alert the police? Why? Why not? Would it make any difference if the physician knew the parents and had been to their home for a social event?

2. What is the most serious form of physical child abuse? Why?

3. If a child has been seriously injured by his or her mother, should that child ever be returned to her care? Why?

4. If a mother has a criminal record of physically abusing her two young children, should a judge have the power to order her to take birth control measures so as to prevent the birth of another child? Why? Why not?

5. Should a convicted child abuser be required to inform all social partners of his crimes? What if he is dating someone who has small children and his date asks him to watch the children while she goes to work for the day?

Suggested Readings

Almond, L., ed. *Child Abuse (Current Controversies)* (Greenhaven Press, Farmington Hills, Mich., 2006).

Cloitre, M., L. Cohen, and K. Koenen. *Treating Survivors of Childhood Abuse: Psychotherapy for the Interrupted Life* (Guilford Press, New York, 2006).

Cole, T. *Splintered Emotions: Aftermath of Child Abuse* (Oberpark Publishing, Indianapolis, Ind., 2006).

DePanfilis, D., and M. K. Salus. *A Coordinated Response to Child Abuse and Neglect.* DHHS Pub. No. (ACF) 92–30362. (U.S. Department of Health and Human Services, Washington, D.C., 1992).

Gerber, G., C. Ross, and E. Zigler, eds. *Child Abuse: An Agenda for Action* (Oxford University Press, New York, 1980).

Gil, D. G. *Violence against Children: Physical Child Abuse in the United States* (Harvard University Press, Cambridge, Mass., 1973).

Helfer, R., and C. H. Kempe, eds. *The Battered Child*, 2nd ed. (University of Chicago Press, Chicago, 1974).

Justice, B., and R. Justice. *The Abusing Family* (Human Services Press, New York, 1976).

Koster, K., ed. *Child Abuse: Opposing Viewpoints* (Greenhaven, San Diego, Calif., 1994).

Martin, H. P., ed. *The Abused Child* (Ballinger, Cambridge, Mass., 1976).

Seidel, H., J. Ball, J. Dains, and G. Benedict, eds. *Mosby's Guide to Physical Examination*, 2nd ed. (Mosby–Year Book, New York, 1991).

Sorel, N. C. *Ever since Eve: Personal Reflections on Childbirth* (Oxford University Press, New York, 1984).

Tardieu, A. *Etude medico-legale sur les services et mauvais traitements exercés sur des enfants.* In S. M. Smith, ed., *The Battered Child Syndrome* (Butterworths, London, 1975). (Originally published in 1860.)

Thelan, L., J. Davie, and L. Urden. *Textbook of Critical Care Nursing* (Mosby, St. Louis, Mo., 1990).

Tower, C. C. *Understanding Child Abuse and Neglect*, 2nd ed. (Allyn & Bacon, Needham Heights, Mass., 1993).

Van Hasselt, V. B. et al., eds. *Handbook of Family Violence* (Plenum, New York, 1988).

Endnotes

1. A. Tardieu, *Etude medico-legale sur les services et mauvais traitements exercés sur des enfants*, in S. M. Smith, ed., *The Battered Child Syndrome* (Butterworths, London, 1975). (Originally published in 1860.)

2. J. Caffey, "Multiple Injuries in the Long Bones of Infants Suffering from Chronic Subdural Hematoma," *American Journal of Roentgenology* 56 (1946), pp. 163–173.

3. C. H. Kempe et al., "The Battered Child Syndrome," *Journal of the American Medical Association* 118 (1962), pp. 105–112.

4. Ibid, p. 23.

5. See *State v. Byrd*, 309 N.C. 132, 305 S.E.2d 724, 729 (1983).

6. See, for example, V. B. Van Hasselt et al., eds., *Handbook of Family Violence* (Plenum, New York, 1988).

7. C. T. Wang and J. Holton. *Total Estimated Cost of Child Abuse and Neglect in the United States* (Prevent Child Abuse America, Chicago, 2007), p. 2.

8. S. Radbill, "A History of Child Abuse and Infanticide," in R. Helfer and C. H. Kempe, eds., *The Battered Child*, 2nd ed. (University of Chicago Press, Chicago, 1974).

9. C. F. Potter, "Infanticides," in M. Leach, ed., *Dictionary of Folklore, Mythology and Legend*, vol. 1 (Funk & Wagnalls, New York, 1949).

10. N. C. Sorel, *Ever since Eve: Personal Reflections on Childbirth* (Oxford University Press, New York, 1984).

11. This material is based on *Current Trends in Child Abuse Reporting and Fatalities: The Results of the 1996 Annual Fifty State Survey* (National Committee to Prevent Child Abuse, Chicago, April 1997). Reprinted with permission.

12. N. Peddle and Ching-Wang, *Current Trends in Child Abuse Prevention, Reporting, and Fatalities: THE 1999 FIFTY STATE SURVEY* (National Center on Child Abuse Prevention Research, Chicago, Revised August 28, 2001).

13. Ibid., p. III.

14. N. Peddle et al., *Current Trends in Child Abuse and Fatalities, THE 2000 FIFTY STATE SURVEY* (National Center on Child Abuse Prevention Research, Chicago, September 2002).

15. Ibid., p. 12.

16. Ibid., p. 19.

17. Ibid.

18. U.S. Department of Justice, Bureau of Justice Statistics, *Criminal Victimization in the United States, 1987* (Government Printing Office, Washington, D.C., 1989). See Table 4.

19. P. Rondell and J. Parker, "Factitious Disorder by Proxy and the Abuse of a Child with Autism," *Educational Psychology in Practice* 13(1) (1997), p. 39.

20. C. C. Tower, *Understanding Child Abuse and Neglect*, 2nd ed. (Allyn & Bacon, Needham Heights, Mass., 1993).

21. B. Justice and R. Justice, *The Abusing Family* (Human Services Press, New York, 1976), p. 37.

22. See J. D. Delsordo, "Protective Casework for Abused Children," *Children* 10 (1963), pp. 213–218.

23. H. P. Martin, ed., *The Abused Child* (Ballinger, Cambridge, Mass., 1976).

24. M. Lynch, "Risk Factors in the Child: A Study of Abused Children and Their Siblings," in H. P. Martin, ed., *The Abused Child* (Ballinger, Cambridge, Mass., 1976), pp. 43–56.

25. See R. T. Ammerman, V. B. Van Hasselt, and M. Hersen, "Maltreatment in Handicapped Children: A Critical Review," *Journal of Family Violence* 3 (1988), pp. 53–72.

26. R. Loeber, D. K. Felton, and J. Reid, "A Social Learning Approach to the Reduction of Coercive Processes in Child Abuse Families: A Molecular Analysis," *Advances in Behavior Research and Therapy* 6 (1984), pp. 29–45.

27. Problems with reported cases of child abuse range from reporting bias—poor and minority families are more likely to be reported as maltreating—to the position that reported cases are only a portion of the total incidents of child abuse. For a discussion of reporting bias, see R. L. Hampton and E. H. Newberger, "Child Abuse Incidence and Reporting by Hospitals: Significance of Severity, Class, and Race," *American Journal of Public Health* 75 (1995), pp. 56–60. For a review of the issue regarding underreporting, see National Center on Child

Abuse and Neglect, *Study Findings: Study of National Incidence and Prevalence of Child Abuse and Neglect: 1988* (U.S. Department of Health and Human Services, Washington, D.C., 1988).

28. American Association for Protecting Children, *Highlights of Official Child Neglect and Abuse Reporting 1986* (American Humane Society, Denver, 1988).

29. National Center on Child Abuse and Neglect. *Study Findings: National Study of the Incidence and Severity of Child Abuse and Neglect.* DHHS Publication No. OHDS 811–30325 (Government Printing Office, Washington, D.C., 1981); and National Center on Child Abuse and Neglect, *Study Findings: National Study of the Incidence and Severity of Child Abuse and Neglect: 1988* (U.S. Department of Health and Human Services, Washington, D.C., 1988).

30. D. G. Gil, *Violence against Children: Physical Child Abuse in the United States* (Harvard University Press, Cambridge, Mass., 1973).

31. R. J. Gelles and M. A. Straus, "Is Violence toward Children Increasing? A Comparison of 1975 and 1985 National Survey Rates," *Journal of Interpersonal Violence* 2 (1987), pp. 212–222.

32. M. A. Finkel and L. R. Ricci, "Documentation and Preservation of Visual Evidence in Child Abuse," *Child Maltreatment* 2(4) (1977), p. 322.

33. *State v. Jones*, 59 Wash. App. 744, 801 P. 2d 263 (1990).

34. See *Estelle v. McGuire*, 112 S. Ct. 475 (1991).

35. In *People v. Turner*, 193 Ill. App. 152, 549 N.E.2d 1309, 1313 (1990), the defendant first stated to the paramedics that the child was not breathing as a result of a fall. She later changed her story to indicate she had put the child to bed and upon checking her found that she was not breathing.

36. H. Schmitt, "The Child with Nonaccidental Trauma," in R. Kempe and R. Helfer, eds., *The Battered Child*, 4th ed. (University of Chicago Press, Chicago, 1987), p. 178.

37. Ibid., p. 186.

38. *State v. Jones*, 59 Wash. App. 744, 801 P.2d 263 (1990), and ibid., p. 180.

39. H. Schmitt, "The Child with Nonaccidental Trauma," p. 186.

40. *Coagulation* is the process of clotting. Coagulation of the blood depends on the presence of several substances. For further information, see C. L. Thomas, ed., *Taber's Cyclopedic Medical Dictionary*, 14th ed. (Davis, Philadelphia, 1981), pp. 302–303.

41. H. Seiden et al., eds., *Mosby's Guide to Physical Examination*, 2nd ed. (Mosby–Year Book, New York, 1991), p. 115.

42. J. Showers and K. M. Garsion, "Burn Abuse: A Four-Year Study," *Journal of Trauma* 28 (1988), p. 1581.

43. Based on S. Bilchik, *Burn Injuries in Child Abuse* (U.S. Department of Justice, Washington, D.C., May 1997).

44. D. B. Kessler and P. Hyden, "Physical, Sexual, and Emotional Abuse of Children," *Clinical Symposia* 43(1) (1991), p. 10.

45. *State v. Church.* 99 N.C. App. 647, 394 S.E.2d 468, 470 (1990).

46. K. W. Feldman, "Child Abuse by Burning," in R. Helfer and R. Kempe, eds., *The Battered Child* (University of Chicago Press, Chicago, 1997).

47. See *State v. Williams*, 541 N.W.2d 886, 888 (Minn. Ct. App. 1990), for a case dealing with cigarette burns to a child.

48. Feldman, "Child Abuse by Burning," pp. 205–206.

49. Based on Bilchik, *Burn Injuries in Child Abuse.*

50. See, for example, D. P. Jones, "The Syndrome of Munchausen by Proxy," *Child Abuse and Neglect* 18 (1994), p. 769.

51. See P. Randall and J. Parker, "Factitious Disorder by Proxy and the Abuse of a Child with Autism," *Educational Psychology in Practice* 13(1) (1997).

52. See *Diagnostic Statistical Manual*, 4th ed. (American Psychological Association, Washington, D.C., 1994), p. 725.

53. E. J. Kudsk and J. A. Nolan, "Munchausen Syndrome by Proxy: The Case for Adult Victims," paper presented at the Annual Meeting of Academy of Criminal Justice Sciences, Boston, March 1995.

54. H. A. Schreier, "The Perversion of Mothering: Munchausen Syndrome by Proxy," *Bulletin of the Menninger Clinic* 56(4) (1992), pp. 421–437.

55. J. Money, "Munchausen's Syndrome by Proxy: Update," *Journal of Pediatric Psychology* 11(4) (1986), p. 583, discussing an earlier article that appeared in the *Bulletin of the American Academy of Psychiatry and the Law* in 1976.

56. R. Meadow, "Munchausen Syndrome by Proxy: The Hinterland of Child Abuse," *The Lancet* 13(2) (1977), p. 351.

57. S. J. Boros and L. C. Brubaker, "Munchausen Syndrome by Proxy," *FBI Law Enforcement Bulletin* 61(6) (1992), p. 16.

58. D. Hall et al., "Evaluation of Covert Video Surveillance in the Diagnosis and Munchausen Syndrome by Proxy: Lessons from 41 Cases," *Pediatrics* 105(6) (2000), pp. 1305–1312.

59. C. Bartsch et al., *Munchausen Syndrome by Proxy: An Extreme Form of Child Abuse with a Special Forensic Challenge*, www.sciencedirect.com, accessed October 3, 2006. See also B. Vennemann et al., "A Case of Munchausen Syndrome by Proxy with Subsequent Suicide of the Mother," *Forensic Science International* 158 (2006), p. 195.

60. See S. Bilchik, *Child Neglect and Munchausen Syndrome by Proxy* (U.S. Department of Justice, Washington, D.C., September 1996).

61. Ibid., p. 20.

62. For an excellent discussion of this form of abuse, see T. F. Parnell and D. O. Day, eds., *Munchausen by Proxy Syndrome* (Sage, Thousand Oaks, Calif., 1988).

63. Kessler and Hyden, "Physical, Sexual, and Emotional Abuse of Children."

64. For an excellent discussion of this type of injury, see L. Thelan, J. Davie, and L. Urden, *Textbook of Critical Care Nursing* (Mosby, St. Louis, Mo., 1990), pp. 543–549.

65. Ibid., p. 546.

66. Ibid., p. 545.

67. D. L. Chadwick, S. Chin, C. Salerno, J. Landsver, and L. Kitchen, "Deaths from Falls in Children: How Far Is Fatal?" *Journal of Trauma* 31 (1991), p. 1353.

68. A. C. Duhaime et al., "Current Concepts: Nonaccidental Head Injury in Infants—The "Shaken-Baby Syndrome," *New England Journal of Medicine* 338 (June 1998), p. 1822.

69. N. Miehl, "Shaken Baby Syndrome," *Journal of Forensic Nursing*, 1/3 (Fall 2005), p. 111.

70. J. Showers, *Never Never Never Shake a Baby: The Challenges of Shaken Baby Syndrome* (National Association of Children's Hospitals and Related Institutions, Alexandria, Va., May 1999).

71. C. Haberman "Shaken Baby Syndrome: A Diagnosis That Divides the Medical World." *New York Times* (September 13, 2015), C-1.

72. D. Cenziper "Prosecutors Build Murder Cases on Disputed Shaken Baby Syndrome Diagnosis," *Washington Post* (March 20, 2015), A1.

73. N. Kellogg, "Oral and Dental Aspects of Child Abuse and Neglect," *Pediatrics* 116 (6) (2005), p. 1566.

74. Ibid., p. 1566.

75. *National Child Abuse and Neglect Date System: 1990 Summary Data component*, Working Paper 1 (National Center on Child Abuse and Neglect, U.S. Department of Health and Human Services, Washington, D.C., 1990).

76. D. Finkelhor, *Out of Darkness: Contemporary Perspectives on Family Violence* (Sage, Thousand Oaks, Calif., 1997).

77. M. Overpeck et al., "Risk Factors for Infant Homicide in the United States," *New England Journal of Medicine* 339 (1998), p. 1211.

78. S. R. Kaplin, *Child Fatalities and Child Fatality Review Teams* (ABA Center on Children and the Law, Washington, D.C., 1996).

79. P. Mones, "Parricide: Opening a Window through the Defense of Teens Who Kill," *Stanford Law & Policy Review* 7 (Winter 1995–1996), p. 61.

80. P. Mones, *When a Child Kills: Abused Children Who Kill Their Parents* (Simon & Schuster, New York, 1991).

81. S. Post, "Adolescent Parricide in Abusive Families," *Child Welfare* 61(7) (1982), p. 445.

82. K. M. Heide, *Why Kids Kill Their Parents*, 2nd ed. (Sage, Thousand Oaks, Calif., 1995), p. 6.

83. A. Weigall, *Nero: The Singing Emperor of Rome* (Garden City, New York, 1939).

84. Ibid.

85. M. R. Carlisle, "What Made Lizzie Borden Kill?" *American Heritage* 43 (1992), pp 66–72.

86. Ibid.

87. P. Mones, *When a Child Kills.*

88. K. M. Heide, *Why Kids Kill Their Parents.*

89. R. Inman, *The Case of the People v. Lyle and Erik Menendez*, www.cyberspace.com/sidebar2.html, accessed September 17, 1996.

90. B. F. Corder et al., "Adolescent Parricide: A Comparison with Other Adolescent Murder," *American Journal of Psychiatry* 133(8) (1976), pp. 957–961.

91. P. Mones, *When a Child Kills.*

6

Child Sexual Abuse

CHAPTER OBJECTIVES

After studying this chapter, you should be able to:

- Define and explain the leading issues involving child sexual abuse;
- Describe the acts that are needed to legally constitute child sexual abuse;
- List the various types of intrafamilial sexual abuse;
- Distinguish between intrafamilial and extrafamilial child sexual abuse;
- Recognize the signs of child sexual abuse.

Detailed Look at What You Should Know About Child Sexual Abuse

- Child sexual abuse is one of the most emotional topics in the field of family violence.
- The U.S. population has a widespread interest in child abuse. However, the true magnitude of this problem is difficult to establish.
- **Child sexual abuse** is sexual exploitation or sexual activities with a child under circumstances that indicate that the child's health or welfare is harmed or threatened.
- **Intrafamilial sexual abuse** includes incest and refers to any type of exploitative sexual contact occurring between relatives.
- **Extrafamilial sexual abuse** refers to exploitative sexual contact with perpetrators who may be known to the child (neighbors, babysitters, live-in partners) or unknown to the child.
- From a legal perspective, harm to the victim is not an element of the crime of child sexual abuse. If certain physical acts occur, the crime is complete. In criminal proceedings, it is not necessary to prove that the perpetrator intended to harm or actually harmed the child.

- Child sexual abuse can be distinguished from rape in that the perpetrator may use a variety of "techniques" to achieve the objective of sexual gratification.

- Numerous studies indicate that child abusers do not fit any stereotype.

- The motivation to abuse a child sexually includes emotional congruence, sexual arousal, and blockage.

- Traditionally, the abuser is thought of as a male and the victim as a young female. However, studies indicate that boys may be the victims of sexual abuse at a higher rate than it was previously thought.

- The high-risk years for child sexual abuse range between four and nine years old.

- Contrary to popular belief, the actual physical attractiveness of the female child has little, if anything, to do with whether she becomes a victim of molestation.

- Children are at a higher risk of sexual abuse if they are socially isolated or left alone and unsupervised.

- Early warnings of sexual abuse may take the form of indirect statements made by the child or acted out in play.

- Although not all behavioral patterns will be present in every sexual abuse case, any professional who observes these symptoms should be alert to the possibility of child sexual abuse.

- Physical characteristics may suggest that a child has been, or currently is, a victim of sexual abuse. However, a lack of any physical findings only means that the acts did not leave any physical evidence.

- Unlike rape, few children are brought into an emergency room right after a sexual assault. A child may exhibit behavioral, physical, and/or medical symptoms of abuse, and professionals must be aware of these characteristics. Only by recognizing these indicators of sexual abuse can it be prevented.

- No clearly defined pattern or course of conduct leads to sexual child abuse.

- **Pedophilia** is a term used to describe a sexual fixation on young children that is usually translated into sexual acts with the victim.

- One of the most common consequences of child sexual abuse is the exhibition of stress. Stress may be classified as acute, secondary, or tertiary.

INTRODUCTION

Despite education and training, which specifies how to perform our professional roles, each of us has personal reactions to our work. Child sexual abuse probably arouses more personal reaction than many of the problems we encounter. . . . After all, if we had no emotional reaction to the plight of a sexually abused child or a father facing a life sentence in prison, something would be wrong with us. (Kathleen Faller, 1993, p. 1i)

Child sexual abuse is one of the most emotional topics in the field of family violence. Repeated media stories report accounts of both long-term and situational incidents of children being sexually abused by family members, caretakers, or strangers. Unlike the definition for child physical abuse or neglect, the definition of child sexual abuse is relatively easy to understand. What is hard to accept is why a middle-aged adult would want to engage in sexual activities with a prepubescent child.

This chapter examines several major aspects of child sexual abuse. As with the other forms of child abuse, this is not a pleasant topic. However, child sexual abuse is a harsh reality, and professionals must understand what it is, know the factors—both physical and behavioral—that may indicate its existence, and be familiar with the procedures utilized to prove it occurred.

The U.S. population has a widespread interest in child abuse. However, the true magnitude of this problem is difficult to establish.[1] The general agreement among both scholars and professionals in the field is that the incidence of child abuse reporting is understated.[2] Estimates on the number of child sexual abuse cases vary from source to source. Finkelhor's 1979 study of 796 college students indicated that 19 percent of females and 9 percent of males had been subjected to sexual abuse as children.[3] A later study by Finkelhor of 521 Boston parents indicated that 15 percent of females and 6 percent of males had been sexually abused by the age of sixteen.[4] Russell's survey of 930 San Francisco women found that 28 percent had been victims of child sexual abuse before the age of fourteen.[5] In 1985, the *Los Angeles Times* conducted a random survey of 2,627 adults across the United States. The survey revealed that 27 percent of women and 16 percent of men survey participants had been molested as children. The total percentage (combining men and women) for those who suffered child sexual abuse was 22 percent.[6] In 1991, researchers concluded that as many as 10 to 15 percent of all boys and 20 to 25 percent of all girls had experienced at least one instance of sexual abuse prior to the age of eighteen.[7]

Rape in America, published by the National Victim Center, indicates that sexual violence occurs at a much higher rate than it was previously expected.[8] This study will be discussed in more detail in Chapter 13 dealing with women and sexual violence, but it illustrates that sexual violence is still a major problem in the United States. On the basis of this study, the National Victim Center estimates that there are at least 12.1 million women in the United States who have been subjected to sexual violence as a child or an adult.

In January 2001, David Finkelhor and Lisa Jones published a remarkable article that addressed the issue of child sexual abuse.[9] In "The Decline in Child Sexual Abuse Cases," the authors pointed out that substantiated cases of child sexual abuse decreased from a national estimate of 149,800 in 1992 to 103,600 in 1998. This represents a 31 percent decline. This decline has occurred in the majority of the states, with no clear regional patterns. Although cases of other types of child maltreatment have also declined, the decrease in child sexual abuse cases has been more significant. Possible explanations for this decline could be an actual decline in the incidence of child sexual abuse, or changes in policies, attitudes, and standards that have reduced the amount of child sexual abuse that is being reported, or a combination of both factors. Even if child sexual abuse has declined in recent years, it still represents a serious threat to our children and our society. Although the figures vary from study to study regarding the types and incidences of child sexual abuse, there is some agreement among researchers that the following classification of offenders is a valid estimate:

Strangers as the offender	Approximately 8–10%
Family members as the offender	Approximately 47%
Acquaintances as the offender	Approximately 40%[10]

Child sexual abuse is an unfortunate fact of life. One of the best ways to deal with it is to understand what it is and who the perpetrators and victims are of this form of child maltreatment. The following sections will examine these issues.

DEFINITIONS

Child sexual abuse is sexual exploitation or sexual activities with a child under circumstances that indicate that the child's health or welfare is harmed or threatened.[11] This definition includes inappropriate sexual activities between children and adults. The inappropriate behavior may be between family members or between a stranger and the victim. **Intrafamilial sexual abuse** includes incest and refers to any type of exploitative sexual contact occurring between relatives. **Extrafamilial sexual abuse** refers to exploitative sexual contact with perpetrators who may be known to the child (neighbors, babysitters, live-in partners) or unknown to the child.[12]

One of the major problems with this definition is the requirement that the child may be harmed. From a legal perspective, harm to the victim is not an element of the crime of child sexual abuse. If certain physical acts occur, the crime is complete. In criminal proceedings, it is not necessary to prove that the perpetrator intended to harm or actually harmed the child. However, this definition is useful for exploring the consequences of child sexual abuse, and retaining the requirement of an injury to the child will allow for such a discussion.

The following acts are examples of child sexual abuse: exposing one's sexual organs to the child, voyeurism, touching the sex organs of the child, mutual or self-masturbation with the child, oral sex, intercourse, and anal sex. In addition, allowing the child to view or participate in pornographic or obscene movies is considered child abuse.

Child sexual abuse can be distinguished from rape in that the perpetrator may use a variety of different techniques to achieve the objective of sexual gratification. Rape normally involves sexual acts as the result of force or fear. Child abuse offenders may also use force or fear. However, they also employ other pressures or influences to accomplish their goal. These actions include manipulation of the child (psychologically isolating the child from other loved ones), coercion (using adult authority or power on the child), force (restraining the child), and threats or fear (informing the child that if he tells, no one will love him).[13]

THE ABUSER AND THE ABUSED

This section deals with who the abusers are rather than why they abuse. Scholars agree that at this stage in our research and understanding of child sexual abuse, the latter question cannot be answered. However, studying the abusers may lead to an understanding of why these acts occur.

Focus

What Is Child Sexual Abuse?

At the extreme end of the spectrum, sexual abuse includes sexual intercourse or its deviations. Yet all offences that involve sexually touching a child, as well as nontouching offenses and sexual exploitation, are just as harmful and devastating to a child's well-being.

Touching sexual offenses include:

- Fondling;
- Making a child touch an adult's sexual organs; and
- Penetrating a child's vagina or anus no matter how slight with a penis or any object that doesn't have a valid medical purpose.

Nontouching sexual offenses include:

- Engaging in indecent exposure or exhibitionism;
- Exposing children to pornographic material;
- Deliberately exposing a child to the act of sexual intercourse; and
- Masturbating in front of a child.

Sexual exploitation can include:

- Engaging a child or soliciting a child for the purposes of prostitution; and
- Using a child to film, photograph, or model pornography

Source: American Humane Web site, www.americanhumane.org, accessed July 28, 2009.

The Abuser

Numerous studies indicate that child abusers do not fit any stereotype.[14] The common perception that all abusers are ugly old men who prey on children is simply not true. Nevertheless, researchers have attempted to find a common thread or factor that connects all child abusers. They have examined the degree of violence, the age of the victim, the age and education of the offender, preoffense social and occupational adjustment, alcohol abuse, physiological responses of offenders, and aggression. Conti reviewed the literature in this area and describes the following factors that were considered important when evaluating the characteristics of abusers:[15]

1. Measurement of sexual arousal is essential to discriminate between various categories of sexual offenders.
2. The role of sexual fantasies with children is important because of its connection to deviant sexuality. Fantasies about children coupled with masturbation during these fantasies serve as a form of rehearsal for contact with the victims.
3. The type of rationalizations used by adult offenders who have sexual relations with children is a crucial point. These rationalizations commonly take the form of statements or thoughts to the effect that "A child who does not resist really wants to have sex," "Having sex with a child is the best way to teach her about sex," or "You become closer to the child when you share sex with him."

In addition to the various forms of psychopathology present in child abuse, Finkelhor has established four factors involved in sexual abuse.[16] He calls this theory the

four preconditions model of sexual abuse. This model establishes preconditions that create a personal and social context for expressing sexually abusive behaviors. These preconditions include the motivation to sexually abuse, overcoming internal inhibitors, factors predisposing to overcome external inhibitors, and factors predisposing to overcome the child's resistance.

PRECONDITION I: MOTIVATION TO ABUSE SEXUALLY.   The motivation to abuse a child sexually includes emotional congruence, sexual arousal, and blockage. Emotional congruence involves satisfying an emotional need by relating to the child in a sexual manner. Sexual arousal occurs when the child becomes the source of sexual gratification. Blockage occurs when other alternative forms of sexual satisfaction are not present, not available, or less satisfying. The motivation to abuse a child is based on individual as well as sociological grounds. Individual explanations include the need for power and control, unconscious reenactment of a childhood trauma, and biological abnormality. Sociological reasons include the male-oriented society that demands male dominance, child pornography, and erotic portrayal of children in the media.

PRECONDITION II: OVERCOMING INTERNAL INHIBITORS.   The perpetrator must overcome internal controls that would prevent him from sexually abusing the child. Some of these controls are overcome by the use of alcohol or drugs, an existing psychosis, the inability of the offender to identify with the needs of the victim, weak criminal sanctions against offenders, and child pornography.

PRECONDITION III: FACTORS PREDISPOSING TO OVERCOME EXTERNAL INHIBITORS.
These conditions are outside the control of the perpetrator. These factors include social situations such as the type and amount of supervision a child receives, the lack of a parental figure close to or protective of the victim, and unusual sleeping or living arrangements. In

---

Focus

═══

Who Commits Child Sexual Abuse?

- Most often, sexual abusers know the child they abuse, but are not family. For example, the abuser might be a friend of the family, babysitter, or neighbor. About 6 out of 10 abusers fall into that group.
- About 3 out of 10 of those who sexually abuse children are family members of the child. This includes fathers, uncles, or cousins.
- The abuser is a stranger in only about 1 out of 10 child sexual abuse cases.

- Abusers are men in most cases, whether the victim is a boy or a girl.
- Women are the abusers in about 14 percent of cases reported against boys and about 6 percent of cases reported against girls.
- Child pornographers and other abusers who are strangers may make contact with children using the Internet.

Source: U.S. Department of Veterans Affairs-National Center for PTSD Web site at www.ptsd.va.gov/public/types/violence/child-sexual-abuse.asp, accessed September 7, 2015.

addition, the lack of social support for mothers, barriers to equality, and erosion of the family's social networks contribute to the ability of the offender to overcome external inhibitors.

PRECONDITION IV: FACTORS PREDISPOSING TO OVERCOME CHILD'S RESISTANCE. These factors concern the victim's ability to resist the sexual advances. The child may be emotionally insecure, deprived, or lacking in sexual experience or knowledge. The victim may feel powerless, or a situation of trust may exist between the offender and the victim.

There is no distinct or clear answer as to why adults sexually abuse children. The offender may commit these acts for a variety of reasons. Both psychological forces and the social structure enter into this complex mesh that allows individuals to engage in sexual activities with young children.

The Abused

Traditionally, the abuser is thought of as a male and the victim as a young female. However, studies indicate that boys may be the victims of sexual abuse at a higher rate than it was previously thought. One study in San Jose, California, indicates a rise in the reported incidents of sexual abuse of boys.[17] Between 1970 and 1975, only 5 percent of the reported victims of sex abuse were boys. However, this figure rose to over 22 percent by 1986.[18] A study by Snyder confirms that of all sexual assaults on children reported to law enforcement agencies, 31 percent of the victims under the age of six were males.[19]

Boys who are victims of abuse may not report the acts or incidents for several reasons. First, boys may not want to be viewed as victims or sissies or perceived as weak. Second, boys normally do not have to account for their movements and are given greater degrees of freedom and less protection through supervision; parents, therefore, may not notice any unusual behavior that may indicate sexual abuse. And third, our stereotypes lead us to look for abuse with girls, not with boys.[20] One scholar pointed out that sexual abuse of boys may lead to certain psychological responses, such as anxiety, denial, dissociation, and self-mutilation. Some male victims may decide that life is not worth living and plan suicide.[21]

The high-risk years for child sexual abuse range between four and nine years old.[22] At the former age, children are naive and sexually curious, and by the time they reach nine, their loyalty, desire to please, and trust of adults are traits manipulated by offenders to accomplish their goal of molestation. Generally, sexual abuse is terminated by the time the child reaches fourteen. This termination occurs because the victim may threaten the offender with disclosure or engage in activities such as running away that would lead authorities to suspect abuse.[23]

Contrary to popular belief, the actual physical attractiveness of the female child has little if anything to do with whether she becomes a victim of molestation. In addition, the seductiveness of the female child is now discounted as a contributing factor in sexual abuse situations. Although research has dispelled certain stereotypes about female victims, there needs to be more research on the issue of male victims. Two scholars have isolated at least one factor that may clarify why certain male children are molested. Finkelhor and Porter suggest that less assertive boys are more likely to be victims of sexual abuse.[24]

Focus

Proving Child Sexual Abuse

Excerpts from *People v. Patrick Charles Villwock, Defendant and Appellant.*

(Court of Appeal, Fourth District, Division 2, California, decided May 17, 2012)

Between the ages of 6 and 11, Jane Doe's mother was married to Patrick Charles Villwock, the defendant. During that time, on a weekly basis, defendant engaged in sexual abuse of Jane Doe involving oral copulation, digital penetration, and masturbation. After a jury trial, defendant was convicted of continuous sexual abuse of a child, and sentenced to 12 years in prison. He appealed.

Jane Doe and her mother originally lived in Utah for the first five or six years of Jane Doe's life. Jane Doe's mother worked in a county jail in Utah, where defendant worked on the LiveScan fingerprinting machinery. When Jane Doe's mother and defendant became involved in a relationship, Jane Doe and her mother moved to Temecula, California, to live with him. At first they lived in an apartment for approximately one year, and later, when Jane Doe was six years old, they moved into a house.

The jury found that after the family moved into the house, defendant started to touch her inappropriately. Approximately once a week, the defendant entered Jane Doe's bedroom at night, asked her to undress, took off his own clothes, and orally copulated her as she lay across the bed, with Jane Doe's head towards his privates. He would also grab Jane Doe's hand and make her masturbate him or orally copulate him until he ejaculated. If he ejaculated in her mouth, she ran to the bathroom to throw up. Some incidents occurred on the couch in the living room, where Jane Doe would be sitting on the couch and defendant would kneel in front of her, orally copulating her.

When Jane Doe was approximately 11 years old, Jane Doe learned that it was not normal to be touched the way defendant touched her. She told defendant she did not want to do it anymore, and she told her mother about the abuse, but her mother did not believe her. Jane Doe had been in therapy and counseling during some of the time she was abused, but she never mentioned the abuse to any counselors. However, Jane Doe did tell her best friend Rebecca about the abuse. Rebecca, whose family lived across the street, was the first person to whom Jane Doe mentioned the abuse, because defendant had told Jane Doe that if she ever said anything, he would lose his job, the family would lose their house, Jane Doe would lose her cat, and Jane Doe and her mother would be living on the streets.

After hearing Jane Doe's report, Rebecca told her parents about the abuse, after which Rebecca's parents went to Jane Doe's house to confront the defendant. Defendant denied committing any abuse and stated Jane Doe was lying, as she always did. Jane Doe's mother asked Jane Doe why she would say such things, but Jane Doe did not provide any details, she just told her mother not to leave her alone with defendant. Jane Does' mother told Jane Doe she was lying, and made Jane Doe go over to Rebecca's house to apologize to Rebecca's family.

Jane Doe's mother felt Jane Doe was lying because Jane Doe had gone over to Rebecca's house after having a heated argument with defendant. Jane Doe also had a history of lying, which made it difficult for her mother to believe the allegations. However, Jane Doe's mother had a gut feeling defendant was not telling her the truth because he enjoyed pornography. Nevertheless, the only time Jane Doe's mother had seen defendant touch Jane Doe was when she was six years old and had a yeast infection. Defendant had applied medication on Jane Doe's vaginal area, which made her mother leery, but she allowed it to happen on rare occasions because she trusted defendant.

(continued)

That same year, while Jane Doe was 11 years old, Jane Doe expressed a desire to be adopted by defendant. Prior to the adoption, and during the pre-adoption investigation, Jane Doe did not mention any sexual abuse; instead, she said great things about defendant. The adoption went through even though defendant lost his job during the process. The sexual abuse continued until Jane Doe was 12 years old.

The financial problems that ensued from defendant's unemployment caused strain on the relationship between Jane Doe's mother and defendant. They eventually divorced and mother returned to Utah with Jane Doe in 2004. Jane Doe's behavior was still problematic, so her mother put her into counseling a few months after moving back to Utah. After Jane Doe's mother explained the behavior problems to the counselor, and informed the counselor of Jane Doe's accusations against defendant, the counselor spoke with Jane Doe, and then informed the mother that Jane Doe could not be making it up and that she had been correct.

Subsequently, Jane Doe was interviewed by a social worker and the police about the incidents. Jane Doe also underwent a forensic medical examination where a colposcope was used to look for vaginal tears. The examination revealed a normal hymen, with no evidence of tears, although one would expect to find tears if a child had been penetrated 200–300 times with two or three fingers.

Jane Doe 2 first met Jane Doe when she was nine or 10 years old, in either 2000 or 2001. When Jane Doe 2 was either 11 or 12, she spent the night at Jane Doe's house. After they ate dinner and put the dishes away, they watched television. While they were on the couch, defendant reached over from behind the couch and started tickling both girls, going from under their armpits to their hips. Jane Doe 2 thought this behavior was kind of weird but went along with it.

The next day, the two girls decided to go sit in the jacuzzi. Because Jane Doe 2 did not have a swimsuit, she wore shorts and a T-shirt.

Jane Doe 2's leg was stretched across the jacuzzi. Defendant joined them in the jacuzzi, felt Jane Doe 2's leg, rubbing it along the back of the calf. He lifted her leg out of the water, telling Jane Doe 2 that her legs were very smooth. Defendant moved his hand down to her foot and Jane Doe 2 moved her foot.

The girls got out of the jacuzzi and went inside where they played piano. Jane Doe played the piano first, and then Jane Doe 2 played the piano. As Jane Doe 2 messed around on the piano, defendant was laying down on the couch with Jane Doe laying on top of him on her stomach. Defendant held Jane Doe like one would hold a baby, with his hand on her back. Jane Doe 2 thought this, too, was weird, and felt very uncomfortable, so she suggested to Jane Doe that they go to her room. Then Jane Doe 2 decided to call her father to pick her up, locking herself in the bathroom till her father arrived to get her. Jane Doe acted like it was normal, but Jane Doe 2 felt uncomfortable. Although Jane Doe 2 remained good friends with Jane Doe, she never went back to the latter's house because she did not want to be around the defendant.

Jane Doe 3 is Jane Doe's cousin. Jane Doe 3 met defendant when she was 12, and Jane Doe was about eight years old. Jane Doe 3 recalled an incident that made her uncomfortable that occurred when she was 14, when Jane Doe and her family were visiting Utah. The incident occurred at the visitor's center of the Latter Day Saints (LDS) church in Salt Lake City, when Jane Doe's family visited a monument there. Jane Doe 3 had been having problems with her family and discussed them with the defendant while they sat on a bench. Defendant started rubbing her leg near the knee, but gradually he moved his hand up to her upper thigh, within a half inch or an inch of her private part, moving his hand back and forth from outer thigh to inner thigh. He did this for approximately 30 seconds, at which time Jane Doe 3 began to feel pretty uncomfortable. At that point, Jane Doe 3 got up and walked away.

(continued)

On another occasion when Jane Doe 3's family visited Jane Doe's family in California, defendant got into the hot tub where Jane Doe, Jane Doe 3 and defendant's son were sitting. Jane Doe got out of the hot tub, followed by the defendant's son, leaving Jane Doe 3 alone in the jacuzzi with the defendant. Defendant moved his hand and began to rub her leg just like he had done on the earlier occasion, making her feel uncomfortable. Jane Doe 3 moved to the outside of the hot tub, and eventually defendant's son came back into the hot tub.

Jane Doe 3 recalled defendant as being "touchy," hugging longer than other uncles, and rubbing her shoulders and neck, which Jane Doe 3 found to be a little weird. Later, when Jane Doe 3 was about 17 or 18, and wanted to run away from home, defendant invited her to live with him in California.

Defendant was charged by way of information with continuous sexual abuse of a child under the age of 14. Following a jury trial, he was convicted of that charge, and was sentenced to state prison for a term of 12 years. Defendant timely appealed.

Discussion

Defendant argued that the trial court abused its discretion in admitting evidence pertaining to Jane Doe 3, because the acts were not sexual and the probative value of the evidence was outweighed by prejudice. We disagree.

Before admitting propensity evidence of a prior sex offense, a trial court must engage in a careful weighing process considering facts that include relevance, similarity to the charged offense, the certainty of commission, remoteness, and the likelihood of distracting or inflaming the jury. No specific time limits have been established for determining whether an uncharged offense is so remote as to be inadmissible. Substantial similarities between the prior offenses, or between the victims, may balance out the remoteness of the prior offenses.

Here, the evidence was highly relevant to show defendant's propensity to commit sexual offenses against girls of the same age as Jane Doe. Contrary to defendant's argument, the acts committed against Jane Doe 3 were sexual in nature despite the fact they did not constitute substantial sexual conduct. The Penal Code does not require any touching, but does require conduct that a normal person would unhesitatingly be irritated by, and conduct motivated by an unnatural or abnormal sexual interest in the victim.

The rubbing of Jane Doe 3's leg, which made her so uncomfortable that she moved away, satisfied the elements of annoying or molesting a minor within the meaning of Penal Code section 647.6. The jury was correctly instructed on the elements of that crime. The evidence was relevant and admissible as propensity evidence. The trial court did not abuse its discretion in admitting the evidence of the prior sexual offense against Jane Doe 3.

Children are at a higher risk of sexual abuse if they are socially isolated or left alone and unsupervised. If the mother is absent from the home for long periods, either because of work or other commitments, the child is more likely to be abused. Some authorities theorize that the presence of a stepfather in the home adds to the risk of sexual abuse.[25] These factors establish situations that make the child vulnerable to the perpetrator.

Professionals are still researching and learning about the characteristics of those who abuse and why certain children are chosen for abuse over others. Misconceptions and stereotypes have contributed to the confusion in this very important area. Although researchers do not have all the answers to why children are abused and who commits child sexual abuse, they have developed a fairly comprehensive list of factors that may indicate whether a child is the victim of sexual abuse.

INDICATIONS OF SEXUAL ABUSE

Victims of child sexual abuse may disclose the fact that they have been sexually abused at different times during their lives, and this disclosure may take many forms. Early warnings of sexual abuse may take the form of indirect statements made by the child or acted out in play. These signals can be subtle, such as a child describing a sexual event without identifying himself as the victim or naming the offender.[26]

Children may also make direct statements to their friends or to adults about being molested. Children sometimes say odd things to observe the adult's reaction before proceeding any further. These odd or partial statements are designed to test the water before saying anything else. Many times, the victim is told by the perpetrator that bad things will happen if the abuse is ever discussed. If the adult fails to pick up on the signals or reacts negatively to the statements, the child may not proceed any further. Refer to the next section for a list of behavioral changes or patterns that are most commonly associated with child sexual abuse.

Behavioral Indicators

Although not all behavioral patterns will be present in every sexual abuse case, any professional who observes these symptoms should be alert to the possibility of child sexual abuse. Once alerted to this situation, the professional should begin a careful inquiry into the facts.

Physical Indicators

Physical characteristics may suggest that a child has been, or currently is, a victim of sexual abuse. However, the lack of any physical findings only means that the acts did not leave any physical evidence. A child, depending on his or her age, may be the victim of an ongoing series of sexual acts and not exhibit any physical signs. The following is a list of physical signs of sexual abuse:

- Difficulty in walking or sitting;
- Torn, stained, or bloody underwear;
- Genital/anal itching, pain, swelling, or burning;
- Genital/anal bruises or bleeding;
- Frequent urinary tract or yeast infections;
- Pain on urination;
- Poor sphincter control;
- Venereal disease;
- Pregnancy;
- Chronic unexplained sore throats;
- Frequent psychosomatic illnesses;
- Loss of appetite.[27]

Knowledge of physical indicators of possible child sexual abuse is especially important for those professionals who come into daily contact with the child. School personnel, including nurses and teachers, should always be alert to the message these symptoms send.

Medical Indicators

Although medical evidence may not be present in all cases, when such facts are present they provide strong evidence of abuse. As indicated, simply because there is no physical evidence or injuries, sexual abuse cannot automatically be ruled out. Testimony from physicians can assist the jury in understanding this fact. A study of pregnant adolescents revealed that only two out of thirty-six had any evidence of penetration.[28]

Most authorities agree that medical evidence of sexual abuse is found in only 10 to 50 percent of all cases.[29] In one study, 382 children were evaluated for sexual abuse. Seventy-one percent did not display any medical signs or symptoms of abuse. This 71 percent figure included 48 percent who had a history of sexual penetration.[30]

Child sexual abuse victims may be seen by pediatricians as a result of a number of circumstances: (1) The victim is taken to the physician because of a statement about abuse or because abuse has been witnessed; (2) the victim is brought to the physician by law enforcement or child protective services for a nonacute medical evaluation for possible sexual abuse as part of an ongoing investigation; (3) the child is brought to an emergency room after suspected acute sexual abuse for a medical examination, evidence collection, and crisis management; (4) the child is taken to the physician, because a caretaker suspects sexual abuse after observing behavioral or physical symptoms; or (5) the child is brought in for a routine examination, and signs of sexual abuse are detected.[31]

Indicators of Child Sexual Abuse

Sexual abuse may result in physical or behavioral manifestations. While a few manifestations (e.g., gonorrhea of the throat in a young child) are conclusive of sexual abuse, most manifestations require additional investigation.

Early efforts at cataloging indicators of sexual abuse were problematic. Often, they indicated situations that were extremely rare, such as finding blood in a child's underpants and students who come early to school and leave late. These signs could be indicative of many problems or no problem at all. Present in detecting signs of sexual abuse are far more helpful.

Physical and Psychosocial Indicators

Presently, the indicators of child sexual abuse are grouped into either physical or psychosocial indicators. While physical indicators may be noted by any one, a definitive determination is generally reserved for persons in the medical profession. Similarly, anyone may observe psychosocial indicators; however, generally a mental health professional is responsible for forming an opinion that the symptoms are indicative of sexual abuse.

A differentiation is also made between indicators that indicate a high or low probability of sexual abuse. Some indicators are diagnostic of sexual abuse, whereas others may only be suggestive of sexual abuse but could indicate other circumstances or conditions as well.

In the majority of sexually abused children, there are no physical findings. The physical indicators, particularly vaginal ones, are generally most useful with prepubertal victims. As children become older, the possibility of consensual sexual activity needs to be considered. In addition, changes that occur with puberty render some insignificant indicators that have great significance in young children.

(continued)

Nonsexual Behavioral Indicators of Possible Sexual Abuse

The reason that nonsexual behavioral symptoms are lower probability indicators of sexual abuse is because they can also be indicators of other types of trauma. For example, these symptoms can be a consequence of physical maltreatment, marital discord, emotional maltreatment, or familial substance abuse. Nonsexual behavioral indicators can arise because of the birth of a sibling, the death of a loved one, or parental loss of employment. Moreover, natural disasters such as floods or earthquakes can result in such symptomatic behavior.

As with sexual behaviors, it is useful to divide symptoms into those more characteristic of younger children and those found primarily in older children. However, there are also some symptoms found in both age groups.

Nonsexual Behavioral Indicators in Young Children

The following symptoms may be found in younger children:

- sleep disturbances;
- enuresis;
- encopresis;
- other regressive behavior (e.g., needing to take transitional object to school);
- self-destructive or risk-taking behavior;
- impulsivity, distractibility, difficulty concentrating (without a history of nonabusive etiology);

- refusal to be left alone;
- fear of the alleged offender;
- fear of people of a specific type or gender;
- firesetting (more characteristic of boy victims);
- cruelty to animals (more characteristic of boy victims); and
- role reversal in the family or pseudomaturity.

Nonsexual Behavioral Indicators in Older Children

- eating disturbances (bulimia and anorexia);
- running away;
- substance abuse;
- self-destructive behavior (e.g., suicidal gestures, attempts, and successes and self-mutilation);
- incorrigibility;
- criminal activity; and
- depression and social withdrawal.

Nonsexual Behavioral Indicators in All Children.

Three types of problems may be found in children of all ages:

- problems relating to peers;
- school difficulties; and
- sudden noticeable changes in behavior.

Source: K. Faller. *Child Sexual Abuse: Intervention and Treatment Issues User Manual* (U.S. Department of Health and Human Services, Washington, D.C., 1993), and updated by Child Welfare Information Gateway, www.childwelfare. gov/pubs/usermanuals/sexabuse/sexabusec.cfm, accessed July 27, 2009.

Some medical scholars now believe that child sexual abuse is a recognized medical diagnosis.[32] For a physician to come to this conclusion, a complete medical evaluation is recommended. This evaluation should include a medical history, physical examination, and laboratory tests.

A medical history includes the chief complaint, history of the present illness, past medical history, family history, psychosocial history, and review of the physical systems. For children, this information is many times obtained from adults. The medical history allows the physician to exclude or confirm a diagnosis. The history may also indicate whether the offender still has access to the child, thus indicating whether the child is still at risk. The history assists the physician in determining what laboratory tests to order.

The physical examination should cover the entire body of the victim. The genitals and anal opening must be examined with care and in detail. As mentioned previously, sexual abuse often occurs without leaving any physical evidence. Contrary to popular belief, sexual intercourse may occur without damage to the hymen.[33] Many laypersons do not understand how a small hymenal opening could accept an object as large as an erect penis. The adult penis averages 3.5 centimeters at the glans, while the normal size of the vaginal opening at puberty is 0.7 to 1.0 centimeters. The vaginal opening and hymen are flexible and able to distend. Thus, penetration can occur without damage to the hymen. In addition, certain types of child abuse involve neither anal nor vaginal intercourse. These acts include fondling, kissing, fellatio, cunnilingus, or mutual masturbation.

Laboratory tests may provide confirmation of sexual abuse. If the sexual abuse is recent, tests may indicate the presence of ejaculate or phosphatase. Acid phosphatase is a chemical found in ejaculate even in the absence of sperm. In addition, laboratory tests may confirm the presence of certain venereal diseases—almost a presumptive sign of abuse. Gonococcal or

Focus

Can a Memory Be Forgotten and Then Remembered? Can a "Memory" Be Suggested and Then Remembered as True?

According to the American Psychological Association (APA), this question central in evaluating the memory of childhood abuse. While there are experts in the field that can provide some answers, clearly more study and research is needed.

According to the APA, both memory researchers and clinicians who work with trauma victims agree that both phenomena occur. However, experienced clinical psychologists state that the phenomenon of a recovered memory is rare. Although laboratory studies have shown that memory is often inaccurate and can be influenced by outside factors, memory research usually takes place either in a laboratory or some everyday setting. For ethical and humanitarian reasons, memory researchers do not subject people to a traumatic event in order to test their memory of it. Since the issue has not been directly studied, we do not know whether a memory of a traumatic event is encoded and stored differently from a memory of a non-traumatic event.

Some clinicians theorize that children understand and respond to trauma differently from adults. Some furthermore believe that childhood trauma may lead to problems in memory storage and retrieval. These clinicians contend that dissociation is a likely explanation for a memory that was forgotten and later recalled. Dissociation means that a memory is not actually lost, but is for some time unavailable for retrieval. That it is in memory storage, but cannot for some period of time actually be recalled. Some clinicians believe that severe forms of child sexual abuse are especially conducive to negative disturbances of memory such as dissociation or delayed memory. Many clinicians who work with trauma victims believe that this dissociation is a person's way of sheltering himself or herself from the pain of the memory. Many researchers argue, however, that there is little or no empirical support for such a theory.

Source: American Psychological Association Web site, accessed September 6, 2015 at www.apa.org/topics/trauma/memories.aspx

syphilitic infections can only be contracted through sexual activity. Other infections such as the herpes virus or lymphogranuloma (venereal warts) may be transmitted other than sexually, and therefore further inquiry is necessary.

Unlike rape, few children are brought into an emergency room right after a sexual assault. A child may exhibit behavioral, physical, and/or medical symptoms of abuse, and professionals must be aware of these characteristics. Only by recognizing these indicators of sexual abuse can it be prevented.

SEXUAL ABUSE

No clearly defined pattern or course of conduct leads to sexual child abuse. When a father bathes his two-year-old daughter, this does not necessarily lead to sexual urges or acts. Nor do specific relationships cause molestation. Sexual acts may be committed by fathers, mothers, stepparents, uncles, siblings, babysitters, and, of course, strangers. The consequences of sexual abuse to children are still being researched. However, professionals know that the effects of sexual acts last far beyond the time of the molestation. This section will examine the dynamics of child sexual abuse, including the various types of sexual relationships and the consequences of sexual abuse on the child's development and growth.

Forms of Sexual Abuse

PEDOPHILIA. **PEDOPHILIA** is a term used to describe a sexual fixation on young children that is usually translated into sexual acts with the victim. The psychiatric definition of a pedophile requires the following three conditions: Over a period of at least six months, the person has recurrent intense sexual urges and sexually arousing fantasies involving sexual activity with a prepubescent child (generally aged thirteen or younger), the person has acted on these urges or is markedly distressed by them, and the person is at least sixteen years old and at least five years older than the child.[34]

Numerous studies have been conducted about why certain individuals molest children. Groth's research concentrated on convicted sex molesters. He concluded that there were two types of perpetrators: the fixated offender and the regressed offender.[35] The *fixated offender* is usually attracted to male children, and he is unable to form a heterosexual relationship with someone his own age. His compulsive premeditated acts are based on the need to repeat his own victimization. The *regressed offender* primarily chooses young females as his victims. He is able to maintain the appearance of a heterosexual relationship with someone his own age.

Although it would be convenient to accept a classification such as Groth's, clinicians have found that such stereotyping does not fit everyday experiences.[36] Many molesters have combined characteristics from both categories. Other researchers continue to classify offenders on the basis of distinct differences. Some scholars argue that whereas an incestuous father may establish a long-term sexual relationship with his victim, the pedophile loses interest in the child once the victim passes into puberty.[37] In addition, it was once thought that an offender who molested in the home or family circle did not actively engage in sex outside the home. However, there is some authority to believe that incestuous fathers may also molest victims outside the family.[38]

The conflict regarding pedophiles and their sexual habits continues to be debated in professional circles.[39] What is certain is that some males have an obsession for children—male or female—and that they prey on them sexually. This molestation can be perpetrated by a stranger who kidnaps a child or by a family member who sexually molests a blood relative. The latter form of sexual abuse is known as **incest**.

INCEST.   Incest has a long and varied history in our society. It has various definitions, however. One of the more accepted definitions states that *incest* is sexual relations between blood relatives. It is prohibited in many cultures and accepted as normal in others. The prohibition against incest may be classified into five major categories: psychological, biological, familial, feminist, and multidimensional. Each of these theories offers a rationale for the prohibition against sexual relations with family members.

The *psychological theory* holds that the taboo against incest is a method of preventing family members from engaging in unconscious sexual desires with other family members. Sigmund Freud accepted this justification of the prohibition against incest because he believed that male family members had deep-seated unconscious desires to have sex with their mothers and daughters. Freud wrote an article titled "The Etiology of Hysteria," which discussed the effects of family molestation on patients he treated. He theorized that the hysteria suffered by the patients was the result of sexual abuse by family members.[40]

International Perspectives

Child Sexual Abuse

Whom can you trust? The United Nations Children's Fund (UNICEF) is a member of an international committee, which examines various aspects of child sexual abuse. This committee recently examined the sexual abuse of refugee and internally displaced women and children by those who we think of as their protectors—*humanitarian workers and peacekeepers*.

Conflict and displacement erode and weaken many of the social and political structures that are designed to protect members of a community. Displaced populations are often fleeing violence and turmoil in their community or nation, and sadly they often encounter violence during the course of their displacement. Resources available for displaced persons are often scarce, especially in third-world countries, and mechanisms for their protection are not given sufficient priority.

The lack of economic opportunities for displaced persons may result in commercial and exploitative sex, being one of the few options for earning income necessary to meet basic needs. Women and girls are often at risk for sexual abuse, but it is important to remember that young boys may face this same threat.

There are no standards or codes of conduct for humanitarian workers. Furthermore, there is no commonly agreed-on system for accountability for the humanitarian community. There need to be specific standards that are enforceable by the international community in the area of humanitarian assistance.

Source: Based on *Report of the Task Force on Protection from Sexual Exploitation and Abuse in Humanitarian Crises*, www.unicef.org, accessed September 3, 2002.

However, Freud later changed his position and repudiated his theory, stating that the patient's memories were fantasies.

The *biological theory* holds that prohibiting sexual relations between family members is a method of ensuring survival of the human race, and that such activity causes recessive or defective genes to multiply, resulting in deformity. This theory stresses the harmful effects of inbreeding.[41] One of the leading proponents of this theory is L. H. Morgan.[42] He based his assumptions on the experiences of animal breeders who discovered that inbreeding caused physical and mental deformities and disabilities. There were several flaws in Morgan's approach, and it has generally been discredited. Today, however, modern science accepts that although inbreeding may produce physical and mental disabilities, it may also be capable of producing a superior species.[43]

The *familial theory* against incest holds that the taboo creates order, unity, and cooperation among family members. The taboo establishes roles within the family that would otherwise be blurred by sexual involvement of its members. Without such a taboo, there would be disorder, disruption, and confusion within the family system.[44]

The *feminist theory* regarding incest holds that this taboo establishes the father as the authority figure in the family and preconditions women to accept this domination in society.[45] The authority granted the father establishes a patriarchal social system that discriminates against women. Under the feminist theory of taboo, men have the ability to restrict access to certain women, thereby increasing their own authority, power, and domain.

The *multidimensional approach* combines a number of the preceding theories to explain the incest taboo. Several authorities have argued that the incest taboo was and is important to the family structure and the child's development. Talcott Parsons believed that the taboo forced the child to develop autonomy and social roles necessary to leave the family. Carl Jung theorized that the incest prohibition was a necessary part of the child's development as a distinct individual.

Each of these theories has its proponents and opponents. Although they are helpful in understanding differing views as to why incest is considered bad or harmful, evidence to support their conclusions is lacking. As a result, none of them have been accepted by all scholars in the field.

As mentioned earlier, not all cultures accept incest as an immoral or illegal act. Some societies accept sexual activity between family members, including father-daughter liaisons, as natural, healthy, and proper.[46] Even in the United States, there are groups referred to as the pro-incest lobby "that believe that sexual activity with young girls is an acceptable lifestyle.[47] One organization, the René" Guyon Society, has a slogan: "Sex before eight, or else it's too late."[48] This group lobbies legislatures for the abolition of incest laws. The society claims to have more than 5,000 members, each of whom has filed an affidavit stating that the individual has deflowered a male or female child under the age of eight.[49] The group argues that the laws prohibiting incest are unenforceable because it is so prevalent, that the intervention by law enforcement agencies causes more harm than the "consensual" sexual act, and that the prohibition is old-fashioned and not in tune with the new sexual freedom in our society.

Child Pornography. Child pornography is another form of child sexual abuse that is alive and flourishing in the United States. In New York City, one shelter that cares for runaway children discovered that out of 5,000 runaways in one year, 2,000 of them had been involved in child pornography.[50]

Children who run away from home are prime targets for child pornography rings. The adults who control these rings recruit and maintain these children using a variety of techniques, including material and psychological rewards. Ann Burgess has studied various child pornography rings and found that different structures exist in these rings depending on their purpose. *Solo rings* are typified by an individual who keeps the sexual activity and pornographic material secret and does not inform or involve other adults. *Transition rings* are impromptu gatherings that come together for the purpose of selling photos and trading sex, and victims may be traded among members at this time. *Syndicated rings* are well-organized businesses that recruit and peddle children to customers who desire certain types of sexual activity. Syndicated rings are very structured and engage in child pornography, prostitution, and other sexual activities.[51] Also, the commercial exploitation of children in sex movies continues to be a highly emotional and legal problem. The stakes are high, and enormous profits are made from the publishing of these types of movies and videos. Child pornography has developed into a highly organized, multimillion-dollar industry that operates on a nationwide scale.[52]

Child pornography is really an inaccurate term. Pornography is any form of expression that deals with explicit sexual activity that is not considered obscene. The First Amendment to the Constitution protects our freedom of expression. This includes the right to make, sell, and view sexually explicit material so long as it does not cross over the line and become obscene. Although the First Amendment protects freedom of speech and expression, not all such activity is protected. The U.S. courts have determined that certain speech-related activity does not warrant First Amendment protection. This means that the states are free to regulate and make it a crime. This is the case with obscenity. The U.S. Supreme Court has defined **obscenity** as requiring a finding of all three of the following elements:

1. An average person, by applying contemporary community standards, would find that the work, taken as a whole, appeals to mainly prurient interest in sex.
2. The work depicts or describes sexual conduct in a patently offensive way.
3. The work, taken as a whole, lacks serious literary, artistic, political, or scientific value.[53]

Thus, the Supreme Court has established the principle that regulates obscene movies. Clearly, a movie that depicts a minor involved in sex acts with another person falls within this category. Therefore, such activity is not protected under the First Amendment. As a result, state and federal statutes can and have made it a crime to involve a minor in a sexually explicit movie.

The widespread use of the Internet has changed the face of obscenity. Recent advances in computer technology and in the manipulation of images have resulted in what some authorities are calling virtual child pornography.[54] This form of obscenity or pornography is composed of images that do not depict real children, but use youthful-looking actors or digital computer images that seem to show children engaging in sexual activities. In response to these virtual displays, Congress passed the Child Pornography Act of 1996.[55]

This law prohibited images that appeared to display real children engaging in sexually explicit acts or conveyed the impression that real children were engaged in sexual activities.

In *Ashcroft v. Free Speech Coalition*, the U.S. Supreme Court struck down Congress's attempt to regulate these images unless either they are obscene or they constitute actual images of children engaging in sexual activities.[56] The Court examined the Child Pornography Act and found that it did not meet the three-prong test established in Miller. Thus, unless the digital image actually shows real children engaging in sexual activities, it cannot be declared obscene. Even though portions of the Child Pornography Act have been declared unconstitutional, this is just the beginning of our response to cyber obscenity.

Child sexual abuse takes numerous forms. It may occur within or outside the family. No matter what its type is, the consequences to the victim are long-lasting and severe. The next section examines some of these consequences.

Consequences of Sexual Abuse

The impact of sexual molestation on children has been studied and researched by numerous authorities. Conti sets forth the following reasons for the wide range of interpretations and differing results from the various studies of child sexual abuse.[57] These differences can be attributed to several factors:

1. *Differential impact:* Some victims of sexual abuse are affected more than others, and this issue has caused trouble for researchers. However, a wide range of factors contributes to this problem: age of the victim, use of force, duration of the molestation, and other variables all contribute to methodological problems.
2. *Substantive implications:* Some of the substantive implications of sexual abuse focus on the behavioral and psychological effects on the victim. The presence of force, duration, and age of the victim at the time of the last incident are all associated with negative effects.
3. *Political contexts:* The continuing debate over the effects or lack of them adds to the confusion in this area. As discussed earlier, some groups advocate sex with children, versus the vast majority of U.S. citizens, who argue such acts cause harm to the children.
4. *Methodological issues:* Studies of the consequences of child sexual abuse have been criticized as drawing samples from special populations, such as prostitutes, college students, prison inmates, and other non-representative populations.

Although scholars differ on mythology and variables, certain consequences to the victim should be examined. However, because of the special impact of sexual molestation on victims, all should be aware of some of the major consequences of sexual abuse on children and their development.

These consequences may be classified into different aspects or reactions. Any set or classification of traits may be used to judge the impact of sexual abuse on the victim. One of the most common consequences of child sexual abuse is the exhibition of stress. Stress may be classified as acute, secondary, or tertiary.

Acute stress symptoms may appear at the onset of the abuse or when the acts are disclosed to others. Physical or emotional actions by the victim could be symptoms of acute stress. The child may exhibit any of the symptoms listed in the section discussing indications of sexual abuse.

Secondary stress symptoms may occur if abuse has continued for a long period of time. The victim has adapted to the situation and is able to function normally, at least on the surface. Some scholars argue that shame, guilt, and low self-esteem are secondary stress symptoms found in sexually abused children. However, these conclusions are subject to criticism by other authorities who argue that these findings do not always hold up. Suicide attempts and self-mutilating behavior appear to be higher with these victims than with the general population.[58] Fear, anxiety, a feeling of isolation, and stigma have been found to be present in some follow-up studies of victims of child sexual abuse.[59] Other secondary stress symptoms include difficulty with interpersonal relations and sexual maladjustment.

Tertiary stress symptoms include situations in which the victim identifies with the offender. Many times, there will be no outward symptoms of tertiary stress.

Tower sets forth various factors affecting the degree of stress or trauma a child victim experiences:

1. *The type of abuse:* Some victims of incest appear to be more affected by the acts than do victims of stranger molestation. However, if the nonfamily member engaged in sadistic or violent acts, this can have profound effects on the victim.
2. *The identity of the offender:* When the molester is known and close to the victim, the trauma appears to be greater than that from sexual molestation by a stranger. This trauma is based on feelings of a betrayal of trust by the known abuser.
3. *The duration of the abuse:* Most incestuous relationships last from one to three years. Long-term abuse of this nature seems to cause more stress than a one-time event. The exception to this rule is the one-time event that involves violence.
4. *The extent of the abuse:* The more intrusive or progressive the abuse, the more trauma suffered. Intercourse, sodomy, and oral copulation cause more trauma than fondling or masturbation.
5. *The age the abuse started:* Children develop incrementally. When the abuse begins, it will cause different types of problems, depending on the child's age.
6. *The reactions of others to disclosure of the abuse:* When the child tells other adults of the abuse, their reaction may affect how the child perceives himself or herself. If the adult discounts the abuse or blames the child, the child may not discuss the incidents until adulthood. Keeping the abuse secret does in fact add to the trauma suffered by the victim.
7. *The personality of the child:* Each person is a distinct individual. Each victim will react in a different way to the abuse and suffer different types and forms of trauma.[60]

Hartman and Burgess have developed a conceptual framework for understanding the linkage between sexual abuse and the victim's level of adjustment.[61] This process has two aspects: the phases of sexual abuse and recovery and the concepts for processing traumatic life events. The first phase discusses the experiencing, disclosing, and recovering from child sexual abuse. The second phase addresses how the child views the event and adjusts to the fact of abuse.

The first aspect of this conceptual framework is composed of four distinct phases: preabuse conditions, processing the event, revealing the event, and patterned responses to the event.

PHASE 1: PRETRAUMA—PREABUSE CONDITIONS.   As the title implies, this is the period before the sexual activity. The total sum of the victim's experiences and emotional makeup give an indication of the child's vulnerabilities and risk factors for maladjustment. These experiences include the quality of relationships with siblings and adults, early socialization experiences, and other resources. Preexisting beliefs and values are critical to coping with the abuse.

PHASE 2: TRAUMA ENCAPSULATION—PROCESSING THE EVENT.   This phase encompasses the actual sexual activity and disclosure of the abuse. The activity may be a one-time event or a series of acts. Factors such as the relationship of the molester to the victim, the degree of violence or force used during the assault, the type of defensive mechanisms used by the victim during the abuse, and the child's age all contribute to the level of stress encountered during this phase.

PHASE 3: DISCLOSURE—THE PROCESS OF REVEALING THE EVENT.   The disclosure phase deals with stress factors associated with external forces outside the child's control. How the system responds to the victim's disclosure will affect the amount of stress imposed on the child. Physical examinations, interviews with adults in the criminal justice system, and family members all exert pressure and stress on the child. Different forms of stress will occur, depending on whether the assailant is a family member or a stranger. If the molester is a family member, how others react to the disclosure will affect the child. If the molester is a stranger, whether the stranger is in custody or free will strongly influence the child's stress level.

PHASE 4: POSTTRAUMA OUTCOME—PATTERNED RESPONSES TO THE EVENT.   This phase extends at least two years after the criminal action and/or therapy. How is the child adjusting to the situation? Is the child and family discussing the abuse and responding to the child's reactions to it? How the immediate family handles this time period will affect the stress the child feels.

The second phase of processing the sexual molestation involves examining the victim's postabuse reactions. The details of the abuse are retained in active memory until the victim can transfer it to a distant memory. Therapy assists in processing this event. This processing of information and storage of unpleasant memories allows the child to function in society. The ability of the child to adjust to sexual molestation is dependent on a number of factors. Professionals are still learning how children cope with abuse and how they adjust to the trauma of sexual molestation.

Summary

Child sexual abuse is one of the most emotional areas of family violence. It is a crime that occurs in secret and may last only moments or for years. Even the definition of child sexual abuse is shrouded in controversy. Although professionals cannot explain why it occurs, some scholars have established certain profiles or characteristics of both the abuser and the abused.

Unlike other forms of child abuse, sexual molestation may not leave scars that are visible to other persons. However, certain symptoms should raise the suspicion of any professional. Physical, behavioral, and medical indicators may lead a professional to uncover incidents of sexual abuse. As with all indicators, these must be viewed with caution. Concerning medical indicators, the general public must be made aware that certain commonly held beliefs may be misleading. For example, it is possible to have a completed act of intercourse and still retain an intact hymen in young girls.

Child sexual abuse takes many forms. Incest is an act of sexual activity with blood relatives. In some countries, this is accepted as normal. In the United States, however, it is both a crime and a moral wrong.

Child pornography is alive and well in the United States. It is a multimillion-dollar business that preys on unsuspecting children. The U.S. Supreme Court has established a definition of obscenity, and films depicting children engaged in sexual activity clearly fall within it. However, child pornography continues as a profitable business despite severe criminal sanctions and public condemnation.

The consequences of child sexual abuse are traumatic and long-lasting, and various scholars have attempted to study the ramifications of this type of child maltreatment. Although there is disagreement among these authorities, all agree that it is a serious problem that must be studied. Hopefully, a solution can be found to ease the pain of the survivors of sexual abuse.

Key Terms

child sexual abuse—sexual exploitation or sexual activities with a child under circumstances that indicate that the child's health or welfare is harmed or threatened.

intrafamilial sexual abuse—includes incest and refers to any type of exploitative sexual contact occurring between relatives.

extrafamilial sexual abuse—exploitative sexual contact with perpetrators who may be either known or unknown to the child.

four preconditions model of sexual abuse—establishes preconditions that create a personal and social context for expressing sexually abusive behaviors.

pedophilia—a sexual fixation on young children, usually translated into sexual acts.

incest—sexual relations between blood relatives.

obscenity—material that an average person, by applying contemporary community standards, would find that taken as a whole, appeals to mainly prurient interest in sex; depicts or describes sexual conduct in a patently offensive way; and taken as a whole, lacks serious literary, artistic, political, or scientific value.

Discussion Questions

1. On the basis of your reading of this chapter, can you provide a more comprehensive definition of child sexual abuse? What about a more specific definition?
2. Can you list at least two reasons why offenders sexually abuse children? Justify your answer.
3. What in your opinion are the strongest physical, behavioral, and medical indicators of child abuse? Why?
4. If you were a professional working in an environment that included young children and you observed a child exhibiting symptoms that led

you to suspect child sexual abuse, what would you do?

5. Which should be punished more strongly, incest or stranger sexual abuse? Why?

6. Should we punish or treat child molesters? Some argue that pedophiles can never be cured. Does this mean they should be locked up for life?

7. Should experts be used in child abuse cases? Is the use of paid professionals subject to abuse by the highest bidder?

Suggested Readings

Ammerman, R. T., and M. Hersen, eds. *Treatment of Family Violence* (Wiley, New York, 1990).

Burgess, A. W. *Child Pornography and Sex Rings* (Lexington Books, Lexington, Mass., 1984).

Cicchetti, D., and V. Carlson, eds. *Child Maltreatment* (Cambridge University Press, Cambridge, Mass., 1989).

Draucker, C. B., and D. Martsolf. *Counseling Survivors of Childhood Sexual Abuse* (SAGE, Thousand Oaks, Calif., 2006).

Finkelhor, D. *Sexually Victimized Children* (Free Press, New York, 1979).

Finkelhor, D. *Child Sexual Abuse: New Theories and Research* (Free Press, New York, 1984).

Ford, H. *Women Who Sexually Abuse Children* (John Wiley & Sons, New York, 2006).

Fox, R. *The Red Lamp of Incest* (Dutton, New York, 1980).

Groth, A. N. *Men Who Rape* (Plenum, New York, 1979).

Herman, J. *Father–Daughter Incest* (Harvard University Press, Cambridge, Mass., 1981).

Justice, F., and R. Justice. *The Broken Taboo: Sex in the Family* (Human Services Press, New York, 1979).

Lederer, L., ed. *Take Back the Night* (Morrow, New York, 1980).

Lewis, P. *Delayed Prosecution for Childhood Sexual Abuse* (Oxford University Press, New York, 2006).

Pence, D., and C. Wilson. *Team Investigation of Child Sexual Abuse* (SAGE, Thousand Oaks, Calif., 1994).

Pipe, M., ed. *Child Sexual Abuse: Disclosure, Delay, and Denial* (Lawrence Erlbaum Associates, Florence, Ky., 2007).

Porter, E. *Treating the Young Male Victims of Sexual Assault* (Safer Society Press, Syracuse, New York, 1986).

Russell, D. *Rape in Marriage* (Macmillan, New York, 1982).

Van Hasselt, V. B., R. L. Morrison, A. S. Bellack, and M. Hersen, eds. *Handbook of Family Violence* (Plenum, New York, 1988).

Wortley, R., and S. Smallbone, eds. *Situational Prevention of Child Sexual Abuse* (Criminal Justice Press, Devon, United Kingdom, 2006).

Endnotes

1. T. Luster and S. Small, "Sexual Abuse History and Problems in Adolescence: Exploring the Effects of Moderating Variables," *Journal of Marriage and the Family* 59(1) (1997), p. 131.

2. C. R. Hartman and A. W. Burgess, "Sexual Abuse of Children: Causes and Consequences," in D. Cicchetti and V. Carlson, eds., *Child Maltreatment* (Cambridge University Press, Cambridge, 1989), p. 98.

3. D. Finkelhor, *Sexually Victimized Children* (Free Press, New York, 1979).

4. D. Finkelhor, *Child Sexual Abuse: New Theories and Research* (Free Press, New York, 1984).

5. D. Russell, *Rape in Marriage* (Macmillan, New York, 1982).

6. L. Timnick, "22% in Survey Were Child Abuse Victims," *Los Angeles Times*, August 25, 1985, p. 1.

7. W. Friedrich, P. Grambsch, D. Broughton, J. Kuiper, and R. L. Beilke, "Normative Sexual Behavior in Children," *Pediatrics* 88 (1991), p. 456.

8. D. G. Kilpatrick, C. N. Edmonds, and A. K. Seymour, *Rape in America: A Report to the Nation* (National Victim Center, Arlington, Va., 1992).

9. L. Jones and D. Finkelhor, *The Decline in Child Abuse Cases*, Juvenile Justice Bulletin, OJJDP, Washington, D.C. (January 2001).

10. T. E. Hartman and A. Burgess, "Sexual Abuse of Children: Causes and Consequences," pp. 98–99. See also Howard N. Synder, *Sexual Assault of Young Children as Reported to Law Enforcement: Victim, Incident, Offender Characteristics* (Bureau of Justice Statistics, Washington, D.C., July 2000).

11. This is a shortened version of the definition contained in the Child Abuse Prevention and Treatment Act of 1974, which is one of the most widely adopted statutes defining child sexual abuse.

12. D. A. Wolfe, V. V. Wolfe, and C. L. Best, "Child Victims of Sexual Assault," in V. B. Van Hasselt et al., eds., *Handbook of Family Violence* (Plenum, New York, 1988).

13. J. R. Conti, "Victims of Child Sexual Abuse," in R. T. Ammerman and M. Hersen, eds., *Treatment of Family Violence* (Wiley, New York, 1990), pp. 64–65.

14. S. D. McIlwaine, "Interrogating Child Molesters," *FBI Law Enforcement Bulletin* (June 1994), pp. 1–4.

15. See J. Conti, "The Effects of Sexual Abuse on Children: A Critique and Suggestions for Future Research," *Victimology: An International Journal* 10 (1985), pp. 110–130; and J. Conti, I. Berliner, and J. Schurman, "The Impact of Sexual Abuse on Children: Final Report," available from the authors at the University of Chicago, 969 E. 60th Street, Chicago, Ill. 60637.

16. D. Finkelhor, *Child Sexual Abuse.*

17. E. Porter, *Treating the Young Male Victims of Sexual Assault* (Safer Society Press, Syracuse, New York, 1986).

18. Ibid.

19. Howard N. Synder, *Sexual Assault of Young Children as Reported to Law Enforcement: Victim,* *Incident and Offender Characteristics* (Bureau of Justice Statistics, Washington, D.C., June 2000).

20. A. N. Groth, *Men Who Rape* (Plenum, New York, 1979).

21. S. V. Valente, "Sexual Abuse of Boys," *Journal of Child and Adolescent Psychiatric Nursing* 18(1) (2005), pp. 10–16.

22. D. J. Gelinas, "The Persisting Negative Effects of Incest," *Psychiatry* 46 (1983), pp. 312–322.

23. C. A. Courtios, "Studying and Counseling Women with Past Incest Experience," *Victimology: An International Journal* 5 (1980), pp. 322–334.

24. D. Finkelhor, *Child Sexual Abuse*, and E. Porter, *Treating the Young Male Victim of Sexual Assault.*

25. D. Finkelhor, *Child Sexual Abuse.*

26. S. Petronio, "Disclosure of Sexual Abuse by Children and Adolescents," *Journal of Applied Communication Research* 24(3) (1996), p. 181.

27. Based on R. Laymen, *Current Issues: Vol. I. Child Abuse* (Omnigraphics, Detroit, 1990), p. 36. Originally circulated by the Children's Safety Project in Manhattan.

28. N. D. Kellogg, S. W. Menard, and A. Santos, "Genital Anatomy in Pregnant Adolescents: Normal Does Not Mean Nothing Happened," *Pediatrics* 113(1) (2004), p. 67.

29. A. R. De Jong and M. Rose, "Frequency and Significance of Physical Evidence in Legally Proven Cases of Child Sexual Abuse," *Pediatrics* 84 (1989), p. 1022.

30. W. Marshall, T. Puls, and C. Davidson, "New Sexual Abuse Spectrum in an Era of Increased Awareness," *American Journal of Diseases of Children* 142 (1988), p. 664.

31. N. Kellogg, "The Evaluation of Sexual Abuse in Children," *Pediatrics* 116(2) (2005), p. 506.

32. H. Dubowitz, M. Black, and D. Harrington, "The Diagnosis of Child Sexual Abuse," *American Journal of Children* 146 (1992), p. 688.

33. W. Enos, T. B. Conrath, and J. C. Byer, "Forensic Evaluation of the Sexually Abused Child," *Pediatrics* 78 (1986), pp. 385, 395.

34. See Classification 302.2, *Diagnostic Criteria*, DSM-IV (American Psychiatric Association, Washington, D.C., 1994), pp. 527–528.

35. J. N. Groth, *Men Who Rape.*

36. J. Conti, "The Effects of Sexual Abuse on Children."

37. B. Justice and R. Justice, *The Broken Taboo: Sex in the Family* (Human Services Press, New York, 1979).

38. J. Conti, "The Effects of Sexual Abuse on Children."

39. F. A. Johnston and S. A. Johnson, "A Cognitive Approach to Validation of the Fixated—Regressed Typology of Child Molesters," *Journal of Clinical Psychology* 53(4) (1997), p. 361.

40. S. Freud, "The Etiology of Hysteria," in *The Complete Psychological Works of Sigmund Freud*, trans. James Strachey, standard ed. (Hogarth, London, 1896).

41. G. Lindsey, "Some Remarks Concerning Incest, the Incest Taboo and Psychoanalytic Theory," *American Psychologist* 22 (1967), pp. 1051–1059.

42. L. H. Morgan, *Ancient Society* (Kerr, Chicago, 1877).

43. K. Meiselman, *Incest* (Jossey-Bass, San Francisco, 1978).

44. B. Malinowski, *Sex and Repression in Savage Society* (Routledge & Kegan Paul, London, 1927).

45. J. Herman, *Father–Daughter Incest* (Harvard University Press, Cambridge, Mass., 1981).

46. R. Fox, *The Red Lamp of Incest* (Dutton, New York, 1980).

47. B. Demott, "The Pro-Incest Lobby," *Psychology Today* (March 1980), p. 12.

48. R. Summit and J. Kryso, "Sexual Abuse of Children: A Clinical Spectrum," *American Journal of Orthopsychiatry* 48(2) (1985), p. 242.

49. J. Densen-Gerber, "Child Prostitution and Child Pornography: Medical, Legal, Societal Aspects of the Commercial Exploitation of Children," in K. MacFarlane, B. B. Jones, and L. L. Jenstrom, eds., *Sexual Abuse of Children: Selected Readings*, GPO Pub. No. 78–30161. (Department of Health, Education and Welfare, Washington, D.C., 1980), pp. 77–81.

50. L. Lederer, ed., *Take Back the Night* (Morrow, New York, 1980), pp. 77–78.

51. A. W. Burgess, *Child Pornography and Sex Rings* (Lexington, Mass., 1984).

52. S.R. Rep. No. 438, 95th Cong., 2nd Session (1978).

53. *Miller v. California.* 413 U.S. 881 (1973).

54. See Gary D. Marts, "First Amendment and Freedom of Speech—'It's OK—She's a Pixel, Not a Pixie': The First Amendment Protects Virtual Pornography. Ashcroft v. Free Speech Coalition," 535 U.S. 234 (2002), 25 *U. Ark. Little Rock L. Rev.* 717 (2003).

55. 18 U.S.C. Section 2256 (2000).

56. 535 U.S. 234 (2002).

57. J. R. Conti, "Progress in Treating the Sexual Abuse of Children," *Social Work* 22 (1984), pp. 258–263.

58. J. Briere, "The Effects of Childhood Sexual Abuse on Later Psychological Functioning: Defining a Post–Sexual-Abuse Syndrome," paper presented at the Third National Conference on Sexual Victimization of Children, Washington, D.C., 1984.

59. Herman, *Father–Daughter Incest.*

60. C. C. Tower, *Understanding Child Abuse and Neglect*, 2nd ed. (Allyn & Bacon, Needham Heights, Mass., 1993), pp. 146–147.

61. C. R. Hartman and A. W. Burgess, "Sexual Abuse of Children: Causes and Consequences," in D. Cicchetti and V. Carlson, eds., *Child Maltreatment* (Cambridge University Press, New York, 1989), pp. 114–122.

7

Child Neglect

CHAPTER OBJECTIVES

After studying this chapter, you should be able to:

- Explain the dynamics of child neglect;
- Define the types of child neglect;
- Discuss the important aspects of the Child Abuse Prevention and Treatment Act;
- Explain what constitutes medical neglect;
- Discuss the effects on children when they observe violence being committed on other family members.

Detailed Look at What You Should Know About Child Neglect

- Child neglect is considered as the most common form of maltreatment of children.
- **Child neglect** is the negligent treatment or maltreatment of a child by a parent or by a caretaker under circumstances, indicating harm or threatened harm to the child's health or welfare.
- Child neglect covers a wide range of activities or omissions that impact on the physical and emotional well-being of a child.
- Simply being poor does not make a neglectful parent.
- The **economic theory of child neglect** suggests that neglect is caused by stress as a result of living in poverty.
- The **ecological theory of child neglect** views family behavior and neglect as a result of social causes.

- The **personalistic theory of child neglect** attributes child neglect to individual personality characteristics of the caretakers.

- **Child Abuse Prevention and Treatment Act (CAPTA)**—(42 U.S. Code 5116, as amended in 2003) provides the foundation for a national definition of child abuse and neglect.

- No single set of factors establishes a clearly defined line dividing neglect and poor parenting. Any list must be viewed with caution.

- Certain physical acts by children should alert teachers, nurses, social workers, and others to look for the reasons for these actions. Individual acts may appear and, in many instances, are simply normal childhood activities.

- Professionals should not only be alert to physical indications of neglect, but also watch for emotional or psychological indications that may signal child neglect or maltreatment. These factors may be normal stages of childhood development or may indicate a darker secret that should be examined.

- *Failure to thrive* is an identifiable medical diagnosis. This designation classifies children whose development is deficient in relation to the established norms and whose physical condition is incompatible with viability and growth.

- *Emotional neglect* consists of acts or omissions that are judged by community standards and professional expertise to be psychologically damaging to the child.

- Drug and alcohol neglect is a serious form of child maltreatment.

- **Medical neglect** is the refusal of a parent or a caretaker to obtain acceptable medical services for the child.

- In *Heinemann's Appeal* in 1880, the courts established the principle that when parents fail to provide medical care for their children, the state may intervene to do so.

- One of the most emotional and hard-fought battles dealing with medical neglect concerns the conflict between parents' religious beliefs that may prevent them from seeking and accepting medical care and the state's interest in protecting children.

- **Abandonment** is parental conduct that indicates a conscious rejection of the obligations of parenthood. It may take many forms and is usually established by presenting evidence of the parents, leaving the child without proper care or custody.

- Children who observe family violence exhibit a number of different responses.

INTRODUCTION

Some scholars have stated that child neglect is the most common form of maltreatment. According to Arthur Green, in New York the reported cases of neglect outnumbered those of physical abuse by eleven to one in 1987.[1] In 1998, there were an estimated 903,000 victims of child maltreatment nationwide. More than half of the victims (53%) suffered from neglect.[2] Another more recent study confirms prior research that neglect is more prevalent than other forms of child abuse. In 2002, the Prevent Child Abuse (PCA) America issued a joint report with the Centers for Disease Control and Prevention (CDC) that indicates that in 2000 there were 879,000 cases of child maltreatment with 515,800 (63%) categorized as neglect.[3]

Not all abuse of a child is physical.

Child neglect is an important topic that all professionals should understand. Neglect is less obvious than physical or sexual abuse, and it may continue for years without any outsiders ever being aware that the child they see daily is a victim. It has many faces, forms, and appearances. There are serious cases in which a child's life is threatened and more mundane acts where the child is simply neglected on a daily basis. This chapter explores some of the more common forms of child neglect.

In the past twenty years, numerous textbooks, articles, and studies have been published that deal with neglect. The literature runs the gamut, from examining assessment techniques of neglect[4] to listing all the different forms of this abuse.[5] Except for rare instances, such as the *Home Alone* case, child neglect does not receive the public attention that child sexual and physical abuse generates.[6] Part of the reason for this lack of emphasis may lie in the definition and nature of child neglect.

DEFINITION

Child neglect is the negligent treatment or maltreatment of a child by a parent or by a care-taker under circumstances indicating harm or threatened harm to the child's health or welfare. Although this appears at first glance to be a simple and straightforward statement, it covers a wide range of activities or omissions that impact on the physical and emotional well-being of a child.

At what point does mere inattention or lack of knowledge translate itself into child neglect? The definition given earlier would require an act or omission that results in harm or threatens to cause harm to a child's health or welfare. This act or omission may be physical or psychological. A strict interpretation of this definition would require that parents or caretakers guard their children like prisoners. However, this approach is unrealistic because children are mobile, getting into drawers, cabinets, and every corner in the house and yard. More useful, therefore, is a continuum that stretches from momentary inattention to gross inaction.

Somewhere along this line, acceptable parenting ends and child neglect begins. The following sections define the circumstances that professionals and courts have agreed on as clear cases of child neglect.

CAUSES OF NEGLECT

Are poor children neglected and rich children well cared for? Unfortunately, a substantial number of people in society equate poverty with neglect, but simply being poor does not make a neglectful parent. There are children who live at the edge of poverty or below the poverty level and are loved and nurtured. On the other hand, there are children who live in million-dollar homes but are neglected or psychologically abused on a daily basis. The causes of neglect are varied and wide ranging.

Polansky and his colleagues, in their classic textbook *Damaged Parents: An Anatomy of Child Neglect*, established three major causes of neglect: economic causes, ecological causes, and personalistic causes.[7] The **economic theory of child neglect** suggests that neglect is caused by stress as a result of living in poverty. The **ecological theory of child neglect** views family behavior and neglect as a result of social causes. The **personalistic theory of child neglect** attributes child neglect to individual personality characteristics of the caretakers.

Numerous studies have indicated that poverty is an important factor in the parents' ability to care for their children, and the question must be asked whether poverty causes neglect or whether poverty is the result of the parents' inability to function.[8]

Some scholars have indicated that families who neglect their children live in an environment that is unfriendly and characterized by low morale and hopelessness.[9] As indicated earlier, the issue is whether the environment causes neglect or is a characteristic of the parents' inability to function.

Focus

Child Abuse Prevention and Treatment Act

Child Abuse Prevention and Treatment Act (CAPTA)—(42 U.S. Code 5116, as amended in 2003) provides the foundation for a national definition of child abuse and neglect. CAPTA defines child abuse and neglect as "at a minimum, any recent act or failure to act on the part of a parent or caretaker, which results in death, serious physical or emotional harm, sexual abuse or exploitation, or an act or failure to act which presents an imminent risk of serious harm."

CAPTA was reauthorized on December 20, 2010, by the CAPTA Reauthorization Act of 2010 (P.L. 111–320).

Purpose

1. To support community-based efforts to develop, operate, expand, enhance, and, where appropriate to network, initiatives aimed at the prevention of child abuse and neglect, and to support networks of coordinated resources and activities to better strengthen and support families to reduce the likelihood of child abuse and neglect; and

2. To foster an understanding, appreciation, and knowledge of diverse populations in order to be effective in preventing and treating child abuse and neglect.

(continued)

American Bar Association Statement on CAPTA

[Excerpts from the American Bar Association director Thomas M. Susman's, July 15, 2009, letter to U.S. Senate and House committee members]

Dear Mr. Chairman Harkin and Ranking Member Cochran:

Your Subcommittee will soon consider Fiscal Year 2010 appropriations recommendations for the Departments of Labor, Health and Human Services, and Education. On behalf of the American Bar Association, I am writing to urge your support for funding for programs under the Child Abuse Prevention and Treatment Act (CAPTA) at the authorized levels of $84 million in FY 2010 for CAPTA basic state grants and $80 million for CAPTA Title II community-based prevention grants. In addition, we urge funding for the CAPTA discretionary research and demonstration grants at the level of $37 million.

CAPTA funding helps states improve the child protective services infrastructure for screening, assessing, and investigating each year more than three million reports of possible abuse and neglect of children. Although the most recent data, released this month by the Department of Health and Human Services, shows decrease in the number of substantiated cases of child abuse and neglect to 794,000 in 2007, child maltreatment-related deaths rose 15.5 percent in that same period. In 2007, 1,760 American children, nearly three-quarters of whom were under four years of age, died as a result of abuse or neglect. During that same year, child protective services agencies received nearly 3.2 million reports of child maltreatment and were able to screen 62 percent of these reports for investigation. In short, our nation's child welfare system is stretched far beyond capacity. Only by fully funding CAPTA can we hope to give our children the prevention and treatment services they deserve.

A more reasoned approach seems to be that of the personalistic theories. In this approach, neglect is viewed as being caused by complex maladaptive interactions and/or lack of essential caretaking behaviors that are influenced by the level of parental skill, knowledge deficits, and other stress factors.[10]

Other models profile personalities of neglectful parents or caretakers, and no study or theory has gained universal acceptance. However, certain factors have been established that indicate when a child is or may be neglected.[11] The following section examines those factors.

Major Federal Legislation Concerning the Protection of Children from 1974 to Present:

2015 P. L. 114–22— Justice for Victims of Trafficking Act of 2015: (Authorized programs to provide justice for the victims of trafficking, including grants to States to combat trafficking, child abuse investigation and prosecution programs, services for victims of child pornography, and domestic child human trafficking deterrence programs)

2012 P. L. 112–275—Protect Our Kids Act of 2012: (An Act to establish a commission to develop a national strategy and recommendations for reducing fatalities resulting from child abuse and neglect)

2010: P.L. 111–320—CAPTA Reauthorization Act of 2010

2008: P.L. 110–351—Fostering Connections to Success and Increasing Adoptions Act of 2008

2006: P.L. 109–288—Child and Family Services Improvement Act of 2006

2006: P.L. 109–248—Adam Walsh Child Protection and Safety Act of 2006

2006: P.L. 109–239—Safe and Timely Interstate Placement of Foster Children Act of 2006

2003: P.L. 108–36—Keeping Children and Families Safe Act of 2003

2001: P.L. 107–133—Promoting Safe and Stable Families Amendments of 2001

(continued)

2000: P.L. 106–279—Intercountry Adoption Act of 2000

2000: P.L. 106–177—Child Abuse Prevention and Enforcement Act of 2000

1999: P.L. 106–169—Foster Care Independence Act of 1999

1997: P.L. 105–89—Adoption and Safe Families Act of 1997

1996: P.L. 104–235—Child Abuse Prevention and Treatment Amendments of 1996

1994: P.L. 103–382—Multiethnic Placement Act of 1994

1993: P.L. 103–66—Family Preservation and Support Services Program Act of 1993

1992: P.L. 102–295—Child Abuse, Domestic Violence, Adoption, and Family Services Act

1988: P.L. 100–294—Child Abuse Prevention, Adoption, and Family Services Act of 1988

1984: P.L. 98–457—Child Abuse Amendments of 1984

1980: P.L. 96–272—Adoption Assistance and Child Welfare Act of 1980

1978: P.L. 95–608—Indian Child Welfare Act (ICWA) of 1978

1978: P.L. 95–266—Child Abuse Prevention and Treatment and Adoption Reform Act of 1978

1974: P.L. 93–247—Child Abuse Prevention and Treatment Act (CAPTA) of 1974

As can be noted from the above list, the federal government has been very active in passing legislation involving the protection of children. The reader who wants more information on one of the above acts may simply do an Internet search using either the Public Law designation or the title of the act.

Practicum

Situation 1: Howard is babysitting his eight-month-old daughter while his wife works nights. Howard is a smoker and has run out of cigarettes. He checks the baby, sees that she is sleeping, walks over to the neighborhood store, and buys a pack of cigarettes. Has Howard committed child neglect?

Situation 2: Jane has had to battle a weight problem all her life. She is determined that her two-month-old baby will not have the same problem. Therefore, Jane only feeds the baby six bottles of nonfat milk a day. (A traditional feeding of a two-month-old baby is approximately thirty-two ounces of formula a day.) The baby is losing weight and is constantly crying. Has Jane committed child neglect?

Situation 3: Karen is a housewife who lives in an expensive four-thousand-square-foot home. While talking to a friend on the phone, Karen's two-year-old son went into the backyard and climbed over the fence surrounding the swimming pool. He fell into the pool and would have drowned except that their dog jumped in and pulled him out. Has Karen committed child neglect?

Situation 4: Bill was watching television when his eighteen-month-old child walked into the kitchen and fell on the tile floor. She cut her lip and required three stitches. Has Bill committed child neglect?

Characteristics of Parents or Caretakers Who Neglect Their Children

Inability to plan

These parents lack the ability to establish goals, objectives, and direction. They may have low frustration levels and little ability to delay gratification.

(continued)

Lack of knowledge	Lack of motivation
Parents have little or no knowledge about children's needs, housekeeping skills, cooking, and so on.	Parents lack energy, have little desire to learn, and have no other standard of comparison. These parents are apathetic and futile in that they are withdrawn and feel that nothing is worth doing.
Lack of judgment	
Parents may leave a young child alone and unsupervised.	

Source: Based on H. B. Contwell, "Child Neglect," in C. H. Kempe and R. E. Helfer, eds., *The Battered Child* (University of Chicago Press, Chicago, 1980), pp. 183–197.

INDICATIONS OF CHILD NEGLECT

No single set of factors establishes a clearly defined line dividing neglect and poor parenting. Any list must be viewed with caution. However, any professional who observes certain characteristics in young children should be suspicious. At the very least, professionals need to reassure themselves of the welfare of the child. Initial suspicion may lead to verification of child neglect. On the other hand, further checking may indicate a situational fact pattern that can or will cure itself without the intervention of public agencies.

Certain physical acts by children should alert teachers, nurses, social workers, and others to look for the reasons for these actions. Individual acts may appear and, in many

Physical Indicators	Behavioral Indicators
Poor growth pattern	Developmental lags
Constant hunger, malnutrition	Begs or steals food, forages through garbage; always hungry
Poor hygiene, body odor, and lice; inappropriate clothing	Destructive to self and/or others; extremes in behavior—aggressive and withdrawn; hyperactive
Constant fatigue; listlessness; falls asleep in class	Assumes adult responsibilities or acts in pseudomature fashion; exhibits infantile behavior; delinquent behavior
Consistent lack of supervision, especially for long periods or in dangerous conditions	
Unexplained bruises or injuries as a result of poor supervision	Depressed/apathetic; states "no one cares"
Unattended physical problems or medical needs such as lack of proper immunizations, gross dental problems, needs glasses/ hearing aids	Frequent school absences or chronic tardiness; seeks attention and/or affection
	Hypochondria

Source: Based on R. Layman, *Current Issues—Volume 1: Child Abuse* (Omnigraphics, Inc., Detroit, 1990), p. 37. Originally circulated by the Children's Safety Project in Manhattan.

Focus

Parents Who Reject Their Children

According to medical researchers Angelo Giardino and Eileen Giardino there are parents who reject their children. They refuse to touch or show affection to their children and do not acknowledge the childrens' presence or accomplishments. Parental rejecting behavior includes:

- Refusing to allow a child to get needed psychological or medical treatment;

- Constantly belittling and ridiculing the child;
- Purposefully and continually embarrassing the child;
- Singling the child out for punishment or criticism;
- Undermining the child's attachment to others;
- Routinely rejecting the child's ideas and desires.

Source: A.Giardino and E. Giardino. *Recognition of Child Abuse for the Mandated Reporter*, 3rd ed. (G.W. Medical Publishing, St. Louis, 2002), pp. 66–67.]

instances, are simply normal childhood activities. However, if more than one of these acts continue, the professional should begin to look for a possible pattern of neglect.

Professionals should not only be alert to physical indications of neglect, but also watch for emotional or psychological indications that may signal child neglect or maltreatment. These factors may be normal stages of childhood development or may indicate a darker secret that should be examined.

Physical or emotional indicators may assist in determining whether a child is suffering from neglect. One form of child neglect occurs prior to the preschool years and can be life threatening. The next section discusses this serious form of child neglect.

FAILURE-TO-THRIVE SYNDROME

Failure to thrive is a term that has generated controversy among scholars and medical professionals. The term has come to mean different things to different groups. One perspective states that failure to thrive is a result of the parents' failure to meet the nutritional needs of their children. The child exhibits a low height and weight and small head circumference when compared with other children.[12] Ruth Kempe and Richard Goldbloom argued that the term *failure to thrive* is misleading. They have used the term *malnutrition and growth retardation* or *growth failure without other disease* to describe the same or similar symptoms.[13] Kempe and her colleagues believe that the term *failure to thrive* is misleading in that the condition may be caused either by a disease or by a nonorganic cause. Many authorities believe that these distinctions are mutually exclusive. Kempe argues that clinical evidence supports her position. However, numerous scholars and medical professionals continue to identify the symptoms of malnutrition and growth retardation as *failure to thrive*. By whatever name this form of neglect is called, it can have devastating consequences for the infant.

Definition

Failure to thrive is an identifiable medical diagnosis. This designation classifies children whose development is deficient in relation to the established norms and whose physical condition is incompatible with viability and growth.[14] What is not so clear is the cause of this condition. It may be disease based or organically caused or may be attributed to nonorganic or family causes.

Nonorganic failure to thrive (NFTT) has been defined as a condition found in infants and diagnosed by the presence of two factors: The infant is under the fifth percentile in both height and weight, and the infant at one time weighed and was of a height within the expected norm.[15] Failure to treat this condition can result in the death of the infant. The child simply wastes away and dies.

Characteristics

Children suffering from NFTT exhibit emaciation, paleness, weakness with little subcutaneous fat, and decreased muscle mass. Most of the children appear listless, apathetic, and motionless.[16] The responding professional must be careful not to confuse NFTT with other physical ailments. Diseases such as chronic renal disease, food allergies, or congenital heart disease may cause a child to fail to grow and gain weight. NFTT is a complex medical condition that requires even physicians to carefully examine the child.

Although the Focus discussing a medical response to failure to thrive lists some characteristics indicating this form of neglect, other authorities have provided a more in-depth list of risk factors. Block lists the following risk factors that should alert a pediatrician to the possibility of neglect as the cause of NFTT:

- Parental depression, stress, marital strife, divorce;
- Parental history of abuse as a child;
- Mental retardation and psychological abnormalities in the parents;
- Young and single mothers without social supports;
- Domestic violence;
- Alcohol or other substance abuse;
- Previous child abuse in the family;
- Social isolation and/or poverty;
- Parents with inadequate adaptive and social skills;
- Parents who are overly focused on career and/or activities away from home;
- Failure to adhere to medical regimens;
- Lack of knowledge of normal growth and development;
- Infant with low birth weight or prolonged hospitalization.[17]

Although the main cause for this condition is the lack of adequate calories, the roots of NFTT can normally be associated with the lack of parent–child relationship. The inability of the parents to respond to the physical needs of the child is a symptom of their lack of parenting skills that may manifest itself in other ways. The lack of parenting skills may prevent the parents from recognizing and responding to the child's emotional and developmental needs. Simply providing the infant with the necessary nutritional supplements

Focus

Failure to Thrive—A Medical Response

The following is an example of a medical protocol for emergency room physicians.

EMERGENCY DEPARTMENT ASSESSMENT OF FAILURE TO THRIVE

1. *Failure to thrive* (FTT) can be defined as an underweight (malnourished) condition in a young child. The causes of FTT are 50 percent due to neglectful underfeeding, 30 percent organic, and 20 percent accidental underfeeding.

   Assessment of FTT in an emergency department is difficult because diagnosis requires historical documentation of prenatal and birth, past medical, family, nutritional, social, and developmental histories. Diagnosis is confirmed only when a child who has not been able to gain weight at home easily gains weight in a hospital.

2. When should a child (eighteen months and younger) seen in an emergency department who is under the 5 percent-in-weight category be reported to the child abuse registry (CAR) as suspected FTT?

   When any of the following risk factors are present, call CAR immediately:

   a. Child displays a ravenous appetite, deprivational behaviors, or wrinkled skin from severe malnutrition.

   b. Family does not have a regular source of medical care for the child (should be able to provide name/address of physician or clinic).

   c. Child has not seen a doctor in the past six months for well-child care.

   d. Child has not had immunizations.

   e. Caretaker is vague about child's nutritional intake.

   f. Caretaker is oblivious or disinterested in child's condition.

   g. Caretaker appears to be under the influence of alcohol or drugs or is emotionally unstable.

   h. Family is residing in a temporary (i.e., in friends' or relatives' home) or transient (i.e., car, park, motel) residence.

3. Special Considerations

   a. Organic causes include chromosomal, gastrointestinal, renal, cardiac, and endocrine disorders, as well as prenatal, central nervous system abnormalities, chronic infections, cystic fibrosis, and idiopathic short stature.

   b. Ten percent of nonorganic FTT have fractures from physical abuse.

   c. Mixed etiology of FTT occurs frequently.

   d. Hospitalization is frequently the only realistic means to provide the child with protection while assessment for FTT occurs.

   e. Blood tests may be helpful in assessing for nutritional anemia.

Source: Based on Dr. James Williams's (Children's Hospital, Oakland) presentation entitled "Medical Evidence," *Physical Child Abuse Prosecution* (California District Attorneys Association, Sacramento, Calif., 1992), p. 30.

does not solve the problem of NFTT. Professionals should work with family members to improve their ability to interact with each other and the child. This approach does not work overnight. It is a time-consuming and prolonged treatment program that must be carefully monitored.

The consequences of NFTT on the child are substantial. Even if the child is initially treated and the original symptoms disappear, the long-term effects of NFTT are not easily remedied. Several follow-up studies have been conducted on children who were initially hospitalized for NFTT. These studies indicated continued growth problems, school failure, and psychological problems, including retardation.[18] Failure to thrive is a physical condition that results from the parents' inability to care physically for the child. The next section discusses emotional neglect and explores the parents' inability to respond to the child emotionally.

EMOTIONAL NEGLECT

Emotional neglect is used as a definition to distinguish this type of abuse from physical maltreatment. Some scholars use the latter term to include all forms of neglect. However, emotional neglect is a specific form of abuse that should be examined independently. Unlike child abuse or certain types of child neglect, there may not be any physical signs on a child who is suffering from emotional abuse. Rather, the "scars" are implanted on the child's mind as a result of the caretaker's actions or inactions. Many jurisdictions require proof that the psychological injury to the child is a direct result of emotional abuse. Consequently, this is one of the most difficult forms of child neglect to prove. Whereas emotional abuse may cause adverse physical reactions in the child, these responses are caused by acts of the caretakers that affect the child's psyche.

Characteristics

Emotional abuse may be considered as nonphysical behavior or attitude that controls, intimidates, subjugates, demeans, punishes, or isolates another person by using degradation, humiliation, or fear. Yelling, screaming, and name-calling are all forms of emotional abuse. More subtle tactics include actions such as refusing to be pleased with anything, isolating an individual from family and friends, and invalidating another's thoughts and feelings. A few examples of emotionally abusive behaviors include:

- Humiliating and degrading the child;
- Accusing and blaming the child for every minor mistake or transgression;
- Isolating the child from other children;
- Withholding affection and emotional support;
- Dismissive, disapproving, or contemptuous looks, comments or behavior toward the child;
- Threatening to harm or damage the child's pets, toys, possessions, or person.

Common effects of emotional abuse are often debilitating. They include depression, confusion, difficulty concentrating and making decisions, overwhelming feelings of worthlessness, hopelessness, and poor physical health.

Definition

Emotional neglect consists of acts or omissions that are judged by community standards and professional expertise to be psychologically damaging the child. These acts are traditionally committed by caretakers who are in a position of power over the child. This power differential

Practicum

Emotional Neglect or Bad Parenting?

Situation 1: Both Sally and Bob work nights. Sally's mother watches Billy, aged two years, at night. After they pick up the baby, they are in need of sleep, so they put Billy in his room and tie the door shut so that they can sleep for six to eight hours.

Situation 2: Jill and Howard believe in nudity within the home. They also undress their three-year-old daughter. They eat, watch television, and do housework undressed.

Situation 3: Liz and Jeff do not believe in corporal punishment. Instead of spanking their four-year-old son, they tell him that unless he is good, they will leave him and the night monsters will eat his legs.

may be based on any number of characteristics, including age, status, position, or relationship. These acts affect the child's psychological stability. This in turn may cause behavioral, cognitive, or physical problems in the child.[19]

As indicated previously, a child suffering from emotional abuse will not have a visible bruise, scar, burn, or broken bone. However, the child's mind may suffer a more terrible and long-lasting injury. Children who are emotionally abused may suffer from feelings of inadequacy, isolation, or being unwanted or unloved. They may have low self-esteem and consider themselves unworthy.[20]

Emotional neglect is hard to detect precisely because there are no physical scars, but it may be manifested by numerous acts or actions. While the definition of emotional neglect may appear simple, describing the characteristics or acts of the caretaker that comprise this form of neglect is more difficult. The following section briefly examines some of the more common forms of this type of child neglect.

Characteristics

Which, if any, of the situations in the Practicum are examples of emotional neglect or simply inexperienced or bad parenting? Clearly, situations 1 and 3 would fall within the definition set forth earlier. Situation 2 may well be acceptable depending on the activities engaged in by the father and mother, or it might fall into the classification of sexual abuse discussed in the previous chapter.

Hart and Brassard in their seminal study identified specific categories of emotional neglect.[21] These acts form a pattern of behavior that includes the following:

Spurning or rejecting the child: The caretaker refuses to acknowledge the child's worth or emotional needs. Examples of spurning include treating the child differently than his or her siblings or calling the child stupid, weak, or worthless.

Isolating the child: The caretaker refuses to allow the child to interact with others. Examples of isolation include locking the child in a room, closet, or other confined space for an extended period of time and denying the child complete access to other adults or children.

Terrorizing the child: The caretaker establishes a state of extreme fear, fright, or dread in the child. Examples of terrorizing include threatening to hurt, mutilate, or abandon the child or placing the child in a frightening environment.

Corrupting the child: The caretaker engages in antisocial behavior with the child. Examples of corrupting the child include requiring him to stay home and act as a servant instead of attending school, involving the child in sexual acts with adults or siblings, and exploiting the child by using him in pornographic movies.

Denying the child emotional responses: The caretaker fails to provide emotional responses necessary for the healthy psychological development of the child. Examples of this form of emotional neglect include mechanical responses to the child, lack of touching and caring, and no eye contact with the child.

Although one act in the above categories may not establish emotional neglect, when engaged in for prolonged periods of time, emotional injury to the child is almost inevitable. Other scholars have established comparable types of categories for emotional neglect.[22] The National Center on Child Abuse and Neglect (NCCAN) established a similar set of categories for its National Incidence Studies in 1980 and 1986. Emotional abuse is also referred to as psychological abuse or maltreatment. It is receiving more and more attention as scholars and researchers continue to study this form of violence. Max Lesnik-Oberstein and his associates in the Netherlands have conducted research on psychologically abusive mothers and concluded that mothers who have high levels of hostility are more likely than other parents to commit psychological abuse.[23] Other scholars, such as Davis, are examining whether the threat of physical punishment (spanking) is a form of emotional abuse.[24] Still other researchers are attempting to validate a method of measuring emotional abuse. Two examples of such tools are the *Psychological Maltreatment Inventory* and the *Child Abuse and Trauma Scale.*[25]

Other authorities have researched the long-term psychological effects of emotional abuse. Simeon conducted an excellent literature review and analysis of the effects of emotional abuse. She acknowledged that there was very little research in this area as compared with physical or sexual abuse. However, her research and review did point out significant findings relating to the long-term psychological effects of emotional abuse. Her research indicated that patients with borderline personality disorder remember both parents as less caring and more controlling. Adults with major depression reported significantly greater emotional abuse and neglect. These patients also reported physical abuse. Finally, when dealing with women suffering from bulimia nervosa, the most distinct difference between those patients and the control group was in the psychological maltreatment suffered by those with eating disorders.[26]

Whether a caretaker is engaging in emotional neglect may vary according to the culture of the family. For example, in some Asian cultures shame is an accepted technique to reinforce family behavior within and outside of the family.[27] Other cultures have their own methods of raising children that are not viewed as abusive by either the parents or the child and therefore do not psychologically damage the child. In our own cultures, many of us have experienced the use of guilt by parents, siblings, loved ones, and others to induce us to respond in certain ways.

The distinction between the use of normal child-rearing techniques and emotional neglect is the psychological damage that is inflicted on the child. If the child suffers as a

Characteristics of Children Who Have Been Emotionally Neglected

Clingy and indiscriminate attachment	Antisocial, destructive behavior
Fearfulness—exaggerated	Enuresis and encopresis
Depressed, withdrawn, apathetic	Habit disorders (biting, rocking, whining, picking at scabs)
Sleep, speech, or eating disorders	
Substance abuse	

Source: Based on Dr. James Williams's (Children's Hospital, Oakland) presentation entitled "Medical Evidence," *Physical Child Abuse Prosecution* (California District Attorneys Association, Sacramento, Calif., 1992), p. 10.

result of the caretaker's acts or omissions and if that suffering is beyond the accepted norm in society, those actions may be labeled as emotional neglect.

OTHER TYPES OF CHILD NEGLECT

The preceding sections briefly discussed some of the more common forms of child neglect. Unfortunately, those types of neglect are not the only types of acts or omissions that result in child neglect. This section examines other types of neglect that threaten the welfare of the child.

Dirty Homes

Dirty homes are those living situations that expose the child to injury or life-threatening illness.[28] The term **dirty home** is used in lieu of *unsafe home environment* to identify a specific form of neglect. Examples of dirty homes include those living arrangements that have exposed wiring, shattered or broken glass, animal feces, lice or rodents, and other situations in which children might injure themselves. The Home Accident Prevention Inventory was developed to measure the safety of the home environment. It evaluates fire and electrical hazards, suffocation risks, and the presence of firearms and poisons.[29]

Simply having a sink full of dirty dishes and soapwater for several days does not raise a household to the level of this form of neglect. A home may be unclean and chock-full of dirty clothes and unwashed dishes and still provide a loving environment for children. Some parents simply do not have money or time to do the laundry or wash dishes on a daily basis.

The discovery of dirty homes may be made by police officers, welfare workers, social workers, nurses, or teachers paying a home visit. Once these professionals are aware of the situation, they should alert the proper agency to evaluate whether the child should be removed from the home or the parents should be given assistance in learning how to maintain a safe and healthy living situation for the child. Sometimes, the dirty home is a result of extreme poverty and the resulting hopelessness that accompanies it. On other occasions, the landlord simply is not responding to requests from low-income tenants. In these situations, intervention by social service agencies may be sufficient to remedy the problem. A dirty home is often a symptom of more serious underlying family problems, such as incest and sexual abuse. Occasionally, authorities will discover a dirty home that results from the parents' inability to cope with everyday life. In these situations, long-term counseling may be required. In the event that the decision is made to remove the child from the home, a critical aspect of the court case will be a description of the home environment. This may come in the form of a narrative, diagrams, or photographs.

A special type of unsafe home environment involves children living in homes that are being used to produce methamphetamines. Children living in these homes face acute risks. The manufacture of methamphetamines involves risks of fires and explosions as well as exposure to toxic chemicals. Producers of methamphetamines many times use common household items, such as kitchen utensils, dishes, sheets, and other linen. In addition, toxic chemicals are frequently discarded outdoors near areas where children play. Children may absorb chemicals into their bodies via ingestion, inhalation, skin contact, or accidental injection.[30]

Dirty-home cases normally require an expert witness to testify to specifics in the home that place the child at risk. Doctors, public health nurses, and in some instances building code

---

Focus

When Should a Child Be Removed from the Home?

In *re G.J. v. Maria H.* (Cal. App. 2d Dist. 2009)

Before the court may order a minor physically removed from his or her parent, it must find, by clear and convincing evidence, the minor would be at substantial risk of harm if returned home and there are no reasonable means by which the minor can be protected without removal (§ 361, subd. (c)(1)). A removal order is proper if it is based on proof of parental inability to provide proper care for the minor and proof of a potential detriment to the minor if he or she remains with the parent (In re Jeannette S. (1979) 94 Cal.App.3d 52, 60 re Jeannette S. (1979) 94 Cal.App.3d 52, 60). The parent does not need to be dangerous, and the minor does not need to have been actually harmed before the removal is appropriate. The focus of the statute is on averting harm to the child.

***B.T. v. M.T.* (Cal. App. 4th Dist. 2008)**

A removal order is proper if it is based on proof of (1) parental inability to provide proper care for the minor and (2) potential detriment to the minor if he or she remains with the parent. The parent does not need be dangerous, and

the minor does not need to have been harmed before removal is appropriate. The focus of the statute is on averting harm to the child.

In *Re Henry V.*, 119 Cal. App. 4th 522, 531 (Cal. App. 1st Dist. 2004)

Our dependency system is premised on the notion that keeping children with their parents while proceedings are pending, whenever safely possible, serves not only to protect parents' rights but also to protect children's and society's best interests. Our society does recognize an "essential" and "basic" presumptive right to retain the care, custody, management, and companionship of one's own child, free of intervention by the government. Maintenance of the familial bond between children and parents—even imperfect or separated parents—comports with our highest values and usually best serves the interests of parents, children, family, and community. Because we so abhor the involuntary separation of parent and child, the state may disturb an existing parent–child relationship only for strong reasons and subject to careful procedures.

inspectors may provide the necessary testimony to establish that the living environment is injurious to the child's well-being.

Drugs and Alcohol

Caretakers who use drugs or alcohol in excess are emotionally unavailable to parent and may not be able to properly supervise their children. In addition, the child may find some portion of a narcotic, ingest it, and suffer serious injury or death. Studies have indicated that substance-abusing parents are highly resistant to changing their behavior.[31] This type of neglect requires long-term intervention by social service agencies.

Another aspect of drug and alcohol neglect concerns mothers who use drugs while pregnant or during nursing. Infants may be born addicted and suffer withdrawal immediately after birth if the mother ingested drugs during her pregnancy. In either situation, the infant is at risk.

If the mother uses drugs during pregnancy, they will readily cross the placenta into the fetus's body. Some parents expose children to drugs in other manners. Prenatal abuse of drugs can cause a wide variety of serious medical complications to the child, including neurological and physical defects, growth retardation, premature delivery, and long-term developmental abnormalities.[32] One source states that one in every ten newborns in the United States has been prenatally exposed to drugs.[33] Another authority estimates that 20 percent of all newborns in California have been prenatally exposed to drugs.[34] Cocaine has been used as a topical anesthetic on sore nipples; bottles and pacifiers have accidentally been contaminated with drugs; and some parents use drugs as an intentional method to soothe an irritable infant.

Cocaine may cause a variety of problems during and after pregnancy.[35] It may lead to spontaneous abortions and increase the chances of premature labor. Neonates exposed in utero suffer a variety of problems, including cardiac and central nervous system abnormalities, hyperactivity, and persistent irritability. These problems may appear at birth or later, during the infant's childhood.

Mothers who smoke marijuana more than once a month have an increased risk of delivering a preterm, low-weight infant. It has been reported that the use of marijuana has a stronger effect on newborns than smoking twenty cigarettes each day during pregnancy.[36] However, other scholars reported no long-term effects from the use of marijuana during pregnancy.

Controversies continue regarding the effects of drugs and/or alcohol on the fetus. Despite these limitations and the lack of clearly accepted research, states have enacted a number of laws mandating the reporting of newborns who have been exposed to drugs.[37] For example, Wiese and Daro report that by 1994 twenty-seven states mandate reporting of newborns who have been exposed to drugs.[38]

Alcohol is one of the most commonly abused substances in the United States. It may be one of the leading causes of mental retardation in children. Mothers who are alcoholic or drink excessively during pregnancy may have babies who suffer from fetal alcohol syndrome (FAS). This is a condition in which the alcohol ingested by the mother crosses the placenta, causing the fetus to have the same blood alcohol level as the mother. The infant will exhibit alcohol withdrawal within the first few days of birth. These signs may include hyperactivity, tremors, seizures, and difficulty in feeding and sleeping. Children who have been exposed to alcohol in utero and who as a result suffer from FAS have an average IQ of 63.[39] Growth failure and abnormalities in the heart, kidneys, ears, and skeletal system have also been reported. It should be noted that not all mothers who have an occasional drink give birth to children suffering from FAS, of which we are just beginning to study the extent and dynamics. Scholars estimate that between one and three infants out of 1,000 newborns suffer from FAS.[40]

Clear legal authority exists for courts to remove the child from the custody of the mother immediately after birth in these situations. In the *Matter of Baby X*, the Michigan Court of Appeals stated:

> Prenatal treatment can be considered probative of a child's neglect. . . . We hold that a newborn suffering narcotics withdrawal symptoms as a consequence of prenatal maternal drug addiction may properly be considered a neglected child within the jurisdiction of the . . . court.[41]

Drug and alcohol neglect is a serious form of child maltreatment. The child may be exposed to these substances during or after pregnancy. Normally, these situations involve action or omissions on the part of the caretakers. Just as there is a controversy surrounding the effect of drugs and/or alcohol on newborns, so is there a raging debate regarding the appropriate remedy or action once this condition is discovered. Some authorities urge the removal of the child from the custody of the mother to ensure that the child is properly cared for. Others claim that such activities infringe on the mother's constitutional right of privacy.[42] Still others argue for the treatment of the pregnant mother in hopes of rehabilitating the mother and keeping the mother and child together.[43] The next section explores medical neglect, which is a type of neglect that occurs when the parents refuse to act.

Medical Neglect

Medical neglect is the refusal of a parent or a caretaker to obtain acceptable medical services for the child. This chapter has indicated that parents and caretakers must provide their children with food, clothing, and shelter. Failure to do so may be classified as neglect. It is equally clear that failure to obtain necessary lifesaving medical care is also neglect.

In *Heinemann's Appeal* in 1880, the courts established the principle that when parents fail to provide medical care for their children, the state may intervene to do so.[44] In that case, the father refused to seek medical care for his wife and three of his children, who were all suffering from diphtheria. All four died as a result of his failure to act. The maternal grandmother sought guardianship of the two remaining children, alleging that she was afraid the same fate would befall them. The Pennsylvania Supreme Court upheld the lower court's granting of the guardianship, stating that the deceased children had been shamefully neglected in regard to their medical treatment.[45] The authority for the state to intervene in neglect cases is based on the state's inherent *parens patriae* authority to protect children.[46]

One of the most emotional and hard-fought battles dealing with medical neglect concerns the conflict between parents' religious beliefs that may prevent them from seeking and accepting medical care and the state's interest in protecting children. When care is necessary to protect the child's life, the state's interest in the welfare of the child will normally prevail. This is based on the constitutional distinction between the right to believe in a religion and the freedom to act in accordance with that belief.

In *Prince v. Massachusetts*, the U.S. Supreme Court set forth a well-reasoned opinion laying out the distinction between the right of belief and the liberty to act on that belief:

> Acting to guard the general interest in youth's well being, the state as *parens patriae* may restrict the parent's control by requiring school attendance, regulating or prohibiting child labor, and in many other ways. Its authority is not nullified merely because the parent grounds his claim to control the child's course of conduct on religion or conscience. Thus, he cannot claim freedom from compulsory vaccination for the child more than for himself on religious grounds. The right to practice religion freely does not include liberty to expose the community or the child to communicable disease or the latter to ill health or death. . . .
>
> Parents may be free to become martyrs themselves. But it does not follow they are free, in identical circumstances, to make martyrs of their children before they have reached the age of full and legal discretion when they can make that decision for themselves.[47]

Since 1944, when this decision was rendered, its reasoning has been consistently followed by both the Supreme Court and state courts. Numerous court decisions uphold the state's right to intervene and order medical treatment over the parent's objections when the alternative might be a life-threatening illness or injury to the child.

When parents refuse medical care that might be advisable but is not essential to the life of the child, courts are divided on whether the state has the same authority to intervene. The greater the threat of harm to the child, the more likely courts will authorize medical treatment. In addition to evaluating the degree of harm or threat to the child, courts will examine whether the medical condition is progressive or stable. If the medical condition is stable, some courts will not allow the state to intervene. Some courts will also consider the child's preferences if he or she is old enough to express a knowing and intelligent answer.

The failure of a parent to obtain medical treatment for a child is clearly a form of child neglect. The state has a right and obligation to protect its citizens and, especially, children who cannot make informed decisions for themselves. The controversy of medical neglect due to failure to treat based on religious grounds is an emotional and sometimes heartbreaking process for both professionals in the field and the parents.

Abandonment

Abandonment is parental conduct that indicates a conscious rejection of the obligations of parenthood. It may take many forms and is usually established by presenting evidence of the parents leaving the child without proper care or custody. Almost everyone has read in newspapers or seen on television cases of newborn babies found in trash containers or on doorsteps of social service agencies. The identity of the mother or the father is almost always unknown. These are clear-cut cases of abandonment.

The sanction for abandonment of a child may be a termination of the parental rights. This is accomplished by either the state or the party with whom the child was placed filing a petition requesting that the parents' rights and obligations to the child be terminated. In the trash container-type case mentioned earlier, courts will hesitate to grant such a petition.

In other situations, the issue of abandonment is not so clear. What if a parent leaves the child with caretakers and does not communicate with them or the child for a two-year period? The caretakers may file a petition to terminate parental rights. At the hearing, the parent shows up and states that he or she would like custody of the child. A parent may abandon a child and then evidence intent to reestablish the parent–child relationship. The question to be asked in the factual situation presented above is whether the parent indicated a conscious rejection of the obligations of parenthood. Some courts will examine all the facts before finding that the child has been abandoned and terminating the parent's rights. Factors such as why the parent left the child, the parent's expressed intentions to care for the child now, and whether the parent attempted to communicate with the child during the separation are all important considerations in determining whether the parent abandoned the child. Abandonment of a child is a form of child neglect, and the state will intervene to protect the child. This intervention may take the form of termination of parental rights.

Children Exposed to Violence

For a number of years, we have been concerned about the effects on children who are exposed to or witness violence either in the home or within society at large. In 1997, the National Institute of Justice released a report by Kilpatrick and Saunders indicating that a significant number of U.S. youth have witnessed incidents of violence.[48] Of the 22.3 million adolescents (aged twelve to seventeen) in the United States, approximately nine million have witnessed

---

Focus

National Center for Children Exposed to Violence (NCCEV)

The National Center for Children Exposed to Violence (NCCEV) was created by grants from the U.S. Departments of Justice, Health and Human Services, U.S. Department of Homeland Security, Office of Domestic Preparedness, and the Urban Area Security Imitative Program in an effort to reduce the incidence and impact of violence on children and families; to train and support the professionals who provide intervention and treatment to children and families affected by violence; and to increase professional and public awareness of the effects of violence on children, families, communities, and society.

The Center is designed to serve as a primary national resource center for anyone seeking information about the effects of violence exposure on children and initiatives addressing these issues, including a dynamic body of literature, Internet resources, and a bibliographic database.

The present information on the center is available from:

National Center for Children Exposed to Violence (NCCEV) [www.nccev.org] or at Yale University, Child Study Center

230 South Frontage Road, New Haven, CT 06520-7900 USA

Source: NCCEV Web site.

some form of serious violence. Although the effects of witnessing violence as a youth are difficult to predict, many researchers believe that there is a correlation between this form of abuse and the development of posttraumatic stress disorder (PTSD).[49]

Wolak and Finkelhor report that children who observe family violence exhibit a number of different responses.[50] These reactions to violence include behavioral (aggression, cruelty to animals, acting out, immaturity, delinquency), emotional (anxiety, anger, depression, and low self-esteem), social (peer rejection, inability to empathize), cognitive (language lag, poor school performance), and physical (difficulty sleeping, poor motor skills, bedwetting). The authors point out that not all children will exhibit these symptoms, nor are researchers sure at this time whether these symptoms are due only to witnessing of family violence or to other factors or difficulties in the home.

Finally, in an excellent review of the literature in this area, Edelson analyzed eighty-four studies that evaluated the effects of witnessing adult domestic violence on the social and physical development of children.[51] Having determined that only thirty-one of these research projects met the requirements of valid research, he examined these projects to determine the effects of violence in the home on children. Significantly, Edelson concluded that children from homes in which their mothers were victims of intimate partner abuse have shown less skill in understanding how others feel and examining situations from others' perspectives when compared to children from nonviolent homes. Research in this area provides strong evidence for the position that children who witness intimate partner abuse in the home may exhibit a variety of behavioral, emotional, cognitive, and long-term developmental problems. However, like other researchers, Edelson concluded that a significant number of children who had witnessed violence in their homes did not display any developmental problems, and he cautioned against assuming that witnessing violence automatically leads to negative outcomes in children.

As a society we have become more aware of the effects visited on children who witness violence in the home. Law enforcement agencies have published training manuals on this topic, and major foundations such as The David and Lucile Packard Foundation have funded continuing research in this area. In a handbook for police who train officers about the effects

What will be the effects on this young child after listening to a violent argument between his parents?

on children exposed to violence, it was pointed out that children who are exposed to domestic violence may experience increased psychological, behavioral, and social problems.[52]

Similar to other authorities, Baker and her associates point out that not all children exposed to domestic violence have problems in adjusting as adults. However, Baker does identify certain facts that influence future adjustment. These factors include the following:

- The nature of the violence (its intensity, proximity, and duration);
- The child (age, gender, developmental stage);
- The child's immediate and broader social context (parent–child relationships, social connections, financial resources).

How a child reacts to witnessing domestic violence is related to a variety of factors. Factors that may help a child cope with exposure to violence in the family include the following:

- The existence of a strong caring relationship with an adult (parent, teacher, relatives);
- Community safe havens (churches, schools);
- A child's own internal resources (intelligence, interpersonal skills).[53]

This is still a developing area within the newly recognized realm of family violence. It is ripe for further research and the development of protocols and responses when we come across children in a violent home. Care must be taken to protect the children and at the same time not to simply react to the situation.

Summary

This chapter has examined the various types of child neglect. In many instances, no clear line exists between poor parenting and neglect. Each situation must be evaluated on its own merits, and professionals must look at the totality of the circumstances to determine whether the child is a victim of neglect.

The causes of neglect are varied and do not simply rest on the assumption that poverty is the cause. The rich and famous can and do subject their children to acts that are clearly child neglect. Although there is no complete or all-inclusive list of physical or behavioral actions that signal a child is a victim of neglect, there are indicators that should raise suspicion in any professional. Caution must be exercised, and care must be taken not to react to a situation that may not be neglect.

Failure to thrive is one of the more serious forms of child neglect. However, there are other valid medical reasons for a child to be under the 5 percent category in height or weight. Medical personnel must carefully evaluate any child who is suspected of suffering from failure to thrive to ensure that they do not misdiagnose the cause.

Emotional neglect is one of the hardest forms of child neglect to define and evaluate. Many parents yell at their children. Has anyone not experienced or heard a parent raising his or her voice to a young child? The key to emotional neglect is the degree of injury the child suffers from the caretaker's actions. Normal parenting may require a caretaker to raise his voice to a child, but when this act becomes the norm and the child is terrorized, threatened, or worse, the situation clearly becomes one of emotional neglect.

Numerous other forms of child neglect exist. Some of the more common types include dirty homes, drug abuse, medical neglect, and abandonment.

Key Terms

child neglect—the negligent treatment or maltreatment of a child by a parent or by a caretaker under circumstances indicating harm or threatened harm to the child's health or welfare.

economic theory of child neglect—suggests that neglect is caused by stress as a result of living in poverty.

ecological theory of child neglect—views the family behavior and neglect as a result of social causes.

personalistic theory of child neglect—attributes child neglect to individual personality characteristics of the caretakers.

nonorganic failure to thrive (NFTT)—a condition found in infants and diagnosed by the presence of

two factors: The infant is under the fifth percentile in both height and weight, and the infant at one time weighed and was of a height within the expected norm.

emotional neglect—acts or omissions that are judged by community standards and professional expertise to be psychologically damaging to the child.

dirty home—those living situations that expose the child to injury or life-threatening illness.

medical neglect—the refusal of a parent or a caretaker to obtain acceptable medical services for the child.

abandonment—parental conduct that indicates a conscious rejection of the obligations of parenthood.

Discussion Questions

1. Based on your reading, what is the single most important cause of neglect? Why?
2. Should professionals rely on charts that list possible indicators of neglect? What are the dangers inherent in these lists?
3. How can physicians and nurses protect themselves from charges that they misdiagnosed a child as a failure to thrive? If they are unsure of the medical condition, should they allow the child to return

home with the parents? What are the advantages and disadvantages of this approach?

4. Emotional neglect is a gray area in family violence. Can you list absolute factors that in your mind establish a fact pattern for emotional neglect?
5. If a mother is found to be addicted to and using drugs during her pregnancy, should the court order the child removed from her custody before it is born? Why? Why not?

Suggested Readings

Ammerman, R., and M. Hersen, eds. *Case Studies in Family Violence* (Plenum, New York, 1991).

Ammerman, R. T., and M. Hersen, eds. *Assessment of Family Violence* (Wiley, New York, 1992).

Feerick, M., ed. *Child Abuse and Neglect: Definitions, Classifications, and a Framework for Research* (Brookes Publishing Company, Baltimore, Md., 2006).

Garbarino, J., E. Guttmann, and J. W. Seeley. *The Psychologically Battered Child* (Jossey-Bass, San Francisco, 1986).

Giardino, A., and E. Giardino. *Recognition of Child Abuse for the Mandated Reporter*, 3rd ed. (G.W. Medical Publishing, St. Louis, 2002).

Horwath, J. *Child Neglect* (Palgrave Macmillan, Hampshire, UK, 2007).

Johnson, C. *Model on Child Abuse and Neglect* (Authorhouse, Bloomington, Ind., 2006).

Katz, S. N. *When Parents Fail* (Beacon, Boston, 1971).

Kempe, C. H., and R. E. Helfer, eds. *The Battered Child* (University of Chicago Press, Chicago, 1980).

Knudsen, D. D, and J. L. Miller, eds. *Abused and Battered: Social and Legal Responses to Family Violence* (Aldine Transaction, New Brunswick, N.J., 2007).

Myers, J. *Evidence in Child Abuse and Neglect*, 2nd ed. (Wiley, New York, 1992).

Polansky, N., M. Chambers, E. Buttenwieser, and D. Williams, eds. *Damaged Parents: An Anatomy of Child Neglect* (University of Chicago Press, Chicago, 1981).

Sherman, P. *Child Protective Services' Response to Child Neglect* (Proquest/UMI, Ann Arbor, Mich., 2006).

Weisz, V. G. *Children and Adolescents in Need* (SAGE, Thousand Oaks, Calif., 1995).

Young, L. *Wednesday's Children* (McGraw-Hill, New York, 1964).

Endnotes

1. A. H. Green, "Child Neglect," in R. Ammerman and M. Hersen, eds., *Case Studies in Family Violence* (Plenum, New York, 1991), p. 135.

2. *Child Maltreatment 1998: Reports from the States to the National Child Abuse and Neglect Data System* (U.S. Department of Health and Human Services, Washington, D.C., 2000).

3. *Monitoring Child Neglect: Summary of Discussions at a Meeting Co-Sponsored by the Centers for Disease Control and Prevention and Prevent Child Abuse America* (Prevent Child Abuse America and Centers for Disease Control and Prevention, Chicago, March 29, 2002).

4. R. T. Ammerman and M. Hersen, *Assessment of Family Violence* (Wiley, New York, 1992).

5. P. Cowen, "Child Neglect: Injuries of Omission," *Pediatric Nursing* 25(4) (1999), p. 401.

6. H. Dubowitz and L. Berliner, "Neglecting the Neglect of Neglect," *Journal of Interpersonal Violence* 4(9) (1994), pp. 556–561.

7. N. Polansky et al., *Damaged Parents: An Anatomy of Child Neglect* (University of Chicago Press, Chicago, 1981), p. 21.

8. See L. Young, *Wednesday's Children* (McGraw-Hill, New York, 1964); and S. N. Katz, *When Parents Fail* (Beacon, Boston, 1971).

9. I. Wolock and B. Horowitz, "Child Maltreatment and Maternal Deprivation among AFDC Families," *Social Service Review* 53 (1979), pp. 175–184.

10. D. J. Hansen and V. M. MacMilian, "Behavioral Assessment of Child Abuse and Neglectful Families: Recent Developments and Current Issues," *Behavior Modification* 14 (1990), pp. 225–278.

11. Compare N. A. Polansky, N. D. Borgman, and C. DeSaix, *Roots of Futility* (Jossey-Bass, San Francisco, 1972); and C. Hally, N. F. Polansky, and N. A. Polansky, *Child Neglect: Mobilizing Services* (National Center on Child Abuse and Neglect, U.S. Department of Health and Human Services, Washington, D.C., 1980).

12. *Child Abuse Prevention Handbook* (Office of the Attorney General, Crime Prevention Center, Sacramento, Calif., 1982), p. 9.

13. R. S. Kempe and R. B. Goldbloom, "Malnutrition and Growth Retardation (Failure to Thrive) in the Context of Child Abuse and Neglect," in R. E. Helfer and R. S. Kempe, eds., *The Battered Child*, 4th ed. (University of Chicago Press, Chicago, 1987), pp. 312–332.

14. J. Giovannoni, "Definitional Issues in Child Maltreatment," in D. Cicchetti and V. Carlson, eds., *Child Maltreatment* (Cambridge University Press, Cambridge, 1989), pp. 12–13.

15. See P. C. English, "Failure to Thrive with Organic Reason," *Pediatric Annuals* 7 (1978), pp. 774–780.

16. Kempe and Goldbloom. "Malnutrition and Growth Retardation," p. 318.

17. R. W. Krebs and N. F. Krebs, "Failure to Thrive as a Manifestation of Child Neglect," *Pediatrics* 116(5) (2005), p. 1234.

18. I. W. Hufton and R. K. Oates, "Nonorganic Failure to Thrive: A Long Term Follow-up," *Pediatrics* 8 (1977), pp. 73–77; and R. K. Oates, A. Peacock, and D. Forrest, "Long Term Effects of Nonorganic Failure to Thrive," *Pediatrics* 75 (1985), pp. 36–40.

19. M. Rorty, J. Yager, and E. Rossotto, "Childhood Sexual, Physical, and Psychological Abuse and Their Relationship to Comorbid Psychopathology in Bulimia," *International Journal of Eating Disorders* 16(4) (1994), pp. 317–335.

20. R. D. Krugman and M. K. Krugman, "Emotional Abuse in the Classroom," *American Journal of Diseases of Children* 138 (1984), pp. 284–286.

21. S. N. Hart and M. Brassard, "Developing and Validating Operationally Defined Measures of Emotional Maltreatment: A Multimodal Study of the Relationships between Caretaker Behaviors and Child Characteristics across Three Developmental Levels." Grant No. DHHS 90CA1216-01 (Department of Health and Human Services and the National Center on Child Abuse and Neglect, Washington, D.C., 1986).

22. See J. Garbarino, E. Guttmann, and J. W. Seeley, *The Psychologically Battered Child* (Jossey-Bass, San Francisco, 1986).

23. M. Lesnik-Oberstein, A. J. Koers, and L. Cohen, "Parent Hostility and Its Sources in Psychologically Abusive Mothers: A Test of the Three-Factor Theory," *Child Abuse & Neglect* 19(1) (1995), p. 33.

24. P. W. Davis, "Threats of Corporal Punishment as Verbal Aggression: A Naturalistic Study," *Child Abuse and Neglect* 20(4) (1996), p. 289.

25. See M. L. Engels and D. Moisan, "The Psychological Maltreatment Inventory: Development of a

Measure of Psychological Maltreatment in Childhood for Use in Adult Clinical Settings," *Psychological Reports* 74 (1994), p. 595; and B. Sanders and E. Becker-Lausen, "The Measurement of Psychological Maltreatment: Early Data on the Child Abuse and Trauma Scale," *Child Abuse and Neglect* 315 (1995).

26. D. Simeon, "Emotional Maltreatment of Children: Relationship to Psychopathology," *Psychiatric Times* 29 (June 1, 2006).

27. M. K. Ho, "Social Work Practices with Asian Americans," in A. Morales and B. W. Sheafor, eds., *Social Work: A Profession of Many Faces* (Allyn & Bacon, Needham Heights, Mass., 1989).

28. See D. J. Hansen and J. E. Warner, "Child Physical Abuse and Neglect," in R. T. Ammerman and M. Hersen, eds., *Assessment of Family Violence* (Wiley, New York, 1992).

29. Ibid., p. 134.

30. *Children at Risk* (U.S. Department of Justice, Washington, D.C., July 2002).

31. R. Famulara, R. Kinscherff, D. Bunshaft, G. Spivak, and T. Fenton, "Parent Compliance to Court-Ordered Treatment Interventions in Cases of Child Maltreatment," *Child Abuse and Neglect: A Guide for Intervention* (U.S. Department of Health and Human Services, Washington, D.C., April 1993).

32. D. Petitti and M. Coleman, "Cocaine and the Risk of Low Birth Rate," *American Journal of Public Health* 80(1) (1990), p. 25; and D. R. Weston et al., "Drug-Exposed Babies: Research and Clinical Issues," *National Center for Clinical Infant Programs Bulletin* 9(5) (1989), p. 7.

33. A. Toufexis, "Innocent Victims," *Time*, May 13, 1991, p. 56.

34. E. Atkins, "Reporting Fetal Abuse through California's Child Abuse and Neglect Reporting Act," *Southwestern University Law Review* 21(1) (1992), pp. 105–123.

35. Ibid., p. 883.

36. E. E. Hatch and M. B. Bracken, "Effect of Marijuana Use in Pregnancy on Fetal Growth," *American Journal of Epidemiology* 124 (1986), p. 986.

37. D. Wiese and D. Daro, *Current Trends in Child Abuse Reporting and Fatalities: The Results of the 1994 Annual Fifty State Survey* (National Committee to Prevent Child Abuse, Chicago, 1995).

38. Ibid.

39. J. Bays, "Substance Abuse and Child Abuse," *Pediatric Clinics of North America* 37(4) (1990), p. 881.

40. B. B. Little et al., "Failure to Recognize Fetal Alcohol Syndrome in Newborn Infants," *American Journal of Diseases of Children* 144 (1990), pp. 1142–1146.

41. 293 N.W.2d 736 at 739 (1980). See also *In the Matter of Stefanel Tyesha C.*, 157 A.D.2d 322, 298 N.Y.S.2d 280 (1990), involving a mother who used drugs during her pregnancy in which the court held it did not have to wait until the child suffered a broken bone or shattered psyche before it acted.

42. F. E. Garrity-Rokous, "Punitive Legal Approaches to the Problem of Prenatal Drug Exposure," *Infant Mental Health Journal* 15 (1994), p. 218.

43. A. Finnegan et al., "Comprehensive Care of the Pregnant Addict and Its Effect on Material and Infant Outcome," *Contemporary Drug Problems* 1 (1992), p. 795.

44. 96 Pa. 112 (1880).

45. 96 Pa. 112 (1880), p. 115.

46. See *Prince v. Massachusetts*, 321 U.S. 158 (1944), where the U.S. Supreme Court stated that the state has a wide range of power for limiting parental freedom and authority in things affecting the welfare of a child.

47. 98 U.S. at pp. 166–167, 170 (footnotes omitted).

48. D. Kilpatrick and B. Saunders, "Prevalence and Consequences of Child Victimization," *Research Preview* (National Institute of Justice, U.S. Department of Justice, Washington, D.C., 1997).

49. For more information on PTSD, see Chapter 1, "Characteristics and Consequences of Family Violence."

50. J. Wolak and D. Finkelhor, "Children Exposed to Partner Violence," in J. L. Jasinski and L. M. Williams, eds., *Partner Violence: A Comprehensive Review of 20 Years of Research* (Sage, Belmont Park, Calif., 1998).

51. J. Edelson, "Problems Associated with Children's Witnessing of Domestic Violence," *Violence against Women Online Resources*, www.vaw.umn.edu (rev. ed., April 1999).

52. L. L. Baker et al., *Children Exposed to Violence: A Handbook for Police Trainers to Increase Understanding and Improve Community Responses* (Centre for Children and Families in the Justice System of the London Family Court Clinic, London, Ontario, Canada, 2002).

53. Ibid., p. 19.

8

Sibling Abuse

CHAPTER OBJECTIVES

After studying this chapter, you should be able to:

- Explain why sibling abuse is generally believed to be the most common form of family violence;

- Discuss what constitutes sibling abuse;

- List and discuss the effects of sibling abuse;

- Explain how to detect sibling abuse;

- Discuss the laws designed to prevent or reduce sibling abuse.

Detailed Look at What You Should Know About Sibling Abuse

- Sibling abuse is probably the most common form of family violence in the United States.

- No one has accurate figures on the nature, type, or extent of sibling abuse.

- Many acts of sibling abuse occur when the older or more powerful sibling has care or control over the victim.

- **Sibling abuse** is any form of physical, mental, or sexual abuse inflicted by one child in a family unit on another. This definition covers the various types of abuse that will be discussed later. In addition, it does not require that the child be related by birth; in some situations, for example, children from different marriages end up in the same household.

- As with other types of family violence, sibling abuse can be divided into three distinct forms of abuse: physical, emotional, and sexual.

- **Intrafamilial sexual abuse** is defined as incest and refers to any type of exploitative sexual contact occurring between relatives.

- The effects of sibling sexual abuse are different and distinct from the effects of stranger or acquaintance abuse. Many times, the abuser and the victim live together, and the victim may feel trapped by the abuser over a long period of time.

- One characteristic that is similar to other forms of sexual abuse is that the victim will feel powerless to stop the abuse.

- Sibling abuse occurs at a higher rate among children in families in which both child abuse and intimate partner abuse are present.

- Sibling assaults are higher in families with child abuse than in those with intimate partner abuse.

- Although boys are more likely than girls to engage in sibling abuse, both sexes participate in this form of family violence.

- Sibling abuse crosses all racial and socioeconomic lines.

- Sibling abuse is highest in multiassaultive families.

- **Serial abuse of siblings** occurs when the perpetrator who is a member of the family first abuses one child and then abuses another sibling.

- State courts have upheld the termination of parents' rights on the basis of their abuse of siblings.

INTRODUCTION

Sibling abuse is probably the most common form of family violence in the United States. Gelles and Cornell stated this fact in another manner when they wrote that the most commonly victimized family members are siblings.[1] If sibling abuse is in fact the most common form of family violence, why is there such a reluctance on the part of society and professionals to discuss it? Very few textbooks are devoted exclusively to this topic. Most academic articles dealing with child abuse may include as an afterthought a discussion of sibling abuse. Two areas of sibling abuse that are being examined in some detail are incest and the abuse of a sibling by parents.

A variety of reasons exist for this lack of discussion regarding sibling abuse. Many people consider sibling aggression to be a normal part of growing up. Everyone has heard excuses for sibling aggression—they are common refrains in families with more than one child. Society tends to minimize sibling aggression. Yet, early studies in New York and Philadelphia indicated that 3 percent of all homicides committed in those cities were committed by siblings against siblings.[2] In another classic study of sibling abuse, Steinmetz found that parents did not consider their children's physical aggression toward siblings as abuse. They would even talk with friends, neighbors, and relatives about the aggression, viewing it as an inevitable part of growing up.[3] Whipple theorizes that violent families often face multiple problems that include chaos and deprivation. She believes that sibling abuse may be more likely to occur in such overburdened families because parents who are overwhelmed with multiple stressors may selectively ignore what they perceive as normal sibling rivalry when in fact such acts are sibling abuse.[4]

Some possible signs of sibling abuse include:

- One child always avoids his or her sibling;
- A child has changes in behavior, sleep patterns, eating habits, or has nightmares;
- A child acts out abuse in play;
- A child acts out sexually in inappropriate ways.

EXTENT OF THE PROBLEM

No one has accurate figures on the nature, type, or extent of sibling abuse. The popular media first addressed this issue in 1979 with a report in *U.S. News and World Report* that stated that 138,000 children aged three to seventeen years had used a weapon on a sibling within the last year.[5] In a 1980 study, Straus, Gelles, and Steinmetz reported that 82 percent of parents of children surveyed considered sibling violence to be the most common form of intrafamily violence.[6] In another 1981 study, Steinmetz found that a clear majority of children used physical violence to resolve conflicts with their siblings.[7]

In 1988, Pagelow presented the findings of her study of 1,025 college students at three university campuses in Southern California at the annual meeting of the Pacific Sociological Association. Pagelow's survey revealed that almost half the siblings living at home at the age of twelve were either aggressors or victims of violent acts, including kicking and punching. Ten percent said their siblings beat them up, and 4 percent stated that their siblings had threatened them with a gun or a knife or used a gun or a knife against them.

Focus

When Siblings Become Abusive

Vernon Wiehe, coauthor of *Perilous Rivalry: When Siblings Become Abusive*, states that as many as fifty-three out of every one hundred children abuse a brother or sister, higher than the percentage of adults who abuse their children or their spouse. According to Wiehe, what some kids do to their brother or sister inside the family would be called assault outside the family.

List of symptoms or warning signs that abuse is taking place or may have taken place.

- Failure to thrive
- Weight loss/gain

- Anxiety and/or depression
- Listlessness
- Phobias or irrational/inexplicable fears
- Personal space/privacy issues
- Difficulty with authority
- Passivity
- Low self-esteem
- Nightmares
- Anger
- Emotional outbursts
- Frequent illness
- Withdrawal
- Sympathy issues
- Difficulty sleeping/insomnia or fear of the dark.

Source: V. Wiehe and T. Herring. *Perilous Rivalry: When Siblings Become Abusive* (Lexington Books, Lexington, Mass, 1991).

Focus

Sibling Abuse and Excuses

How many of the following excuses have you heard used to justify one sibling's acts toward another?

- Don't worry about it; it's just normal sibling rivalry.
- They were just playing doctor.

- Kids will be kids.
- He really didn't mean to hurt his sister. He loves her.
- It's just normal childhood curiosity.
- Kids are always calling each other names.
- I told him not to hit her again.
- They will grow out of it.

In 1992, Carson and Daane presented the results of their study of 3,357 students in an Indiana school district at the annual meeting of the American Sociological Association. Seventy-four percent of the students approved of hitting their sibling if they were reacting to being hit first. Forty-three percent approved of striking their sibling if he or she broke their stereo. Thirty-eight percent believed that it was appropriate to hit their sibling if that sibling made fun of the student in front of friends. Almost one-quarter of all the students surveyed approved of hitting their sibling if there was an argument and the other sibling did not listen to reason. In discussing sibling abuse, the University of Michigan Health System Web page points out an estimate that three children in every hundred are "dangerously violent" toward a brother or sister.[8]

These and other studies indicate that sibling abuse is indeed a common form of family violence. Its existence can no longer be denied. However, researchers are still studying its nature, causation, and extent. As with many other forms of family violence, there is no single definition of sibling abuse.

DEFINITION

Clearly, sibling abuse falls within the definition of family violence discussed in Chapter 1: any act or omission by persons who are cohabitating that results in serious injury to other members of the family. The question then must be whether a separate definition of sibling abuse is needed or whether other definitions within this textbook cover most if not all the situations in which children commit acts of violence toward their siblings.

In an earlier chapter, *physical child abuse* was defined as any act that results in a non-acci-dental physical injury caused by a person who has care, custody, or control of a child. Many acts of sibling abuse occur when the older or more powerful sibling has care or control over the victim. However, some acts of sibling abuse take place within the home when parents are present but unaware of the acts of the abusing sibling. Therefore, the definition of physical child abuse does not cover all situations that might arise in sibling abuse. Although it is possible to draft a broad definition of child abuse that would cover acts of sibling abuse by defining it as a separate and distinct form of child abuse, its importance in any study of family violence is highlighted.

Sibling abuse is any form of physical, mental, or sexual abuse inflicted by one child in a family unit on another. This definition covers the various types of abuse that will be discussed later. In addition, it does not require that the child be related by birth; in some situations, for example, children from different marriages end up in the same household. Finally, the definition uses the term *child*, which requires further explanation. There are reported incidents of one sibling abusing the other after they have both reached the age of eighteen. However, it appears that most abuse occurs before the victim and/or the abuser reaches adulthood. Therefore, **child** is defined as a person under the age of legal majority, which is typically stated to be eighteen. It should be clear that this definition does not include abuse of different children within the same family by an adult member of the household. That particular form of family violence is discussed later in this chapter.

SIBLINGS AS PERPETRATORS

Professionals within the service fields must understand that children, even at relatively young ages, can be violent toward their siblings. To automatically discount sibling abuse by a five- or

---

Focus

Indicators of Sibling Sexual Abuse

Behavioral sibling sexual abuse may be indicated by:

- Siblings who behave like boyfriend and girlfriend;
- A child who fears being left alone with a sibling;
- Siblings who appear embarrassed when found alone together;
- One sibling antagonizing the other but the other not retaliating (through fear, or fear of exposing the secret), or in some cases the threat of blackmail.

Physical Indicators of Child Sexual Abuse

Some sexually abused children also come to attention because of physical indicators:

- Bruises, bleeding, or other physical trauma in genital or rectal area. There may be pain or problems with urination/defecation or blood-stained and/or torn underwear.

The physical discomfort may cause the child to limp, perform poorly at sports, drop out of strenuous play activities, or perhaps even have difficulty in sitting still.

- Foreign bodies in genital, rectal, or urethral openings;
- Abnormal dilation of the urethral, vaginal, or rectal openings;
- Itching, inflammation or infection of urethral, vaginal, or rectal openings;
- Presence of semen;
- Trauma to breasts, buttocks, lower abdomen, or thighs;
- Unusual odors from the vaginal area;
- Sexually transmitted diseases;
- Pregnancy, especially when the child refuses to reveal any information about the father of the baby and/or complete denial of the pregnancy by the child and/or her family;
- Psychosomatic illness; e.g., abdominal pain, nightmares.

Source: R. Weisberg-Ross "Sibling Abuse: Children Abusing Other Children," (March 8, 2010). Posted on Good Therapy Web site at www.goodtherapy.org/blog/sibling-abuse, accessed September 7, 2015.

six-year-old committed against his younger brother or sister is to ignore the realities and dynamics of family violence. This section examines more characteristics of sibling abuse.

Types of Abuse

As with other types of family violence, sibling abuse can be divided into three distinct forms of abuse: physical, emotional, and sexual. The dynamics involved in each type of abuse are similar if not the same as those interactions that occur with other forms of abuse. The critical difference in this type of family violence is that the perpetrator is a sibling.

Physical abuse of a sibling includes any of the acts or omissions discussed in Chapter 5. Striking, kicking, punching, and the use of instruments such as sticks, appliances, and other items as weapons are common. Wiehe conducted an extensive study of physical, emotional, and sexual abuse of siblings.[9] His definition of physical abuse is similar to the one used in this textbook, with one significant distinction: Wiehe reports that prolonged tickling is also used by siblings as a form of prolonged physical abuse.

Emotional abuse of siblings includes those acts or omissions discussed in Chapter 7. While Wiehe acknowledges the more accepted definition of emotional abuse discussed previously; he narrows its scope in his research to include name-calling, ridicule, degradation, exacerbating a fear, destroying personal possessions, and torture or destruction of a pet. Defining concepts is one of the existing controversies in family violence. Therefore, rather than establishing a series of distinct definitions for each separate form of violence, it may be more acceptable to use a single definition if it can be applied to the facts. Because all these acts conform to the previously established definition of emotional abuse, there is no need to add an additional definition at this time.

The third type of sibling abuse is sexual abuse. Chapter 6 defined **child sexual abuse** as sexual exploitation or sexual activities with a child under circumstances that indicate that the child's health or welfare is harmed or threatened. **Intrafamilial sexual abuse** was defined as incest and refers to any type of exploitative sexual contact occurring between relatives. Clearly, sibling sexual abuse falls within these definitions. In some situations, however, certain activities may be considered simple curiosity; in others, it is sexual abuse.

Depending on what other facts are added to the Practicum "Curiosity or Sexual Abuse?" what appears to be simple curiosity may be sibling sexual abuse. Situation 1 may indicate normal curiosity that many children experience regarding body differences.[10] Situation 2 may be simple curiosity but is more likely to be sexual abuse, depending on the difference in age and the type of activities engaged in by the siblings. Clearly, situation 3 is sexual abuse.

The effects of sibling sexual abuse are different and distinct from the effects of stranger or acquaintance abuse. Many times, the abuser and the victim live together, and the victim may feel trapped by the abuser over a long period of time. In addition, the victim had an established relationship and trusted the abuser and will feel betrayed by the fact that a brother or sister is hurting them. One characteristic that is similar to other forms of sexual abuse is that the victim will feel powerless to stop the abuse.

Early thinking characterized sibling sexual abuse as relatively benign. Professionals have rejected this view, and most authorities now accept the proposition that sibling sexual abuse can be coercive and have serious long-term consequences for the victim.[11] Laredo established a continuum of motivations of perpetrators of sibling sexual abuse.[12] At one end

Practicum

Curiosity or Sexual Abuse?

Situation 1: Both curious	Both "consent"*	Same age—under four
Situation 2: One curious	Both consent	Different ages
Situation 3: One curious	One consents	Same or different ages

*Consent in this context focuses on mutual agreement by the minors and does not deal with the legal issue of consent. Legally, as was pointed out in other chapters, persons under the age of eighteen cannot consent to sexual activities.

is the relatively common childhood activities of exploration, and at the other is power and control.

Laredo explained that exploration often takes the form of play or games. Retribution is common in sibling sexual abuse and is used to get even with younger siblings for perceived or actual past slights or injuries to the abusing sibling. Third, power and control, common ingredients in family violence, also play a major role in sibling sexual abuse.

O'Brien studied various forms of adolescent sexual abuse, including sibling sexual abuse, and found that siblings committed more serious types of sexual abuse than other adolescent offenders.[13] O'Brien theorized that this increased sexual activity was based on two factors: the easy and continuing access the sibling had to the victim and the secrecy that surrounds the activities of the family unit.

Characteristics of Sibling Abuse

Even though sibling abuse has been studied for over forty years, an absence of information regarding its characteristics remains. What is known has come from small samples and is subject to debate. The lack of adequate research should not reflect negatively on the researchers because the size of the sample is obviously limited to family units that have more than one child.

Hotaling and his associates used the two National Family Violence Surveys and a survey of university students to construct a profile of sibling abuse.[14] These researchers established the following characteristics of sibling abuse:

- Sibling abuse occurs at a higher rate among children in families in which both child abuse and intimate partner abuse are present.
- Sibling assaults are higher in families with child abuse than in those with intimate partner abuse.
- Although boys are more likely than girls to engage in sibling abuse, both sexes participate in this form of family violence.
- Sibling abuse crosses all racial and socioeconomic lines.
- Sibling abuse is highest in multiassaultive families.

These professionals conclude that the data cannot be used to establish a relation between sibling abuse and other forms of family violence. In addition, no concrete data from these studies establish the fact that violence in families causes sibling abuse. However, more recent studies suggest that brothers and sisters who fight with each other while growing up may continue their aggressive acts toward their dates.[15]

Factors That May Contribute to Sibling Abuse

This is an under-researched area. Research is needed to determine how and why sibling abuse happens. Some probably risk factors include:

- Parents are mostly absent from home.
- Parents are not involved in their children's lives.
- Parents are not emotionally available to the children.
- Parents see sibling rivalry as part of family life, rather than working to minimize it.
- Parents do not stop children when they are violent.
- Parents encourage competition among children by playing favorites, comparing children, and labeling or type-casting children.
- Parents have not taught children about sexuality and about personal safety.
- Parents and children are in denial that there is a problem.
- Children have inappropriate family roles; for example, they are burdened with too much care-taking responsibility for a younger sibling.
- Children are exposed to violence.
- Children have been sexually abused or witnessed sexual abuse.
- Children have access to pornography.

Gelles and Cornell's research confirmed another commonly held belief—namely, that as siblings grow older, the abuse decreases.[16] A number of reasons have been advanced for this phenomenon. First, as a child ages, his or her verbal and coping skills increase. Also, as the child victim reaches adolescence, he or she becomes able to spend more time out of the home and away from the abusing sibling. Finally, as parents become more sensitive to aggressive behavior between siblings, its incidence may decrease.

Focus

Difficult Choices

Sex Crime or Abuse of Power

Often we think of sibling sex abuse as a sex crime, but more and more researchers are beginning to consider the crimes as a crime of power and authority. Power is common to child abuse, spouse abuse, and sibling abuse. Abuse is the weapon to achieving power and control, and is the general motive in sibling sexual abuse.

It is noted that older children who sexually abuse their younger brothers and sisters frequently abuse them in other ways as well. The other type of abuse that includes persistent putting down, teasing, or belittling younger children about their size, gender, or other personal characteristics is called emotional abuse. Scaring younger children in dark rooms, telling them that no one loves them, or that terrible things are going to happen to them are also examples of emotional abuse.

Another form of sibling abuse continues nevertheless to defy any effort to stop it or find a reason for its existence. The serial abuse of siblings within the family unit is examined in the next section.

SERIAL ABUSE OF SIBLINGS

The Focus "Difficult Choices" illustrates one of the dilemmas facing professionals in the area of sibling abuse. What should they do when they discover that one sibling has been abused? Should they remove any other siblings from the custody of the parents to prevent further abuse? Can or should they recommend birth control measures to abusing parents to prevent them from conceiving and abusing other children? This section examines these issues and offers some guidelines to consider when making decisions regarding intervention in child abuse cases involving siblings.

Overview

Social workers, probation officers, police, attorneys, and judges have all heard stories of the sibling who was left behind with the abusive family and suffered death or serious injury. This situation is a nightmare that haunts all professionals who work in the area of family violence. **Serial abuse of siblings** occurs when the perpetrator who is a member of the family first abuses one child and then abuses another sibling. The type of abuse inflicted on a sibling may be physical, emotional, sexual, or a combination of various types of abuse. Either or both parents or caretakers may participate in this form of family violence. This abuse may take place within a matter of months of abusing the first child, or the perpetrator may wait years until the younger sibling reaches a certain age before beginning the abuse.

As discussions in previous chapters have illustrated, professionals have been unable to agree on specific characteristics, forces, and factors that cause parents to abuse their children. With such disagreement, how can professionals attempt to predict with any accuracy that a parent or a caretaker who has abused one child will abuse a sibling or siblings? When a person is accused of child abuse, professionals may assume that other children are also being abused or will be abused in the future. In addition, many professionals will argue that proof of abuse of one child indicates that the parent or the caretaker is unfit to care for the siblings.

The question of serial abuse of siblings has generated both controversy and continued research. In 1981, Farrell determined that 53 percent of female children whose siblings were infected with gonorrhea also contracted the disease.[17] In 1989, the Tennessee Department of Human Services conducted a study of all children who were closely associated with a victim of sexual assault and exposed to the perpetrator.[18] This study revealed that 58 percent of these girls also admitted to being victims of sexual abuse. In 1992, Gutman and her associates examined the sexual abuse of children exposed to offenders carrying the human immunodeficiency virus (HIV).[19] They determined that 50 percent of twenty-two cohabiting children were confirmed to have been sexually abused by the perpetrator. Of these children, two were determined to be HIV-positive and thirteen HIV-negative. These two children were thought to have acquired their infections through vertical transmission because their mothers were HIV-positive. However, acquisition by sexual abuse could not be ruled out.

Sexual abuse of children is not the only form of serial abuse of siblings. Herrenkohl and his associates found that in 45 percent of all families studied, more than one child was abused.[20] Alexander and his associates studied babies who were seen at hospitals and clinics in Iowa with the diagnosis of shaken baby syndrome.[21] He concluded that the risk of abuse to siblings may be approximated by the findings that in 33 percent of families with more than one child, two or more siblings had experienced abuse or neglect. Because of the nature of the study,

---

Focus

What Causes One Sibling to Abuse Another?

1. Acting out anger at parents on sibling, or acting out anger at an older sibling on a younger sibling.
2. Parents overwhelmed by their own problems are not paying attention.
3. Inappropriate expectations—older sibling given too much responsibility or freedom.
4. Mirroring parents' behavior.
5. Viewing the behavior as normal by parents.
6. Socialization of males as dominant over females.
7. Contribution of victim. Some researches contend that the behavioral patterns of the abused child tend to invite further abuse.
8. The interactional cycle of violence theory. Note: this theory does not blame the victim. Rather it identifies a pattern in order to treat and help prevent further abuse.

Source: R. Weisberg-Ross "Sibling Abuse: Children Abusing Other Children," (March 8, 2010). Posted on Good Therapy Web site at www.goodtherapy.org/blog/sibling-abuse, accessed September 7, 2015.

Alexander cautions that this figure was most likely an underestimate of the true extent of serial sibling abuse. Newlands and Emery found that the names of families on the child abuse register in Derbyshire, England, were the same as the names of families who were reporting deaths of other siblings. She found that approximately 10 percent of the children whose deaths were reported as accidental also had siblings who had been abused by their families.[22]

Interventions

Removal of an abused child from the care and custody of the parents is a serious step for any professional to take. This form of intervention is discussed in detail in Chapter 11, which deals with responses to child abuse. This section examines other, more controversial forms of intervention—removal of children from a home based on abuse of a sibling and sterilization of the mother to prevent further births.

Removal of a sibling from the home of the abusing parents or caretakers is an obvious form of intervention. It is designed to protect both the abused child and any siblings from future injury.

Many courts have upheld the removal of a child with a showing that another sibling has been abused. The District of Columbia Court of Appeals stated:

> a substantial number of decisions in other jurisdictions support the proposition that trial judge may legitimately find, on the basis of a parent's abusive conduct towards one child, that the child's siblings are also in danger of abuse and should be removed from the home for their own safety.[23]

Removing a child from a home is one form of intervention. The child may be placed with another relative or in a foster home while the abusing parents seek counseling or other forms of assistance. However, sometimes the abuse is so serious that courts will consider another more serious form of intervention—terminating the parental rights of the abusing parent.

Some state statutes authorize removal from the home and termination of parental rights without a showing of abuse to a sibling. In 1991, the Florida Supreme Court upheld that state's statute authorizing such action. In *Padgett v. Department of Health and Rehabilitative Service*, the department sought to terminate the parental rights of Mary and Tom Padgett to their child, identified as W. L. P.[24] On a previous occasion, Mary's parental rights to a newborn infant had been terminated on the basis of acts of physical child abuse. Tom's parental rights to five children from a previous marriage had also been terminated. Two days after W. L. P.'s birth, the department filed a petition asking the court to terminate the parents' rights. This petition was based on three grounds: Another child had been removed from the parents' custody, Mary was mentally ill, and she had tried to perform an abortion on herself by using a pair of scissors to terminate the birth of W. L. P. In upholding the trial court's order terminating the parents' rights, the Florida Supreme Court stated that to require a child to suffer abuse in those cases where mistreatment is virtually assured is illogical and directly adverse to society's fundamental policy of preserving the welfare of its youth.[25]

Other jurisdictions have upheld the termination of parents' rights on the basis of their abuse of siblings. In the California case of *In re Luwanna*, an appeals court upheld the termination of the parental rights of Luwanna's parents on the basis of evidence that her younger brother had been repeatedly beaten with a stick.[26] The appeals court affirmed the termination of parental rights of both children even though there was no evidence that Luwanna's father had beaten her. In Missouri, the state filed for termination of parental rights to a daughter, C. M. W., on the basis of the abuse of a sibling.[27] In *C. M. W. v. P. W.*, the state had terminated the parental rights for C. M. W.'s older brother, C. C., on the basis of a showing of severe physical and sexual abuse by the father and the mother's uncle. The Missouri court upheld the termination of parental rights because the conditions that led to the abuse of the older brother still existed. Termination of parental rights is a harsh but sometimes necessary act if children are to be protected from abuse. A more controversial method of intervention is to request or demand that the abusing parent undergo sterilization to prevent giving birth to more children, who might then be abused.

Numerous courts have attempted to deal with the issue of parents who abuse their children and the issue of future births of siblings who might suffer the same or similar fates. The use of involuntary sterilization raises the specter of ethnic cleansing and Nazi Germany. Compulsory sterilization is a highly emotional and controversial subject. In addition, the U.S. Supreme Court has ruled that parents have a "right to procreate."[28] However, that same court has ruled that in limited situations the state may involuntarily sterilize a person. In the still controversial decision of *Buck v. Bell* in 1927, the Supreme Court upheld a Virginia statute allowing superintendents of various state mental institutions to order the sterilization of any patient if the sterilization served the best interests of the patient and the society.[29]

All states provide for the termination of parental rights of parents of children who have been abused, and a number of these states authorize the termination of parental rights on the basis of sibling abuse. Termination of parental rights is one method of intervention that attempts to prevent further injury to siblings. Sterilization of abusing parents will continue to be a hotly debated topic.[30] Although many trial court judges have conditioned probation for abusing parents on acceptance of sterilization, no modern appellate court has approved such a remedy.

Summary

Sibling abuse is the most common form of family violence. Society often accepts violence between siblings as normal. Sibling abuse can have long-term consequences for its victims.

Two types of sibling abuse have been discussed: those acts perpetrated against another child in the family unit by a sibling and abuse visited on a child by an adult who has abused that victim's sibling. Professionals must be aware of both types of sibling abuse. Sibling abuse may include physical, emotional, or sexual abuse by either male or female children. Like other forms of family violence, it crosses all socioeconomic lines and may be present in the homes of the rich and the famous as well as those who live in abject poverty.

Serial abuse of siblings presents another aspect of sibling abuse. Professionals must determine how they are going to intervene to protect not only the abused child but also the welfare and best interests of other siblings. Many states authorize the termination of parental rights to siblings on the basis of the abuse of another child in the family. Another controversial alternative is the sterilization of women to prevent the conception and birth of other children who might be subjected to abuse.

Key Terms

sibling abuse—any form of physical, mental, or sexual abuse inflicted by one child in a family unit on another.

child—a person under the age of legal majority, which is typically stated to be eighteen.

child sexual abuse—sexual exploitation or sexual activities with a child under circumstances that indicate that the child's health or welfare is harmed or threatened.

intrafamilial sexual abuse—incest; refers to any type of exploitative sexual contact occurring between relatives.

serial abuse of siblings—occurs when the perpetrator who is a member of the family first abuses one child and then abuses another sibling.

Discussion Questions

1. How serious is sibling abuse? Do you believe that it is more serious than rape? Why?
2. When does normal childhood curiosity become abuse?
3. What should we do with children who abuse their siblings? What if the perpetrator is eight years old and has sexually molested his five-year-old sister? What if he were twelve years old and molested his six-year-old sister?
4. If a father sexually abuses his ten-year-old daughter, should we remove his eight-year-old daughter? What about his five-year-old son?
5. Should certain people be sterilized? Who? Justify your answer.

Suggested Readings

Bard, M. "The Study and Modification of Intra-family Violence." In J. L. Singer, ed., *The Control of Aggression and Violence* (Academic Press, New York, 1971).

Caffaro, J. *Sibling Abuse Trauma: Intervention Strategies for Children, Families, and Adults* (Haworth Press, Binghamton, N.Y., 1998).

Gelles, R. J., and C. P. Cornell. *Intimate Violence in Families*, 2nd ed. (Sage, Newbury Park, Calif., 1990).

Hotaling, G. T., A. Strauss, and A. J. Lincoln. "Intra-family Violence and Crime and Violence Outside the Family." In Straus and Gelles, eds., *Physical Violence in American Families* (Transaction, New Brunswick, N.J., 1990).

Kempe, R. S., and C. H. Kempe. *The Common Secret: Sexual Abuse of Children and Adolescents* (Freeman, New York, 1984).

Laredo, C. "Sibling Incest." In S. Sgroi, ed., *Handbook of Clinical Intervention in Child Sexual Abuse* (Lexington Books, Lexington, Mass., 1982).

Mitchell, J. *Siblings: Sex and Violence* (Policy Press, Bristol, U.K., 2003).

Mott, S. R., S. R. James, and A. M. Sperhac. *Nursing Care of Children and Families* (Addison-Wesley, Redwood City, Calif., 1990).

Steinmetz, S. K. *The Cycle of Violence: Assertive, Aggressive, and Abusive Family Interaction* (Praeger, New York, 1971).

Straus, M., R. Gelles, and S. Steinmetz. *Behind Closed Doors: Violence in the American Family* (Doubleday, New York, 1980).

Wiehe, V. *What Parents Need to Know about Sibling Abuse* (Bonneville Books, Springville, Vt. 2002).

Wiehe, V. R. *Sibling Abuse* (Lexington Books, New York, 1990).

Wolfgand, M. *Patterns in Criminal Homicide* (Wiley, New York, 1958).

Endnotes

1. R. J. Gelles and C. P. Cornell, *Intimate Violence in Families*, 2nd ed. (SAGE, Newbury Park, Calif., 1990), p. 85.

2. See M. Bard, "The Study and Modification of Intra-Family Violence," in J. L. Singer, ed., *The Control of Aggression and Violence* (Academic Press, New York, 1971), for the study of homicides in Philadelphia; and M. Wolfgand, *Patterns in Criminal Homicide* (Wiley, New York, 1958), for the study of homicides in New York.

3. S. K. Steinmetz, *The Cycle of Violence: Assertive, Aggressive, and Abusive Family Interaction* (Praeger, New York, 1971).

4. E. E. Whipple and S. E. Finton, "Psychological Maltreatment by Siblings: An Unrecognized Form of Abuse," *Child and Adolescent Social Work Journal* 12(2) (1995), pp. 135–146.

5. "Battered Families: A Growing Nightmare," *U.S. News & World Report*, January 15, 1979, pp. 60–61.

6. M. Straus, R. Gelles, and S. Steinmetz, *Behind Closed Doors: Violence in the American Family* (Doubleday, New York, 1980).

7. S. Steinmetz, "A Cross-Cultural Comparison of Sibling Violence," *International Journal of Family Psychiatry* 2(3/4) (1981), pp. 337–351.

8. www.med.umich.edu/1libr/yourchild/sibabuse.htm, accessed March 14, 2007.

9. V. R. Wiehe, *Sibling Abuse* (Lexington Books, New York, 1990).

10. S. R. Mott, S. R. James, and A. M. Sperhac, *Nursing Care of Children and Families* (Addison-Wesley, Redwood City, Calif., 1990), pp. 224–225.

11. R. S. Kempe and C. H. Kempe, *The Common Secret: Sexual Abuse of Children and Adolescents* (Freeman, New York, 1984).

12. C. Laredo, "Sibling Incest," in S. Sgroi, ed., *Handbook of Clinical Intervention in Child Sexual Abuse* (Lexington Books, Lexington, Mass., 1982).

13. J. O'Brien, *Characteristics of Male Adolescent Sibling Incest Offenders* (Safer Society Program, Orwell, Vt., 1989).

14. G. T. Hotaling, M. A. Straus, and A. J. Lincoln, "Intrafamily Violence and Crime and Violence outside the Family," in Straus and Gelles, eds., *Physical Violence in American Families* (Transaction, New Brunswick, N.J., 1990).

15. "Sibling Violence Leads to Violent Dating," *The Futurist* 38(5) (2004), p. 7.

16. Gelles and Cornell, *Intimate Violence in Families.*

17. M. K. Farrell et al., "Prepubertal Gonorrhea: A Multidisciplinary Approach," *Pediatrics* 67(1) (1981), pp. 151–153.

18. D. Muram, P. M. Speck, and S. S. Gold, "Genital Abnormalities in Female Siblings and Friends of Child Victims of Sexual Assault," *Child Abuse and Neglect* 15 (1991), pp. 105–110.

19. L. T. Gutman et al., "Sexual Abuse of Human Immunodeficiency Virus-Positive Children: Outcomes for Perpetrators and Evaluations of Other Household Children," *American Journal of Diseases of Children* 146 (1185) (October 1992).

20. R. C. Herrenkohl et al., "The Repetition of Child Abuse: How Frequently Does It Occur?" *Child Abuse and Neglect* 3 (1979), pp. 67–72.

21. R. Alexander et al., "Serial Abuse in Children Who Are Shaken," *American Journal of Diseases of Children* 144(1) (1990), pp. 58–60.

22. M. Newlands and J. L. Emery, "Child Abuse and Cot Deaths," *Child Abuse and Neglect* 15 (1991), pp. 275–278.

23. *In re S. G.*, 581 A.2d 771, 778 (D.C. Ct. App. 1990).

24. 577 So. 2d 565 (Fla. 1991).

25. 577 So. 2d 565 (Fla. 1991), p. 570.

26. 107 Cal. Rptr. 62 (1973).

27. *C. M. W. v. P. W.*, 813 S.W.2d 331 (Mo. Ct. App. 1991).

28. *Skinner v. Oklahoma*, 316 U.S. 535 (1942).

29. 274 U.S. 200 (1927). In that decision, a highly regarded justice, Oliver Wendell Holmes, uttered his now infamous statement that "three generations of imbeciles is enough."

30. E. T. Blum, "When Terminating Parental Rights Is Not Enough: A New Look at Compulsory Sterilization," *Georgia Law Review* 28 (Summer 1994), p. 977.

9

Child Exploitation

CHAPTER OBJECTIVES

After studying this chapter, you should be able to:

- Explain why child exploitation is a severe form of violence;
- Define the concept of child exploitation;
- List and explain the forms of child labor that violate international social norms;
- Discuss the issues involved in preventing child pornography;
- Explain the key points in the Model State Anti-Trafficking Criminal Statutes.

Detailed Look at What You Should Know About Child Exploitation

- Child exploitation is a severe form of violence against children.
- Lack of scientific research, different social and legal perspectives both nationally and internationally, and ineffective efforts to combat this form of violence all contribute to misunderstandings about child exploitation.
- The exploitation of children both by their families and by strangers has existed since the beginning of time.
- Child exploiters use the Internet to maintain their anonymity. The Internet also poses risks to children who use it.
- Child sex tourism is the commercial sexual exploitation of children by men or women who travel from one place to another, usually from a richer country to a poorer, less-developed country, and engage in sexual acts with children.
- Debt bondage is a form of enslavement in which a person must work as a means of replaying the advancement of funds for a loan or service such as transporting a person to a location for the purposes of employment.

- Exploitation includes use of persons for prostitution and other forms of sexual activities, forced labor or services, slavery or practices similar to slavery, servitude, or the removal of organs.

- *Human smuggling* is a contractual agreement in which one person (the smuggler) agrees to take, guide, or transport another person from one location to another. Smuggling usually involves consent of the parties.

- *Trafficking* means the recruitment, transportation, transfer, harboring, or receipt of persons by means of a threat or use of force or other forms of coercion for the purpose of exploitation. Trafficking may occur within one country or across national borders.

- Three forms of child labor violate international social norms, laws, and treaties: all work done by children under the minimum legal age for that type of work; work that endangers the health, safety, and morals of a child; and the worst forms of child labor, defined as slavery, trafficking, bonded labor, forced recruitment into armed conflict, prostitution, pornography, or other illegal activities.

- **Child pornography** is really a misnomer.

- Materials depicting children engaging in explicit sexual activities fall within the definition of obscenity, and therefore those who exploit children for this purpose may be prosecuted.

- Under federal law, child pornography is defined as any visual depiction of any kind, including a drawing, cartoon, sculpture, painting, photograph, film, video, or other images, whether made or produced by electronic, mechanical, or other means, of sexually explicit conduct.

- Other forms of extreme child exploitation are child prostitution, child sex tourism, begging, and trafficking.

- A variety of factors contribute to child exploitation. Countries have different cultures and situations, some of which allow for children to be exploited. These factors include poverty, desire for a better life, ignorance, lack of schools, family violence, consumerism, and gender and ethnic discrimination.

- The use of children as soldiers is a very special form of child exploitation that is not often linked directly to trafficking.

- There are several common characteristics of children who have been trafficked. Each victim is manipulated through the act or threat of violence. Each victim is a displaced person in foreign circumstances that increase his or her dependence on the trafficker.

- The Model State Anti-Trafficking Criminal Statute attempted to address a number of problems that faced states in their efforts to prosecute traffickers.

INTRODUCTION

"There can be no keener revelation of a society's soul than the way in which it treats its children." Nelson Mandela[1]

"Given the current statistics surrounding child pornography, we are living in a country that is losing its soul." Judge John Adams[2]

Child exploitation is an especially severe form of violence against children. It is included in this textbook to give the reader an opportunity to compare this form of violence with other forms of violence that occur within the family. An additional reason for including this discussion is because in many countries, parents actually contribute to or actively aid in the exploitation of their children. Finally, a number of experts have requested that this chapter be included to educate both students and service providers about this form of violence.

The study of child exploitation, like many other aspects of family violence, is surrounded by a number of controversies. Lack of scientific research, different social and legal perspectives both nationally and internationally, and ineffective efforts to combat this form of violence all contribute to misunderstandings about child exploitation. One aspect of child exploitation is clear: The types of child exploitation blur, and victims of one form often become victims of another form. For example, a child who is forced to work as a child laborer may end up being forced to become a prostitute and have his or her pictures distributed across the Internet as a form of child pornography. The child victim may grow up to become an adult victim of sexual exploitation. Therefore, it is incumbent on all researchers to remember that child exploitation may include many different acts against children.

The exploitation of children both by their families and by strangers has existed since the beginning of time. In recent years, this severe form of violence has been impacted by the use of technology to aid in the exploitation of children. Although many students, faculty, and researchers are intimately familiar with the Internet and its capabilities, many do not understand how this and other technologies are used to exploit children.

TECHNOLOGY AND THE EXPLOITATION OF CHILDREN

Advancing technology is making our world smaller as well as allowing for improvements in education, increasing effectiveness in the workplace, and encouragement of interpersonal relationships. However, technology also has a dark side. It is being used by those who exploit children.[3]

Child exploiters use the Internet to maintain their anonymity. By using pseudonyms in chat rooms, false names on e-mails, and software that prevents tracing of e-mails, they attempt to cover their tracks and true identity from both victims and law enforcement agencies. Furthermore, the Internet is a unique contact point and communication space whose social dynamics as well as psychological implications are not yet fully understood. We know that child exploiters also use the Internet to find others who agree with their values and practices. They may trade or purchase pictures of young victims. In one case, 50,000 images of child pornography were found on a server based in Moscow but directed by e-mails from the

---

Focus

Child Exploitation and Obscenity Section Web Site

In 1987, the U.S. Department of Justice established the Child Exploitation and Obscenity Section (CEOS) Web site. Its mission is to protect the welfare of America's children and communities by enforcing federal criminal statutes relating to the exploitation of children and obscenity. The Web site may be accessed at www.justice.gov/criminal/ceos/.

Focus

Domestic Sex Trafficking of Minors

- Although comprehensive research to document the number of children engaged in prostitution in the United States is lacking, it is estimated that about 293,000 American youth are currently at risk of becoming the victims of commercial sexual exploitation.
- The majority of American victims of commercial sexual exploitation tend to be runaway or thrownaway youths who live on the streets who become victims of prostitution.
- Other young people are recruited into prostitution through forced abduction, pressure from parents, or through deceptive agreements between parents and traffickers.
- Once these children become involved in prostitution, they are often forced to travel far from their homes and as a result are isolated from their friends and family.
- Few children in this situation are able to develop new relationships with peers or adults other than the person who is victimizing them.
- The lifestyle of such children revolves around violence, forced drug use, and constant threats.
- Among children and teens living on the streets in the United States, involvement in commercial sex activity is a problem of epidemic proportion.
- Approximately 55 percent of street girls engage in formal prostitution.
- Of the girls engaged in formal prostitution, about 75 percent worked for a pimp.
- Pimp-controlled commercial sexual exploitation of children is linked to escort and massage services, private dancing, drinking and photographic clubs, major sporting and recreational events, major cultural events, conventions, and tourist destinations.
- About one-fifth of these children become entangled in nationally organized crime networks and are trafficked nationally. They are transported around the United States by a variety of means—cars, buses, vans, trucks, or planes, and are often provided with counterfeit identification to use in the event of arrest.
- The average age at which girls first become victims of prostitution is twelve to fourteen years.
- It is not only the girls on the streets who are affected—for boys and transgender youth, the average age of entry into prostitution is eleven to thirteen years.

Source: Excerpts from Child Exploitation and Obscenity Section, U.S. Department of Justice Web site at www.usdoj.gov/criminal/ceos/prostitution, accessed August 2, 2009.

United States. The owner charged $100 per month to download these images. Authorities agree that there has been an astronomical growth of pornographic images of children in the past decade. The numbers used by some police forces have gone from the hundreds to the millions.

The Internet also poses risks to children who use it. Teenagers and younger children many times use the Internet without parental supervision. They are also likely to participate in online discussions with others. On the basis of a study of 1,501 teens and preteens, approximately one in five received a sexual solicitation or approach over the Internet. Less than 10 percent of these solicitations were reported to law enforcement agencies.[4]

Child exploitation is increasing on the Internet. As technology expands, so does the availability of access to the Internet. Mobile phones and handheld game consoles now offer instant access.[5] The Internet is being used to promote child sex tourism, child pornography, child prostitution, and other forms of child exploitation. Although many authorities focus on the Internet and child exploitation, it is important to acknowledge that other forms of modern technology such as text messaging and picture sending can be used to exploit children. The following sections examine various aspects of child exploitation in our modern and evolving society.

DEFINITIONS

Uniform definitions are lacking in this area of family violence. Definitions have been established by nongovernmental organizations (NGOs), international organizations such as the United Nations, and independent countries. This lack of uniformity and inability to agree on standard definitions also results in underreporting of the amount and type of child exploitation that is occurring within countries. However, a review of the literature indicates that there are certain areas or classifications that many scholars, NGOs, countries, and international organizations agree on. These include among others human smuggling, trafficking, debt bondage, prostitution, pornography, and child sex tourism. Other issues that are raised in this area include the definition of *child* and use of the word *consent*. There are a number of NGOs that are doing outstanding work in educating, caring for, and responding to child exploitation. One of the most well-known NGOs in this area is ECPAT (End Child Prostitution, Child Pornography, and Trafficking of Children for Sexual Purposes), which is a network of international organizations with its secretariat in Bangkok, Thailand. ECPAT has groups in numerous countries around the world and is very active in trying to stamp out child exploitation. Many of the following definitions have been based on an outstanding textbook, *Semantics or Substance*, which ECPAT edited:[6]

- *Child* is any person under the age of eighteen. This definition is based on a number of international protocols and conventions. However, some regions of the world define adulthood as occurring when a child reaches the age of thirteen, whereas others require the child to reach the age of twenty-one.
- *Child sex tourism* is the commercial sexual exploitation of children by men or women who travel from one place to another, usually from a richer country to a poorer, less-developed country, and engage in sexual acts with children.
- *Consent* is the legal agreement to do or refrain from doing certain acts. Children as a matter of law cannot consent.
- *Debt bondage* is a form of enslavement in which a person must work as a means of replaying the advancement of funds for a loan or service such as transporting a person to a location for the purposes of employment. It is the status or condition of a debtor arising from a promise by the debtor for his or her personal services as the security for a debt or condition.
- *Exploitation* includes use of persons for prostitution and other forms of sexual activities, forced labor or services, slavery or practices similar to slavery, servitude, or the removal of organs.

- *Human smuggling* is a contractual agreement in which one person (the smuggler) agrees to take, guide, or transport another person from one location to another. Smuggling usually involves consent of the parties. Smuggling may, however, become a form of trafficking if force or duress is introduced.
- *Child pornography* is any representation, by whatever means, of a child engaged in real or simulated explicit sexual activities or representation of the sexual parts of a child for a sexual purpose.
- *Prostitution* is an act of engaging or offering the services of a child to a person to perform sexual acts for money or other consideration with that person or any other person.
- *Trafficking* means the recruitment, transportation, transfer, harboring, or receipt of persons by means of a threat or use of force or other forms of coercion for the purpose of exploitation. Trafficking may occur within one country or across national borders.

Semantics or Substance was published because of the differing definitions used by parties across the world. No one definition is accepted by all parties or countries. This disparity in definitions obviously has ramifications for the study of child exploitation because different regions using different definitions will have difficult attitudes toward the same activities.

NATURE AND SCOPE OF THE PROBLEM

Accurate reporting of the extent of child exploitation is hindered by several factors.[7] The first and most obvious is that it is criminal and therefore secret. Persons engaged in this activity do not publicize their activities. Second, victims are mobile and are moved from one location to another. This movement might be from one country to another, within a country, or a combination of movements within one country and then into another country. The third factor is simply a result of differences among governments regarding the definitions of child exploitation. Fourth, accurate reporting is affected by corruption or purposeful deception in some governments. Some purposely underreport the nature and extent of child exploitation, either because of corruption or because accurate reporting by these governments might impact international tourism or result in loss of aid from other countries. The fifth factor involves a perception by many law enforcement agencies that the victims are prostitutes instead of trafficking victims. This attitude affects the number of cases that are reported. It is critical to understand that not all prostituted children are trafficked and not all trafficked children are prostituted. The last factor is very similar to the definitional issue in that it involves not reporting or underreporting for political reasons.

The *Trafficking in Persons Report, 2006*, published by the U.S. Department of State, cites figures from the United Nations estimating 12.3 million victims of **trafficking,** enduring forced labor, bonded labor, forced child labor, and sexual servitude at any given time.[8] The *Trafficking in Persons Report* is an annual mandatory report submitted by the U.S. Department of State to Congress. It is intended to raise global awareness of trafficking. What is interesting is that the report does not discuss trafficking in the United States.

The report classifies countries based on their efforts to combat or eliminate trafficking. Tier 1 countries are those that fully comply with the Trafficking Victims Protection Act

Focus

Burma (Myanmar): A Tier 3 Country

Burma, or Myanmar as it is officially known as in the international community, is a source country for women and men trafficked for the purposes of forced labor and sexual exploitation. Burmese men, women, and children are trafficked to Thailand, the People's Republic of China (PRC), Bangladesh, Malaysia, Korea, and Macau for sexual exploitation, domestic service, and forced labor—including commercial labor. A significant number of men, women, and children from Burma are economic migrants who wind up in forced labor, bonded labor, and forced prostitution. Burma is also a country for transit as well as a destination for women trafficked from the PRC for sexual exploitation. There are also some cases of other countries using Burma for transit purposes. Internal trafficking of persons occurs primarily for labor in industrial zones and agricultural estates. Internal trafficking of women and children for sexual exploitation occurs from villages to urban centers, truck stops, fishing villages, border towns, mining camps, and military installations. Burma's large trafficking problems are a result of the military junta's economic mismanagement, human rights abuses, and its policy of using forced labor.

Significant state use of forced labor continues, especially by the military. The military is directly involved in trafficking of forced labor, and there are reports of some children who are forced into the Burmese Army. Although the Burmese government passed an antitrafficking law in 2005, it has made minimal efforts to enforce the law.

Source: Based on *Trafficking in Persons Report, 2006* (Department of State, Washington, D.C., June 2006).

of 2000. Tier 2 countries are those whose governments do not fully comply with the Act's minimum standards but are making significant efforts to bring themselves into compliance with those standards. Tier 2 Watch List countries are those whose governments do not fully comply with the Act's minimum standards but are making some efforts to bring themselves into compliance with those standards. These countries still have a significant number of trafficking victims, or there is a failure to combat severe forms of trafficking, but their classification is based on commitments to improve their efforts against trafficking in the next year. Tier 3 countries are those who do not fully comply with the minimum standards and are not making significant efforts to do so.

TYPES OF CHILD EXPLOITATION

Child Labor

The International Labour Office in Geneva, Switzerland, lists three forms of child labor that violate international social norms, laws, and treaties:

- All work done by children under the minimum legal age for that type of work;
- Work that endangers the health, safety, and morals of a child;
- The unconditionally worst forms of child labor, defined as slavery, trafficking, bonded labor, forced recruitment into armed conflict, prostitution, pornography, or other illegal activities.[9]

Many countries accept the practice of having children work as domestic helpers. The performing of chores in someone's home is often considered part of the child's socialization and development. Although not all domestic labor a child performs is child labor, there is a close line between the two and it is many times crossed over by greedy, unscrupulous people. Child domestic work is carried on behind closed doors, and children are particularly vulnerable to exploitation, including long hours with little or no pay, physical and sexual abuse, and being denied the ability to go to school.[10]

Children working on the streets represent one of the most visible groups of child laborers. They engage in a variety of different tasks, including peddling goods, preparing and selling food, polishing shoes, cleaning car windows, and scavenging for recyclables or other resalable items from garbage cans or dumpsites. These "street children" may also be involved in prostitution, drug dealing, or other illegal activities. The work street children perform varies from country to country. Sometime they live with their parents at night, and in other countries or locations, they may live on the streets. They may work as part of a family enterprise, an informal network, or be self-employed.[11]

Child Pornography

Child pornography is really a misnomer. The U.S. Constitution protects freedom of expression, and the courts have ruled that simple pornography is protected under the First Amendment. However, the courts have also ruled that obscene material is not protected, and its possession, sale, or distribution can be prosecuted. What is pornographic and what is obscene have generated controversy for decades. The U.S. Supreme Court in *Miller v. California* established a comprehensive definition of obscenity.[12] The Court held that a material may be considered obscene if it meets the following three criteria:

- The average person, applying contemporary community standards, must find that the work, taken as a whole, appeals to the prurient interest.
- The work depicts or describes, in a patently offensive way, sexual conduct.
- The work, taken as whole, lacks serious literary, artistic, political, or scientific value.

Each of the elements above has definitional problems. For example, what is contemporary? Must the material have been produced within the last several years to meet this requirement? Another hurdle that must be overcome is the requirement that the work is "taken as a whole"; this means that one scene may not be taken out of the context of the entire work. Finally, and what gives many scholars, professionals, and prosecutors problems, is the requirement that the work must lack serious literary or political or scientific value. In many adult obscenity cases, the defense calls expert witnesses to establish that the work, although offensive, does have some literary, political, or scientific value.

Even with these problems or hurdles to overcome, this definition allows prosecutors to charge and convict those who possess obscenity. Many states define obscenity using those three prongs. For example, California defines obscene matters as "matters taken as a whole, that to the average person, applying contemporary statewide standards, appeals to the prurient interest, that, taken as a whole, depicts or describes sexual conduct in a patently offensive way, and that taken as a whole, lacks serious literary, artistic, political, or scientific value."[13]

However, it is clear that materials depicting children engaging in explicit sexual activities fall within the definition of obscenity, and therefore those who exploit children for this purpose may be prosecuted. Under federal law, child pornography is defined as any visual depiction of any kind, including a drawing, cartoon, sculpture, painting, photograph, film, video, or other images, whether made or produced by electronic, mechanical, or other means, of sexually explicit conduct that depicts one of the following:

- A minor engaging in sexually explicit conduct that is obscene;
- An image of a minor engaging in bestiality, sadistic, or masochistic abuse;
- An image of sexual intercourse involving a minor, whether between persons of the same or different sex, if such depiction lacks serious literary, artistic, political, or scientific value.[14]

A major setback in the war against child pornography occurred when the U.S. Supreme Court struck down a segment of the definition that classified child pornography as including virtual acts or actions such that virtual depictions of children engaging in sexual activity were prohibited. The Court held that this ban on virtual child pornography was overbroad and unconstitutional under the First Amendment.[15]

Researchers and law enforcement officials believe that the crime of child pornography is increasing, and much of that increase can be attributed to the growing use of the Internet.[16] One study estimates that approximately 20 percent of all pornographic activity on the Internet may involve children.[17] Such estimates are hard to verify for a number of obvious reasons, including unreported incidents, secrecy of the networks and perpetrators, unknown or unidentified victims, and other methodological reasons. Another study indicates that the United States has the highest percentage of illegal Web sites containing child pornography. The *New Scientist* claims the United States has 40 percent of the Web sites, followed by Russia with 28 percent, and the remainder of Europe with 13 percent.[18] This startling claim is subject to the same methodological flaws as the estimates dealing with child pornographic material. Other sources indicate that Japan is the largest producer and consumer of child pornography, and the United States remains a major market for child pornography.[19]

Research is lacking regarding the motivations or characteristics of those who possess child pornography. However, one in-depth study established the following typology of perpetrators based on motivation or intent:

- Sexually interested in prepubescent children (pedophiles) or young adolescents (hebephiles) who use pornography for sexual fantasy and gratification;
- Sexually indiscriminate perpetrators who are constantly looking for new sexual stimulation;
- Sexually curious, downloading a few images to satisfy that curiosity;
- Sexual profiteers who profit by selling images or establishing child pornography Web sites.[20]

Other sources give a profile of those who possess child pornography. Those who are arrested for this crime are typically male, white (91%), older than twenty-five years (86%), and most are unmarried at the time of their arrest. Most of the perpetrators had images of prepubescent children and images graphically depicting sexual penetration.[21] Most of the incidents involving child pornography occur in private residences and homes, which is also the location where sexual abuse tends to occur.[22] The new National Incident-Based Reporting System (NIBRS), which is replacing the Uniform Crime Reports, collects statistics regarding reported cases of child pornography. Currently, the NIBRS data are available from only a small fraction of law enforcement agencies across the nation. Using this small fraction of reporting agencies, the NIBRS extrapolates that 2,900 incidents of child pornography were discovered by law enforcement agencies in 2000.[23] Of the identifiable victims, 62 percent were females and 25 percent were members of the offender's family. The ages of the victims were as follows:

12–17 years old	59%
6–11 years old	28%
Younger than 6 years old	13%

It should be obvious that it is impossible to produce child pornography without abusing or exploiting children. Given the demand and ease of obtaining child pornography by purchasing images online, the market for child pornography is growing. The fact is that there are those who make huge profits from this form of child exploitation. This in turn means that there is an economic demand for more victims.

Child pornography is a continuing problem, not only in the United States, but around the world. The Internet has given rise to an explosive growth in child pornography. Law enforcement agencies around the world continue to fight its existence, spread, and effects on young victims.

Child Prostitution

Another form of extreme child exploitation is **child prostitution.** This section will examine prostitution from both domestic and international perspectives. Domestic prostitution is present in every state in the United States, but how children become prostitutes in the United States differs from the process in many foreign countries. The next sections will examine child prostitution from both perspectives.

DOMESTIC PROSTITUTION.   Prostitution in the United States is defined by state and federal statutes and court decisions, but usually involves offering, agreeing, or performing a sexual act for any money, property, token, object, article, or anything of value.[24] Therefore, child prostitution may be defined as an act of engaging or offering the services of a child to a person to perform sexual acts for money or other consideration with that person or any other person.[25]

The true extent of child prostitution is subject to debate among law enforcement officials, professionals, and researchers. The nature of the act makes it hard to study, since in all jurisdictions it is a crime and therefore is hidden from view. However, data from service providers and other sources give us some indication of the scope of this activity. In 1996, one report indicated that up to 300,000 children who engage in prostitution live on the streets of the United States.[26] Many of these children are eleven or twelve years old, with some entering prostitution at the age of nine. The average age of entry into prostitution is fourteen years old.[27]

Prostitution takes many forms. It may range from sexual activities for approval or attention to sexual activities for food, shelter, or money. There are a variety of ways that children become involved in prostitution. Children may be trafficked domestically and then exploited through prostitution. One of the most common methods of entry into prostitution involves young vulnerable girls in search of love and acceptance on the streets. Often a pimp or someone working for a pimp will approach one of these girls and pretend to be a friend and supporter. The pimp will befriend the victim and provide companionship, financial support, and intimacy. The pimp may then demand that she must have sex with a friend as proof of her love for him. Soon the victim must continue prostituting herself as a condition of retaining the pimp's affection. Once the victim has been "turned," the pimp may use violence to control her. The pimp's relationship with the victim in many ways parallels the relationship an abuser has with his spouse or girlfriend.

Child pornography is another means by which pimps control their victims. They may take photographs or videos of the victims engaging in sexual acts and then threaten to send them to their families and friends. Pornography also tends to humiliate the victims and break their spirit. Pimps may also show photographs to the users, and the users themselves may want to take pictures of the victims. With the use of modern technology, these records of abuse can be made available to thousands of people. Domestic child prostitution continues to be a serious and ongoing problem within the United States.

INTERNATIONAL PROSTITUTION.   International child prostitution has many of the same characteristics as domestic child prostitution; however, there are some dramatic differences. The prostitution of children is closely connected with the trafficking of children for sexual purposes. Family members may knowingly sell their children to pimps or unwittingly sell them to persons claiming to be legitimate employment agents who in fact are traffickers. Other children are simply kidnapped and trafficked. These victims are usually from the poorest segments of undeveloped countries.

Once in the custody of the traffickers, child victims are beaten, raped, and forced to engage in various acts of prostitution. One report indicates that child prostitutes serve between two and thirty clients per week. This results in an estimate of between 100 and 1,500 users per year, per child.[28] They suffer from poor diets, lack of hygiene, and as a result end up with serious and sometimes life-threatening illness and diseases.

International child prostitution has become a multimillion-dollar-a-year business. For example, in 1997, the United Nations International Children's Educational Fund (UNICEF) reported that more than one million children are forced into prostitution each year, with the majority being in Asia.[29] International child prostitution, however, is not confined to Asia. Many countries, such as India, Pakistan, Russia, and Poland, among others, are involved in child prostitution.

Some countries promote prostitution in general and look the other way when the prostitute is a child because it is an economic boon to the country. Some government policies have led to child prostitution because of disparities in income and social status, causing poorer families to allow their children to become prostitutes as a means of survival, especially in the absence of any other social safety nets.[30]

International prostitution has a system of procurement, movement, and use. The illegal recruitment and sale of children within countries and across national borders is an organized industry that ranges from small loosely knit organizations to organized crime networks.[31]

Child Sex Tourism

"On this trip, I've had sex with a 14-year-old girl in Mexico and a 15-year-old in Colombia. I'm helping them financially. If they don't have sex with me, they may not have enough food. If someone has a problem with me doing this, let UNICEF feed them."

Source: Retired U.S. Schoolteacher, Posted on Child Exploitation and Obscenity Section, U.S. Department of Justice Web site at www.usdoj.gov/criminal/ceos/prostitution, accessed August 2, 2009.

Child sex tourism is another form of child exploitation. However, it has special characteristics that necessitate it being discussed separately. As indicated earlier in this chapter, child sex tourism is the commercial sexual exploitation of children by men or women who travel from one place to another, usually from a richer country to a poorer less-developed country, to engage in sexual acts with children. Although women commit such acts, they represent less than 5 percent of the sexual offenders.[32] Women can also be the procurers or arrangers by bringing or taking care of the children.

According to some reports, Americans make up 38 percent of all sex tourists in Cambodia and 80 percent in Costa Rica.[33] Other source countries include Japan, South Korea, countries of Western Europe, Australia, and New Zealand.

The persons who travel to a foreign country or within their own country with the intent of engaging in sex with a child are known as preferential child sex tourists.[34] These make up the minority of child sex tourism offenders. Many child sex tourists may not have a specific preference for children as sex objects or sexual partners, but will take advantage of such children if they are made available to them. These child sex tourists may be known as situational exploiters and are the majority of users in child sex tourism. The situational exploiter may rationalize his or her actions in a number of distorted ways. For example, he or she may believe that they are helping the children better themselves and their families. Others argue that sex with a child is culturally acceptable in the country they are visiting. Finally, others are simply racist and do not believe that the welfare of children in these countries is important.[35] Although sex with a child may be illegal, in many developing countries the authorities decline to take any action because of the economic benefit to the country.[36] Countries may also be unable to take action because they lack the resources—either because of economic circumstances or because existing resources are diverted to deal with other matters such as civil unrest or natural disasters.

Much international media attention on child sex tourism has focused on Thailand and other Southeast Asian countries. However, other countries regularly engage in this form of child exploitation as well: One estimate indicates that in San Jose, Costa Rica, there are more than 2,000 child prostitutes.[37]

Child sex tourism is a dynamic and ever-shifting problem—it occurs where the right circumstances combine. When one country accelerates action on the issue, it may spread elsewhere, as happened when much of the problem moved from Thailand to Cambodia and is seen increasingly in Vietnam. Similarly, when Brazil began coping with a major child sex tourism problem and stepped up its efforts, other countries in the region, such as Peru and Colombia, faced increased child sex tourism. The problem has also developed in Eastern

Europe, and yet just a few years ago, child sex tourism was unheard of in these countries. This problem is not a static one that will be easily solved.

The stereotype of sexual users of children may be middle-aged fat men on a tour who engage in sex with underaged minors. There are some companies that promote tours for the purpose of allowing their clients access to children for sexual purposes. While tours offering sex with children may still occur on a regular basis, many acts of child sex tourism happen outside the confines of a regularly scheduled tour. Indeed, opportunities for independent travel continue to grow, especially with the emergence of low-cost airline carriers, more Internet tour operators, expanding travel routes, and increased accommodations establishments. In other words, there are more opportunities for wealthy tourists to be in direct contact with poorer communities and children.

The U.S. Department of State estimates that each year more than one million children are exploited in the world as part of the commercial sex trade.[38] Over the last ten years, NGOs and governments have begun to respond to this form of child exploitation. In 1999, the World Tourism Organization, ECPAT, and certain Nordic tour operators created a "Code of Conduct for the Protection of Children from Sexual Exploitation in Travel and Tourism." The World Tourism Organization is the leading international organization in the field of tourism and has actively pushed for the adoption of the Code of Conduct in the past. It has 141 member states and 304 affiliate members representing the operational sector of tour groups. The Code of Conduct establishes six principles that revolve around the concept of protecting children from sexual exploitation as a result of tourism. These principles include establishing an ethical policy regarding commercial sexual exploitation of children, training personnel in the country of origin, introducing a clause in contracts stating a common repudiation of commercial sexual exploitation of children, providing information to travelers about sexual exploitation of children, providing information to local persons at destinations, and filing an annual report.[39] The main partner for signatory travel and tourism companies in the implementation of these principles is ECPAT country groups as well as UNICEF country offices. Together, they conduct tourism staff training, develop informational materials to distribute to tourists, monitor tourism developments, which may place children at risk, and launch awareness campaigns.

Individual countries have responded to this form of child exploitation in various ways. Thailand has passed a law that allows for prosecution of those who engage in child sexual activities. Those who have sex with a girl fifteen years old or younger are subject to seven to twenty years in prison. If the victim is younger than thirteen years, the sentence is life imprisonment. Germany passed a law making it a crime to engage in sexual activities with a child who is younger than fourteen years no matter where the act occurred. Australia criminalizes sex with someone who is younger than sixteen years old by citizens traveling outside of Australia.[40]

In 2003, Congress passed the Prosecutorial Remedies and Other Tools to End the Exploitation of Children Today (PROTECT) Act and the Trafficking Victims Protection Reauthorization Act. These laws allow for imprisonment of persons who engage in child sex tourism. The PROTECT Act makes it a crime to travel to another country for the purpose of having sex with a child.

These laws are examples of extraterritorial legislation. This type of legislation allows a country to prosecute its citizens for crimes committed against children even if they were committed outside the country. To date, thirty-two countries have enacted extraterritorial legislation designed to protect children.

Even with extraterritorial legislation criminalizing child sex tourism, authorities face numerous obstacles when conducting investigations and prosecuting offenders under these laws. For example, collection of evidence and testimony depends on the cooperation of the local police agencies. Differences in language, customs, and attitude toward commercial sexual exploitation of children may lead to a lack of cooperation by local authorities.[41]

Progress is being made in the battle against child sex tourism. Education, enactment of laws, and more focused law enforcement activities are fighting this form of child exploitation.

Other Child Exploitation (Such as Begging)

There are additional forms or variations of child exploitation. Some children are kidnapped from their families and used as forced labor. When they are not actually working in the factories, they may be forced to sit on the streets and act as beggars. Still other children are used strictly as beggars when they are very young and then are sent to factories as they grow older. Begging involves sitting on the street in extremely hot or cold or rainy weather and asking for money from strangers. Some begging rings work their location twenty-four hours a day and actually have shifts that bring in new beggars at regular hours. Their begging spot or location is jealously guarded against other independent beggars who would attempt to take over what may be viewed as a prime location for begging. In some cases, children may have to pay a fee to a beggar master for the begging spot. These could be subway or other mass transit locations, roads, or sidewalks used by tourists, and other heavy traffic areas. These begging masters take the money gathered by the child and control the actions of the child.

THE TRAFFICKERS AND USERS

Within most of the other areas of family violence, there are information and data on the perpetrators. For example, earlier chapters in this textbook discussed various characteristics of child abusers. However, in the area of child exploitation, there is a very limited body of literature dealing with both traffickers and users.

One excellent study classified traffickers into four distinct roles. Stulhofer and Raboteg-Saric's typology included the organizers, the middlemen, the business operators, and the aides.[42] This typology concerned Croatian sex trafficking, but Kelly argues that it is a valid typology that applies to all trafficking. Although Kelly's use of this typology focused on the trafficking of women, it can easily be adapted to the trafficking of children.[43] The organizers are those who organize the network. They are at the beginning of the chain, but may be responsible for maintaining its integrity. The middlemen are the recruiters of the victims. They transport the victims and are also responsible for selling the victims. The business operators include the brothel and nightclub owners and the pimps. These parties are actively involved in the selling of the victim's product—either her body or the results of her acts such as pornographic media. The aides, governmental officials or police, assist the business operator by overlooking trafficking or even take an active part in catching any fleeing victim and returning her to the operators. However, this typology does not include a fifth and critical part of the chain of child exploitation, that of the users. Therefore, a suggested modification of Stulhofer and Raboteg-Saric's typology would be a fifth classification that includes the users of children. Users are the demand side of the supply and demand equation in child exploitation. To call them customers validates their status as reasonable, law-abiding citizens. That is simply not the case. To call them clients implies a relationship on a professional level, but child prostitution cannot be considered a profession. The users are exploiters of children. They are the middle-aged men or women who travel to a foreign country to have sex with underaged children. They are the average-looking male who purchases child pornography for his personal use. They are any person or persons who use the results of child exploitation. Therefore, the modified typology would include five classifications:

> *Organizers:* those who organize and maintain the trafficking chain or routes
>
> *Middlemen:* recruiters and transporters
>
> *Business Operators:* brothel owners, nightclub operators, and pimps
>
> *Aides:* those officials who overlook trafficking
>
> *Users:* those who pay to use the victim.

There is a continuing controversy regarding who are the traffickers of children. At one time, trafficking was believed to be completely controlled by organized crime. Now many researchers believe that individuals and small organized groups are also involved in trafficking. Some of these groups recruit or kidnap victims and then rely on organized crime to use its networks to move the victims to the destination country. There are some Asian traffickers that consist of small groups of entrepreneurs with organizational and international business skills that traffic victims.[44]

FACTORS THAT CONTRIBUTE TO CHILD EXPLOITATION

A variety of factors contribute to child exploitation. Countries have different cultures and situations, some of which allow for children to be exploited. These factors include poverty, desire for a better life, ignorance, lack of schools, family violence, consumerism, gender, and ethnic discrimination. There are other factors that pull children into situations in which they can be or are exploited. These include the demand for children, the growing tourist industry, lack of enforcement laws and inadequate implementation of existing laws, and the growth of the sex industry.

Poverty is probably one of the major causes of child exploitation. In many countries, there is a wide separation between the poor and the rich. Wars, natural disasters, and other factors contribute to poverty and a feeling of helplessness. Desire for a better life is closely tied to poverty, and families may give their children to others in the belief that the child will have a better life or that the child will earn money and allow the family to have a better life. Ignorance of the consequences of giving their children away or ignorance of the intent of those who take the children under the guise of offering the child a job contributes to child exploitation. Lack of schools or educational opportunities, especially for females, may lead to a situation in which children are exploited. Family violence or the existence of a dysfunctional family may allow for children to be given away or encourage children to run away from home. Gender discrimination places less value on protecting or caring for female children. Ethnic discrimination in some countries encourages the trafficking of children in an attempt to find a better life.

Focus

Factors That Increase a Child's Vulnerability to Trafficking

Supply Factors	Demand Factors
Poverty	Lack of schools or ability to attend them
Desire for a better life	Family violence
Ignorance by parents and children of the consequences	Consumerism
of leaving home to work	Gender discrimination
Demand for cheap migrant labor	Ethnic discrimination
Size of the tourist industry	
Lack of implementation and enforcement of laws	
Growth of sex industry	

Source: Based on "Facts on Trafficking of Children," International Programme on the Elimination of Child Labor, www.ilo.org/childlabour, accessed September 10, 2006.

Focus

Federal Efforts to Combat Interstate Sex Trafficking of Minors

It has been a federal crime to transport minors over state lines for the purpose of committing illegal sex acts since 1910. The most recent initiative to combat this crime has been sponsored by the FBI Crimes Against Children Division in conjunction with CEOS and with the National Center for Missing and Exploited Children. Operation Innocence Lost, announced in early 2003, is a nationwide initiative to focus on child victims of interstate sex trafficking in the United States. Four primary statutes, 18 U.S.C. § 1591 and 18 U.S.C. §§ 2421–2423, criminalize prostituting minors in interstate commerce. In summary, 18 U.S.C. § 1591 makes it illegal to recruit, entice, obtain, provide, move, or harbor a person or to benefit from such activities knowing that the person will be caused to engage in commercial sex acts where the person is under eighteen or where force, fraud, or coercion exists. This statute does not require that either the defendant or the victim actually travel.

The statute defines *Commercial Sex Act* as any sexual act for which something of value is given or received. 18 U.S.C. § 1591(c)(1). *Coercion* is defined as (1) actual threats of harm, (2) scheme intended to cause the victim

to believe harm would result, or (3) threats of legal repercussions against the victim 18 U.S.C. § 1591(c)(2). Statutory penalties for violating Section 1591 are quite severe. In instances where no force, fraud, or coercion is used and in which the victim is between fourteen and eighteen years of age, the statutory maximum penalty is up to forty years imprisonment. If the victim has not attained the age of fourteen, or in instances when force, fraud, or coercion can be proved, the statutory maximum penalty is any term of years or life imprisonment.

An individual who engages in interstate sex trafficking of minors may also be charged with violations of 18 U.S.C. §§ 2421–2423. In order to obtain federal jurisdiction, the statutes require proof of actual travel in interstate commerce, or a specific use of the channels of interstate commerce for illegal sexual activity.

Eighteen United States Code, Section 2421 criminalizes the knowing transportation of any individual in interstate or foreign commerce, or in any territory or possession of the United States, with the intent that such individual engage in prostitution, or in any sexual activity

(continued)

for which any person can be charged with a criminal offense. The maximum term of imprisonment under this statute is ten years. Eighteen United States Code, Section 2422 applies to defendants who coerce or entice either adults or minors to engage in illegal sexual activity:

a. Whoever knowingly persuades, induces, entices, or coerces any individual to travel in interstate or foreign commerce, or in any territory or possession of the United States, to engage in prostitution or in any sexual activity for which any person can be charged with a criminal offense, or attempts to do so, shall be fined under this title or imprisoned not more than twenty years, or both;

b. Whoever, using the mail or any facility or means of interstate or foreign commerce or within the special maritime and territorial jurisdiction of the United States, knowingly persuades, induces, entices, or coerces any individual who has not attained the age of eighteen years, to engage in prostitution or any sexual activity for which any person can be charged with a criminal offense, or attempts to do so, shall be fined under this title and imprisoned not less than five years and not more than thirty years.

18 U.S.C. § 2422. The PROTECT Act, passed in April 2003, raised the maximum sentence under Section 2422(a), and both established a mandatory minimum sentence and raised the maximum sentence under Section 2422(b).

The statute criminalizing interstate or international transportation of minors for illegal sexual activity is 18 U.S.C. § 2423. This statute, too, was recently amended in the PROTECT Act. The newly revised statute provides the following:

a. *Transportation with intent to engage in criminal sexual activity:* A person who knowingly transports an individual who has not attained the age of eighteen years in interstate or foreign commerce, or in any commonwealth, territory, or possession of the United States, with the intent that the individual engage in prostitution, or in any sexual activity for which any person can be charged with a criminal offense, shall be fined under this title and imprisoned not less than five years and not more than thirty years.

b. *Travel with intent to engage in illicit sexual conduct:* A person who travels in interstate commerce or who travels into the United States, or a U.S. citizen or alien admitted for permanent residence in the United States who travels in foreign commerce, for the purpose of engaging in any illicit sexual conduct with another person shall be fined under this title or imprisoned not more than thirty years, or both.

c. *Engaging in illicit sexual conduct in foreign places:* Any U.S. citizen or alien admitted for permanent residence who travels in foreign commerce and engaged in any illicit sexual conduct with another person shall be fined under this title or imprisoned not more than thirty years, or both.

d. *Ancillary offenses:* Whoever, for the purpose of commercial advantage or private financial gain, arranges, induces, procures, or facilitates the travel of a person knowing that such a person is traveling in interstate commerce or foreign commerce for the purpose of engaging in illicit sexual conduct shall be fined under this title, imprisoned not more than thirty years, or both.

e. *Attempt and conspiracy:* Whoever attempts or conspires to violate subsection (a), (b), (c), or (d) shall be punishable in that same manner as a completed violation of that subsection.

f. *Definition:* As used in this section, the term *illicit sexual conduct* means (1) a sexual act (as defined in Section 2246) with a person under eighteen years of age that would be in violation of chapter 109A if the sexual act occurred in the special maritime and territorial jurisdiction of the United States or (2) any commercial sex act (as defined

(continued)

in Section 1591) with a person under eighteen years of age.

g. *Defense:* In a prosecution based on illicit sexual conduct ad defined in subsection (f) (2), it is a defense that the defendant must establish by a preponderance of the evidence, that the defendant reasonably believed that the person with whom the defendant engaged in the commercial sex act had attained the age of eighteen years.

The PROTECT Act specifically implemented several amendments in connection with sex tourism and commercial sexual exploitation: (1) In the area of sex tourism, new provision 2423(c) makes it sufficient to show that a U.S. citizen or lawful permanent resident traveled abroad and engaged in any illicit sexual conduct with a minor, regardless of what his intentions may have been when he left the United States; (2) the addition of 2423(d) specifically reaches any person who knowingly "arranges, induces, procures, or facilitates the travel" of an individual he knows is traveling for the purpose of engaging in illicit sexual conduct, when he engages in facilitating the travel for the purpose of commercial advantage or private financial gain; (3) new provision 2423(e) punishes an attempt or conspiracy to violate any of the provisions in 2423; (4) the definitions contained in 2423(f) broaden the prohibited conduct under the statute to include commercial sex acts (as defined in 18 U.S.C. § 1591(c)(1)) with persons under eighteen of age; and (5) for defendants charged under the sex tourism provision, 2423(c) an affirmative defense was added for defendant who "reasonably believed" that person who had engaged in the commercial sex act was eighteen years old. The defendant bears the burden of proving the affirmative defense by a preponderance of the evidence.

The PROTECT Act also changed the sentencing scheme for 18 U.S.C. § 2423. For 18 U.S.C. § 2423(a) (traveling for criminal sex act), the maximum sentence was upgraded to thirty years imprisonment. Formerly, the equivalent provision had a maximum sentence of fifteen years. A mandatory minimum sentence of five years was also enacted. In the revision to section 2423(b), the maximum sentence was also upgraded from fifteen to thirty years imprisonment.

Source: Child Exploitation and Obscenity Section, U.S. Department of Justice Web site at www.usdoj.gov/criminal/ ceos/prostitution, accessed August 2, 2009.

On the other side, there are at least four factors that increase child exploitation. Demand for children in the workforce and the sex trade makes child exploitation economically successful. Growth of the tourist industry feeds the demand for children who are exploited. Lack of enforceable laws allows for the kidnapping and continued exploitation of children. Growth of the sex industry encourages child exploitation with its need for more and more young children.

Children as Soldiers

The use of children as soldiers is a black mark against humanity.[45] This is a very special form of child exploitation that is not often linked directly to trafficking. The effects and consequences of children being used as weapons of war last for generations.[46] Almost all civilized nations publicly agree that they should not use children as soldiers. The great majority of these nations are signatories to various treaties, conventions, and protocols that prohibit or condemn the use of children as soldiers. However, many of them as well as other nonsignatories continue to use children as soldiers both in external and internal conflicts. In addition, rebel groups routinely recruit or abduct children for use as soldiers. These children, both boys and girls, experience violence, intimidation, and sexual abuse by their so-called leaders.

The major international standards that prohibit the use of children as soldiers are the Convention on the Rights of the Child, the Optional Protocol to the Convention, the Rome Statute of the International Criminal Court, and additional protocols to the four Geneva conventions.[47]

The Convention on the Rights of the Child contains specific prohibitions that attempt to protect children from serving as soldiers by prohibiting recruitment of children under the age of fifteen. A number of nations decided to build on the principles of the convention and worked to raise the minimum age for recruitment and participation in the armed forces to eighteen years of age. The Protocol to the Convention on the Rights of the Child was adopted by the U.N. General Assembly on May 25, 2000, and became effective on February 12, 2002. By 2005, this protocol had been signed by 115 countries and ratified by 63 countries. It outlaws compulsory recruitment of children under the age of eighteen by government or nongovernment forces. It raises the age that children may volunteer for the armed forces to sixteen years old and requires nations to establish methods to prove that the child's acts were in fact voluntary. It further requires that any nation that does accept volunteers under the age of eighteen ensure that those children do not take part in direct combat operations. Finally, it outlaws the recruitment or participation of any person under the age of eighteen in any insurgency groups or rebel forces under any circumstances.[48] The Rome Statute of the International Criminal Court classifies conscription, enlistment, or use in hostilities of children below the age of fifteen in internal or external conflicts as a war crime.

Although the United Nations has information that indicates child soldiers are being used in more than thirty countries, the Security Council actions were limited to six armed conflicts, with five of them being in Africa. It appears that members of the Security Council are reluctant to interfere with the actions of other sovereign states or have declined to incur the cost of enforcing sanctions against those nations that violate various international agreements.[49]

Who are child soldiers? The treaties, conventions, and protocols define them by age. The Coalition to Stop the Use of Child Soldiers defines them as any person under the age of eighteen who is a member or attached to government forces or any other regular or irregular force or armed group.[50] However, some nations allow young people to join the armed forces with the consent of their parents. In many cases, these are truly voluntarily acts by the parents and the young persons. Therefore, it would seem a better definition might be the following: "Child soldiers are any persons under the age of sixteen who, without the voluntary consent of their parents, become members or are attached to government forces or any regular or irregular force or armed group. In no event shall any person under the age of eighteen be allowed to participate directly or indirectly in armed combat." This definition will undoubtedly raise concern and controversy, but it addresses the realities and practices of modern industrialized nations, many of whom allow sixteen- or seventeen-year-old children to join their armed forces with the consent of their parents. Great Britain and the United States are two examples of nations that allow persons under the age of eighteen to enlist in their armed forces with the consent of their parents.

The true extent of the problem is unknown, because like many other issues addressed in this chapter, in many nations recruitment and use of children as soldiers is shrouded in secrecy and outsiders are barred from examining this issue. However, the Coalition to Stop the Use of Child Soldiers estimates that there are more than 120,000 children under the age of eighteen currently participating in armed conflicts in Africa alone. Children are used as solders in other countries, including those of the Mideast. Some of these children are not more than seven or eight years old.[51] Other estimates state that more than 500,000 children under the age of eighteen have been recruited by state or nonstate armed forces or groups in more than eighty-five countries.[52] A third source, Amnesty International, USA, states that approximately 300,000 children under the age of eighteen are participating in armed conflicts in thirty different countries.[53] As can be seen from these figures, well-meaning and dedicated organizations and/or agencies have different figures and facts regarding the extent of the problem of child soldiers. What is clear is that it is a persistent problem that affects our most valuable resource—children.

Children become soldiers in a variety of ways. Some children are drafted or conscripted, others are kidnapped, and others are forced to join armed groups to protect their family from retaliation. The kidnapping may occur in a variety of ways; they may be seized off the street or taken while attending school or living in orphanages. Hunger, poverty, or fear may drive parents to offer their children for service, especially when the armed group offers to pay the child's wages to the family instead of giving it to the child. Sometimes, children may "voluntarily" join the armed groups because they may perceive it as the only way to survive.[54]

Children may participate in armed conflict at ages as young as seven years old. They may act as porters who carry food or ammunition for the actual fighters. They also act as runners or scouts, sex slaves, cooks, or spies. Girls are especially vulnerable as child soldiers. Many are sexually assaulted, forced to engage in prostitution, or forced to be "wives" of adult combatants. When they reach the age of ten, their roles may change and they may be given rifles and become soldiers.[55]

Focus

What Is the Appropriate Age for a Soldier?

The discussion and definition of a child soldier raises complex social and cultural issues. In the United States, a person at the age of seventeen may enlist with parental approval. In the United Kingdom, a person at the age of sixteen may enlist in the armed forces.

- What is the appropriate age for a person to become a soldier in the armed forces?
- Does it make any difference that a person who is sixteen years old cannot drive in many states?
- How about the fact that a person seventeen years old has only been driving for one year?

- Does your opinion change if the person joining the armed forces is doing so to get out of a ghetto and make a better life?
- Would your opinion change if they were allowed to join the military but were prohibited from directly or indirectly being involved in an armed conflict?
- What about the fact that in many states you may join the armed forces at the age of eighteen, but cannot drink in a bar or vote?
- Would your answer be different if instead of joining a formal recognized military, the person was joining a rebel group?

Many commanders like using children as soldiers because they are so young that they view combat as a game or are not afraid of death. They are also viewed as a consumable quantity to be used up instead of the more dependable adult combatants. Because they are considered so expendable, many of them never receive any training and are often massacred during combat. In addition, they are easier to mold into effective fighters. Finally, in some countries, there is a shortage of eligible men, so the combatants widen the recruitment base by accepting or abducting children.

Child soldiers have been witnessed committing atrocities during and after combat. Sometimes, these acts are committed under the influence of drugs or alcohol or at the urging of the adult soldiers. However, drugs or alcohol alone are not responsible for these acts. A more likely cause of the majority of the atrocities stems from the fact that the children have suffered systematic abuse by adult combatants and have lived in a pervasive culture of killing and violence. This environment, coupled with threats of deadly retaliation if they do not conform to the beliefs of their adult leaders, is probably the major reason that children are involved in acts of mutilations, killings, and rapes. Some of these acts include beheading a captive and playing catch with her head or gouging out the eyes of one victim and then proceeding to cut off his hands and feet.[56]

The consequences of children serving as soldiers have been explored by a number of different authorities. Daya Somasundaram has examined the long-term civil war in Sri Lanka and explains that child soldiers suffer brutalization, deprivation, institutionalized violence, and various brutal sociocultural factors. Psychological injuries include somatization (physical illness resulting from psychological injuries), depression, posttraumatic stress disorder, and even severe psychosis.[57]

CONSEQUENCES OF TRAFFICKING

There are several common characteristics of children who have been trafficked. Each victim is manipulated through the act or threat of violence. Each victim is a displaced person in foreign circumstances that increase his or her dependence on the trafficker. Each victim represents a profit for the trafficker and yet is also expendable. Language barriers, lack of social networks, and constant fear entrap the victim. Finally each victim lives in a situation outside the rules of law.[58] There are human and social costs of trafficking in general that also apply to child exploitation. These include human rights violations, social breakdown, organized crime, depriving countries of human capital, public health problems, and erosion of governmental authority.[59]

> *Human rights:* Trafficking in persons violates accepted universal rights of life, liberty, and freedom. Trafficking of children violates a child's right to grow up in a safe and secure environment.
>
> *Social breakdown:* The loss of family and community support makes the child vulnerable to the trafficker's demands and threats. The loss of educational opportunities reduces the victim's economic potential. Victims who try to return to their communities are many times viewed as outcasts and stigmatized.
>
> *Organized crime:* The profits from trafficking provide funds for other criminal activities. Human trafficking is closely associated with money laundering, drug trafficking, and human smuggling.

Depriving countries of human capital: Trafficking has an adverse impact on labor markets by contributing to the loss of people in the workforce in source countries. Some effects of trafficking include depressed wages, loss of productivity, and loss of an educated workforce. It can suppress wages in a country due to the availability of cheap trafficked labor. Trafficking reinforces the cycle of poverty in a country.

Public health: There are serious public health consequences for child victims of trafficking. They may be classified into six different categories:

1. Infectious diseases, such as HIV and TB;
2. Noninfectious diseases, such as skin diseases and malnutrition;
3. Reproductive problems, including forced abortions and high-risk pregnancies;
4. Substance abuse, including drugs and alcohol;
5. Mental health problems, including depression and posttraumatic stress disorder;
6. Violence, including physical and sexual assault by users and pimps.

Erosion of governmental authority: Trafficking undermines the national government's authority. Many governments are unable to protect segments of their populations, including women, children, and certain minorities within their borders.

Understanding the consequences of child exploitation will allow NGOs and governmental agencies to develop scientifically based intervention programs. Hopefully, this knowledge can also be used to establish effective prevention programs that will lessen or do away with child exploitation.

UNIFORM LAWS ON TRAFFICKING

In the United States, one of the methods that we are using to lessen or do away with child exploitation is the adoption of laws that punish the offenders. Whereas Congress has enacted various laws attempting to combat child exploitation, a great majority of the states have not enacted effective antitrafficking laws, which could be used to fight child exploitation. In an attempt to remedy this situation, the U.S. Department of Justice drafted a Model State Anti-Trafficking Criminal Statute.[60]

The Model State Anti-Trafficking Criminal Statute attempted to address a number of problems that faced states in their efforts to prosecute trafficking. These challenges include failure at the state and local levels to understand the complexity and seriousness of human trafficking. For instance, many trafficking rings have been overlooked for years simply because they were hidden under the cover of simply being cases of prostitution. In these cases, law enforcement officials may view the victims of trafficking as coconspirators or willing participants in the crime. In addition, it may be difficult for local investigators to penetrate trafficking groups that are ethnically based.

The Model State Anti-Trafficking Criminal Statute points out that many states already have laws on their books that address trafficking. For example, kidnapping and prostitution statutes could be used against traffickers. However, these crimes are listed in different parts of most criminal statutes, and it may be unclear to prosecutors that the perpetrators may be engaged in trafficking and should be charged as such. The Model State Anti-Trafficking Code indicates that more comprehensive statutes are needed to combat trafficking. It sets forth a series of definitions, establishes penalties, and provides for restitution and protections of victims.

Several years after the Model State Anti-Trafficking Criminal Statute was introduced by the Department of Justice, a group of lawyers and service providers who work with victims of trafficking drafted the State Model on Protection for Victims of Human Trafficking.[61] Similar to the Department of Justice statute, the Model State Code acknowledges that the federal government cannot combat trafficking by itself. It points out that state and local authorities are more often likely to encounter victims of trafficking while engaged in routine arrests, inspections of buildings, factories, and farms. The State Model points out that the Department of Justice statute, while very good, contains some gaps and inconsistencies.

Both these efforts indicate a growing awareness of the problem of trafficking and a resolve at both the federal and state levels to combat it. With increased laws, more education, and better understanding, progress will be made in the fight against this heinous form of slavery.

Focus

Executive Summary of the U.S. Attorney General's Report to Congress on Child Exploitation

August 2010

[The following executive summary provides an excellent discussion of the problems in policing child exploitation and the federal government's efforts to combat these crimes.]

The sexual abuse and exploitation of children rob the victims of their childhood, irrevocably interfering with their emotional and psychological development. Ensuring that all children come of age without being disturbed by sexual trauma or exploitation is more than a criminal justice issue, it is a societal issue. Despite efforts to date, the threat of child sexual exploitation remains very real, whether it takes place in the home, on the street, over the Internet, or in a foreign land.

Because the sexual abuse and exploitation of children strikes at the very foundation of our society, it will take our entire society to combat this affront to the public welfare. Therefore, this National Strategy lays out a comprehensive response to protect the right of children to be free from sexual abuse and to protect society from the cost imposed by this crime.

In the broadest terms, the goal of this National Strategy is to prevent child sexual exploitation from occurring in the first place, in order to protect every child's opportunity and right to have a childhood that is free from sexual abuse, trauma, and exploitation so that they can become the adults they were meant to be. This Strategy will accomplish that goal by efficiently leveraging assets across the federal government in a coordinated manner. All entities with a stake in the fight against child exploitation—from federal agencies and investigators and prosecutors, to social service providers, educators, medical professionals, academics, nongovernmental organizations, and members of industry, as well as parents, caregivers, and the threatened children themselves—are called upon to do their part to prevent these crimes, care for the victims, and rehabilitate the offenders.

Background

In 2008, Congress passed and the president signed the Providing Resources, Officers, and Technology to Eradicate Cyber Threats to Our Children Act of 2008 (the "PROTECT Our Children Act" or the "Act"). This Act requires the Department of Justice (the "Department") to formulate and implement a National Strategy to combat child exploitation. The Act also

(continued)

requires the Department to submit a report on the National Strategy (the "National Strategy" or "Report") to Congress every other year. The Act mandates that the National Strategy contain a significant amount of information, including: (1) an assessment of the magnitude of child exploitation, (2) a review of the Department and other state and federal agencies' efforts to coordinate and combat child exploitation, and (3) a proposed set of goals and priorities for reducing child exploitation.

In this inaugural National Strategy report, the Department describes its first-ever threat assessment of the danger that faces the nation's children, its current efforts to combat child exploitation, and posits some goals and plans to fight the threats that are facing our nation's children.

The Threat Assessment

This Report attempts to marshal a massive amount of information about the nature of the child exploitation problem and the significant efforts being undertaken by federal, state, and local agencies to address this epidemic. To evaluate the extent and forms of child exploitation, between approximately February 2009 and February 2010, the National Drug Intelligence Center (NDIC) prepared a threat assessment (the "Threat Assessment" or "Assessment") that is summarized in this Report. In conducting the Threat Assessment, the NDIC interviewed over a hundred prosecutors, investigators, and other experts in the field; conducted interviews to collect information; reviewed thousands of pages of documents from investigations, cases, relevant research; and analyzed data from the National Center for Missing and Exploited Children. In addition to conducting the Threat Assessment, the Department and the Library of Congress have gathered and reviewed an extensive amount of studies and research relevant to the field of child exploitation to help inform the Department and its partners of the most recent information available from academia on this subject.

The Threat Assessment research indicates that the threat to our nation's children of becoming a victim of child exploitation is a very serious one. For example, investigators and prosecutors report dramatic increases in the number, and violent character, of the sexually abusive images of children being trafficked through the Internet. They also report the disturbing trend of younger children depicted in these images, even including toddlers and infants. Furthermore, offenders have become proficient at enticing children to engage in risky behavior, like agreeing to meet for sexual activity, or even to display themselves engaging in sexual activity through images or webcams. In addition, the offenders have been able to master Internet technologies to better mask their identities.

To address the threat to our nation's children, the National Strategy focuses on the following types of child sexual exploitation: (1) child pornography, often called images of child sexual abuse; (2) online enticement of children for sexual purposes; (3) commercial sexual exploitation of children; and (4) child sex tourism.

Child Pornography

The expansion of the Internet has led to an explosion in the market for child pornography, making it easier to create, access, and distribute these images of abuse. While *child pornography* is the term commonly used by lawmakers, prosecutors, investigators, and the public to describe this form of sexual exploitation of children, that term largely fails to describe the true horror that is faced by hundreds of thousands of children every year. The child victims are first sexually assaulted in order to produce the vile, and often violent, images. They are then victimized again when these images of their sexual assault are traded over the Internet in massive numbers by like-minded people across the globe.

The anonymity afforded by the Internet makes the offenders more difficult to locate, and makes them bolder in their actions. Investigations show that offenders often gather in communities over the Internet where trading of these images is just one component of a larger relationship that is premised on a shared sexual interest in children. This has the effect of eroding

(continued)

the shame that typically would accompany this behavior, and desensitizing those involved to the physical and psychological damage caused to the children involved. This self-reinforcing cycle is fueling ever greater demand in the market for these images. In the world of child pornography, this demand drives supply. The individual collector who methodically gathers one image after another has the effect of validating the production of the image, which leads only to more production. Because the Internet has blurred traditional notions of jurisdiction and sovereignty, this urgent crime problem is truly global in scope, and requires a coordinated national and international response.

Online Enticement of Children

Child predators often use the Internet to identify, and then coerce, their victims to engage in illegal sex acts. These criminals will lurk in chat rooms or on bulletin board Web sites that are popular with children and teenagers. They will gain the child's confidence and trust, and will then direct the conversation to sexual topics. Sometimes they send the child sexually explicit images of themselves, or they may request that the child send them pornographic images of themselves. Often, the defendants plan a face-to-face for the purpose of engaging in sex acts.

The Commercial Sexual Exploitation of Children

Children are being recruited and coerced into the world of prostitution in our own cities. Teen runaways—who are often trying to escape abusive homes—may turn to prostitution as a means of survival. They also frequently fall prey to "pimps" who lure them in with an offer of food, clothes, attention, friendship, love, and a seemingly safe place to sleep. Once the pimps gain this control over the children, they often use acts of violence, intimidation, or psychological manipulation to trap the children in a life of prostitution. Pimps will also cause the children to become addicted to drugs or alcohol (or will increase the severity of a pre-existing addiction) in order to ensure complicity. These children are taught to lie about

their age and are given fake ID. They are also trained not to trust law enforcement and to lie to protect their pimps. As a result, these victims are often not recognized as victims, and may be arrested and jailed. The dangers faced by these children—from the pimps, from their associates, and from customers—are severe. These children become hardened by the treacherous street environment in which they must learn to survive. As such, they do not always outwardly present as sympathetic victims. These child victims need specialized services that are not widely available given that they often present with illnesses, drug additions, physical and sexual trauma, lack of viable family and community ties, and total dependence—physical and psychological—on their abusers, the pimps.

Child Sex Tourism

Child sex tourism refers to Americans or U.S. resident aliens traveling abroad for the purpose of sexually abusing foreign children (usually in economically disadvantaged countries). Americans, capitalizing on their relative wealth and the lack of effective law enforcement in the destination countries, easily purchase access to young children to engage in illicit sex acts, sometimes for as little as $5. Like child pornography and other Internet-facilitated crimes against children, the Internet has revolutionized the child sex tourism industry. As a result, a new, emboldened crop of offenders are finding the navigation of travel in developing countries much easier than in the past. Additionally, the Internet allows like-minded offenders to gather and exchange information on how and where to find child victims in these foreign locations, making the offenders better informed about where sex tourism is prevalent and where law enforcement is lax. Numerous countries in Southeast Asia are so well-known for child sex tourism that there are entire neighborhoods that are considered brothels, and there are open-air markets where children can be purchased for sex.

In short, the threat of sexual exploitation faced by children today is very real.

(continued)

Brief Overview of the Nation's Efforts to Combat Child Exploitation

While the threat has increased, so, too, have the resources dedicated to addressing this issue. This Report provides an overview of the significant efforts of the Department and numerous other federal, state, and local agencies that are working to prevent and interdict child exploitation. The efforts are multi-faceted, and many of these groups work cooperatively to address this ever-expanding problem.

The Department has a number of components, offices, and agencies that devote personnel, resources, and time to the issue of preventing, investigating, and prosecuting child exploitation, as well as to providing services to victims and families. These components include, but are not limited to, the Office of the Deputy Attorney General (ODAG), the Federal Bureau of Investigation (FBI), the U.S. Marshals Service, Interpol Washington, the U.S. Attorney's Offices, the Criminal Division's Child Exploitation and Obscenity Section (CEOS), and the Office of Justice Programs (OJP).

The ODAG helps to direct all of the Department's efforts to combat child exploitation. The Department has appointed a National Coordinator for Child Exploitation Prevention and Interdiction, who is an official within the Office of the Deputy Attorney General.

The FBI leads the Department's investigative efforts and as a part of that mandate created the Innocent Images National Initiative, which focuses on technology-facilitated child exploitation. Between 1996 and 2007, there was a 2,062 percent increase in child exploitation investigations throughout the FBI. In 2004, the FBI launched the Innocent Images International Task Force, which has brought dozens of investigators from all over the world to train with the FBI and foster international cooperation in the global fight against child exploitation.

The Marshals Service is tasked under the Adam Walsh Act with the primary responsibility for locating and apprehending sex offenders who have failed to register on a sex offender registry. As part of the Adam Walsh Act, the Marshals Service has three principle responsibilities: assisting state, local, tribal, and territorial authorities in the location and apprehension of noncompliant and fugitive sex offenders; investigating violations of the Adam Walsh Act for federal prosecution; and assisting in the identification and location of sex offenders relocated as a result of a major disaster. Dozens of Deputy U.S. Marshals lead task forces of federal, state, and local partners to track down and apprehend these offenders. In addition, the Marshals Service has formed a Sex Offender Investigations Branch. In Fiscal Year 2009, this Branch arrested more than 10,000 fugitives, wanted for failing to register and/or actual sex offenses, and conducted thousands of compliance checks.

Interpol

Washington is the official U.S. representative to the International Criminal Police Organization (INTERPOL). As the national point of contact for INTERPOL in the United States, INTERPOL Washington routinely exchanges criminal investigative data with international counterparts on behalf of the more than 18,000 federal, state, local, and tribal law enforcement agencies in the United States. In addition to providing support to the National Center for Missing and Exploited Children, Immigrations and Customs Enforcement, and the FBI, INTERPOL Washington tracks sex offenders who travel overseas, and coordinates a number of international alerts relating to child exploitation.

The ninety-four U.S. Attorney's offices prosecute federal child exploitation cases throughout the country and coordinate Project Safe Childhood within their districts, the Department's 2006 national initiative to marshal federal, state, and local resources to prevent and interdict child exploitation. Since 2006, the number of cases and defendants prosecuted by the U.S. Attorney's offices has increased by 40 percent, with 2,315 indictments against 2,427 defendants filed in Fiscal Year 2009.

CEOS, situated within the Department's Criminal Division, consists of approximately

(*continued*)

twenty attorneys and a six-person High Technology Investigative Unit (HTIU). CEOS leads the Criminal Division's campaign against the sexual exploitation of children by investigating and prosecuting the most challenging child sexual exploitation cases, and then by drawing from those experiences to shape domestic and international policy, launch nationwide investigations against the worst offenders, and provide guidance and training to other prosecutors and agents, both within and outside the federal government. CEOS is able to leverage a small amount of resources into extraordinary results. For example, in the last three years CEOS has spearheaded eighteen national operations that have resulted in the investigation of more than 2,000 individuals. Since 2001, the number of cases and investigations handled by CEOS Trial Attorneys has increased by 1,100 percent.

The OJP oversees the disbursement of millions of dollars in grants to federal, state, and local agencies to aid in the fight against child exploitation. OJP's efforts help provide communication and coordination to dozens of groups, including the Internet Crimes Against Children (ICAC) Task Force Program, which is a fundamental component to our nation's fight against child exploitation. Since 1998, the Department, through OJP, has funded the ICACs, which are a collection of sixty-one separate task forces throughout the country, with at least one in each state, that work to coordinate federal, state, local, and tribal investigative and prosecution agencies to coordinate efforts to interdict child exploitation. Since 1998, ICAC task forces have arrested nearly 17,000 offenders.

Moreover, there are numerous other federal agencies that are partners in the fight against child exploitation. This includes the U.S. Postal Inspection Service, the Department of Homeland Security through Immigration and Customs Enforcement and the U.S. Secret Service, the Department of Health and Human Services, the Department of Defense, the Department of State, the Department of Labor, and the Department of Commerce.

Nongovernmental organizations work alongside federal, state, local, and tribal partners to combat child exploitation as well. These include the National Center for Missing & Exploited Children, Child Help, Darkness to Light, Girls Educational and Mentoring Services, Inc., Enough is Enough, i-Safe, Kristi House, Inc., Nevada Child Seekers, Paul and Lisa Program, Inc., Web Wise Kids, San Diego Police Foundation, Self-Reliance Foundation, Washtenaw Area Council for Children, INOBTR, Tech Mission Youth Program, PROTECT, ECPAT-USA, and many others.

One of the chief mandates of the Act was that the Department expand its efforts to coordinate and cooperate with federal, state, local, and international organizations and agencies to combat this scourge. While the Department has long coordinated with all levels of government within the United States and with law enforcement internationally to fight child exploitation, additional high-level working meetings have begun between the Department and other federal government agencies, as well as state, local, and international partners. The Department already belongs to several interagency working groups related to child exploitation, like the Federal Inter-Agency Task Force on Missing and Exploited Children. Additionally, the Department provides funding for the Amber Alert program, many child advocacy centers, and many state and local agencies through grants and funding administered by the Office of Juvenile Justice and Delinquency Prevention, the Bureau of Justice Assistance, the National Institute of Justice, the Office for Victims of Crime, and others.

The Continuing Fight against Child Exploitation

As outlined in this Report, the Department is diligently working to combat child exploitation. For example, the Department has increased the number of agents and prosecutors dedicated to child exploitation cases. The FBI has increased the digital forensic capacity at Regional Computer Forensics Labs, which will lead to more expeditious

(continued)

reviews of the critical evidence in these cases. The Department has funded, and will continue to fund, the ICAC Task Force Program. CEOS advises and provides training to the nation's prosecutors, and also conducts high-tech and complex investigations. The U.S. Marshals pursue and have successfully captured thousands of individuals who abscond from their responsibility to register as sex offenders and those who offend and become fugitives. However, as the Threat Assessment evidences, more work must be done to combat the expanding number of predators and, more importantly, to prevent them from harming a child in the first instance.

At its core, the goal of this National Strategy is to reduce the incidence of the sexual exploitation of children. This goal is the guiding principle for all the Department's current and future efforts. The Department's approach for achieving this goal is multifaceted and includes: (1) an overarching statement of broad goals that will be used to direct the National Strategy, (2) more specific goals to address the dangers identified by the Threat Assessment, (3) programmatic goals that can provide some measurable information and results to help guide the Strategy going forward, and (4) individualized goals by relevant Department components that are designed to support both the broad goals of the Strategy and the programmatic goals of the Department.

The following broad goals will direct the effort of the National Strategy going forward.

1. The Department will continue to partner closely with state, local, tribal, and nongovernmental entities, as well as other federal agencies and the private sector to implement the National Strategy in a coordinated fashion.
2. The Department will increase its commitment to a leadership role in finding a global solution to the transnational problem of the sexual exploitation of children.
3. The Department will continue to partner with Industry to develop objectives to reduce the exchange of child pornography.
4. The Department will explore opportunities to increase the education and awareness of federal, state, local, and tribal judges of the difficult issues involved in child sexual exploitation.
5. The Department will work toward improving the quality, effectiveness, and timeliness of computer forensic investigations and analysis.
6. The Department will increase its commitment to effective and sophisticated training for prosecutors and investigators.
7. The Department will build on the success of the Project Safe Childhood initiative.

Beyond these broad goals, this National Strategy seeks to best marshal all of the Department's resources in a more coordinated, integrated, and strategic way. As outlined in this Report, the Department, in partnership and cooperation with other federal, state, local, tribal, and international partners, is aggressively pursuing those who would steal the innocence from the soul of our children. Thousands of federal, state, and local investigators and prosecutors, without fanfare or even adequate public recognition of the difficulty of their work, fight this battle fiercely every day. Dedicated professionals in nongovernmental organizations, child protective services, and child advocacy centers devote massive time and energy to protecting children, again largely without society fully recognizing the importance of their work.

This National Strategy outlines how we will, and must, act together as a nation to protect our children and provides a unique opportunity for us to act together as a nation to protect, as Nelson Mandela said, our society's soul by vigorously pursuing those who violate our children.

[The entire report may be downloaded from: ovc.ncjrs.gov/Publications.aspx?TopicID=]

Source: U.S. Department of Justice, *National Strategy for Child Exploitation Prevention and Interdiction: A Report to Congress* (NCJRS Photocopy Services, Rockville, Md, August 2010, NCJ 231333).

Focus

Operation Predator

U.S. Immigration and Customs Enforcement's (ICE) Homeland Security Investigations (HSI), Web site describes "Operation Predator" as follows:

> ICE, the largest investigative agency in the Department of Homeland Security, places a high priority on enforcing laws that combat the sexual exploitation of children. Under Operation Predator, the agency's flagship initiative targeting child sex predators, ICE has made more than 8,000 criminal arrests since 2003.
>
> Each year, millions of children fall prey to sexual predators. Experts estimate that one in five girls and one in ten boys in the United States will be sexually exploited before they reach adulthood. These young victims are left with permanent psychological, physical, and emotional scars. Operation Predator identifies, investigates, and arrests child predators. Operation Predator draws on ICE's unique investigative

and enforcement authorities to safeguard children. Coordinated nationally and internationally, this initiative brings together an array of ICE disciplines and resources to target these child sex abusers. As part of the effort:

- ICE created the National Child Victim Identification System in partnership with the National Center for Missing & Exploited Children, the FBI, the U.S. Postal Inspection Service, the U.S. Secret Service, the Department of Justice, the Internet Crimes Against Children task forces, and other agencies.
- ICE agents stationed internationally work with foreign governments, Interpol, and others to enhance coordination and cooperation on crimes that cross borders.
- ICE is a member of the Virtual Global Taskforce, joining law enforcement agencies around the world to fight child exploitation information and images that travel over the Internet.

Source: U.S. Immigration and Customs Enforcement's (ICE) Homeland Security Investigations Web site at www.ice.gov/factsheets/predator, accessed September 8, 2015.

Summary

The exploitation of children is as old as civilization. Modern technology has made children more vulnerable and allowed easier access to those who would use them. In addition, it has made exploitation of children more financially profitable. There continues to be a controversy regarding the extent of the problem, but governments, international organizations, and NGOs all agree it is a serious problem.

Although there are various types of child exploitation, many of them form a continuum in which a child victim may suffer many different forms of exploitation over his or her life. The consequences of these victimizations are severe for individual countries and the individual victims.

A variety of responses to this form of violence against children are occurring. Governments and NGOs are issuing reports and guidelines for countries, businesses, and individuals. Model codes and statutes are being circulated in an attempt to help governments respond to this form of violence. This fight must be continued until children in this country and other countries are safe.

Key Terms

exploitation—use of persons for prostitution and other forms of sexual activities, forced labor or services, slavery or practices similar to slavery, servitude, or the removal of organs.

trafficking—the recruitment, transportation, transfer, harboring, or receipt of persons by means of a threat or use of force or other forms of coercion for the purpose of exploitation; trafficking may occur within one country or across national borders.

child pornography—any representation, by whatever means, of a child engaged in real or simulated explicit sexual activities or representation of the sexual parts of a child for a sexual purpose.

child prostitution—act of engaging or offering the services of a child to a person to perform sexual acts for money or other consideration with that person or any other person.

child sex tourism—the commercial sexual exploitation of children by men or women who travel from one place to another, usually from a richer country to a poorer, less-developed country, to engage in sexual acts with children.

Discussion Questions

1. Should children's use of the Internet be monitored and controlled, so they do not enter chat rooms?
2. Why do you think we do not hear more about child exploitation on the news?
3. What is the most severe form of child exploitation? Why?
4. If an eighteen-year-old female decides to become a prostitute to help her poor family, is this valid consent? Would it matter if the girl were seventeen?
5. What is the biggest factor or cause that contributes to child exploitation?
6. Should child exploitation be strictly a federal crime instead of a state crime and a federal crime?

Suggested Readings

Farley, M., ed. *Prostitution, Trafficking, and Traumatic Stress* (Haworth Press, Binghamton, New York, 2004).

Farr, K. *Sex Trafficking: The Global Market in Women and Children* (Worth Publishers, New York, 2004).

Kile, D., and R. Koslowski, eds. *Global Human Smuggling: Comparative Perspectives* (The Johns Hopkins University Press, New York, 2001).

King, G., and E. Clift. *Woman, Child for Sale: The New Slave Trade in the 21st Century* (Chamberlain Bros., London, 2004).

Laczko, F., and E. M. Gozdziak, eds. *Data and Research on Human Trafficking: A Global Survey* (United Nations, New York, 2005).

McGill, C. *Human Traffic: Sex Slaves and Immigration* (Vision Paperbacks, London, 2003).

Moghadam, V. *Globalizing Women: Transnational Feminist Networks* (The Johns Hopkins University Press, New York, 2005).

Obokata, T. *Trafficking of Human Beings from a Human Rights Perspective: Toward a Holistic Approach* (Martinus Nijhoff, Boston, 2006).

Seabrook, J. *No Hiding Place: Child Sex Tourism and the Role of Extraterritorial Legislation* (Zed Books, London, 2000).

Seabrook, J. *Children of Other Worlds: Exploitation in the Global Market* (Pluto Press, London, 2001).

Smith, R. G., P. Grabosky, and G. Urbas. *Cyber Criminals on Trial* (Cambridge University Press, London, 2004).

Sorajjakool, S. *Child Prostitution in Thailand: Listen to Rahab* (Haworth Press, Binghamton, New York, 2002).

Weston, B. H. *Child Labor and Human Rights: Making Children Matter* (Lynne Rienner Publishers, Boulder, Colo., 2005).

Endnotes

1. As reported by U.S. Attorney General Eric Holder in August 2010, *The National Strategy for Child Exploitation Prevention and Interdiction: A Report to Congress*, available at www.justice.gov/criminal/ceos/additionalresources.

2. Statement of Judge Adams, the Northern District of Ohio in his decision in *U.S. v. Cunningham, 1:09-CR-00154-JRA.*

3. This section is based on an outstanding publication by C. Livingston, ed., *Protecting Children Online: An ECPAT Guide*, 2nd ed. (ECPAT International, Bangkok, Thailand, May 2002).

4. D. Finkelhor, K. J. Mitchell, and J. Wolak, *Online Victimization: A Report to the Nation's Youth* (National Center for Missing and Exploited Children, Alexandria, Va., 2000).

5. D. Muir, *Violence against Children in Cyberspace* (ECPAT International, Bangkok, Thailand, September 2005).

6. Subgroup against Sexual Exploitation of Children, NGO Group for the Convention on the Rights of the Child, Geneva, Switzerland (January 2005).

7. For an excellent discussion of the factors affecting underreporting, see E. J. Schauer and E. M. Wheaton, "Sex Trafficking into the United States: A Literature Review," *Criminal Justice Review* 31(2) (2006), p. 146.

8. *Trafficking in Persons Report, 2006* (U.S. Department of State, Washington, D.C., 2006).

9. *Helping Hands or Shackled Lives? Understanding Child Domestic Labour and Responses to It* (International Labour Office, Geneva, Switzerland, no date).

10. *Facts on Child Domestic Labour*, International Programme on the Elimination of Child Labour, www.ilo.org/childlabour, accessed September 10, 2006.

11. *Facts on Children Working in the Streets*, International Programme on the Elimination of Child Labour, www.ilo.org/childlabour, accessed September 10, 2006.

12. 413 U.S. 15 (1973).

13. California Penal Code Section 311 (2006).

14. 18 U.S.C. Section 1466A and 18 U.S.C. Section 2256 (2006).

15. *Ashcroft v. Free Speech Coalition*, 122 S. Ct. 1389 (2002).

16. E. J. Klain, H. J. Davies, and M. A. Hicks, *Child Pornography: The Criminal-Justice System Response* (National Center for Missing and Exploited Children, Alexandria, Va., March 2001) (hereinafter cited as *Response*).

17. *Response* citing Allotted Day on Child Pornography, 36th Parliament, 1st Session, Edited Hansand 1, No. 172, February 2, 1999, p. 12.

18. "Child Abuse on the Web," 189(189) *New Scientist* (1) (March 11, 2006), p. 25.

19. M. L. Voss, *Commercial Sexual Exploitation of Children: An Overview*, ECPAT USA, www.ecpa-tusa.org, accessed June 23, 2006.

20. J. Wolak, D. Finkelhor, and K. Mitchell, *Child-Pornography Possessors Attested in Internet-Related Crimes: Finding from the National Juvenile Online Victimization Study* (National Center for Missing and Exploited Children, Alexandria, Va., 2005), p. x.

21. Ibid., p. vii.

22. D. Finkelhor and R. Ormrod, *Child Pornography: Patterns from NIBRS* (Office of Justice Programs, U.S. Department of Justice, Washington, D.C., December 2004).

23. Although significant in numbers, the number of 2,900 incidents of child pornography is very small when compared with an estimates number of 269,000 sex crimes committed against children during the same time period. See Finkelhor and Ormrod.

24. *What Is the Prostitution of Children?* National Center for Missing and Exploited Children, www.missingkids.com, accessed June 23, 2006.

25. UN NGO Group for the Convention on the Rights of the Child, Semantics or Substance? Towards a Shared Understanding of Terminology Referring to the Sexual Abuse and Exploitation of Children, www.comminit.com/printversion.cgi?url=www.comminit.com/strategicthinking/st2005/thinking-1298.html, accessed August 9, 2007.

26. *Report of the Special Rapporteur on the Sale of Children, Child Prostitution, and Child Pornography*, United Nations Economic and Social

Council, Commission on Human Rights, 52nd Session, Agenda Item 20, Paragraph 35, U.N. Doc. E/CN.4/1996/100 (1996).

27. E. J. Klain, *Prostitution of Children and Child-Sex Tourism: An Analysis of Domestic and International Responses* (National Center for Missing and Exploited Children, Alexandria, Va., April 1999).

28. S. Nair, "Child Sex Tourism, Child Exploitation and Obscenity Section," U.S. Department of Justice, www.usdoj.gov/criminal/ceos/sextour.html, accessed September 9, 2006.

29. C. Bunch, "The Intolerable Status Quo: Violence against Women and Girls," www.unicef.org/pon97/women1.htm, accessed September 5, 2006.

30. M. L. Voss, *Commercial Sexual Exploitation of Children: An Overview*, ECPAT USA www.ecpatusa.org, accessed on June 23, 2006.

31. Ibid.

32. UN NGO Group for the Convention on the Rights of the Child, *Semantics or Substance? Towards a Shared Understanding of Terminology Referring to the Sexual Abuse and Exploitation of Children*, www.comminit.com/printversion.cgi?url=www.comminit.com/strategicthinking/st2005/thinking-1298.html, accessed on August 9, 2007.

33. M. B. Farrell, "Global Campaign to Police Child Sex Tourism," *The Christian Science Monitor*, www.csmonitor.com, accessed April 22, 2004.

34. S. Song, "Children as Tourist Attractions," *Global Child Sex Tourism* (Youth Advocate International Program, Washington, D.C., no date).

35. S. Nair, "Child Sex Tourism, Child Exploitation and Obscenity Section," U.S. Department of Justice www.usdoj.gov/criminal/ceos/sextour.html, accessed September 9, 2006.

36. UN NGO Group for the Convention on the Rights of the Child, *Semantics or Substance? Towards a Shared Understanding of Terminology Referring to the Sexual Abuse and Exploitation of Children*, www.comminit.com/printversion.cgi?url=www.comminit.com/strategicthinking/st2005/thinking-1298.html, accessed on August 9, 2007.

37. *What Is Child Sex Tourism*, National Center for Missing and Exploited Children, www.missing-kids.com, accessed June 23, 2006.

38. *Trafficking in Persons Report, 2006* (U.S. Department of State, Washington, D.C., 2006).

39. www.thecode.org, accessed September 9, 2006.

40. E. J. Klain, *Prostitution of Children and Child-Sex Tourism: An Analysis of Domestic and International Responses* (National Center for Missing and Exploited Children, Alexandria, Va., April 1999).

41. "The Protection of Street Children," *ECPAT International Newsletters* 47 (April 1, 2004), www.ecpat.net/eng/Ecpat_inter.

42. A. Stulhofer and Z. Raboteg-Saric, *Sex Trafficking in Croatia: An Assessment Study* (International Organization for Migration, Geneva, 2002).

43. E. Kelly, "Journey of Jeopardy: A Review of Research on Trafficking and children in Europe," *IOM Migration Research Series* (November 2002).

44. S. X. Zhang and K. Chin, "Enter the Dragon: Inside Chinese Human Smuggling Organizations," *Criminology* 40(4) (2002), pp. 737–768.

45. D. Coday, "Pope Prays for Child Soldiers," *National Catholic Reporter* 40 (23) (April 9, 2004), p. 7.

46. "The Hidden Health Trauma of Child Soldiers," *The Lancet* 363 (9412) (2004), p. 831.

47. www.child-soldiers.org/resources/internationalstandards, accessed September 2006.

48. http://irinnews.org/webspecials/childsoldiers/print/intro.asp, accessed September 2006.

49. *Child Soldiers Global Report 2004*, Coalition to Stop the Use of Child Soldiers, London (2004).

50. www.child-soldiers.org/resources/global-reports, accessed August 9, 2007.

51. www.child-soldiers.org, accessed September 2006.

52. irinnews.org/webspecials/childsoldiers/print/intro.asp, accessed September 2006.

53. www.amnestyuse.org/child_soldiers/index.do, accessed September 2006.

54. www.un.org/rights/concerns.htm, accessed August 9, 2007.

55. "Tens of Thousands of Girls Fighting on the Front Lines," *Women in Action* 1 (April 2004), p. 6.

56. www.releifweb.int/library/documents/chilsold.htm, accessed August 9, 2007.

57. D. Somasundaram, "Child Soldiers: Understanding the Context," *British Medical Journal* 324 (7348) (2002), p. 126.

58. J. R. Miller, "Slave Trade: Combating Human Trafficking (Underground Markets)," *Harvard International Review* 27(4) (Winter 2006), p. 70.

59. This section has been based on an excellent discussion of the consequences of human trafficking contained in *Trafficking in Persons Report, 2006* (U.S. Department of State Washington D.C., 2006).

60. V. Suveiu and B. Uekert, "Human-Trafficking: A Growing Crime to Hit State Courts," *Future Trends in State Courts, 2005*, www.nsconline. org, accessed September 14, 2006.

61. State Model on Protection for Victims of Human Trafficking, 2005, www.freedomnetworkusa.org, accessed September 14, 2006.

10

Special Issues in Child Abuse

CHAPTER OBJECTIVES

After studying this chapter, you should be able to:

- Discuss the issues involved with ritualistic child abuse;
- Define ritualistic child abuse;
- List and discuss the emotional, behavioral, medical indicators in a child who is being ritualistically abused;
- Explain the concept of dissociative identity disorder;
- Explain the issues involved when investigating possible ritualistic child abuse;
- Explain the effects on children of seeing violence events.

Detailed Look at What You Should Know About Special Issues Concerning Child Abuse

- Child abuse, neglect, and sexual molestation are difficult to accept, but satanic ritualistic abuse not only causes harm to children but also strikes a chord in the collective consciousness as to the evil perpetrated by humanity.
- A controversy exists as to the validity of many of the claims made by these survivors and to the extent of their abuse.
- To understand this ritual abuse, it is necessary to understand the growth and development of the satanic movement.
- Satanism is the worship of Satan. Satan's name is derived from early Egyptian theology in which Set, the killer of Osiris, represented the forces of disharmony and disorder.
- Ritual abuse is not a new problem, but society is only just beginning to recognize the gravity and scope of this problem.

- *Ritual abuse* is defined as the psychological, sexual, spiritual, and/or physical assault on an unwilling human victim, committed by one or more people whose primary motive is to fulfill a prescribed ritual in order to achieve a specific goal or to satisfy the perceived needs of their deity.

- Recognition of ritualistic abuse is a critical aspect of this form of family violence. What may appear to be a rather simple form of child abuse or child sexual abuse may turn out to be just the tip of the iceberg.

- The emotional, behavioral, and medical indicators present in a child who has been sexually abused may also indicate that the child has been ritualistically victimized.

- Dissociative identity disorder is the existence within a person of two or more distinct personalities or personality states in which at least two of these personalities recurrently take full control of the person's behavior.

- Probably the most famous case involving child care takers and ritual abuse of children is the "McMartin Preschool Case." One positive factor in the case is that psychologists and police investigators changed their methods of interrogating young children.

INTRODUCTION

"The evidence is rapidly accumulating that the problem of ritual abuse is considerable in scope and extremely grave in its consequences."[1]

Almost daily, the press releases stories of horror and disgust involving children being victimized in so-called satanic cults. Adults who were victims are coming forward to shed light on this new form of family violence. Like the slow acceptance of the fact that fathers were molesting their young daughters, society is hesitant to believe that many of the described practices of ritualistic abuse actually occur. Child abuse, neglect, and sexual molestation are difficult to accept, but satanic ritualistic abuse not only causes harm to children but also strikes a chord in the collective consciousness as to the evil perpetrated by humanity.

During 2001 to 2011, the police in greater London had investigated at least eighty-three incidents of child abuse and torture linked to witchcraft and other religious rituals. Of these children, four were murdered during ritualized violence. One London police official stated that the ritual abuse of children is a hidden and unreported crime. The police in London have established a special unit to probe this type of crime, and many of them believe that they have only scratched the surface.[2]

Professionals in recent years began to treat survivors of ritualistic abuse.[3] However, a raging controversy exists as to the validity of many of the claims made by these survivors and to the extent of their abuse. Other scholarly works in the field are silent or only briefly touch on this issue.[4] Even though this is a relatively new form of family violence and professionals are still researching its causes and consequences, it is included in this textbook to familiarize students with the general nature and types of ritualistic abuse.

During the 1970s, a movie titled *Rosemary's Baby* became a smash hit. This tale involved a young couple who moved into an apartment next door to a supposedly friendly elderly couple who turned out to be followers of Satan. The young wife had intercourse with a beast-like creature and eventually gave birth to a monster who was Satan's child. The moviegoers shivered in delight because they understood that this could never actually happen. Unfortunately, stories are beginning to surface that individuals, groups, or cults may in fact be engaging in ritualistic abuse. Although a great deal of controversy exists regarding the nature and extent of satanic worship and child abuse, there is sufficient evidence to support more study and research in this area. To understand this phenomenon, it is necessary to review the growth and development of the satanic movement.

HISTORICAL BACKGROUND

Stories of Satan and satanic worship are interspersed throughout history.[5] There is no simple definition of satanism. For purposes here, however, **satanism** is the worship of Satan. Satan's name is derived from early Egyptian theology in which Set, the killer of Osiris, represented the forces of disharmony and disorder.[6] During the third and fourth centuries, a group identified as the Phibionites was discovered. They were promiscuous, consumed semen during the sacrament, and practiced abortion. This early group had much in common with modern-day cults in that the masses were held in secret, semen was used ritualistically, and they subscribed to other practices abhorred by modern religions.[7]

During the fourteenth century, nature itself aided in the development of the satanic movement. The climate began to change, crops failed, and the population began to starve—perfect conditions for the spread of the bubonic plague, which was also known as the Black Death. Beginning in 1348 and continuing until the start of the sixteenth century, the Black Death was responsible for the demise of more than one-third of the entire population of Europe, thereby decimating the labor force.[8] The ensuing labor shortage set the stage for workers to demand higher wages and more freedom. Both the church and the state responded brutally in an attempt to restore order. Governments attempted to set the prices of goods and services. The ensuing legislation of economics made large families an economic liability.[9] As a result, large families became an economic burden, and the population responded with a brutal form of contraception—infanticide.

As the populace struggled to survive with only death and poverty surrounding them, they began to search for explanations to the chaos that existed in their lives. The belief in powers that could be manipulated began to take hold. In this environment, magic and magical powers became an accepted alternative to traditional beliefs and religions. The populace began to view the Catholic Mass and its transformation of bread and water into the body and blood of Christ as another form of magic. Once the population had accepted the sacrament as simply a form of magic rather than a religious experience, the stage was set for the acceptance of other unnatural phenomena. Thus, witches, warlocks, and magic could become a part of society.

In France during the 1680s, Catherine Deshayes, also known as La Voisin, practiced magic and astrology for the French aristocrats. She subsequently joined forces with Abbé Guibourg, and the two of them routinely sacrificed children to Astaroth and Asmodeus for the Black Mass.[10]

During the 1800s, theosophy began to gain acceptance. This belief system accepted Lucifer as a benign force and required believers to answer for their earthly actions. It was founded by Helena Blavatsky and borrowed from Hindu and Gnostic concepts. Theosophy made occultism more acceptable by portraying Lucifer as benign and was responsible for introducing the concept of *white magic.*

During the early twentieth century, Aleister Crowley, author of *Magick in Theory and Practice*, became one of the most important figures in the development of magic and mysticism.[11] Crowley's book was a "how to" for neophytes who wanted to experiment with magic. It told them what to do, what to say, and how to feel. For those who were unable to achieve the desired psychological state, Crowley recommended the use of various drugs, including hashish, mescaline, and cocaine.

The 1960s and 1970s were decades of rebellion in the United States. The concept of mind-expanding drugs gained widespread acceptance. During this period of change, it was popular to question authority and beliefs. The advent of birth control, the first stirrings of the women's movement, and the breakdown of traditional roles all combined to force change in the United States. Magic, free love, and drugs were accepted tenets.

During this period, Anton LaVey established the Church of Satan and drafted *The Satanic Bible.* Although denounced as a fraud by some, LaVey had a far greater impact than most people were willing to admit. He took the position that individuals could make a conscious choice to live in a world without God, and then he thrust this idea on the general public.[12] It should be stressed that the Church of Satan does not condone ritualistic child abuse. It is listed in the telephone directory and has its headquarters, or Grotto, in San Francisco. LaVey continued to publish controversial books, including one entitled *The Satanic Rituals*, which was listed as a companion to *The Satanic Bible.* In *The Satanic Rituals*, LaVey sets forth the Black Mass, including the requirements for its performance as well as the exact language it must be used.[13]

In 1980, the reading public was shocked by a book that brought the specter of satanism and ritualistic abuse into grim reality. In *Michelle Remembers*, a book written by psychiatrist Lawrence Pazder, Michelle Smith recounts a tale of satanism and ritualistic abuse that occurred to her as a child at the hands of a satanic cult in Victoria, Canada.[14] The book describes how Michelle recovered her memories during therapy. She claimed that she was to be a designated bride to Satan and was to be presented to him at a ceremony during the Year

Focus

Excerpts from the Report of the Ritual Abuse Task Force, Los Angeles County Commission for Women

Ritual abuse is a serious and growing problem in our community and in our nation. Ritual abuse is not a new problem, but society is only just beginning to recognize the gravity and scope of this problem. We are all in need of education on this issue. Parents need to be educated about the hallmarks of this abuse occurring in preschools and day care centers. Many professionals are seeing victims of ritual abuse and not yet recognizing the patterns of this abuse. The concept of ritual abuse, that groups of adults would terrorize and torture children in order to control them, is frightening and controversial, raising for all of us problems of denial and fear of the consequences of such information.

(continued)

1. Threats of punishment, torture, mutilation, or death of the victim, the victim's family or pets. Threats are heightened by carrying out killings of animals or human beings in the presence of the victim, sometimes with the victim's forced participation. Told that it would be futile to disclose because "no one will believe you."

2. Threats against the victim's property, including threats that his/her house will be broken into or burned down if s/he discloses the abuse.

3. Told that family or other loving and protective figures are secretly cult members who intend to harm the victim. Or made to believe that parents not only know, but also have chosen that their child be ritually abused. Told that s/he is no longer loved by family or by God.

4. Told that his/her family is not the "real" family, that the abusers are in fact the child's "real" family. Victim is told that s/he will be kidnapped and forced to live with the abusers, apart from his/her family. Or told that parents no longer want the child and approve of the cult becoming the child's "new family."

5. Tied up or confined to a cage, closet, basement, isolation house, or other confined space. Told that s/he is being left there to die. Some are placed in coffins and told to "practice being dead." For some, this includes mock burials in which the victim is buried and told s/he is being left to die. Sometimes a cult member seems to rescue the child from these terrifying situations, and thus the distraught child reaches out gratefully and bonds to the cult member.

6. Tied up or confined in space with insects or animals. Told that they will harm him/her, or tricked into believing that frightening insects or animals are present. Confined with or hung upside down in a hole with a dead body or the mutilated body parts of an animal or a human being.

7. Humiliated or degraded through verbal abuse. Forced nudity in front of the group. Body of the victim smeared or covered with urine or feces. Forced ingestion of urine, feces, or semen.

8. Photographed in sexually provocative poses. Photographed while being physically or sexually assaulted, or while physically or sexually assaulting someone else. Forced participation in the production of pornography used in the intimidation and humiliation of the victim as well as to financially profit the abusers.

Less Detectable Examples

- Pins or "shots" inserted into sensitive areas of the body, especially between digits, under fingernails, or in genital areas. Electric shock to these body areas.
- Being hung by hands or upside down by feet for extended periods of time. Sometimes hung from crosses in mock crucifixions. Sexual abuse while in such positions.
- Submerging victim in water with perception of near drowning.
- Withholding of food or water for several hours.
- Sleep deprivation and activities aimed at inducing exhaustion.

More Detectable Examples

- Physical beatings.
- Use of cuts, tattoos, branding, burns, often to sensitive body areas.
- Withholding food, water, or sleep for days or weeks.
- Removal of body parts (e.g., digits).

Sexual Abuse

The sexual abuse of ritual victims is unusually brutal, sadistic, and humiliating. It is far more severe than that which is usually inflicted by a pedophile or in the context of intrafamilial sexual abuse (incest). It seems intended as a means of gaining total dominance over the victim, as well as being an end in itself.

(continued)

1. Repeated sexual assaults by men, women, and other children, often occurring in a group, may be associated with the marriage ritual, repeated fondling, oral copulation, rape, and sodomy.
2. Assaults include the use of instruments for penetration of body orifices, including symbolic objects (e.g., crucifix or wand) or weapons (e.g., knife or gun).

3. Sexual assault coupled with physical violence. Participation in rituals in which sexual assault is associated with death. Forced sexual contact with dead or dying people.
4. Forced to sexually perpetrate against children and infants.
5. Forced sexual contact with animals.

Source: Report posted at www.mindcontrolforums.com/ritualab.htm, accessed August 1, 2009.

of the Beast, which occurs in every twenty-eight years. One of the most controversial portions of *Michelle Remembers* details how, with the help of the Virgin Mary, she resisted Satan's attempts to claim her.

On October 25, 1988, millions of people across the United States watched a prime-time Geraldo Rivera special on NBC entitled "Devil Worship: Exposing Satan's Underground." It was one of the most widely watched documentaries of the season. By 1993, ritualistic child abuse had become such a common topic that the *New Yorker* magazine published a lengthy two-part series entitled "Remembering Satan," which detailed the accounts of a family in Olympia, Washington, accused of ritualistic child abuse.[15]

To explain satanism as the creation of a deranged mind would be easy. Doing so would permit researchers to dismiss it as something undeserving of serious consideration. That approach, however, would not allow for a complete understanding of this form of family violence. Although historians still dispute the historic nature and extent of satanism, and many present-day scholars continue to discount stories of ritualistic child abuse, more and more people are coming forward and claiming to be victims of this type of abuse. It is therefore imperative that professionals in the field have a general understanding of ritualistic abuse.

Focus

What Is Ritual Abuse?

A ritual is an act that is repeated according to a specific procedure. One simple superstitious example is throwing of a pinch of salt over your shoulder after you have spilled some salt. Societies have many rituals related to major life passages, like birth, marriage, and death. *Ritual abuse* is defined as the psychological, sexual, spiritual, and/or physical assault on an unwilling human victim, committed by one or more people whose primary motive is to fulfill a prescribed ritual in order to achieve a specific goal or satisfy the perceived needs of their deity. Ritual abuse is also known as cult-related abuse, satanic ritual abuse (SRA), ritualized abuse, occult ritual abuse (ORA), and sadistic ritual abuse (SRA).

Source: Religious Tolerance Organization at www.religioustolerance.org/ra.htm, accessed August 1, 2009.

DEFINITION

The definition of **ritualistic child abuse** is still evolving. One of the most cited definitions was established by the Los Angeles County Commission for Women in 1989. This commission set forth the following definition of ritual abuse:

A brutal form of abuse of children consisting of physical, sexual, and psychological abuse, and involving the use of rituals. Ritual does not necessarily mean satanic. However, most survivors state that they were ritually abused as part of satanic worship for the purpose of indoctrinating them into satanic beliefs and practices. Ritual abuse rarely consists of a single episode. It usually involves repeated abuse over an extended period of time.[16]

As the definition states, ritualistic child abuse does not have to involve religion. However, most of the survivors claim that the ritualistic abuse was definitely tied to satanic worship. All rituals are not evil. The word *ritual* is defined as the established form for a ceremony, a system of rites, or any formal and customarily repeated act or series of acts.[17] It is only when ritual is combined with abuse that society can intervene. As stated previously, ritualistic child abuse involves long-term repeated abuse of the most severe form. These abuses may be inflicted (and believed justified) because of certain religious tenets held by the cult or organization.

Kahaner has developed a typology of three distinct types of satanic groups.[18] Langone and Blood have also developed a very similar typology. However, this includes individuals or psychopaths who act alone and adopt the more violent forms of satanism as a way of expressing their own beliefs and actions.[19] In dealing with groups that engage in ritualistic child abuse, Kahaner's definitions seem more appropriate. Kahaner's typology includes the following classifications of satanic groups:

1. *Publicly known cults.* These groups deny that they engage in any abusive conduct and are generally accepted as operating within the bounds of the law. The Church of Satan and the Temple of Set are examples of these groups.
2. *Self-styled satanists.* These are loosely knit groups of individuals who band together occasionally to dabble in magic and the occult. They include teenagers who are attracted to this behavior by heavy-metal music, easy-to-read books, and fantasy role-playing games.
3. *Formal satanists.* These groups are highly organized and secretive. They may have national or international connections with other similarly organized cults.

Although both law enforcement officials and scholars are skeptical regarding the extent of satanic cults and ritualistic child abuse, others accept their existence because of the similarity of stories related by survivors. However, it must be restated that the study of ritualistic child abuse is still in its infancy. As more is learned about this modern-day problem, professionals will begin to understand more about the structure, functioning, and beliefs of the satanic cults that practice this form of family violence. In addition, fact will eventually separate from fantasy in dealing with actual survivors and those who only believe they were victims. Professionals in the field will gain the knowledge and the ability to evaluate and treat individuals who have been victims of ritualistic child abuse.

TYPES OF RITUALISTIC ABUSE

Professionals in the field must understand the different aspects of ritualistic abuse. This knowledge will aid in identifying victims, apprehending offenders, and treating survivors of this type of abuse. Ritualistic abuse can take many different forms and variations. The following sections examine satanic beliefs and activities as they relate to ritualistic child abuse.

Satanic Beliefs and Practices

All cultures, societies, and religions have certain formalities that must be observed. Some fraternal organizations, for example, employ candles, oaths of secrecy, and pledges of allegiance to the group. Satanic cults follow this practice. One of the most commonly shared beliefs among these cults is the belief in magic. **Magic** is a method of harnessing the secret powers of nature to influence events for one's own purpose. It is believed that magic empowers all living entities with a source of power. Ancient civilizations called this power different names. The Chinese named it *qi*, the Hindus call it *prana*, and the Polynesians call it *mana.*

Satanism usually embraces the opposite of Christianity. The Bible prohibits incest, the worship of idols, magic, the sacrifice of children, and the drinking of blood. On the other hand, satanic cults adopt these practices as a method of gaining power and practicing magic. Other well-known reversals of Christianity include the use of an inverted cross, backward prayers, and of course the Black Mass, the purpose of which is to blaspheme the sacrament of Christ.[20]

The use of sacrifices is based on the theory that all living things contain energy. When the animal or human is killed, this energy is liberated. Crowley states in *Magick in Theory and Practice:*

> It was the theory of the ancient magicians that any living being is a storehouse of energy varying in quantity according to the size and health of the animal, and in quality according to its mental and moral character. At the death of the animal this energy is liberated suddenly.[21]

If the killing is done inside a certain type of circle, the energy is contained and concentrated within that circle for use by the magician. The animal or human should be healthy, young, and a virgin so that its internal energy and power is strong. The magician is then able to use this energy to make magic.[22]

A common prelude to the actual sacrifice is torture or sexual activities. Torture and sex are common ways to arouse the victim emotionally and thereby extract the greatest amount of life force at the time of death. One authority points out that during the practice of "white magic," the witch engages in flogging the "victim" to overload the nervous system and thereby transcend normal consciousness, which the high priestess calls the ecstasy of magic.[23] Survivors of ritualistic child abuse have confirmed the use of torture and sex during satanic rituals.

Another common belief in satanic cults is the theory of **transmission.** This is the belief that the qualities of objects or beings can be transmitted from them to another person. Some ancient societies ate the hearts of their enemies; African tribesmen once ate the hearts of lions to obtain the animal's courage; and British Columbian Indians used to rub the body of a beaver on a young female baby to make her industrious. Black magic and voodoo rites include obtaining a portion of an enemy's body, such as nail clippings or hair, and using it to harm the intended victim. Being aware of these ancient beliefs, it is easy to understand how satanic cults could engage in cannibalism or the drinking of blood, semen, and other body fluids as a form of transmission.

Magic, witchcraft, sorcery, and the occult often employ symbols to represent certain forces.[24] Therapists treating survivors have reported various satanic or occult symbols that have been burned, cut, or tattooed on various portions of the victims' bodies. **Pentagrams and hexagrams** are common symbols of the occult and satanism. In the form of squares or five- or six-pointed stars, these figures are believed to form the mystical system that links together all parts of the universe.[25] Colors are also often used as symbols during cult ceremonies. Black represents death, darkness, and evil. White is the symbol of purity or truth. Red represents blood, vitality, and sexual potency.

Many of the rituals carried out in satanic cults are contained in handbooks or grimoires. These instruction manuals are guarded by the cult leader and passed down from one generation to another. Every **grimoire** will have a critical section in the rituals omitted or transposed, to ensure that the uninitiated do not accidentally come on to the source of power of the cult.[26]

One final aspect of satanic practices needs to be examined. As mentioned earlier, all groups have certain rites or ceremonies for admission into the organization. They may be formal, as in the case of a professional or social fraternity or sorority, or informal, as it occurs when joining a service organization.

Any former Marine will tell you that Marine Corps boot camp builds character and forms a sense of esprit or loyalty to the corps. This form of indoctrination is deemed necessary by senior Marine officers. They believe, on the basis of more than 200 years of experience, that Marines must be conditioned to react because they may not have time to think in combat. In many cases, they must blindly and faithfully follow the orders of their officers. This type of training has proven successful, and many former Marines believe that it kept them alive in combat. They would not view boot camp as a ritual or evil—they would argue that although it may have been abusive at the time, it was for their own good.

A similar indoctrination occurs in law school. The experience of law school can be compared to a form of boot camp. Young students are taught to question and think in ways they have not experienced. Their minds are changed or conditioned to view a set of facts differently from other people. This is not a painless experience. Many law students are humiliated

---

Focus

Black Magic, Voodoo, and Zombies

In Wade Davis's classic work *The Serpent and the Rainbow*, he exposed the existence of secret societies that practice black magic in Haiti. These groups worship an evil deity known as Samedi. Davis was able to show that truth may really be more scary than fiction.

Davis relates how these groups take criminals or persons who have violated certain norms, convince them that they have been turned into zombies, and sell them to plantation owners as slaves. The victim is given a drug that induces an almost trancelike state. The sorcerer then buries the victim, digs him up, and sells him into slavery.

Source: Based on W. Davis, *The Serpent and the Rainbow* (Simon & Schuster, New York, 1985).

in front of their peers by professors intent on ensuring that they learn how to think on their feet logically.

The same type of conditioning that occurs at Marine boot camp or law school is used in satanic cults that engage in ritualistic abuse. However, the difference is the degree and the resulting injury to the survivors. The indoctrination goes beyond the bounds of the law and results in severe emotional trauma.

Many survivors describe rituals involving death and rebirth as a member of the cult. These ritualistic deaths may involve being buried and "born anew" into the cult. Various techniques include being physically and sexually abused and then placed in a coffin with a dead animal and brought forth as a new member of the cult community. One reported case involved a child being placed inside a dead or dying animal, sewing the animal closed, then reopening the carcass and telling the child that she is now reborn as evil and a member of the cult.

Another characteristic of cult indoctrination includes the use of guilt. Being forced to participate in killing animals and group sex with other children and adults impairs the child's self-worth. Adult cult members explain to the child that he is bad, evil, and not good. This constant downgrading of the child affects the child's ability to resist further demands from the cult.

As with other forms of abuse, isolation and the feeling of helplessness are also important characteristics of satanic cults and ritualistic abuse. Children are often threatened that members of the cult will find them and kill them, their parents, or any other loved one if the child ever tells anyone about the cult. Survivors are informed that their every move can be watched, which only adds to their paranoia. The cult members become all-powerful and invulnerable. The child is helpless to fight against them.

All these techniques involve modifying the victim's thinking and behavior. Many of the actions cause the victim to confront past or existing values. This in turn causes an extreme conflict within the personality of the victim. Because of the nature of the acts, the impact on the victim can be greater and more severe than that of a victim of incest or other forms of sexual or physical abuse. The next section examines satanic activity and the different types of ritualistic abuse.

Satanic Activity

The true extent of ritualistic child abuse is unknown. Intermingled with true accounts of abuse by survivors of past ritualistic abuse are accounts by persons suffering from mental illness and other mental problems. Some of the stories of survivors are so horrible and outlandish that many people have a great deal of difficulty accepting them as true. However, humanity is capable of incredible acts of savagery. A quick review of history, especially the Holocaust, indicates that we can kill, torture, and abuse millions of people only because of their religious belief. Some groups today, however, still argue that the Holocaust did not really happen.

Satanic ritualistic abuse basically involves three distinct abuses: physical, sexual, and psychological. Each of these abuses is repeated over an extended period of time, and they are often intermingled so that the victim is exposed to psychological, sexual, and physical abuse simultaneously. The following is a brief summary of each of these forms of abuse.

Physical. Ritualistic physical abuse can take many different forms. Cutting, branding, or tattooing symbols onto the victim's body is one clear example of this type of abuse. This establishes the cult's ownership of the victim and is a symbol that reinforces the image of ownership and loss of the victim's individual identity. Forcing the victim to drink contaminated water, urine, semen, or even eat feces are other forms of physical abuse. Ingesting raw meat and cannibalism have also been reported in ritualistic physical abuse cases. Burning portions of the body with branding irons, flames, or acid is another method of breaking down the victim's resistance. Deprivation of sleep, food, or water causes the child to become more confused and suggestible to cult demands and threats. Drugs and torture are common. All of these forms of physical abuse create instability in the victim's psyche. The addition of sexual abuse accelerates the destruction of the child's personality.

Sexual. Sexual abuse is more than simple intercourse. The victim may have to engage in group sex with other children of the same or different sex. Adult members of the cult may use the child sexually either in a group or individually. Pictures or videos of these acts may be taken and shown to the victim. Sex with animals has been reported by survivors of ritualistic abuse. Sexual abuse may continue for hours at a time, with the victim subjected to repeated sexual assaults by other children, adults, or animals, all within the period of a day. These acts may occur each day for days at a time. The use of urine, semen, blood, and other body fluids during sexual abuse is not uncommon. The child may be sexually stimulated while being forced to watch the killing of animals, thus planting the thought in the child's mind that he enjoyed the killing. Some survivors have related being impregnated for the purpose of giving birth to a child who is to be sacrificed by the cult.

Psychological. Psychological abuse involves a destruction of the child's personality and the ability to resist. Sleep deprivation and isolation are two of the fastest ways to indoctrinate any person. Prisoners of war report that this method of torture is often the hardest to resist. Survivors have reported being bound and placed in coffins for long periods. Being enclosed in a dark box or other small space with insects, spiders, or snakes is another form of psychological torture that rapidly breaks down the will.

Forcing children to engage in physical and sexual acts that run counter to their morality can cause a loss of identity. Victims are told that the cult always knows what they are doing and that, if they ever tell anyone, revenge will be swift and severe.

Victims may also have to participate in killing animals. This may cause guilt and shame, which is then used by the cult members to point out how bad and evil the victims have become. The children are then told that because they have now participated in, committed, or witnessed these unspeakable acts, only the cult will accept them as people. A feeling of total dependency and despair overwhelms the children's psyches.

Each of these forms of abuse is severe by itself. Combining them places an incredible strain on the child and may lead to dissociation episodes. Some survivors develop multiple personalities or other forms of mental illness in an effort to cope with the ritualistic abuse. The consequences of this form of abuse are long-lasting and may require long-term therapy.

RESPONDING TO RITUALISTIC ABUSE

As stated earlier, a great deal of controversy surrounds the existence and extent of ritualistic abuse.[27] Its very existence is questioned by a number of educated, well-intentioned professionals. Affirming the existence of ritualistic abuse means that there are groups of individuals who practice some of the most bizarre forms of abuse known. If this is the case, it would seem only reasonable that at least one satanic cult practicing ritualistic abuse would have been discovered and prosecuted by law enforcement agencies. That trial, like the McMartin day care center trial, would have made national and international news. But so far, no such trial has occurred. Had these cults operated according to the survivors' statements, skeletal remains, remnants of clothing, or some other form of physical evidence should have been discovered.

Skeptics of ritualistic abuse abound. They argue that the survivors are not victims of satanic cults but instead have been victimized by sophisticated sex rings similar to the ones discussed in Chapter 6. Others allege that overzealous therapists put these ideas in the minds of their patients. Still others explain that these stories are simply the delusions of the mentally ill persons.

Jones sets forth three explanations that should be examined in assessing the validity of claims of ritualistic abuse: The events did in fact occur as described; the events did not occur, and children or adult survivors are mistaken or telling lies; and some of the events did in fact happen, and others did not.[28] He points out that the problem with the first alternative is the lack of physical evidence to support the victim's claims. A second problem deals with the dynamics of conspiracies. Law enforcement agencies know that the longer a conspiracy continues, the more likely one of the coconspirators will break from the conspiracy and disclose the activity or crime. In terms of ritualistic abuse, no coconspirator has come forward and testified. However, the counter to this argument is the depth of the cult's indoctrination of its members. This indoctrination and the nature of the activity that occurs during ritualistic abuse may make it very difficult for a coconspirator or member to break away and discuss these acts with law enforcement officials. Also, the survivors may have been drugged, and their recollection of dates and places may be inaccurate; therefore, no evidence would be found at the location they specify.

The second possibility is that the allegations are false. This flies in the face of the belief that children do not normally fabricate stories of sexual or physical abuse. Jones points out that mechanisms such as mass hysteria, contamination from one source to another, leading and suggestive questions by interviewers, child fantasies that are fed by video and movies containing scenes of the occult, and horror movies may explain some of these stories.[29] However, all these explanations cannot account for all the statements made by all the various victims.

The final possibility is that some events did in fact occur and that others did not. The use of physical, sexual, and psychological abuse may be so overwhelming as to distort the child's memory and may account for some of the inaccuracies.

The controversy surrounding ritual abuse continues unabated. For example, in 1995, when this textbook was originally published, only a few references to ritualistic child abuse existed. In 2000, a search of the World Wide Web revealed a number of Web sites either dealing with the existence of ritual abuse or claiming that it did not exist. For example, a Web site listed as Witchhunt lists a number of cases of "false claims regarding ritual abuse."[30] Witchhunt has links to other sites that are skeptical of cases or incidents involving ritualistic child abuse. On the other hand, the Ritual Abuse, Ritual Crime, and Healing Homepage site has a list of support groups for survivors of ritualistic abuse.[31] This site has also compiled an impressive list of 200 articles and journals on ritualistic abuse and ritual crime. Unlike some resources on the World Wide Web, this list is composed of articles written by a number of respected researchers.

A recent study examined the different resources that addressed ritualistic child abuse.[32] It compared and contrasted academic resources, professional or trade publications, and Web sites that examined ritualistic child abuse. It was found that the literature in all three areas continues to grow and expand. As of 2005, an online search resulted in a total of 488 academic articles that addressed ritualistic child abuse. Professional or trade publications totaled 210, while Internet resources returned an astounding 81,295 references. Yamamoto correctly points out that each resource has its own advantages and disadvantages. Academic articles, although more scientifically valid, are many times limited to those who work on university campuses, whereas trade or professional publications are not referred to and may contain some inaccuracies, and Internet resources can be placed by anyone with the interest and time to do so. However, it is interesting to note the continued interest, growth, and research that continue in this controversial area.

No single theory explains all the variations of ritualistic abuse. More research is necessary before the nature and extent of ritualistic abuse can be determined. However, there are too many stories and statements by survivors of ritualistic abuse to deny completely the existence of this form of family violence.[33] This section is included in this textbook because of the special trauma suffered by survivors of ritualistic abuse. If ritualistic abuse does in fact exist, professionals must be able to recognize the symptoms and understand how to respond to victims of this type of abuse.

Focus

The Need to Follow Laws and Regulations in Taking Responsive Action

In re Tex. Dep't of Family & Protective Servs., 255 S.W.3d 613, 614 (Tex. 2008)

The Yearning for Zion Ranch was a 1,700-acre complex near Eldorado, Texas, and was home to a large community associated with the Fundamentalist Church of Jesus Christ of Latter Day Saints. On March 29, 2008, the Texas Department of Family Protective Services received a telephone call reporting that a sixteen-year-old girl named Sarah was being physically and sexually abused at the ranch. On April 3, about 9:00 P.M., the department investigators and law enforcement officials entered the ranch, and throughout the night they interviewed adults and children and searched for documents. Concerned that the community had a culture of polygamy and of

directing girls younger than eighteen years to enter spiritual unions with older men and have children, the department took possession of all 468 children at the ranch without a court order. The court described this case as "the largest child protection case documented in the history of the United States." It never located the girl Sarah, who was the subject of the March 29 call.

On that April 3 night, the department investigators and law enforcement personnel conducted 19 interviews of girls aged 17 or below, as well as 15 to 20 interviews of adults. In the course of these interviews, the department learned that there were many polygamist families living on the ranch; a number of girls under the age of eighteen living on the ranch were

(continued)

pregnant or had given birth; both interviewed girls and adults considered no age too young for a girl to be "spiritually" married; and the ranch's religious leader, "Uncle Merrill," had the unilateral power to decide when and to whom they would be married. In addition, in the trial court, the department presented "Bishop's Records"—documents seized from the ranch—indicating the presence of several extremely young mothers or pregnant "wives" on the ranch: a sixteen-year-old "wife" with a child, a sixteen-year-old pregnant "wife," two pregnant fifteen-year-old "wives," and a thirteen-year-old wife who had conceived a child. The testimony of Dr. William John Walsh, the families' expert witness, confirmed that the Fundamentalist Church of Jesus Christ of Latter Day Saints accepts the age of "physical development" (i.e., first menstruation) as the age of eligibility for "marriage." Child psychologist Dr. Bruce Duncan Perry testified that the pregnancy of the underage children on the ranch was the result of sexual abuse, because children of the age of fourteen, fifteen, or sixteen are not sufficiently, emotionally mature to enter a healthy consensual sexual relationship or a "marriage."

Thirty-eight mothers petitioned the court of appeals for review of the orders terminating custody and seeking return of their 126 children. The record reflects that at least 117 of the children are under 13, and that two boys are 13 and 17. The ages of the other seven, at least two of whom are boys, are not shown.

The appellate court noted that the Texas Family Code defines "abuse" to include "sexual conduct harmful to a child's mental, emotional, or physical welfare"—as well as "failure to make a reasonable effort to prevent sexual conduct harmful to a child." The court noted that in determining whether there is a "continuing danger to the health or safety" of a child, the Family Code explicitly permits a court to consider "whether the household to which the child would be returned includes a person who ... has sexually abused another child."

The court held that notwithstanding this evidence of a pattern or practice of sexual abuse of pubescent girls on the ranch, that the trial court abused its discretion in awarding temporary conservatorship to the department because the department failed to attempt legal steps, short of taking custody, to protect the children. The court suggests, consistent with the mothers' arguments in the court of appeals below, that the department failed to adequately justify its failure to seek less-intrusive alternatives to taking custody of the children, namely, seeking restraining orders against alleged perpetrators or other temporary orders under section 105.001 of the Family Code. The appellate court noted that the trial court could grant other appropriate relief to protect the children.

As a trial judge, what orders would you grant or what conditions would you impose prior to returning the children to their mothers?

Recognition of Ritualistic Abuse

Recognition of ritualistic abuse is a critical aspect of this form of family violence. What may appear to be a rather simple form of child abuse or child sexual abuse may turn out to be just the tip of the iceberg. The emotional, behavioral, and medical indicators present in a child who has been sexually abused may also indicate that the child has been ritualistically victimized. The symptoms described in this section may be observed by law enforcement officers, social workers, medical personnel, or teachers. Each professional should be aware that the symptoms observed may indicate a need to evaluate the situation from the perspective of ritualistic abuse. At the same time, extreme care must be used not to plant ideas in the victim's mind or to suggest factual situations that the victim may adopt as his own. This issue is still unresolved, and more research is being done on recall and ritualistic abuse. Caution should be exercised, and professionals should not jump to the conclusion that every child is a victim of ritualistic abuse, nor should they turn away from that possibility.

One of the most extensive lists of symptoms of ritualistic abuse was written by Catherine Gould in "Diagnosis and Treatment of Ritually Abused Children," in Sakheim and Devine's *Out of Darkness*.[34] Although many of these symptoms are exhibited by children who have been sexually or physically abused, the extent and nature of these indicators should alert the professional to the possibility that the child may have been ritually abused. The following is a shortened version of Gould's analysis:

1. ***Strange or unusual sexual behavior or beliefs.*** A child may have knowledge of sexual activities far beyond his normal developmental stage. These activities may include unusual or bizarre sexual practices or activities. The child may act out sexually in an aggressive manner toward other children. The child may report that she is married. Discussions of group sex and of sex with children and adults or even with animals are indications of possible ritual abuse.

2. ***Unusual distress regarding bowel movements or body wastes.*** The child may speak of drinking urine or eating feces. Some children spread urine or feces on their body or consume it. Whereas many children discuss toilet training, the ritualistically abused child is more compulsive and less innocent in discussing this body function.

3. ***Belief in the supernatural, rituals, occult symbols, and religion.*** Many ritually abused children state that they have been married to Satan or are Satan's bride. They have been indoctrinated to believe that the cult has spies everywhere and knows what they do. They will have an unusual knowledge of satanic symbols or methods. They may draw pentagrams, hexagrams, or other symbols and signs associated with ritualistic abuse.

4. ***A fear of enclosed or small spaces.*** As indicated earlier, many children are buried and reborn into the cult. The child may become tense or even hysterical at being enclosed in a confining space or location. They may also act out these fears by trying to confine a pet, sibling, or even the therapist.

5. ***A preoccupation with death and dying.*** The child may believe she has died or will die soon. Concern that the child's parents, siblings, or friends will die is sometimes present. The child may ask questions regarding death and have strange or bizarre beliefs about death and dying.

6. ***Other strange or unusual beliefs or actions.*** The child may have a preference for certain colors associated with satanic practices. Fear of police and other authority figures is not uncommon. Familiarity with cemeteries, mortuaries, and other locations that children normally do not visit is another indication of ritualistic child abuse.

If a professional has reason to believe that a person is or has been a victim of ritualistic abuse, he or she must proceed very carefully. The consequences of this type of family violence are still being determined, researched, and studied, as the next section suggests.

Consequences of Ritualistic Abuse

Extreme caution must be used in making a diagnosis of ritualistic abuse. Because research in this area is still evolving, professionals must be careful not to jump to any unfounded conclusions simply because a person describes what is believed to be satanic abuse. As with any child abuse case, extreme care must be taken not to plant ideas in the mind of the victim. Not only would this be poor therapy, but it could also destroy the credibility of the victim during any court proceedings.

If a professional comes to the conclusion that a child has been a victim of any form of abuse, including ritualistic abuse, this suspicion must be reported to the local authorities. This aspect of family violence is examined in detail in later chapters. Once the report is made, child protective services (CPS) and law enforcement agencies enter the picture. Their responsibility is not to treat the victim but to prove or disprove that criminal actions have occurred or, in the case of CPS, to determine whether the child is at risk and, if so, to remove him or her from that situation.

The investigation of ritual crimes is a specialty within law enforcement agencies.[35] These kinds of offenses are similar to serial murders or other complex and difficult crimes. They should be handled with care and sensitivity. If the victim can identify individuals, caution must be used in interviewing potential witnesses or defendants. Compounding the problem of investigating this type of crime is the fact that the victim may have been drugged during the abusive acts. Persons, places, times, and dates may be hazy at best.

If the scene of the ritualistic abuse can be located, it must be carefully checked for evidence such as blood, semen, candle wax, fibers or hair from animals, and signs of fire. In the event the victim is able to identify a specific residence, business, or location, law enforcement officials should attempt to obtain a search warrant. Any search warrants must be based on probable cause and should include lists of items that, although not directly tied to the abuse, may provide corroboration to the victim's testimony. Some of the more common items that should be included on any search warrant dealing with ritualistic abuse include occult games; ashes from any fires; robes; stands that might have been used for altars; swords; knives; animal masks or trophies; gloves (especially right-handed gloves); incense; body paint (especially red or black); animal bones or remains; any books dealing with satanism or the occult; all drugs (prescription or not); any handwritten notes or diaries; and any videos on witchcraft, the occult, or devil worshipping.

The criminal justice process is one aspect of ritualistic child abuse. Another aspect concerns the impact of this form of family violence on the survivor. This is not a textbook in abnormal psychology. However, a brief discussion of some of the mental and emotional problems that survivors of this form of abuse face is considered necessary to inform professionals fully of the repercussions of these types of offenses.

Posttraumatic stress disorder (PTSD) came into the lexicon as a result of the Vietnam War. Returning veterans reported flashbacks, severe depression, and other symptoms. PTSD is now recognized as a mental disorder. The *Diagnostic and Statistical Manual of Disorders*, fourth edition (DSM-IV) states that the essential feature of this disorder is the development of characteristic symptoms following a psychologically distressing event that is outside the range of usual human experience. The stressor is usually experienced with intense fear, terror, and helplessness. The characteristic symptoms involve flashbacks where the patient relives the experience, avoidance of stimuli associated with the event, and numbing of general responsiveness.[36] Some authorities have concluded that PTSD is a frequently observed symptom of sexually abused children.[37]

Dissociative disorders include several recognized mental illnesses. These disorders are characterized by changes in consciousness, identity, or memory so that the individual becomes impaired. These changes may be sudden or gradual. The impairment may be amnesia, affecting memory. Impairment of identity occurs when the patient's normal identity is replaced by an alternate or satellite identity. There are four types of dissociative disorders: multiple personality disorder (MPD), depersonalization disorder, psychogenic amnesia, and psychogenic fugue. *Depersonalization disorder* occurs when a patient's feeling of reality is lost and is replaced with a feeling of unreality. *Psychogenic amnesia* involves a sudden loss of memory in which the person is unable to remember important personal information. *Psychogenic fugue* occurs with a sudden flight from one's workplace or home and the subsequent assumption of a new identity with no memory of the past identity. The one disorder currently receiving the most attention is MPD.

During the 1970s and 1980s, the diagnosis of MPD was considered quite rare and carried with it overtones of "another self."[38] It was considered an almost nonexistent mental illness. Today, it is one of the most talked-about disorders. The cluster of symptoms was once known as multiple personality disorder, but the DSM-IV now describes it as **dissociative identity disorder** (DID).

Some professionals claim that the number of DIDs is exaggerated. Others believe that people are claiming to be DIDs to avoid responsibility for their actions. Similar to ritualistic abuse, the diagnosis of DID is a controversial subject.

DID is the existence within a person of two or more distinct personalities or personality states in which at least two of these personalities recurrently take full control of the person's behavior.[39] *Personality* in this context is the relatively enduring pattern of perceiving, relating to, and thinking about the environment and one's self that is exhibited in a wide range of social and personal settings. The DSM-IV states that the predisposing factor included in nearly all cases is the fact that the disorder has been preceded by abuse (often sexual) or by another form of severe emotional trauma in childhood.[40]

One of the most dramatic cases of MPD was reported in the book *Sybil*, which detailed the variety of interests and characters that may exist in this disorder.[41] Sybil was a young woman who was eventually diagnosed as having at least sixteen distinct personalities. Another popular book dealing with MPDs was *The Three Faces of Eve*, which chronicled the story of Mrs. Chris Sizemore.[42] Eve, as she was known in the book, had twenty-two personalities that always manifested themselves in sets of three. *The Three Faces of Eve* was published in 1957. In 1975 Mrs. Sizemore publicly revealed herself to be Eve and subsequently wrote an autobiography, *I'm Eve.*

Researchers are continually learning about ritualistic child abuse and the impact it has on its victims. More study and research needs to be done in this area.[43] At present, very little academic work is available that deals with the long-term effects of this type of abuse. Young and his associates conducted an analysis of thirty-seven patients who claimed to be victims of ritualistic abuse. Although some criticism exists of their methodology and conclusion, the study does provide an overview of some of the possible or potential effects of ritualistic abuse.[44]

Focus

The McMartin Preschool Abuse Trials

Probably the most famous child abuse case was the McMartin Preschool Abuse Trial. It was at the time the longest and most expensive criminal trial in American history. The government spent seven years and $15 million dollars investigating and prosecuting the cases with no convictions.

More important, the McMartin cases resulted in a large number of emotionally damaged children and the ruined careers for members of the McMartin School staff. Ray Buckey, one of the principal defendants, spent five years in jail awaiting trial for a crime that most people agreed today that he never committed.

One juror stated that the trial experience taught her to be more cautious. She said that she now realizes how easily something can be said and misinterpreted and blown out of proportion. Another juror blamed the "experts." The juror stated that in his opinion, some of the expert testimony about the children told you more about the expert than the child. The McMartin investigation started when a telephone call was received by the police in Manhattan Beach, California, by the mother of a two-and-a-half-year-old son who attended the preschool in 1983. The mother stated in her call that school aide, Ray Buckey, the twenty-five-year-old son of the owner of the preschool, had molested her son. Even though the young boy was unable to identify Buckey from photos and medical investigations of the boy showed no signs of sexual abuse, the police conducted searches of his home, confiscating such "evidence" as a rubber duck, a graduation robe, and Playboy magazines. Buckey was arrested in September 1983.

After the arrest, the police chief mailed letters to the McMartin Preschool parents telling them that Buckey was suspected of child abuse. The letter requested the parents to question their child to see if he or she has been a witness to any crime or if he or she has been a victim. The letter listed the possible criminal acts under investigation. The listed acts included oral sex,

fondling of genitals, buttock or chest area, and sodomy, possibly committed under the pretense of "taking the child's temperature." The letter also stated that photos may have been taken of children without their clothing. And to provide the police with any information from their child regarding having ever observed Buckey to leave a classroom alone with a child during any nap period, or if they have ever observed Ray Buckey tie up a child.

The chief's letter requested the parents to keep the investigation confidential because of the nature of the charges and the highly emotional effect it could have on the community. Parents were instructed not to discuss the investigation with anyone outside of immediate family. Despite this request for confidentially, the information regarding the investigation was widely discussed or printed by the media.

The chief's letter led to new accusations and demands from parents for a full-scale investigation of doings at the McMartin Preschool. The reports of misbehavior included a report that Ray's mother was involved in satanic practices: She was said to have taken a child to a church, where the boy was made to watch a baby being beheaded, and then was forced to drink the blood. One mother insisted that Ray Buckey had sodomized her son while his head was in the toilet, and had taken him to a car wash and locked him in the trunk. It was also stated that Ray pranced around the preschool in a cape and a Santa Claus costume, and that other teachers at the school chopped up rabbits and placed "some sort of star" on one child's bottom.

Parents were encouraged to allow their children to be interviewed by an expert. The expert interviewed about 400 children using a series of leading questions and the offer of rewards, to report instances of abuse at McMartin. Children generally denied seeing any evidence of abuse at first, but eventually many gave the stories that the expert wanted to hear.

(continued)

After the interviews, the expert told parents that their children had been abused, and described the nature of the alleged abuse. By March 1984, 384 former McMartin students identified as having been sexually abused.

In addition to interviews, 150 children received medical examinations. The medical doctor concluded that 80 percent of the children she examined had been molested. For the most part, she based her findings not on physical evidence, but on medical histories and her belief that any conclusion should validate the child's history.

On March 22, 1984, a grand jury indicted seven of the preschool staff, including Ray Buckey and Peggy Buckey (Ray's mother), on 115 counts of child sexual abuse. Two months later, additional 93 indictment counts were added. Bail for Peggy Buckey was set at one million dollars. Ray Buckey was held without bail.

At a pretrial hearing on the case in August 1984, the prosecutor told the media that the seven defendants committed 397 sexual crimes and that thirty additional individuals associated with the McMartin Preschool were under investigation.

Searches of the preschool and the homes of defendants failed to produce much incriminating evidence. No nude photographs of children were discovered, despite the insistence of investigators and parents that such photographing was commonplace at McMartin. No evidence was found of the secret rooms where massive instances of sexual abuse were said to have taken place.

The testimony of children at the preliminary hearing was shockingly bizarre, and often riddled with inconsistencies and contradictions. Children testified that sexual assaults took place on farms, in circus houses, in the homes of strangers, in car washes, in store rooms, and in a "secret room" at McMartin accessible by a tunnel. One boy testified that the students were taken to a cemetery where the kids were forced to dig up coffins. Once the coffins were removed

from the ground, they would be opened and the teachers would begin hacking the bodies with knives.

By September 1985, and well over a year into the preliminary hearing, members of the prosecution's own team began to express doubts about the case. One prosecutor was quoted as saying that the expert could make a sixth month old baby say he was molested. The two co-prosecutors in the case urged dropping all charges against five of the seven defendants, and pushing ahead with prosecution only for Ray Buckey and Peggy Buckey. In December 1985, the District Attorney's Office dropped charges against all defendants except Ray and Peggy Buckey.

Prior to the first trial, independent filmmakers producing a documentary on the McMartin trial turned over to both the California A. G.'s office and to defense attorneys copies of a taped interview with one of the McMartin prosecutor. In the interview, the prosecutor acknowledged that children began "embellishing and embellishing" their stories of sexual abuse. The prosecutor also admitted on tape that prosecutors withheld potentially exculpatory information from defense attorneys, including evidence concerning the mental instability of the original complainant in the case.

Jury selection for the first trial took weeks. The twelve finally selected included eight men and four women. Half of the jurors were white, three African American, two Asian, and one Hispanic. All but two jurors had at least some college education. The prosecution presented sixty-one witnesses, including nine child witnesses, a jailhouse informant, parents, medical specialists, therapists, and even a woman who had sexual relations with Ray Buckey.

On November 2, 1989, after nearly thirty months of testimony, the case went to the jury. The jury spent another two-and-a-half months deliberating its verdicts. On fifty-two of the sixty-five charges against the

(continued)

two defendants, including the charges against Peggy Buckey, the jury returned an acquittal. On the remaining charges against Ray Buckey, the jury announced that it was hopelessly deadlocked.

Child protection groups and parents pressured the district attorney to retry Ray Buckey on the charges on which the first jury deadlocked. About 500 people marched through the streets of Manhattan Beach carrying signs, such as "We believe the children." A television poll showed 90 percent of respondents thought the Buckeys were guilty.

Two new prosecutors were assigned to the case. The second trial also saw a different trial judge, following a successful motion by defense to remove the first judge from the case.

The second trial involved only eight counts of molestation and three children. The prosecution presented its entire case in just thirteen days and called only eleven witnesses. The jury ended its deliberations deadlocked on all eight counts. Following the mistrial, the district attorney Reiner chose not to retry Buckey a third time and all charges against him were dismissed.

The effects of the trial extended nationwide. Day care providers resisted the temptation to hug or touch children—contact almost all child experts say children need—out of a fear that their actions might be interpreted as signs of abuse. Many day care centers were forced to close their doors after insurance companies dramatically raised liability insurance rates. Early publicity surrounding the McMartin investigation also spawned a rash of charges against day care providers elsewhere, many of which proved to be unsubstantiated.

One of the positive things that resulted from the investigation was the need to refrain from using leading questions and the need to use professional techniques in questioning children. As one expert noted, young children are vulnerable to "suggestive questioning," in which the interviewer coaches a child into saying things that incriminate the accused person.

Sources: J. Earl, "The Dark Truth about the 'Dark Tunnels of McMartin': Section IV: Children's Institute International," *Issues in Child Abuse Accusations (Institute for Psychological Therapies)* 7(2) (1995); C. Hubert and S. Stanton, "McMartin Preschool Abuse-Case Fiasco Led to New Child Interview Techniques," *Sacramento Bee*, July 21, 2011, p. 1A; K. Zirpolo and D. Natha. "I'm Sorry: A Long-delayed Apology from One of the Accusers in the Notorious McMartin Pre-School Molestation Case," *Los Angeles Times Magazine*, October 10, 2005; and W. J. Wyatt, "What Was Under the McMartin Preschool? A Review and Behavioral Analysis of the 'Tunnels' Find," *Behaviour and Social Issues* 12(1) (Fall/winter 2002), pp. 29–39.

OBSERVING VIOLENCE

Children are exposed to or experience family violence in many ways. They may hear one parent/caregiver or partner threaten the other, observe a parent who is out of control or reckless with anger, see one parent assault the other, or live with the aftermath of a violent assault. Many children are affected by hearing threats to the safety of their caregiver, regardless of whether it results in physical injury. Children who live with domestic violence are also at increased risk to become direct victims of child abuse. In short, domestic violence poses a serious threat to children's emotional, psychological, and physical well-being, particularly if the violence is chronic.[45]

While different children react differently and are not exposed to violence equally or in the same ways, the reactions discussed in this section may vary. Exposure to family violence

**A child hiding her ears to keep from seeing and hearing
her parents fight and argue.**

has been linked to poor school performance, impaired ability to concentrate, difficulty in completing school work and lower scores on tests that measure verbal, motor, and social skills.[46]

According to the Wisconsin Coalition Against Domestic Violence, children who live with domestic violence are affected by the experience. The nature and extent of the effects vary greatly. Some children are severely traumatized, particularly if they are among the many who are also victims of child abuse. Others are able to cope well, and go on to live healthy, productive lives. Children are not just eye witnesses to battering. They are actively involved in trying to understand the abuse, predict when it will happen, protect themselves, their mother, or their siblings, and worrying about the consequences. They live in homes where the dynamics of their households are governed by domestic violence. Fear and secrecy dominate family relationships, and survival becomes the primary goal of non-abusing family members.[47]

A child's immediate reaction to family violence may include:

- generalized anxiety
- sleeplessness
- nightmares
- difficulty concentrating
- high levels of activity
- increased aggression
- increased anxiety about being separated from a parent
- increased worry about safety
- feeling to blame for the violence.

The long-term effects may include:

- physical health problems
- behavior problems

- emotional difficulties later in adulthood
- suicide
- addiction problems.

The Effect of Domestic Violence on Children

Children who witness domestic violence frequently develop serious emotional, behavioral, developmental, or academic problems. Often they become violent themselves, or withdraw. Many act out at home or school; others try to be the perfect child. Children from violent homes are frequently depressed and have low self-esteem.

As the children grow up, those who grow up with domestic violence in the household are:

- more likely to use violence at school or in the community in response to perceived threats;
- more likely to attempt suicide;
- more likely to use drugs;
- more likely to commit crimes, especially sexual assault;
- more likely to use violence to enhance their reputation and self-esteem;
- more likely to become abusers in their own relationships later in life.

ARREST OF PARENTS

Similar to the situation of a child observing violence is the situation where the child observes his or her parents being arrested by law enforcement. The arrest of a parent generally will result in a significant impact on a child whether or not the child is present at the time of the arrest. The degree of the impact depends to some extent on the age and quality of the child's relationship with the parent. Frequently the child will feel shock, immense fear, anxiety, or anger towards the arresting officers or law enforcement in general. Since the 1990s, the Bureau of Justice Assistance (BJA) has been increasing emphasis on examination of the effects of these events on children of various ages and the ways in which law enforcement can make sure that an involved child doesn't "fall through the cracks." According to the BJA, research clearly indicates that such events can and often do have a negative impact on a child's immediate and long-term emotional, mental, social, and physical health. Symptoms such as sleep disruptions, separation anxiety, irritability, and even more serious disorders or posttraumatic reactions have been documented. In addition, later problems with authority figures in general and law enforcement in particular can arise if officers or other service providers do not take the time to address the needs of the child.[48]

According to the BJA, time taken with a child under these trauma producing circumstances is time well spent. The kindness and assistance of an officer with a child creates lasting impressions even among very young children. Treating a child with compassion and thoughtfulness is not only the proper thing to do, it is also a hallmark of good policing that can have long-term positive benefits for the child and the community.

A 2014 study sponsored by the BJA concluded that unfortunately, enforcement procedures, or training that specifically address actions that should be taken to reduce and prevent trauma associated with the arrest of a parent. For example, a seven-year study of all local California law enforcement agencies found that two-thirds of responding agencies did not have written policies outlining officer responsibilities for a child at the time of a parent's arrest. Additionally, about half of responding child welfare agencies had no written protocols describing how to minimize trauma that may occur. The majority of those jurisdictions suggest that both law enforcement and community partner organizations who share responsibility for child welfare in arrest situations lack the training or preparation necessary to respond appropriately.

The BJA's report contends that law enforcement when arresting a parent has a duty to ensure that the children of arrested parents are properly cared for. The report concludes that in many cases law enforcement because of the lack of and procedures reflects a lack of awareness by many departments concerning the process surrounding, and sufficiency of, the care that should be provided.

The BJA report states that the child of an arrested parent needs to understand that he or she is not to blame and has done nothing wrong. Placing the child with a trusted and familiar adult or family member may add a level of stability to the situation and help the child cope with the other changes occurring during the period of stress.

The BJA recommends that law enforcement personnel be trained to identify and respond effectively to a child, present or not present, whose parent is arrested in order to help minimize potential trauma and support a child's physical safety and well-being following an arrest.

Summary

A complex and controversial form of family violence, ritualistic child abuse is a distinct form of child abuse that involves repeated, multifaceted forms of physical, sexual, and psychological violence over an extended period of time.

Some argue that the extent and nature of ritualistic abuse is exaggerated, pointing to the fact that there has never been one successful prosecution of a satanic cult engaged in ritualistic abuse. However, the number of survivors who claim to be victims, their strikingly similar but independent statements, and the proven existence of individuals who have engaged in satanic crimes support the position that this type of abuse may exist. The exact nature and extent of this form of family violence will continue to be discussed, researched, and debated for the foreseeable future. Professionals must be able to recognize the symptoms of ritualistic abuse. They should be able to distinguish these indicators from the types observed in physical and sexual abuse. Care must be taken to ensure that ideas are not planted in the victim's mind. Law enforcement agencies must attempt to obtain evidence that will support a conviction in a court of law. Medical personnel must ensure that the child is no longer at risk and must begin the arduous process of long-term treatment in an attempt to bring the survivor back into society.

Key Terms

satanism—the worship of Satan.

ritualistic child abuse—a brutal form of abuse of children, adolescents, and adults, consisting of physical, sexual, and psychological abuse and involving the use of rituals. Ritualistic does not necessarily mean satanic. However, most survivors state that they were ritually abused as part of satanic worship for the purpose of indoctrinating them into satanic beliefs and practices. Ritual abuse rarely consists of a single episode. It usually involves repeated abuse over an extended period of time.

magic—a method of harnessing the secret powers of nature to influence events for one's own purpose.

transmission—the belief that the qualities of objects or beings can be transmitted from one person to another.

pentagrams and hexagrams—common symbols of satanism and the occult.

grimoires—instruction manuals setting forth the rituals of satanic cults.

dissociative identity disorder—the existence within a person of two or more distinct personalities or personality states in which at least two of these personalities recurrently take full control of the person's behavior.

Discussion Questions

1. Does ritualistic abuse exist?
2. Take a position on satanism and justify your answer.
3. How long has ritualistic child abuse existed?
4. Is a sex ring a form of ritualistic abuse? Why or why not?
5. Should we enact special laws that enhance punishment for those convicted of ritualistic abuse?

6. What type of education or information should be supplied to children regarding ritualistic abuse? If we educate them regarding this form of family violence, are we programming or predisposing them to believe that they have been ritually abused?
7. Do you believe in the diagnosis of multiple personality disorder?

Suggested Readings

Ammerman, R. T., and M. Hersen, eds. *Case Studies in Family Violence* (Plenum, New York, 1991).

Cavendish, R. *The Black Arts* (Putnam, New York, 1967).

Crowley, A. *Magick in Theory and Practice* (Dover, New York, 1924, reprinted in 1976).

Davis, W. *The Serpent and the Rainbow* (Simon & Schuster, New York, 1985).

Frankfurter, D. *Evil Incarnate: Rumors of Demonic Conspiracy and Satanic Abuse in History* (Princeton University Press, Princeton, N.J., 2006).

Gallagher, B. J. *The Sociology of Mental Illness*, 2nd ed. (Prentice Hall, Upper Saddle River, N.J., 1987).

Gottfried, R. S. *The Black Death: Natural and Human Disaster in Medieval Europe* (Free Press, New Work, 1983).

Hill, D., and P. Williams. *The Supernatural* (New American Library, New York, 1965).

Investigation of Ritualistic Abuse Allegations: Think Tank Report (National Resource Center on Child Sexual Abuse, Huntsville, Ala., 1989).

Kahaner, L. *Cults That Kill* (Warner, New York, 1988).

King, F. *Sexuality, Magic, and Perversion* (Citadel, Secaucus, N.J., 1971).

LaVey, A. *The Satanic Bible* (Avon, New York, 1969).

Nobitt, J., and P. Perskin. *Cult and Ritual Abuse: Its History, Anthropology, and Recent Discovery in Contemporary America* (Praeger, Westport, Conn., 2000).

Ofshe, R., and E. Watters. *Making Monsters: False Memories, Psychotherapy, and Sexual Hysteria* (Scribner's, New York, 1994).

Perimutter, D. *Investigating Religious Terrorism and Ritualistic Crimes* (CRC, Boca Raton, Fla., 2003).

Rasche, G. *Painted Black: Satanic Crime in America* (Harper & Row, San Francisco, 1990).

Rhodes, H. T. F. *The Satanic Mass* (Citadel, Secaucus, N.J., 1954).

Ryder, D. *Breaking the Circle of Satanic Ritual Abuse* (CompCare, Minneapolis, 1992).

Sakheim, D. K., and S. E. Devine. *Out of Darkness* (Lexington, New York, 1992).

Schreiber, F. R. *Sybil* (Warner, New York, 1973).

Singer, M. *Cults in Our Midst: The Continuing Fight against Their Hidden Menace* (John Wiley & Sons, New York, 2003).

Smith, M., and L. Pazder. *Michelle Remembers* (Congdon & Lattes, New York, 1980).

Thigpen, C., and H. Cleckley. *The Three Faces of Eve* (McGraw-Hill, New York, 1957).

Valiente, D. *An ABC of Witchcraft Past and Present* (Phoenix, Custer, Wash., 1973).

Endnotes

1. C. Gould "Denying Ritual Abuse of Children," *The Journal of Psychohistory* 22(3) (1995), p. 14.

2. S. Laville, "The Underreported Crime," *The Guardian*, March 1, 2012, p. A-2.

3. S. J. Ireland and M. J. Ireland, "A Case History of Family and Cult Abuse," *Journal of Psychohistory* 21(4) (Spring 1994), pp. 417–428.

4. See D. Cicchetti and V. Carlson, eds., *Child Maltreatment* (Cambridge University Press, Cambridge, 1989); C. C. Tower, *Understanding Child Abuse and Neglect*, 2nd ed. (Allyn & Bacon, Needham Heights, Mass., 1993); R. T. Ammerman and M. Hersen, *Assessment of Family Violence* (Wiley, New York, 1992), which does not discuss ritual abuse; and compare C. C. Kent, "Ritual Abuse," in R. T. Ammerman and M. Hersen, eds., *Case Studies in Family Violence* (Plenum, New York, 1991); and D. K. Sakheim and S. E. Devine, *Out of Darkness* (Lexington, New York, 1992), which covers the entire realm of ritualistic abuse.

5. G. C. Feldman, "Satanic Ritual Abuse: A Chapter in the History of Human Cruelty," *Journal of Psychohistory* 22(3) (Winter 1995), p. 340.

6. C. Rasche, *Painted Black: Satanic Crime in America* (Harper & Row, San Francisco, 1990), pp. 140–141.

7. S. Hill and J. Goodwin, "Satanism: Similarities between Patient Accounts and Pre-Inquisition Historical Sources," *Dissociation* 2(1) (1989), pp. 39–43.

8. R. S. Gottfried, *The Black Death: Natural and Human Disaster in Medieval Europe* (Free Press, New York, 1983), p. 100.

9. Ibid., p. 133.

10. H. T. F. Rhodes, *The Satanic Mass* (Citadel, Secaucus, N.J., 1954), pp. 113–122.

11. A. Crowley, *Magick in Theory and Practice* (Dover, New York, 1924, reprinted in 1976).

12. C. Raschke, *Painted Black: Satanic Crime in America* (Harper & Row, San Francisco, 1990), p. 123.

13. A. S. LaVey, *The Satanic Rituals* (Avon Books, New York, 1972).

14. M. Smith and L. Pazder, *Michelle Remembers* (Congdon & Lattes, New York, 1980).

15. L. Wright, "Remembering Satan," *The New Yorker*, May 17 and 24, 1993.

16. *Ritual Abuse: Definitions, Glossary, the Use of Mind Control* (Ritual Abuse Task Force, Los Angeles County Commission for Women, Los Angeles, September 15, 1989).

17. *Webster's Ninth New Collegiate Dictionary* (Merriam-Webster, Springfield, Mass., 1987), p. 1018.

18. L. Kahaner, *Cults That Kill* (Warner, New York, 1988).

19. M. D. Langone and L. O. Blood, *Satanism and Occult Related Violence: What You Should Know* (American Family Foundation, Weston, Mass., 1990).

20. D. Valiente, *An ABC of Witchcraft Past and Present* (Phoenix, Custer, Wash., 1973).

21. Crowley, *Magick in Theory and Practice*, pp. 94–95.

22. R. Cavendish, *The Black Arts* (Putnam, New York, 1967), p. 272.

23. F. King, *Sexuality, Magic, and Perversion* (Citadel, Secaucus, N.J., 1971), pp. 8, 163.

24. The author has been contacted by "right-handed" witches who use some of these symbols and do not engage in ritualistic abuse.

25. D. Hill and P. Williams, *The Supernatural* (New American Library, New York, 1965), pp. 107–108.

26. Ibid., pp. 110–111.

27. J. Fine, "Seeking Evil: The Hell of Prosecuting Satanic Ritual Abuse," *California Lawyer* 14(7) (1994), pp. 50–55.

28. D. P. H. Jones, "Ritualism and Child Sexual Abuse," *Child Abuse and Neglect* 15 (1991), pp. 163–170.

29. Ibid., p. 168.

30. See www.geocities/CapitalHill/Embassy/9062/witchhunt, accessed August 10, 2000.

31. See www.xroads.com/rahome, accessed August 10, 2000.

32. S. Yamamoto, *Ritualistic Child Abuse: A Comprehensive Analysis of Academic, Professional, Web-Based Literature of Ritualistic Child Abuse* (submitted in partial fulfillment of the requirements for the degree of Master of Science in Criminology) (California State University, Fresno, Calif., December 2005).

33. See L. S. Gonzalez et al., "Children's Patterns of Disclosures and Recantations of Sexual and Ritualistic Abuse Allegations in Psychotherapy," *Child Abuse and Neglect* 17 (1993), p. 281, for an excellent discussion of how disclosure occurs with victims of abuse.

34. D. K. Sakheim and S. E. Devine, *Out of Darkness* (Lexington, New York, 1992), pp. 210–216.

35. P. Jenkins, "Investigating Occult and Ritual Crime: A Case for Caution," *Police Forum, Academy of Criminal Justice Sciences* 2(1) (1992), pp. 1–7.

36. *Diagnostic and Statistical Manual of Mental Disorders*, 4th ed. revised (DSM-IV-R) (American Psychiatric Association, Washington, D.C., 1994), p. 424.

37. See E. Deblinger et al., "Post-Traumatic Stress in Sexually Abused, Physically Abused, and Non-abused Children," *Child Abuse and Neglect* 13 (1993), p. 403.

38. B. J. Gallagher III, *The Sociology of Mental Illness*, 2nd ed. (Prentice Hall, Upper Saddle River, N.J., 1987), pp. 117–119.

39. *Diagnostic and Statistical Manual of Mental Disorders*, 4th ed. (DSM-IV) (American Psychiatric Association, Washington, D.C., 1987), pp. 484–487.

40. Ibid., p. 485.

41. F. R. Schreiber, *Sybil* (Warner, New York, 1973).

42. C. Thigpen and H. Cleckley, *The Three Faces of Eve* (McGraw-Hill, New York, 1957).

43. M. R. McMinn and N. G. Wade, "Beliefs about the Prevalence of Dissociative Identity Disorder, Sexual Abuse, and Ritual Abuse among Religions and Nonreligious Therapists," *Professional Research and Practice* 26(3) (1995), pp. 257–261.

44. F. W. Putnam, "The Satanic Ritual Abuse Controversy," *Child Abuse and Neglect* 15(1991), p. 175.

45. National Child Traumatic Stress Network at www.nctsn.org, accessed July 28, 2015.

46. Ibid.

47. Wisconsin Coalition Against Domestic Violence Web site at www.wcadv.org, accessed July 28, 2015.

48. Bureau of Justice Assistance, "Safeguarding Children of Arrested Parents" (Washington, D.C., August 2014).

11

Professionals and Their
Response to Child Abuse

CHAPTER OBJECTIVES

After studying this chapter, you should be able to:

- Explain the goals of intervention;
- Discuss the major statutes that have been enacted by the states and federal government to protect children;
- Discuss and list the reporting requirements in suspected child abuse cases;
- Discuss the issues involved when interviewing a child witness;
- Explain the sex offender registration requirements.

Detailed Look at What You Should Know About Professionals and Their Response to Child Abuse

- The goal of intervention is to protect the child from abuse. The child's safety and health must be the overriding issue in any decision to intervene.
- All states in the United States have enacted statutes with the specific goal of protecting abused children by mandating the reporting of suspected child abuse cases to the authorities.
- No uniform reporting code has been adopted by all states in this area of the law. However, most states have passed legislation that contains similar characteristics that include when reporting is required, who must report, and the consequences of reporting.
- The reporting statutes require that certain classes of professionals who normally come into contact with children report cases of suspected child abuse. The theory is that a young child cannot speak for himself or herself, and therefore intervention and protection from a dangerous situation is necessary.

- A suspicion based on the professional's education and training is sufficient to trigger the reporting mandate.

- The statutes apply to most professionals who might have regular contact with young children. Physicians, nurses, social workers, teachers, psychologists, psychiatrists, and counselors are normally covered by these laws and are therefore required to report cases of suspected child abuse.

- The reporting statutes require incidents of suspected child abuse to be reported even when confidential relationship exists. In essence, this privilege is waived for purposes of reporting. Most of these reporting laws authorize agencies to remove the child from the custody of the parents if there is reason to believe that the child is in imminent danger.

- All states have laws requiring sex offenders to register with a department or a law enforcement agency.

- Once any professional suspects that a child has been a victim of abuse, the interview process takes on an entirely different perspective. The questions asked, the environment in which the interview is conducted, and the motives of the interviewer could have a direct impact on any court intervention.

- One of the most important aspects of interviewing child abuse victims is their ability to recall the incident or incidents.

- Children's memory can be classified into two types: recognition and free recall.

- **Recognition memory** occurs when the child is cued or is able to perceive an object or event that was first perceived at an earlier time. For example, showing a child a photographic lineup and having the child identify the perpetrator is a form of recognition memory.

- **Free recall memory** occurs when the child can recollect the event without the aid of cues or other assistance. This is the most complex form of memory. This type of memory is used most often in court proceedings. Questions such as "What happened on that night?" would trigger free recall.

- From a legal perspective, the most acceptable form of questioning of an abused child is using open-ended questions. An **open-ended question** does not suggest or imply an answer. Examples of open-ended questions are "Did anything happen to you?," "Were you doing anything?," and "Where was your daddy?"

- A **leading question** is one that suggests the answer to the witness. The rationale behind prohibiting leading questions is to remove the ability of the interviewer to suggest answers to the victim.

INTRODUCTION

The previous chapters have focused on specific incidents of family violence. Because children cannot speak for themselves when they are in an abusive situation, courts have determined that others must act on their behalf. This chapter explains what must occur once child abuse has been discovered.

Once students graduate from college or university and enter certain professions, there is a high probability that they will come into contact with a child who has been neglected or

Focus

Issues Learned from a Recent Child Sex Abuse Case

The child sex abuse case of Jerry Sandusky is discussed later in this chapter, but there are some key observations that are apparent in the course that need to be stressed to each individual who investigates reports of child sexual abuse. Those observations include:

- Child sexual abusers generally are not skuzzy looking strangers in trench coats. For the most part, they are individuals who have cloaked themselves with a high degree of respectability in the community.

They are coaches, teachers, priests, or other highly respectable individuals in the community.

- Child sexual abuse victims are very reluctant to report the abuse.
- Eye witnesses to such events are also reluctant to get involved.
- Institutions such as churches and schools tend to close ranks and try to take corrective action without reporting or engaging law enforcements.

abused. Every state has passed laws that mandate certain actions on the part of any professional who has reason to believe that a child is abused. Before these laws were passed, numerous children became victims of the system that was supposed to protect them.

Many states and counties in the United States have demanded that professionals who deal with abused children become more sensitive to children's special needs and requirements. In fact, all states in the United States have enacted statutes that have a specific goal of protecting abused children by mandating the reporting of suspected child abuse cases to the authorities.

NATIONAL CHILD ABUSE AND NEGLECT DATA SYSTEM (NCANDS)

To help understand the extent of child abuse, the National Child Abuse and Neglect Data System (NCANDS) was developed. The data collection system is a federally sponsored effort that collects and analyzes annual data on child abuse and neglect. The Child Abuse Prevention and Treatment Act (CAPTA) of 1988 (P.L.100-294) directed the U.S. Department of Health and Human Services to establish a national data collection and analysis program. The Children's Bureau in the Administration on Children, Youth and Families, Administration for Children and Families, U.S. Department of Health and Human Services, collects and analyzes the data.

The data are submitted voluntarily by the states, the District of Columbia, and the Commonwealth of Puerto Rico. The first report from NCANDS was based on data for 1990; this report for federal fiscal year (FFY) 2010 data is the twenty-first issuance of this annual publication.

NCANDS data are used for the Child Maltreatment report. The Child Maltreatment reports are available on the Children's Bureau Web site at www.acf.hhs.gov/programs/cb/stats_research/index.htm# or by contacting the Child Welfare Information Gateway at info@childwelfare.gov or 1–800–394–3366.

In addition, restricted use files of the NCANDS data are archived at the National Data Archive on Child Abuse and Neglect (NDACAN) at Cornell University. Researchers who are

Focus

Children Exposed to Violence May Respond Differently to Law Enforcement

Repeated exposure to traumatic events during childhood can have dramatic and long-lasting effects. Presently, we are beginning to understand the effects on children who are being repeatedly traumatized by violence. The effects include problems in the growth and development of preadolescent children, especially when such traumatized children lack a nurturing and protective parental figure that might mitigate the impact of the trauma. A recent research report by Dr. Richard G. Dudley, a medical doctor, summarized the current understanding of the effects of ongoing trauma on young children, how these effects impair adolescent and young adult functioning, and the possible implications of this for policing.

The combination of repeated childhood trauma and the absence of parental nurture, support, and protection can result in the development of multiple psychiatric and neuropsychiatric disorders. Repeated violent traumatization of children in the absence of parental protection

can permanently rewire their brains, which do not become fully developed until early adulthood. This influences the structure and the functioning of the brain so as to create symptoms that were previously thought to be purely psychological.

Understanding the effects of such childhood trauma and the behaviors that these individuals are likely to exhibit as a result has practical implications for police operations in three areas:

- First, where police deal with violence and children are victims or witnesses;
- Second, where police encounter individuals already affected by childhood trauma who exhibit behaviors often attributed to aggressiveness and callousness; and
- Third, when a suspect in police custody or under interrogation manifests behaviors symptomatic of a history of trauma, case officers need to recognize those symptoms and make appropriate referrals, as they would for any other mental disorder.

Source: Dudley, R. G., Jr. "Childhood Trauma and Its Effects: Implications for Police." NCJ 248686. *New Perspectives in Policing Bulletin* (Washington, D.C.: U.S. Department of Justice, National Institute of Justice, 2015).

interested in using these data for statistical analyses can contact NDACAN by phone at 607–255–7799, by e-mail at ndacan@cornell.edu, or on the Internet at www.ndacan.cornell.edu.

Source: NCANDS Web site, www.ndacan.cornell.edu.

REPORTING

No uniform reporting code has been adopted by all states in this area of the law. However, most states have passed legislation that contains similar characteristics that include when reporting is required, who must report, and the consequences of reporting.

Elements of Reporting Laws

State reporting laws have as their ultimate goal the protection of the child from violence or abuse within the home or family. To accomplish this, statutes require that certain classes of professionals who normally come into contact with children report cases of suspected child

Stopping child abuse should be a priority goal of law enforcement.

abuse. The theory is that a young child cannot speak for himself or herself, and therefore intervention and protection from a dangerous situation is necessary.

DEFINITION OF ABUSE. Most statutes define child abuse from a physical, neglectful, and sexual perspective. Some states include emotional abuse within this area. The professional does not need to prove that the child was actually abused. A suspicion based on the professional's education and training is sufficient to trigger the reporting mandate.

Focus

Who Reports Child Maltreatment?

For 2010, three-fifths of reports of alleged child abuse and neglect were made by professionals. The term *professional* means that the person had contact with the alleged child maltreatment victim as part of the report source's job. This term includes teachers, police officers, lawyers, and social services staff. "Other" and unknown report sources submitted 13.7 percent of reports. The remaining reports were made by nonprofessionals, including friends, neighbors, and relatives:

- The three largest percentages of report sources were from such professionals as teachers (16.4%), law enforcement and legal personnel (16.7%), and social services staff (11.5%).
- Anonymous sources (9.0%), other relatives (7.0%), parents (6.8%), and friends and neighbors (4.4%) accounted for nearly all of the nonprofessional reporters.

Source: Child Maltreatment Report (U.S. Department of Health & Human Services, Administration for Children and Families, Administration on Children, Youth and Families Children's Bureau, 2012). Available at their Web site www.acf.hhs.gov/programs/cb/stats_research/index.htm#can

PERSONS COVERED.   These statutes apply to most professionals who might have regular contact with young children. Physicians, nurses, social workers, teachers, psychologists, psychiatrists, and counselors are normally covered by these laws and are therefore required to report cases of suspected child abuse.

FILING OF THE REPORT.   The report must be made to a specific agency named in the law. Normally a social service agency or department is tasked with conducting the initial investigation of the alleged child abuse.[1] Some jurisdictions require the report to go both to a social service agency such as CPS and to the local law enforcement agency.[2] Many states have standardized forms that the professional must use in filing the report. These forms may be a combination of fill-in boxes and a narrative summary of the facts surrounding the suspected abuse.

WAIVER OF PRIVILEGE.   Many professional relationships establish a confidential relationship between the patient or client and the professional offering treatment. The reporting statutes require incidents of suspected child abuse to be reported even when this confidential relationship exists. In essence, this privilege is waived for purposes of reporting.

TIMELY INVESTIGATION.   These statutes mandate that the professional who suspects or has reason to believe child abuse has occurred or is occurring must report that information within a certain period of time from the discovery of the abuse. Once the report has been made, an investigation must be commenced within a certain period of time, normally forty-eight hours, and concluded usually no later than six months after the receipt of the report.

EMERGENCY REMOVAL.   Most of these reporting laws authorize agencies to remove the child from the custody of the parents if there is reason to believe that the child is in imminent

---

Focus

Failures in the System

When Joseph Bellamy's parents were reported for child neglect, social workers failed to follow the case. When his mother was turned in for beating Joseph two months later, one social worker figured it was a hoax. Joseph Bellamy by sixteen months old was brain damaged from a series of savage shakings.

Experts within and outside the government continue to call "to do something" about child protective services (CPS). One group of child welfare experts concluded that there were five concerns about the current operation and procedures of CPS agencies: (1) overinclusion—the involvement of families in CPS referrals that shouldn't be, (2) capacity—the number of families referred exceeds the agency's capacity to respond, (3) underinclusion—some families are not referred when they should be, (4) service orientation—an authoritative approach in some agencies does not work with some families, and (5) service delivery—many families do not receive the services they need.

Sources: Based on *President's Child Safety Partnership: Final Report* (Washington D.C., 1987); and D. J. English et al., "Alternative Responses to Child Protective Services: Emerging Issues and Concerns," *Child Abuse and Neglect* 24 (2000), p. 375.

danger. Emergency removal is usually valid for up to forty-eight hours and must normally be based on specific evidence from a professional that the child is in a dangerous situation. At the end of this time period, there must be a judicial review of the agency's actions to continue the separation of the child from his parents.

EMERGENCY TREATMENT.   Most state statutes authorize emergency medical treatment of the child to protect his or her health. Once the child's condition is stabilized, however, any further medical treatment must be authorized by the court after notice to the parents and an opportunity for them to respond to the request for treatment.

IMMUNITY.   These laws establish immunity from civil lawsuits for any professional who acted in good faith. This provision is present to encourage professionals to report without fear of facing an expensive lawsuit by the parents after the incident is concluded. This immunity is a defense to any civil action and allows the professional to move for dismissal of the lawsuit at an early stage in the proceedings.

PENALTIES.   Most statutes establish both civil and criminal penalties for failing to report suspected child abuse. Some statutes hold the professional liable for any damages or injuries that occur to the child as a result of the professional's failure to report. Most states authorize the filing of misdemeanor charges against the party who did not report. As a result, a professional may face fines or incarceration if found guilty of violating these statutes.

Reporting statutes provide a valuable tool in the fight against child abuse. They mandate that professionals who have reason to believe or suspect that a child is a victim of abuse report such information to agencies tasked with the responsibility of investigating child abuse. On occasion, a professional will have to disclose confidential information received from clients or patients in order to comply with these reporting mandates.

Confidentiality

A **confidential communication** is information that is made under circumstances in which the speaker intends that the statement be shared only with the recipient of the information.[3] This communication is protected by a privilege that prohibits the recipient from disclosing the communication to any unauthorized person. Normally, confidential communications are based on state statutes that establish certain categories of relationships that society has deemed require or need such confidentiality. Typical relationships include spouses, physician–patient, confessor–penitent, and others who are involved in a professional relationship with persons.

From early times, certain information relayed to a physician was considered confidential. The Hippocratic Oath states that whatever a physician hears or sees in the course of his or her profession shall not be disclosed and that he or she will never divulge this information, holding such things to be holy secrets. Many professions have adopted ethical standards or codes that make communication between patients or clients confidential. For example, the American Medical Association requires physicians (and psychiatrists) to safeguard patient's communications within the constraints of the law.[4]

In addition to ethical considerations, all states have adopted statutes that make certain information privileged if disclosed in a professional relationship that the law has established as

Focus

Sandusky Child Sex Abuse Scandal Raised Questions Regarding State Reporting Laws

The investigations that resulted in the 2012 trial of former Penn State University Assistant Football Coach Jerry Sandusky raised some serious questions about state sexual abuse reporting requirements. According to the investigative reports, numerous individuals at Penn State University suspected the assistant coach of child sexual abuse but failed to report their suspicions to the police.

After the case made the media, many states reviewed their reporting requirements of the statutes and expanded the mandatory reporting requirements. Presently while in some states the reporting requirements apply only to professionals like doctors and teachers, in eighteen states the mandatory reporting requirements apply to all adults.

There is a conflict of opinion among experts as to whether increasing the number of mandatory reporters will make the public more vigilant or does it merely add more work to an overloaded child welfare system? Critics of the mandatory reporting statutes claim that such laws force child welfare workers to investigate an endless flow of inconsequential complaints. It is often stated by these critics that we do not have problem with underreporting, the public already overreports.

Prior to the breaking of the news on the Sandusky case, the State of New Jersey hot line for child sexual abuse received about 400 calls a day. In the months after the case was in the media, the number of calls increased to about 750 per day. In Pennsylvania, the number of child abuse reports more than doubled after the case went public. Other states faced similar increases.

While as of July 2012, eighteen states required all adults to report suspected child sexual abuse, other states vary as to which professionals are included in the mandatory reporting requirements. The list includes teachers, school nurses, doctors, day care workers, coaches, and camp counselors.

One of the problems is that many of the state mandatory reporting statutes have no specific sanctions for those who failed to comply with the laws. And others have penalties that are rarely enforced unless the case is particularly heinous or deadly.

An interesting question that will only be decided by time is whether or not the state university will be held liable and be required to pay damages to the victims based on the failure of certain university personnel to report suspected child abuse by the assistant coach?

Source: "Sandusky Child Sex Abuse Scandal Raises Questions about State Laws," Christian Science Monitor Web site, www.csmonitor.com, accessed July 12, 2012.

being confidential. If a privileged communication has occurred, the law normally prevents the recipient from disclosing the content or substance of any information. This prohibition against disclosure includes all information obtained during the professional relationship. Many of these statutes prevent the professional from identifying the person who transmitted the information.

The person who communicates the information to the professional is the holder of the privilege and can bar disclosure or waive it as deemed necessary but cannot be forced to waive this privilege. The professional who has received the confidential information cannot, absent certain statutory exceptions, disclose this information to any other person. Most statutes authorize professionals to communicate with other professionals if necessary to treat or work with the client. For example, a medical doctor may be authorized to inform a nurse or specialist about a patient's conditions so as to provide the necessary treatment to the patient. Many states provide that professionals may or must disclose this information if they receive a duly executed court document such as a subpoena for records. Absence of such a court-sanctioned process, the information cannot be divulged to unauthorized third parties.

This privilege, however, is not absolute. Under certain circumstances, state statutes hold that the privilege or communication is not confidential and may or must be disclosed without the necessity of service of court papers. This is the case when a professional encounters a situation in which there is reason to believe or suspect that a child may be a victim of abuse. As discussed previously, certain professionals are mandated to report incidents of suspected child abuse. Although the statutes mandate reporting, this does not end the professional's duty and obligation to the child. There should be an attempt to obtain information regarding the incident, and interview the child if necessary. This process is critical; if improperly conducted, it may result in the child being returned to the abusive situation.

SEX OFFENDER COMMUNITY NOTIFICATION (MEGAN'S LAW)

A large population of prison inmates are sexual offenders.[5] Although community programs and agencies exist that specialize in treating sex offenders, few incarcerated sex offenders receive any treatment. In addition, the debate continues regarding the effectiveness of treatment for the various types of sex offenders.[6]

A series of highly publicized violent sex offenses committed on unsuspecting victims by newly released sex offenders heightened the general public's awareness of this type of offender.[7] One of the most famous cases concerned a recently released sex offender who raped and murdered seven-year-old Megan Kanka in 1994. Her family became one of the guiding forces behind the adoption of the sex offender notification law in New Jersey. The movement by victims and their families to prevent these types of offenders from committing new crimes gained momentum. As a result of these forces, by August 1995, forty-three states had adopted laws requiring offenders to register with a department or law enforcement agency. The 1994 Violent Crime Control and Law Enforcement Act may result in the enactment of registration laws by all states because failure to do so may result in loss of funding from the federal government.

By 2000, all states had adopted laws requiring notification to individuals and organizations. These so-called Megan's laws reflect a community perception that registration alone is inadequate to protect the public against these types of sexual predators. Those in favor of notification laws believe that such a process allows neighbors to take action to protect themselves from sex offenders by keeping themselves and their children out of harm's way.[8] Proponents of notification also believe that these statutes improve public safety because the community will be on alert for risky or suspicious behavior (loitering around school grounds, talking with children in the park, etc.) that might escalate to criminal acts if left unchecked.

The existing notification statutes vary in their scope and level of detail. However, four models have emerged that typify existing laws:

1. An agency is identified as determining the level of risk posed by the offender and then implements the notification plan on the basis of that level of risk. Frequently, the notification plan has three levels or requirements, depending on the offender risk:

- The first level may involve notification of only selected organizations.
- The second level adds community residents.
- The third level includes the media.

2. Some state statutes stipulate which type of offender is subject to notification and what notification methods to use. Under this model, a state agency may carry out the notification but plays no role in how notification will be implemented.
3. The offenders must do the actual notification, although they may be supervised by a criminal justice agency.
4. The burden is on the community organizations and individuals to take the initiative to request information about whether a sex offender is living in their community.

A wide variety of registration and notification procedures are in place in existing state statutes.[9] Recent data from the Bureau of Justice Statistics indicate that we have increased the number of registered sex offenders.[10] In April 1998, there were 277,000 registered sex offenders. By February 2001, that number had increased to 386,000 registered sex offenders. California had the largest number of offenders with 88,000, while Texas had the second largest number with 30,000. Twenty-two of the states indicated that DNA samples are collected and maintained as part of the registration process.

In 2006, President George W. Bush signed the Adam Walsh Child Protection Act of 2006.[11] This new law creates a national public sex offender database and implements measures that will improve the tracking of convicted sex offenders. Existing laws allowed sex offenders to slip through the system without any accountability. The wide disparity that existed among the various state laws allowed sex offenders to move to states with less control and thereby live in relative anonymity. Others simply moved and failed to register in the new state. The Adam Walsh law remedies many of the problems that existed in a state-by-state registration format. First, it provides that all sex offenders will be subject to the same registration requirements in all states. Second, it toughens penalties for failure to comply with the law. Third, it allows law enforcement officers to track sex offenders nationwide.[12]

At this time, no empirical evidence suggests that notification increases public safety or assists law enforcement agencies in their investigations of sex offenses. However, many professionals believe that notification can serve as a basis to educate the community further about sex offending and offenders. Notification must be considered as only one of a number of techniques that must be employed in our quest for a community free from the threat of sexual violence.

INTERVIEWING

Once any professional suspects that a child has been a victim of abuse, the interview process takes on an entirely different perspective. The questions asked, the environment in which the interview is conducted, and the motives of the interviewer could have a direct impact on any court intervention. All professionals must keep in mind that their actions will be reviewed and judged by others who have not had their training or expertise. This review or judgment of the professional and the interview of the child victim occurs in court and is conducted by both the prosecutor and the attorney representing the person accused of abusing the child.

Focus

Examples of Two States' Approaches to Megan's Law

	Texas	Washington
Offenders required to register	Adult and juvenile sex offenders	Adult and juvenile sex offenders
Information collected	Full name, each alias, date of birth, sex, race, height, weight, eye color, hair color, social security number (SSN), driver's license number, shoe size, home address, photograph, fingerprints, type of offense the person committed, the age of the victim, the date of conviction, and the punishment and current status	Full name, fingerprints, photograph, SSN, date of birth, type of offense the person committed, date of conviction, place of employment, and place of conviction
Time frame for registration	Within 7 days of arriving at intended residence or 7 days of changing residence or before intended move	Within 24 hours of release; immediately if not confined; 30 days after becoming a state resident; within 24 hours of moving to a new county
Verification of address	Twice-convicted offenders—every 90 days. First conviction—annually	Annually
Access to information	Registry data are public information, but the street address, SSN, phone number, driver's license number, and photo are not released. Citizens may write to local agencies for information. Preparation of a CD-ROM is under discussion.	Limited information is disseminated to the public and only in response to a written request. Based on offender's risk level, local agencies may notify the neighbors and community groups. Some agencies have Internet sites.
Percentage of compliance	89	81

Source: Information obtained and based on KlassKids Foundation, www.classkids.org-legmeg.htm, accessed August 27, 2000.

The Interview Process

During the 1970s and 1980s, a common defense tactic was to attack the child's credibility by inferring or stating that the child was lying about the incidents. When dealing with children under the age of seven, these attacks centered on the child's inability to remember specific facts, distinguish between truth and falsehoods, and the intermingling of fact and fantasy in the child's mind. Older children were accused of being spiteful and seeking revenge for real or imagined discipline by the parents. Soon, however, defense attorneys began to realize that jurors and judges were capable of evaluating the truthfulness of children, and for the most

Focus

Possible Murder Charges?

In 1995, John Choate spent nine months in jail for assaulting his three-month-old son. After the assault, the severely brain-damaged boy spent twenty-one years in hospital beds before he died in October 2014 as a ward of the State of Missouri.

In May 1993, the parents brought the infant to the emergency room of the hospital for unexplained seizures and vomiting. On examination, it was discovered that the infant had broken ribs, a broken leg, and severe brain injuries.

At the trial in 1995, the doctors testified that the infant's injuries did not match the explanation his parents had provided for the injuries. At trial, the mother refused to answer questions about her son's injuries. She was not charged with a crime. The father was charged with first-degree assault. The father entered a plea of guilty to second-degree assault. He did not admit guilt but acknowledged that prosecutors had enough evidence to convict him. He served nine months of his three-year sentence and was paroled in September 1995.

According to the *St. Louis Post Dispatch*, the boy received few, if any, visits from relatives over the years. When he died in 2014, the medical examiner ruled his death a homicide stemming from the assault when he was three months old. After his death, the police reopened the investigation and sought new charges against the father in 2015. The St. Louis County Prosecutor, however, concluded that most of the evidence in the original case has been destroyed and that the boy's parents had denied hurting the infant.

Should the parents be liable for the death of their son twenty-one years after the alleged assault?

In a similar case in Missouri in 2011, a babysitter was charged with manslaughter after the delayed death of a teenage girl who was violently shaken as an infant by the babysitter in 1994. The babysitter was sentenced to fourteen years on the manslaughter charge.

Source: J. Currier "No new charges against man in son's death," *St. Louis Post Dispatch* (July 29, 2015), p. 1.

part there were very few cases in which children engaged in lying regarding incidents of physical or sexual abuse. As a result of this almost universal acceptance of the credibility and lack of bias on the part of children, the defense establishment moved from attacking the child directly to attacking those who interact with the victim before trial.

Today, one of the most commonly raised issues in child abuse cases is the validity of out-of-court interviews with the victim. Charges are levied against professionals that suggestions or memories have been planted in impressionable young minds. The interviewer is accused of being biased and unprofessional. Defense attorneys will further claim that the interviewer has brainwashed or tainted the recollection of the child, and therefore that the victim's testimony should be considered untrustworthy.[13]

The fact that defense attorneys and others may second-guess an interviewer's professionalism should not deter those charged with safeguarding victims of abuse from carrying out their duties. However, all professionals must be aware of the possibility of these accusations being levied against them and conduct the interview in an unbiased manner. Interviews with victims of abuse should not be dreaded; rather, they must be approached with the understanding that the ultimate goal is safeguarding the child.

As any professional knows, children are not small adults. They have different perceptions, abilities, and needs than adults. Understanding how children react to events is critical in conducting a valid interview.

One of the most important aspects of interviewing child abuse victims is their ability to recall the incident or incidents. Scholars and professionals generally accept that children have the ability to recall events and relate details concerning those events.[14] Although there is some debate whether stressful events promote or impair memory, most authorities agree that the child will remember the substance of the event, if not all the details.[15]

Children's memory can be classified into two types: recognition and free recall. **Recognition memory** occurs when the child is cued or is able to perceive an object or event that was first perceived at an earlier time. For example, showing a child a photographic lineup and having the child identify the perpetrator is a form of recognition memory.[16] **Free recall memory** occurs when the child can recollect the event without the aid of cues or other assistance. This is the most complex form of memory.[17] This type of memory is used most often in court proceedings. As discussed in more detail later in this section, questions such as "What happened on this night?" would trigger free recall. These types of questions do not prompt or cue the witness.

Researchers have determined that when children are asked questions that prompt free recall memory, they relate fewer details than adults.[18] Although the information they do remember is as accurate as that from adults, it is not as detailed.[19] And even though children may be as accurate as adults in recalling recent events, their memories fade faster on points of detail than those of adults. This is especially the case with very young children.[20]

Most interviews are not conducted in a random manner. There is usually a reason for talking with the child. It may be part of a normal medical interview, a discussion at school regarding why the child is acting in a certain manner, or in response to a request for assistance from the child. Professionals conducting interviews should have as much information as possible prior to the interview.[21]

Simply having this information does not prejudice the interviewer. In fact, an argument can be made that, armed with this information, the person conducting the interview is able to ask questions in such a manner as to avoid making suggestions or improperly influencing the child. The type of questions asked of child abuse victims is a critical aspect of the interview.

Depending on the dynamics of the interview, the professional may attempt to gain information from the victim in a variety of ways. This may require that questions be posed in different forms, and there are several types of questions that may be used in any interview of an abused child. These questions range from open-ended to coercive.

From a legal perspective, the most acceptable form of questioning of an abused child is using open-ended questions. An **open-ended question** does not suggest or imply an answer. Examples of open-ended questions are "Did anything happen to you?," "Were you doing anything?," and "Where was your daddy?"

After receiving certain information from the victim, the interviewer will need to obtain more specific facts. Often focused questions are used when this need arises. A **focused question** narrows the scope of inquiry and requires the witness to answer within certain parameters. Examples of focused questions are (after establishing that the father entered the child's bedroom) "When your daddy walked into the room, what did he do?," (after the child states that he was hurt at a particular time) "On the morning you were hurt, where was your mother?," and (when the child has indicated that the father touched her genitals) "Did your daddy say anything before he touched you?"

A **leading question** is one that suggests the answer to the witness.[22] It is a question that includes the desired reply within it, or it may be a statement posed to the witness under the guise of being a question. The rationale behind prohibiting leading questions is to remove the ability of the interviewer to suggest answers to the victim. Examples of leading questions are "Your daddy touched your private parts, didn't he?," "Did your mother hit you every day when she drank?," and "Is it true that you saw your brother being hit by your mother?"

The final form of questioning involves the use of coercive questions. *Coercive questions* promise rewards or threaten punishment for certain answers. Coercive questions should never be used when interviewing children. They are normally employed in court with a hostile witness. An example of coercive questions is "Are you aware that telling a lie is considered perjury and subjects you to criminal sanctions?"

Once a professional interviews the child, the process has just begun. There will be other interviews and other persons who interact with the child along the way, but one of the most critical interviews is that conducted by the prosecuting attorney. This final prefiling interview will determine whether the prosecutor believes there is sufficient evidence to go forward with the case. This interview is conducted in the same manner as other interviews, and its goal is to allow the prosecutor to determine the competency and credibility of the victim and how the judge or jury will react to the child's testimony.

As the previous discussion illustrates, different types of questions may be used when interviewing child abuse victims. No clear-cut rule exists as to when an open-ended question is more appropriate than a focused question. This will depend on the dynamics of the interview, the age of the child, the trauma of the incident, and the experience of the interviewer. What is clear is that all interviewers must guard against influencing or suggesting certain answers or stories to the child. They must be prepared to explain why they chose certain questions over others and what their purpose or intent was when they used those questions.

Evidentiary Issues

Knowledge of the rules of evidence and what courts consider important will assist the professional in conducting these interviews. Although this is not intended as a law school textbook, certain legal and procedural aspects of questioning witnesses and using their responses should be discussed.

HEARSAY.   Hearsay is one of the simplest and most complex subjects in the area of evidence. Numerous textbooks, articles, and treatises have been written about it, dealing with the nuances and exceptions to the hearsay rule.[23] Simply stated, **hearsay** is any out-of-court statement that is offered in court for the truth of the matter stated. This definition can be broken down further into three distinct areas:

1. Any out-of-court statement
2. Offered in court
3. For the truth of the matter stated.

ANY OUT-OF-COURT STATEMENT.   These may be statements made by the victim or the suspect. For example, the child may have told a nurse in a hospital emergency room,

"My daddy hurt me." When the nurse attempts to repeat or testify to the statement in court, she is stating something that occurred outside the presence of the judge and jury. Thus, any statement that is made outside the courtroom agrees with this element of the hearsay rule.

OFFERED IN COURT.   The second element of the hearsay rule requires that the out-of-court statement be offered as testimony or evidence in a court proceeding. In the previous example, if the nurse were to repeat the statement to a police officer who responded to the call for assistance at the emergency room, simply telling the officer what the child said would not be hearsay because the repeating of the statement did not occur in court.

FOR THE TRUTH OF THE MATTER STATED.   The statement when offered in court must be offered as true. In other words, it is not offered for any other reason than to show that the child stated, "My daddy hurt me." If it is offered for any other reason, the final element of the hearsay rule has not been satisfied. This might be the situation in which the statement is offered to show that the officer had probable cause to arrest the suspect and not to show that the child was in fact molested or abused.

For a statement to be objectionable on hearsay grounds, all three of these elements must be present. Courts have traditionally been reluctant to admit out-of-court statements because they lacked reliability, and many times offering such a statement in court denied the

---

Focus

Interviewing Children

Excerpts from
People v. Michael Luis Grant
2012 WL 1437453 (Cal.App. 6 Dist. 2012)

Dr. Abbott testified that open-ended questions are better for eliciting information from children. Research shows that "yes" or "no" questions tend to lead to more errors with respect to the information that is provided because children tend to simply answer "yes" or "no" rather than providing more detailed information. Moreover, to the extent the "yes" or "no" question contains false information, "it increases the probability of a child assenting to false or misleading information that may be contained in the question." In addition, children are generally more susceptible to coaching or leading questions coming from adults than from other children. Even if the information conflicts with the child's recollection of the event, the child will "often acquiesce to what the adult says because [children] put so much trust in what adults think and what adults say." The child may then incorporate that false or misleading information into the child's memory of the events. Repeating the same question to a child also raises an issue. "Typically when children are asked the same question more than once in an interview, there is a tendency for them to interpret the repeat question as their answer being wrong to the earlier question." Thus the information provided by the child to the repeat question may be inaccurate. False information may also be provided by a child due to "negative stereotyping." If the interviewer or another person related to the child provides negative information about the suspect, "children will often elaborate on their recall of the event with false information consistent with the negative stereotype that's being presented about the suspect."

defendant the opportunity to confront and cross-examine the person who made the statement. In addition, because these statements were not made under oath, there was a judicial inclination not to accept them as trustworthy.

Some commentators argue that the hearsay rule has been consumed by the number of exceptions written into statutes by legislatures. These exceptions allow certain types of out-of-court statements to be admitted as truthful. The major exceptions to the hearsay rule that are of interest to professionals dealing with family violence are the following:

1. Excited utterance
2. Admissions
3. Declarations against interest
4. State of mind
5. Statements made to medical professionals
6. Statements made by victims of abuse.

EXCITED UTTERANCE.   Excited utterances are also known as spontaneous declarations. An **excited utterance** is a statement made whenever a person is excited or under stress as a result of a traumatic event. Many of us have hit our hand with a hammer and without any conscious effort uttered a curse word or two. These curse words were not planned or thought out; they just happened as a result of the pain we suffered when the hammer struck our hand. The theory behind admitting such statements is that the person making the statement has had no opportunity to fabricate a false story. Suspects or the victims of child abuse may make these same types of statements. For a statement to be classified as an excited utterance, it must meet the following criteria: There must have been some events startling enough to produce this excitement and render the statement spontaneous and unreflecting, the utterance must have been made before there was an opportunity to contrive and misrepresent any feelings, and the utterance must relate to the circumstances of the occurrence preceding it.[24]

ADMISSIONS.   An **admission** is a statement or conduct of a party in the action that is offered against him in the trial. The theory behind admitting such evidence is that the party who made the statement is present in court and can testify and explain the comments or action. An admission may occur as a result of a person's actions. For example, a classic form of admission is flight from the scene of the crime. This flight shows a "consciousness of guilt" and can be introduced during trial to indicate that the party who fled had something to hide or was trying to get away and avoid apprehension.[25]

DECLARATIONS AGAINST INTEREST.   Declarations against interest are very similar to admissions except they are not made by a party to the action. A **declaration against interest** is a statement by a nonparty that is against his or her own interest. The theory behind admitting such statements is that a person will normally not speak against his or her own interest unless it is true. For the statement to be admitted, several conditions must be satisfied: The declarant, or person making the statement, must not be available as a witness, and the statement must be against the person's pecuniary or proprietary interest or subject him or her to civil or criminal liability as a result of the statement.

For the unavailability requirement to be met, the person making the statement must be insane, dead, or absent from the jurisdiction of the court. The declaration must be against the declarant's financial, property, civil, or criminal interests and of such a nature that a reasonable person would not have made the statement unless he or she believed it to be true.

STATE OF MIND.   A **state-of-mind** statement relates a fact regarding the declarant's mental or emotional condition. The theory behind admitting these statements is that a person would not normally tell a falsehood about his or her state of mind. This area is one of the most complex areas in the exceptions to the hearsay rule. For these types of statements to be admissible as an exception to the hearsay rule, they must be offered to prove the declarant's state of mind at the time when it was an issue in the action or when the statement is offered to prove or explain the conduct of the declarant. For example, a person's statement to a friend, "When I get home, I'm going to beat her blue for breaking that dish," would be admitted to show the declarant's state of mind or explain his subsequent behavior if he did batter his child. Some jurisdictions allow statements that pertain to previously existing as well as present states of mind to be admitted into evidence.

STATEMENTS MADE TO MEDICAL PROFESSIONALS.   Closely related to the state-of-mind exception are the statements made to medical professionals. The theory behind this exception is that spontaneous statements describing present pain or other physical conditions are likely to be true. A **statement made to medical professionals** is information given for purposes of diagnosis or treatment of a medical condition. The Federal Rules of Evidence allow statements made to medical professionals to be admitted as an exception to the hearsay rule when they are made for purposes of medical diagnosis or treatment and describe medical history, past or present symptoms, pain or sensations, or the general character of the medical problem.[26]

STATEMENTS MADE BY VICTIMS OF ABUSE.   Some jurisdictions have amended their evidence code statutes to provide specifically for an exception to the hearsay rule for statements made by victims of abuse. The U.S. Supreme Court upheld the concept underlying this exception to the hearsay rule in *Idaho v. Wright* when it stated that judges could consider the totality of the circumstances surrounding the making of the statement to determine whether it was reliable and therefore admissible under this type of exception.[27]

The previous discussion has briefly examined the hearsay rule and some of its more common exceptions. Professionals need to be familiar with these technical rules to understand the importance of information received from victims of child abuse. Clearly documenting the circumstances surrounding statements made to the professional may provide the necessary factual information that will allow these statements to be admitted as evidence in court proceedings.

COMPETENCY.   Another aspect of the legal system professionals must understand deals with the concept of competency. For a witness to testify in a court of law, a determination must be made that the witness is competent. In most cases, the judge will make an initial ruling and allow the jury to give whatever weight it desires to that witness's testimony. **Competency** is

Focus

The Prosecution's Interview

The following are guidelines followed by prosecutors when interviewing children who have been sexually abused.

1. Be yourself.
2. Introduce yourself, tell the child your name, and ask the child his name and whether he has a nickname.
3. Demonstrate a genuine interest in the child by inquiring about the child's interests, family and friends, school, pets, and so on.
4. Find out whether the child knows why she is there to see you. Explain who you are and what you do in simple terms. Let her know you have talked to other children who have had similar things happened to them.
5. Find out from the child what he thinks should happen to the suspect. Does the child love or hate the suspect? The child's feelings toward the suspect will enable you to better assess the case.
6. Determine the child's capacity for understanding "telling the truth."

    a. "Do you know the difference between right and wrong?"
    b. "Do you know what it is to tell a lie?"
    c. "If I said it was Christmas today, would that be a truth or a lie?"
    d. "What happens when you lie?"
    e. "Do you promise to tell me only things that really happened?"

7. Use open-ended questions. Do not lead the child. Never confront the child. Instead, ask the child to explain her statement in more detail. Let the interview flow on the child's level.

    a. Can you tell me what happened?"
    b. "Have you ever been touched in a way that made you feel funny or uncomfortable?"
    c. "What kind of touching was it?"
    d. "Who touched you?"
    e. "How/when did it start?"

    f. "What happened next?"
    g. "What did he/she touch you with?"
    h. "Where did he/she touch you?"
    i. "How were you feeling?"
    j. "What did he/she say?"
    k. "Who was the first person you told?"

8. Do not use accusatory questions when interviewing the child.

    a. "Why didn't you tell someone right away?"
    b. "Why did you let this go on?"
    c. "You should have told Mommy. Tell me why you didn't. Don't you trust her?"

9. Remember that children can be very literal and think in concrete terms.
10. If you sense that the child is fearful, confront her fears.
11. Remember that abused children are guilt ridden and feel that they are somehow responsible for what had happened to them. Relieve the guilt of the child. Tell the child that he did nothing wrong and won't get in trouble for telling. Tell them that it is not your job or their job to punish the defendant; that is the job of the judge.
12. Let the child draw pictures or play with dolls. (See the discussion of the use of anatomical dolls later in this chapter.) Some children find it easier to answer more difficult questions when it appears that they are occupied with other things.
13. Show the child the courtroom. Introduce him to the staff. Let him go up to the witness stand and play with the microphone if he wishes. Make him comfortable in this environment.
14. End the interview by thanking the child for helping you understand what had happened. Do not mislead the child about the judicial process.

Source: Based on Susan Etezadi, "Interviewing and Preparing the Child Witness for Court," *Introduction to Sexual Assault Prosecution* (California District Attorneys Association, Sacramento, 1991).

the ability of the witness to testify accurately to events. This requirement involves two distinct elements: Does the witness understand the nature of the proceedings, and can the witness accurately relate what transpired? Both these elements must be satisfied before a witness is considered competent. For adult victims or witnesses, these requirements are simple to meet: They understand that they are testifying under oath in a criminal proceeding, and they can describe what they saw or did not see.

The issue of competency is much more complex when dealing with children. The child must understand that he or she is swearing or affirming to tell the truth, and the child must be able to testify accurately as to the events in question.

The first element requires that the child understand that he or she must tell the truth. Depending on the age of the child, the concept of truthfulness becomes a critical issue in determining competency to testify. Many authorities have studied the ability of children to distinguish between truth and falsehood and have concluded that children under the age of seven are unlikely to be successful in telling a lie. However, by the time they reach fourth or fifth grade, they can tell lies.[28] Other scholars have concluded that although children and adults both engage in lying, no evidence supports the assumption that children lie more than adults.[29]

The second element requires that a child accurately testify as to what occurred. This requirement not only raises issues of memory but also issues of fact versus fantasy. The world of make-believe and the fantasy play that all children engage in as they mature are normal functions of growing up. A common defense ploy is to argue that the child is testifying about an imaginary event. A tactic that many defense attorneys employ in sexual abuse cases is to say that the child is not bad or evil but cannot distinguish fact from normal childhood fantasy. Numerous scholars, however, have established that children can tell the difference between imaginary and real-life events.[30]

Closely related to the concept of competency is the issue that someone may have implanted memories in the child's mind. As was discussed earlier in this chapter, this is a favored defense tactic. If defense attorneys can convince the judge or jury that the treating professional or another party, such as a parent, has manipulated the child's memory and planted false memories in the child's mind, those accused of molesting or abusing the child may walk away free. Therefore, the manner and type of questions asked of child victims are important and should be framed to solicit what the child recalls, not what the professional expects the child to remember.

INTERVIEW TECHNIQUES.   A number of different techniques are used in interviewing children who have been victims of abuse. Two of the most well-known methods involve anatomical dolls and videotaping the interview. The use of anatomical dolls during the interview process is one of the most highly debated techniques.

Anatomical Dolls.   Anatomical dolls are used by CPS, law enforcement officers, and therapists during interviews with children who may have been victims of abuse.[31] These dolls assist professionals in a number of ways:

1. Dolls allow the child to explain what had occurred by referring to the doll rather than themselves. By using the doll, the child does not have to identify his or her

genital area but can instead point to the doll's genitals. This allows the interview to be less stressful from the child's perspective.

2. The child's interaction with the doll may provide clues for the interviewer as to what occurred during the molestation and therefore allow the professional to focus the questions that are asked of the child.

3. Anatomical dolls allow the child to communicate by using toy-like objects that he or she is familiar with. This facilitates the communication process by placing the child in a familiar environment with familiar toys.

The use of anatomical dolls during the interview process has been both condemned and endorsed. Defense attorneys argue that the use of these dolls is suggestive and may lead the child to make untrue statements or act out in their play in sexually explicit ways. Researchers believe that there is no evidence to support this contention and that exposure to these dolls does not cause the child to fantasize or engage in sexual play.[32]

The use of anatomical dolls during the interview process should be documented as to reasons the dolls were used, a clear description or picture of the dolls, and a detailed narrative summary of what the child did with the dolls. Although subject to criticism, the use of anatomical dolls may allow the interviewer to obtain information from a victim that might not otherwise be available. Perhaps the best use of dolls during the interview process is as an aid in allowing the child to communicate. If they are used in this manner, defense charges of fantasy or sexual play may be discounted.

Videotape. The second interview technique involves videotaping the child's statements for future use in the courtroom. Similar to the use of anatomical dolls, this method of interviewing has both its supporters and critics. Supporters of video interviewing claim that it preserves evidence and rebuts charges of programming. Critics of videotaping claim that the process itself is subject to manipulation.

The use of videotaping varies from jurisdiction to jurisdiction. Some agencies require all sexual abuse cases to be videotaped, whereas others do not engage in this practice at all.

Videotaping child abuse victims has both advantages and disadvantages. The advantages include reducing the number of times a child has to repeat his or her story to different people within the criminal justice system. A videotape can be played for different parties without requiring the child to go through the trauma of telling the story over and over again. A second advantage is that it allows for an assessment of the child's credibility by a number of people at one time as they view the videotape. Third, the tape can be replayed and critical statements be reviewed and evaluated without having the child repeat portions of the story numerous times. Fourth, videotaping preserves the interaction between the interviewer and the child so that the defense cannot raise the issue of programming or leading the child to a certain result or statement. Fifth, interviews can be scheduled to accommodate the child witness and be viewed later by prosecutors or other parties who may be involved in the decision-making process. Finally, interviewers can watch other videotapes and engage in peer reviews of techniques, thereby improving their own abilities to interview future victims of child abuse.

Significant disadvantages exist as well in videotaping interviews, however. First and most important, children seldom recount all the details of a molestation during a single interview. Therefore, if one interview is taped, all subsequent interviews must be taped. This

Focus

Recovered Repressed Memories

One of the more controversial issues facing professionals in the field today is recovered repressed memories. This condition is known by a variety of names, including *repressed memory, delayed recall memory*, and *false memory syndrome*. It has resulted in families suing each other; claims of sexual abuse surfacing years, even decades, after the incidents; and lawsuits against therapists who treated survivors of abuse.

In a relatively short period of time since the 1992 founding of the False Memory Syndrome Foundation (FMSF), claims and counterclaims regarding the accuracy of recovered memory have reached new heights. A valid concern exists regarding the validity of recovered repressed memories and the damage that can result when false accusations of abuse are levied against someone.

To interpret some of the dynamics in this area, it is important to understand that long-term memory, rather than being a reliable tape recording, is a reconstruction that is subject to distortions based on later experience and influence. It has also been established that the accuracy of the memories cannot be established by the confidence of the subject in the reality of the memory. Otherwise, we would have to accept the reality of abduction and abuse of humans by aliens in UFOs—a claim that has never been proven.* However, we can also accept the fact that in certain situations memory blockage does in fact occur. This process is better described as a continuum where people experience varying degrees of access to different parts of memory at different points of time. There are documented situations in which, because of a harrowing event, a person suffers trauma-induced amnesia. In certain combat situations, veterans suffered battle-induced amnesia that was later recovered during therapy.

A number of court cases have dealt with repressed memories that have been reported in the national media. These have ranged from reports of daughters witnessing the killing of playmates by their father to cases of long-term sexual molestation by family members. In addition, courts have allowed those who have been accused of these incidents to sue the therapists.

A variety of claims have been made against the validity of recovered memories, including Holmes, who believes that there is a complete lack of research support for the concept of repression. On the other hand, widespread support exists for the theory of repressed memories by other scholars. For example, Briere and Conti, in a study of 450 adult victims of child sexual abuse, found that 59 percent of these survivors had at some point prior to their eighteenth birthdays been unable to recall the abuse.

In summary, there is some evidence that may support the existence of the repressed and false memories. At this time, no consensus exists among scholars and researchers regarding the prevalence of either type of memory. This will continue to be a controversy in the field, and professionals who work with victims of family violence must understand both sides of this debate.

Sources: Based on K. S. Pope, "Memory, Abuse, and Science, Questioning Claims about the False Memory Syndrome Epidemic," *American Psychologist* 51 (September 1996), p. 957; A. D. Reisner, "Repressed Memories: True or False?" *The Psychological Record* 46 (1996), p. 563; C. G. Bowman and E. Mertz, "A Dangerous Direction: Legal Intervention in Sexual Abuse Survivor Therapy," *Harvard Law Review* 109 (1996), p. 551; C. Fisher, "Amnestic States in War Neurosis: The Psychogenesis of Fugues," *The Psychoanalytic Quarterly* 14 (1945), p. 437. See, for example, *Sullivan v. Cheshler*, 846 F. Supp. 654 (N.D. III. 1994); D. S. Holmes, "The Evidence for Repression: An Examination of Sixty Years of Research," in J. L. Singer, ed., *Repression and Dissociation* (University of Chicago Press, Chicago, 1992), p. 85; and J. Briere and J. Conti, "Self-Reported Amnesia for Abuse in Adults Molested as Children," *Journal of Traumatic Stress* 6 (1993), p. 21.

*A claim of abduction by aliens might be considered evidence of a psychotic disorder that is based on delusions rather than a repressed memory, depending on whether you believe in the existence of aliens.

may allow the defense to argue that the child was programmed off camera and that subsequent interviews are invalid because the child was simply repeating what he or she had been instructed to repeat. A second disadvantage is the cost of the video machine and equipment. Even with modestly inexpensive palm-sized recorders, the equipment is too expensive for many financially burdened agencies. Moreover, not only must the equipment be purchased, but someone must be trained to operate it, and the film must be cataloged and stored for future use. Third, videotaping interviews takes some of the feeling of the interview away from the people who must assess the credibility of the child. In essence, they are watching a movie instead of evaluating a live victim. Finally, if the first recorded interview results in a denial of abuse by the child, it must be preserved and turned over to the defense. The initial interview will then be used in any subsequent court proceeding as proof that the child is being untruthful.

Another critical aspect of the use of video cameras and recording equipment concerns the use of closed-circuit cameras during criminal proceedings. The U.S. Constitution has been interpreted to require that a defendant has a right to confront and cross-examine all witnesses against him or her. However, this right is not absolute. As the discussion of hearsay indicated, in some instances statements of another person may be admitted against the defendant even though he or she does not have the opportunity to cross-examine the person making those statements. The Supreme Court addressed the issue of closed-circuit television in child abuse cases in *Maryland v. Craig*.[33]

In October 1986, a Howard County grand jury charged Sandra Ann Craig with a number of child abuse offenses. The victim, Brooke, was a six-year-old girl who from August 1984 to June 1986 attended a kindergarten and prekindergarten center owned and operated by Craig. In March 1987, before the case went to trial, the state sought to invoke a Maryland statute that allowed the judge and jury to view the victim via closed-circuit television. The victim was to be located in a separate room outside the presence of the defendant. Although the defendant and her attorney could view the television and ask questions, they would not be allowed to confront the victim physically.

In support of its motion, the state presented expert testimony that Brooke, as well as a number of other children who were allegedly abused, would suffer serious emotional distress such that they could not reasonably communicate if required to testify in the courtroom and face the defendant. Another expert testified that Brooke would probably stop talking and would withdraw and curl up into a ball if she were in the same room with the defendant. The trial court ruled that because of the possible distress that the victim would suffer in seeing the suspect, the closed-circuit television would be authorized.

In upholding such a procedure, the Supreme Court held that a strict reading of the confrontation clause would do away with every hearsay exception and that this was too extreme a result. Therefore, the court held that the confrontation clause reflects a preference for face-to-face confrontations at trial, but that the preference must occasionally give way to considerations of public policy and the necessities of the case. Thus, the holding in *Maryland v. Craig* allows the use of closed-circuit television under certain circumstances in child abuse cases. Specifically, there must be a state statute that authorizes such a procedure, and the state must establish that the child is unable to face his or her molester in person.

Interviewing child victims is a critical aspect of any professional involved in this area of family violence. It must be conducted in a fair and unbiased manner with regard to the

Focus

The Emotional Effects of Testifying on Sexually Abused Children

Child sexual abuse presents complicated issues of physical, emotional, and psychological trauma for its victims. This is especially true for child victims who are thrust into a process with adult rules and values. These victims are required to testify about intimate details that are embarrassing to them.

The National Institute of Justice (NIJ) and the Office of Juvenile Justice and Delinquency Prevention (OJJDP) awarded three grants to examine the emotional effects of the court process on sexually abused children. These studies occurred in North Carolina and Denver and as part of the Child Victim as Witness Research and Development Program (see the table). This research resulted in a variety of findings, points of similarity, and conclusions that are of interest to those who work with victims of child sexual abuse.

The three studies appear to agree with three basic conclusions: (1) That at the initial testing, prior to their involvement in the court process, children score high on measures of stress and anxiety; (2) that most children tend to improve with time, regardless of their experience in court; and (3) that maternal support is associated with improvements in these children's mental health. Perhaps the most compelling difference among these studies is the context of the children's testimony. The children in North Carolina testified in CPS proceedings in a juvenile court setting, whereas the other studies occurred in a criminal court environment. The experience of testifying in a juvenile court proceeding is vastly different from the experience of testifying in criminal court. These findings indicate that we need to examine

	State of North Carolina	Denver, Colorado	Child Victim Witness Research and Development Program
Number of children examined	62–100	218	256
Ages	6–17	4–17	4–17
Characteristics of cases	Victims of intrafamilial abuse	Victims primarily of extrafamilial abuse	Victims primarily of extrafamilial abuse
Nature of proceedings	CPS hearing in juvenile court	Criminal court prosecutions	Criminal court prosecutions
Number of mental health assessments	After case accepted by CPS 5 months later	After case accepted for prosecution 3 months after testifying	After case referred for prosecution 7–9 months later
	18 months later	7 months after testifying After case disposition	

Source: Based on D. Whitecomb et al., "The Emotional Effects of Testifying on Sexually Abused Children," *Research in Brief* (National Institute of Justice, Washington, D.C., April 1994). One hundred completed the first interview, seventy-six completed the second interview, and sixty-two completed the third interview.

(continued)

courtroom procedures and, consistent with constitutional requirements, relax rules of evidence and procedure in criminal cases. In addition, the number of hearings in which the child is required to testify should be limited.

On the basis of these studies, it cannot be stated with any certainty that testifying is either harmful or beneficial to sexually abused children. One consistent and encouraging finding is that all children improved emotionally regardless of their experience in court. At worst, testifying may impede the improvement process for some children. Even if current research does not reveal substantial long-term negative effects on child witnesses in the criminal justice system, professionals must continue to be sensitive and supportive of these vulnerable victims.

The stop child abuse sign signifies that we need to take strong actions to prevent child abuse.

child's best interests. Many times, the initial interview forms the basis for intervention into the family's privacy.

INTERVENTION

The goal of intervention is to protect the child from abuse. The child's safety and health must be the overriding issue in any decision to intervene. The child's future safety and well-being

Focus

Child Sexual Abuse Accommodation Syndrome (CSAAS)

Excerpts from *People v. Michael Luis Grant*
2012 WL 1437453 (Cal.App. 6 Dist. 2012)

At trial, R. testified that she loves defendant and wants to continue being married to him. R. testified that she had lied to the police and that she also told her daughter M. and her sister I. to lie to the police. R. testified that she was angry and upset after learning that defendant was seeing Lisa Duncan, and expressed her feelings to M. while I. was present. R. wanted defendant to "get in trouble" and wanted him "away from Lisa." She testified that she "made" the girls "believe that it happened." According to R., defendant would wrestle and tickle the girls and nothing improper occurred. However, she told the girls that defendant was doing "nasty things" to them and putting his "'private part. . . on your private part.'" She further told I. to tell their mother.

R. testified that she later felt "bad" about "making the girls believe that [defendant] molested them" when she heard "something about" defendant facing a 25-year-to-life sentence. The first time that R. disclosed that she had influenced the girls was during the meeting in defense counsel's office. She was scared of her mother learning that she had put the girls up to this.

R. testified that she talked to defendant frequently while he was in jail. It was common for him to call her two to four times a day, and they would talk for the entire time allowed. R. paid for all of defendant's calls to her. At trial, she admitted that she lied on jail visitation logs by writing down the name of defendant's cellmate when in fact she was visiting defendant.

R.'s cousin testified that she talked "quite a bit" with R. and that, after defendant was arrested, she talked to R. almost every day. R. initially told her cousin that she believed the girls. R. also told her cousin about an incident involving defendant. R. had left the two girls with defendant at a condominium. When R. returned, she walked into a room and saw defendant behind I., who was bent over. When defendant saw R. walk into the room, he "jumped off I. and adjusted his penis."

Carl Lewis, a private investigator and retired police officer, testified as an expert on CSAAS. Lewis did not know defendant or the specific charges in the case, and had not been told about the specific facts of the case. Lewis testified about the five categories of CSAAS: secrecy, helplessness, entrapment and accommodation, delayed conflicted unconvincing disclosure, and retraction. Lewis cautioned that the categories are not present in every case of abuse, and that CSAAS is not a tool for discerning whether a child is telling the truth about being abused. He explained that CSAAS is "background information" and is "intended to dispel some commonly held myths about child sexual abuse as an occurrence and child sexual abuse victims in particular."

Jenny August Adler, volunteer and counseling coordinator at the YWCA of Silicon Valley Rape Crisis Center, testified as an expert in "coping behaviors of victims and intimate partner and family battering and its effects." She did not read any reports or listen to any tapes in defendant's case, and she did not know anything about the facts of the case.

Adler explained that there is a "cycle of violence" in a "domestic abuse relationship." The relationship starts with a "hearts and flowers" stage where both parties put their best foot forward. Tension builds in the relationship, leading to an explosion and the display of some type of violence. The abuser will often apologize and make promises, leading to the hearts and flowers stage again.

In domestic abuse relationships, one partner continuously has more power and control in all the different areas of the relationship, whereas in most relationships, the partners have

(continued)

power and control in different areas, such as finances and the social calendar, but ultimately there is equality. Power and control may be taken away from a partner in different ways, including through physical or verbal abuse. This power dynamic may occur in a dating relationship and may occur between family members.

Jealousy is part of many domestic abuse relationships and may be used as an excuse to monitor or isolate the victim from others. The victim may also be jealous of the abuser, "because of insecurity created by the power and control difference." Victims often have very low self esteem because of the abuse, and "frequently they feel like they aren't worth anything unless they are with the abuser."

It is very common for domestic violence victims who report violence within the family to later deny it, downplay it, or lie for the abuser. Statistics reflect that a victim leaves an abusive relationship seven times before the victim is able to really disconnect from that relationship. In the cycle of abuse, when the victim is reconciling with the abuser, very often they're going back into that hearts and flowers stage and the victim does not want to look at the abuse that the victim previously experienced. There may also be a lack of support for the victim and the charges of abuse when those in the victim's social circle know the abuser but are unaware of the abuser's negative side or controlling side.

In a domestic violence relationship, coping strategies include "learned helplessness," which refers to a person who has experienced ongoing abuse, is unsuccessful in getting away from the abuse, and stops trying to get away.

At trial, Lewis testified about the five categories of CSAAS. First, secrecy "describes the fact that sexual abuse of a child occurs almost exclusively when the offender is alone or somehow isolated with the child." Second, helplessness describes a child's feelings as the child is unable to stop the abuse by an adult. Third, entrapment and accommodation refers to a child "trapped by the circumstances of sexual abuse but accommodat[ing] that circumstance by a variety of means," such as acting as if nothing is wrong or engaging in antisocial behavior. Fourth, delayed conflicted unconvincing disclosure describes the fact that there is usually a delay between the time the child suffers the abuse and when it is disclosed, the child experiences internal conflict in determining whether to disclose, and the disclosure is "usually done at a time or in a manner that makes the child seem unconvincing," such as when the child is being punished. Fifth, retraction may occur as the disclosure results in a "great deal of chaos and attention" to the child and the family, such as by child protective services, law enforcement, the criminal justice system, and the medical field, and the child feels "very uncomfortable" from all the attention.

As we explained, the trial judge instructs the jury that an expert's testimony about CSAAS "is not evidence that the defendant committed any of the crimes charged against him," and that the jury "may consider this evidence only in deciding whether or not the victim's conduct was not inconsistent with the conduct of someone who has been molested, and in evaluating the believability of the victim's testimony." In this case, Lewis readily acknowledged the limits of CSAAS and did not offer an opinion about the specifics of defendant's case. Lewis testified that CSAAS is "not a tool for discerning whether a child is telling the truth" about being abused. He further admitted that CSAAS is "not a diagnosis" and that, for example, a child might retract a claim of abuse because there actually had been no abuse. Lewis explained that CSAAS is simply "background information" and is "intended to dispel some commonly held myths." He also testified that he did not know defendant and had not been told about the specific facts of the case. Lewis's testimony concerning CSAAS was accordingly general and not directed to a particular child in this case. Defendant's own expert witness, Dr. Abbott, similarly testified that CSAAS is not a "diagnostic tool" and "cannot be used to diagnose whether a child has been sexually abused or not." We believe that this testimony by both experts in the case eliminated any risk that the jury might misuse or misapply the CSAAS evidence.

(continued)

Excerpts from *People v. James Edmond Daly* 2009 WL 757337 (Cal.App. 6 Dist.)

Dr. Anthony Urquiza testified as an expert in the area of child sexual abuse. He described the components of the child sexual abuse accommodation syndrome as secrecy, helplessness, entrapment and accommodation, delayed and unconvincing disclosure, and retraction. Dr. Rahn Minagawa, a psychologist who has worked extensively in the field of child sexual abuse, testified that the child sexual abuse accommodation syndrome was "intended specifically for clinical use" and "was never intended to be used in a forensic arena." He agreed with Dr. Urquiza that "anywhere between two to possibly eight percent of allegations about sexual abuse from children or adolescents was false." He said, "Fictitious allegations appear to occur in two populations. . . . One is coached children in custody disputes. And the second, adolescents who make up convincing reports out of boredom, infatuation or in an effort to retaliate."

must also be considered in evaluating the type of intervention. Finally, any decision to intervene should also consider that children need positive parenting models after which they can bond and model their actions.[34]

At a certain point, a professional will make a decision to inject himself or herself into the family to protect a child. This decision should not be made lightly, nor should professionals hesitate to do so if they have reason to believe that the child may be in danger. A delicate balance must be maintained between the parents' right to raise their children without interference and society's obligation to protect those who cannot speak for themselves. Because a professional may disagree with a certain type of lifestyle does not mean that the official can intrude into the family without facts that indicate that the child is in danger of neglect or physical or sexual abuse. The decision to intervene normally starts with an investigation.

Investigation

An investigation of child abuse does not occur in a vacuum.[35] It involves different parties and affects various interests. The child's family, medical, educational, and social services, as well as law enforcement agencies, are all involved and interact in a child abuse investigation.

MEDICAL PROFESSIONALS.   The medical professionals have a number of roles to play in the investigative process. They must report suspected incidents of child abuse, they provide information on the nature and extent of physical injuries, and they are responsible for healing those injuries. As indicated in previous chapters, doctors were traditionally hesitant to invade the privacy of the home. However, individuals such as John Caffey and C. Henry Kempe brought startling evidence of the nature and extent of child abuse to the attention of physicians in the United States. This knowledge, coupled with continuing education and mandated reporting laws, has dramatically increased the "suspicion index" of the general medical community.[36]

Physicians are not the only members of the medical profession who are involved in the investigative process. Nurses are also required to report suspected cases of child abuse. Many statutes require them to report such cases even if the treating physician is reluctant

Focus

Intervention by Americans When They Witness Child Abuse?

Three out of every ten Americans have witnessed an adult physically abuse a child, and another two have witnessed acts of neglect by an adult to a child. Prevent Child Abuse America surveyed a representative sample of Americans to determine what they do when they observe a child being abused. Astonishingly, 44 percent of those who saw a child being abused or neglected failed to do anything about it. The reasons for failing to act included the following:

- Didn't think it was any of my business;
- Didn't know what the proper response was;
- Afraid other people might interpret response as overreacting;

- Concerned for own personal safety;
- Thought parent's actions might be justified.

Prevent Child Abuse America points out that some responses may do more harm than good (e.g., giving the parent a dirty look may incite him or her to anger and more aggression toward the child). To educate the public, Prevent Child Abuse America is working with corporate sponsors such as Target to provide brochures and posters offering advice on positive parenting and how to respond effectively when a child is abused in public.

Source: Kevin Kirkpatrick, *Fifty Percent of Americans Do Nothing When They Witness Child Abuse or Neglect: 1999 Public Awareness Survey* (Prevent Child Abuse America, Chicago, 2000).

to do so. Nurses have taken on an expanded role within the medical profession, and the advent and growing popularity of the nurse practitioner will undoubtedly further expand the role of nurses in the area of child abuse reporting and investigation. Because nurse practitioners receive special education and training that allows them to treat patients without a physician's direct supervision, they may be the only person to have contact with the abused child.

Psychiatrists and mental health workers may also have an occasion to report suspected cases of child abuse. The information may come from an adult patient who is in therapy or from a child in treatment. As discussed earlier, many states classify emotional abuse as child abuse and therefore require the treating professional to report these cases to the appropriate agency.

Expert Witnesses and Child Sexual Abuse

Sexual abuse of children is a multifaceted phenomenon. There may be a progression of activities that lead up to the molestation. It can take many forms and can involve family members or strangers. Its consequences leave a scar on the victim that may not heal for years. By its very nature, child sexual abuse occurs in secret with no witnesses. Many times, the child will not be a credible witness. Child sexual abuse may therefore require a special form of intervention: expert witnesses.

Earlier in this textbook, the medical aspects of child abuse were reviewed. Medical evidence by its very nature involves the use of expert witnesses.[37] This section examines the use of these expert witnesses in child abuse cases. Most people are familiar with the university professor with multiple degrees who can testify as an expert regarding a specific subject. However, a person with specialized experience and little, if any, formal education beyond a bachelor's degree may also qualify as an expert witness in certain situations.

ADMISSION OF EXPERT WITNESS OPINIONS.   For a person to testify as an expert, the court must determine whether he or she is qualified to render an expert opinion. Federal Rules of Evidence Rule 702 is a representative statute that sets forth the requirements of admission of expert opinion in court:

If scientific, technical, or other specialized knowledge will assist the trier to understand the evidence or to determine a fact in issue, a witness qualified as an expert by knowledge, skill, experience, training, or education may testify thereto in the form of an opinion or otherwise.

When the court is determining the admissibility of certain expert opinions, it looks at whether the testimony will assist the jury.[38] It should be emphasized that expert opinion is admitted not only in highly technical cases but also in any case in which the testimony can assist the jury in understanding the evidence or determining a fact that is in issue.[39] Before a court will admit expert testimony, it must establish that the person offering the testimony has "knowledge, skill, experience, training, or education" to qualify as an expert on the matter before the jury.[40] The party utilizing experts calls them to the stand, has them sworn in, and asks a series of questions regarding their education, training, and experience that would qualify them in the area of child sexual abuse.

Once qualified as experts, the party calling them to the stand proceeds to question them regarding their opinion. This opinion may take various forms and can carry either a great deal or little weight. The next section examines the bases and forms of expert opinions in child sexual abuse cases.

TYPES OF EXPERT OPINIONS.   The facts an expert relies on in forming an opinion may come from many different sources. Sometimes the expert may have personal knowledge about the abuse from treating or interviewing the child. On other occasions, the expert may rely on reports from other professionals as the basis for the opinion. The expert does not need to have personal knowledge in order to form an opinion. Federal Rules of Evidence Rule 703 states:

The facts or data in the particular case upon which an expert bases an opinion or inference may be those perceived by or made known to the expert at or before the hearing. If of a type reasonably relied upon by experts in the particular field in forming opinions or inferences upon the subject, the facts or data need not be admissible in evidence.

The latter section of the federal rule allows an expert to base the opinion on evidence that would normally not be admissible in court. These facts or data may be written and/or oral hearsay. Writings include medical records, police reports, and psychological reports. Verbal statements by the child or by the caretaker are often critical in proving sexual abuse.

Expert testimony may take three distinct forms in child sexual abuse: opinion, dissertation, and answers to hypothetical questions. Each of these forms of expert testimony serves a distinct purpose.

Focus

Qualifying a Witness as an Expert in Child Sexual Abuse Cases

State your full name and spell it for the record.

What is your present occupation?

What is your education that qualifies you for this position?

Are you licensed by this or any other state to practice (medicine, etc.)?

Do you have any specialized training in the area of child sexual abuse? Please list that training.

Explain your experience in treating sexually abused children.

Are you familiar with the current literature in the area of child abuse? Specifically, are you familiar with the literature in the area of child sexual abuse?

Are you a member of any professional organizations that focus on sexual abuse of children?

Please list those organizations and your activities in them.

Have you presented any papers at any professional conferences that deal with sexual child abuse? Please list them and the dates.

Have you published any articles in professional journals regarding sexual child abuse? Please describe those articles.

Have you qualified in court on previous occasions as an expert witness in child sexual abuse? How many times?

The most common form of expert testimony in child sexual abuse cases is the rendering of an opinion. An expert might testify, for example, that certain behavioral symptoms displayed by the child are consistent with incest. Although there is no requirement to do so, an advisable practice is to ask experts to state those facts that caused them to form the opinion. This technique assists the trier of fact in understanding the basis of the opinion. Experts do not have to establish any level of proof for their opinions. In other words, they do not have to testify, "I am certain beyond a reasonable doubt and to a moral certainty that the child was sexually molested." The jury must determine how much weight to give an expert opinion, and in many jurisdictions the court instructs the jury that it may give the expert's testimony whatever weight it desires or that it may completely disregard the opinion. Normally, experts will be asked questions that allow them to testify from the point of view of their professions. For example, a medical doctor might be asked, "Do you have an opinion based on reasonable medical grounds that the child is a victim of sexual abuse?" This allows the opinion to be based on medical reasons and not on legal grounds.

A **dissertation** is expert testimony that does not include an opinion but sets forth scientific facts or other principles relevant to the case that allows the triers of fact to draw their own conclusion. In this situation, the expert might not testify that the victim has been molested but would testify to certain medical or psychological indicators of abuse. The jury would then apply these principles to the actions of the child and determine whether it should give the expert's opinion any weight.

A **hypothetical question** sets forth certain facts and asks the expert to give an opinion on the basis of these facts. The facts may not have been admitted into evidence at the time the expert testifies. Many authorities argue that hypothetical questions confuse the lawyers, the court, and the jury.[41]

Various forms of expert testimony exist in child sexual abuse cases. The most traditional expert opinions are either medical or psychological. Medical opinions are provided by doctors, nurses, and other qualified personnel. Psychological opinions are rendered by psychiatrists, psychologists, and in some instances social workers. Medical opinions may be based on physical examinations, laboratory results, and a medical history. For example, if a child has a certain type of venereal disease, child sexual abuse is the only rational explanation. Psychological opinions are based on certain tests, interviews, and observations. One of the most controversial areas in the field of psychological opinions deals with the delayed discovery of abuse. Some victims have suppressed the acts, and once they are free of the abuser and out of the situation that allowed the abuse to occur, they may remember the acts. There are cases in which the victim suddenly remembered acts of abuse from ten or twenty years ago. This topic is discussed in more detail in Chapter 10, which examines ritualistic child abuse.

Experts serve a valuable purpose in child sexual abuse cases. They assist the trier of fact in understanding this often complex and emotional area of family violence. A good expert opinion can shed light on what would otherwise be a confusing and difficult area.

EDUCATION PROFESSIONALS.   Teachers, principals, advisers, coaches, and school nurses are mandated to report suspected cases of child abuse. Unlike members of the medical professions, they may not be directly involved in the treatment of the victim but may discover evidence of abuse in a variety of ways. Discussions with the student or the student's classmates may lead them to conclude that the child is a victim of abuse. Teachers are in a unique position in our society because they are in close personal contact with children for several hours at least five days of the week. This contact allows them to observe the child over extended periods of time and note any changes in behavior or physical appearance that may indicate child abuse.

Unfortunately, many educational professionals do not feel comfortable in reporting suspected incidents of child abuse. Some believe in corporal punishment, and others have not received the proper training to allow them to recognize cases of child abuse. To correct this perception, many states require education professionals to undergo specialized training in child abuse or neglect prior to receiving their credentials that authorize them to be employed in a school district.

As the investigation proceeds, educators may assist the law enforcement agency and CPS by reporting the academic progress or any marked changes in the child's behavior. This information may be critical in determining how the child is adapting to the situation and helpful in deciding where the child should be placed.

SOCIAL SERVICES.   Welfare departments, housing authorities, and other agencies that deliver social services may have the occasion to observe incidents of suspected child abuse. These situations can range from physical or sexual abuse to incidents of dirty homes. Once these situations are discovered, these professionals should not only report the incident to the appropriate agency but also document the facts to support the case because they may be the only ones who have the authority to do so. Photographs or diagrams of dirty homes may be invaluable in assisting the prosecution in filing and proving the case.

Most reporting statutes mandate that the information be forwarded either to the local law enforcement agency or to CPS, the latter of which in many jurisdictions is mandated to conduct the initial investigation. A trained social worker may contact the reporting party and develop additional information requiring emergency removal of the child from the home. In some jurisdictions, CPS has this authority, although in other states CPS is required to contact a law enforcement officer and request that the officer remove the child from the home. In either event, social workers are an important part of the entire process, and their ability to assess a situation is critical to protecting the child from further harm. It is a heavy burden that CPS workers bear on a daily basis. They must evaluate the degree of risk a child faces if the child remains in the home. If the risk is low, treatment should be offered in a manner that protects the integrity of the family system. Services provided to the parents and child while they remain in their own home would be the treatment of choice. If the risk is high, the child must be removed, which causes emotional scars on both the child and the family because involuntary separation can have drastic emotional consequences for all concerned. On the other hand, failure to remove the child from a hazardous situation could result in further abuse and possible death. Each case must be fully evaluated, and the final decision must always be weighted on the side of protecting the child from further injury.

CHURCHES.   Pastors and other spiritual advisers many times hear members of their congregation list a number of religious reasons why they have to stay in an abusive relationship. Some of the more common justifications include (1) the victim can't leave an abusive spouse because it would be a sin to destroy the marriage; (2) if she prays more, the beatings will stop; and (3) the belief that she should simply turn the other cheek and forgive the batterer. Churches are responding to such rationalization by addressing these issues in a number of ways.

Churches are printing literature for their pastors and advisers who denounce intimate partner abuse. The Catholic Church has issued a "Pastoral Response to Domestic Violence against Women" in which U.S. bishops condemn domestic violence as never being justified.[42] In St. Louis, Project Tamar, an ecumenical counseling agency, is training hundreds of clergy members on how to respond to domestic violence. Other religious groups are preparing resource kits for their church members that offer recommendations about leaving an abusive relationship.

LAW ENFORCEMENT.   These professionals are tasked with gathering evidence that will support a dependency petition or criminal charges. Many large jurisdictions have specialized teams of detectives who are assigned full-time to this area. Other jurisdictions require that the patrol officer carry out this function. Law enforcement officers may have to remove the child from the custody of her parents and interview the parents in an attempt to find out exactly what had happened. In many cases, the investigating officer can compare statements made to him or her with information gained from other professionals and determine whether there are any inconsistencies. Once the law enforcement officer has finished the initial investigation, it will be forwarded to the prosecutor's office for a determination as to whether to file dependency or criminal charges.

FAMILY.   The child's family is an integral part of this process. As discussed earlier, on occasions a spouse may be incapable of leaving the abusive partner. The intervention of certain

Practicum

When Does Law Enforcement Become Liable for Failing to Investigate?

Ortega v. Sacramento County Dept. of Health & Human Services, 161 Cal. App. 4th 713, 714 (Cal. App. 3d Dist. 2008)

Plaintiff, a minor, sued a child protective services agency and two social workers who had participated in releasing her to her father. Police had arrested her father because he was screaming uncontrollably in the street and around his apartment and was violently banging on a refrigerator. A urine test showed the father was under the influence of phencyclidine. Four days after the minor was returned to her father's custody, the father, who had a history of domestic violence and substance abuse, stabbed the minor in the heart and lung. The trial court granted summary judgment in favor of the child protective services and the social workers, relying in part on the immunity for discretionary acts of government employees.

The Court of Appeal affirmed the judgment. The court concluded that the minor had failed to show breach of a mandatory duty under Gov. Code, § 815.6. The agency and social workers complied with the duties imposed by the statute by conducting an investigation, even though the investigation was "lousy," and by making a determination about the potential risk of returning plaintiff to her father.

They were entitled to summary judgment because they showed a complete defense to the minor's causes of action, to wit, that they were immune from liability pursuant to Gov. Code, § 820.2. Section 820.2 immunity applied to a 48-hour investigation conducted by a social worker. The court rejected the minor's argument that the social worker failed to exercise any discretion in reaching a considered decision as to how to carry out her investigation. The record reflected that the social worker made a considered decision by balancing risks and advantages, even though the decision was based on woefully inadequate information.

> Had the social workers failed to conduct an investigation, they would have been liable for the minor's injuries. Why then if the investigation is "lousy" aren't they also liable?

The court noted that the duty to conduct an investigation was mandatory, but once the investigation was conducted the determination as to whether it was sufficient and actions to be taken based on the investigation were judgmental decisions and not mandatory duties. And that the care providers were immune, based on the California statute, from civil suit because of the errors in judgment.

professionals may provide this spouse with the resources to leave the abuser and begin a new lifestyle. The loss of custody of a child, even on a temporary basis, is a traumatic event for the family, affecting not only the child but also the parents. The decision to remove should not be made lightly, but neither should it be stayed simply because the parents may be upset or hurt.

Understanding who the parties are in an investigation is merely the first step in the process. The investigative function in child abuse cases is a multifaceted process that involves various stages leading to the decision by the prosecutor whether to file a petition or criminal charges. The investigative process includes reporting, investigation by CPS and/or law enforcement agencies, and referral to the prosecutor or county attorney for filing of charges.

Once one of the professionals mandated to report suspected child abuse files a report, the investigative process begins. The professional who files this report should be aware that his or her actions will be scrutinized by the prosecutor, defense attorney, and court. Therefore, it is incumbent on that professional to maintain accurate records of all events, conversations, and other pertinent data involving the decision and the status of the child. This information may be included in the standard medical protocol, school records, or other information maintained by the reporting party. No matter where it is maintained, the professional filing the report should be able to testify at a later date that it was accurate when recorded. Small details, such as the type of clothing worn by the child when admitted to the emergency room, may turn out to be important during any subsequent hearing.

The second phase of the investigative process involves the actual investigation by CPS or law enforcement agencies. Once notified that a child has been abused, these workers will review the report and may conduct an initial investigation to determine whether the child is in immediate peril. This initial investigation may entail no more than reviewing the report and discussing the matter with the reporting professional. On the basis of information received from the initial report and the reporting official, CPS workers may decide to remove the child immediately from the parental custody. This is normally done in all cases of suspected sexual abuse and in those physical abuse cases where it is demonstrated that the child is in imminent danger in the existing home environment.

If CPS does not immediately remove the child from the care and custody of his or her parents, it begins an investigation to determine whether it is necessary to file a petition with the appropriate court. This investigation normally involves interviewing the parents to determine whether the situation can be corrected that placed the child in danger without the intervention of the law enforcement agency or a court order. Many times, simply informing the parents of the resources available in the community is sufficient to alleviate a problem in the home. In more serious situations, the worker can develop a written service agreement with the parents identifying what needs to be corrected and who needs to do what to achieve the desired changes. Services would be provided to satisfy the conditions of the plan, and the progress of the family would be monitored. In the absence of progress, CPS may come to the conclusion that voluntary services have not worked and request that a petition be filed.

Filing a petition involves presenting evidence to either the prosecuting attorney or the county attorney who appears in juvenile court. In some jurisdictions, prosecuting attorneys or district attorneys make the decision as to whether to file dependency petitions, and in other jurisdictions county counsels or county attorneys represent CPS in these matters. These attorneys evaluate the facts to determine whether there is sufficient evidence to proceed and may request further information from the reporting professional, CPS worker, or law enforcement officers. Sometimes these attorneys are tasked with evaluating the case from both the civil and the dependency aspects as well as deciding whether to file criminal charges against the parents. Once the decision to file formal court documents is made, the next stage, the hearing process, begins.

The Hearing Process

If the investigation has resulted in removing the child from the home, the judicial process begins. Basically, two forums are used in child abuse cases. Civil proceedings may be filed in family or juvenile court, whose objectives are protecting the child from further injury. Criminal proceedings are filed in courts of general jurisdiction with the purpose of punishing the offender for committing a crime against the state (this process is explained in more detail in Chapter 3, which discusses law enforcement responses to partner violence). On occasion, both civil and criminal processes will be initiated. These are completely separate hearings with different purposes and procedures.

Depending on the jurisdiction, a civil proceeding may be initiated in courts known as family or juvenile courts. These courts originated in the state of Massachusetts in 1870 with the passage of legislation that required separate hearings for juveniles.[43] However, it was not until 1899, when the state of Illinois passed the Illinois Juvenile Court Act, that the juvenile court system as known today came into existence.[44] This statute separated the juvenile court system from the adult criminal system. It labeled minors who violated the law as delinquents rather than criminals and required that juvenile court judges determine what "is in the best interest of the minor" in rendering their decisions.

The juvenile court system is guided by five basic principles:

1. The state is the ultimate parent of all children within its jurisdiction.
2. Children are worth saving, and the state should use nonpunitive measures to do so.
3. Children should be nurtured and not stigmatized by the court process.
4. Each child is different, and justice should be tailored to meet the individual needs and requirements of each child.
5. The use of noncriminal sanctions is necessary to give primary consideration to the needs of the child.[45]

Although these principles were originally adopted for delinquents or minors who committed criminal acts, they have been broadly applied to proceedings involving children who are victims of abuse. Juvenile courts have jurisdiction over three types of minors: delinquents, status offenders, and dependent children. **Delinquents** are those minors who have committed criminal offenses. **Status offenders** are minors who are truant from school, have run away from home, or are considered incorrigible. **Dependent children** are those who are in need of state intervention because of neglect or abuse by their caretakers.

The juvenile court process is normally initiated by filing a petition with the court. A **petition** is a formal pleading that alleges that the parents or custodians endangered the health or welfare of the child. The petition may allege neglect or physical, emotional, or sexual abuse of the child and gives the juvenile court authority to act.

Once the petition is filed, many jurisdictions hold a show-cause, or detention, hearing. This hearing is usually conducted within twenty-four to forty-eight hours after filing the petition or the emergency removal of the child. The **detention hearing** requires CPS or police to produce evidence justifying the emergency removal of the child or to present evidence that would allow the court to order the removal of the child if he or she is still in the custody of the parents. The parents may also admit or deny the allegations contained in the petition at this hearing. If they admit the allegations, the court orders CPS to conduct an investigation to determine where the child should be placed as a result of the admissions by the parents. If the parents deny the allegations, the court sets a date for an adjudicatory or jurisdictional hearing. Pending this hearing, the court may order the child temporarily placed in a living arrangement outside the home.

An **adjudicatory or jurisdictional hearing** is used to determine whether there is sufficient evidence to find that the allegations in the petition are true. At the conclusion of this hearing, the court will render its decision. If the petition is upheld, the court sets a date for a dispositional hearing. If the petition is not upheld, the child is returned to the parents and the case is dismissed.

During the adjudicatory hearing, the state presents evidence to support its claim that the child has been abused. This may take the form of having the child testify to the incident, or experts employed by the state may render their opinions regarding the facts surrounding the case. The state is represented by a prosecutor, county counsel, or other government attorney. The parents have a right to cross-examine witnesses and present any evidence they desire in rebuttal to the state's evidence. At the end of the hearing, both parties may present arguments in favor of their positions.

The burden of proof to uphold the petition is the same as in civil cases. In civil trials, the plaintiff has the burden of proving the case by a preponderance of the evidence. This is normally defined as more than 50 percent. A criminal case requires proof beyond a reasonable doubt. This is not proof beyond all doubts but proof of the material facts to a moral certainty that they did occur. In juvenile dependency cases, in order to remove the child from the custody of his or her parents, some jurisdictions require proof by clear and convincing evidence. This is more than a preponderance of the evidence but less than beyond a reasonable doubt.[46]

Once the adjudicatory or jurisdictional hearing concludes, the next hearing to occur is the **dispositional hearing,** which determines where the child should be placed. The court will decide whether the child should be immediately returned to his parents or placed in an out-of-home environment for a period of time. The guiding principle in this hearing is the child's best interest. If the court orders the child to be placed outside the home, it may schedule periodic reviews to determine whether or when the child will be reunited with the parents.

From the beginning of the intervention process until the final dispositional hearing and beyond, every party in the action has certain rights. Both the parents and the child have

---

Focus

Nosey Neighbor Situation

Consider the following scenario: Nancy is a very nosey neighbor who likes to spread gossip. She overhears her neighbors discussing the possibility of their son being sexually abused. Nancy reports to the police that she thinks that the neighbor's son is being abused by his mother. There is no substance to her report. The neighbors sue her in civil court for damages to their reputation. Should they recover? [While the actual results will mainly depend on state laws and state court decisions, the majority rule is discussed below.]

In most states as long as Nancy honestly believed that sexual abuse was occurring, the answer is that Nancy is not liable for the false report. For example, California Penal Code Section 11172 (a typical state statute in this area) provides that members of the general public who voluntarily report incidences of child abuse are also protected. Their immunity from civil or criminal liability is not absolute. They are not protected if they make a report with knowledge of its falsity or with reckless disregard of its truth or falsity. The limitation on the immunity for false or negligent reports is necessary to prevent a vindictive former spouse or neighbor from making a knowingly false report.

distinct rights that must be observed and protected. These rights involve notice, an opportunity to be heard, and effective representation by an attorney.

In a dependency hearing, the rights of a child include appointment of an attorney who will speak on behalf of the child. This attorney must represent what he or she believes is in the best interest of the child regardless of what CPS or the parents advocate. In some jurisdictions, this is a county attorney and in others a private attorney appointed by the court to represent the child. Depending on the case, the attorney may side with the parents and argue for return of the child to their care, or the attorney may take the position that it is in the best interest of the child to be removed from the custody of the parents. Even if the child is removed temporarily from the custody of his or her parents, the child has a right to reunification efforts after a reasonable time.

During dependency hearings, parents have a right to notice of the hearing and an opportunity to be present at that hearing and to be represented by an attorney. They may present any evidence they desire to rebut the charges. If the child is removed from their custody, they have the right in most jurisdictions to a reunification plan that will allow them to regain custody of the child once they have finished treatment or counseling.

In criminal proceedings, the child is normally not appointed an attorney but may be represented by a child advocate whose mission is to assist the child and represent his or her best interests. The parents have a right to an attorney and all other rights accorded those accused of committing crimes against society.

Summary

Child abuse is a serious form of family violence. It is an accepted fact that parents or caretakers do abuse children, and, as a result of efforts of concerned citizens and professionals, every state has adopted mandatory reporting laws. These laws require certain individuals who come into contact with children to file reports with designated agencies if they have reason to believe that a child is the victim of abuse.

These reporting laws require immediate reporting, waive any privilege that may have existed between the caretakers and the professionals, and mandate that CPS or law enforcement agencies conduct an investigation into the circumstances surrounding the abuse. These laws also authorize the emergency removal of the child if there is reason to believe that he or she is in imminent danger.

Interviewing a child is more an art than a science. Questions should be phrased in certain ways to avoid charges that the professional programmed or suggested the answer to the child. Understanding the basics of the hearsay rule will allow professionals to ask children and their caretakers the right types of questions.

The intervention process involves both an investigation and a court hearing. The purpose of both these activities is to protect the child. If the nature of the abuse is serious, civil and criminal actions may be initiated against the parents. In many jurisdictions, the juvenile court is tasked with the responsibility of conducting dependency hearings aimed at protecting the child from further abuse. These courts have the power to remove the child from the custody of his or her parents and order placement outside the home.

Key Terms

confidential communication—information offered under circumstances in which the speaker intends that the statement be shared only with the recipient of the information.

recognition memory—occurs when the child is cued or is able to perceive an object or event that was first perceived at an earlier time.

free recall memory—occurs when the child can recollect the event without the aid of cues or other assistance.

open-ended question—does not suggest or imply an answer.

focused question—narrows the scope of inquiry and requires the witness to answer within certain parameters.

leading questions—promise rewards or threaten punishment for certain answers.

hearsay—any out-of-court statement that is offered in court for the truth of the matter stated.

excited utterance—a statement made whenever a person is excited or under stress as a result of a traumatic event.

admission—a statement or conduct of a party in the action that is offered against him or her in the trial.

declaration against interest—a statement by a non-party that is against his or her own interest.

state-of-mind—statement relates a fact regarding the declarant's mental or emotional condition.

statement made to medical professionals—information given for purposes of diagnosis or treatment of a medical condition.

competency—the ability of the witness to testify accurately to events.

dissertation—expert testimony that does not include an opinion but sets forth scientific facts or other principles relevant to the case that allows the triers of fact to draw their own conclusion.

hypothetical question—sets forth certain facts and asks an expert to give an opinion on the basis of these facts.

delinquents—those minors who have committed criminal offenses.

status offenders—minors who are truant from school, have run away from home, or are considered incorrigible.

dependent children—those who are in need of state intervention because of neglect or abuse by their caretakers.

petition—a formal pleading that alleges that the parents or custodians endangered the health or welfare of the child.

detention hearing—requires child protective services or police to produce evidence justifying the emergency removal of the child or present evidence that would allow the court to order the removal of the child if still in the parents' custody.

adjudicatory or jurisdictional hearing—used to determine whether there is sufficient evidence to find that the allegations in the petition are true.

dispositional hearing—used to determine where the child should be placed.

Discussion Questions

1. If you could revise the elements of the reporting laws discussed in this chapter, what would you add or delete? Why?

2. What is the single most important aspect of the existing reporting laws?

3. Can you list any other professionals who should be mandated to report suspected cases of child abuse? Who are they? Why should they be included?

4. Should we waive the privilege that many professionals have with their clients or patients? Why? Why not? If individuals know that whatever they tell certain professionals may end up in a police report, will they be truly candid?

5. Should all cases of child abuse be referred automatically to the district attorney for filing of criminal charges? What does this do to the family and the child?

Suggested Readings

Fox, S. *Modern Juvenile Justice: Cases and Materials* (West, St. Paul, Minn., 1972).

Johnson, T. A. *Introduction to the Juvenile Justice System* (West, St. Paul, Minn., 1975).

McCloskey, P. L., and R. L. Schoenberg, eds. *Criminal Law Advocacy* (Bender, New York, 1986).

Sagatum, I. J., and L. P. Edwards. *Child Abuse and the Legal System* (Nelson-Hall, Chicago, 1995).

Spencer, J. R., and R. Flin. *The Evidence of Children: The Law and Psychology* (Blackstone, London, 1990).

Tower, C. C. *Understanding Child Abuse and Neglect* (Allyn & Bacon, Needham Heights, Mass., 1993).

Zaragoza, M. S., J. R. Graham, G. C. N. Hall, R. Hirschman, and Y. S. Ben-Porath, eds. *Memory and Testimony in the Child Witness* (SAGE, Thousand Oaks, Calif., 1995).

Endnotes

1. Approximately thirty states mandate that reports be filed with local child protective agencies. For example, see Florida Statutes Annotated Section 415.504(2)(a) (West Supp. 1990) and New York Social Services Law Section 415 (McKinney supp. 1990).

2. See Iowa Code Annotated Section 232.70(2) (West 1985).

3. *Black's Law Dictionary*, 6th ed. (West, St. Paul, Minn., 1990), p. 298.

4. *Principles of Medical Ethics* (American Medical Association, Washington, D.C., 1989).

5. This section has been based on Peter Fin, "Sex Offender Community Notification," *Research in Brief* (National Institute of Justice, Washington, D.C., February 1997).

6. R. A. Prentky, R. A. Knight, and A. F. S. Lee, "Child Sexual Molestation," *Research Issues* (National Institute of Justice, Washington, D.C., March 1997).

7. P. Davis, "The Sex Offender Next Door," *New York Times Magazine*, June 28, 1996, pp. 20–43.

8. P. L. Petrucelli, "Megan's Law: Branding the Sex Offender or Benefitting the Community?" *Seton Hall Constitutional Journal* 5 (1995), pp. 1127–1169.

9. A. R. Bedarf, "Examining Sex Offender Community Notification Laws," *California Law Review* 83(3) (1995), p. 885.

10. Based on D. B. Adams, *Summary of State Sex Offender Registries, 2001* (Bureau of Justice Statistics, Washington, D.C., March 2002).

11. HR 4472, The Adam Walsh Child Protection and Safety Act of 2006.

12. *The Front Line, Special Legislative Edition, 2006* (National Center for Missing and Exploited Children, Washington, D.C., 2006).

13. T. Weidlich, "False Memory, Big Award," *The National Law Journal* 17(19) (1995), p. A6.

14. R. J. Flush, T. Grey, and F. A. Fromhoff, "Two-Year-Olds Talk about the Past," *Cognitive Development* (2) (1987), p. 393.

15. G. S. Goodman et al., "Children's Memory for Stressful Events," *Merrill-Palmer Quarterly* 37 (1990), p. 109.

16. N. W. Perry, "Child and Adolescent Development: A Psycholegal Perspective," in J. E. B. Myers, ed., *Child Witness Law and Practice* (Wiley, New York, 1987).

17. Ibid.

18. K. J. Saywitz et al., "Children's Memories of Physical Examinations Involving Genital Touch: Implications for Reports of Sexual Abuse," *Journal of Consulting and Clinical Psychology* 59 (1991), p. 682.

19. J. R. Spencer and R. Flin, *The Evidence of Children: The Law and Psychology* (Blackstone, London, 1990).

20. Ibid., p. 250.

21. N. G. Fieldings and S. Conroy, "Interviewing Child Victims: Police and Social Work Investigations of Child Sexual Abuse," *Sociology* 16(1) (1992), pp. 103–125.

22. P. L. McCloskey and R. L. Schoenberg, eds., *Criminal Law Advocacy* (Matthew Bender, New York, 1986), vol. 4, pp. 3–5.

23. See E. Swift, "Abolishing the Hearsay Rule," *California Law Review* 75 (1987), p. 495.

24. See *Federal Rules of Evidence* 803(2), which requires the statement to relate to a startling event or conditions made while the declarant was under the stress of the excitement caused by the event.

25. Some states have statutes that provide for introduction of this form of admission. California Penal Code Section 1127c provides that the jury shall be instructed as follows: "The flight of a person immediately after the commission of a crime, or after he is accused of a crime that has been committed is not sufficient in itself to establish his guilt, but is a fact which if proved, the jury may consider in deciding his guilt or innocence. The weight to which such circumstance is entitled is a matter for the jury to determine."

26. *Federal Rules of Evidence* 803(4).

27. 110 S. Ct. 3139 (1990).

28. K. M. Quinn, "The Creditability of Children's Allegations of Sexual Abuse," *Behavioral Science and Law* 6 (1988), p. 181.

29. Spencer and Flin, *The Evidence of Children*, p. 270.

30. A. B. Sivan, "Preschool Child Development: Implications for Investigation of Child Abuse Allegations," *Child Abuse and Neglect* 15 (1991), p. 485.

31. J. R. Conti et al, "Evaluating Children's Reports of Sexual Abuse: Results of a Survey of Professionals," *American Journal of Orthopsychiatry* 61 (1991), p. 428.

32. M. D. Everson and B. W. Boat, "Sexualized Doll Play among Young Children: Implications for the Use of Anatomical Dolls in Sexual Abuse Evaluations," *Journal of the American Academy of Children and Adolescent Psychiatry* 29 (1990), p. 736.

33. 110 S. Ct. 3157 (1990).

34. C. C. Tower, *Understanding Child Abuse and Neglect* (Allyn & Bacon, Needham Heights, Mass., 1993).

35. For an excellent discussion of child abuse investigations, see D. Pence and C. Wilson, *The Role of Law Enforcement in Response to Child Abuse and Neglect* (U.S. Department of Health and Human Services, Washington, D.C., 1992).

36. The term *suspicion index* was used by Dr. David Chatwick in conversations with the author.

37. For an excellent discussion of controversies surrounding the use of experts, see D. L. Chadwick and H. F. Kraus, "Irresponsible Testimony by Medical Experts in Cases Involving Abuse and Neglect of Children," *Child Maltreatment* 2(4) (1977).

38. See *State v. Lindsey*, 149 Ariz. 472, 273, 720 P.2d 73, 74 (1986) regarding the admission of expert testimony describing the behavior of incest victims.

39. *State v. Moran*, 151 Ariz. 378, 380, 728 P.2d 248, 250 (1986).

40. *State v. Higgins*, 61 Ohio App. 3d 414, 572 N.E.2d 834, 837 (1990).

41. *Ingram v. McQuiston*, 261 N.C. 392, 134 S.E.2d 705 (1964), which sets forth an example of misuse of hypothetical questions.

42. See *The Faces and Facts of Family Violence* (Christopher News Notes, New York, October/November 1999).

43. T. A. Johnson, *Introduction to the Juvenile Justice System* (West, St. Paul, Minn., 1975), p. 3.

44. S. Fox, *Modern Juvenile Justice: Cases and Materials* (West, St. Paul, Minn., 1972), p. 47.

45. See R. G. Cadwell, "The Juvenile Court: Its Development and Some Major Problems," *Juvenile Delinquency: A Book of Readings* (Wiley, New York, 1966), p. 358.

46. See D. V. Otterson, "Dependency and Termination Proceedings in California—Standards of Proof," *Hasting Law Journal* 30 (1979), p. 1815.

12

Special Populations and Family Violence

CHAPTER OBJECTIVES

After studying this chapter, you should be able to:

- Discuss the issues involved with victims with HIV/AIDS;
- Discuss the problems of family violence in the military;
- Explain the types of victims involved when considering special victims population;
- Understand the role that mental issues may play in family violence;
- Recognize the issues involved with spiritual abuse.

Detailed Look at What You Should Know About Special Populations and Family Violence

- HIV/AIDS is the black plague of modern times.
- AIDS is the acronym for the medical term *acquired immune deficiency syndrome.*
- There are two primary types of HIV: HIV-1, which is the most common and deadly, and HIV-2, which reproduces more slowly.
- HIV is a spectrum virus, in that it has various phases that run along a spectrum.
- HIV/AIDS is a medical condition and therefore is considered confidential information.
- Special victims population includes victims of rape, children, family violence victims, and victims with disabilities.
- Family violence in the military is a problem for the military services.
- Another type of abuse is spiritual abuse.
- Mental issues may be a factor or contributing factor in family violence incidents.
- Mental disorder is difficult to define.

- DSM-5 is the bible on mental issues.

- Mental disorders include psychotic disorders, bipolar and related disorders, depressive disorders, anxiety disorders, and trauma and stress related disorders.

VICTIMS WITH HIV/AIDS

HIV/AIDS is the black plague of modern times.[1] It causes many normally rational professionals to become emotional at the thought that they may have been exposed to AIDS. We are still learning the consequences of this disease, but one factor remains constant: Persons with AIDS eventually die, and at present there is no known cure. It is therefore critical that professionals in this area understand how to respond to victims who have been exposed to this disease.

Medical and Psychological Aspects of HIV/AIDS

AIDS is the acronym for the medical term *acquired immune deficiency syndrome.* The "acquired" portion of the term means that the condition is not a birth defect but was acquired after birth from another person. "Immune deficiency" indicates that the immune system is repeatedly attacked by infections and diseases until it becomes so weak that it cannot perform its job. The "syndrome" part of the term means that a series of signs or symptoms occurs together and characterizes this particular abnormality. The term *AIDS* should normally be used only when the person has become seriously ill and fulfilled the Centers for Disease Control and Prevention's (CDC's) criteria for a formal diagnosis of AIDS. Otherwise, the more correct description is "HIV+," or "HIV-positive," for persons who have the HIV infection.[2]

Human Immunodeficiency Virus (HIV) is the virus that causes AIDS. While many viruses can be controlled by the immune system, HIV targets and infects the same immune system cells that are supposed to protect us from illness. These are a type of white blood cell called CD4 cells. AIDS is the most advanced stage of HIV infection, which is caused by HIV attacking the immune system's soldiers—the CD4 cells. When the immune system loses too many CD4 cells, it is less able to fight off infection, and serious, often deadly, infections can develop. These are called *opportunistic infections* (OIs) because they take advantage of the body's weakened defenses. When someone dies of AIDS, it is usually OIs or other long-term effects of HIV infection that cause death. AIDS refers to the body's immune-compromised state that can no longer stop OIs from developing and becoming so deadly.

Two primary types of HIV are HIV-1, which is the most common and deadly, and HIV-2, which acts in the same way as HIV-1 but reproduces more slowly. Almost all infected persons in the United States suffer from HIV-1. Once a person is infected with HIV, there is no known cure. The progression of the disease can be slowed with medication but cannot be stopped. Most cases result in death, but some persons, known as *nonprogressive long-term survivors*, have the virus, but it does not destroy their immune systems and they do not become sick and die from the disease. Researchers continue to study these individuals in an attempt to learn why the virus affects them differently than most of the infected population.[3]

HIV is a spectrum virus; that is, it has various phases that run along a spectrum, from wellness to illness.[4] Normally, the virus replicates itself in the lymph glands and then begins to dump copious amounts of itself into the bloodstream, setting the stage for progression of AIDS. There are five phases in the HIV infection:

Phase 1. The *asymptomatic incubation period* lasts from four to six weeks. Phase 1 is often called the *window period* because the infected person has HIV present and replicating in the blood but generally no detectable symptoms. This is a dangerous period because the infected person has no idea that he or she is contagious. At some point during this phase, the first antibody is produced, and the person converts from HIV-negative to HIV-positive. This conversion is called the *seroconversion*.

Phase 2. The *acute primary infection* lasts from one to two weeks. During phase 2, the person will experience some symptoms of early infection but may not recognize the cause of the symptoms. For example, the person may attribute aches, pains, and swollen glands to the flu. The infected person has sufficient antibodies in his or her system to detect the HIV virus during this phase.

Phase 3. The *asymptomatic phase* lasts three to fifteen years. This phase is characterized by seeming good health while HIV continues to replicate in the blood and certain tissues and begins slowly to erode the body's immune system. The length of this phase will vary from person to person, depending on a number of factors, including the person's overall general health, the way the person cares for himself or herself, and the medical treatment received.

Phase 4. The *symptomatic phase with persistent generalized lymphadenopathy* lasts one to three years. Serious symptoms signal the beginning of phase 4. Infections that a normal healthy person would fight off will make an HIV-positive person ill. The symptoms for this phase include fever, night sweats, diarrhea, enlargement of the lymph glands, weight loss, oral lesions, fatigue, rashes, and cognitive slowing.

Phase 5. The *AIDS phase* lasts from one to three years. This condition meets the CDC's criteria for the definition of AIDS. As the person approaches death (end-stage AIDS), it is common for him or her to have multiple symptoms. The person dies as a result of infections and disease.[5]

HIV is not transmitted by animals or insects or by using swimming pools or hot tubs. It cannot be transmitted after contact with an infected person's clothes or by using the same toilet seat, eating utensils, drinking glasses, or telephone. There has never been a case in which HIV was transmitted by kissing or receiving cardiopulmonary resuscitation. For HIV to be passed from one person to another, there must be an infected party, an uninfected party, and a route of entry to get particles of the virus from the donor to the recipient. The fact that HIV has been found in blood, semen, saliva, serum, urine, tears, breast milk, vaginal secretions, lung fluid, and cerebrospinal fluid does not mean that it is transmissible through those fluids. The three most common routes of HIV transmission are sexual transmission, blood-to-blood transmission, and mother-to-child transmission.

Most cases of HIV transmission occur as a result of sexual activities. Anal intercourse carries the highest risk of transmission, because the fragile tissues of the anus and rectum may tear as a result of the friction of intercourse. Vaginal intercourse is also a high-risk practice with an infected person. Oral sex with a man or a woman, although lower in risk than anal or vaginal intercourse, may also transmit the virus. Because of the violent nature of most sex crimes, there is much concern that victims may be exposed to HIV.

Blood-to-blood transmission can also occur in a variety of ways. For example, using infected needles can transmit the disease. This method of transmission is common among drug users and is of concern to health workers who receive needle sticks during their work with patients. The virus may be transmitted with contaminated blood or body fluids that come into contact with open wounds. This is an area of concern in domestic violence cases in which one party may get infected blood in an open wound of another person.

Mother-to-child transmission occurs when the virus is transmitted to the fetus of a pregnant women. This is the most common form of pediatric transmission. A newborn child may also become infected as a result of breast feeding from his or her HIV-positive mother.

Both AIDS and HIV present social, psychological, and medical problems. AIDS has changed our view of public health and affected how we judge others. People with HIV disease respond like all others in a crisis situation. Learning that one has HIV is a severe stressor because of the inevitable result: death. Service providers must understand that there is no right or wrong way to respond to this life-threatening disease.

When a person learns that he or she is infected with HIV, he or she may react with a wide range of emotions similar to those experienced by victims of crime. After passing through these emotions, he or she must face the physical, social, and psychological aspects of living and dying with this disease. As death becomes more imminent, AIDS victims begin to plan for death. This process becomes difficult and sometimes impossible because the victim may be coping with HIV-related dementia.

Dementia as a result of HIV is judged to be the direct pathophysiological consequence of the virus. The major features of this type of dementia are forgetfulness, slowness, poor concentration, and difficulties with problem solving. The infected person may also exhibit apathy and social withdrawal and occasionally experience delirium, delusions, or hallucinations.[6]

Professionals must remember that AIDS is a medical disease that has additional social and psychological aspects. Because some victims of crimes may become infected with the virus, professionals must be knowledgeable regarding the disease and be prepared to address sensitive issues. The next section examines some of these concerns.

Service Issues

Once society acknowledged the existence and impact of HIV, victim service providers have attempted to deal with the impact of this disease on the victims they serve. Most service providers focused solely on victims of rape. However, with the passage of time and the expansion of knowledge regarding the disease, victim service professionals now must understand how HIV affects victims of child sexual abuse and other forms of family violence. Service providers must also be ready to deal with persons who are infected with the disease and who are victimized. In addition, they must respond to family members, friends, and colleagues of these victims who all bring their own concerns, biases, and feelings to their interactions with victim service providers.

HIV/AIDS is a medical condition and is therefore considered confidential information. Victim service providers must always remember that they cannot disseminate the medical

Focus

Domestic Abuse and the Presence of HIV/AIDS

The presence of HIV/AIDS in an abusive relationship often includes specific forms of abuse. The forms include:

- Outing or threatening to tell others that the victim has HIV/AIDS;
- An HIV + abuser suggesting that she or he will sicken or die if the partner ends the relationship;
- Preventing the HIV + partner from receiving needed medical care or medications;

- Taking advantage of an HIV + partner's poor health status, assuming sole power over a partner's economic affairs, create the partner's utter dependency on the abuser;
- An HIV + abuser infecting or threatening to infect a partner.

Source: National Coalition Against Domestic Violence Web site at www.uncfsp.org, accessed August 27, 2015.

status of persons with this disease without their express permission. Victim service professionals must be capable of explaining the consequences to victims of disclosing or not disclosing their condition to others.

A critical first step in responding to these victims' special needs is to create a safe and open environment in which a victim, family member, friend, or colleague will feel secure enough in raising the HIV/AIDS issue. By creating this safe environment, the victim will receive a message that he or she is with someone who has some knowledge of the disease and is open to discussing it. Victims must be reassured that the professional is not sitting in judgment of them or their lifestyle.

The displaying of AIDS awareness posters in the office may assist in establishing this open environment. These posters can be obtained from local AIDS service organizations, county health departments, and the CDC. Information regarding the disease should be made available in brochures. Many victims have found lists of local AIDS service organizations very helpful.[7]

Raising the issue of HIV/AIDS with a victim who may be at risk may be one of the most difficult tasks undertaken by a service provider. Victims may not want to discuss this topic for a variety of reasons: They may not realize that they are at risk, they may understand that they are at risk but fearful of discussing the risk with anyone, or they may already know that they are infected and decide not to disclose that fact.

Victim assistance professionals should take the time to review the victim's risk of infection and motivation for being tested. They should explain the testing process, including the various test results. They may need to consider a collaborative response to a victim's inquiry by using a local AIDS service provider. Victim service providers should never deliver the victim's HIV/AIDS test results. This would possibly introduce an uncomfortable aspect to an already existing relationship as the victim service professional might become a constant reminder of the moment the positive results were delivered to the victim.[8]

One of the most controversial issues in the criminal justice field today involves involuntary testing of offenders. In recent years, several states have passed laws that give victims of sexual assault access to information about the HIV status of their offender.[9] These laws apply to those arrested or convicted or who have pled guilty to crimes involving sexual penetration or other exposure to an offender's bodily fluids. At the federal level, sexual assault victims can request an order requiring the HIV testing of the defendant if the court finds probable cause that the defendant committed the offense, that the victim has received appropriate counseling, and that the information is necessary for the health of the victim.

If the offender is positive, it does not mean that the victim will have contracted the virus, but simply learning of the offender's status may cause the victim unnecessary emotional upheaval. The victim must also be tested to be absolutely sure that the virus was or was not transmitted. Other professionals fear that imposing mandatory testing on offenders will lead to mandatory testing of other groups or professions. This continues to be a hotly debated topic.[10] Some wonder, for example, if we adopt mandatory testing of offenders and other groups for HIV/AIDS, isn't it also reasonable to test those groups for additional diseases, such as all other sexually transmitted diseases?[11]

Professionals in this field normally work with persons who have already experienced the trauma of victimization. Most victim assistance providers do not encounter a person who has a life-threatening illness such as the HIV/AIDS virus. When they work with these victims, it is with the knowledge that the victim will surely die as a result of this disease. It is therefore critical that everyone in the criminal justice system understand the effect and consequences of victims with HIV/AIDS.

Specific Victim Populations

Victim service providers must not only understand HIV/AIDS but also be able to relate to specific victim populations that might be exposed to the disease. This section focuses on those victims for whom HIV/AIDS is a particularly significant concern, including victims of rape, children, family violence victims, and HIV-positive persons.

VICTIMS OF RAPE.   Many rape victims, and their consensual sexual partners, are concerned regarding possible exposure to HIV.[12] There is a continuing controversy surrounding the transmission of HIV during a rape. This is not to say that such a transmission has not occurred, only that at present the CDC, which officially tracks AIDS cases, does not classify cases by consensual or nonconsensual sex.

Even as enlightened as we like to think our society is about crime and victimization, victims of rape are still reluctant to report such assaults. Whereas many victims have experienced difficulty in disclosing their rapes to their significant partners, the additional factor of possible exposure to the HIV virus may make disclosure even more difficult. The grieving process that normally occurs after a rape may now be extended and deepened because of the added fear regarding the HIV virus.[13] All these issues will continue to confront victim service providers as they work with victims of rape until we find a cure for HIV/AIDS.[14]

CHILDREN.   The CDC reports that there were 4,883 pediatric cases of AIDS in the United States as of the end of 2004. Children who are sexually assaulted are considered to be at higher risk than adult victims of sexual assault. This increased risk is based on two factors: (1) Child

Practicum

Who Should Undergo Mandatory Testing for HIV/AIDS?

Sexual predators

Physicians, dentists, nurses

Members of the military

Professional athletes

Law enforcement personnel

All persons above the age of fifteen

victims may be repeatedly assaulted over a long period of time by the same perpetrator, and (2) children are at a greater risk of injury during penetration, and as a result there is a higher likelihood of transmission of the virus during the sexual act.

Victim service professionals must assist parents in making informed decisions regarding how much information to give to a young child who has been sexually assaulted by an HIV-positive perpetrator. The victim service professional should work closely with the AIDS service provider regarding counseling and other support techniques for both the child and the parents.[15]

FAMILY VIOLENCE VICTIMS. **Family violence** occurs every day, from the mansions of Brentwood to the slums of New York. This type of violence crosses all ethnic, social, and sexual boundaries, and its victims include whites, blacks, Hispanics, Asians, and homosexuals. Some family violence victims are forced to participate in drug usage with the abuser and his friends. In addition, the abuser may be using drugs or engaging in sexual acts with multiple partners that exposes him to the disease. He then can pass the virus along to his partner during "consensual" sexual relations. The victim's request for use of a condom or other device may be met with violence by the abuser.

Shelters for battered women have traditionally been places of sanctuary for these victims. The spread of HIV/AIDS has added another complication to the heavy burden carried by these shelters. Victim service providers must ensure that staff working in the shelters understand the medical and legal aspects of the disease so as not to further traumatize those residents who are HIV-positive.

HIV-POSITIVE PERSONS. Persons who are HIV-positive are no different from the rest of society as it relates to becoming a victim of a violent crime. What is different is that some persons have been victimized merely because of their real or perceived HIV status. Other HIV-positive victims must decide whether they are going to disclose their status to authorities when reporting crimes of violence.

Violence related to HIV covers a wide spectrum of acts, including simple verbal abuse, harassment, job discrimination, and actual physical attacks. The person's appearance may suggest that they are at risk of carrying the HIV virus. Certain groups, such as homosexuals, drug users, and those wearing AIDS support ribbons and other symbols, have suffered HIV-related violence.

A person who is living with the HIV virus must expend a great deal of energy on day-to-day survival, including taking medications, attending medical appointments and treatment sessions, and going to support groups. Suffering criminal victimization with its attendant responsibilities of reporting the crime, participating in interviews with law enforcement officers, attending court, and facing the perpetrator can add a tremendous amount of stress to the victim's life. This increased stress can dramatically affect his or her health. For this and other reasons, HIV-positive victims may decide not to pursue reporting victimization. Still others may report, but as the burdens of appearing in court increase they may opt to drop the charges. Victim service providers must be aware of the dynamics of this form of victimization and respond accordingly by supporting the victim.

VICTIMS WITH DISABILITIES

People with disabilities have the same rights as any other victim, but they remain one of the largest categories of victims to be neglected by our criminal justice system.[16] This is because they are not afforded the same type of access, legitimacy, or respect as other victims. For example, as the Practicum in this section shows, although some material in the criminal justice system is in several different languages, very few agencies may have information in Braille.

Crime against persons with developmental and other severe disabilities is a problem similar to other forms of violence.[17] Some research indicates that the level of violence against children and adults with developmental and other severe disabilities is as much as five times higher than that against the general public, that such crimes are reported at a much lower rate, and that there are indications of lower rates of prosecution and conviction.[18]

One of the first issues confronting victim service providers is how to respond to victims of family violence who also have a disability.[19] Each type of disability may require a different response on the part of the victim service provider. For example, a victim with a hearing impairment will have different needs than a victim with a sight impairment. However, certain rules apply to all family violence victims who have disabilities:

- Do look directly at the victim when addressing him or her. Deliberately averting your eyes is impolite and can be uncomfortable.
- Do feel free to ask a victim with disabilities how you should act or communicate most effectively with him or her if you have any doubts about correctness in the situation.
- Do address and speak directly to the person with disabilities, even if he or she is accompanied or assisted by a third-party person without disabilities.
- Do feel free to offer physical assistance to a person with disabilities, such as offering your arm if the need arises, but do not assume that he or she will need it or accept it.
- Do ask a victim with disabilities whether he or she has any needs that will require special services or arrangements and then attempt to make arrangements to meet those needs.
- Don't stare, and avoid looking at a visible disability or deformity or expressing sympathy to the victim with disabilities.
- Don't tell the victim with disabilities that you admire his or her courage or determination for living with the disability. The person with disabilities doesn't want to be thought of as a hero.
- Don't avoid humorous situations that occur as a result of a disability. Take your cue from the victim.[20]

Practicum

Disability and Crime

It was late in the evening when Jane was returning home from the local convenience store with a carton of milk and some other groceries. It was cold and rainy, and Jane was hurrying as fast as she could to reach her apartment when two persons grabbed her from behind and pulled her into an alley.

They took her purse, trashed her bag of groceries, and proceeded to rape her. Several other people walked by the alley but did nothing to render assistance. The perpetrators fled only when they heard a police siren. Jane was taken to the local emergency room where she received a medical examination. She gave a report to the police and was informed by the investigating officer of her right to contact the local victim/witness office. Several days later, Jane went downtown to the office. She had to ride ten stories in a crowded elevator and was late for the scheduled appointment. Once inside the office, she was asked to have a seat and then waited about thirty minutes before she finally was interviewed regarding her victimization. After the interview with a victim service volunteer, Jane wanted to take some of the information home so that she could study her rights as a victim more closely. Unfortunately, the office did not have any pamphlets in her language—Jane was blind.

What are the issues faced by a victim service provider in this situation? What problems did Jane encounter? How would you attempt to solve those problems? (Assume that you have no additional funds in your agency.)

These tips should be used as guidelines when working with persons with disabilities. Victim service professionals must understand that the person with disabilities, just like all other victims, is an individual, and each must be approached and interacted with as an individual. For years, people with disabilities tolerated discrimination and hardship as a result of society's reaction to their disability. Congress finally addressed this issue when it enacted the Civil Rights Act of 1964 and the Americans with Disabilities Act of 1990 (ADA).

Legal Issues

About forty-three million Americans have one or more disabilities, be they mental, physical, or both. They may be congenital (occurring at birth) or adventitious (occurring after birth). As indicated earlier in this chapter, a **person with disabilities** is one who has a physical or mental impairment that substantially limits one or more of the major life activities of that individual, one who has a record of such impairment, or one who is regarded as having such an impairment. This definition is founded on the language contained in the ADA, which is one of the most comprehensive pieces of civil rights legislation ever passed by Congress since the Civil Rights Act of 1964. The ADA was enacted by Congress to protect the employment and accessibility rights of persons suffering from disabilities. Any agency receiving any type of government funding (federal, state, or local) must comply with the provisions contained in the ADA.

Some authorities state that persons with developmental and other severe disabilities represent about 10 percent of the U.S. population (1.8% developmental disabilities, 5% adult-onset brain impairment, and 2.8% severe major mental disorders). As many as 30 to

40 percent of all families may have loved ones or close friends with developmental or other severe disabilities. These numbers may increase as the U.S. population ages. Fifteen percent of Americans above the age of fifty-five have cognitive disabilities, and 25 percent of those above the age of seventy-five suffer from this form of disability.[21]

Disabilities covered by the law include physical and mental impairments. Physical disabilities include physiological disorders or conditions, disfigurement, or loss of the use of any body system. Specific examples include cerebral palsy, epilepsy, multiple sclerosis, AIDS/HIV infections, cancer, heart disease, and diabetes. Mental impairments include any mental or psychological disorder, such as mental retardation, organic brain syndrome, emotional or mental illness, and specific learning disorders.

Focus

Memory and Victims with Disabilities

Children who are victims of sexual assault have been accused of fabricating the events. Others claim that these child victims have been programmed or had false memories implanted in their minds by social workers, counselors, law enforcement officers, or others in the criminal justice system. [This topic is addressed in more detail in Chapter 6.] Whereas interviewing children takes a special kind of expertise, interviewing victims with disabilities takes the same skills plus a great deal of empathy.

Ann Craft has pointed out that professionals who work with victims with disabilities are becoming more aware of their lack of skills in assisting these persons to give accounts of what happened to them. In an early study, Pear and Wyatt studied the reliability of testimony from child victims with disabilities. They found that these children's unprompted recall was reliable and that prompted recall was much less reliable than recall from children with normal intelligence.

Dent found that interviewing children with disabilities poses a real dilemma for professionals

in this field: On the one hand, child victims with disabilities are in need of prompts to access their memory, but on the other hand, their recall may be influenced by the nature of the prompts used. She examined on children with disabilities the effects of three types of questions: free recall, specific, and general. Free-recall questions consisted of a request for an unprompted narration in which any cues contained in the instructions were given in all conditions. Specific questions took the form of "What color was the man's hair?" whereas general questions took the form of "What did the man look like?" Dent found that specific questions were the least accurate, free-recall questions were higher in reliability than specific questions, and general questions were the most accurate. However, other scholars have questioned Dent's conclusion regarding the validity of specific questions. Bull argues that specific questions are not necessarily more suggestive than general questions. What all authorities agree on is that more research needs to be conducted in this newly emerging area of family violence.

Sources: A. Craft, "NAPSAC in Context," in *Newsletter of the National Association for the Protection from Sexual Abuse of Adults and Children with Learning Disabilities* (Nottingham, UK, 1981); T. Pear and S. Wyatt, "The Testimony of Normal and Mentally Defective Children," *Journal of Psychology* 3 (1914), p. 388; H. R. Dent, "Experimental Study of the Effectiveness of Different Techniques of Questioning Mentally Handicapped Child Witnesses," *British Journal of Clinical Psychology* 27 (1986), pp. 13–17; and R. Bull, "Innovative Techniques for the Questioning of Child Witnesses, Especially Those Who Are Young and Those with Learning Disability," in M. S. Zaragoza et al., eds., *Memory and Testimony in the Child Witness* (SAGE, Thousand Oaks, Calif., 1995).

Service providers must anticipate serving victims with disabilities. They must work with local government agencies and be prepared to provide a wide variety of services. They should also become familiar with the ADA and be spokespersons for victims with disabilities within the criminal justice system.

Types of Victimization

People with disabilities can be victimized in the same way as other persons are, but their response to crime is different than other victims. Crimes against these individuals are under-reported for a number of reasons: There may be communication and mobility barriers; the person may be unable to report the crime because of a mental or developmental reason, or he or she may depend on others to do so; and some reporting agencies fail to record the fact that the victim was a person with disabilities.[22]

One researcher reported that 60 percent of all persons who have mental disabilities become victims of crime sometime during their lives and that 60 percent of all hearing-impaired women will be victims of sexual assault.[23] Another source indicates that many people with disabilities do not receive any form of sex education and that some of them are socialized to obey others without question. Consequently, they do not complain or report acts of sexual maltreatment.[24] Individuals with disabilities in institutions are twice as likely as those in the community to be abused.[25]

Although the data are extremely limited, there is some reason to believe that substantial numbers of persons with disabilities are victims of domestic abuse. These studies also indicate that hearing-impaired females have a high probability of becoming victims of domestic violence.[26] For years professionals have acknowledged that there is a higher risk of child abuse if the child has a disability.[27]

Emerging Issues

The realization that victims with disabilities present unique challenges to those in the criminal justice system is just now being acknowledged in local, state, and federal jurisdictions. California has assembled a task force to study these issues, and this group has formulated a series of recommendations regarding the treatment of crime victims with disabilities (summarized in the following sections).[28] These suggestions still need study and revision, but they represent an important first step in this newly emerging area of victimization of the person with disabilities.

THE LEGAL PROCESS.   Each service provider should have a criminal justice coordinator. Knowledgeable service professionals and disability advocates should be available to assist the police, prosecutors, and courts. Each developmental disabilities regional center and other primary care or case management service agencies should have a twenty-four-hour phone number to respond to requests for information on an emergency basis. Criminal justice organizations should have specialized staff for cases involving persons with disabilities. This will allow for the gathering of information and building of expertise by those in the system. It will also provide a single point of contact for service organizations. There should be sentence enhancements when persons with disabilities are victims to protect those who cannot protect themselves. Regular and relatively comprehensive training on victims with disabilities should occur for police, prosecutors, judges, defense attorneys, probation officers, victim witness offices, and others in the criminal justice system.

Reporting laws should be amended to require mandatory reporting of possible crimes against people with disabilities. Persons who deal with this population regularly should receive training in recognizing criminal acts against these victims and how to report them. Multidisciplinary teams that include victims with disabilities should be formed in all local jurisdictions and meet on a regular basis. They should also review sudden unexpected deaths or major traumatic injuries to the persons with disabilities when the death or injury occurs in an institution, residence, or other service facility.

VICTIM SUPPORT.   Each community should develop multidisciplinary teams to cooperatively provide victim support. As a minimum, each team should include victim service providers, sexual assault advocates, and service providers who work with the persons with disabilities. All case management agencies should have a designated staff person to serve as an advocate for victims with disabilities. There should be a coordinated public relations campaign to encourage such victims to report all crimes committed against them.

RISK REDUCTION/PREVENTION.   Curricula and required training for residential programs, vocational training, day programs, recreational programs, and special education should be modified to include personal safety training skills for persons with disabilities. This training should include self-defense skills, individual rights, assertiveness training, social skills, and training about the criminal justice system. All education and service plans for clients with disabilities should include a personal safety plan as a component. Crime prevention should involve the client, service providers, family, and friends. Special training should be conducted for family members on how to overcome isolation, facilitate attachments, support family relationships, and increase and improve communication skills of the client and family members. Safer living environments are necessary to prevent victimization of the persons with disabilities. The more connected and integrated these persons are with their community, the lower the risk of victimization. Steps should be taken to break down the traditional barriers that exist between the persons with disabilities and the community. Adult protective service agencies should have adequate resources to investigate reported abuse of people with disabilities.

INSTITUTIONAL ABUSE.   There is a critical need to improve standards for screening and hiring of staff in institutions that serve the people with disabilities. Staff training in institutions needs to be improved and updated. Use of the "buddy system" for mentoring new and problem employees should be implemented. Advocacy systems that are independent of any institutional provider are needed. Ombudsperson programs need to be expanded to address these concerns. Administrators and professional staff must be actively present in all institutions to monitor and supervise staff and the clients. Management staff must be held accountable for abuse that occurs in their institutions, yet they must be encouraged to report such abuse. They must look beyond individual cases and accept their moral and professional responsibility to care for these individuals.

Cultural Issues

The United States has traditionally been a melting pot of different peoples who have come to its shores and taken their unique place in our society. We pride ourselves on our diversity and multiculturalism. New refugees, recent immigrants, and other minority groups often face misunderstanding and confusion when our traditional values conflict with their beliefs and customs. These groups may encounter an almost overwhelming task when attempting to understand the expectations regarding family behavior in the criminal or civil justice system. Victim service providers need to be aware of these issues when dealing with these individuals.

Introduction

Simply saying to those who work in the criminal justice system that a victim comes from a different culture and is different from the rest of us does not automatically guarantee sympathetic treatment and/or an understanding response to that person's special needs. Stereotyping must be guarded against, and relying on third-hand information when responding to the needs of minority populations should be avoided. Different cultures may not be as homogeneous as they appear on the surface, and care should be taken not to attribute characteristics to special populations on the basis of conversations or interactions with one member of the group. The person being interviewed may be advocating his or her personal beliefs, which may not represent the feelings of other members of that particular culture. It is essential that professionals working in the criminal justice profession be both culturally sensitive and careful to validate their information if possible.

Focus

The Exorcist—Guilty or Innocent?

On April 16, 1997, Los Angeles Superior Court Judge James Albright found two Korean Christian ministers guilty of involuntary manslaughter (the commission of an act, ordinarily lawful, which involved a high degree of risk of death or great bodily injury, without due caution and circumspection) for beating to death one of their wives during an exorcism. The prosecution had asked for second-degree murder, and the defense had argued for an acquittal for the two defendants, Jae-Whoa Chung and Sung Soo Choi.

The defendants decided to go forward with the exorcism because Chung's wife had become spiritually arrogant and at times had refused to obey her husband. These acts supported their beliefs that she was possessed by a demon named Gundae.

The exorcism involved both defendants slapping the woman's face, holding her down, and pushing on her abdomen with their fingers, knuckles, and feet. She died as a result of blunt force trauma, and her injuries included sixteen broken ribs and crushed internal organs. It was conceded that the husband loved his wife.

The judge stated that the case involved a collision of California law with honestly held Christian beliefs influenced by Korean shamanist practices.

Source: M. D. Havies, "Priests Found Guilty in the Exorcist Case," *Los Angeles Daily Journal*, April 17, 1997, p. 1.

Culture awareness can be defined as the understanding that an individual has regarding different cultures. The term *culture* includes different races, religions, genders, ages, and physical disabilities as well as gay or lesbian issues. Therefore, culture awareness encompasses a wide range of issues, any of which may confront those working in this field.

FAMILY VIOLENCE IN THE MILITARY

The War in Iraq brought the violence of war into our living rooms at breakfast, lunch, and dinner. Many in our nation were, and are, proud of our soldiers, sailors, marines, and air crews for serving our country. However, over the last several years, we have learned of a darker, more private side to service in the military. Within the last five years, reports of abuse and intimate violence have surfaced in the media regarding members of the military. It should be stated that family violence in the military is not a new phenomenon; rather, as we as a society have become more aware of family violence in general, more and more victims are stepping forward to report it. This is what appears to be happening in the military.

Unfortunately, the stories set forth in the Focus are not isolated incidents that have been blown out of proportion by a sensation-seeking press. They are tragic examples of a problem that must be overcome within the military. To understand the dynamics of family violence within the military, it is necessary to discuss the structure and functioning of our military forces.

THE MILITARY STRUCTURE. One might question why such a specialized "narrow" topic is included in a text dealing with family violence. The answer is simple: The Department of Defense (DOD) is the nation's largest and busiest company. The mission of the DOD is to

---

Focus

Intimate Partner Abuse in the Military

- Four Army soldiers in North Carolina killed their spouses in a six-week period in 2002. All the soldiers were assigned to Fort Bragg, N.C., and three had just recently returned from combat duty in Afghanistan. At the time, Army spokespersons denied there was any connection between the stress of a life in the military and the abuse.
- Female cadets at the U.S. Air Force Academy were victims of sexual harassment and dozens of sexual assaults that went without

any formal response by the leadership of the Academy.
- Suzy was a member of the U.S. Air Force. The abuse began the week after she married a fellow construction engineer. He threw her down a flight of stairs. When she reported the incidents, the command ordered her into joint counseling, where she kept quiet because she knew he would beat her more if she told.

Sources: "'Disturbing': Veterans of Afghanistan Kill Wives at Fort Bragg," *NewsMax.com Wires*, July 27, 2002; "The War at Home Is Still Raging," stamp.org/domestic-abuse.html; and Faye Fiore, "Academy Culture Blamed in Sex Abuse," *The Fresno Bee*, A5, June 20, 2003.

provide the military forces needed to deter war and to protect the security of our country. The DOD is a cabinet-level organization that has three military departments reporting to it. The Army, Navy, and Marine Corps were established in 1775 during the American Revolution. The precursor to the Defense Department, the War Department, was established in 1789. In 1947, Congress established the DOD and ordered that all military branches report to the newly created civilian Secretary of Defense.

In 2003, the department had approximately 1.4 million men and women on active duty. The military are located in more than 150 countries. The president is the commander-in-chief and works through the secretary of defense, who in turn tasks the various military departments, the chairman of the Joint Chiefs of Staff, and the unified commands. The Army defends the landmass of the United States, its territories and possessions, and operates in more than fifty countries. The Navy maintains, trains, and equips combat-ready maritime forces capable of winning wars, deterring aggression, and maintaining freedom of the seas. The Marine Corps maintains ready expeditionary forces, sea-based and integrated air-ground units for contingency and combat operations. The Air Force provides rapid, flexible, and when necessary, lethal air and space capability that can deliver forces anywhere in the world in less than forty-eight hours. The Coast Guard provides law and maritime safety enforcement and military naval support.

The military has its own law enforcement, corrections, family service structure, and legal system. Military justice is governed by the Uniform Code of Military Justice. This law contains the substantive and procedural laws governing the military justice system. Investigations of serious crimes that are committed on a military reservation are conducted by military law enforcement personnel. In very minor offenses, the immediate commanding officer will conduct a preliminary investigation. Military commanders exercise a great deal of discretion in deciding whether an offense should be charged and how the offender should be punished. Serious charges are referred to courts martial. There are three levels of courts martial: summary, special, and general courts martial. A summary courts martial is designed to handle minor offenses. An individual officer presides over these cases. A special courts martial is an intermediate level and has either a military judge or three service members and a military judge. A general courts martial is the military's highest trial court. It handles the most serious violations of law, including capital cases. The trial in a court martial is very similar to the criminal trials that occur in civilian jurisdictions.

The DOD has a number of victim and witness programs. It established a DOD Directive that implements requirements for victims and witnesses from initial contact through investigation, prosecution, and confinement. The Directive includes a Bill of Rights that closely resembles the Federal Crime Victims' Bill of Rights. In providing services and assistance to victims, the DOD programs emphasize an interdisciplinary approach including law enforcement, criminal investigators, chaplains, family advocacy personnel, emergency room personnel, family service center personnel, equal opportunity personnel, judge advocates, unit commanding officers, and corrections personnel. Each branch of the service has issued regulations to further implement victim and witness programs and assign responsibility to appropriate commands.

The DOD maintains an Equal Opportunity Program to address complaints of discrimination and sexual harassment. It also provides training of all personnel on how the complaint system functions and the protection against reprisal it affords individuals making complaints.

Each branch of the service has a family advocacy program designed to prevent and treat child and intimate partner abuse. These programs are designed to prevent abuse by early identification and intervention and to provide programs of rehabilitation and treatment for child and spouse abuse problems. Each branch of the service maintains a central registry containing data on alleged child and intimate partner abuse.

The DOD has acknowledged the existence of a number of barriers to reducing family violence. These obstacles include lack of awareness within the military community of the dynamics of family violence, lack of training about available resources, inconsistent command response to various acts of family violence, and unit deployment schedules that deny full participation in and completion of treatment programs.[29] Another major factor complicating the problem is the military mindset or military perspective.

THE MILITARY PERSPECTIVE.   The military operates on a formal chain of command. This chain of command requires juniors to obey the orders of any person superior to them in rank. Failure to obey one's superiors can result in formal charges being filed against the disobeying person. Obedience and conformity are prized characteristics in many commands within the military. Many of the service boot camps teach immediate obedience to any order as well as train recruits in controlled violence necessary for survival in combat operations. Persons who have never experienced violence are taught to use their hands, feet, and weapons to kill or maim the "enemy." While many of these skills are valuable and even necessary for survival in a combat situation, they sometimes cannot simply be left at the door when that military member walks into his or her home.

CHILD ABUSE AND INTIMATE PARTNER ABUSE IN THE MILITARY.   As indicated earlier, the military is a culture that in many instances is closed to outsiders. We do not understand their language, their lifestyles, or their social structure. Similar to many other closed cultures, it is difficult to obtain valid data on the nature and source of abuse within the military. However, as discussions about family violence are becoming more common in our society, researchers are gaining access to databases that contain information regarding various forms of family violence in the military.

There have been a number of studies regarding family violence in the military. Acord studied child abuse and neglect in the Navy and Marine Corps.[30] Myers published a short article on child abuse and neglect in the Air Force.[31] Raiha and Soma analyzed child abuse in the Army.[32] These inquiries examined physical abuse, sexual abuse, emotional neglect, and neglect. In 1999–2000 (fiscal year 2000) more than 10,500 physical and/or sexual assaults of a spouse were substantiated within the U.S. military. Of the 10,500 incidents, more than 5,200 active duty personnel were identified as the perpetrators.[33]

A review of these articles as well as an analysis of other databases indicates that although minor physical child abuse and neglect have shown small decreases over the past ten years, the extent of major physical abuse has remained the same, and sexual and emotional abuse have shown sharp fluctuations.[34]

Other scholars have attempted to determine if there is more child abuse in the junior enlisted ranks than in the senior enlisted ranks. Soma found that child abuse was more common among the E-3s than the more senior E-7s. The abuse rate decreased as rank of the service member increased.[35]

Focus

Department of Defense Family Advocacy Program

In 1984, Department of Defense (DOD) Directive 6400.1 established the Family Advocacy Program (FAP) to address family violence in military families. The FAP consists of coordinated efforts designed to prevent, identify, report, and treat all aspects of child abuse and neglect and domestic abuse. The DOD FAP recommends policy and program guidance to assist the Military Service FAPs, which are available locally at installations with command-sponsored families. The Service FAPs have a major role in addressing family violence at the local level through outreach, prevention, and intervention efforts. Because abuse can take many forms and some forms of abuse can be much more severe than other forms, FAP provides a wide range of services geared toward the specific needs of families. FAP staff works closely and collaboratively with military command, military law enforcement personnel, medical staff, family center personnel and chaplains, as well as civilian organizations and agencies, to prevent family violence and help troops and families develop healthier relationships.

Family Advocacy Program Goals

- Promote the prevention, early identification, reporting, and treatment of child abuse and neglect and domestic abuse.
- Strengthen family functioning in a manner that increases the competency and self-sufficiency of military families.
- Preserve families in which abuse has occurred without compromising the health, welfare, and safety of the victims.
- Collaborate with state and local civilian social service agencies.
- Provide effective treatment for all family members when appropriate.

Department of Defense Definitions

Child abuse and neglect includes physical injury, sexual maltreatment, emotional maltreatment, deprivation of necessities, or combinations for a child by an individual responsible for the child's welfare under circumstances indicating that the child's welfare is harmed or threatened. The term encompasses both acts and omissions on the part of a responsible person. A *child* is a person under eighteen years of age for whom a parent, guardian, foster parent, caretaker, employee of a residential facility, or any staff person providing out-of-home care is legally responsible. The term *child* means a natural child, adopted child, stepchild, foster child, or ward. The term also includes an individual of any age who is incapable for self-support because of a mental or physical incapacity and for whom treatment in a medical treatment facility is authorized.

Domestic abuse includes domestic violence or a pattern of behavior resulting in emotional/psychological abuse, economic control, and/or interference with personal liberty when such violence or abuse is directed toward a person of the opposite sex who is a current or former spouse, a person with whom the abuser shares a child in common, or a current or former intimate partner with whom the abuser shares or has shared a common domicile.

Reporting Child Abuse

If a military service member suspects that someone is abusing or neglecting a child, he/she is required by federal and state laws and by DOD policy to report it to FAP immediately. Suspected child abuse or neglect may also be reported by contacting the appropriate state child abuse hotline.

Suspected child abuse in a DOD-sponsored out-of-home care facility, including child development centers, family child care, youth programs, or DODDS/DDESS schools, can be reported to FAP or the DOD Child Abuse Safety and Violation Hotline at 1-800-336-4592. (OCONUS service members should access the AT&T operator first.)

(continued)

Stop the Violence

If you are in an abusive relationship, contact Military OneSource at 1-800-342-9647 to locate a victim advocate in your area.

You may also contact the National Domestic Violence Hotline at 1-800-799-7233 or 1-800-787-3224 (TTY).

Source: Department of Defense Family Advocacy Program at www.defenselink.mil/fapmip/, accessed August 3, 2009.

Family violence in the military, like its civilian counterpart, crosses all ethnic, social, and economic lines. A private in the Army can molest his stepdaughter, a chief in the Navy can batter his spouse, a sergeant in the Air Force or a captain in the Marine Corps may also be perpetrators. It can occur in on-base housing or wherever the family lives off base.

POLICIES AND PROCEDURES. The DOD and the various branches of the military under its control are beginning to respond to the problem of family violence. The DOD has issued a policy statement requiring commanders at every level to take appropriate steps to prevent domestic violence, protect victims, and hold those who commit these acts accountable.[36] Each branch of the military has followed up with its own policy statement to its members. For example, Commandant of the Marine Corps, General J. L. Jones issued an order to all marines in the Marine Corps on February 12, 2002, reiterating the DOD policy and further stating that commanders at all levels shall initiate administrative or disciplinary proceedings to hold domestic violence offenders accountable for their actions. The Commandant went on to emphatically state that such behavior is an offense to our core values.[37]

PROMISING TRENDS AND PRACTICES. In 2000, Congress passed laws establishing a Defense Task Force on Domestic Violence. It would evaluate family violence in the military and make recommendations to the Secretary of Defense. The Task Force was established and issued reports to Congress during 2001, 2002, and 2003.

The Task Force stressed the importance of preventing domestic violence, protecting victims, and holding offenders accountable. Its recommendations included a "zero tolerance" memorandum that states that domestic violence is a pervasive problem and that it will not be tolerated in the DOD. Other recommendations include the development of standardized guidelines to assist commanders in addressing domestic violence and the use of full-time DOD liaison personnel to work with local law enforcement agencies to be the link between military installations and civilian agencies responding to domestic violence.[38]

Its final report was released in 2003 and set forth a strategic plan for addressing family violence in the military. Among the Task Force recommendations was a list of principles that all military intervention programs should follow. The following is a summary of those principles:

- Respond to the needs of victims and provide for their safety;
- Hold offenders accountable;
- Consider multicultural and cross-cultural factors;
- Consider the context of the violence and provide a measured response;

What Is a Military Protective Order?

A military protection order (MPO) is issued by a commander to an active duty service member to protect a victim of domestic abuse or child abuse and to control the behavior of the alleged abuser. A victim, victim advocate, installation law enforcement agency, or FAP clinician may request a commander to issue a MPO.

Among other things, a MPO may order the service member to surrender his or her government weapons custody card or may order the service member abuser to stay away from the family home if they are living on the installation. Commanders may tailor their orders to meet the specific needs of a victim.

A MPO is only enforceable while the service member is attached to the command that issued the order. When the service member is transferred to a new command, the order will no longer be valid. If the service member is being transferred to a new command, and the victim still believes that the MPO is necessary to keep him or her safe, the victim, a victim advocate, or a FAP staff member may ask the commander who issued the MPO to contact the new commander to advise him or her of the MPO and the circumstances within the family.

If an abusive service member violates the MPO, he or she can be disciplined under the Uniform Code of Military Justice. Depending on a number of factors, a violation of a MPO may result in non-judicial punishment, court-martial proceedings, or other disciplinary measures.

- Coordinate military and civilian response;
- Involve victims in monitoring domestic violence services;
- Provide early intervention.

By 2013, the DOD has taken steps to implement the recommendations. Further research will be needed to determine if the steps taken have reduced domestic violence in the military.

Spiritual Abuse

The following Focus points out incidents involving sexual abuse and other forms of abuse that occur in a religious environment or because of spiritual pressure. Some would argue that spiritual abuse is similar to stranger rape or other forms of violence perpetrated by strangers and it doesn't fit within the definition of a family. Yet, many of the definitions in this textbook include acts by strangers or caretakers. In many of the spiritual abuse cases, the pastor, priest, or religious leader was in a caretaker role with the victim. It is therefore appropriate that this form of family violence be examined in this textbook.

The Focus also asks the question of whether spiritual abuse is a new form of family violence. However, it then presents situations dating back twenty or more years that involved abuse by spiritual leaders. What is new about spiritual abuse is the widespread acknowledgment by media, scholars, and other professionals that it exists and must be addressed. Another aspect of this form of abuse is the relatively recent revelations regarding sexual abuse by members of the Catholic priesthood.

Exactly what is spiritual abuse? There are a number of definitions that different groups or professionals use when discussing this form of family violence. For example, Pope John Paul II stated, "The sexual abuse of children by some priests is not only a crime against society but also a sin in the eyes of God."[39] Rusher discusses three forms of sexual abuse in the Catholic Church: priestly misbehavior with girls and women, clergy misbehavior with men and boys, and consensual sex with a young person who has reached the age of consent.[40] Martinez defines religious abuse as the crushing inner psychological, spiritual, and emotional damage suffered by members of authoritarian communities of faith whenever their spiritual authority is twisted by spiritual leaders to achieve a desired goal through unethical, cruel, and damaging means.[41] For the purpose of this textbook, *spiritual abuse* will be defined as *physical, emotional, or sexual abuse committed by a person using the authority of, or under color of, spiritual beliefs.* This definition includes those who exercise control in religious groups, such as pastors, faith healers, and priests, as well as those who supervise others in religious settings and act for the spiritual leader.

What must be understood as we discuss this topic is that it is not an indictment of all religious activities or groups. Religious beliefs, activities, and groups have been with us for centuries. Many of these beliefs and activities have served as sources of strength and comfort to millions upon millions of those who embrace them. It is only a very, very small percentage of individuals within these religious groups who have used their authority to commit spiritual abuse on the group's members or believers.

Religious abuse can involve physical beatings or floggings, brainwashing, sexual acts with children, and even result in death. Religious abuse can erupt in splinter groups and result in the death of hundreds of followers, or it can occur in traditional religions such as the present-day scandal involving sex abuse and the Catholic Church. The following sections will examine abuse by splinter or nontraditional religious groups.

SPLINTER GROUPS: DEATHS AND SUICIDE. There are a number of religious groups whose spiritual abuse actions have made headlines over the years. The following is a brief summary of some of the more famous or infamous of these groups.

MOVEMENT FOR THE RESTORATION OF THE TEN COMMANDANTS OF GOD. This group is located in Uganda, and information about its activities is limited. Its leaders preached the end of the world. They moved the date back several times and finally told the believers that the Virgin Mary would appear on March 17, 2000. In anticipation of the appearance, the members held a feast and entered their church to celebrate. About 5:30 in the morning, an intentionally set fire consumed their church in Kanungu, Uganda. Local police estimate at least 330 persons,

---

Focus

A New Form of Family Violence?

Daily news reports detail scandalous behavior by members of one of the world's most recognized religions. Many of these sexual acts are alleged to have occurred when the victims were young trusting children. Is this a newly discovered form of family violence, or has it been with us in other sinister forms? Consider the following examples:

- Members of a religious sect are killed or commit suicide in Africa.
- Sect members plot and carry out deadly gas attacks on innocent victims in a Tokyo subway.
- Parents allege that a religious group has kidnapped their daughter and is holding her against her will.

including 78 children, died in the blaze. The reported leader, Joseph Kibweteere, is alleged to have lured the members inside the church, boarded up the windows, and nailed the doors shut before using gasoline to start the fire.[42] Police also located five pit latrines sealed with cement, which contained more dead bodies that appeared to have been strangled or poisoned.

AUM SHINRI KYO (SUPREME TRUTH). This is a religious group located in Japan that combines the teaching of Buddhism and Christianity. It has been rejected as a legitimate Buddhist group by leaders of the Buddhist faith in Japan. The leader of the group, Shoko Asahara, was born partially blind in 1955. After traveling to the Himalayas to study Buddhism and Hinduism,

Asahara formed Aum Shinri Kyo in 1987. Using the Book of Revelation and the writings of a famous sixteenth-century astrologer Nostradamus, Asahara predicted the end of the world. On March 20, 1995, members of the group spread Sarin, a deadly nerve gas, in a Tokyo subway station. The gas killed 12 passengers and injured more than 5,000 people. Asahara and hundreds of his members were arrested and charged with murder.[43]

HEAVEN'S GATE. This group was located in California. The group combined elements of Christianity with beliefs about UFOs. Their beliefs about the nature of UFOs came from passages in the Four Gospels and the Book of Revelation. Members looked upon themselves as monks and nuns and lived in a large rented home in San Diego County. They believed that by committing suicide at the correct time, they would leave their bodies and their souls would unite with a representative of the level above humans. Starting on March 23, 1997, for three successive days eighteen men and twenty-one women committed suicide to follow their beliefs.

THE PEOPLE'S TEMPLE. This group moved from the United States to Guyana. It was founded by James (Jim) Warren Jones. The group was initially set up as an interracial mission for the sick, homeless, and jobless. During the 1950s, the group had more than 900 members in Indianapolis, Indiana. Jones moved the location of the temple several times during the ensuing years, from Ukiah to San Francisco to Los Angeles. In the mid-1970s, as a result of increasing negative press coverage, Jones moved some of the temple membership to Jonestown, Guyana. During November 1978, a U.S. Congressman, Leo Ryan, and several others visited Jonestown on a personal inspection tour. On November 18, the group was at Port Kiatuma Airfield preparing to leave with sixteen members of the temple who requested to be allowed to travel with them. Jones's security group arrived at the airport and started shooting at the group. They killed Congressman Ryan and four others, including members of the press. Jones and the remaining members discussed several options and decided on mass suicide. That evening 914 persons committed suicide, were shot, or were killed by injection at the temple. Several members managed to flee into the jungle and survived.[44]

CATHOLIC CHURCH AND SEXUAL ABUSE. The Catholic Church is not the only traditional religious organization whose religious leaders have committed spiritual abuse on its members. Other mainstream religious groups have experienced situations where pastors, preachers, rabbis, lay ministers, and others have used the trust and confidence placed in them by congregation members to take sexual advantage of young children or others. The Catholic Church is simply the most recent example of this type of abuse and provides insight into the ongoing struggle between the Church's hierarchy, its members, and the victims.

During the summer of 2001 in Boston, more than eighty persons came forward claiming that Catholic priest John Geoghan had molested them.[45] Cardinal Bernard F. Law admitted that when he took over the Boston Archdiocese post in 1984, he was aware that Geoghan had already molested seven boys. Claims of priests molesting young children began surfacing across the United States. Many of these claims resulted in criminal charges being filed against the priests because of changes in the statute of limitations that allowed survivors of sexual assault to file claims up to twenty years after the incident.

Another complication in the ongoing criminal actions involving priests was the U.S. Supreme Court decision of *Stogner v. California*.[46] In *Stogner*, the court held an unconstitutional law that retroactively extended the time for filing of criminal charges against perpetrators. *Stogner* has caused an uproar in the prosecution of clergy sex-abuse cases. California state prosecutors reported that more than 800 criminal cases, including hundreds of convictions, will be overturned as a result of the Supreme Court case.

Survivors have also filed civil damages lawsuits against the Catholic Church, claiming the church hierarchy knew about these crimes and covered them up by transferring the priests to other posts without taking any other action. The rationale of *Stogner* may also affect these civil lawsuits because many states amended their civil statute of limitations to allow for these types of lawsuits. High-ranking members of the Church are threatening to challenge these civil lawsuits using the rationale set forth in *Stogner*.[47]

The leadership of the Church reacted in various ways: Some dioceses began checking their records and dismissing sexually abusive priests, American bishops met to discuss the crisis, and still other segments of the church refused to admit the seriousness of the situation. The Church settled some lawsuits and in the summer of 2003 was still fighting other lawsuits.

The Catholic Church has to contend not only with allegations of sexual abuse of young boys by their priests, but also with a disturbing study raising issues of sexual abuse of nuns by priests and other nuns.[48] A national survey completed in 1996 estimated that 34,000 Catholic nuns, or approximately 40 percent of all nuns in the United States, have been victims of sexual abuse at some time in their life. The study analyzed responses of a fifteen-page survey that was returned by 1,164 nuns representing 123 distinct religious orders throughout the United States. Of these, 18 percent of the nuns reported having been sexually abused as a child, and 6 percent of those reported that the sexual abuse was instigated by priests, with another 3 percent occurring by nuns. When specially asked about sexual exploitation, exploitation, or harassment as an adult, 11 percent of all respondents reported such activity. The study was conducted by researchers at the Jesuit-run St. Louis University. The results of the study were published in two scholarly journals of low and specialized circulation in 1998, but did not receive any special public attention until the *St. Louis Post Dispatch* published the study results in January 2003. A Catholic spokesperson stated that the study validates the fact that religious women are subjects of the same types of abuse and exploitation as women in general.

It is not surprising that nuns have been sexually abused. We know this form of family violence crosses all economic, social, and religious boundaries. What is awkward for the Catholic Church is to face these allegations at the same time as it is dealing with abuse of young children by priests.

CHARACTERISTICS OF RELIGIOUS GROUPS THAT ABUSE. As the preceding discussion indicates, there has been a number of religious organizations that have caused harm to their members. Do these churches have any common characteristics that we can use to identify them? One authority has attempted to establish a profile of religious groups that abuse their members. LeVonne Neff examines characteristics of religious groups that establish unhealthy or abusive situations.[49] The following is a brief statement of these characteristics as set forth by Neff:[50]

1. *Does a member's personality generally become stronger, happier, more confident as a result of contact with the group?* In abusive churches, guilt, fear, and intimidation are used to control members. This is likely to result in low self-image, the feeling of being beaten down, and a general change in personality, usually in the negative direction.

2. *Do members of the group seek to strengthen their family commitments?* Nearly all abusive churches attempt to cut off contact with the family. The member is told he or she has a new spiritual family. Loyalty to the church is deemed more important than loyalty to the family.

3. *Does the group encourage independent thinking and the development of discernment skills?* Control-oriented groups tend to dictate what members think and use religion as the basis so that members rarely realize what is happening.

4. *Does the group allow for individual differences of belief and behavior, particularly on issues of secondary importance?* A rigid, legalistic approach that demands immediate keeping of the rules and staying within prescribed boundaries is usually present in unhealthy religious organizations.

5. *Does the group encourage high moral standards both among members and between members and nonmembers?* In unhealthy religious organizations, there may be different standards for the leaders and the members. This may result in confusion and unhealthy relationships for the members.

6. *Does the group's leadership invite dialogue, advice, and evaluation from outside its immediate circle?* Authoritarian religious leaders are usually threatened by different opinions and expressions of belief. Dissent is carefully controlled or crushed.

7. *Does the group allow for development in theological beliefs?* These religious groups do not tolerate any belief system that is different from their own. Many of these groups will adopt an "us-versus-them" attitude.

8. *Are group members encouraged to ask hard questions of any kind?* A dominant characteristic of these groups is the attitude of not asking questions, or "making waves." Disagreement is considered disloyalty. Those who ask too many questions may face sanctions from the leadership.

9. *Do members appreciate truth wherever it is found, even if it is outside their group?* Abusive churches believe that they are superior to other Christian groups. This allows them to adopt a religious elitism that disallows any outside influence.

10. *Is the group honest in dealing with nonmembers, especially as it tries to win them to the group?* Some groups have one perspective or position for its members and another position for those outside the church. A healthy organization should have no problems exposing its beliefs to the general public.

11. ***Does the group foster relationships and connections with the larger society that are more than self-serving?*** Abusive churches usually encourage activities that promote dependency instead of relationships outside the church.

This section has explored the emerging issue of religious abuse. This is a new form of family violence that will continue to expand as time passes. We must continue to research this form of abuse, its extent, and the consequences suffered by the survivors of this form of family violence.

MENTAL ISSUES AND DOMESTIC ABUSE

While certain mental issues were discussed elsewhere in the text, in this section we will take a coordinated examination of the mental issues and domestic violence. Clearly mental disorders affects the lives of many individuals and their partners. We can assume that in many domestic violence incidents that a mental disorder caused or encouraged the actions of one of the partners or both that lead to the violence. In this section, we will examine briefly mental disorders that may affect a domestic situation.

The exact number or even an accurate estimation of the number of individuals with mental disorders is unknown. Some studies suggest that about one-third of the U.S. adult population suffers from some degree of mental disorder.[51]

One reason that so many individuals are classified with mental disorders is probably because the classification categories are very broad and include many disorders that are not of serious consequences.[52] Defining mental disorder is a difficult task. To many psychiatrists a mental disorder is any disorder that causes a person to deviate significantly from the expected norm. Others tend to use a more narrow definition. Unfortunately, the *Diagnostic and Statistical Manual of Mental Disorders* (DSM-5) fifth edition does not attempt to define the disorder. Cockerham provides us with a working definition for the purposes of our examination of the issues. He defines mental disorder as "a significant deviation from a person's past behavior, thought processes, and emotions that result from an abnormal disturbance in his or her state.[53] Another issue to keep in mind is that the concepts of mental disorders change as modern medicine advances. For example until the 1970s, the DSM considered homosexuality as a mental disorder.

Psychotic Disorders

According to the DSM-5, psychotic disorders are illnesses that disrupt how someone thinks and understands what he or she sees or hears. These disorders involve a psychosis that makes it difficult for a person to know what is real, to think clearly, and to communicate or relate with others. In other words, an individual with this disorder is unable to feel normal emotions.

Schizophrenia is the most common psychotic disorder. Other psychotic disorders include delusional disorder, brief psychotic disorder, and catatonia. While the symptoms of psychotic disorders may vary from person to person. One or more of the five listed key features will be present in a diagnosis of psychotic disorder:

- False delusions that do not change even with proof that the beliefs are not true. This type of delusion is often referred to as bizarre because it is far-fetched and is not based on beliefs of a person's culture.

- The individual suffers from hallucinations that appear to be real to the individual. The hallucinations refer to seeing, smelling, feeling, or hearing things that are not there.
- The individual suffers from disorganized thinking and speech. The person does not think clearly and does not appear logical when he or she is talking.
- The individual experiences disorganized or abnormal motor behavior by making movements that seem nervous, restless, or frantic and without a clear purpose.
- The person has negative symptoms or an absence of energy, may not speak, and has little or no interest in past activities.

Psychotic disorders seldom appear in children. They almost always begin in the late teens or early 20s. While there is no complete care, treatment can improve the symptoms. Individuals with psychotic disorders generally lose tract with reality and have problems knowing what is real and in thinking clearly.[54]

Bipolar Disorders

Bipolar disorders are brain disorders that cause extreme shifts in a person's mood, energy, and ability to function. The American Psychiatric Association (APA) estimates that more than ten million Americans suffer from a bipolar disorder. The disorder contributes to damaged relationships, causes problems with work, school, or partner relations. It can even lead to suicide. The DSM-5 divides the disorders into three different conditions:

- Bipolar I-This disorder is diagnosed when a person has had a major episode. The manic episode can come either before or after a hypomanic episode or a major depressive episode.
- Bipolar II-This disorder is diagnosed when an individual has had at least one hypomanic lasting at least four days and one depressive episode lasting at least two weeks.
- Cyclothymic-This disorder is a milder form of bipolar illness in which there are many mood swings with hypomania and depressive symptoms occur often on a constant basis.

The three bipolar conditions share many of the same symptoms, but differ in severity and intensity. While the disorders are lifelong once they begin, proper treatment can relieve or lessen the symptoms. The symptoms cause great stress and problems with social relationships and other key aspects of life. They are not due to drug abuse or medication.

Key bipolar issues include:

- Individuals with bipolar disorders have extreme and intensive mood swings. Often switching between being very happy with high energy to feeling very low and out of energy.
- Often individuals with these disorders feel out of control and are ruled by their extreme moods and behaviors.
- Bipolar symptoms may change over time and therefore treatment may need to be varied.

Depressive Disorders

Depressive disorders include major depressive disorder, persistent depressive disorder, premenstrual dysphoric disorder, and disruptive mood dysregulation disorder. Depressive disorders can be caused by certain medications, alcohol and other drugs, and some medical conditions, such as thyroid disease. Depression is not the same as normal sadness or grief caused by an event such as the loss of a dear one. Depression can cause someone to feel hopeless, worthless, or guilty for months and even years. Depressive disorder is a major medical issue that can result in deep and profound impact upon a person's safety, well-being, and social relationships.

Treatment for depressive disorders is generally successful about 80 percent of the time. Treatment may include medication and psychotherapy i.e., talk therapy or both.

Major depressive disorder can cause a person to feel deeply sad or wholly absence of feelings the majority of time and last for at least two weeks. Individuals with major depressive disorder generally lose interest in activities that they once enjoyed. Frequently they have major changes in their sleep patterns, find it hard to think or focus, and have a feeling of worthlessness.

Persistent depressive disorder, formerly called dysthymic disorder, refers to a person with chronic and long-lasting type of depression in which the person's moods are often low for a long time. Symptoms may last for at least two years or longer. The symptoms cause great distress are impaired social relations, work, or other key aspects of living.

Premenstrual dysphoric disorder (PMDD) has finally been recognized as a disorder. A woman with this disorder may have severe symptoms of depression, irritability, and tension one week before menstruation begins. Some women may have premenstrual syndrome (PMS) which condition describes a broad range of emotional and physical symptoms but the symptoms are not serious enough to disrupt daily life. Women suffering this disorder may experience sudden mood swings, irritability, anger, or increased conflict with others. The risk of this disorder is increased by a history of trauma, cultural beliefs about the distinct roles for women, seasonal changes, and genetics.

Disruptive mood dysregulation disorder is a new disorder added to DSM-5. It is generally diagnosed in children who are severely irritable or angry and have frequent temper outbursts. Generally the symptoms for this disorder start before the child reaches the age of ten.

Premenstrual syndrome (PMS) is believed to affect up to 90 percent of women of reproductive age. A small subset of women have been identified who actually experience psychotic symptoms in the premenstrual phase of their cycles. PMS has been offered as a defense for criminal acts. The defense has generally fared poorly in the United States

In the United Kingdom, PMDD or in general PMS has been used as a defense to criminal charges since the 1980s. For example, Anna Reynolds, an 18-year-old, was accused of murdering her mother. Her defense used PMS as a mitigating factor. The court reduced her sentence from murder to manslaughter. Nicola Owen, who claimed that she committed arson occurred during her PMS plunges over which she had little or no control of, was acquitted of arson. Sandie Craddock committed a dozen criminal offenses, including the murder of a barmaid. Each of her convictions, along with her suicide attempts, were spread out in 29-day intervals and in sync with her menstrual cycle. The court concluded that she wasn't in control of her faculties. Craddock's charge was reduced to manslaughter as she was placed on probation provided that she remained on hormone therapy.

In the United States, PMS or PMDD has not generally been recognized as a defense to criminal behavior. However in *People v. Santos*, Shirley Santos, a 24-year-old single mother of six, was charged with beating her 4-year-old daughter when the child refused to be quiet. The child was examined and it was noted that the child was covered with bruises and welts. Miss Santos, distraught and remorseful, explained that she had just gotten her menstrual period. When Santos was charged with child battering, she raised the defense of premenstrual syndrome (PMS) in a pretrial hearing. Santos presented the first opportunity for an American court to consider PMS in a criminal case. Plea bargaining reduced the felony charge to a misdemeanor and Santos pleaded guilty. Accordingly, there was no legal test of the controversial defense. Increased publicity and recognition of PMS, however, may prompt more criminal defendants to assert the PMS defense.

Probably the first successful PMS defense in the U.S. occurred in a Virginia court in 1991. Geraldine Ritter, a 42-year-old orthopedic surgeon, was acquitted of driving erratically with three children in her car. She failed a breathalyzer test for blood-alcohol content. Her defense included the fact that she was suffering from PMS at the time of the incident. An expert witness testified that her conduct was consistent with PMS symptoms. After she was acquitted by the trial judge, many people criticized the trial judge based on the contention that it was a renaissance of old myths about "raging hormones" and could be used as an excuse for denying women high-level jobs.

Anxiety Disorders

Anxiety disorders are the most common diagnosed mental health problem in the United States. Anxiety disorders feature extreme fear and anxiousness with people usually experiencing the first episode in their early 20s. Separation anxiety disorder pertains to persons under the age of eighteen years who suffer abnormal anxiety following a separation from their home with people with whom they share a strong emotional bond. Panic disorders generally consist of reoccurring attacks of anxiety or panic. The attacks are characterized by a sudden onset of extreme misapprehension, fear, and terror usually associated with a feeling of doom. Agoraphobia is an abnormal fear of leaving home or being in a closed or crowded space.

Specific phobia disorder is an irrational fear of an object, activity, or situation. While this fear is usually recognized as unrealistic, the person goes to great lengths to avoid the objects or situation. Another anxiety disorder is social anxiety disorder (social phobia). This disorder results in an excessive fear of public speaking, eating in public, using public laboratories, and other frightening exposures to people.

The generalized anxiety disorder occurs when a person has a chronic worry or anxiety that does not resemble the other anxiety disorders. The final disorder that we will look at is substance-induced anxiety disorders. These are disorders caused by the direct physiological effects of drug abuse. The effects include prominent anxiety, panic attacks, or obsessions and compulsions and cannot be accounted for by an anxiety disorder that is not substance-induced.

Obsessive Compulsive Disorders

The principal characteristics of obsessive-compulsive disorders is the reoccurrence of sessions and compulsions that are foreign to the individual's personality. Common examples include obsessions of doubts, violence, and contamination. Common forms include repetitive hand washing, counting, checking, and touching.

Trauma and Stress Related Disorders

Trauma and stress disorders are most commonly experienced by people who have lived through some traumatic event. They are a new group of disorders listed in DSM-5. Generally these disorders are caused by events or circumstances that overwhelm the person, often threatening or causing serious injury, neglect, or death.

Posttraumatic stress disorder (PTSD) symptoms vary from person to person. People with PTSD frequently relive the experience through sudden disturbing memories that repeat and involve the horrible incident they saw, felt, heard, or smelled as if the event was happening again. Frequently people with PTSD have at least one other mental disorder. The most common other stress or trauma related disorders are depressive, bipolar, anxiety, and substance abuse disorders. It has been estimated that approximately one-half of the U.S. combat veterans from Iraq and Afghanistan wars have experienced some form of PTSD.

People with PTSD disorder may require different types of help at different stages. Many recover with the help of family, friends, or clergy but many do not. A range of treatment methods for this disorder include medication, cognitive behavior therapy, hypnosis, and exposure therapy. The medium onset of this disorder is twenty-three years of age.

Although the symptoms for Acute Stress Disorder are the same, a diagnosis of PTSD cannot be issued, according to DSM-5, until one has suffered the symptoms for 30 days. Even if a trauma survivor suffers greatly with severe symptoms following the trauma, they cannot receive a PTSD diagnosis or treatment until reaching the 30-day point.

The major difference between Acute Stress Disorder and PTSD is time. Like PTSD, acute stress disorder occurs for some people after they have experienced traumatic events. Generally they symptoms for acute stress disorder last for a shorter time than for PTSD. People with acute stress disorder frequently relives the traumatic event. When the symptoms last longer than one month, the disorder can progress to PTSD.

The symptoms for both PTSD and Acute Stress Disorder include:

- Reexperiencing Symptoms: upsetting thoughts or memories, nightmares, flashbacks, strong responses to reminders of the traumatic event.
- Avoidance Symptoms: avoiding thoughts, conversations, feelings, places, and people that remind us of the event; loss of interest, feeling distant, difficulty remembering parts of the event.
- Hyperarousal Symptoms: sleep problems, irritability, outbursts of anger, difficulty concentrating, and/or jumpiness.

RURAL VICTIMS

Although rural crime rates have traditionally been lower than urban crime rates, patterns of rural crime now indicate both the exporting of urban problems to rural areas and problems that are unique to rural areas.[55] Although far less research has been conducted on rural than on urban family violence, the National Institute of Justice, in its publication *Rural Crime and Rural Policing*, indicates the following characteristics and dimensions of rural versus urban family violence:

- Recent studies indicate that children in rural communities are as likely, and possibly more likely, to be abused or neglected than children in cities.

- Crimes such as homicide, rape, and assault are more likely to occur among acquaintances in rural areas than in urban areas.
- Although a limited number of surveys of the level of rural domestic violence have been conducted, an Ohio study found that the highest rates for domestic violence disputes were in the least populated jurisdictions.
- Although rural families face the same drug, alcohol, poverty, and stress problems as families living in a metropolitan area do, rural communities typically have fewer resources.[56]

Many rural counties have very low populations. Currently, one out of three rural counties (850) has fewer than 10,000 residents. This presents a challenge to establishing even basic services for crime victims, such as counseling for child abuse victims and shelters for battered women. Many rural domestic violence victims face the additional problem of not only having to leave their homes but also their communities to find safety. Often, the nearest shelter may be several communities and many miles away. Not only are these victims forced to leave whatever support network was available, but their children must be taken out of school to reach safety.

Promising Practices

Special Populations

The Midwest LEAD Institute (MLI)—Leadership Through Education and Advocacy for the Deaf. The Institute has developed a program to provide culturally and linguistically appropriate crisis intervention and counseling services to deaf victims of domestic violence. With support from VOCA funds, MLI provides volunteer sign language interpreters for shelters and agencies, and has established a twenty-four-hour 1-800 crisis line for deaf victims of violence.

The Bronx Independent Living Services (BILS) Crime Victims and Domestic Violence Program, Bronx, New York. The BILS Crime Victim Program provides assistance to all types of crime victims with disabilities. Victim Assistance services include crisis intervention: assistance with state crime victim compensation applications, assistance with housing, supportive counseling, and information and referral to community service programs.

Domestic Violence Access Project, State of Hawaii. Using Violence Against Women Act grant funding, the Hawaii Attorney General's Office supports a statewide effort to link domestic violence programs with programs that serve individuals with disabilities. The linkages are designed to enable shelter programs to receive training on disabilities and make accommodations to increase accessibility to programs.

Enhancing Your Interactions with People with Disabilities. This American Psychological Association (APA) brochure targets victim service providers, mental health providers, advocates, and psychologists and assists them in the development of improved communications skills with people with disabilities.

Source: National Victim Assistance Text (U.S. Department of Justice, Washington, D.C., 2003).

Problems and Issues

Federal victims of family violence who reside in rural areas face serious problems. Many victims must travel long distances to a U.S. courthouse. Often, these victims face similar attitudinal problems that other victims face, such as a lack of understanding of the impact of distance and an absence of support services. In addition, rural federal crime victims are skeptical about seeking assistance from the U.S. attorney general, feeling that the federal official is really not "one of the locals." This feeling may arise because the U.S. attorney general is not elected by the populace, as are most county attorneys.

Violence on Native American tribal lands is one of the most pressing issues in modern society. Feelings of alienation and rage are common among members of various tribes. Victims of family violence on tribal lands face unique problems that are not duplicated elsewhere in the United States. In addition, confusing jurisdictional boundaries among state, federal, and tribal laws are nowhere more evident than in victims' rights. For example, in a statewide survey of Wyoming's victim services, domestic violence victims who received orders of protection on the reservation had to file for similar protection orders in the local county in order to be protected from their abusers when they left the reservation. Often, their batterers would wait until the victims left the reservation to shop at the grocery store to intimidate, threaten, and harm them.

Although a tremendous amount of research is being funded and conducted in this area and excellent support from the Office for Victims of Crime is being offered to local tribal victim assistance programs, very few of these projects have adopted a multisystems approach to researching and understanding issues of tribal victims of crime.

Economic problems facing rural areas increasingly affect the nature and extent of crime. The impact on the resources available to communities to respond to crime and to assist victims cannot be underestimated. In sentencing offenders, often the only option for judges to select is jail because few community sentencing programs exist in rural areas.

The effects of geography also pose serious problems for rural family violence victims. Distance affects the response time and the speed with which law enforcement and emergency services respond to victims' calls for assistance. Whereas urban areas judge emergency response time in minutes, access to medical treatment in rural areas takes longer, resulting in higher death rates for rural victims suffering the same injuries as those living in urban environments. In addition, rural law enforcement waits longer for backup, forcing decisions of responding to dangerous situations alone or the delay of critical emergency responses, such as on domestic violence reports.

For many rural family violence victims, simply traveling to the local police station to make a report takes on special significance because of the distance, lack of transportation, and time involved in making such a trip. Transportation issues are especially critical for elderly victims and children going to therapy sessions. Travel to criminal justice agencies is exacerbated for tribal crime victims who participate in the federal justice system. Many tribal crime victims have to travel hundreds of miles to participate in the criminal justice process. One crime victim from the Wind River Reservation in Wyoming had to travel more than 500 miles to present a victim impact statement at the federal courthouse—and was told of the sentencing hearing the day before!

In addition, aspects of the rural culture may affect the willingness of family violence victims to report this violence and to participate in the criminal justice system. One study found that shoplifting and employee theft were rarely reported to the police; rather, the cases were handled informally. One criminal justice official said, "I simply can't get people to tell me things. I hear about them two or three weeks later, and when I ask them why they didn't come to see me about it, they say, 'Oh, I took care of it myself.' We simply can't get people to take advantage of the services of this office."

Overall, the issues of rural family violence and rural justice have not received national attention in the development of policies and protocol for law enforcement or other areas of the criminal justice system. For example, in the 447-page book *Local Government Police Management*, considered by most law enforcement officers to be the definitive reference on municipal police administration, the distinction between rural and urban policing is covered in a brief one-page section.[57] Moreover, this one-page overview does not even appear in updated editions. Family violence in rural areas is an important topic that warrants further study. We must provide services in these areas if we are ever going to stop this form of violence.

FETAL ALCOHOL SYNDROME DISORDER (FASD)

"Of all the substances ingested during pregnancy, alcohol produces the most long-ranging damage to the brain. Children and youth within the justice system are disproportionately affected by fetal alcohol spectrum disorder (FASD), with ramifications for a variety of cases, including delinquency, abuse and neglect, and education."[58]

Fetal alcohol syndrome disorder (FASD) is a unique form of child abuse. It is difficult to find an appropriate place to discuss this issue. Clearly it is one of the most severe forms of child abuse. As noted by the previous quote from the American Bar Association, its damage to the child is the most damaging.

According to the CDC, there is no known safe amount of alcohol to drink while pregnant. There is also no safe time during pregnancy to drink and no safe kind of alcohol. The CDC urges pregnant women not to drink alcohol any time during pregnancy.

The CDC advises that women should not drink alcohol if they are planning to become pregnant or are sexually active and do not use effective birth control. This is because a woman could become pregnant and not know for several weeks or more. In the United States, half of all pregnancies are unplanned. The CDC states that FASDs are 100 percent preventable. If a woman doesn't drink alcohol while she is pregnant, her child cannot have an FASD.

The CDC notes that when a pregnant woman drinks alcohol, so does her unborn baby. Alcohol in the mother's blood passes through the placenta to the baby through the umbilical cord. Drinking alcohol during pregnancy can cause miscarriage, stillbirth, and a range of lifelong disorders, known as FASDs. Children with FASDs might have the following characteristics and behaviors:

- Abnormal facial features, such as a smooth ridge between the nose and upper lip (this ridge is called the philtrum);
- Small head size;

- Shorter-than-average height;
- Low body weight;
- Poor coordination;
- Hyperactive behavior;
- Difficulty paying attention;
- Poor memory;
- Difficulty in school (especially with math);
- Learning disabilities;
- Speech and language delays;
- Intellectual disability or low IQ;
- Poor reasoning and judgment skills;
- Sleep and sucking problems as a baby;
- Vision or hearing problems;
- Problems with the heart, kidney, or bones.[59]

Summary

Family violence within special populations continues to increase. Because the United States is becoming more diverse, victim service professionals need to become aware of and sensitive to the needs of these special family violence victims. More important, they need to act as the spokespersons for these victims to individuals and agencies within the criminal justice system.

Both HIV and AIDS have deadly consequences for any infected person. Victims of crimes may suffer a second trauma if there is the possibility that they were exposed to the virus during the commission of the crime. Victim service providers must be sensitive to these special needs.

Victims with disabilities are only one example of the many special populations that exist in the United States. However, their victimization carries special problems and issues that must be addressed by those within the criminal justice system. Because of their status, these victims may not report incidents of family violence. In addition, they may be victimized a second time during the criminal justice process.

Family violence in the military is one of the more recent topics of research by academics and professionals. The military, like other special populations, is a culture that lives apart from other segments of our society. We are just now learning of the nature and extent of family violence in the military and are beginning to address some of the issues surrounding this type of violence.

Another form of violence that has occupied our nation's conscience is the sexual abuse committed by leaders of religious groups on congregation members. This type of abuse has existed for years, but with the disclosures surrounding members of the priesthood, it has taken on a new importance. It will be years before we completely understand the causes, effects, and consequences of this form of family violence.

Clearly mental disorders affects the lives of many individuals and their partner. We can assume that in many domestic violence incidents that a mental disorder caused or encouraged the actions of one of the partners or both that lead to the violence. Mental disorder may be defined as a significant deviation from a person's past behavior, thought processes, and emotions that result from an abnormal disturbance in his or her state.

Rural victims of family violence also face special problems when interacting with the criminal justice system. Something as important as filing a protective order may become an overwhelming task simply because of the distance between the victim's home and the courthouse. Victim service professionals must be aware of these potential problems when dealing with these special populations.

Key Terms

family violence—any act or omission by persons who are cohabitating that results in serious injury to other members of the family.

person with disabilities—one who has a physical or mental impairment that substantially limits one or more of the major life activities of that individual, who has a record of such impairment, or who is regarded as having such an impairment.

culture awareness—the understanding that an individual has regarding different cultures.

Discussion Questions

1. Should victims who are HIV-positive be treated any differently than other victims? Why?
2. Should a person with HIV/AIDS be required to disclose that fact to family members? To sexual partners? To workplace associates? To friends?
3. Should there be stiffer criminal penalties for perpetrators who commit crimes while HIV-positive? What if they were unaware of their infection?
4. Explain how you would work with a sight-impaired victim, a hearing-impaired victim, and a victim who uses a wheelchair. What problems or issues do you see that they will face in the criminal justice system?
5. Compare the problems facing rural and urban family violence victims. What is the most striking difference?

Suggested Readings

American Psychiatric Association, "Understanding Mental Disorder." (American Psychiatric Publishing), Washington, D.C., 2015).

Bickel, B., and S. Jantz. *World Religions and Cults 101: A Guide to Spiritual Beliefs* (Harvest House Publishers, Irvine, Calif., 2005).

Cockerham, W. *Sociology of Mental Disorder*, 9th ed. (London, Routledge, 2015)

Fontes, L. A., ed. *Sexual Abuse in Nine North American Cultures* (SAGE, Thousand Oaks, Calif., 1995).

Levin, J., and J. McDevitt. *The Rising Tide of Bigotry and Bloodshed* (Plenum, New York, 1993).

Nichols, L. A., G. Mather, and A. J. Schmidt. *Encyclopedic Dictionary of Cults, Sects, and World Religions*, Revised and Updated Edition (Zondervan, Grand Rapids, Mich., 2006).

Randel, W. P. *The Ku Klux Klan: A Century of Infamy* (Chilton, New York, 1965).

Sipe, A. *Sex, Priests, and Power: Anatomy of a Crisis* (Brunner/Mazel, London, 1995).

Weisheit, R. A., D. Falcone, and L. E. Wells. "Rural Crime and Rural Policing." *Research in Brief* (National Institute of Justice, Washington, D.C., October 1994).

Zaragoza, M. S., J. R. Graham, G. C. N. Hall, R. Hirschman, and R. S. Ben-Porath, eds. *Memory and Testimony in the Child Witness* (SAGE, Thousand Oaks, Calif., 1995).

Endnotes

1. This section has been based on *HIV/AIDS and Victim Services: A Critical Concern of the 90s,* sponsored by a grant from the Office for Victims of Crime (National Victim Center, Arlington, Va., February 1996), Chapters 2, 3, and 4.

2. *HIV/AIDS and Victim Services,* pp. II-1–II-2.

3. *HIV/AIDS and Victim Services,* pp. II-3–II-4.

4. *HIV/AIDS and Victim Services,* p. II-5.

5. *HIV/AIDS and Victim Services,* pp. II-5–II-8.

6. *HIV/AIDS and Victim Services,* pp. II-30–II-32.

7. *HIV/AIDS and Victim Services,* p. III-3.

8. *HIV/AIDS and Victim Services,* p. III-5.

9. See, for example, Florida Code Section 960.003 (1) (1994).

10. *HIV/AIDS and Victim Services,* p. III-18.

11. See *People v. Adams,* 97 *Daily Journal D.A.R.* 4854 (April 16, 1995), in which a California appellate court held that transmitting genital herpes is an aggravating sentencing factor and that AIDS testing is not unconstitutional.

12. *HIV/AIDS and Victim Services,* pp. IV-1–IV-2.

13. *HIV/AIDS and Victim Services,* p. IV-7.

14. *HIV/AIDS and Victim Services,* pp. IV-21–IV-30.

15. Department of Health and Human Services, Centers for Disease Control and Prevention, *Fact Sheet: HIV/AIDS among Youth in 2004,* www.cdc.gov/, accessed August 9, 2007.

16. Much of the material in this section has been based on *Focus on the Future: A Systems Approach to Prosecution and Victim Assistance,* sponsored by a grant from the Office for Victims of Crimes, U.S. Department of Justice, Washington, D.C. (National Victim Center, Arlington, Va., 1992).

17. K. Wolfe, "Bashing the Disabled: The New Hate Crime," *The Progressive* 9(11) (1995), p. 24.

18. This paragraph was based on the *Draft Report: Criminal Justice Task Force for Persons with Developmental Disabilities, Victim of Crime Section* (Office of Criminal Justice Planning, Sacramento, Calif., October 1, 1996), p. 1 (hereinafter cited as *Task Force for Persons with Developmental Disabilities*).

19. L. Merkin and M. J. Smith, "A Community-Based Model Providing Services for the Deaf and Deaf-Blind Victims of Sexual Assault and Domestic Violence," *Sexuality and Disability* 13(2) (1995), pp. 97–106.

20. "Eight Do's and Don'ts in Working with Disabled Victims of Crimes," *Focus on the Future: A Systems Approach to Prosecution and Victim Assistance* (National Victim Center, sponsored by a grant from the Office for Victims of Crimes, U.S. Department of Justice, Washington, D.C., 1992), p. C-13.

21. Based on *Task Force for Persons with Developmental Disabilities,* p. 1.

22. C. G. Tyiska, "Responding to Disabled Victims of Crime," *NOVA Network Information Bulletin,* no. 8–12 (NOVA, Washington, D.C., 1990), p. 10.

23. G. M. Worthington, "Sexual Exploitation and Abuse of People with Disabilities," *Response to Violence in the Family and Sexual Assault* 7(2) (1994), p. 43.

24. *Sexual Exploitation of Handicapped Students: Teachers Training Manual* (Seattle Rape Relief Disabilities Project, Seattle, Wash., 1981).

25. C. McPherson, "Bringing Redress to Abused Disabled Persons," *NOVA Network Information Bulletin,* no. 8–12 (NOVA, Washington, D.C., 1990), p. 14.

26. L. Melling, "Wife Abuse in the Deaf Community," *Response to Violence in the Family and Sexual Assault* 7(1) (1984), p. 12.

27. D. Aiello and L. Capkin, "Services for Disabled Victims: Elements and Standards," *Response to Violence in the Family and Sexual Assault* 7(5) (1984), p. 14.

28. Based on *Task Force for Persons with Developmental Disabilities,* pp. 11–22.

29. C. Hansen, "A Considerable Service: An Advocate's Introduction to Domestic Violence and the Military," *Domestic Violence Report,* 6(4) (2001), pp. 262–290.

30. L. D. Acord, "Child Abuse and Neglect in the Navy," *Military Medicine* 142 (1977), pp. 862–864.

31. S. S. Myers, "Child Abuse and the Military Community," *Military Medicine* 144 (1979), pp. 23–25.

32. N. K. Raiha and D. J. Soma, "Victims of Child Abuse and Neglect in the Army," *Child Abuse & Neglect* 8 (1997), pp. 759–768.

33. "Domestic Violence," Department of Defense Memorandum, November 19, 2001.

34. J. E. McCarroll et al., "Trends in Child Maltreatment in the U.S. Army, 1975–1997," in P. J. Mercer and J. D. Mercer, eds., *Battle Cries on the Home Front: Violence in the Military Family* (Charles C Thomas, Springfield, Ill., 2000).

35. D. J. Soma, "An Analysis of Rank Effects on Child Maltreatment in the United States Army," in P. J. Mercer and J. D. Mercer, eds., *Battle Cries on the Home Front: Violence in the Military Family* (Charles C Thomas, Springfield, Ill., 2000).

36. "Domestic Violence," Department of Defense Memorandum, November 19, 2001.

37. ALMAR 008/02, J. L. Jones, Commandant, Washington, D.C. signed 02/12/2002.

38. Linda D. Kozaryn, "DOD Task Force Seeks Better Domestic Violence Response," News Release, American Forces Press Service, March 9, 2001.

39. John Paul II, "Address of John Paul II to the Cardinals of the United States," www.vatican.va, 2002.

40. William Rusler, "The Catholic Church's Three Problems," *Conservative Chronicle*, V. 17 (April 3, 2002), p. 23.

41. Rafael Martinez, "What Is Religious Abuse," www.spiritwatch.org, accessed June 18, 2003.

42. Gavin Pattison, "235 Doomsday Believers Perish by Uganda Fire," Reuters, www.reuters.com/com, accessed March 18, 2000.

43. D. E. Kaplin and A. Marshall, *The Cult at the End of the World: The Terrifying Story of the Aum Doomsday Cult, from the Subways of Tokyo to the Nuclear Arsenals of Russia* (Crown Publications, New York, 1996). Author's note: There are some who dispute the material in Kaplin's book. For example, see Timoth3y [with a 3] Romero, "Lies at the End of the World," www.dotco.com/t3/Aum/Kaplin.

44. C. Wessinger, ed., *Millennialism, Prosecution, and Violence: Historical Cases* (Syracuse University Press, Syracuse, New York, 2000); and D. Layton, *Seductive Poison: A Jonestown Survivor's Story of Life and Death in the People's Temple* (Anchor Publishing, Wilmington, N.C. 1998).

45. Thomas Farragher, "The Cardinal Resigns," *The Boston Globe*, p. A15, December 14, 2002.

46. 2003 DJDAR 6986 (June 26, 2003).

47. See J. Anderson, "Church Mulls Challenge to Sex-Abuse Law," *LA Daily Journal*, p. 1, July 17, 2003.

48. J. Filteau, "Study Says Two-Fifths of U.S. Nuns Suffered Some Form of Sexual Abuse," *Catholic News Service*, January 8, 2003, cns@catholic-news.com.

49. L. Neff, "Evaluating Cults and New Religions," in R. Enroth et al., eds., *A Guide to Cults and New Religions* (Intervarsity Press, Downers Grove, Ill., 1983), republished in R. Enroth, *Recovering from Churches That Abuse* (Zondervan Publishing House, Grand Rapids, Mich., 1994).

50. It must be noted that many attribute these characteristics to Enroth. However, a careful reading of his latest textbook, *Churches that Abuse*, clearly reveals that he is citing Neff from an earlier work he edited.

51. World Health Organization (WHO), "Improving Health Systems and Services For Mental Health" (Geneva, Switzerland, 2011).

52. W. C. Cockerham, *Sociology of Mental Disorder*, 9th ed. (London, Routledge, 2014).

53. Ibid, p. 4.

54. American Psychiatric Association, "Understanding Mental Disorder." *American Psychiatric Publishing* (Washington, D.C., 2015).

55. This section has been based on H. Wallace and C. Edmunds, *America's Forgotten Crime Victims*, a federal grant proposal to the Office for Victims of Crimes, U.S. Department of Justice, Washington, D.C., July 1, 1995.

56. R. A. Weisheit et al., "Rural Crime and Rural Policing," *Research in Brief* (National Institute of Justice, Washington, D.C., October 1994).

57. Ibid

58. American Bar Association Web page that advertised a webinar on Fetal Alcohol Spectrum, www.apps.americanbar.org/cle/programs, accessed June 1, 2012.

59. See the CDC Web site, www.cdc.gov/, accessed June 1, 2012.

13

Sexual Violence

CHAPTER OBJECTIVES

After studying this chapter, you should be able to:

- Discuss what should be considered as sexual violence;
- Explain the history of aggression and violence against women;
- List the theories involved in explaining sexual violence;
- Explain the various forms of sexual violence;
- Define sexual harassment;
- Discuss the issues involved with date rape.

Detailed Look at What You Should Know About Sexual Violence

- While sexual violence is generally perpetrated against a woman, men have also been victims of sexual violence.
- Certain types of acts or actions are specific to women and contribute to violence against women both within and outside the family.
- Power in the feminist analysis is not police or political power; rather, it is defined in terms of a relationship that structures the interactions between men and women. Power, therefore, is not a property right but a personal force that establishes male control and dominance over females.
- A review of history indicates that the use of aggression and violence against women has existed for eons.
- Only recently has society begun to recognize other forms of sexual violence. It is now acknowledged that spouses may be raped, and acquaintance rape has become a common term.

- Sexual violence can take the form of a single act or a long and protracted series of incidents. It can also involve aggression and/or discrimination against women.

- Sexual violence can happen to any person, at any time, and in any place. No one is completely secure from this type of assault.

- One of the major problems in the area of women and sexual violence is the lack of agreement among scholars, researchers, and professionals on definitions and research methodology.

- The average age at the time of arrest for rapists was thirty-one years, with sex offenders being slightly older, at age thirty-four. About one in four rapists and sexual assault offenders had a prior conviction for violent crimes.

- As with other forms of family violence, a number of theories exist regarding this form of aggression, but the exact cause of sexual violence is undetermined.

- Researchers have now developed different typologies of rapists in an effort to streamline and define this type of personality. One authority states that there are more than fifty different types of rapists.

- On the basis of the limited data available, it has been estimated that 100 to 132 million girls and women have been subjected to female genital mutilation worldwide.

- Carnal knowledge of a female was one of the first terms used to connote sexual violence.

- Rape carries with it certain physical, mental, and legal consequences. Many times, during a rape the offender will perform or attempt to perform a variety of acts, including vaginal, oral, and anal sex.

- Intimate sexual violence includes marital and acquaintance rape. These forms of assault are not isolated incidents that occur to only a few women.

- For centuries, society has believed that a man is entitled to have sex with his wife. In the eighteenth century, a man could not be charged or convicted of raping his wife in England.

- The marital exemption for rape can be traced to Sir Matthew Hale, a seventeenth-century English jurist.

- Blackstone, the great English legal scholar, stated that the legal existence of a woman is suspended during marriage or at the very least incorporated into that of her husband.

- Just as there are a number of theories as to why intimate partner abuse and stranger rape occur, so there are a variety of theories dealing with factors that encourage or promote marital rape.

- Rape drugs make it easy for perpetrators to gain control of the victim. Two drugs were consistently reported in these types of cases of acquaintance rape: gamma-hydroxybutyrate (GHB) and flunitrazepam (Rohypnol).

- Sexual harassment is the overall umbrella under which specific forms of sexual violence take place. Although it is true that men have been targets of sexual harassment, most victims are women.

INTRODUCTION

This is a textbook on family violence; however, sexual violence both within and outside the family is included because when a person is a victim of sexual violence, the violence also significantly affects the family unit. Generally sexual violence is a crime in which women are the victims, but men may also be victims. Some acts involving sexual violence could have been examined in earlier chapters. They are so distinctive and important, however, that they have been placed in a separate chapter for emphasis and expanded discussion.

Many of the previous acts of violence involved husbands, lovers, or other significant individuals in a family situation. This chapter examines abusive actions that are perpetrated by those persons as well as strangers or persons with whom women have professional rather than personal relationships. Some of these acts are allowed by a society that permits certain forms of expression to continue that are degrading to women. Others involve coworkers and supervisors who treat women as inferiors or sexual playthings. Still others involve forced sexual activities either by a stranger or by a person known to the woman. All these actions or situations are sexually abusive in nature.

It's little wonder that sexual violence is still present in today's society, considering Western history. Sigmund Freud, the father of psychoanalysis who invented the concept of primacy of the penis, declined to explore the concept of rape.[1] Marx and Engels, who developed the theory of economic determinism of crime, were silent concerning the exploitation of women by the act of rape.[2]

Three works by feminist authors and researchers set the stage for advancing the awareness of sexual violence against women. Millett's *Sexual Politics*, Griffin's "Rape: The

Focus

Sexual Violence in America

State of Florida v. William Kennedy Smith involved allegations of rape brought against a member of the Kennedy family. The victim alleged that Willie Smith picked her up and took her to a beach house where he raped her against her will. The nation watched on live television as defense attorneys questioned the virtues and motives of the victim. While Mr. Smith was acquitted on all charges, the specter of something called "date rape" became a common topic throughout the United States.

State of Indiana v. Mike Tyson involved a black beauty contestant and the former heavyweight champion of the world. She claimed that he raped her in his hotel room. Mr. Tyson was convicted and sentenced to prison even though he maintained that the sexual acts were consensual.

One of the premier military educational universities, the U.S. Air Force Academy, was exposed as an institution that did not respond to allegations of sexual assault. In 2003, the Secretary of the Air Force reported more than fifty-four cases of sexual violence in the last ten years. The resulting crisis involved three congressional investigations into the nature and extent of sexual harassment and sexual assault at the academy. There were forced resignations, and new policies were put in place to address issues of sexual violence at the academy.

Anita Hill was a tenured law school professor when she heard that a former employer of hers, Clarence Thomas, had been nominated for the U.S. Supreme Court. She appeared before a subcommittee of the Senate and testified to certain sexually oppressive acts that she alleged Mr. Thomas committed when she worked for him. Ms. Hill was accused of being psychotic and of lying. Mr. Thomas was subsequently appointed to the Supreme Court.

All-American Crime," and Brownmiller's *Against Our Will* each raised the collective consciousness regarding the domination of women by men.[3]

Sexual Politics examines the concept of patriarchy, which Millett claims is a social and political system used by men to control women. She argues that patriarchy is a feature of all past and present societies and exists across cultures and socioeconomic systems today. Millett concludes that power and coercion are central features of patriarchy and are used to control women's sexuality.

Griffin's short article "Rape: The All-American Crime" contains numerous themes. One of the most important concerns is the nature of the crime of rape. She argues that rape is not a sexual act; rather, it is a violent political act. Griffin concludes that the threat of rape is used as a method of social control that affects all women.

Brownmiller discusses the history of rape, maintaining that rape is an act used by men to maintain their dominance over women by the use of force. She expands on both Millett's and Griffin's work and concluded that the threat of rape creates a climate of fear, and this fear acts as a form of social control that benefits men.

Kelly, in her book *Surviving Sexual Violence*, reviews these early feminist approaches to sexual abuse and concludes that sexual violence is based on three concepts: power, sexuality, and social control.[4]

Power in the feminist analysis is not police or political power; rather, it is defined in terms of a relationship that structures the interactions between men and women. Power, therefore, is not a property right but a personal force that establishes male control and dominance over females. This power is multifaceted and complex. It not only is present in interpersonal relationships but also extends to society's social structure and beliefs.

Sexuality has two aspects. First, male control of women's sexuality is a key factor in women's oppression. Second, sexuality is defined by men's experiences, which legitimatize

---

Focus

Some Startling Facts about Rape

- Most rapes and sexual assaults against females were not reported to the police.
- The National College Women Sexual Victimization (NCWSV) study, a National Institute of Justice-funded telephone survey of 4,446 women attending two- or four-year colleges, found victimization rates for completed and attempted rapes at 35.3 per 1,000 college women during the academic year 1996–1997. For both completed and attempted rapes, the victims knew their offenders in nine out of ten incidents.
- In 2005, the rate of rape was 0.8 per 1,000 persons aged twenty-one or older. This was a 68.6 percent drop in the rate of rape in 1993.

Sources: Rape and Sexual Assault: Reporting to Police and Medical Attention 1992–2000 (Bureau of Justice Statistics, Washington, D.C., August 2002); *Criminal Victimization, 2002* (Bureau of Justice Statistics, Washington, D.C., August 2003); *National Victim Assistance Text* (U.S. Department of Justice, Washington, D.C., 2003); and S. M. Catalano, *Criminal Victimization, 2005* (Bureau of Justice Statistics, Washington D.C., September 2006).

the use of force or coercion in intimate relationships. Some conflict exists among feminists regarding the issue of sexuality and whether it has the same significance for women in all cultures.

Social control is the outcome of power and sexuality. The mere threat of sexual violence may result in women developing strategies for self-protection that will limit their mobility, work, or advancement. The reality of sexual violence not only impacts women in intimate relationships but also spills over to the campus setting. Numerous colleges and universities provide "escort services" for female students who attend evening classes. This speaks volumes for the fear that exists regarding sexual violence, even on campuses in the United States.

These feminists laid the foundation that allows a greater understanding of the concept of sexual violence and women. The following sections examine this type of violence and explore some of the more common theories regarding its causes and consequences.

DEFINITION

Exactly what do the terms *rape, marital rape, acquaintance rape*, and *sexual violence* mean? Should they be defined strictly from a legal perspective, a medical view, a psychological point of view, or a combination of all the foregoing? Each discipline has valid reasons for defining sexual violence in a certain manner.

A review of history indicates that the use of aggression and violence against women has existed for eons. Sexual violence against women traditionally has been viewed as stranger rape, a violent forceful sexual assault on a female. Only recently has society begun to recognize other forms of sexual violence. It is now acknowledged that spouses may be raped, and *acquaintance rape* has become a common term. In addition, other forms of sexual violence are more subtle but just as damaging; sexual harassment and sexual discrimination are still rampant in the United States. To define sexual violence by any one of these acts is to do

---

Focus

Male Rape Victims: A Symbol of an Unhealed Congo

The headlines of the *New York Times* on August 5, 2009, stated "male rape victims were the latest tragic symbol of an unhealed Congo." According to the news report, the Human Rights Watch and United Nations officials are concerned over the rapid rise in the number of men raping men. One aid worker in attempting to explain the sudden spike in male rape cases stated that sexual violence against men is yet another way for armed groups to humiliate and demoralize Congolese communities into submission. One United Nations official stated that eastern Congo is the rape capital of the world. The official noted that hundreds of thousands of women have been sexually assaulted by the various armed groups haunting the hills and that this area is going through one of its bloodiest periods in years. The American Bar Association, which runs a sexual violence legal clinic in Goma, reported that more than 10 percent of the cases in June 2009 involved men as victims.

Source: Jeffery Gettleman, "Latest Tragic Symbol of an Unhealed Congo: Male Rape Victims," *New York Times*, August 5, 2009, p. A-1.

injustice to the whole concept that women are equal to men. A legal definition of sexual violence focuses on certain conduct that is prohibited and strictly defined. A medical definition views sexual violence as injury to the body. A psychological evaluation of sexual violence examines the effect on the mind and the emotions of the victim. Each of these approaches has certain strengths and weaknesses.

Sexual violence can take the form of a single act or a long and protracted series of incidents. It can also involve aggression and/or discrimination against women. For purposes of this discussion, **sexual violence** is any intentional act or omission that results in physical, emotional, or financial injury to another person. The term *financial injury* is included to cover sexual harassment situations in which women have been terminated from employment for refusing to engage in sexual acts with their supervisors. Sexual violence does not include the termination of a romantic relationship. The ritual of courting, dating, and marriage in the United States commonly results in one person being hurt or heartbroken when the relationship ends. Although painful, it does not rise to the level of sexual violence. Some might argue that this definition is too comprehensive, but to narrow it would be to exclude certain types of acts that result in harm to women.

Focus

Rape and Sexual Assault Among College-age Females, 1995–2013

Two researchers Lynn Langton and Sofi Sinozich, compared the characteristics of rape and sexual assault victimization against females ages 18 to 24 who are enrolled and not enrolled in college. Their report examined the relationship between the victim and offender, the involvement of a weapon, location of the victimization, reporting to police, perceived offender characteristics, and victim demographics. Their data was taken from the National Crime Victimization Survey (NCVS), which collects information on nonfatal crimes, reported and not reported to the police, against persons from a nationally representative sample of U.S. households. The report also discusses methodological differences between the NCVS and other surveys that measure rape and sexual assault victimization and the impact of these difference on rape and sexual assault estimates.

Highlights of their report:

- The rate of rape and sexual assault was 1.2 times higher for nonstudents (7.6 per 1,000) than for students (6.1 per 1,000).
- For both college students and nonstudents, the offender was known to the victim in about 80 percent of rape and sexual assault victimizations.
- Most (51%) student rape and sexual assault victimizations occurred while the victim was pursuing leisure activities away from home, compared to nonstudents who were engaged in other activities at home (50%) when the victimization occurred.
- The offender had a weapon in about one in ten rape and sexual assault victimizations against both students and nonstudents.
- Rape and sexual assault victimizations of students (80%) were more likely than nonstudent victimizations (67%) to go unreported to police.

Source: L. Langton and S. Sinozich "Rape and Sexual Assault Among College-age Females, 1995–2013" NCJ 248471, (December, 2014). Available online at www.bjs.gov/index.cfm?ty=pbdetail&iid=5176, accessed September 1, 2015.

Sexual violence can happen to any person, at any time, and in any place. No one is completely secure from this type of assault. The following sections examine different aspects of this form of sexual violence.

EXTENT OF THE PROBLEM

How many women are raped each year? Exactly what is involved in the act of **rape**? Is sexual assault the same as rape? Should statisticians determine whether a woman has been raped once in a lifetime or only attempt to determine how many rapes occur each year? These are legitimate questions that surface any time the study and research of sexual violence is undertaken. Determining the exact nature and extent of sexual violence is a complex and difficult process.

One of the major problems in the area of women and sexual violence is the lack of agreement among scholars, researchers, and professionals on definitions and research methodology. Depending on which article, paper, or textbook one reads, the estimates regarding the incident of rape will vary. This disparity has caused problems and confusion within the professions from the outset. There are a number of reasons for the different figures and definitions within this area of family violence. The following list summarizes some of the more common problems encountered when this phenomenon is studied:

Definitional issues: Some scholars use the term *rape*, others use *sexual assault*, and still others define each of the foregoing terms differently. For example, one researcher may define *rape* as vaginal intercourse accomplished by use of force or fear, whereas other researchers may define *rape* as vaginal, oral, or rectal intercourse accomplished by force or fear. The simple addition of two terms changes the entire results of any study.

Professional issues: Various professionals approach rape from different perspectives. Attorneys view rape in a certain legalistic way, physicians treat it as a medical problem, and psychologists approach it from a mental health point of view.

Gathering of information: Problems in the screening techniques, formation of questions, context of questioning, and issues of confidentiality all impact the validity and type of response that the researcher will receive.[5] Koss compiled many of the various studies on rape, and her work illustrates the different approaches various researchers have used when attempting to determine the incidence of sexual violence against women in the United States.[6]

Sexual Violence and Women

One of the most important studies of sexual violence was conducted by the National Victim Center entitled *Rape in America: A Report to the Nation*, and it caused an uproar across the United States when it was released in April 1992.[7] The National Victim Center relied on a comprehensive study titled "The National Women's Study" to gather its information. This report was based on a national sample of 4,008 women who were interviewed regarding their experience with rape. The report indicated that rape occurred at a much higher incidence than previously thought.

One of the most controversial rape studies was conducted by Mary Koss, who was then a professor at Kent State University. In 1985, Koss was contacted by *Ms. Magazine* and commissioned to conduct a national rape survey. Koss and her associates interviewed more than 3,000 women nationwide. They concluded that 15.4 percent of the respondents had been raped, and 12.1 percent were victims of attempted rape. This equaled a total of 27.5 percent who were victims of sexual assault. This percentage in turn led to the "one in four" victims of rape slogan. Koss's study became one of the most widely cited articles on rape. It also became and still is one of the most controversial articles on rape.[8]

In 1997, the U.S. Department of Justice released one of the most comprehensive studies of sexual violence in the United States.[9] This report, titled *Sex Offenses and Offenders*, draws on more than two dozen data sets maintained by the U.S. Department of Justice in an effort to provide a comprehensive overview about the incidence of sexual assault, the response by the criminal justice system to such crimes, and the characteristics of both the offenders and the victims. The report drew on the National Crime Victimization Survey (NCVS), the Uniform Crime. Reporting Program, the National Incident Based Reporting System, the National Judicial Reporting Program, and the Supplemental Homicide Reporting (SHR) Program.

The 2004 National Crime Victimization Survey reveals a drop in the number of rapes and sexual assaults between 1996 and 2003.[10] In 1996, there were a total of 291,820 sexual assaults, and in 2004 there was a decline to 207,240, a 29 percent decrease.

Even though the numbers of rapes or sexual assaults have declined in recent years, these types of violent crimes remain an unsolved crisis in our society. These crimes can occur at any place and at any time.

Overall, about 91 percent of all victims of rape or sexual assault were female. About 60 percent of all the offenses were found to occur between 6 p.m. and 6 a.m. About 60 percent of all the incidents occurred in the victim's own home or at the home of a friend, neighbor, or relative. More than half of the rapes and/or sexual assaults occurred within one mile of the victim's home or at his or her home. About 90 percent of all incidents involved a single offender. About 75 percent of the single offenders had a prior relationship as a family member, intimate, or acquaintance. When multiple offenders engaged in rape or sexual assaults, about 72 percent of the victims were unknown to these offenders.[11]

About 74 percent of all victims reported that they took some form of self-protective action during the crime. The most common form involved resisting the attack or attempting to chase and capture the offender. Among those victims who took some form of self-protective action, more than half felt that their actions had helped the situation.

Every other year, the Bureau of Justice Statistics obtains information on felony defendants from the nation's seventy-five most populous counties. Information from this survey indicates that 48 percent of all defendants charged with rape were released from detention prior to the adjudication of their cases. The most common method used by those charged with rape for obtaining their release was to post a bond. About two-thirds of all defendants convicted of the crime of rape received a prison sentence. Nineteen percent served their sentence in jail, and the remaining 13 percent received a sentence of probation. For those defendants sentenced to state prison, the average term was 146 months, or just under fourteen years. The average term for those defendants sentenced to jail was eight months, and the average probationary period was six years.

The average age at the time of arrest for rapists was thirty-one years, with sex offenders being slightly older, at age thirty-four. About one in four rapists and sexual assault offenders

TABLE 13.1 Number and Percent Distribution of Incidents, by Type of Crime and Victim–Offender Relationship

Type of Crime	All Incidents		Percent of Incidents Involving Strangers		Percent of Incidents Involving Nonstrangers	
	Number	Percent	Number	Percent	Number	Percent
Rape/sexual assault	381,400	100	129,890	34.1	251,510	65.9
Rape/attempted rape	200,880	100	61,110	30.4	139,770	69.6
Rape	141,070	100	32,900	23.3	108,160	76.7
Attempted rape[a]	59,810	100	28,210*	47.2*	31,600	52.8
Sexual assault[b]	180,530	100	68,780	38.1	111,750	61.9

Note: Detail may not add to total shown because of rounding.
*Estimate is based on about ten or fewer sample cases.
[a]Includes verbal threats of rape.
[b]Includes threats.

had a prior conviction for violent crimes. Ten percent of those incarcerated for rape had prior convictions for rape or sexual assault. Violent sex offenders reported that two-thirds of their victims were under the age of eighteen. Table 13.1 supports the proposition that rape occurs much more often between those who know each other than between strangers. About 30 percent of the rapists and less than 15 percent of the sexual offenders reported that their victims had been strangers.

The FBI collects additional information about murder in its annual SHR Program. In this program, local law enforcement agencies provide a monthly report that includes a wide variety of information regarding homicides in their jurisdictions. Murder that was classified as involving rape or other sexual offenses accounted for 1.5 percent of all reported homicides in which the circumstances of the crime were known to investigators. Sexual assault murder victims differ from other murder victims in that they were substantially more likely than other murder victims to be female and white. The weapon of choice in sexual homicides was a knife.

The preceding figures indicate that rape in the United States is more common than previously thought, and rape is only one form of sexual violence that is perpetrated against women.

THEORIES ON SEXUAL VIOLENCE

As with other forms of family violence, a number of theories exist regarding this form of aggression, but the exact cause of sexual violence is undetermined. The following section examines some of the theories regarding the possible etiology of this violent act of aggression.

Causes of Rape

No single factor can be highlighted as the cause of rape. Just as there are many forms of sexual violence, so there are a multitude of theories on causes of sexual aggression toward women.

Some of the more common theories on the causes of rape include the following: sexual moti-vation, socialization, machoism, biological factors, psychological forces, and the culture of violence.

> *Sexual motivation:* Most current research dismisses this theory of rape. It is not viewed as a sexual act; rather, it is an act of violence, aggression, and power by the male.

> *Socialization:* This concept holds that in society young boys are taught to be aggressive, forceful, tough, and a winner in any sport or activity. This socialization creates aggres-sors and can spill over into the sexual arena, where men are taught to sexually conquer as many women as possible. This aggressive attitude encourages and gives consent to men to engage in rape.[12]

> *Machoism:* This theory holds that men who believe in male machoism will be more aggressive toward women. Machoism is a set of beliefs that includes a view of women as objects simply to be added to a numerical list of sexual conquests. These conquests may include the act of rape.[13]

> *Biological factors:* This view argues that rape is a male instinctive reaction that is a drive to perpetuate the species. Symons believes that men still have a genetic holdo-ver that impels them to have sex with as many women as possible, and he argues that rape is closely linked to sexuality and violence.[14] Other scholars discount this position.[15]

> *Psychological forces:* This theory purports that men rape because they suffer from some sort of personality disorder or mental illness. Studies have attempted to define the dynamics of convicted sex offenders and identify exactly what mental condition causes them to rape. To date, there is no conclusive profile of a rapist.

> *Culture of violence:* The culture of violence theory states that society is a violent envi-ronment that encourages some men to use violence to obtain sex. The use of violence and aggression is expected, and these individuals view women as legitimate targets of sexual aggression. These men believe that women want to be dominated and overpow-ered by an aggressive male.[16]

Types of Rape

Although there are many causes of rape and sexual violence, studies in the past have failed to clearly define or predict who will rape. Researchers have now developed different typologies of rapists in an effort to streamline and define this type of personality. One authority states that there are more than fifty different types of rapists.[17]

Groth and his associates conducted a study in Massachusetts of 133 convicted rapists and ninety-two victims. This classic study, "Rape: Power, Anger and Sexuality," established that issues of power, anger, and sexuality are important concepts in understanding the various types of rape. In addition, this was one of the first research efforts to recognize that rape is a crime of violence and not a sexual act.[18] Groth and his associates classified rape types into two major categories: power and anger.

Power rapes involve the offender seeking power and control over his victim by the use of force or threats. The sexual assault is evidence of conquest and domination. The perpetrator will plan and fantasize about the rape, believing that the victim will respond to his advances after initially resisting. Power rapes may be further classified as power-assertive rapes or power-reassurance rapes. The *power-assertive* rapist views the assault as an expression of his virility, mastery, and dominance. The *power-reassurance* rapist, on the other hand, commits rapes to resolve doubts about his masculinity and sexual adequacy.

Anger rapes involve the expression of anger, rage, contempt, or hatred toward the victim. The objective of this type of rapist is to vent his rage on the victim and retaliate for rejections or perceived wrongs that he has suffered in the past by other women. Anger rapes may be categorized as anger–retaliation or anger–excitation rapes. In *anger–retaliation* rapes, the rape is an expression of hostility and rage toward women. *Anger–excitation* rape occurs as a result of the offender's desire to obtain pleasure, thrills, and arousal secondary to the suffering of the victim during the assault.

Two years after their initial publication, Groth and Birnbaum established a more refined version of the original typology. In *Men Who Rape*, they established three categories of rapists and determined that there were three types of rape offenses: anger rapes, power rapes, and sadism rapes.[19]

The new definitions of anger and power rapes are very similar to those in the earlier study, and the sadistic rapist is obsessed with ritual during the rape. He may tie up his victim, torture her, or humiliate her, becoming intensely excited during the act. This type of rape is

International Perspectives

Rape in Other Countries and Cultures

In Dubai, a French businesswoman who was a victim of gang rape was charged with adultery. The victim was raped by three men who offered her a ride home from a nightclub. She immediately reported the attack to the Dubai police. The police investigated the incident and interviewed one of the attackers, who claimed the sexual acts were consensual. The police arrested her rather than the attackers. The woman, aged thirty-nine, was charged under the Emirate's law, which declares that any sexual relationship outside of marriage is illegal. Her passport was confiscated, and she could not leave Dubai.

The U.S. Department of State reports that the Myanmar military have systematically raped ethnic minority women and children as a weapon of war in its ongoing campaign to bring ethnic minority states under its control. Myanmar, also known as Burma, has been investigated by human rights groups as well as by an official from the State Department. Both investigations confirm that Burmese soldiers gang-raped young girls as well as pregnant women in an effort to subdue the ongoing rebellion in the ethnic states Burma claims to control.

For many girls and women in other countries, sexual violence can take place in a variety of contexts, including the home. Studies conducted in a number of countries have reported rates as high as 46 percent of adolescent women and up to 20 percent of adolescent men who have reported sexual coercion at the hands of family members, teachers, boyfriends, or strangers.

Sources: Based on Philip Delves, "Gang Rape Victim Faces Jail on Adultery Charges," *The Daily Telegraph*, January 3, 2003, p. 1; "Report Details Mass Rapes," *The Fresno Bee*, December 26, 2002, p. A14; and "Sexual Violence," World Health Organization, www.who.in/en, accessed September 21, 2003.

very traumatic, and Groth found that victims of this type of rape needed long-term psychiatric counseling.

Sexual violence continues to be researched, and perhaps one day rapists will be identified by a series of tests or events. However, until that time arrives, sexual violence will continue to be a serious problem that must be evaluated and treated.

Consequences of Rape

Although this section deals specifically with the consequences of rape, it should be noted that it does not cover the entire range of possible consequences and treatment for all forms of sexual violence. This discussion instead focuses on the psychological damage that is a result of this act of aggression.

One of the first longitudinal studies of rape victims' reactions indicated that certain fears are more severe than those suffered by nonvictims.[20] However, fear is not the only symptom suffered by rape victims. Resick reports that rape victims suffer a variety of reactions, including the following: fear and anxiety, posttraumatic stress disorder (PTSD), depression, social maladjustment, decreased self-esteem, and impaired sexual functioning.[21]

> *Fear and anxiety:* These are the most common reactions to the crime of rape. Burnam conducted a survey of 3,132 households and found that rape victims reported significantly higher levels of phobias and panic disorders than nonvictims.[22] Rape victims suffer a higher level of anxiety than victims of other violent crimes such as robbery.[23]
>
> *Posttraumatic stress disorder:* This mental disorder has already been touched on when the consequences of ritual abuse on children were discussed. **Posttraumatic stress disorder** (PTSD) is defined as the development of characteristic symptoms following a psychologically distressing event that is outside the range of usual human experience. The characteristic symptoms involve reexperiencing the traumatic event, avoidance of stimuli associated with the event or numbing of general responsiveness, and increased agitation.[24] Victims of rape also have reported or been diagnosed as suffering from PTSD. Rothbaum's study found that 94 percent of rape victims displayed classic

---

Focus

Movies, Books, Celebrities, and Sexual Violence

Is it any wonder that sexual violence is accepted in American culture? *Gone with the Wind* is famous for the scene in which Rhett Butler sweeps a protesting Scarlet off her feet and carries her up the stairs to the bedroom. The next morning finds Scarlet happy and fulfilled with her darling husband.

The classic play *A Streetcar Named Desire* involves Stanley raping his sister-in-law while his wife is in the hospital giving birth to their child.

The matinee hero of the 1940s and 1950s Errol Flynn was constantly overpowering resisting women who halfway through the first kiss gave up and responded just as passionately. People have been raised on a diet of male machismo and women who give in after a brief but half-hearted struggle. This has led to a certain mind-set toward sex and women.

symptoms of PTSD one week after the assault. This figure dropped to 47 percent twelve weeks after the incident.[25] Kilpatrick and colleagues' study, *Rape in America*, reported that 11 percent of all women raped still suffer from PTSD, and the authors estimated that 1.3 million women in the United States are currently suffering from PTSD as a result of a rape or multiple rapes.[26]

Rape crisis syndrome is very similar to PTSD. **Rape crisis syndrome** occurs when the victim experiences feelings of shame, humiliation, disjointedness, anger, inability to concentrate, and withdrawal.[27]

Depression: A number of studies have found that rape victims suffer from depression as a result of their experiences, with classifications ranging from moderate to severely depressed. *Rape in America* states that 33 percent of all rape victims thought seriously about suicide compared to 8 percent of nonvictims.[28]

Self-esteem: The issue of self-blame on the part of rape victims has been commented on by a number of authorities. However, no conclusive study indicates that rape victims as a class suffer from lower self-esteem than other victims or nonvictims. Although Resick and her associates found that there were long-term problems with self-esteem in rape victims, it is also clear that this area needs further study.[29]

Social adjustment: Victims of rape often suffer from economic, social, and leisure adjustment. Studies indicate that marital and family adjustments may be more difficult for rape victims than for nonvictims.[30]

International Perspectives

Female Genital Mutilation

Based on the limited data available, it has been estimated that 100 million to 132 million girls and women have been subjected to female genital mutilation worldwide. Each year, approximately two million more girls will undergo some form of female genital mutilation. Female genital mutilation is known to be practiced in twenty-eight African countries, a few countries of western Asia, and some minority communities in other Asian countries.

Female genital mutilation is defined as all procedures that involve partial or total removal of the external female genitalia or other injury to the female genital organs, whether for cultural or any other nontherapeutic reasons. This definition covers a wide range of activities, including excision of the prepuce with or without excision of the clitoris and cauterization of the clitoris by burning it and its surrounding tissues.

In spite of medical risks and serious and certain physical and psychological damage, the practice continues, and many women support their daughters undergoing it. The reason most often given for this decision is to maintain social acceptance and to protect girls' reputations. The United Nations has issued a statement condemning this practice, suggesting methods by which countries can eliminate female genital mutilation.

Source: The World's Women: 2000 Trends and Statistics (United Nations, New York, 2000).

Sexual functioning: it is clear that rape is now accepted as a physical assault in which sex is used to dominate or control the victim. Women who have been raped report continuing problems in sexual functioning. Sexual dysfunctions are one of the most long-lasting effects of rape with the most common reaction by rape victims being the avoidance of sex.

Other psychological reactions to rape: Other psychological problems may arise as a result of a rape. These include but are not limited to obsessive-compulsive disorders, anger, hostility, fatigue, and confusion.

Although the physical act of rape may last minutes, hours, or, in some cases, days, the effects and consequences to the victims may linger for months, years, or a lifetime. The rape is only the beginning of the suffering that the victim will endure. During the criminal justice system's response to this act of aggression, the victim will relive the trauma several times as she testifies in court.

STRANGER RAPE

A number of myths persist regarding the crime of rape. These myths apply to stranger, marital, or acquaintance rape situations.

Definition

Carnal knowledge of a female was one of the first terms used to connote sexual violence. It was defined as *penile-vaginal penetration.*[31] *Black's Law Dictionary* defines *carnal knowledge* as "Coitus; copulation; the act of a man having sexual bodily connections with a woman; sexual intercourse."[32]

Traditional penal codes reflected this bias and misunderstanding of the crime of rape. Criminal codes are enacted by each state and the federal government and set forth various definitions of crime. This has resulted in a patchwork of different definitions applied to basically the same act. In an effort to establish uniformity within the area of criminal law, a distinguished group of scholars and attorneys worked together for several years in drafting a Model Penal Code (MPC). The purpose of this code was to set forth the most reasoned thinking on various crimes and encourage states to adopt these definitions so that uniformity would be established throughout the United States. The MPC defines rape as follows:

A male who has sexual intercourse with a female, not his wife, is guilty of rape if:

1. he compels her to submit by force or by threat of imminent death, serious bodily injury, extreme pain, or kidnapping to be inflicted on anyone, or
2. he has substantially impaired her power to appraise or control her conduct by administering or employing without her knowledge drugs, intoxicates, or other means for the purpose of preventing resistance, or
3. the female is unconscious, or
4. the female is less than ten years old.

Rape is a felony of the second degree unless (1) in the course thereof the actor inflicts serious bodily injury on anyone, or (2) the victim was not a voluntary social companion of the actor on the occasion of the crime and had not previously permitted him sexual liberties, in which case the offense is a felony of the first degree.[33]

The drafters of the MPC were not purposefully discriminating against women. However, it is clear that the MPC perpetuated the bias of the times. First, a reading of the MPC reveals several flaws: The statute is gender biased, does not punish acquaintance rape as seriously as stranger rape, and does not provide for marital rape. The MPC prohibits only males from raping women. It makes no provision for female rape of a male. Second, although it "allows" that an acquaintance might rape his companion, this form of rape is not as serious as stranger rape; therefore, it will not be punished as harshly. Finally, it would not be a crime for a husband to rape his wife under the code.

Some states adopted the provisions of the code, and others have modernized their criminal statutes relating to the crime of rape. Many statutes now provide that the crime of rape is defined as an unlawful act of sexual intercourse with another person against that person's will by force, fear, or trick.[34] This statute is gender-neutral; either a male or a female may commit the crime. Also, the very definition allows for the charging and prosecution of marital rape. Finally, a person may be prosecuted for acquaintance rape under this statute. The only area that is not covered by this statute is the insertion of an object into the vagina during the assault.

Some authorities define rape as the penetration by a penis or other object into the mouth, vagina, or anus by force or fear.[35] There is a small but growing movement among the states to adopt this more modern definition of rape. Part of the rationale for the expanded definition is that rape is not a sexual crime; rather, it is a violent assault on the victim, and any type of forced penetration should be punished. This definition attempts to punish all forms of sexual assault. In addition, it attempts to provide uniformity in an area where each state has adopted differing statutes regarding sexual violence. Other authorities suggest doing away with the term *rape* and using instead *sexual assault* or *sexual battery* and prohibiting oral, vaginal, or anal penetration by force or fear.[36]

Someday the law may move toward a more comprehensive definition of this type of sexual violence, but at present most statutes define rape in a manner similar to that discussed previously. This definition in turn triggers reporting requirements by professionals in certain instances. Therefore, the definition set forth earlier will be used for purposes of clarity and conformity with existing statutes. This should not give the impression that forcible anal intercourse or oral copulation is not a crime in most states. Under most statutes, these are considered separate offenses that are distinct from the crime of rape.

Victim Selection

As with so many other aspects of sexual assault, we are not certain why certain rapists select certain victims. This is one of the many subjects in this area that needs further research. One study did attempt to answer this question by interviewing convicted sexual predators. Stevens used other convicted felons to conduct a survey of sixty-one sexual offenders incarcerated in a maximum-security prison.[37] Stevens trained thirteen incarcerated violent offenders enrolled in his class at a maximum-security prison as student-interviewers. They conducted interviews with convicted sexual predators and ended up with sixty-one valid interviews.

Promising Practices

Women and Sexual Violence

The Rape Treatment Center (RTC) at Santa Monica–UCLA Medical Center is nationally recognized for its exemplary treatment, education, and prevention programs. Established in 1974, the RTC has provided care for more than 24,000 sexual assault victims. In April 1999, the RTC created a new state-of-the-art clinic to enhance the treatment of victims in the immediate aftermath of a sexual assault. Historically, rape victims have received emergency services in hospital emergency rooms, where they are often subjected to long waits and a chaotic environment; as a result, the victim's trauma may be compounded, and critical evidence may deteriorate. The RTC's new clinic was designed to remedy these problems. Located within the hospital in a safe, private, therapeutic environment, the clinic is a twenty-four-hour facility dedicated exclusively to sexual assault victim care. It is staffed by advanced-practice nurse practitioners and professional therapists. The clinic uses advanced forensic equipment and technologies. In addition to medical and evidentiary services, victims receive crisis intervention and other advocacy and support services. Special health-related educational materials are provided. All of the services are free. In the development of the clinic and in its ongoing operations, the clinic has collaborated with law enforcement agencies, crime laboratories, and other victim service providers.

In Montgomery County, Maryland, rape counselors were unable to find a rape crisis videotape in Spanish, so they developed their own. The twelve-minute video, produced with a $30,000 state grant and introduced publicly during 1999 National Crime Victims' Rights Week, features Spanish-speaking people (a police officer, prosecutor, and rape counselor, among others) to explain what happens to the victim who reports a sexual assault.

The Anonymous and Confidential Internet Support Counseling Service was initiated in March 1997 by the Brazos County Rape Crisis Center (BCRCC) in Bryan, Texas. It gives victims/survivors of sexual abuse or assault, their friends, and/or family members an opportunity to seek anonymous support counseling that is provided by a trained support counselor at the BCRCC. Victims and/or survivors anywhere in the world can access this technology and service. This technology allows users to "write" electronically to the BCRCC at any time (twenty-four hours a day, seven days a week) to request information or to seek help. Through the secure server, the user's identity and location are protected and confidential. It allows users to tell or talk about their sexual abuse/assault without the fear of someone knowing who they are or from where they are calling.

Source: Based on U.S. Department of Justice, *National Victim Assistance Academy Text* (Washington, D.C., 2003).

The average respondent was thirty-two years old and had served seven years in prison at the time of the interview. The average rapist had attended eighth grade and was employed in a menial type of job before his arrest. The subjects averaged 3.4 prior adult arrests. Fifty-six percent of the sample was black; 42 percent, white; and 2 percent, Hispanic.

The author cautions against accepting the word of criminals. However, the data do show some interesting results: The most common characteristic for selecting victims was that the victims were perceived as "easy prey," meaning that the victims were thought to be vulnerable. In other words, these predators selected victims who they thought could not or would not resist an attack, or an opportunity presented itself that allowed them to attack the victim.

Some of the predators viewed young females as easy prey. Another predator talked about attacking sixty or seventy victims by scouting financial districts and looking for middle-class working females. Still other predators found that female shoppers were easy prey. They identified them by their demeanor. One predator stated, "If she's not watching what's happening all around her, then [she] doesn't know how to handle herself, how to use the things around her to hurt me, or get me caught." Finally, other predators wait for situations to develop in which the victim puts herself in a vulnerable position. For example, one predator attacked a female in the parking lot by threatening to harm her young child unless she cooperated. More study and research is needed in this area so that we can identify "risk patterns" that will allow us to avoid this type of violence.

Legal Aspects

Rape carries with it certain physical, mental, and legal consequences. Many times, during a rape the offender will perform or attempt to perform a variety of acts, including vaginal, oral, and anal sex. As mentioned earlier, each of these acts is considered a separate and distinct crime.

The crime of rape requires penetration of the penis into the vagina. The offense is complete on the slightest entry into the victim; therefore, it is possible for a woman to be raped and still retain her hymen. There is no requirement that the offender ejaculate for the crime to be complete.

As indicated previously, rape may be committed by force, fear, or trick. Forcible rape involves the offender using brute force to overpower the victim. He may use his fists, clubs, or other objects to strike the victim prior to raping her. The second situation occurs when the offender threatens the victim and she submits out of fear for her safety. This type of rape may not leave any physical scars, torn clothing, or other signs of physical violence. The third type of rape occurs when the offender tricks the victim. This is a broad category that includes sex with incompetents as well as the use of drugs and alcohol to render the victim incapable of consenting.

Sodomy or *forcible anal intercourse* is defined as the unlawful sexual penetration of the penis of one person into the anus of another committed by use of force or fear.[38] Similar to the crime of rape, no emission or ejaculation is required. The offense is complete on the slightest penetration of the victim's anus.

Oral copulation is the unlawful act of copulating the mouth of one person with the sexual organs or anus of another by use of force or fear.[39] Oral copulation does not require emission or ejaculation for the act to be completed. Penetration is not required for this crime. If the victim is forced to place her mouth on any part of the penis, the crime is complete. She does not have to place the penis in her mouth for this crime to occur.

Once the crime is complete and if the victim reports the offense to the authorities, the criminal justice system begins its slow and methodical prosecution of the offender. The rape victim will have to testify in open court about the incident. As late as the early 1960s, rape victims were treated as the criminals in sexual assault cases, and defense attorneys were allowed to ask questions regarding the victims' previous sexual experiences.[40] A variety of theories allowed for admission of this type of evidence. Two of the more common theories

Focus

Did She Consent When She Asked Him to Wear a Condom?

One of the most common defenses in rape cases is that the victim consented. This is especially true in fear or trick rapes in which the victim suffers no outward physical injuries.

In Texas, a rape trial caught the attention of the media. The victim was single and lived alone. One evening after she returned from a friend's party, she looked up and saw the defendant who had entered through a sliding glass door with a knife in his hand. He approached her and demanded sex. The victim, fearing for her life, consented and asked the offender to wear a condom, which she supplied. The defendant was later arrested and tried for the crime of rape. He claimed that the act was consensual in nature and pointed to the victim's supplying him with a condom as proof of his assertion. The jury did not believe his story and convicted him of rape.

involved the victim's reputation: Because she had intercourse with other persons, she was therefore likely to have consented during this act, and this was proof that she was a person of loose morals and meant that she was willing to have sex with anyone, including this defendant. These antiquated and biased rules are no longer accepted in the judicial system. All fifty states and the federal government have adopted **rape shield laws**. These statutes prohibit the defendant or his attorney from questioning the rape victim regarding her previous sexual history or introducing any other evidence concerning her past sexual practices.[41]

Stranger rape is a violent physical assault on women. However, it is not the most common form of sexual assault. Recent studies have indicated that more women are raped by persons they know than by strangers. The next section examines two forms of this sexual violence: marital rape and acquaintance rape.

MARITAL AND ACQUAINTANCE RAPE

The article featured in the Focus "Marital Rape and the Medical Community's Response" goes on to discuss various forms of family violence with subsequent recommendations from the Council on Scientific Affairs that the American Medical Association undertake a campaign to sensitize its members to family violence. The recommendation includes training and dissemination of protocols on identifying and treating victims of family violence. The medical community is slowly becoming aware of the need to respond to intimate sexual violence. Although there is now more awareness of marital and acquaintance rape primarily because of the media, many people, including professionals, have difficulty with the concept that a man can be accused and convicted of raping his wife or that a date who "consented" the evening before cannot raise the specter of rape the next day. Although the perception is slowly changing, those remain who believe that sex is a matter of right in marriage and in other intimate relationships.

The Problem

Intimate sexual violence includes marital and acquaintance rape. These forms of assault are not isolated incidents that occur to only a few women. *Rape in America* reports that only

Focus

Marital Rape and the Medical Community's Response

The medical community along with the criminal justice system is the most likely to see women victims and as such constitutes a front line of identification and intervention. However, physicians and other medical staff are rarely provided with training or specific protocols to aid in dealing with these cases. The cost of the failure to identify and intervene in violence is incalculable, particularly in violence by intimates because assaults tend to be repeated over time, produce more injuries than assaults by strangers, and have complicated sequelae with implications for further violence.

Although a neglected topic in the areas of both family violence and medicine, empirical research has shown that marital rape is an integral part of marital violence. Sexual abuse is a serious form of marital violence. It is possible to inflict an intense level of physical pain over a long period and cause a wide range of injuries, from superficial bruises and tearing to internal injuries and scarring. The psychological impact of assault by an intimate partner can also be extreme. Yet, except for child sexual molestation, this type of violence is least likely to be reported by victims. An awareness of the potential for forcible sexual assault in marriage, particularly in cases in which other types of physical abuse have been identified, will enable the clinician to sensitively assess the cause of observed symptoms.

Source: Based on Council of Scientific Affairs, "Violence against Women," *Journal of the American Medical Association* 267(23) (1992), pp. 3184–3185.

22 percent of all women raped were sexually assaulted by someone they had never seen before or did not know.[42] Nine percent of all victims were raped by their husbands or ex-husbands, 10 percent by boyfriends or ex-boyfriends, and 21 percent by other nonrelatives such as friends or neighbors. The remaining percentages were made up of fathers, stepfathers, other relatives, and a not-sure category of 3 percent. This report indicates that approximately 683,000 women were raped in a one-year period. Using the figures provided in this report, it means that in one year 61,470 women were raped by their husbands or ex-husbands, 68,300 women were raped by their boyfriends or ex-boyfriends, and 143,430 women were raped by other acquaintances.

Marital Rape

For centuries, society has believed that a man is entitled to have sex with his wife. In the eighteenth century, a man could not be charged or convicted of raping his wife in England. Wives were considered chattel and clearly subordinate to the husband.[43] Fathers had a property right or interest in their daughters' virginity and husbands in their wives' fidelity. The rape of an unmarried woman destroyed her value as a suitable bride and sexual mate. The rape of a married woman was an infringement on the property rights of her spouse and a disgrace to her husband.

The marital exemption for rape can be traced to Sir Matthew Hale, a seventeenth-century English jurist. Sir Hale was the chief justice of King's Bench from 1671 to 1675. A book based on his writing was published after his death in 1736.[44] Geis in his review of early English common law indicates that Sir Hale's statement on rape helped establish a precedent for spousal immunity from rape when he held, "The husband cannot be guilty of rape committed by himself upon his lawful wife, for by their mutual matrimonial consent and contract the wife hath given up herself in this kind unto the husband which she cannot retract."[45]

Blackstone, the great English legal scholar, helped to perpetuate this reasoning. He stated that the legal existence of a woman is suspended during marriage or at the very least incorporated into that of her husband. Blackstone's argument served to continue the legal fiction of unity of the person on marriage. Therefore, a wife was deemed to have irrevocably consented to sex whenever and wherever her husband wished.[46] This philosophy continued in England and elsewhere into modern times. Martin points out that Winston Churchill's mother could not refuse her husband's sexual advances even though he was suffering from incurable syphilis.[47]

The feminist movement in the 1970s sought to change the laws to allow for charges to be brought against a husband who raped his wife. It was not an easy victory. State and congressional elected officials made comments such as, "But if you can't rape your wife, who can you rape?" and "[T]he Bible doesn't give the state permission anywhere in the Book for the state to be in your bedroom."[48] Unbelievable as it may seem now, there was a great deal of resistance to passage of any laws that would delete spousal immunity from the books and thus allow a wife to charge her husband with rape. Through the efforts of several dedicated groups and individuals, laws began to be amended to define marital rape as a specific crime.

As mentioned earlier, many rape statutes now allow for the prosecution of a husband who rapes his wife. Therefore, there is no separate legal definition of marital rape. However, for purposes of explaining and distinguishing this form of sexual violence from stranger rape, **marital rape** is defined as the unlawful sexual intercourse with a spouse or ex-spouse against her will by means of force or fear.

Finkelhor and Yllo have conducted extensive research in the area of marital rape and classify marital rapes into three categories: force-only rapes, battering rapes, and obsessive rapes. *Force-only* rapes occur when the husband attempts to gain control over the type and frequency of sexual activity within the marriage. Finkelhor and Yllo compare this type of rape to Groth and Birnbaum's power rapes. *Battering* rapes involve the husband attempting to humiliate and degrade his wife. These types of marital rapes are very similar to Groth and Birnbaum's anger rapes. The last type of marital rape, *obsessive* rape, involves sexual sadism, fetishes, and forcible anal intercourse. This type of rape is similar to Groth and Birnbaum's classification of sadistic rapes.[49]

Just as there are a number of theories as to why intimate partner abuse and stranger rape occur, so there are a variety of theories dealing with factors that encourage or promote marital rape. Previous chapters have discussed factors that increase the risk of family violence, including child physical and sexual abuse, intimate partner abuse, and marital rape. The following discussion focuses on factors and forces within society that specifically encourage or contribute to marital rape. These factors include the historical perspective toward the family, spousal immunity, economics, and Western culture's preoccupation with violence.

Historical perspective toward the family: For generations, the family has been viewed as the last stronghold of absolute privacy. What happened in the wedding bed was believed to be no one else's business. This concept of family privacy has caused delays and problems in researching issues such as marital rape. In addition, women were raised with beliefs that they had to submit to their husband's sexual advances. Only recently have we begun to study the dynamics within the family bedroom, and women now understand that they do not owe sex on demand to their spouses.

Spousal immunity: As mentioned earlier, early common law established the proposition that a husband could not be accused of raping his wife. Rape of a stranger was considered a violent and unspeakable act; however, rape of a wife was unknown. The wife was considered to be part of the husband, and he was therefore immune from any charges of rape brought by his spouse. Only recently have spouses been able to bring charges of rape against their husbands.

Economics: Similar to other causes of family violence, economics and dependency play a role in promoting marital rape. Both spouses are aware of the wife's economic dependency. Some men argue that they provide the paycheck, so the wife must take care of the home. This "taking care of the home" includes, in the male's mind, sex on demand—any kind of sex.

Preoccupation with violence: Violence and its effect on family violence have been discussed in detail earlier in this textbook. Because some films, books, and television programs devalue women, it is easier for males to use violence as an acceptable form of sexual expression.

Although none of these factors may be the single cause of marital rape, they contribute along with other factors to a general climate of violence in the United States that promotes sexual violence against women.

Focus

When Is It Rape?

1. A couple attending college decides to break up. They have been intimate for three years, engaging in oral, anal, and vaginal sexual activities. One week after they separate, the male arrives at the female's apartment intoxicated and states that they are going to have sex. The female insists that the relationship is over; however, the male gets angry, punches the wall, and demands sex. The female knows that he will not hit her and is therefore not frightened for her own safety but gives in, and they engage in sexual relations.

2. On a third date, the male double-shots his date's drinks. She is not an experienced drinker and passes out while they are engaged in heavy petting. The male proceeds to have intercourse with her.

3. A couple has been dating for three weeks. They both have had several drinks and are intoxicated. They engage in heavy petting, and the girl responds physically but says, "Please, darling, no." The male continues his sexual advances, and the girl continues to respond physically but also continues to say, "No." They finally engage in intercourse.

4. The female initially consents to intercourse but, during the act, changes her mind and tells the male to stop. He continues with the act until orgasm.[50]

Are any of these acquaintance rape? Why? Who is responsible in these situations? Are both parties at fault?

Acquaintance Rape

Consider the Focus "When Is It Rape?" Some males and defense attorneys would argue that situations 1 and 3 were clearly not rape and that a male should not be responsible for getting inside the mind of his date. Depending on what further facts are added, situation 1 may have involved the use of force and therefore qualify as a sexual assault and rape. Situation 2 is clearly a rape-by-trick situation in which the victim was unable to give consent. Situation 3 may be classified as rape because many authorities argue that when a female says "no," the advances by the male must stop. Others argue that it may or may not be rape, depending on the victim's state of mind.[51]

Sexual violence in dating relationships is not a new topic to social scientists and other professionals. As early as 1957, Eugene Kanin studied college students' sexual aggression. He found that more than half of all college women (50% to 60%) reported being the target of sexual aggression, whereas only 20 to 30 percent of college men admitted to such aggressive behavior.[52] This indicates a serious lack of empathy on the part of male college students as to what is appropriate behavior. Although most women found the acts aggressive, only 20 to 30 percent of the males found them to meet their definition of sexual aggression. Other researchers have confirmed these percentages and come to the conclusion that the double standard still exists in the United States.[53] This attitude in turn leads to situations in which date rape can and does occur.

A more recent study of acquaintance rape was conducted by the Bureau of Justice Statistics.[54] The authors utilized the National College Women Sexual Victimization Study, which had a sample of 4,446 women who were attending a two- or four-year college or university. The study found that 2.8 percent of the sample had experienced a completed rape or attempted rape. This equaled 27.7 rapes per 1,000 female students during the academic year. This statistic would place the numbers at one in thirty-six female college students. However, the authors point out that these statistics are misleading. First, the data are only for 6.91 months instead of a full year. This in turn may lead to the conclusion that nearly 5 percent of college women are victimized in any given calendar year; and because a college career now typically lasts five years, the percentage of rapes or attempted rapes in colleges and universities could be as high as one-fifth or one-quarter.

Although sexual aggression in dating relationships has been studied for more than thirty years, people still have problems in accepting the concept of rape by a person known to the victim.[55] Some individuals want to believe that rape is committed only in some dark alley by a sadistic monster and that only "nice girls" who resist and whose resistance was overcome by physical force can be raped.

Stranger rape, at one time, was thought to be the most common form of sexual violence. However, we now understand that intimate violence is more frequent than suspected. One survey reported that on a midwestern campus, 100 percent of the rapists knew their victims.[56]

Similar to marital rape, date or acquaintance rape situations are covered by the general definition of rape set forth earlier. However, for purposes of explaining this special type of sexual violence, **acquaintance rape** is defined as unlawful sexual intercourse accomplished by force or fear with a person known to the victim who is not related by blood or marriage.

The following actual cases illustrate the continuing problems facing victims of acquaintance rape:

- A young woman reports to the police that she was kidnapped and raped by a former boyfriend. He had beaten her in the past, leading to his arrest on at least one occasion. The prosecutor resists bringing rape charges because of the victim's prior relationship with her assailant and offers the man a plea to reduced charges—a misdemeanor assault for which the attacker receives a six-month sentence and eighteen months probation. Less than a year later, the attacker brutally rapes and almost kills another woman.
- A group of young men meet a woman in a bar at night; they surreptitiously slip a tablet of LSD in her drink on leaving the bar. At the home of one of the young men, they slip her four more doses of LSD. The woman is then repeatedly raped with objects as a group cheers and takes pictures, which are later destroyed. One of the assailants stops the attack when someone suggests raping the woman with a statue of Christ. Three of the attackers are given immunity for providing statements helpful to the prosecution. One defendant pleads guilty to evidence tampering and delivery of illegal drugs; he serves three months of an eight-month sentence in jail with eight years probation. Not one of the defendants is convicted of sexual assault.
- A woman breaks off her engagement with a man. Several weeks later, he goes to her house, and they get into an argument in his car. She tells the police that he dragged her into the back seat of the car and raped her. After the attack, she goes to the hospital and files a police report. The prosecutor in the case accepts the defendant's plea to unlawful restraint—a fourth-degree felony with a two-year sentence—saying, "It's not like she didn't have sex with him before." The attacker serves six months and one day in jail.[57]

We are beginning to address acquaintance rape and sexual assault on campus. Starting in 1990, Congress has enacted laws requiring institutions of higher education to prevent and respond to sexual assault on campus. The Student Right-to-Know and Campus Security Act of 1990 (the Clery Act) requires that schools annually disclose information about crime, including sexual assaults in and around campus.[58] In addition, Congress passed the Campus Sexual Assault Victims' Bill of Rights of 1992. This law requires schools to develop prevention policies and provide certain assurances to victims.[59]

Acquaintance rape will continue to be a serious problem in the United States as long as we socialize men to view women as inferior members of society who really want to be chased, conquered, and dominated.

Drugs and Acquaintance Rape

We began acknowledging acquaintance rape during the 1960s and 1970s. However, during the 1980s and 1990s, law enforcement and rape crisis centers started to receive reports about victims who had been drugged or unconscious during the rape. Two drugs were consistently reported in these types of cases of acquaintance rape: gamma-hydroxybutyrate (GHB) and flunitrazepam (Rohypnol).[60]

Both of these drugs produced unconsciousness and the inability to recall recent events. Victims of these drugs report feeling sensations of drunkenness that do not correspond to the amount of alcohol ingested, unexplained physical trauma normally associated with sexual assault, and loss or altered states of consciousness.[61]

Gamma-hydroxybutyrate was first discovered in the 1920s and was under development as an anesthetic agent in the 1960s. It was banned by the Food and Drug Administration in

1990.[62] Rohypnol is part of a class of drugs that produce sedation, sleep or muscle relaxation, and retrograde amnesia. The latter characteristic is important because persons will respond to commands or requests at the moment but on wakening have no memory of the acts. During surgery, this is a desired and sometimes needed reaction by the patient, but when used during sexual assault, it allows the perpetrator to control the victim and have the victim do his bidding. This characteristic also raises questions regarding sexual assault and the Internet. With the advent of digital cameras and the ability to make instant CDs, research needs to be conducted regarding the recording and sale of sexual assaults via the Internet of unsuspecting victims of acquaintance rape.

Rape drugs make it easy for perpetrators to gain control of the victim. They do not have to gain physical control or threaten the victim, nor do they have to be concerned about the victim screaming for help or trying to attract attention. Because the victim's outward behavior will many times be consistent with drunkenness, the perpetrator may appear as a helper or rescuer who is assisting the victim when in reality he is leading her to a location to commit the rape.

This form of sexual assault is further complicated by the victim's reluctance to report the rape. While many victims of acquaintance rape have difficulty in deciding to report the offense, a drug-related victim of sexual assault may have additional feelings of guilt and confusion about what really happened. She may be hesitant to make an accusation when she does not clearly remember what occurred.

SEXUAL HARASSMENT

Sexual harassment is the overall umbrella under which specific forms of sexual violence take place. Although it is true that men have been targets of sexual harassment, most victims are women.[63] Because sexual harassment is a form of violence against women, it is included in this chapter to allow for comparison between sexual violence within the family and sexual violence in the workplace. Only by understanding the full spectrum of sexual violence can professionals begin to respond appropriately to it.

Discrimination has existed in the United States since its founding. President Lincoln began the process of doing away with discrimination when he freed the slaves, and for decades U.S. courts have held that one citizen should not discriminate against another because of skin color. However, that battle goes on today in coffee shops that refuse to serve people of color, in banks that decline to make home loans to persons living in certain locations, and in many service-related businesses such as automobile dealers who simply ignore persons of different races. Discrimination against women because of their sex is one bias that is also gaining attention. One of the most offensive forms of this discrimination is sexual harassment. Employment-based sexual harassment is dehumanizing, and it changes the focus of employment from the woman's work performance to her sex. In addition, it degrades women by reinforcing their traditionally inferior role in the workplace. The following sections provide a brief overview of sexual harassment.

Introduction

Sexual harassment is a widespread phenomenon. One of the first work-related surveys of 9,000 women found that 9 out of 10 women reported instances of sexual harassment.[64] Probably the most comprehensive survey of sexual harassment ever done was conducted by the U.S. Merit System Protection Board in 1980. The board surveyed 23,000 federal employees and reported that 42 percent of all women stated being the subject of some form of sexual harassment.[65]

The demands for sexual favors in exchange for continuing employment have long been a common abuse of personal power in the workplace. The clandestine squeeze on the factory floor, the stolen kiss in the copy room, or the lewd suggestion regarding sex have been commonplace in U.S. businesses for years. Until recently, the victim of such sexual violence has had two choices: agree to the demands or lose her job. In addition, she was led to believe that the activities that she found offensive were in reality common practice in the workplace. There was no legal recourse for victims of sexual harassment until the 1980s.

In 1964, the United States began the long process of outlawing all forms of discrimination. Congress passed Title VII of the Civil Rights Act of 1964, which prohibited employment discrimination based on race, color, religion, sex, pregnancy, or national origin.[66] Title VII provides the following:

> It shall be an unlawful employment practice for an employer—
>
> 1. to fail or refuse to hire or to discharge any individual, or otherwise to discriminate against any individual with respect to his compensation, terms, conditions, or privileges of employment, because of such individual's race, color, religion, sex, or national origin; or
> 2. to limit, segregate, or classify his employees or applicants for employment in any way that would deprive or tend to deprive any individual of employment opportunities or otherwise adversely affect his status as an employee, because of such individual's race, color, religion, sex, or national origin.[67]

Even though the language of the statute was clear, women continued to be exposed to discrimination either because they were pregnant at the time or because they might become pregnant in the future. This continuing discrimination caused Congress to pass the Pregnancy Discrimination Act of 1978, which prohibited discrimination based on pregnancy, childbirth, or other related medical conditions.[68]

Many scholars believe the Civil Rights Act of 1964 was the basis for the current prohibition against sexual harassment. However, Congress never directly addressed that issue when it passed the Civil Rights Act. In fact, sex was added as a prohibited classification in a last-minute attempt to block passage of the legislation.[69] Rather, courts and administrative agencies have used the Civil Rights Act as the foundation on which to base their rulings regarding sexual harassment.[70]

Definitions

Several definitions of sexual harassment exist. From a traditional perspective, **sexual harassment** is a demand that a subordinate, usually a woman, grant sexual favors to retain a job benefit.[71] A more encompassing definition defines it as the imposition of any unwanted condition on any person's employment because of that person's sex. Under this definition, harassment includes jokes, direct taunting, disruption of work, vandalism or destruction of property, and physical attacks.[72] Sexual harassment occurs in a wide variety of forms, including rape, pressure for sexual favors, sexual touching, suggestive looks or gestures, sexual joking or teasing, and the display of unwanted sexual material.

Sexual harassment may occur in either of two forms: quid pro quo harassment or hostile environment harassment. These are not mutually exclusive situations. Many times, they will overlap, and both forms may be present in the workplace.

Quid pro quo harassment occurs when an agent or supervisor of the employer uses his position to induce a female employee to grant him sexual favors. The exchange of continued employment or job benefits for sex suggests the name "quid pro quo." The essence of a quid pro quo harassment is that the victim must choose between suffering economic disadvantage and enduring sexual advances.[73]

Hostile environment harassment occurs when unwelcome conduct of a sexual nature creates a hostile working environment. The conduct usually involves a series of incidents rather than a single episode of harassment. The essence of a hostile environment form of harassment is that an individual is forced to work in a context that, although not causing direct economic detriment, results in psychological or emotional harm or humiliation.

Barnes v. Costle established the principle that sex-based assignments or sexual advances in which the employer enforces the demand by threat of discharge or other adverse economic consequences violates Title VII of the Civil Rights Act.[74] In this case, the plaintiff alleged that she was hired as an administrative assistant to the director of the agency's Equal Employment Opportunity Division at the Environmental Protection Agency. Shortly after commencing employment, the director solicited her to join him after hours at social functions and stated that if she cooperated with him in a sexual affair, her employment status would be enhanced. She refused these advances, and her position was abolished. The appellate court held such actions to be a clear violation of Title VII of the Civil Rights Act.

In 1980, the Equal Employment Opportunity Commission (EEOC) adopted regulations in the form of guidelines that prohibited discrimination based on sex. These guidelines

---

Focus

Attitudes Regarding Sexual Harassment

In October 1997, NBC released the results of a poll it had conducted regarding equity in the workplace. The network polled 1,019 adults in September in an effort to determine their views regarding whether society is doing enough to promote equality, especially in the workplace.

The pollsters found confusion among men and women about what is considered appropriate or offensive behavior in the workplace. This confusion occurred not as much by gender as by age. Younger women were less offended than older women regarding compliments about their appearance from male coworkers. This was especially true if the younger women had worked outside the home for a period of time.

This poll also pointed out that sexual harassment is still a major problem in the workplace. One in every five working women reported incidents of sexual harassment within the last two years. Both men and women reported making comments that were inappropriate and "crossed the line" to a coworker of the opposite sex within the last five years.

Source: Associated Press, "Men, Women Divided on Equality," *The Fresno Bee*, October 20, 1997, p. A-4.

specifically state that an individual's response to unwelcome conduct of a sexual nature may not be made the basis of any adverse employment decision.[75] Although the EEOC guidelines are not binding, they have been held to constitute a body of experience and informed judgments to which courts and litigants may properly resort for guidance.[76]

It wasn't until 1986 that a case of sexual harassment based on a hostile working environment was decided. In *Meritor Savings Bank v. Vinson*, the U.S. Supreme Court held that a working environment that is hostile to women may violate Title VII of the Civil Rights Act even without any question of economic detriment.[77] In this case, the victim was hired by the bank as a teller and eventually advanced to the position of assistant branch manager. She alleged that a supervisor subjected her to sexual harassment in excess of four years. This harassment included sexual intercourse, fondling her in front of other employees, exposing himself to her, and even following her into the ladies' restroom. The Supreme Court upheld the victim's claim of sexual harassment on the basis of the theory that the actions of the aggressor established a hostile working environment.

In 1993, the Supreme Court further clarified the meaning of sexual harassment when it decided *Harris v. Forklift Systems Inc.*[78] Teresa Harris worked as a manager at Forklift Systems Inc., an equipment rental company, from April 1985 to October 1987. Charles Hardy, Forklift's president, often insulted Teresa because of her gender and made unwelcome sexual innuendos. Hardy told Harris several times in front of other employees that she was a woman who didn't know anything and what the company needed was a male manager. He also suggested that they go to the local hotel and negotiate Harris's salary. On other occasions, he threw objects on the ground and asked Harris to pick them up. Hardy also asked Harris and other female employees to get coins from his front pants pocket.

Harris finally complained to Hardy, who claimed that he was only joking and apologized. He further promised not to engage in that behavior again. However, several weeks later he asked Harris whether she had slept with a customer to get that customer to sign a contract. Harris quit and filed a lawsuit, alleging violations of Title VII.

The Supreme Court ruled that there was no requirement that the conduct be so severe as to cause the victim to become physically ill or psychologically distressed. The Court stated that victims of sexual harassment had met their burden if they proved that the environment was perceived as hostile or abusive. An environment is considered hostile or abusive by looking at all the circumstances, including the frequency of the conduct; whether it is physically threatening, humiliating, or a mere offensive remark; and whether it unreasonably interferes with an employee's work performance.

Tangri, Burt, and Johnson established three models or types of sexual harassment: the natural/biological model, the organizational model, and the sociocultural model.[79] Using data from the initial Merit Systems Protection Board 1980 survey, they partially tested these models.

The *natural/biological model* assumes that sexual behavior in the workplace is an extension of human sexuality. It is assumed that men and women possess strong sex drives, but the man whose sex drive is stronger takes the role of the aggressor. From this perspective, sexual harassment is not discriminatory in nature; it is simply the result of natural biological mating urges. This model presupposes that all sexual advances are mutual in nature and part of courtship or mating behavior. Researchers now understand that all advances are not in fact part of courtship, and therefore this model fails to explain sexual harassment.

The *organizational model* is a result of a workplace environment that provides opportunities for sexual aggression. From this perspective, sexual harassment becomes an issue of power, not sex. This power is derived from the formal roles in an organizational context. For this model to be valid, only those women in positions of low hierarchical power would be targets of sexual harassment. Women who hold a variety of positions have been harassed, some of whom were considered high on the organizational scheme. Therefore, this model does not adequately explain sexual harassment.

The *sociocultural model* views sexual harassment as reflecting the more dominant position of men in Western culture, where they are the source of economic and political power. This model suggests that sexual harassment is the result of a patriarchal power system in which men rule society. Power is an important factor in sexual harassment. The male aggressor may control advancement, benefits, and continued employment.

Sexual harassment does not exist only in the workplace. It has been called one of the best-kept secrets on college campuses, and some feminists are concerned that some professors have used their positions of power to obtain sexual favors from students. Dziech and Weiner list the following actions that they consider as inappropriate behavior by professors:

Staring, leering, or ogling. These behaviors may be surreptitious or obvious. Professors who by the very nature of their occupation look at and observe students should not cross the boundaries of reason.

Frequently commenting on the student's personal appearance. In an academic setting, professors should refrain from discussing apparel and physical characteristics of female students.

Touching out of context. Touching of students should be minimal and only to the extent necessary to carry out certain types of instruction.

Excessive flattery and praise for the student. This behavior, coupled with others listed here, is especially seductive to female students with low self-esteems or high expectations. By convincing the student that she is exceptional, the professor gains psychological access to her.

Injecting a "male v. female" tone into discussions with the student. This type of disparaging remark about women and their abilities is a clear signal of a bias or negative perception on the part of the professor.

Persistently emphasizing sexuality in all contexts. Pervasive emphasis on sex in or outside the classroom is inappropriate.[80]

This discussion should not be construed as labeling every professor as a potential sexual harasser. However, even in academia the controversy over professor–student relationships continues to be debated. In April 1993, the University of Virginia Faculty Senate was considering a policy that would prohibit faculty members from dating students. Representatives of the American Civil Liberties Union (ACLU) questioned the appropriateness of the actions, remarking that the university might be infringing on privacy and associational rights of teachers. The ACLU recommended that the university enhance its sexual harassment codes instead. The faculty senate proceeded to approve the no-dating policy. Many universities have sexual harassment codes, and some are beginning to adopt a no-dating policy between students and faculty members. The relationship between students and faculty members is one of power. When a professor uses his position to extract sexual favors from a student, this becomes a serious quid pro quo form of sexual harassment.

Simply having agencies and courts establish procedures and processes to handle sexual harassment cases does not do away with this behavior. The perception of women must be changed, and they should be viewed as equals instead of sex objects. Only when women are approached as partners and equals will sexual harassment stop.

Summary

Sexual violence is a complex and far-ranging topic. The study of sexual violence has been and will continue to be hindered by a lack of agreement among the different professions on terminology and research methodology. All professionals agree that sexual violence continues to be a serious problem. Recent studies have indicated that women are more at risk from someone they know than from a stranger lurking in the darkness. Also, the consequences of any type of sexual violence are severe and in many instances long-lasting.

Professionals are slowly advancing in their perception of rape victims. No longer can only "nice girls" be raped, and professionals have accepted that rape is a violent physical assault that has very little if anything to do with sexual gratification. Legislatures have passed rape shield laws that now provide some protection to rape victims. These laws bar questions to the victim that require her to explain her previous sexual experiences to the judge and jury. As long as men rape women, consent will be raised as a defense. However, as society becomes more educated, that rationalization will stop bearing credibility. Sexual harassment continues to be a form of sexual violence in the United States and will persist as long as men view women as sexual trophies or playthings instead of equals. Only through ongoing education can this form of sexual violence be put to an end.

Key Terms

sexual violence—any intentional act or omission that results in physical, emotional, or financial injury to a women; sexual violence does not include the termination of a romantic relationship.

rape—an unlawful act of sexual intercourse with another person against that person's will by force, fear, or trick.

posttraumatic stress disorder—the development of characteristic symptoms following a psychologically distressing event that is outside the range of usual human experience. The characteristic symptoms involve reexperiencing the traumatic event, avoidance of stimuli associated with the event or numbing of general responsiveness, and increased arousal.

rape crisis syndrome—occurs when the victim experiences feelings of shame, humiliation, disjointedness, anger, inability to concentrate, and withdrawal.

carnal knowledge of a female—penile-vaginal penetration.

sodomy—the unlawful sexual penetration of the penis of one person into the anus of another committed by use of force or fear.

oral copulation—the unlawful act of copulating the mouth of one person with the sexual organs or anus of another by use of force or fear.

rape shield law—prohibits the defendant or his attorney from questioning the rape victim regarding her previous sexual history or introducing any other evidence concerning her past sexual practices.

marital rape—unlawful sexual intercourse with a spouse or ex-spouse against her will by means of force or fear.

acquaintance rape—unlawful sexual intercourse accomplished by force or fear with a person known to the victim who is not related by blood or marriage.

sexual harassment—the imposition of any unwanted condition on any person's employment because of that person's sex.

Discussion Questions

1. Based on your reading of this chapter, draft a definition of rape. Justify why your definition is better than the one given in the textbook.

2. Which of the causes of rape is the most important? Why? Can we do anything as a society to diminish the chances of a woman being raped? What?

3. Which is the most severe type of rape—stranger, marital, or acquaintance rape? Why? Should all forms of rape be punished the same, or should we have more harsh penalties for certain forms? Why?

4. How would you respond if a married friend of yours informed you that her husband had raped her last night? The husband is a good friend of yours. What are the options available to you?

5. Is the male always at fault in acquaintance rape situations? Why? Why not?

6. List at least ten types of sexual harassment. Explain why you think they qualify as sexual violence.

Suggested Readings

Brownmiller, S. *Against Our Will: Men, Women, and Rape* (Penguin, New York, 1975).

deKoster, K. *Rape on Campus* (Greenhaven, San Diego, Calif., 1995).

Epstein, J., and S. Langenbahn. *The Criminal Justice and Community Response to Rape* (National Institute of Justice, U.S. Department of Justice, Washington, D.C., May 1994).

Finkelhor, D., and K. Yllo. *License to Rape* (Holt, Rinehart & Winston, New York, 1985).

Freud, S. *New Introductory Lectures on Psychoanalysis.* J. Strachey, ed. (Norton, New York, 1965).

Gilder, J. L. *Acceptance of Acquaintance: Attitude and Personality Characteristics of Athletes* (ProQuest, Ann Arbor, Mich., 2006).

Groth, A. N., and J. Birnbaum. *Men Who Rape* (Plenum, New York, 1979).

Jaggar, A. M., and P. S. Rothenberg, eds. *Feminist Frameworks* (McGraw-Hill, New York, 1993).

Juhascik, M. P. *Estimate of the Prevalence of Drug-Facilitated Sexual Assault in the United States* (ProQuest, Ann Arbor, Mich., 2006).

Kelly, L. *Surviving Sexual Violence* (University of Minnesota Press, Minneapolis, 1988).

Landau, E. *Date Violence* (Franklin Watts, London, 2005).

Lindemann, B., and D. D. Kadue. *Sexual Harassment in Employment Law* (Bureau of National Affairs, Washington, D.C., 1992).

Martin, R. E. *The Life of Lady Randolph Churchill* (New York American Library, New York, 1969).

McCaghy, C. *Deviant Behavior, Crime, Conflict and Interest Groups* (Macmillan, New York, 1976).

McGregor, J. *Is It Rape?: On Acquaintance Rape and Taking Women's Consent Seriously* (Ashgate Publishing, London, 2005).

Millett, K. *Sexual Politics* (Abacus, London, 1972).

Phillips, P. *Marx and Engels on Law and Laws* (Barnes & Noble, Totowa, N.J., 1980).

Quigley, A. *Sexual Harassment (Current Controversies)* (Greenhaven Press, Farmington, Mich., 2006).

Russell, D. *The Politics of Rape* (Stein & Day, New York, 1975).

Russell, D. E. H. *Sexual Exploitation* (SAGE, Beverly Hills, Calif., 1984).

Swisher, K. L. *What Is Sexual Harassment?* (Greenhaven, San Diego, Calif., 1995).

Symons, D. *The Evolution of Human Sexuality* (Oxford University Press, Oxford, 1979).

Wallace, H., and C. Roberson. *Principles of Criminal Law*, 4th ed. (Allyn & Bacon, Boston, 2007).

Zippel, K. S. *The Politics of Sexual Harassment: A Comparative Study of the United States, the European Union, and Germany* (Cambridge University Press, Cambridge, U.K., 2006).

Endnotes

1. S. Freud, *New Introductory Lectures on Psychoanalysis.* J. Strachey, ed. (Norton, New York, 1965).
2. P. Phillips, *Marx and Engels on Law and Laws* (Barnes & Noble, Totowa, N.J., 1980).
3. K. Millett, *Sexual Politics.* (Abacus, London, 1972); S. Griffin, "Rape: The All-American Crime," *Ramparts* 10(3) (1971), pp. 26–35; and S. Brownmiller, *Against Our Will: Men, Women, and Rape* (Penguin, New York, 1975).
4. L. Kelly, *Surviving Sexual Violence* (University of Minnesota Press, Minneapolis, 1988).
5. For an excellent in-depth discussion of these issues, see M. P. Koss, "Detecting the Scope of Rape," *Journal of Interpersonal Violence* 8(2) (1993), pp. 198–222.
6. Ibid., pp. 200–203.
7. Personal communication with Christine N. Edmunds, coauthor and project director, National Victim Center, Washington, D.C.
8. C. Sommers, "Researching the 'Rape Culture' of America," LeadershipU, www.leaderu.com/real/ri9502/sommers.html. For a recent review of Internet blogs that reveals continuing dialogue and debate on Koss's methodology and finding, see Archive for the "Mary Koss controversy," www.amptoons.com.
9. This section has been based on Lawrence A. Greenfield, *Sex Offenses and Offenders: An Analysis of Date on Rape and Sexual Assault* (U.S. Department of Justice, Office of Justice Programs, Bureau of Justice Statistics, Washington, D.C., February 1997).
10. *National Crime Victimization Survey, 2004* (U.S. Department of Justice, Washington, D.C., 2004).
11. Ibid.
12. D. Russell, *The Politics of Rape* (Stein & Day, New York, 1975).
13. D. Mosher and R. Anderson, "Macho Personality, Sexual Aggression, and Reactions to Guided Imagery of Realistic Rape," *Journal of Research in Personality* 20 (1987), pp. 77–94.
14. D. Symons, *The Evolution of Human Sexuality* (Oxford University Press, Oxford, 1979).
15. Personal correspondence from Owen D. Jones, professor of law, Arizona State University, Tempe, dated August 27, 1994.
16. C. McCaghy, *Deviant Behavior: Crime, Conflict and Interest Groups* (Macmillan, New York, 1976).
17. J. Rabkin, "Epidemiology of Forcible Rape," *American Journal of Orthospychiatry* 49(4) (1979), pp. 634–647.
18. A. N. Groth, A. W. Burgess, and L. L. Holmstrom, "Rape: Power, Anger, and Sexuality," *American Journal of Psychiatry* 134(11) (1977), p. 1239.
19. A. N. Groth and J. Birnbaum. *Men Who Rape* (Plenum, New York, 1979).
20. D. G. Kilpatrick, L. J. Veronen, and P. A. Resick, "Assessment of the Aftermath of Rape: Changing Patterns of Fear," *Journal of Behavioral Assessment* 1(2) (1979), p. 133.
21. P. A. Resick, "The Psychological Impact of Rape," *Journal of Interpersonal Violence* 8(2) (June 1993), pp. 223–255.
22. M. A. Burnam et al., "Sexual Assault and Mental Disorders in a Community Population," *Journal of Consulting and Clinical Psychology* 56 (1988), pp. 843–850.

23. P. A Resick, "Reactions of Female and Male Victims of Rape or Robbery." Final Report, Grant #85-IJ-CX-0042 (National Institute of Justice, Washington, D.C., 1988).

24. *Diagnostic and Statistical Manual of Disorders,* fourth edition, p. 424.

25. B. O. Rothbaum et al., "A Prospective Examination of Posttraumatic Stress Disorder in Rape Victims," *Journal of Traumatic Stress* 5 (1992), pp. 455–475.

26. D. G. Kilpatrick, C. N. Edmunds, and A. K. Seymour, *Rape in America: A Report to the Nation* (National Victim Center, Arlington, Va., 1992).

27. M. Bard and K. Ellison, "Crisis Intervention and Investigation of Forcible Rape," in L. Brodyaga et al., eds., *Rape and Its Victims: A Report for Citizens, Health Facilities, and Criminal Justice Agencies* (U.S. Department of Justice, Washington, D.C., 1974), pp. 165–171.

28. Kilpatrick et al., *Rape in America.*

29. P. A. Resick et al., "A Comparative Outcome Study of Behavioral Group Therapy for Sexual Assault Victims," *Behavior Therapy* 19 (1988), pp. 385–401.

30. M. H. Thelen, M. D. Sherman, and T. S. Borst, "Fear of Intimacy and Attachment among Rape Survivors," *Behavior Modification* 22(1) (1988).

31. L. B. Bienen, "Rape III—National Developments in Rape Reform Legislation," *Women's Rights Law Reporter* 6 (1981), pp. 171–213.

32. H. C. Black, *Black's Law Dictionary* (West, St. Paul, Minn., 1990), p. 213.

33. Model Penal Code Section 213.1 (American Law Institute, Chicago, 1985).

34. H. Wallace and C. Roberson, *Principles of Criminal Law* (Longman, White Plains, New York, 1994).

35. D. G. Kilpatrick et al., "Rape in Marriage and in Dating Relationships: How Bad Is It for Mental Health?" *Annals of the New York Academy of Sciences* 528 (1988), pp. 335–344.

36. M. P. Koss, "Detecting the Scope of Rape," *Journal of Interpersonal Violence* 8(2) (1993), p. 198.

37. D. J. Stevens, "Predatory Rapist and Victim Selection Techniques," *Social Science Journal* 31(4) (1994), p. 421.

38. Wallace and Roberson, *Principles of Criminal Law.*

39. Ibid.

40. For an excellent discussion of legal, ethical, and professional issues in printing the name of a rape victim, see C. Cooper and V. Whitehouse, "Rape: To Name or Not to Name," *St. Louis Journalism Review* 24(174) (1995), pp. 10–12.

41. See *Michigan v. Lucas,* 111 S. Ct. 1743 (1991), in which the U.S. Supreme Court upheld the constitutionality of these statutes. See also *Vermont Statute,* Title 13, Chapter 72, Section 3255 (3)(A) (B), for an example of a rape shield law.

42. Kilpatrick et al., *Rape in America.*

43. See Comment, "Abolishing the Marital Exemption to Rape: A Statutory Proposal," *University of Illinois Law Review* 201 (1983).

44. M. Hale, *The History of the Pleas of the Crown* (1736). The first American edition of the book was published in 1874. See Comment, "Sexual Assault: The Case for Removing the Spousal Exemption from Texas Law," *Baylor Law Review* 38 (1986), p. 1941.

45. G. Geis, "Rape and Marriage: Historical and Cross-Cultural Considerations," paper presented at the annual meeting of the American Sociological Association, New York, 1980. See also Hale, *The History of the Pleas of the Crown,* p. 629.

46. L. D. Waggoner, "New Mexico Joins the Twentieth Century: The Repeal of the Marital Rape Exemption," *New Mexico Law Review* 22 (1992), p. 551.

47. R. E. Martin, *The Life of Lady Randolph Churchill* (New York American Library, New York, 1969).

48. J. Schulman, "The Marital Rape Exemption in the Criminal Law," *Clearinghouse Review* 13(6) (1980).

49. D. Finkelhor and K. Yllo, *License to Rape* (Holt, Rinehart, & Winston, New York, 1985).

50. B. W. Dziech and L. Weiner, "The Lecherous Professor," in A. M. Jaggar and P. S. Rothenberg, eds., *Feminist Frameworks,* 3rd ed. (McGraw-Hill, New York, 1993), pp. 323–327.

51. In *People v. Roundtree* (2000 *Daily Journal D.A.R.* 897 [January 25, 2000]), a California

court of appeals held that once the act of intercourse has started, the victim may still withdraw her consent and if the male refuses to stop, it is still rape. The court focused on the fact that rape consists of outrage to a person instead of a simple demarcation point in a course of conduct. Others have condemned this approach as unrealistic.

52. R. L. Shotland and B. A. Hunter, "Women's 'Token Resistant' and Compliant Sexual Behaviors Are Related to Uncertain Sexual Intentions and Rape," *Personality and Social Psychological Bulletin* 21(3) (1995), pp. 226–237.

53. E. Kanin, "Male Aggression in Dating-Courtship Relationships," *American Journal of Sociology* 63 (1957), pp. 197–204.

54. M. P. Koss and S. L. Cook, "Date and Acquaintance Rape Are Significant Problems for Women," in R. J. Gelles and D. R. Loseke, eds., *Current Controversies on Family Violence* (Sage, Newbury Park, Calif., 1993).

55. B. Fisher, F. Cullen, and M. Turner, *The Sexual Victimization of College Women* (Bureau of Justice Statistics, U.S. Department of Justice, Washington, D.C., December 2000).

56. P. Pollard, "Rape Reporting as a Function of Victim–Offender Relationships: A Critique of the Lack of Effect Reported by Bachman," *Criminal Justice and Behavior* 22(1) (1995), pp. 74–80.

57. T. Meyer, "Date Rape: A Serious Campus Problem That Few Talk About," *Chronicle of Higher Education*, December 5, 1990, p. A 15.

58. Majority Staff of the Senate Judiciary Committee, *The Response to Rape: Detours on the Road to Equal Justice* (May 1993), pp. 18–19.

59. 20 U.S.C. Section 1092 (1990).

60. *Sexual Assault on Campus: What Colleges and Universities Are Doing about It* (U.S. Department of Justice, Washington, D.C., December 2005).

61. Much of this material has been based on N. Fitzgerald and K. J. Riley, "Assessing Drug-Facilitated Rape," *National Institute of Justice Journal* (April 2000). See also *Rohypnol* (Office of National Drug Control Policy, Washington, D.C., February 2003).

62. See *Fact Sheet: Rohypnol* (Drug Policy Information Clearinghouse, Washington, D.C., 1996).

63. "Date-Rape Drug Turns Deadly, Spurs Call for More Education," *Fresno Bee*, February 7, 2000, p. B-3.

64. J. N. Berdahl et al., "The Harassment of Men: Exploring the Concept with Theory and Data," *Psychology of Women Quarterly* 20(4) (1996), p. 527.

65. C. Safran, "What Men Do to Women on the Job: A Shocking Look at Sexual Harassment," *Redbook* (November 1976), p. 149. *Redbook* received more than 9,000 responses to its questionnaire regarding sexual harassment.

66. "Sexual Harassment in the Federal Workplace—Is It a Problem?" (Merit Systems Protection Board, 1981); see also W. Pollack, "Sexual Harassment: Women's Experience v. Legal Definitions." *Harvard Women's Law Journal* 13 (Spring 1990), p. 35, for a discussion of this and other surveys.

67. 42 U.S.C. § 2000e to 2000e-17 (1964).

68. 42 U.S.C. § 2000e-2(a) (1982).

69. 42 U.S.C. § 2000e(k) (1982).

70. *Wilson v. Southwest Airlines Co.*, 517 F.Supp. 292, at 297, fn. 12 (N. D. Tex.) 1981.

71. *Meritor Saving Bank v. Vinson*, 106 S.Ct. 2399, 2404 (1986).

72. B. Lindemann and D. D. Kadue, *Sexual Harassment in Employment Law* (Bureau of National Affairs, Washington, D.C., 1992).

73. See Note, "The Dehumanizing Puzzle of Sexual Harassment: A Survey of the Law Concerning Harassment of Women in the Workplace." *Washburn Law Journal* 24 (1985), p. 574.

74. See *Barnes v. Castle*, 561 F.2d 983 (D.C. Cir. 1977).

75. 561 F.2d 983 (D.C. Cir. 1977).

76. 29 C.F.R. § 1604.11(a).

77. *Meritor Saving Bank v. Vinson*, 106 S.Ct. 2399, (1986).

78. *Ibid*

79. 510 U.S. 17 (1993).

80. S. Tangri, M. Burt, and L. Johnson, "Sexual Harassment at Work: Three Explanatory Models," *Journal of Social Issues* 38 (1982), pp. 33–54.

14

Stalking

CHAPTER OBJECTIVES

After studying this chapter, you should be able to:

- Explain what constitutes stalking;
- List and discuss law enforcement's responses to stalking;
- Discuss the various types of stalkers;
- Understand why there are questions regarding the constitutionality of anti-stalking statutes;
- Discuss cyberstalking.

Detailed Look at What You Should Know About Stalking

- Stalking is a crime that can happen to anyone at any time.
- Many individuals are stalked by their former husbands, live-in partners, girlfriends, or boyfriends.
- The study of the dynamics of stalking is still in its infancy.
- The term *stalking* has become a buzzword for the media.
- Stalking involves more than simply following another person before committing a crime.
- Stalking involves a complex series of acts that, taken individually, might be normal everyday occurrences.
- The crime of stalking is the knowing, purposeful course of conduct directed at a specific person that would cause a reasonable person to fear bodily injury or death to himself or herself or a member of his or her immediate family.

- Understanding stalking requires more than simply setting forth a definition of the act. Stalking is a course of conduct that may occur in a wide variety of situations.

- The stalker with **erotomania** has a delusional disorder in which the predominant theme of the delusion is that a person, usually of higher status, is in love with the subject.

- The **love obsessional stalker** is similar to the erotomanic in many ways. The subject does not know his or her victim except through the media.

- Unlike the two previous categories, a prior relationship existed between the **simple obsessional stalker** and his or her intended victim.

- A new form of stalking that was not present when this textbook was originally published is becoming more and more common. Cyberstalking is the use of the Internet, e-mail, or other electronic communications devices to stalk another person.

- Stalking laws are a relatively recent phenomenon. California enacted the United States' first stalking legislation in 1990.

- Forty-eight states and the District of Columbia have adopted stalking laws. The remaining two states, Arizona and Maine, use their harassment and terrorizing statutes to combat stalking. States continue to amend their statutes to provide more protection to victims of stalking.

- For stalking laws to withstand a constitutional challenge, they must prohibit specific, clearly defined activity.

- A vague statute fails to provide explicit grounds for enforcement. A statute is vague if a person of common intelligence cannot ascertain the limits of lawful behavior.

- Sanctions for stalking are as different as the statutes that define stalking in the various states. However, most sanctions can be classified into three distinct areas: pretrial release or bail provisions, types of punishment, and civil remedies.

INTRODUCTION

Stalking is a crime that can happen to anyone at any time. It is included in this textbook because many individuals are stalked by their former husbands, live-in partners, girlfriends, or boyfriends. Any professional dealing with family violence must therefore be familiar with this newly emerging course of conduct and know how to respond to victims of this crime. In addition, the study of the dynamics of stalking is still in its infancy. A lack of academic research in this area makes it critical to include a brief overview of stalking in this textbook.

Stalking and domestic violence intersect in a variety of ways. Research indicates that 81 percent of women stalked by an intimate partner have been physically assaulted by that person. Thirty-one percent of women stalked by an intimate partner have been sexually assaulted by that person. Offenders who stalk former intimate partners are more likely to have physically or sexually assaulted them before the relationship ended. Stalking is often a feature of relationships involving domestic violence. Like domestic violence, it is a crime of power and control. Victims report only about half of stalking incidents to the police.[1]

The term *stalking* has become a buzzword for the media. If someone is killed and evidence shows the killer followed the victim on the day of the killing, the media immediately label the offender as a stalker. However, the act of stalking is much more complex than simply following an intended victim before committing a crime. It involves psychological, physical, and legal issues that all converge to form a course of conduct.

Researchers are not fully certain exactly who is or may become a stalker. Professionals are still researching this area, and like so many areas of family violence, they have yet to agree on a single definition of the term *stalker*. For purposes of our discussions, stalking refers to repeated harassing or threatening behaviors that an individual engages in such as following a person, appearing at a person's home or place of business, making harassing phone calls, leaving written messages or objects, or vandalizing a person's property. These actions may be accompanied by a credible threat of serious harm, and they may or may not be precursors to an assault or murder.

In November 1997, the Department of Justice published research regarding the extent of stalking.[2] The National Violence against Women Survey collected data from 8,000 men and women on a broad range of issues involving violence. Of those surveyed, 8 percent of the women and 2 percent of the men responded that they had been stalked sometime during their lives. Using the 1995 estimates of adult population, this translates into 8.2 million women and two million men as stalking victims. Researchers estimate that one million women and 400,000 men are stalked each year. Most victims knew their stalker. Women tended to be stalked by one perpetrator, whereas in 50 percent of the male victimizations, the stalker had an accomplice.

Focus

According to Michelle Garcia, a family violence researcher, 76 percent of the women who are murdered by their current or former intimate partner were stalked by their murderers within the 12 months of the murder.

Source: M. Garcia "Voices from the field: Stalking" *NIL Journal*, No. 266, (2010), p. 14.

A photo of stalking by an ex-girlfriend of her ex-boyfriend with another woman.

DEFINITION

Stalking involves more than simply following another person before committing a crime. If this action were considered stalking, then most street muggings would involve stalking. Stalking also does not have to result in death or injury to another person. Telephone calls, letters, or following the victim are acts that can cause a reasonable person to feel threatened or terrorized. The victim can be a celebrity, an average citizen related to the stalker by marriage or other relationship, or a complete stranger.

As indicated previously, stalking involves a complex series of acts that, taken individually, might be normal everyday occurrences. It has been examined from a psychological perspective, a physical security point of view, and a legal basis. By combining all of these disciplines, the crime of stalking can be distilled down to the following definition: **Stalking** is a knowing, purposeful course of conduct directed at a specific person that would cause a reasonable person to fear bodily injury or death to himself or herself or a member of his or her immediate family. Although the definition may appear simple, it is composed of six distinct elements that must be met before the crime of stalking has occurred:

1. *Knowing:* This requires knowledge that the victim will be placed in fear of injury. Acts that occur without the knowledge of the victim's fear do not meet this criterion. However, this knowledge may be inferred from the perpetrator's actions. If a reasonable person perceives that his acts are placing another in fear, the requirement is satisfied.
2. *Purposeful:* The acts must be done in a conscious course of conduct that a reasonable person would know places another in fear.
3. *Course of conduct:* This element requires more than a single act. Thus, the mugger who follows a victim and then robs her has not engaged in the conduct necessary to be classified as a stalker. However, if an estranged husband followed his former spouse on more than one occasion, and if the other elements are satisfied, he may be guilty of stalking.
4. *Reasonable person:* The victim is judged by what a reasonable person would feel, not what the victim may experience. This poses a problem in the area of family violence because battered spouses are very sensitive to the potential injury from their abuser, and jurors may not understand the victim's level of fear. However, if this standard is interpreted to mean what a reasonable person would feel having undergone what the victim has experienced, then jurors would be exposed to the feelings of a spouse who has been battered and can then place themselves in her position.
5. *Fear of injury or death:* The conduct must be more than simply an annoying series of acts. The victim must fear that she will be injured as the end result of the perpetrator's actions.
6. *Herself or immediate family:* The actions may be directed at the victim or her family. Immediate family is normally considered to be spouses, children, or parents.

Understanding stalking requires more than simply setting forth a definition of the act. Stalking is a course of conduct that may occur in a wide variety of situations. This characteristic makes it difficult to establish a clear typology of stalkers.

Focus

Stalking and the Stars

In July 1989, an obsessed fan, John Bardo, finally met his favorite celebrity. After sending numerous letters and making several long-distance telephone calls to actress Rebecca Schaeffer, costar of the television sitcom *My Sister Sam*, he traveled to Los Angeles. After being turned away at the studio, he hired a private detective who supplied him with her home address. Bardo went to her apartment, and after seeing her the first time, he returned with a .357 magnum and shot her at point-blank range, killing her. The method and manner of her death shocked the entire United States. At the same time, there was little if any understanding of the reasons behind this tragedy.

O.J. Simpson and his wife, Nicole Brown Simpson, were part of the beautiful people that everyone expects to see at Hollywood parties. He was an American dream come true; a poor kid who rose from the ghetto and a troubled childhood to sports, television, movies, fame, and fortune. Few persons could believe that O.J. had beaten his wife so badly that she sustained a black eye, a swollen cheek, a bruise to her forehead, and scratch marks on her neck. Nor could we accept that he would stalk her again and again to the point that she had to repeatedly call the police for assistance. Her death was yet another shock to the public.

TYPES OF STALKING

The study of stalking is still in its infancy. However, several authorities have begun to attempt to classify stalkers according to certain characteristics.[3]

Experts Dr. Michael Zona, Dr. Kaushal Sharma, and Lieutenant John Lane, have conducted an in-depth review of stalkers in the Los Angeles area using the files of the Threat Management Unit (TMU) of the Los Angeles Police Department.[4] This unit is the only one of its kind in the United States. During late 1989, the Los Angeles Police Department became aware of an increase in unsolicited contacts between mentally ill persons and Hollywood celebrities. After a meeting with various entertainment personal managers, the TMU was formed.[5] Los Angeles Police Department Special Order Number 4 sets forth the background and purpose of this unit as follows:

> Obsessed individuals with abnormal fixations on celebrities have recently received a great deal of media attention. However, becoming a victim of harassment, threats, or being stalked could happen to any member of society. Often these situations begin without any specific crime having been committed. If such a case is allowed to escalate, it could end in a tragedy to which law enforcement can only react after the fact. In response to the rapid increase of threats and harassment against a variety of public figures and other community members, the department has developed the Threat Management Unit. This Order establishes the Threat Management Unit within Detective headquarters Division.[6]

Zona and colleagues were able to establish a database of seventy-four subjects who had engaged in stalking behavior. Only cases that were officially opened and investigated by the TMU were considered. Unfortunately, none of the cases involved domestic violence situations. However, situations in which the couple had physically separated and were living apart were included. All the cases were reviewed by a psychiatrist, and a profile was established by classifying stalkers as erotomania, love obsessional, simple obsessional, and false victimization syndrome.

> *Erotomania:* The stalker with **erotomania** has a delusional disorder in which the predominant theme of the delusion is that a person, usually of higher status, is in love with the subject. The victim does not know the stalker and many times will be a public figure or celebrity. The stalker is convinced that the victim, usually of the opposite sex, loves him and would return the affection if not for some external influence. The stalker rejects any contrary evidence and will remain delusional for years.
>
> *Love obsessional:* The **love obsessional stalker** is similar to the erotomanic in many ways. The subject does not know his or her victim except through the media. This stalker may also suffer from delusions. However, the subject has a primary psychiatric diagnosis. These individuals often believe that if the victim would simply acknowledge their existence, then the victim would fall in love with the stalker. These subjects usually engage in a campaign to make their existence known to the victim by writing, telephoning, or otherwise attempting to contact the victim.
>
> *Simple obsessional:* Unlike the two previous categories, a prior relationship existed between the **simple obsessional stalker** and his or her intended victim. This relationship may have been with a former spouse, employer, or neighbor; and in all cases, the stalking began after the relationship had soured or when there was a perception by the subject of mistreatment. The stalking is an attempt to rectify the problem or seek revenge.
>
> *False victimization syndrome:* This is the rarest category of stalkers. These are individuals with a desire to be placed in the victim's role. By insisting that someone is stalking them, they become the victim. There appears to be a similarity between this classification and Munchausen syndrome by proxy (discussed earlier in this textbook). Although this is not truly a "stalker," Zona and his associates included it for purposes of comparison and understanding of the stalking process.

The length of time of stalking varied with the type of stalker studied. The duration for erotomanics was 124 months and that of love obsessional slightly more, averaging 146 months. The simple obsessional stalker maintained contact for 5.1 months. The contact between the stalker and the victim ranged from visiting the subject's home or other locations to mailing letters or making phone calls. In addition, all categories of stalkers made threats to the victim.

Just as we learn more about stalking behavior, it changes and becomes more complex and difficult to prevent. A new form of stalking that was not present when this textbook was originally published is becoming more and more common. Cyberstalking is the use of the Internet, e-mail, or other electronic communications devices to stalk another person.[7] Cyberstalking is a growing problem in the United States and other technologically advanced societies.[8] The attorney general of the United States has predicted that cyberstalking will grow in scope and seriousness as more and more people take advantage of the Internet and other advanced communications technologies. Many of the stalking laws discussed later in this chapter are broad enough to encompass such electronic stalking. Some states such as California are amending their stalking laws to specifically address stalking via the Internet.

Focus

Extent of Stalking

- Approximately one in six women (16.2%) in the United States has experienced stalking at some point in her lifetime in which she felt very fearful or believed that she or someone close to her would be harmed or killed as a result. This translates to approximately 19.3 million adult women in the United States.
- About 4 percent, or approximately 5.2 million women, were stalked in the past twelve months.
- Approximately one in nineteen men (5.2%) in the United States (approximately 5.9 million) has experienced stalking victimization at some point during his lifetime in which he felt very fearful or believed that he or someone close to him would be harmed or killed as a result, and 1.3 percent of men (about 1.4 million) reported being stalked in the past twelve months.
- A variety of tactics were used to stalk victims. More than three-quarters of female stalking victims (78.8%) reported receiving unwanted phone calls, including voice or text messages, or hang ups.
- More than half of female victims (57.6%) reported being approached, such as at their home or work, and more than one-third (38.6%) were watched, followed, or tracked with a listening or other device.

- Similarly, about three-quarters of male victims (75.9%) reported receiving unwanted phone calls, voice or text messages, or hang ups. Just under half (43.5%) reported being approached by the perpetrator. Nearly one-third of male victims (31.0%) reported being watched, followed, or tracked.
- For both female and male victims, stalking was often committed by people they knew or with whom they had a relationship. Two-thirds of the female victims of stalking (66.2%) reported stalking by a current or former intimate partner, and nearly one-quarter (24.0%) reported stalking by an acquaintance. About one in eight female victims (13.2%) reported stalking by a stranger.
- More than half of female victims and more than one-third of male victims of stalking indicated that they were stalked before the age of twenty-five. About one in five female victims and one in fourteen male victims had experienced stalking between the ages of eleven and seventeen. For both female and male victims, more than one-quarter (28.5% and 29.6%, respectively) reported that their first stalking victimization occurred between twenty-five to thirty-four years of age.

Source: The National Intimate Partner and Sexual Violence Survey: 2010 Summary Report (National Center for Injury Prevention and Control of the Centers for Disease Control and Prevention, 2011, Atlanta, Ga.).

MYTHS AND ASSESSMENT OF STALKING

Dr. Kaushal Sharma, a well-respected psychiatrist at the Institute of Psychiatry, Law, and Behavioral Science of the University of Southern California School of Medicine's Psychiatric Hospital, has studied the profile of stalkers and established several myths regarding both stalking and the stalker.[9] He bases the following conclusions on the evaluation and study of numerous referrals of stalkers by mental health professionals and law enforcement officials:

Myth 1: Most stalkers are mentally ill. Some stalkers are mentally ill, but most do not fall within the various DSM-V classifications. Simply being strange is not considered a mental illness.

Myth 2: Most stalkers are dangerous. Less than 5 percent of stalkers commit dangerous acts against their victims.

Myth 3: Psychiatry can help stalkers discontinue their acts. Only a small percentage of stalkers respond to psychiatric treatment.

Myth 4: Most stalkers continue their stalking behavior. Most stalkers will eventually stop their stalking. Most of the individuals who come to our attention are long-term stalkers, but many will stalk their victims for only a short period of time.

Myth 5: Most stalkers look like sleazeballs and have beady eyes. Stalkers can be anyone, including police officers, doctors, judges, and even psychiatrists.

Myth 6: Stalkers are just into stalking. Stalkers commit related and unrelated crimes.

Myth 7: Victims must do something to attract stalking. Anybody can be a victim of stalking.

Myth 8: Stalking is a crime of the young and restless. Stalking is many times a crime of the old and the calm.

Myth 9: Stalking is bad for you. Stalking is bad for the stalker and the victim but has become a big business for the government, security firms, movies, and authors.

Dispelling such myths surrounding this form of family violence allows professionals to offer support and advice to victims of stalking. Family violence practitioners should also be aware of the various factors that can be used in assessing a stalking case. Michael Zona, M.D., is one of the first experts in this area to develop such an assessment protocol. He has established ten factors that should be considered in assessing a stalking case.[10]

The first factor is the history of violence exhibited by the stalker. This, according to Zona, is the single most reliable factor in assessing the danger and propensity for future violent acts. The professional should review criminal records, review school and work histories, and interview family and friends of the stalker.

The second factor is the presence of physical abuse or domestic violence. Domestic violence is often a pattern of behavior and represents poor coping strategies on the part of the stalker. He is less likely to express feelings or frustrations with words and has found that physical violence meets his needs.

The third factor is the presence or absence of **threats.** Verbal or written threats very frequently precede acts of violence by the stalker. Threats also allow the professional an opportunity to understand the suspect by analyzing the content and nature of the threat.

The fourth factor is determining whether the suspect is stalking the same or a similar victim over a period of time. If the stalker is obsessed with a particular victim or a certain type of victim, this represents the greatest risk of harm for the victim. This also provides insight into the nature of the stalking pattern and provides an opportunity to understand the suspect.

The destruction of property is the fifth factor. Those who destroy property represent a greater percentage of stalkers who go on to commit further acts of interpersonal violence. The destruction of property, usually a series of acts of vandalism, represents increasing frustration and desperation on the part of the stalker.

The sixth factor involves access and approach behaviors of the stalker. These behaviors include telephone contact, letter writing, faxing, visits by the stalker to the victim's workplace or home, physical stalking, and face-to-face contacts. Careful assessment of access and approach behaviors can assist in evaluating the risk of danger to the victim. Letter writing is seen as posing less risk of harm to the victim, but a transition into more personal forms of contact increases the risk of violence.

The seventh factor involves the sex and sexual orientation of the stalker. In general, men are more dangerous than women, representing 80 percent of all stalking cases. Both men and women stalkers, however, will commit dangerous acts.

The eighth factor is an evaluation of psychiatric disorders affecting the stalkers. Mood disorders, psychotic disorders, personality disorders, and alcohol or substance abuse are present in many stalkers. Understanding the mental status of a stalker allows treatment plans to be crafted to fit that particular individual.

Investment in the object of the stalking is the ninth factor. The meaning or value the stalker places on the victim is an important assessment tool. This allows for an evaluation of the effectiveness of legal restraints such as temporary restraining orders.

The tenth and last assessment factor is the stalker's insight into the relationship between himself and the victim. This factor may give an indication to the stalker's amenability to treatment.

Experts in the field continue to attempt to establish an accepted typology of stalkers. Disagreement exists among various researchers and other authorities regarding the dynamics of stalking and the categories that should be used when examining this type of individual.[11] However, from a family violence perspective, it is important that professionals understand that stalking does in fact occur and be prepared to offer assistance to victims of this type of family violence.

Different Subtypes of Stalking

Stalking can take many different types of forms. As indicated earlier, it may involve following, calling, and other forms of dangerous or harassing behavior. The following discussion focuses on unique or different types of stalking.

IMMIGRANT STALKING.   All stalking victims face difficult questions when deciding whether or not to report acts of stalking. Immigrants face even more complex questions because of their status. They may be unfamiliar with the legal system and have difficulty understanding the language or the culture of the United States.

The stalker may use cultural barriers to intimidate or control the victim. He may threaten to use the victim's immigration status and her fear of being deported to keep her silent. Because the victim may be alone in the United States, she may have no social network of family or friends to look to for support. If the victim does have family or other friends and associates from his or her own culture present, he or she may fear that reporting the crime may result in shame within his or her own culture.

GANG STALKING.   This is a relatively new and unexplored form of stalking. It involves members of a gang stalking an individual. The reasons for this type of stalking may vary from attempting to control or frighten the victim to using the victim, who may not have done anything wrong, as an example to show others what could happen to them.

TEEN STALKING.   About 12 percent of all stalking victims reported having been stalked before the age of eighteen. One of the difficulties in assessing the nature and extent of teen stalking is that many teens are inexperienced in interpersonal relationships. Many teens began dating between the ages of fourteen and seventeen and are experiencing love for the first time. In addition, many teens are hesitant about reporting crimes and becoming involved with law enforcement officials. Finally, many teens underestimate the dangers of stalking.

CYBERSTALKING.   This is an expanding form of stalking. Although there is no universally accepted definition, **cyberstalking** can be defined as threatening behavior or unwanted advances directed at another using the Internet or other forms of online communication to harass the victim.[12]

A recent study suggests that teens and other victims may be intimidated and emotionally abused by the use of technology. Media used by stalkers include telephones, cell phones, e-mails, instant messaging, chat rooms, and social networking sites. In another study, 10 to

Cyberstalking is becoming one of the most popular forms of stalking.

15 percent of all college students surveyed reported experiencing cyberstalking, including repeated messages that threatened, insulted, or harassed them from strangers, acquaintances, or significant others.[13]

Some states, such as Alaska, Oklahoma, Wyoming, and California, have begun to address this form of stalking and specifically include electronically communicated statements as conduct constituting stalking in their antistalking statutes.

Cyberstalking is different from the techniques used by child predators. Child predators are interested in luring the victim into a situation in which they can get the victim's cooperation in a sexual online activity or get a face-to-face meeting with the victim. Cyberstalkers, on the other hand, are intent on causing fear or punishing or hurting the victim.

Cyberstalking is expected to expand with the increased use of the Internet and cell phones. Law enforcement officials at local, state, and federal levels must become familiar with technology and its use and misuse. Similar to traditional stalking, with time, we will form the necessary responses to this emerging form of violence.

STALKING LAWS

Stalking laws are a relatively recent phenomenon. As a result of the 1989 stalking murder of actress Rebecca Schaeffer and other reports of stalking of high-profile celebrities, California enacted the United States' first stalking legislation in 1990. In retrospect, it is hard to believe that any sane person could oppose legislation that would protect persons from possible danger and harassment. However, proponents of California's stalking law have indicated that there was a great deal of resistance within the legislature to the passage of the proposed law.[14] The statute as finally adopted was very narrow and required the prosecution to prove a credible threat to kill or commit great bodily injury against the victim. Fortunately, California and other states have since adopted a more comprehensive series of stalking laws, which in many instances offer victims of family violence protection where none existed before.

Focus

Federal Stalking Laws

Relevant federal laws on stalking include the following:

- Full Faith and Credit (18 U.S.C. § 2265),
- Interstate Stalking (18 U.S.C. § 2261),
- Interstate Domestic Violence (18 U.S.C. § 2261),
- Interstate Violation of a Protection Order (18 U.S.C. § 2262),
- Federal Domestic Violence Firearm Prohibitions (18 U.S.C. § 922),
- Interstate Communications (18 U.S.C. § 875),
- Harassing Telephone Calls in Interstate Communications (18 U.S.C. § 233(a)(1)(C)).

Note: U.S.C. refers to the U.S. Code. The 18 refers to Title 18 of the U.S.C.

The National Center for Victims of Crime has developed a Model Stalking Code Revisited: Responding to the New Realities of Stalking to assist states that are working to strengthen their stalking laws. www.ncvc.org/ncvc/main.aspx?dbID=DB_ReportsStudies213

Types of Stalking Laws

Forty-eight states and the District of Columbia have adopted stalking laws. The remaining two states, Arizona and Maine, use their harassment and terrorizing statutes to combat stalking. States continue to amend their statutes to provide more protection to victims of stalking. Depending on the jurisdiction, various acts are prohibited. For example, a suspect may not be present, approach, pursue or follow, trespass onto property, lay in wait, intimidate, vandalize, conduct surveillance, harass, show a weapon, restrain, or commit bodily injury against the victim.

Because of this varied patchwork of statutes, in 1993 the National Institute of Justice was asked by Congress to develop a model stalking act.[15] In October 1993, the institute published its findings and recommended a Model Stalking Code for consideration by states when they amend their existing statutes. This model is a well-reasoned approach to stalking and considers the rights of individuals as well as the rights of victims.[16] The code provides that any person who:

1. purposefully engages in a course of conduct directed at a specific person that would cause a reasonable person to fear bodily injury to himself or a member of his or her immediate family or to fear the death of himself or herself or a member of his or her immediate family;
2. has knowledge or should have knowledge that the specific person will be placed in reasonable fear of bodily injury to himself or herself or a member of his or her immediate family or will be placed in reasonable fear of death of himself or a member of his or her immediate family; and
3. whose acts induce fear in the specific person of bodily injury to himself or herself or a member of his or her immediate family or induce fear in the specific person of the death of himself or herself or a member of his or her immediate family is guilty of stalking.[17]

The drafters of the code preferred not to list specific acts of stalking and instead inserted the more encompassing term *course of conduct*. They believed that this would provide for more effective coverage than listing a series of acts and finding out later that another specific act had not been included. Furthermore, the course of conduct provision requires two or more occasions of maintaining visual or physical proximity to the victim or repeatedly conveying threats by words or conduct toward the victim. Part of the problem in enacting any legislation that criminalizes certain types of conduct involving expression of thoughts and ideas is the inevitable confrontation with the rights guaranteed under the Constitution.

Constitutional Issues

Any law that attempts to regulate the exercise of speech is subject to scrutiny by the courts.[18] The First Amendment to the U.S. Constitution states, "Congress shall make no law. . . abridging the freedom of speech."[19] Some scholars argue that the First Amendment is the most important protection within the Constitution.

Stalking laws by their very nature regulate the expression of ideas and thoughts. The stalker may engage in conduct that is intended to express his or her feelings of love or hate toward the victim. This conduct may involve following the victim, sending the victim objects such as flowers, and other conduct that at first glance is clearly protected by the First Amendment. Stalkers may also engage in pure speech activities such as sending letters or phoning the victim proclaiming their undying love for that person. All of these acts raise constitutional issues that must be addressed.

The U.S. Supreme Court has held that certain conduct that is intended as a form of communication is protected by the First Amendment. Demonstrations protesting governmental decisions are examples of such speech-related conduct. However, the courts have held that even First Amendment rights can be regulated. The Supreme Court decision in *Madsen v. Women's Health Center Inc.* illustrates this position.[20] In *Madsen*, the Court stated that abortion protestors were exercising their First Amendment rights; however, other considerations, such as safety of individuals who worked at the clinics and those who desired to use the services of the clinics, were proper factors that the legislature could consider in setting up a zone of protection that the protestors could not enter. Thus, stalking laws may be drafted so as to regulate conduct that otherwise might be protected by the First Amendment.

Another aspect of stalking laws involves punishment for sending letters or making telephone calls. These activities by the stalker are clearly forms of expression. However, the Supreme Court has held that the First Amendment does not prevent the government from regulating speech that contains threats. Threats of violence are outside the protection of the Constitution because they protect victims from a fear of violence and the disruption that such a fear causes.[21] In *Thorne v. Bailey*, the Fourth Circuit Court of Appeals upheld the constitutionality of a statute prohibiting telephone harassment that included a provision against using the phone to make threats against persons or property.[22] The appellate court held that harassment was not protected even though it took the form of speech and involved the use of a telephone.[23]

For stalking laws to withstand a constitutional challenge, they must prohibit specific, clearly defined activity. In the legal profession, this requires that the stalking statute not be overbroad or vague. Each of these requirements involves shades of gray within the realm of constitutional law.

A statute is overbroad if it prohibits both activities that are not constitutionally protected as well as activities that are protected. The Supreme Court has stated several justifications for voiding overbroad statutes. First is the fear that if a statute is overbroad, individuals may refrain from carrying out protected activities as well as regulated activity. The second rationale for voiding overbroad statutes is the fear that an overbroad statute will allow law enforcement agencies to enforce it selectively against unpopular groups or activities. This danger is avoided if the statute is narrowly drafted.

A vague statute fails to provide explicit grounds for enforcement. A statute is vague if a person of common intelligence cannot ascertain the limits of lawful behavior.[24] If a statute is vague, it will be struck down or declared void. This void-for-vagueness doctrine is based on the due process requirements of the Fifth and Fourteenth Amendments.[25] This doctrine demands that all criminal legislation satisfy a two-pronged test. The first prong requires notice and clarity such that ordinary persons can understand what conduct is prohibited. The second prong requires all criminal laws to provide explicit standards to prevent arbitrary and discriminatory enforcement.[26] Similar to overbroad statutes, the danger with a vague statute is the fear that individuals will fail to exercise their right to free speech because of a belief that they will be prosecuted under the statute that regulates unprotected activities. However, the

Supreme Court does not require that words in a statute reach mathematical or scientific precision to be valid and enforceable.[27]

The drafters of the Model Code considered these issues when they proposed their version of a stalking statute. It is drafted to ensure that specific activities are clearly prohibited. Furthermore, it does not attempt to regulate protected speech. Simply drafting or adopting a stalking law, however, does not prevent stalking. Since 1990 to the present, courts have consistently upheld the constitutionality of these laws.

Sanctions

For any statute to be effective, it must provide for sanctions when it is violated. Sanctions for stalking are as different as the statutes that define stalking in the various states. However, most sanctions can be classified into three distinct areas: pretrial release or bail provisions, types of punishment, and civil remedies.

Most state constitutions include provisions that allow for bail of persons awaiting trial or pending appeal of a conviction.[28] The practice of granting bail to accused persons developed in England, where accused persons were otherwise held in disease-infected jails. The right to bail in England was established because of numerous instances where those accused of crimes were not released or the bail was set at such a high level that they could not afford to post it. As a result, when the founding fathers adopted the Constitution, special provisions were included regarding bail. The Eighth Amendment to the U.S. Constitution provides that "[e]xcessive bail shall not be required."[29] In analyzing this amendment, the Supreme Court concluded that there is no absolute right to bail, only that it will not be excessive in those cases where it is proper to grant bail.[30]

Concern for the safety of victims, witnesses, and others prompted Congress to pass the Federal Bail Reform Act of 1984.[31] This act specifically provides for preventive detention of dangerous individuals. As a result, federal courts imposed preventive detention of dangerous offenders in excess of 1,600 times during a one-year period.[32] This provision was challenged in *United States v. Salerno*, in which two defendants were charged with twenty-nine counts alleging various organized crime activities, including mail fraud, extortion, and criminal gambling violations.[33] These defendants were detained pending trial under the dangerous offenders provision of the Federal Bail Act. However, the Supreme Court upheld the provisions of the act, holding that it did not violate the provisions of the Eighth Amendment. Thus, preventive detention is permissible in appropriate situations.

Unfortunately, most state statutes or constitutions dealing with bail mandate reasonable bail for those charged with crimes with the exception of persons charged with capital offenses. Approximately half the states allow the court to detain a suspect pending trial if the offense was violent or a felony and the accused met other requirements, such as a history of prior violence or other factors that definitely indicate his dangerousness.[34] The National Institute of Justice recommends amendment to these statutes or constitutions to allow for the denial of pretrial bail in stalking cases.[35] Some states are following this recommendation and give the court discretion to deny bail. For example, Illinois allows a court to deny bail when the court determines the release of the perpetrator would pose a real and present threat to the safety of the victim.[36] Pending such modifications by all the states, courts should include conditions that the suspect stay away from the victim pending the trial. A violation of this condition would then allow the courts to confine the stalker until the trial.

The second category of sanctions deals with the classification of the crime of stalking. Traditionally, crimes are classified as either felonies or misdemeanors. Felonies are punishable by imprisonment in state prison, and misdemeanors are punishable by incarceration in local jails for no longer than one year. Until recently, most stalking statutes were classified as misdemeanors. The rationale for this appears to be that no physical injury is required for the crime to be complete, and felonies should be reserved for the more serious property or personal crimes. Unfortunately, in numerous instances the stalker seriously wounded or killed his victim.

California has made stalking a felony under certain conditions.[37] In addition, the California statute mandates state prison for a stalker if a temporary restraining order, injunction, or any other court order is in effect at the time of the offense. California was the first state to adopt a stalking law, and other states may follow its lead and revise their statutes to make stalking a felony.

The final category of sanctions involves the use of various civil remedies to prevent stalking. These alternatives include the issuance of temporary restraining orders, injunctions, mental evaluations, and civil commitments. All these options, although available for use by professionals and the courts, are surrounded in controversy.

One of the most controversial civil tools available to victims of stalking is the use of a temporary restraining order. **Restraining orders or protective orders** are court orders that prohibit the offender from having any contact with the victim. Numerous articles have commented on the availability and use of restraining orders in stalking situations.[38] In addition, in many instances issuance of the restraining order may have been a factor in assaultive behavior that ended in serious injury or death to the victim.

Law enforcement officials believe in the use of restraining orders. In California, for example, if the stalking occurs when a restraining order is in effect, the offense is a felony subjecting the suspect to state prison. Other authorities believe that restraining orders may enrage the stalker and cause him to react in a violent and sometimes fatal manner. It is clear that more study needs to be done on the relationship between restraining orders and subsequent violence. However, continuous debate in this area should not stop professionals from recommending that victims of stalking obtain a restraining order. In the proper situation, a restraining order may be effective in deterring or stopping the stalker. One state has taken the concept of a restraining order one step further in its war on stalking. In New Jersey, a conviction for stalking operates as an application for a permanent restraining order. The order can only be dissolved on a motion by the victim.[39]

Mental evaluations are another civil alternative that should be considered. Most states have established procedures that allow for involuntary commitments of short duration for the purpose of evaluating the mental status of those who are a danger to themselves or others. If mental health professionals come to the conclusion that the stalker falls within this classification, they can institute proceedings to have him civilly committed to a mental institution for treatment.

Many states provide for civil commitments of individuals who are a danger to themselves or others. These commitments are normally for a specified period of time, at the end of which the patient must be reevaluated or released. If a stalker is suffering from a mental disease or defect that renders him a danger to himself or others, a civil commitment allows for placement in a mental hospital where he could receive the type of treatment that might cure the disorder. Civil commitments of this type require less proof than criminal convictions and thereby offer professionals another option with which to respond to a stalking situation.

ANTISTALKING MEASURES

Physical Security Measures

A stalking victim can employ many different types of physical security measures.[40] Many of these are commonsense approaches that many people already use to protect their own homes. Others, such as training household staff, are obviously directed at celebrities and the wealthy. Victims of stalking are often so emotionally distraught that they do not think to employ preventive physical security measures. Therefore, this aspect of stalking is included within this textbook. Professionals in the field not only must understand how to assist with the legal and emotional problems but also should be able to offer concrete advice on how the victim can physically protect herself. However, it must be stressed that these are only guidelines, and professionals should ensure that the victim of a stalker does not gain a false sense of physical security simply by using some or all these techniques.

The following series of physical security tactics has been based on material provided by the TMU of the Los Angeles Police Department.

Residence Security

1. Be alert for any suspicious persons.
2. Positively identify callers before opening doors.
3. Install a porch light that cannot be easily removed.
4. Install deadbolts on all outside doors.
5. Keep garage doors locked at all times.
6. Install adequate outside lighting.
7. Trim shrubbery.
8. Keep the fuse box locked.
9. Install a loud exterior alarm bell that can be manually activated in more than one location from within the house.
10. Maintain an unlisted phone number.
11. Any written or telephone threats should be treated as legitimate and should be referred to the appropriate law enforcement agency.
12. Household staff should have a security check prior to employment and be thoroughly briefed on security precautions. Strictly enforce a policy that the staff members do not discuss family matters or movements with anyone.
13. Be alert for any unusual packages, boxes, or devices on the premises. Do not disturb such objects. Call the local law enforcement agency immediately.
14. Install a smoke detector system.
15. Tape emergency numbers on all phones.
16. When away from the residence for an evening, place a light and a radio on a timer.
17. Intruders will attempt to enter unlocked doors and windows without causing a disturbance. Keep all doors and windows locked.
18. Prepare an evacuation plan and ensure that all members of the household are aware of it.

19. A family dog is one of the least expensive but most effective alarm systems.
20. Know the whereabouts of all family members at all times.
21. Children should be accompanied to school or bus stops.
22. Vary all routes and times spent exercising outdoors.
23. Require identification of all repair workers before permitting them entry into the residence.
24. Always park in a secured garage if available.
25. Inform a trusted neighbor regarding the situation. Provide the neighbor with a photograph or description of the suspect and any possible vehicle.

Personal Security

1. Remove your home address from personal checks and business cards.
2. Place real estate in a trust and list the utilities under the name of the trust.
3. Utilize a private mailbox service to receive all personal mail.
4. File for confidential voter status or register to vote utilizing a mailbox address.
5. Destroy discarded mail.
6. Phone lines can be installed in a location other than the person's residence and call-forwarded to the residence.
7. Place residence rental agreements in another person's name.
8. Do not obtain a mailbox with the U.S. Postal Service.
9. All current creditors should be given a change of address card using a mailbox as the new address. Some credit reporting agencies will remove past addresses from credit histories if requested.
10. File a change of address with the Department of Motor Vehicles to reflect the new mailbox address. Obtain a new driver's license with the new address on it.

Vehicle Security

1. Park vehicles in well-lit areas. Do not patronize parking lots where car doors must be left unlocked and keys surrendered. Allow items to be placed in or removed from the trunk only in your presence.
2. When parked in the residence garage, turn the garage light on and lock the vehicle and the garage door.
3. Equip the gas tank with a locking gas cap.
4. Visually check the front and rear passenger compartments before entering the vehicle.
5. Select a reliable service station for vehicle service.
6. Keep doors locked while the vehicle is in use.
7. Be alert for vehicles that appear to be following you.
8. When traveling by vehicle, plan ahead. Know locations of police stations, fire departments, and busy shopping centers.
9. Use a different schedule and route of travel each day. If followed, drive to a police station, fire department, or busy shopping center, and sound your horn to attract attention.
10. Do not stop to assist a stranded motorist (phone in).

These recommendations do not stop the stalker. They merely prevent the stalker from approaching and possibly harming the victim. Other techniques must be employed in an attempt to remove the threat of stalking permanently. The total systems approach is one method that professionals should consider when dealing with a stalking situation.

Total Systems Approach

The previous discussion set forth a number of physical security measures or tactics that a victim can take to protect herself from attack or harassment by the stalker. However, all the experts in this field, including Lieutenant John Lane, Dr. Kaushal Sharma, Dr. Michael Zona, and Gavin de Becker, agree that each case of stalking must be individually evaluated. The actions taken by the victim must be tailored to the tactics and the type of stalker. To be successful, professionals should recommend a total systems approach to stalking.

Focus

Recognizing Stalking

Stalking can be difficult to recognize, investigate, assess, and prevent for many reasons, including the following:

- Stalking is not a single, obvious, easily identifiable crime like assault, robbery, burglary, and most other offenses.
- Stalking, like domestic violence, often is not taken sufficiently seriously because it can involve acts the police may perceive as part of everyday courtship and intimate relationships. The police may mistake repeated telephone calls, letters, cards, and gifts from "would be" lovers for innocent romantic attention. However, when such gestures are part of a course of conduct that instills fear in the victim, they are being used to terrorize.
- There is no single stalker profile to assist investigators.
- When blatant acts of violence occur, a pattern of stalking behavior may not seem significant.
- Effective investigations depend on gathering information from many sources.
- The stalker may commit crimes in different locations and be under investigation in multiple jurisdictions.

- The victim may live in one jurisdiction, work or attend school in another, and seek refuge in yet another.
- If the stalker threatens people connected with the victim, such as coworkers, family members, or friends, or vandalizes their property, different victims' names will appear on complaint reports.
- Stalkers are not easily deterred and tend to be obsessive. Therefore, conventional sanctions, including court orders forbidding contact with victims, may not necessarily make an impact. Many stalkers continue to harass their victims even after conviction; the stalking may escalate if they perceive court sanctions as minor. Others may see their trials as a way to stay in their victims' lives. Because the first prosecution and conviction may not end the stalking, more enforcement is often necessary.
- It is not unusual for an offender to start stalking again before an anniversary, following a stressful event, or after any number of other triggers that renew the stalker's interest in the victim.

Source: National Center for Victims of Crime, *Creating an Effective Stalking Protocol* (U.S. Department of Justice, Office of Community Oriented Policing Services, Washington, D.C., 2002). Available at www.cops.usdoj.gov.

A total systems approach does not rely solely on law enforcement, medical or psychiatric professionals, or the courts to ensure the safety of the victim. Instead, it combines all professional knowledge to craft an individualized response to stalking for a particular victim. Depending on the dynamics involved in the specific stalking situation, the total systems approach may increase physical protection measures and rely less on psychiatric intervention. On the other hand, a particular stalker may respond favorably to mental health treatment but become angry if a restraining order is filed. Thus, each case must be evaluated and treated according to the type of stalker as well as the desires and needs of the victim.

Consideration should be given to forming multidisciplinary committees composed of law enforcement, medical personnel, and prosecutors. Much like existing child abuse coordination councils, these committees could address the stalking issue from an informed total systems approach. By evaluating individual cases of stalking, the best possible intervention strategy could then be implemented.

Professionals involved in stalking situations should use all available resources—law enforcement, medical, and other assistance—to increase the chance of success. The principal objective of intervention is to prevent the victim from being injured or killed. Law enforcement officials should coordinate their activities with the victim and mental health professionals. Occasionally, stalkers may agree to mental health counseling, which may end the problem. More serious cases may involve the decision to obtain a restraining order. Finally, the stalker may be charged criminally for his acts. Treatment programs should be evaluated and modified as more is learned about the dynamics of stalking. No single approach will stop stalking or cure those who engage in this form of family violence.

Summary

Stalking is a complex crime that affects many victims of family violence. Professionals are just beginning to react to this type of activity, and it is imperative that they understand both the dynamics of stalking and the possible alternatives that are available to the victim.

Stalking may occur in a domestic situation, or it may involve a stranger. In either situation, it can be a terrorizing experience for the victim, sometimes resulting in serious injury or death. Numerous typologies of stalkers are beginning to emerge as researchers analyze this type of behavior. To date, no single classification of stalking is accepted as standard by all scholars or authorities in the field of domestic violence.

Stalking laws have been passed that allow law enforcement to act before there is physical injury to the victim, but these statutes need revision in several important areas. Unfortunately, many states continue to allow stalkers to be released prior to trial. Few states treat stalking as a felony, which would subject the stalker to long-term incarceration.

Although debate in this area continues, it may be positive in that it signals an increased awareness of the seriousness of this problem. As long as a person can be terrorized by a phone call in the middle of the night by a former spouse, more work has to be done in this area of family violence. Only by understanding stalking can future injury to its victims be prevented.

Key Terms

stalking—a knowing, purposeful course of conduct directed at a specific person that would cause a reasonable person to fear bodily injury or death to herself or a member of her immediate family.

erotomania—a delusional disorder in which the predominant theme of the delusion is that a person, usually of higher status, is in love with the subject.

love obsessional stalker—does not know his victim except through the media. This stalker may also suffer from delusions; however, the subject has a primary psychiatric diagnosis.

simple obsessional stalker—a prior relationship existed between the stalker and his intended victim. This relationship may have been with a former spouse, employer, or neighbor; and in all cases, the stalking began after the relationship had soured or when there was a perception by the subject of mistreatment.

threat—any offer to do harm, however implausible restraining orders or protective orders—court orders that prohibit the offender from having any contact with the victim.

cyberstalking—threatening behavior or unwanted advances directed at another using the Internet or other forms of online communication to harass the victim.

restraining orders or protective orders—court orders that prohibit the offender from having any contact with the victim.

Discussion Questions

1. What is stalking? What if the victim is unaware that she is being watched and followed? Has the perpetrator committed the crime of stalking? Is it stalking if someone uses a telescope and repeatedly observes the victim from a distance? Has a former spouse committed the crime of stalking if he writes a letter expressing his frustration at the breakup of his marriage? What if he continues to write letters every week demanding that he and his spouse reunite?

2. Based on your reading of this chapter, which typology best explains the categories of stalkers? Why?

3. How can we help dispel the various myths that surround stalking?

4. Do you believe that existing stalking laws are effective in preventing stalking? What else should we do?

5. Are temporary restraining orders an effective legal tool in stalking cases?

6. How does the use of temporary restraining orders in stalking compare with their use in cases of domestic violence?

7. What is the most effective preventive measure that a victim of stalking can use?

8. Should stalkers be treated, punished, or both?

Suggested Readings

Gross, L. *To Have or to Harm* (Warner, New York, 1994).

Hickey, E. W. *Serial Killers and Their Victims* (Brooks/ Cole, Pacific Grove, Calif. 1991).

LaFave, W. R., and A. W. Scott Jr. *Criminal Law*, 2nd ed. (West, St. Paul, Minn., 1986).

Logan, T. K. et al. *Partner Stalking: How Women Respond, Cope and Survive* (Springer Publishing, New York, 2006).

Nicol, B. *Stalking* (Reaktion Books, London, 2006).

Whitebread, C. H., and C. Slobogin. *Criminal Procedure*, 3rd ed. (Foundation Press, Westbury, New York, 1993).

Endnotes

1. *Stalking* (National Center for Victims of Crime, 2004). Available at www.ncvc.org.
2. This information had been based on P. Tjaden, "The Crime of Stalking: How Big Is the Problem?" *Research Preview* (National Institute of Justice, Washington, D.C., November 1997).
3. Holmes reviewed some of the current literature in the area and established six distinct types of stalkers based on their victims (see R. M. Holmes, "Stalking in America," *Law and Order* [May 1994], pp. 89–92).

   Celebrity stalker: The victim of this type of stalker is usually in the entertainment field. Although the victim may be extremely well known, the stalker normally has not had any personal contact with the object of his obsession.

   Lust stalker: This type of stalker is motivated by sex and will stalk one victim after another in a serial fashion. The victim is pursued for sexual gratification. This type of stalker may escalate from a sexual pursuit to more violence, including murder of the victim.

   Hit stalker: This stalker is the paid professional killer who follows his victim to establish the target's habits and then kills for profit. There is no passion or feeling with this type of stalker, nor is he obsessed with his victim.

   Love-scorned: This stalker intends to frighten or injure the object of his hunt. Although this stalker intends violence, it is not normally fatal. He may be a rejected boyfriend, husband, or even a casual acquaintance. The stalker has a deep, abiding love for the victim and believes that if she would just realize how much he cares, then she would return his love.

   Domestic: This stalker is the former husband or boyfriend of the victim. The stalking may take place over an extended period of time, and the motive for the stalking is to get even with the victim. No sexual or fatal violence is involved in this type of stalking, but the stalker may engage in violent acts to terrorize his intended victim.

   Political stalker: The victim of this stalker is an appointed or elected official. The stalker carefully selects his victim, and political ideology usually precipitates the stalking. There is no sexual motivation in this type of stalker.

   Holmes's classification covers all conceivable situations and includes individuals, such as the *hit stalker*, who is a paid assassin and is not motivated by emotion or desire. The victim of a hit stalker is usually not even aware of the stalking until the assassin strikes. Because of a lack of knowledge on the part of the victim, it appears that Holmes's categories, although providing a useful starting point for an overview of stalking, need to be compared with other profiles.

   Geberth established a typology of stalkers based on their mental status (see V. Gerberth, "Stalkers," *Law and Order* [October 1992], p. 138). This approach focuses on the state of mind of the stalker rather than the object of the stalking. Geberth has classified stalkers into two areas:

   Psychopathic personality stalker: This stalker has lost control over the subject and intends violence to the victim. This type is a male offender and represents the largest percentage of stalkers. The object of the stalker is normally a former girlfriend or spouse. According to Geberth, this type of stalker insists on male dominance and exhibits a macho image to hide feelings of inferiority.

   Psychotic personality stalker: This stalker becomes obsessed with an unobtainable love object such as a movie star. This stalker may be either male or female. This stalker has the delusion that the victim also loves the stalker and would respond to his advances except for outside factors. This stalker is a stranger to the victim but has become obsessed with her. He mounts a campaign of harassment to make the victim aware of his existence.

   Various experts in the field of serial killers have established stalking patterns as they relate to stalking and killing. E. W. Hickey, in

Serial Murderers and Their Victims (Brooks/ Cole, Pacific Grove, Calif., 1991, p. 17), examines the dynamics of stalking and serial killers. He devised one category of serial killers based on mobility. These individuals were classified as traveling, local, or fixed serial killers. *Traveling* serial killers often cover thousands of miles each year as they stalk and kill their victims. *Local* serial killers never leave the state they live in when searching for victims. *Fixed* serial killers never leave their homes or places of employment. This last category of killers includes nurses and others who are self-employed who prefer to stay at home and kill rather than go hunting.

Although the body of research in the area of serial killing is growing, many of these incidents involve victims who were not aware that they were the intended prey of the killer, and therefore many serial killers will not fall within the definition of stalking that is being used in this textbook. However, more study is needed in this area to determine whether the dynamics involved in serial killing are the same or similar to the dynamics involved during a stalking.

Dietz and his associates have examined stalkers of celebrities and political officials, reviewing threatening letters and other inappropriate material sent to these high-profile people (see P. E. Dietz et al., "Threatening and Otherwise Inappropriate Letters to Hollywood Celebrities," *Journal of Forensic Sciences* 36 [January 1991], p. 185). Their database for celebrities was drawn from material maintained by Gavin de Becker Inc., a Los Angeles-based security agency. This firm has amassed data on 143,000 items of correspondence, from individuals to entertainment celebrities. Dietz and his associates analyzed the content of 107 stalkers drawn from this sample. In the study of stalking of public figures, the data were drawn from the files of the U.S. Capital Police in Washington, D.C. (see P. E. Dietz, "Threatening and Otherwise Inappropriate Letters to Members of the United States Congress," *Journal of Forensic Sciences* 36 [September 1991], p. 1445). Dietz studied eighty-six stalking cases of members of Congress.

Dietz developed a concept of patronage that classifies the level of attachment the stalker had for the victim: minimal, moderate, or maximal.

Minimal patronage: This level of patronage appears normal. The stalker does what all other persons do—He attends movies and speeches, buys books, or votes in elections for the person he is stalking. The critical difference is that normal persons do this out of a feeling of obligation or attraction for a particular celebrity or public official. Stalkers carry out these acts in an effort to be close to or noticed by the subject.

Moderate patronage: This level of patronage is slightly excessive. The stalker creates an extensive collection of the victim's works, may engage in extensive travel to see the public figure, or may engage in fund-raising or in circulating petitions for the public figure. Similar to the minimal patronage category, normal persons engage in these functions for healthy reasons or ideals, but stalkers engage in these acts out of an overpowering desire or obsession to become close to the victim.

Maximal patronage: This level of patronage is clearly extraordinary in that the stalker may have devoted a room to collecting information, pictures, or other paraphernalia about the victim. In essence, this room may resemble a shrine to the public figure. The stalker is obsessed with the public figure and devotes a significant amount of his daily activities to behavior that is directly related to the public figure.

Dietz and his associates also analyzed the threatening content of the letters sent to celebrities and public figures. A *threat* was defined as any offer to do harm, however implausible. Threats were classified as direct, veiled, or conditional. *Direct* threats were straightforward, explicit statements with an intent to commit harm, such as "I'm going to kill you." *Veiled* threats were indirect or subtle statements suggesting potential harm, such as "There's no saying what might happen." *Conditional* threats portrayed harm and specified that certain conditions must be met to avert the harm.

Gavin de Becker, an expert in security consultations in Los Angeles, established four categories of stalkers based on the relationship between the pursuer and the victim (see G. de Becker, "Intervention Decisions—The Value of Flexibility," paper presented at the Fourth Annual Threat Management Conference, Anaheim, California, June 29, 1994). de Becker's firm has been involved in more than 16,000 cases involving persons who inappropriately pursue other individuals. de Becker's classifications include the pursuit of public figures by the mentally ill persons with no prior relationship, pursuit of public figures by healthy persons with no prior relationship, pursuit of regular citizens with no prior relationship, and pursuit of regular citizens with some prior interpersonal relationship.

Pursuit of public figures by the mentally ill persons with no prior relationship: These are individuals who are suffering from a mental disorder or defect who write letters, attempt to telephone, or otherwise contact public figures even though no prior relationship exists between the stalker and the victim.

Pursuit of public figures by healthy persons with no prior relationship: These individuals may write letters, telephone, or otherwise attempt to contact the public figure. These stalkers may be obsessed with the public figure but do not suffer from a mental illness.

Pursuit of regular citizens with no prior relationship: These victims are not public figures and have no previous relationship with the stalker. The stalker will have selected them for his own reasons. The stalker may be either healthy or suffering from a mental disorder.

Pursuit of regular citizens with some prior interpersonal relationship: In these stalking situations, there was some prior relationship such as romantic, employment, or litigants. The stalker may be seeking revenge for an actual or perceived wrong. He may be either healthy or suffering from a mental disorder.

4. M. A. Zona, K. K. Sharma, and J. Lane, "A Comparative Study of Erotomanic and Obsessional Subjects in a Forensic Sample," *Journal of Forensic Sciences* 38 (July 1993), p. 894.

5. J. C. Lane, "Threat Management Fills Void in Police Services," *The Police Chief* 59 (August 1992), p. 27.

6. Special Order No. 4, Office of the Chief of Police, February 12, 1992.

7. This definition is derived from the U.S. Attorney General's report *1999 Report on Cyberstalking: A New Challenge for Law Enforcement and Industry* (U.S. Department of Justice, Washington, D.C., August 1999).

8. D. Lamplaugh and P. Infield, "Harmonising Anti-Stalking Laws," *George Washington International Review* 34 (2003), p. 853.

9. Presentation at the Fourth Annual Threat Management Conference, Anaheim, California, June 29, 1994.

10. M. A. Zona, "Psychiatric Factors Involved in the Assessment of Stalking Cases," paper presented at the Fourth Annual Threat Management Conference, Anaheim, California, June 29, 1994. The factors set forth in this paragraph are taken from an outline and accompanying speech made by Zona at the conference.

11. F. L. Coleman, "Stalking Behavior and the Cycle of Domestic Violence," *Journal of Interpersonal Violence* 12(3) (1997), p. 420.

12. *Cyberstalking*, The National Center for Victims of Crime, Washington D.C., www.ncvc.org, accessed April 27, 2007.

13. J. Finn, "A Survey of Online Harassment at a University Campus," *Journal of Interpersonal Violence* 19 (2004), p. 468.

14. R. Saunders, Los Angeles Deputy District Attorney, "Legal Tools for Case Management," paper presented at the Fourth Annual Threat Management Conference, Anaheim, California, June 29, 1994.

15. U.S. Departments of Commerce, Justice, and State and the Judiciary and Related Appropriations Act for Fiscal Year 1993, Public Law 103–395, Section 109(b).

16. *Project to Develop a Model Anti-Stalking Code for States* (National Institute of Justice, U.S. Department of Justice, Washington, D.C., October 1993).

17. Ibid., pp. 43–44.

18. H. Wallace, "Stalkers, the Constitution, and Victims' Remedies," *Criminal Justice* 10(1) (Spring 1995), p. 16.

19. U.S. Constitution, Amendment I.

20. 1994 U.S. LEXIS 5087 (June 30, 1994).

21. *R.A.V. v. City of St. Paul, Minnesota*, 112 S. Ct. 2538, 2546 (1992).

22. 846 F. 2d 241 (4th Cir. 1988), cert. denied, 448 U.S. 984 (1976).

23. 846 F. 2d 241 (4th Cir. 1988), cert. denied, 448 U.S. 984 (1976), p. 243.

24. *Winters v. New York*, 333 U.S. 507 (1948).

25. W. R. LaFave and A. W. Scott Jr., *Criminal Law*, 2nd ed. (West, St. Paul, Minn., 1986), section 2.3, pp. 90–91.

26. *Kolender v. Lawson*, 461 U.S. 352 (1983).

27. *Grayned v. City of Rockford*, 408 U.S. 104 (1972).

28. See C. H. Whitebread and C. Slobogin, *Criminal Procedure*, 3rd ed. (Foundation Press, Westbury, New York, 1993), pp. 487–508.

29. U.S. Constitution, Amendment XIII.

30. *Carlson v. Landon*, 342 U.S. 524 (1952).

31. 18 U.S.C. Section 3141–3150 (1984).

32. H. Kurtz, "Detention Law, Further Crowds Prison," *Washington Post*, January 9, 1986, p. A4.

33. 418 U.S. 739 (1987).

34. *Project to Develop a Model Anti-Stalking Code for States*, pp. 55–67.

35. Ibid.

36. 725 Ill. Comp. Stat. 5/110–4.-6.3 (2001).

37. California Penal Code Section 646.9 as amended on September 29, 1993.

38. See K. R. Thomas, "How to Stop the Stalker: State Antistalking Laws," *Criminal Law Bulletin* 29(2) (1993), p. 124; and Karen S. Morin, "The Phenomenon of Stalking: Do Existing State Statutes Provide Adequate Protection?" *San Diego Justice Journal* 1 (1993), p. 123.

39. N.J. Stat. § 2C:12–10.1 (2001).

40. H. Wallace, "A Prosecutor's Guide to Stalking," *The Prosecutor* 29(1) (1995), p. 26.

15

Victims' Issues

CHAPTER OBJECTIVES

After studying this chapter, you should be able to:

- Discuss the losses suffered by victims and their families;
- Explain the various types of civil litigation that a victim may use;
- List and explain the issues involved with victim compensation statutes;
- Recognize the problems involved with victim impact statements;
- Explain the issues involved with court-ordered restitution.

Detailed Look at What You Should Know About Victims' Issues

- Although all authorities acknowledge that those who are abused in an intimate relationship are victims, many researchers tend to focus on the medical or psychological treatment of these victims.
- Many victims of family violence suffer both psychological and physical injuries as well as financial loss.
- The victim of a crime has not always been the forgotten voice in the courtroom.
- Early civilizations accorded victims many more rights than did modern states until the birth of the victims' rights movement in the United States.
- The Victims' Rights Constitutional Amendment faces a long and complex process before it becomes law.
- Restoring the victim's emotional and financial status by using the judicial system cannot occur in a single court hearing. It is a multifaceted process that involves prosecutors, judges, court personnel, and private attorneys.

- There are numerous types of civil litigation; however, one that is of particular importance to victims of domestic violence is called a tort.

- A tort has been defined as a legal wrong committed on the person or property of another independent of contract.

- A tort may occur either as the result of the negligence of another or as the consequence of another's intentional act.

- Torts include actions that result in physical injury or death and damage to one's reputation.

- The same act that may be punished under a criminal code may also give rise to a civil cause of action in tort.

- The growth of victim compensation statutes and restitution of victims in the United States is a relatively recent phenomenon.

- Compensation can be defined as public funds that are paid to victims or their families to recover out-of-pocket expenses for injuries suffered as a result of another's criminal act.

- Victim compensation laws allow those who have suffered economic loss to partially recover funds from a state-supported fund established for that purpose.

- From a family violence perspective, one of the most troubling aspects of some early victim compensation statutes was the prohibition against awarding any funds to victims if they were related to the offender. Under these programs, battered spouses and abused children were deemed ineligible for compensation.

- Restitution is part of a criminal sentence that requires the offender to pay for injuries suffered by the victim. The original rationale for restitution was to require the party that injured the victim to pay for her injuries.

- The ability of courts to order restitution has been a part of the common law in the United States.

- Victim impact statements, in essence, present the victim's point of view to the sentencing authority.

- Victim impact statements may take two distinct forms: victim input at plea agreements and victim impact statements after trial and prior to sentencing.

- The effect of victim impact statements is still being studied and debated. One area being looked at very carefully is victim satisfaction with victim impact statements.

INTRODUCTION

Although all authorities acknowledge that those who are abused in an intimate relationship are victims, many researchers tend to focus on the medical or psychological treatment of these victims. However, another aspect to victimization occurs in family violence situations. Many victims of family violence suffer both psychological and physical injuries as well as financial loss. In the fairly recent past, these injuries were forgotten in the rush to punish the perpetrator or treat the victim. Professionals are beginning to realize that victims should be made whole not only emotionally but financially as well. Victims of all crimes are now accorded certain rights. Understanding these rights will assist in treating victims and allowing them to progress toward complete recovery. The study of family violence in many ways parallels the development of the victims' rights movement in the United States.

HISTORICAL PERSPECTIVE

The victim of a crime has not always been the forgotten voice in the courtroom. Early civilizations accorded victims many more rights than did modern states until the birth of the victims' rights movement in the United States. Early laws were known as **primitive law,** which was a system of rules in preliterate societies. These rules or regulations represent the foundation on which the modern legal system is built. Primitive laws usually contained three characteristics: Acts that injured others were considered private wrongs, the injured party was entitled to take action against the wrongdoer, and this action usually amounted to in-kind retaliation. These types of laws encouraged blood feuds and revenge as the preferred method of making the victim whole.

As society matured, people learned the art of reading and writing. One result of this evolution was the development of written codes of conduct. The Code of Ur-Nammu dates back to the twenty-first century B.C. Other early written codes include the Twelve Tables of Rome, the laws of Greece, and the Mosaic Code. Many of these codes treated certain wrongs such as theft or assault as private wrongs, with the injured party being the victim rather than the state.[1]

International Perspectives

Victims of Torture and War—Victims Without Rights

Thousands of victims of politically motivated torture currently reside in the United States. While the torture occurred in other countries, these victims are seeking treatment and support within the United States. The torture may have ranged from incarceration in jails or prisons without trial to daily beatings and/or mutilation.

The Commission of Human Rights determined that during the conflict in Rwanda in 1994, rape was systematic and was used as a "weapon" by the perpetrators of the massacres. It is believed that rape was the rule rather than the exception. Among those victimized were women, children, the elderly, pregnant women, those who had just given birth, and even corpses. In 1998, violence against women occurred in East Timor by Indonesian security forces. The aggression included rape, forced marriage, forced prostitution, and intimidation of female relatives of suspected activists.

In March 1999, Kosovo became another crisis area that resulted in violations of rights of innocent victims. There were killings, disappearances, torture, ill treatment, and forced expulsions from the country. Human Rights Watch found that rape and other forms of sexual violence were used in Kosovo as weapons of war and instruments of systematic "ethnic cleansing."

Sources: Amnesty International Report 2000 (www.amnesty.org, 2000); *Office for Victims of Crime International Activities* (Office for Victims of Crime, Washington, D.C., July 1999); and *The World's Women: 2000 Trends and Statistics* (United Nations, New York, 2000).

One of the most comprehensive criminal codes was the Code of Hammurabi, which was adopted in 1750 B.C. Although this code was still based on revenge, it required the victim's family and, if necessary, the entire community to take responsibility for making restitution to the victim if the perpetrator escaped or was unable to be found.[2] As the feudal system developed in England, the right to seek redress from a wrongdoer passed from the hands of the victim or his or her family to the state. The state was more concerned about bringing the perpetrator to justice than compensating the victim for any injuries, and this philosophy has continued to modern times.[3]

Previous chapters discussed the slow but growing awareness of family violence. At the same time when society was beginning to acknowledge family violence, so were people beginning to understand that victims of all crimes, including those who suffered abuse in an intimate relationship, should have their day in court. A number of forces have contributed to this development of victims' rights, including the feminist movement, the development of civil rights laws, and a growing conservatism regarding crime.[4]

The feminist movement made plain the plethora of discrimination and violence against women. By speaking out, feminists engendered the realization that women were victims not only from violent crime on the streets of cities but also from sexual harassment within the work environment and family violence in the home. The types of crimes suffered by women are distinct from those suffered by men.

As was discussed in previous chapters, many of these crimes, though sexual in nature, are in fact nothing more than aggressive assaults that have very little to do with sex. Sexual assaults are, in reality, a way for the perpetrator to control, dominate, and humiliate the victim.

The first coordinated effort by feminist groups in the United States to help women who were victims of crimes was the establishment of rape crisis centers in Berkeley, California, and Washington, D.C., in 1972. These centers spread rapidly and are now an accepted part of the criminal justice system. In 1976, the federal government established a research center, the National Center for the Prevention and Control of Rape, within the Department of Health, Education, and Welfare (this agency is now called Health and Human Services). The National Coalition Against Sexual Assault was also established to begin the process of improving communication among victims of sexual aggression, rape crisis centers, and victims' advocates.[5]

The feminist movement not only attacked society's perceptions regarding victims of sexual assault but also focused its efforts on educating the public regarding domestic violence. Although their efforts have been discussed previously, it is important to note that at the same time battered women's shelters were being established, there was a growing awareness that victims of crimes, as a class of citizens, were being treated unfairly by the criminal justice system. This awareness coincided with changes within the judicial system.

During the 1960s and 1970s, a series of U.S. Supreme Court decisions established certain principles regarding the constitutional rights of individuals. These decisions were in the area of both criminal procedure and civil rights. The Supreme Court established constitutional safeguards for those accused of crimes. By interpreting the U.S. Constitution as applying to each and every individual, the Court required that society afford those accused of crimes certain procedural and substantive rights. These rights embraced the entire spectrum of liberties, including freedom from unreasonable search and seizures, the right to an attorney, and fundamental fairness during a criminal trial. By adopting a philosophy that individuals carried with them certain inalienable rights, the Court was poised to expand this concept in the area of civil rights.

The Supreme Court acted to enforce both statutory and constitutional provisions during the 1960s and 1970s in the area of civil rights. These decisions allowed a black man to attend a previously all-white university, held that police officers could be held liable for use of excessive force, and required that all persons be treated equally under the law. As a result of these and other decisions, cases such as *Thurman v. City of Torrington*[6] were decided in favor of victims of family violence.

Another factor that contributed to the awareness of the plight of victims arose as a result of a change in attitude in the United States. In the 1980s and 1990s, citizens became more conservative and concerned about crime in general. This law-and-order movement resulted from citizens becoming more fearful of violent crime, with many groups consequently calling for more stringent punishment of those who violated the law. In addition, the victims' rights movement was gaining momentum, and imprisoning offenders was viewed as a way of vindicating victims of crimes. National organizations composed of victims began lobbying for changes in the criminal justice system. These changes were aimed at making the system more victim-oriented. The rights of victims of family violence began to grow and expand as society became more concerned about crime in general.

In what may become one of the most critical dates in the history of victim rights, on June 25, 1996, President Bill Clinton proposed the Victims' Rights Constitutional Amendment to the Constitution. In a speech made in the Rose Garden announcing the amendment, President Clinton stated:

> Having carefully studied all of the alternatives, I am now convinced that the only way to fully safeguard the rights of victims in America is to amend our Constitution and guarantee these basic rights—to be told about public court proceedings and to attend them; to make a statement to the court about bail, about sentencing, about accepting a plea if the victim is present; to be told about parole hearings to attend and to speak; notice when the defendant or convict escapes or is released; restitution from the defendant; reasonable protection from the defendant; and notice of these rights.[7]

The Victims' Rights Constitutional Amendment faces a long and complex process before it becomes law. It must be approved by Congress and then adopted by three-quarters of the states to become part of the Constitution. It is not something that will happen in a few weeks or months, and already some claim that the proposed amendment is too detailed and should be broadened. No matter what the outcome is, the simple fact that such an amendment has actually been proposed is a significant acknowledgment of the plight of crime victims.

All these combined forces focused an awareness on the plights of crime victims and the dilemma of victims of family violence.[8] As a result, victims began to realize that they could have an effect on sentencing in criminal cases and could pursue civil litigation to recover for damages they suffered as a result of the perpetrator's actions. This twofold approach to making victims whole is the topic of the next section.

VICTIMS AND CIVIL LITIGATION

Restoring the victim's emotional and financial status by using the judicial system cannot occur in a single court hearing. It is a multifaceted process that involves prosecutors, judges, court personnel, and private attorneys.[9] However, before discussing civil and criminal actions against perpetrators of family violence, it is important to understand the development of the discipline that studies victims.

The term **victimology** was coined by Benjamin Mendelsohn.[10] The modern definition of victimology states that it is the study of the victim, the offender, and society. From its inception in the 1940s to the present day, victimology, like family violence, has been an interdisciplinary approach to violence and its effect on victims.

Mendelsohn also developed a typology of victims and their contribution to the criminal act, from the completely innocent victim to the imaginary victim.[11] Specifically, he classified victims into the following six distinct categories:

1. *The completely innocent victim.* This victim may be a child or completely unconscious person.
2. *The victim with minor guilt.* This victim might be a woman who induces a miscarriage and dies as a result.
3. *The victim who is as guilty as the offender.* Those who assist others in suicide or euthanasia fall within this classification.
4. *The victim more guilty than the offender.* These are persons who provoke others to commit a crime.
5. *The most guilty victim.* This victim acts aggressively and kills in self-defense.
6. *The imaginary victim.* These are persons suffering from mental disorders such as paranoia who believe they are victims.

Other scholars have studied the dynamics of victim participation. In an early classic textbook, von Hentig explored the relationship between the "doer," or criminal, and the "sufferer," or victim. He theorized that a large percentage of victims, because of their acts or behavior, were responsible for their victimization.[12] This concept has been repudiated by modern research and studies that have more closely examined the relationship between the victim and the offender.

From 1948 to 1952 in Philadelphia, Wolfgang conducted the first major study of victim precipitation.[13] He focused on homicides and studied both the victim and the offender as separate entities and as "mutual participants in the homicide."[14] Wolfgang evaluated 588 homicides and found that 26 percent (150) of all the homicides studied in Philadelphia involved situations in which the victim was a direct, positive precipitator in the crime—the first to use force during the acts leading to the homicide.[15]

Victimology continued to grow in popularity. Scholars expanded their scope of inquiry and began exploring other aspects of the victim's role in society. Discussing the development of victimology, Karmen has pointed out that this relatively new discipline has three main areas of concentration:

1. Victimologists study the reasons (if any) why or how victims placed themselves in a dangerous situation. This study does not attempt to fix blame on the victim; rather, it examines the dynamics that resulted in the victim being in the risky situation.
2. Victimology evaluates how police, prosecutors, courts, and related agencies interact with the victim. How was the victim treated at each stage in the criminal justice system?
3. Victimologists evaluate the effectiveness of efforts to reimburse victims for their losses and meet victims' personal and emotional needs.[16]

Researchers are still learning about the dynamics of victims' interaction with the judicial system, and victims are learning that they can make a difference within the system. Some jurisdictions have victims' rights advocates who appear with or on behalf of the victim at the sentencing of the offender. These victim advocates also offer advice regarding filing of civil lawsuits against the perpetrator or against other third parties.

As was discussed in previous chapters, in a criminal case the prosecutor represents the people and not the victim. Civil law, however, focuses on the private rights of individuals. Therefore, civil law allows an injured person to file a lawsuit against the injuring party. If successful, the injured party may recover monetary damages from the wrongdoer. In addition, civil law allows for the imposition of certain types of orders regulating conduct such as temporary restraining orders.

There are numerous types of civil litigation; however, one that is of particular importance to victims of domestic violence is called a tort. A **tort** has been defined as a legal wrong committed on the person or property of another independent of contract. A tort may occur either as the result of the negligence of another or as the consequence of another's intentional act.[17] Torts include actions that result in physical injury or death and damage to one's reputation. The same act that may be punished under a criminal code may also give rise to a civil cause of action in tort. For example, the rape of a female is a criminal offense but is also a civil wrong of battery. Battery is an intentional tort that would allow the victim to sue the perpetrator for monetary damages.

Negligence is a civil law concept that holds persons liable for injuries that result from their acts or actions. Negligence is a complex legal theory that gives first-year law students headaches. However, it is necessary to understand this concept in order to grasp the nature of various rights available to victims. *Negligence* consists of the existence of a legal duty owed by one party to another, the breaching or breaking of that duty, a proximate cause or relationship between the breaching of the duty, and the injuries suffered by the injured party and damages. Actions for negligence may be filed against parties such as businesses or government agencies that violated a duty that resulted in injuries to the victim.

Previous chapters examined the criminal process and briefly touched on certain aspects of civil procedures such as dependency or conservatorship hearings. The civil process used to bring an action against a perpetrator for a tort in many ways parallels the criminal process; however, there are significant differences. The following is a brief summary of a trial that a victim would use in pursuing civil damages from the perpetrator.

DETERMINATION THAT A CIVIL ACTION IS AVAILABLE.   The victim of a crime will talk with the prosecutor and testify in court. However, the prosecutor is not her personal attorney, nor will the prosecutor give the victim legal advice regarding her civil remedies. Therefore, the victim may have to consult with a private attorney or a victims' rights organization to determine whether filing a civil lawsuit is advisable. Numerous factors should or will be considered in this determination: the expense and time involved in a civil case, the emotions or mental condition of the victim, the chances of obtaining a verdict in favor of the victim, and the availability of collecting any judgment from the perpetrator. These are critical factors that will be evaluated by any attorney in advising a victim on whether to proceed with a civil action.

FILING OF A PLEADING.   The person filing the complaint is known as the **plaintiff,** and the person who is alleged to have committed the acts that resulted in injury to the plaintiff or victim is called the **defendant.** Filing a civil complaint is the first formal step in the litigation process. The **complaint** is a formal written document stating certain causes of actions that the plaintiff alleges to entitle her to recover damages from the perpetrator. Once the plaintiff has filed the complaint in court and served a copy to the defendant, the defendant must reply or file an answer to the complaint. An **answer** is a formal written document that either admits or denies the allegations contained in the complaint and raises defenses to the charges.

Many times plaintiffs will allege several theories of recovery on the basis of the same set of facts. This is a common practice that allows plaintiffs to file lawsuits early before all the facts are known to them. For example, the plaintiff may allege that the defendant intentionally struck her or, alternatively, that the defendant acted recklessly in striking her, or she may allege that the defendant was negligent and that this resulted in her injury. Once all the facts surrounding the incident are known to the plaintiff, she has the option of dismissing the other causes of action and concentrating on the allegation that most closely fits the facts.

DISCOVERY.   The facts surrounding the incident are determined during the process known as **discovery.** This is a formal method of learning the facts, theories, and positions of opposing parties by means of written or oral questioning. *Depositions* are a form of discovery in which the sworn oral testimony of a person is taken prior to the trial. *Interrogatories* are written questions posed to the other party who must reply in writing and under oath to each of the questions. Discovery is a method to perpetuate or fix the testimony of another party so that he cannot later change his story or testimony. Unlike some television shows, in real life civil attorneys know the answer to almost every question before it is asked, and there are few if any surprises because each side has engaged in extensive and costly discovery prior to trial.

MOTIONS.   Once all the facts have been made available by use of the various discovery techniques, each side may engage in a series of motions designed either to have the case decided or limit the scope of the case. For example, if both sides have engaged in discovery and there is no dispute as to the facts surrounding the incident, the only issue left to be decided is the application of the law to the facts. When this is the case, the parties may submit what is called a *summary judgment motion.* This motion is used when the facts are not in dispute and the parties are asking the judge to apply the law to this set of facts and rule in favor of one party.

TRIAL.   Similar to a criminal case, a civil case may be adjudicated by either a jury or a judge. The trial is conducted in the same manner as a criminal case but with one significant difference. The standard of proof in a civil case is a preponderance of the evidence rather than the much higher criminal standard of beyond a reasonable doubt to a moral certainty.

The perpetrator may be liable to the victim because of intentional or negligent acts. Many criminal acts have counterparts in the civil law that allow a victim to recover independent of the criminal process. Therefore, the same acts that give rise to a criminal complaint may be used in the civil action.

During the trial, responsibility for the injury to the plaintiff will be decided, as will an apportionment of fault if there is more than one defendant. Many times trials are divided, or *bifurcated,* into two phases: liability and damages. During the first phase, the issue before the judge or jury is whether the defendant caused the injuries to the plaintiff. If there is a determination that the defendant did not cause the injuries, the trial is over at that stage. However, if there is determination that the defendant did cause or contribute to the injuries of the plaintiff, the second stage or phase will examine how much money the defendant should pay the plaintiff for his injuries. When the plaintiff asks to be made whole or reimbursed for expenses incurred as a result of an injury, this is known as **compensatory damages**. **Punitive damages** are asked for or awarded to punish the defendant for conduct that is considered outrageous. Punitive damages are also a method of sending a message to others that certain acts will not be tolerated and, if engaged in, will result in financial punishment above and beyond the injury that resulted from the questionable conduct.

RECOVERY.   Simply receiving a favorable verdict does not automatically mean the plaintiff will receive the amount of money set forth in the verdict. Motions for new trials and appeals are likely to occur before any judgment is final. In addition, the perpetrator may not have the financial resources available to pay the judgment.

Prevailing in a civil suit is only half the battle; the plaintiff must also be able to obtain the money awarded by the judge or jury. Even if it can be proved that the perpetrator is at fault, he may not have any funds available to compensate or make the victim whole financially. In an effort to gain compensation for victims of family violence, attorneys have explored different alternatives when filing lawsuits against wrongdoers. For example, civil actions may be brought against the perpetrator, third parties that may have contributed to the victim's injuries such as private businesses or government agencies, the offender's insurance company, and even the victim's insurance company.

Third parties are those individuals or entities that have intentionally or negligently contributed to the injury suffered by the victim. Typical third parties may be businesses that failed to provide a safe working environment for their employees, government agencies or employees who had a duty to protect or serve the victim but failed to do so, and insurance companies that provided insurance coverage to either the perpetrator or the victim. In many jurisdictions, worker compensation statutes are considered the sole source of recovery for workers injured on the job; however, court decisions sometimes allow workers to bring civil lawsuits for job-related injuries.

Businesses may fail to provide adequate protection for their workers. For example, a business may fail to light the parking lot where its employees park. If a female is leaving work late and is assaulted in the parking lot, she may have a civil cause of action against the business for failing to provide proper lighting. She could sue both the perpetrator and the business. The causes of action against the perpetrator might include assault, battery, and intentional infliction of emotional distress, and the causes of action against the business might be based on negligence for failing to fulfill its duty to employees by providing a safe working environment. One of the more famous third-party lawsuits involved the singer Connie Francis. She was in her hotel room at a Howard Johnson's Motor Lodge when an assailant entered through a sliding glass door that was known by the hotel management to be defective. The perpetrator sexually assaulted Ms. Francis, escaped, and was never apprehended. She filed a civil action and in 1976 was awarded $2.5 million against the hotel for failing to provide adequate security.[18]

Focus

Crimes and Torts

Murder or manslaughter	Assault
Criminal assault	Battery
Criminal battery	Assault, battery, and emotional distress
Rape, sodomy, or oral copulation	Same as criminal battery
Child sexual abuse	Intentional torts and negligence
Child neglect	All of the above plus fraud (if the caretaker appropriated the victim's money or property)
Elder abuse	
Wrongful death	

Victims have successfully sued third-party businesses using a variety of legal theories: landlords who have failed to provide adequate security similar to the causes of action alleged in the Connie Francis case, customers against stores,[19] students against private schools, and patients against hospitals.[20] The common thread running though all these actions is the existence of a duty owed by the business to protect the victim and failure to do so that resulted in the victim's being injured by the perpetrator.

Government agencies or their employees have been sued as third parties in situations in which their actions or failure to act contributed to injuries suffered by victims as a result of acts by perpetrators. Several cases involved police officers who stopped to render aid to stranded motorists and then left the victims on the side of the road without protection. When that person was subsequently assaulted, courts have allowed civil lawsuits against both the perpetrator and the government agencies. In these situations, courts have stated that when the officer initially stopped to render aid, a duty to protect the motorist from foreseeable harm was established and the officer breached that duty when the motorist was left alone.

In addition, government agencies may be responsible as third parties for the actions of their employees. If an employee assaults the victim, she may have a cause of action against the government agencies that employed the perpetrator. For example, if the agency knew or should have known that an employee might assault a citizen, it should have taken appropriate steps to prevent those acts or terminate the employee.

However, not all assaults against victims occur as a result of a breach of duty by businesses or government agencies. In these instances, the victim must look elsewhere in her quest to recover finances that would compensate her for injuries. The first and most obvious source of funds is those held by the perpetrator. The victim may attempt to obtain a judgment and levy against the defendant's income or other assets. Many perpetrators may not have sufficient funds available to compensate the victim for all the injuries inflicted. However, they may have automobile or homeowner's insurance. The victim may have a right to recover from these insurance companies for the actions of the perpetrator.

Homeowner's policies are written to protect the owner from injuries that occur on his or her property as a result of an accident or an unintended occurrence. The term *homeowner's insurance* is really misleading because most of these policies provide coverage for accidents or injuries away from the home. Most litigation involves the nature of the acts that resulted in injuries, not the location of where the injuries occurred. Automobile policies are very similar to homeowner's insurance in that they are designed to provide coverage for accidental or unintended events.

Both types of insurance have exclusions for intentional acts committed by the insured. For example, if a homeowner murdered his spouse, insurance policies exclude this type of act from coverage. In many jurisdictions, statutes prevent insuring against criminal conduct of the insured. However, simply because there are exemptions or exclusions for most intentional or criminal acts should not deter the victim from examining the various insurance policies. If it can be proved that the insured owed the victim a duty and that duty was breached, the victim may be able to recover under a theory of negligence.

There is a long-standing judicial and statutory public policy that holds that a person should not be able to obtain homeowner's insurance against his or her own intentional wrong-doing. Courts have struggled with this policy and the desire to compensate victims of crimes by turning to the deep pockets of insurance policies. Some courts have found creative ways to get around the intentional act exclusion by holding that insanity negates the intentional aspect of any offense, and if the perpetrator is insane, the criminal act exclusion does not apply.

In the area of automobile insurance, the issue of coverage is complicated by the fact that there are many different types of insurance, and some states require all owners of cars to maintain certain levels of insurance. Many jurisdictions require drivers to purchase two types of insurance: uninsured motorist and underinsured motorist insurance. Uninsured motorist policies pay for any injuries suffered by the driver or their passengers that are caused by other motorists who have no insurance. Underinsured motorist insurance policies apply when the driver who caused injuries is insured but does not carry enough insurance to cover all the injuries that were inflicted.

Similar to homeowner's policies, automobile insurance applies to accidental injuries and excludes from coverage intentional acts by the insured. In homeowner's insurance, courts look to the perpetrator's state of mind to determine whether the act was intentional and there-fore excluded from coverage. However, in automobile insurance cases, many jurisdictions determine whether the incident was an accident from the victim's point of view. This perspec-tive is a more favorable position to crime victims who are attempting to recover from the perpetrator's automobile insurance company. Courts have allowed victims or their families to recover from automobile insurance companies in cases in which the victim was kidnapped, sexually assaulted, and died when the perpetrator fled with the victim in an automobile;[21] in which the perpetrator used his automobile as a battering ram to strike the victim's car;[22] and in which the accused kidnapped and killed the victim while driving around in a car.[23]

Most of the litigation regarding whether automobile insurance applies is centered around the question of whether the injury arose out of the use, ownership, or maintenance of the car. In several cases, victims left their cars during arguments with other drivers and were attacked by the other driver. Courts have held that the injuries did not arise out of the use of the victim's automobile, and therefore the insurance company was not liable.

Financial rehabilitation of the victim is an often-overlooked area of family violence. Victims, professionals, and others must be educated regarding this important aspect of mak-ing the victim whole. Insurance, both homeowner's and automobile, is one method of provid-ing victims of family violence with the possibility of recovering financially for the inflicted

Focus

Americans Living Overseas Who Experience Domestic Violence

Americans living overseas who experience domestic violence face numerous barriers to accessing victim services. They are probably unfamiliar with the country's legal system and their rights and available resources. In addition, they may not be fluent in the language of the country. Their abusers may keep them from fleeing by hiding or destroying passports, visas, birth certificates, and other essential documents. In some countries, abusers can file for a travel ban so that their victims and children are not permitted to leave the country.

In a few countries, domestic laws do not apply to noncitizens. Frequently, abusers take advantage of child custody laws to pressure their partners. While the Hague Convention on the Civil Aspects of International Child Abduction

may prevent an abuser from returning their children to the foreign country, the Hague Convention has no stated exception for domestic violence in custody disputes, so legal action may be required to resolve cases. Abusers may also use other custody laws, such as the Uniform Child Custody Jurisdiction and Enforcement Act, to gain custody of children.

In response to this critical gap in services, the Office of Victims of Crime, U.S. Department of Justice, established a center to provide a continuum of services to American women and children experiencing family violence while residing in a foreign country. The Americans Overseas Domestic Violence Crisis Center provides domestic violence and child abuse advocacy.

injuries. Civil lawsuits against the perpetrator or his insurance company are an expensive, complex, and drawn-out affair. Many victims do not have the financial ability or emotional stability to endure months and years of protracted litigation. However, civil action against the perpetrator or his insurance company is not the only avenue available to those who have suffered injuries as a result of family violence. All states now allow victims to be compensated from state-supported funds, and most states allow courts to order restitution during sentencing in criminal cases.

COMPENSATION AND RESTITUTION

The growth of victim compensation statutes and restitution of victims in the United States is a relatively recent phenomenon. Much of this slowness to react to the victim's plight was based on our concept of the criminal justice system. As discussed earlier, the victim was viewed as merely one more witness, and the state was the party that was injured when perpetrators committed crimes.

Both compensation and restitution are aimed at making the victim financially whole; however, they are separate and distinct concepts. Victim compensation funds are provided by the state, whereas restitution comes from the perpetrator. Understanding how they operate will assist any professional in advising victims of family violence.

Compensation

Compensation can be defined as public funds that are paid to victims or their families to recover out-of-pocket expenses for injuries suffered as a result of another's criminal act. Victim compensation laws allow those who have suffered economic loss to partially recover

Focus

"In a fundamental sense one who suffers the impact of criminal violence is also the victim of society's long inattention to poverty and social injustice." Former Associate Supreme Court Justice Arthur Goldberg.

Source: A.J. Goldberg. 1970. "Preface: Symposium on Governmental Compensation for Victims of Violence." *Southern California Law Review* 43(1970).

funds from a state-supported fund established for that purpose. Eligible expenses include medical expenses, including the costs of counseling, burial expenses, special services to the victim, and rehabilitation expenses.

The idea that the state should provide financial reimbursement to victims of crime for their losses was initially propounded by English penal reformer Margery Fry in the 1950s. It was first implemented in New Zealand in 1963 and Great Britain passed a similar law shortly thereafter. The early compensation programs were welfare programs providing help to victims in need.

In 1965, California became the first state in the United States to establish compensation funds for victims of crimes. In 1966, New York followed California's lead by setting up a special board to allocate funds to victims. In 1967, Massachusetts organized a procedure whereby the state attorney general grants compensation to victims. Today, all states have a mechanism in place that allows victims of crimes to be compensated for their losses.

Although victim compensation programs vary from state to state, they generally have certain common characteristics:

1. All programs grant aid to innocent victims. Perpetrators who were injured during the commission of the crime are not eligible for compensation under these statutes.
2. Many states have boards or commissions that investigate a victim's claims and eliminate or reduce any award if the victim contributed to his or her injury by participating in or provoking the offender.
3. Most of these programs compensate only the more serious offenses. They do not pay for property that was damaged or stolen in burglaries or robberies.
4. All the states prevent "double dipping," or recovering from more than one source for the same injury. When the victim receives funds from other state agencies, insurance companies, or the perpetrator in the form of a civil judgment or an order for restitution, that amount is deducted from any award.
5. Most states require the victim to report the crime to the police and cooperate with them in any investigation and court proceeding.

From a family violence perspective, one of the most troubling aspects of some early victim compensation statutes was the prohibition against awarding any funds to victims if they were related to the offender. Under these programs, battered spouses and abused children were deemed ineligible for compensation. The rationale for this male-oriented rule was that the offender should not be indirectly rewarded by granting money to the family. Other arguments included the fear that families will conspire to defraud the state by claiming injuries where none exist. Amendments to the Victims of Crime Act required states to provide compensation to victims of family violence.

Although at first glance victim compensation programs appear to provide a long-needed solution to the financial problems faced by victims of family violence, several problems still exist within most programs. As indicated earlier, many of these statutes apply only to victims of violent criminal acts, and as such the financial crimes committed against elders, for example, would not be covered. In addition, some of these statutes reimburse the victim only above a certain minimum level and do not provide compensation above a stated limit.

State compensation is not the only method of making crime victims financially whole. The use of restitution in criminal cases is becoming more common.

Restitution

Restitution is part of a criminal sentence that requires the offender to pay for injuries suffered by the victim. The original rationale for restitution was to require the party that injured the

---

International Perspectives

Crime Victim Compensation

Australia: Crime victim compensation schemes that provide financial assistance to victims of violent crime are state based in Australia. Each state administers its own program in accordance with its state statute. For example, the New South Wales compensation program provides monetary compensation according to a schedule of injuries that specifies the amount payable for a specific injury.

Canada: Crime victim compensation programs provide financial compensation to victims of violent or personal crimes. The programs are administered by the Canadian provinces according to their own rules and standards.

Colombia: This program provides financial compensation to civilian victims of terrorist acts, guerrilla attack, combat, or massacres. Foreign nationals are not eligible for compensation under this program. Colombia does not have a program to compensate victims of violent or personal crime.

Denmark: Crime victim compensation programs provide financial compensation to victims who suffer serious criminal injury.

Israel: This program provides financial compensation to victims of terrorism, including foreign nationals. Israel does not have a program for compensating victims of violent or personal crime.

Italy: Victims of terrorism or organized crime, including foreign nationals, are eligible for financial compensation under this program. Italy does not have a general scheme for compensating victims of violent or personal crime.

Luxembourg: Crime victim compensation programs provide financial compensation to victims for losses resulting from personal crime.

United Arab Emirates: The court system provides financial compensation to victims of violent or personal crime.

Source: Based on *International Crime Victim Compensation Program Directory* (Office for Victims of Crime, Washington, D.C., March 1999).

Promising Practices

Making Restitution Work[24]

Many statutes have attempted to improve collection of restitution by ordering a complete investigation of the assets of the convicted perpetrator before sentencing. A list of the defendant's assets can also assist the victim in his or her collection efforts. In Kansas, for example, the victim has a right to see any information regarding the offender's assets until full restitution is paid.

California and Florida have mandatory entry of an income deduction order at the time restitution is ordered. In Michigan, the probation or parole officer is required to review twice each year every case where restitution has been ordered to ensure that payments are being made.

Finally, many states' prison work programs deduct a portion of the offender's wages for payment of restitution.

victim to pay for her injuries. The ability of courts to order restitution has been a part of the common law in the United States. The increased awareness of the victim's plight resulted in the passage of the Victim Witness Protection Act of 1982. This federal statute specifically authorizes the imposition of an order of restitution in addition to or in lieu of any other sentence in a criminal proceeding. Every state has restitution statutes that allow courts to order the perpetrator to pay the victim for any injuries suffered as a result of the offender's criminal act or acts.

In more than a third of all states, courts are required by statute to order restitution unless there is a compelling reason not to do so. Other states allow restitution but establish broad exceptions with language ordering restitution "whenever possible."[25]

Many states have conflicting restitution statutes. Some states have statutes that require restitution in criminal cases but also have other statutes that leave requiring restitution to the court's discretion.[26] Other states give the victim the right to restitution as mandated by law but fail to mandate the criminal courts to order such restitution.

Restitution statutes, like compensation laws, provide the victims of family violence with some financial relief. However, many of these restitution statutes have shortcomings: Some statutes prohibit restitution for certain types of injuries, such as emotional distress. Other statutes allow the sentencing court not to order restitution if to do so would overly burden the criminal justice system. Still others do not address future costs such as continuing medical expenses.

Restitution and compensation laws provide the victims of family violence with some financial assistance. They are not perfect, but they are a beginning, an acknowledgment that the plight of the victim in the criminal justice system must be considered. One of the most dramatic examples of including the victim in the criminal process is the use of victim impact evidence at sentencing.

VICTIM IMPACT STATEMENTS

A new series of rights is emerging in the judicial system. These rights confer on the victim or the relatives of deceased victims the opportunity to speak out or be heard during various phases of the criminal justice process. As with many rights when they converge on a single point, there is an actual or potential conflict. This section reviews the history of these various rights and examines the rationale behind the current status of the law as it relates to victim impact statements. Victim impact statements may take two distinct forms: victim input at plea agreements and victim impact statements after trial and prior to sentencing.

VICTIM INPUT AT PLEA AGREEMENTS

Recent statistics confirm what any seasoned prosecutor understands very well: Approximately 90 percent of all cases are settled by plea negotiations.[27] This large-scale disposition of cases raises issues for victims of family violence. Unless these victims are afforded an opportunity to be involved in the plea negotiations, most of them will be denied any chance of being involved in the criminal justice process.

Victims of family violence have two opportunities to be involved in plea bargains: one at the time of the negotiations between the prosecutor and defense attorney and a second when the plea is presented to the court for review and acceptance. In at least twenty-two states, victims of family violence have some form of consultation with the prosecutor during the plea negotiations.[28] However, this consultation process varies widely from state to state and may change depending on the type of charges filed against the perpetrator. No state gives the victim the right to veto the prosecution offer or the defense attorney's acceptance of that offer.

Some states hold prosecutors accountable for ensuring that the victim has been consulted during the plea negotiations. Arizona is a state that follows this process. The Arizona statute provides that the court shall not accept a plea agreement unless:

1. The prosecuting attorney advises the court that before requesting the negotiated pleas, reasonable efforts were made to confer with the victim,
2. The prosecuting attorney advises the court that, to the best of the prosecuting attorney's knowledge, notice requirements have been complied with and the prosecutor informs the court of the victim's position, if known, regarding the negotiated plea.[29]

The impact of the offense is an important consideration in sentencing the defendant, and victim impact testimony at the entry of the plea can have an effect on the length and type of sentencing defendants receive. There continue to be misconceptions both by victims and prosecutors regarding victim input in plea negotiations: Some victims believe that consultation gives them the right to veto any plea bargain, and some prosecutors believe that victim input during this process undermines their authority. Neither position is accurate, but in this newly emerging area of rights for victims of family violence, perception is sometimes more important than reality.

The remainder of this section will examine the other type of input by victims: the right of a victim to address the sentencing authority after a criminal trial. During plea negotiations, if the defendant does not like the fact that the victim is involved in the negotiations, the perpetrator can refuse to accept any plea. On the other hand, the concept of victim impact statements is more controversial because impact evidence is presented without the defendant's consent or agreement.

Purpose and Procedure

Victim impact statements, in essence, present the victim's point of view to the sentencing authority. Providing the sentencing authority with all relevant information is not a new phenomenon in the criminal justice system. For many years, courts have received information regarding the defendant prior to imposition of sentence.

Traditionally, judges have used presentence reports to determine the proper punishment for criminal defendants. The report, which is normally prepared by a probation officer, details the defendant's background, education, and prior criminal record. Many of these reports have included information concerning the victim of the crime.[30]

Victim impact evidence is now admitted in sentencing for a wide variety of criminal acts, including those that fall within the realm of family violence. However, the law on admissibility and use of victim impact statements is based on use of this evidence during death penalty cases. To understand the nature of victim impact statements, it is necessary to review how this evidence is used in the most serious criminal cases—those involving capital punishment.

The use of victim impact evidence during the sentencing phase of a criminal trial raises serious constitutional issues. The right to confront witnesses comes against the right to have all relevant evidence placed before the sentencing authority. As will be seen, the use of victim impact statements aroused intense feelings in the Supreme Court when it addressed this issue.

Content

In *Booth v. Maryland*, the Supreme Court initially addressed the issue of the use of victim impact statements in a sentencing jury's determination.[31] In 1983, John Booth and Willie Reed bound and gagged an elderly couple. Believing the couple might be able to identify them, Booth stabbed them numerous times with a kitchen knife. The trial judge in this case allowed the jury to consider a victim impact statement that detailed the family and the community's respect and admiration for the victims as well as the impact of the murder on the victims' family.[32]

The Supreme Court, in reversing the death sentence, held that it was impermissible to allow the jury access to such evidence in the sentencing phase of a death penalty proceeding.[33] In summing up the Court's holding that the introduction of the victim impact statement violates the Eighth Amendment's prohibition against cruel and unusual punishment, Justice Powell commented:

> One can understand the grief and anger of the family caused by the brutal murders in this case, and there is no doubt that jurors generally are aware of these feelings. But the formal presentation of this information by the State can serve no other purpose than to inflame the jury and divert it from deciding the case on the relevant evidence concerning the crimes and the defendant. As we have noted, any decision to impose the death sentence must "be, and appear to be, based on reason rather than caprice or emotion." The admission of these emotionally charged opinions as to what conclusions the jury should draw from the evidence clearly is inconsistent with the reasoned decision making we require in capital cases.[34]

As may be apparent at the time of the decision in *Booth v. Maryland*, the relevant considerations at the sentencing phase of a murder trial were those aspects of a defendant's background or character or those circumstances that extenuate or mitigate the defendant's culpability.

South Carolina v. Gathers followed the rationale of *Booth* in holding as unconstitutional the imposition of a death penalty based on prosecutorial remarks that were considered inflammatory.[35] Demetrius Gather and three companions sexually assaulted and killed Richard Haynes, a man they encountered in a park. During the incident, the perpetrators ransacked a bag the victim was carrying. The bag contained several articles pertaining to religion, including a religious tract entitled "Game Guy's Prayer." During the sentencing phase of the trial, the prosecutor's argument included references to Haynes's personal qualities and included a reading of "Game Guy's Prayer." The Supreme Court reversed the sentence, stating that such references to the qualities of the victim were similar to the *Booth* holding that prohibited victim impact statements. The Court determined that such evidence was likely to inflame the jury and thus violated the defendant's Eighth Amendment rights. In a well-reasoned and logical dissent, Justice O'Conner stated, "Nothing in the Eighth Amendment precludes the community from considering its loss in assessing punishment nor requires that the victim remain a faceless stranger at the penalty phase of a capital case." The dissent by Justice O'Conner was a signal that the winds of judicial temperament might be changing.

In *Payne v. Tennessee*, the Court completely reversed itself and allowed to stand the imposition of a death sentence that was based in part on evidence contained in a victim impact statement. In 1987, Pervis Tyrone Payne entered the apartment of Charisse Christopher and her two children. Payne stabbed Charisse and her two children numerous times with a butcher knife. Charisse and her daughter died; however, three-year-old Nicholas survived.

Payne was caught and convicted for the murders. During the penalty phase, four witnesses testified regarding the defendant's background, reputation, and mental state. All these witnesses urged the jury not to impose the death penalty. In rebuttal, the prosecution called the maternal grandmother who was caring for Nicholas. She was allowed to testify, over the defendant's objection, that Nicholas continued to cry out, calling for his dead mother and sister. The witness was also allowed to testify regarding her personal grief over the loss of her loved ones.

During closing argument, the prosecutor hammered on the pain and suffering that Nicholas and his deceased family had endured:

> But we do know that Nicholas was alive. And Nicholas was in the same room. Nicholas was still conscious. His eyes were open. He responded to the paramedics. He was able to follow their directions. He was able to hold his intestines in as he was carried to the ambulance. So he knew what happened to his mother and baby sister.
>
> There is nothing you can do to ease the pain of any of the families involved in this case. There is nothing you can do to ease the pain of Bernice or Carl Payne, and that's a tragedy. There is nothing you can do basically to ease the pain of Mr. and Mrs. Zvolanek, and that's a tragedy. They will have to live with it for the rest of their lives. There is obviously nothing you can do for Charisse and Lacie Jo. But there is something you can do for Nicholas.
>
> Somewhere down the road Nicholas is going to grow up, hopefully. He's going to want to know what happened. And he is going to know what happened to his baby sister and his mother. He is going to want to know what kind of justice was done.

He is going to want to know what happened. With your verdict, you will provide the answer.[36]

The jury sentenced Payne to death, and the case was appealed to the Supreme Court. Payne contended that the trial court erred when it allowed the maternal grandmother to testify. Relying on *Booth* and *Gathers*, Payne argued that such evidence was a violation of his Eighth Amendment rights.

After reviewing the principles that have guided criminal sentencing over the ages, the Court stated that the consideration of the harm caused by the crime has been an important factor in the existence of the exercise of judicial discretion. The majority opinion went on to state that neither *Booth* nor *Gathers* even suggested that a defendant, entitled as he is to individualized consideration, is to receive that consideration wholly apart from the crime that he had committed.

In setting forth the groundwork for overruling *Booth* and *Gathers*, the Court stated:

> Under our constitutional system, the primary responsibility for defining crimes against state law, fixing punishments for the commission of these crimes, and establishing procedures for criminal trials rests with the States. The state law respecting crimes, punishments, and criminal procedures are of course subject to the overriding provisions of the United States Constitution. Where the State imposes the death penalty for a particular crime, we have held that the Eighth Amendment imposes special limitations upon that process. . . .
>
> The States remain free, in capital cases, as well as others, to devise new procedures and new remedies to meet felt needs. Victim impact evidence is simply another form or method of informing the sentencing authority about the specific harm caused by the crime in question, evidence of a general type long considered by sentencing authorities. We think the *Booth* Court was wrong in stating that this kind of evidence leads to the arbitrary imposition of the death penalty. In the majority of cases, and in this case, victim impact evidence serves entirely legitimate purposes.[37]

Thus, the Supreme Court overruled *Booth* and *Gathers* to the extent that they allowed introduction of evidence or argument regarding the impact of the crime on the victim, families, and the community. In addition, the Court's decision clearly stated that the decision regarding the admission of such evidence was the prerogative of the individual states. The Court ruled that it would not intervene unless the evidence introduced was so unduly prejudicial to render the trial fundamentally unfair.[38] If this occurred, the Court reasoned, the due process clause of the Fourteenth Amendment provides a mechanism for relief.

The decision was not without heated dissent. In a dissenting opinion, Justices Marshall and Blackmun uttered a quote that will continue to be heard in the halls of justice and law school classrooms: "Power, not reason, is the new currency of this Court's decisionmaking."[39] Justices Marshall and Blackmun went on to point out that the court was disregarding the accepted judicial principle of *stare decisis*. In a well-reasoned but emotional conclusion, they state:

> Today's decision charts an unmistakable course. If the majority's radical reconstruction of the rules for overturning this Court's decisions is to be taken at face value—and the majority offers us no reason why it should not—then the overruling of *Booth* and *Gathers* is but a preview of an even broader and more far-reaching assault upon this Court's precedents. Cast aside today are those condemned to face society's ultimate

Focus

Feelings Regarding Victim Impact Statements

"My victim impact statement was the last opportunity I had to let anyone know about my daughter."—A victim
     "I want you to go over each victim impact statement.... You have to live with the stupidity of your behavior for the rest of your life, but you also have to understand what these families have to live with as well."—Judge to a defendant at the time of sentencing.

Source: Based on E. K. Alexander and J. H. Lord, *Impact Statements: A Victim's Right to Speak—A Nation's Responsibility to Listen* (National Victim Center, Arlington, Va., 1992), pp. 10, 17.

penalty. Tomorrow's victims may be minorities, women, or the indigent. Inevitably, this campaign to resurrect yesterday's "spirited dissents" will squander the authority and the legitimacy of this Court as a protector of the powerless.[40]

The decision has also generated controversy in the academic world with a series of articles condemning the Court for both allowing victim impact evidence and appearing to repudiate its acceptance of *stare decisis*.[41] Although the dissent and certain individuals within the academic community may condemn the majority's opinion, it is now clearly the law of the land. In addition, the Supreme Court's decision enhanced the victims' rights movement in the United States. It allowed individual states to determine what is relevant evidence in the death penalty phase of a capital crime.

Some would argue that the decision in *Payne* leaves prosecutors and defense attorneys scrambling to determine what type of evidence is admissible under the guise of victim impact statements. The answer is evidence that does not result in rendering a trial fundamentally unfair. This concept of fundamental fairness is not a new, untested, or ill-defined doctrine.

There is a long history of defining acts that establish the parameters of fundamental fairness, with roots in two early cases. In *Powell v. Alabama*, several black youths were accused of repeatedly raping two young white girls. They were caught, tried, and convicted. Their conviction was overturned on the ground that the failure of the trial court to appoint counsel until the day of the trial was a violation of the defendants' due process.[42] In *Brown v. Mississippi*, a sheriff hung the defendant from a tree and whipped him until he confessed to the murder of a white man. The Supreme Court held that such actions are revolting to the sense of justice, and the confession was suppressed.[43]

The doctrine of fundamental fairness accepts the concept that due process is a generalized command that requires states to provide the defendant with a fair trial. If the admission of the victim impact evidence "revolts the sense of justice" or "shocks the conscience" of the court, such admission would be in error under the due process clause.

Effect of Victim Impact Statements

VICTIM SATISFACTION.   The effect of victim impact statements is still being studied and debated. One area being looked at very carefully is victim satisfaction with victim impact statements. Some authorities believe that impact statements help the victim emotionally deal with the consequences of the crime. Others believe that victims are more satisfied with the criminal justice system if they participate by being allowed to express their feelings in a victim impact statement. This section briefly examines these and other aspects of victim satisfaction and victim impact statements.

In 1981, a National Institute of Justice study revealed that victims' satisfaction with the criminal justice system increased if they believed that they had influenced the process, regardless of whether they really had. For example, victims who had been able to speak to prosecutors and judges were more satisfied with the system than those who believed that they were not able to do so.[44] In 1982, another study indicated that a sense of participation was more critical to victims' satisfaction with the criminal justice process than how severely the defendant was punished.[45] In 1984, another study revealed that victims wanted more information about their cases and the opportunity to tell the prosecutor and judge how the case affected them.[46]

In 1989, Dean Kilpatrick reported the results of his research, which indicated that victim participation not only affected potential cooperation within the criminal justice system but also was critical in promoting victims' recovery from the aftermath of crime by helping them reassert a sense of control over their lives.[47] Kilpatrick stated that a criminal justice system that denies victims a chance to participate fosters a sense of helplessness and lack of control. He pointed out that there is a great danger in promising victims participation in the system and then failing to follow through with that promise because it results in further victimization.

Robert Wells, another noted authority, stated that victim impact statements may promote the psychological recovery of victims. Just as talking about what happened promotes healing, writing about it may also assist victims to emotionally deal with the crime. Allowing victims to tell how they were affected by the crime sends a supportive message that the criminal justice system cares about what happened.[48]

However, other experts claim that the mental and emotional benefits of victim impact statements and victim participation are overrated. In 1985, in a study carried out in Brooklyn, New York, Davis compared the outcome of two court experiments in which victims gave impact statements in one court and no statements were allowed in another court. He found no evidence that victims in the court that mandated impact statements felt a greater sense of participation or increased satisfaction.[49] Davis followed up this research with a 1989 study in the Bronx Supreme Court in New York.[50] The study analyzed 293 victims of robbery, nonsexual assault, and burglary. Each victim was assigned to one of three classifications: Some victims were interviewed and a victim impact statement written and distributed, other victims were interviewed but no impact statement was prepared, or only the name and address of the victim were recorded. A series of interviews was conducted with each victim. The results of this study indicate that victim impact statements are not an effective means of promoting victim satisfaction within the criminal justice system. No data support the theory that victim impact statements led to greater feelings of involvement, greater satisfaction with the criminal justice system, or greater satisfaction with the sentences imposed on the offenders. Davis concluded that more research is necessary regarding the effect of impact statements on victim satisfaction with the system.

As this discussion indicates, a controversy continues over the effect of victim impact statements on victim satisfaction. However, there is sufficient individual and anecdotal evidence of victim approval of the use of impact statements that we should continue using them until definitive studies can be conducted. The next section examines whether victim impact statements affect the outcome of sentencing.

SENTENCING. Limited research exists on the effect that victim impact statements have on judges. On the surface, it would appear that such evidence can only assist the court in rendering its decision and therefore should be readily accepted and consistently used by the judicial system. However, judges, like every other member of the criminal justice system, are understaffed and overworked. Does additional information really help, or does the process simply take more time? Are judges swayed by the emotional appeal of a citizen, or are they bound to render impartial justice to the defendant?

Early research indicates that state trial court judges found financial information contained in a victim impact statement very useful in determining appropriate sentences and restitution orders.[51] Seventy percent of those judges interviewed found the information very useful, and another 20 percent found it useful in terms of restitution orders. Although this research indicates that victim impact evidence is "very useful" to judges, this "usefulness" appears limited to the area of restitution and financial issues, not to other aspects of sentencing the defendant.

In 1990, Erez and Tontodonato produced an important study involving 500 Ohio felony cases and found that the cases in which victim impact statements were taken were more likely than those without statements to result in prison rather than probation.[52] This research has been cited by a number of victim impact statement proponents as authority for the position that such statements have an effect on sentencing. Although this was a significant study, it had several flaws, including a wide disparity in the seriousness of offense among cases that had impact statements. In addition, the authors acknowledged that further research needed to be conducted in this area.

Davis and Smith also researched the effect of impact statements on sentencing. In the same 1989 study that examined victim satisfaction, they evaluated the significance of impact statements on judicial sentencing.[53] They concluded that victim impact statements do not produce sentences that reflect the effects of crime on the victims, nor did they find that sentencing decisions were affected by impact statements once the charge and the defendant's prior record were taken into consideration by the court. They did find that the severity of the charges is a high predictor of sentences. Although judges professed to be interested in impact statements, prosecutors believed that judges only occasionally considered this information when imposing sentences. Conversely, prosecutors claimed that victims should be consulted on a regular basis, but judges stated that prosecutors rarely related impact evidence to them.

Clearly, more research is also needed in this area. In addition, such research must find a way to get around the "political correctness" of advocating the use of victim impact statements. As Davis and Smith's study points out, judges claim that they endorse impact statements, but prosecutors don't believe in them. On the other hand, those same prosecutors claim that they use impact statements, but the judges don't see them. Realistically, in today's climate very few elected or appointed officials within the criminal justice system will admit to anything less than wholehearted endorsement of victim impact statements. What is needed is an in-depth study to determine the impact of such evidence outside the realm of political correctness. Until such research is done, we can only speculate on its real effect.

Victim impact evidence is now an accepted part of the judicial process. The ability of a victim of family violence to inform the court of the impact of the offender's acts on her life can only benefit the victim and continue to educate the public regarding the dynamics of family violence.[54]

Justice for All Act

The Supreme Court's ruling regarding victim impact statements clearly established the right of victims to submit such a statement. However, it was unclear if they had a right to speak at the hearing or simply submit a written statement. In addition, the Court did not grant victims additional rights. This was left for Congress to do. In 2004, Congress enacted the Justice for All Act, which contains major sections relating to rights of crime victims.[55] The Act amends the federal criminal code to provide crime victims certain specified rights:

- The right to be protected from the accused;
- The right to reasonable notice of any public court proceedings, parole hearings, or any release or escape of the accused;
- The right to be heard at any public proceedings involving release, plea, sentencing, or parole hearing.

The Act (1) requires prosecutors to advise victims that they may seek advice of an attorney to enforce their rights and (2) creates several enforcement options that allow the prosecution or the victim to assert these rights in court. However, the Act does not create a separate cause of action to allow the victim to file a lawsuit against the government if the victim believes that his or her rights have been violated.

The Act was soon tested in two important court cases. In *Kenna v. U.S. District Court*, some victims had been denied the right to speak at sentencing. The Ninth Circuit Court of Appeals held that Congress intended to allow victims to speak at sentencing and not just submit victim impact statements. More important, the appeals court held that for victims who were denied this right, the remedy is to have the sentence vacated and a new sentencing hearing held in which they would be allowed to speak.[56] In *United States v. Wood*, the trial court held that a sentencing of a defendant could be delayed because the victims would be out of the country on the scheduled date for sentencing. The court held that the intent of the Act was to make crime victims full participants in the criminal justice system.[57]

It would appear that we are making progress in including victims of crime within the system. Although we have made some progress in addressing the crime victims' needs, much remains to be done.

Focus

The Crime Victims' Rights Act of 2004

Does the Crime Victims' Rights Act of 2004, 18 U.S.C. § 3771, give victims the right to make a statement at the offender's sentencing?

Excerpts from the opinion: In re Kenna, 453 F.3d 1136 (9th Cir. 2006)

Moshe and Zvi Leichner, father and son, swindled scores of victims out of almost $100 million. While purporting to make investments in foreign currency, they spent or concealed the funds entrusted to them. Each defendant pleaded guilty to two counts of wire fraud and one count of money laundering. More than sixty of the Leichners' victims submitted written victim impact statements. At Moshe's sentencing, several, including petitioner W. Patrick Kenna, spoke about the effects of the Leichners' crimes-retirement savings lost, businesses bankrupted, and lives ruined. The district court sentenced Moshe to 240 months in prison.

Three months later, at Zvi's sentencing, the district court heard from the prosecutor and the defendant, as required by Federal Rule of Criminal Procedure 32(i)(4). But the court denied the victims the opportunity to speak. The trial judge stated that he had listened to the victims the last time when Moshe was tried and that he had re-reviewed all the investor victim statements. The trial judge stated that he did not think that there was anything that any victim could say that would have any impact whatsoever on Zvi's sentencing.

Kenna, a victim and petitioner, filed a timely petition for writ of mandamus pursuant to the Crime Victims' Right Act (CVRA), 18 U.S.C. § 3771(d)(3). He sought an order vacating Zvi's sentence, and ordering the district court to allow the victims to speak at the resentencing.

As an appellate justice, how would you rule?

The appellate court granted Kenna's petition and held that the federal district court erred in refusing to allow Kenna and other victims to speak at Zvi Leichner's sentencing hearing. The appellate court stated that if any of the victims file a motion to present information at the hearing, the district court shall conduct a new sentencing hearing and provide the victims the right to speak at the hearing.

Note: The U.S. Courts of Appeal in the Second, Third, and Eleventh Circuits have agreed with the above decision of the U.S. Court of Appeals for the Ninth Circuit. However, the U.S. Courts of Appeal for the Fifth, Sixth, Tenth, and D.C. Circuits have held that crime victims are not entitled to ordinary appellate protection of their rights. See *United States v. Monzel*, 641 F.3d 528, 533 (D.C. Cir. 2011). This is a conflict among the U.S. Courts of Appeal that probably will eventually be decided by the U.S. Supreme Court.

Summary

Victims' rights are an important aspect of family violence. Professionals not only must understand the dynamics of family violence but also must be prepared to offer support and guidance to victims as they move through the judicial system. Repairing the body and spirit is only half the battle; society must be able to make the victims of family violence completely whole. This

effort has to include financial reimbursement from the offender.

Victims must be aware of the various alternatives available to earn financial awards. These alternatives include actions against the perpetrator and his insurance companies. Statutes exist that allow victims of family violence to be compensated by the state for certain types of injuries suffered at the hands of an abuser. In addition, courts routinely order restitution as a part of criminal sentencing. All these mechanisms allow victims to gain greater financial independence.

Society is beginning to accept the fact that victims of crimes in general, and victims of family violence in particular, have rights and need to be active participants in the criminal justice system. This includes giving their input during sentencing of the offender. The use of victim impact statements is a giant step forward for victims of family violence.

Key Terms

primitive law—a system of rules in preliterate societies.

victimology—the study of the relationship between the criminal and the victim.

tort—a legal wrong committed on the person or property of another independent of contract.

plaintiff—the person filing the civil complaint.

defendant—the person who is alleged to have committed the acts that resulted in injury to the plaintiff or victim.

complaint—a formal written document stating certain causes of actions that the plaintiff alleges entitles him or her to recover damages from the perpetrator.

answer—a formal written document that either admits or denies the allegations.

discovery—the formal method of learning the facts, theories, and positions of opposing parties by means of written or oral questioning.

compensatory damages—when the plaintiff asks to be made whole or reimbursed for expenses incurred as a result of an injury.

punitive damages—asked for or awarded to punish the defendant for conduct that is considered outrageous.

third parties—those individuals or entities that have intentionally or negligently contributed to the injury suffered by the victim.

compensation—public funds that are paid to victims or their families to recover out-of-pocket expenses for injuries suffered as a result of another's criminal act.

victim impact statements—presents the victim's point of view to the sentencing authority.

Discussion Questions

1. What is the most important development in the area of victims' rights?
2. What are the advantages and disadvantages of compensation statutes?
3. Is it reasonable to expect a victim of family violence will sue the perpetrator? Why? Why not?
4. What new rights do you believe the victims of family violence will acquire in the near future? Why?
5. Are victim impact statements of any real use in sentencing? Why? Why not?

Suggested Readings

Costanzo, M., and S. Oskamp, eds. *Violence and the Law* (SAGE, Thousand Oaks, Calif., 1994).

Drapkin, I., and E. Viano, eds. *Victimology: A New Focus*, vol. 2 (Heath, Lexington, Mass., 1974).

Dubber, M. D. *Victims in the War on Crime: The Use and Abuse of Victims' Rights* (New York University Press, New York, 2006).

Karmen, A. *Crime Victims: An Introduction to Victimology* (Brooks/Cole, Pacific Grove, Calif., 1984).

Maine, Sir H. S. *Ancient Law*, 10th ed. (Murray, London, 1905).

Miethe, T. D., and R. F. Meier. *Crime and Its Social Content* (State University of New York Press, New York, 1994).

Schafer, S. *The Victim and His Criminal* (Random House, New York, 1968).

von Hentig, H. *The Criminal and His Victim* (Yale University Press, New Haven, Conn., 1948).

Weiner, N. A., and M. E. Wolfgang, eds. *Pathways to Criminal Violence* (Sage, Newbury Park, Calif., 1989).

Wolfgang, M. E. *Patterns of Criminal Homicide* (University of Pennsylvania Press, Philadelphia, 1958).

Woulhter, L. *Victimology: Victimisation and Victims' Rights* (Routledge Cavendish, London, 2006).

Endnotes

1. Sir H. S. Maine, *Ancient Law*, 10th ed. (Murray, London, 1905).

2. S. Schafer, *The Victim and His Criminal* (Random House, New York, 1968).

3. G. O. Mueller and H. A. Cooper, "Society and the Victim: Alternative Responses," in I. Drapkin and E. Viano, eds., *Victimology: A New Focus*, vol. 2 (Heath, Lexington, Mass., 1974), pp. 85–102.

4. A. Karmen, *Crime Victims: An Introduction to Victimology*, 2nd ed. (Wadsworth, Belmont, Calif., 1996).

5. M. Largen, "Grassroots Centers and National Task Forces: A History of the Anti-Rape Movement," *Aegis* 32 (Autumn 1981), pp. 46–52.

6. 595 F.Supp. 1521 (Conn. 1984).

7. "Remarks by the President at Announcement of Victims' Constitutional Amendment," *Press Release* (White House, Office of the Press Secretary, Washington, D.C., June 25, 1996), p. 2.

8. G. D. Gottfredson, "The Experiences of Violent and Serious Victimization," in N. A. Weiner and M. E. Wolfgang, eds., *Pathways to Criminal Violence* (SAGE, Newbury Park, Calif., 1989), pp. 202–234.

9. An excellent source of cases dealing with victims is the National Victim Center's *Crime Victims' Litigation Quarterly* (National Victim Center, Arlington, Va., 1995).

10. B. Mendelsohn, *Rape in Criminology* (Giustizia Penale, Italy, 1940).

11. B. Mendelsohn, "The Origin and Doctrine of Victimology," *Excerpta Criminologica* 3 (June 1963), pp. 239–244.

12. H. von Hentig, *The Criminal and His Victim* (Yale University Press, New Haven, Conn., 1948).

13. M. E. Wolfgang, *Patterns of Criminal Homicide* (University of Pennsylvania Press, Philadelphia, 1958).

14. M. E. Wolfgang, *Analytical Categories for Research in Victimization* (Kriminologische Wegzeichen, Munich, 1967), p. 17.

15. Ibid., pp. 24 and 72.

16. A. Karmen, *Crime Victims: An Introduction to Victimology* (Brooks/Cole, Pacific Grove, Calif., 1984).

17. *Black's Law Dictionary*, 6th ed. (West, St. Paul, Minn., 1990), p. 1489.

18. *Garzilli v. Howard Johnson's Motor Lodge, Inc.* 419 F.Supp. 1210 (E.D.N.Y. 1976).

19. *Jardel Co. v. Hughes*, 523 A. 2d 518 (Del. 1987).

20. *Small v. McKennan Hospital*, 403 N.W. 2d 410 (S.D. 1987).

21. *Harrinton v. New England Mutual Life Insurance Co.*, 873 F 2d 166 (7th Cir. 1989).

22. *State Farm Fire and Casualty Co. v. Tringali*, 686 F 2d 821 (9th Cir. 1982).

23. *Alabama Farm Bur. Mutual Casualty Insurance Co. v. Mitchell*, 373 So. 2d 1129 (1979).

24. This section has been based on *Restitution: Making It Work*, Legal Series Bulletin #5, OVC, Washington, D.C., November 2002.

25. See for example Oregon Rev. Statute Section 137.106 (1999).

26. *Ordering Restitution to the Crime Victim*, Legal Series Bulletin #6, OVC, Washington, D.C., November 2002.

27. J. Brown, P. Langan, and D. Levin, *Felony Sentences in State Courts, 1996* (Bureau of Justice Statistics, U.S. Department of Justice, Washington, D.C., 1999).

28. *Victim Input into Plea Agreements*, Legal Series Bulletin #7, OVC, Washington, D.C., November 2002.

29. Arizona Revised Statutes Section 13–4423 (2000).

30. See P. A. Talbert, "The Relevance of Victim Impact Statements to the Criminal Sentencing Decision," *UCLA Law Review* 36 (1988), pp. 199, 202–211; and Maureen McLeod, "Victim Participation at Sentencing," *Criminal Law Bulletin* 22(501) (1986), pp. 505–511.

31. *Booth v. Maryland*, 482 U.S. 496 (1987).

32. *Booth v. Maryland*, pp. 500–501.

33. *Booth v. Maryland*, p. 509. The Court did, however, carefully note that information typically contained in a victim's statement is generally admissible in noncapital cases and may be considered in capital cases if directly related to the circumstances of the crime. *Booth v. Maryland*, p. 508, n. 10. For example, the Court noted that the prosecution may produce evidence as to the characteristics of the victim to rebut an argument made by the defendant (e.g., victim's peaceable nature to rebut claim of self-defense).

34. *Booth v. Maryland*.

35. 490 U.S. 805 (1989).

36. 115 L.Ed. 728–729.

37. 115 L.Ed. 734–735.

38. 115 L.Ed. 2d 735.

39. 115 L.Ed. 748.

40. 115 L.Ed. 756.

41. See Jimmie O. Clements Jr., "Casenote, Criminal Law—Victim Impact Evidence—The Scope of the Eighth Amendment Does Not Include a Per Se Bar to the Use of Victim Impact Evidence in the Sentencing Phase of a Capital Trial *Payne v. Tennessee*," *St. Mary's Law Journal* 23 (1991), p. 517; A. Alaka, "Note: Victim Impact Evidence, Arbitrariness and the Death Penalty: The Supreme Court Flipflops in *Payne v. Tennessee*," *Loyola University (Chicago) Law Journal* 23 (1992), p. 581; and K. E. Whitehead, "Case Note: Mourning Becomes Electric: *Payne v. Tennessee's* Allowance of Victim Impact Statements during Capital Proceedings," *Arkansas Law Review* 45 (1992), p. 531.

42. *Powell v. Alabama*, 287 U.S. 45, 53 S.Ct. 55, 77 L.Ed. 158 (1932).

43. 297 U.S. 278, 56 S.Ct. 461, 80 L.Ed. 682 (1936).

44. B. Smith and S. Hillanbrand. *Non-Stranger Violence: The Criminal Courts Responses* (National Institute of Justice, Washington, D.C., 1981).

45. D. P. Kelly, "Delivering Legal Services to Victims: An Evaluation and Prescription," *Justice System Journal* 9 (1982), p. 62.

46. J. Hernon and B. Forst, "The Criminal Justice Response to Victim Harm," *Research Report* (National Institute of Justice, Washington, D.C., 1984).

47. D. Kilpatrick and R. K. Otto, "Constitutionally Guaranteed Participation in Criminal Proceedings for Victims: Potential Effects on Psychological Functioning," *Wayne State Law Review* 34 (1989), p. 17.

48. R. Wells, "Victim Impact: How Much Consideration Is It Really Given?" *The Police Chief* (February 1991), p. 44.

49. R. C. Davis, *First Year Evaluation of the Victim Impact Demonstration Project* (Victim Services Agency, New York, 1985).

50. R. C. Davis and B. E. Smith, "Victim Impact Statements and Victim Satisfaction: An Unfulfilled Promise," *Journal of Criminal Justice* 22 (1994), p. 1.

51. S. Hillenbrand, *Victim Rights Legislation: An Assessment of Its Impact on the Criminal Justice System* (American Bar Association, Chicago, 1987).

52. E. Erez and P. Tontodonato, "The Effect of Victim Participation in Sentencing on Sentence Outcomes," *Criminology* 28 (1990), p. 451.

53. R. C. Davis and B. E. Smith, "The Effects of Victim Impact Statements on Sentencing Decisions: A Test in an Urban Setting," *Justice Quarterly* 11(3) (1994), p. 453.

54. For a contrary position, see R. C. Davis and B. E. Smith, "The Effects of Victim Impact Statements on Sentencing Decisions: A Test in an Urban Setting," *Justice Quarterly* 11(3) (1994), which points out that victim impact statements neither increased officials' consideration of harm to victims nor resulted in generally harsher sentencing decisions.

55. *The Justice for All Act*, OVC Fact Sheet, Office for Victims of Crime, Washington, D.C., April 2006.

56. CR-03-00568-JFW (9th Cir., July 5, 2006).

57. CR. No. 05-00072DAE (D. Haw., July 17, 2006).

INDEX

Page numbers in *italic* refer to figures. Page numbers in **bold** refer to tables.